THE NEW INTERNATIONAL COMMENTARY ON
THE NEW TESTAMENT — F. F. BRUCE, *General Editor*

THE EPISTLE
TO THE HEBREWS

THE EPISTLE
TO THE HEBREWS

THE ENGLISH TEXT
WITH INTRODUCTION, EXPOSITION AND NOTES

by

F. F. BRUCE, D.D.

*Rylands Professor of Biblical Criticism and Exegesis in the
University of Manchester*

WM. B. EERDMANS PUBLISHING CO.

GRAND RAPIDS, MICHIGAN

First printing, November 1964
Second printing, March 1967
Third printing, June 1970
Fourth printing, March 1972
Fifth printing, November 1973
ISBN 0-8028-2183-9

PHOTOLITHOPRINTED BY GRAND RAPIDS BOOK MANUFACTURERS, INC.
GRAND RAPIDS, MICHIGAN, UNITED STATES OF AMERICA

To the Memory

of

NED BERNARD STONEHOUSE

CONTENTS

EDITOR'S FOREWORD

On this occasion there is no need for an editorial foreword to introduce a new author to readers of the New International Commentary on the New Testament. It is, rather, the sorrowful duty of a new editor to bid farewell to his predecessor.

The New International Commentary owes the standing which it has secured for itself in the field of New Testament literature to the character and work of its late General Editor far more than to any other factor. Since the project was launched, nearly fifteen years ago, Dr. Stonehouse gave himself and his great abilities unstintingly to its successful realization. The publisher and authors are in the best position to attest how painstakingly and conscientiously he discharged his editorial responsibilities. Every manuscript in the series was submitted to him and read through carefully—how carefully could be estimated from the pages of comments and questions which the author in due course received from him, together with suggestions, tactfully and courteously expressed, for the improvement of the work. Almost invariably the value of these suggestions was immediately apparent to the author, and their substance was embodied in the revision of the manuscript before it went to the printer.

The change in editorship involves no change in the policy of the series. Its aim has been, from its inception, to interpret the New Testament books in accordance with the best standards of Reformed scholarship, in which wholehearted acknowledgment of the divine authority of Holy Writ is combined with the acceptance and presentation of all the light that has been thrown on it by the most recent study and discovery. Anything savoring of mere traditionalism is alien to our purpose; the commentators have no desire to impose a theological system on the biblical text but rather to treat the text as the source of their theology. They recognize the great debt they owe to expositors of previous generations and centuries, and something of their sense of indebtedness comes to expression in the pages of the Commentary; but at the same time they know that "the Lord hath more truth yet to break forth out of His holy word", and hope that some of this truth may be permitted to break forth in the New International Commentary. In the words of Dr. Stonehouse, "the Bible is recognized as being the Word of God, and that Word is given right of way at all times. With the help of this faith, and the disciplines of modern scholarship, the aim of this Commentary is to make for some definite progress in the march of God's truth."

When Dr. Stonehouse died on November 18, 1962, ten volumes in the series had appeared, covering well over half the books of the New Testament. The remaining volumes had been assigned by him to various contributors, who are now engaged on their assignments. To our great loss, Dr. Stonehouse had not been able to complete the commentaries on the two books which he had reserved for himself—Matthew and Revelation—and these have now been assigned to other scholars. In accordance with the original policy, the American Standard Version of 1901 will continue to be used as the basic text for the exposition, while the notes will take the fullest account of the Greek text.

Towards the end of his epistle, the writer to the Hebrews exhorts his readers in these terms: "Remember your leaders, those who spoke to you the word of God; consider the outcome of their life, and imitate their faith" (Heb. 13:7). It is in this spirit that we shall always think, with grateful remembrance, of Ned Bernard Stonehouse.

F. F. BRUCE
General Editor

AUTHOR'S PREFACE

On June 25, 1954, I received an invitation from Dr. Stonehouse to undertake the volume on the Epistle to the Hebrews for the New International Commentary. Since then I have spent a good part of my time with this epistle, and have learned to appreciate increasingly the viewpoint and purpose of its unknown author—still as much unknown by name to me as he was when I embarked on the serious study of his work, but not, I think, completely unknown in other respects.

For many readers the Epistle to the Hebrews is among the more difficult books of the New Testament. Its magnificent style, to which King James's revisers (following in William Tyndale's footsteps) did full justice, can be more easily appreciated than the details of its argument, which call for a greater familiarity with its Old Testament background, and a better understanding of certain phases of first-century biblical exegesis, than most readers possess. Sir Edmund Gosse in *Father and Son* tells of the difficulty which he found in his boyhood in following his father's reading and exposition of the epistle. "The melodious language, the divine forensic audacities, the magnificent ebb and flow of argument which make the 'Epistle to the Hebrews' such a miracle, were far and away beyond my reach, and they only bewildered me."

To many people, it is said, the Epistle to the Hebrews is just "the book about Melchizedek"—although Melchizedek occupies only some twenty out of the epistle's more than three hundred verses. Others find themselves out of their depth when they come across references to "the blood of bulls and of goats and the ashes of a heifer sprinkling the unclean"; and wonder what all this has to do with true religion. The writer to the Hebrews, in fact, is concerned to argue that all this has nothing to do with true religion; but he is dealing with people who had been brought up to think that it had much to do with it. But what has his argument to say to readers today who are not at all disposed to think that animal sacrifices play any part in the worship of God? It has this to say: that true religion or the worship of God is not tied to externalities

xi

of any kind. Our author is insisting on the inwardness of true religion, on the necessity of a purified conscience as the one indispensable condition for offering God acceptable worship in that true sanctuary which no human hands have built.

Moreover, this is the book which establishes the finality of the gospel by asserting the supremacy of Christ—His supremacy as God's perfect word to man and man's perfect representative with God. More than any other New Testament book it deals with the ministry which our Lord is accomplishing on His people's behalf now. In a day of shaking foundations it speaks of the kingdom which cannot be shaken. It reminds Christians that it is no part of their calling to settle down and be content with things as they are, but to press forward continually in God's advancing purpose, along the trail already blazed by the Pioneer of Faith. And when they are tempted to be discouraged and give up the onward march, it revives their drooping spirits and supplies many incentives to press on to that eternal commonwealth which is the true homeland of loyal souls. A book which does all this, no matter what imagery it uses, is a book which speaks to the condition of the church throughout the world in the second half of the twentieth century.

My debt to others in the following pages is enormous, and can be acknowledged only very inadequately. Among previous expositors Calvin and Westcott, James Moffatt and Geerhardus Vos have been of great help. Spicq's encyclopaedic commentary has always been within arm's reach. For drawing out and applying to the conscience the practical lessons of the epistle G. H. Lang has few rivals. And I am not the only writer on the epistle in recent years for whom William Manson has provided it with a more convincing life-setting than anyone else has done. But this list is not exhaustive: others who have helped me clamor for admittance—A. B. Davidson, Riggenbach and Windisch—but the author's preface is not the place for a bibliography.

I must add a word of thanks to the Very Reverend D. E. W. Harrison, Dean of Bristol. In the winter of 1955–56, when he was still Archdeacon of Sheffield and I lived in the same city, he and I jointly conducted a study class on the Epistle to the Hebrews for the Extramural Department of Sheffield University. My understanding of the epistle was very considerably deepened as a result of this happy collaboration with him.

To Dr. Stonehouse my debt of gratitude is great indeed, for the invitation to write this commentary and for many other tokens of friendship and fellowship. In acknowledgment, but by no means in repayment, of this debt the finished work is dedicated to his memory.

August 1963   F.F.B.

ABBREVIATIONS

AG	[Walter Bauer's] *Greek-English Lexicon of the New Testament and Other Early Christian Literature*, translated and adapted by W. F. Arndt and F. W. Gingrich (Chicago, 1957)
Ant.	*Antiquities* of Josephus
ARV	American Revised Version = American Standard Version (1901)
AV	Authorized Version or King James Version (1611)
BA	*The Biblical Archaeologist*
BASOR	*Bulletin of the American Schools of Oriental Research*
BJRL	*Bulletin of the John Rylands Library* (Manchester)
BZAW	*Beiheft zur Zeitschrift für die alttestamentliche Wissenschaft*
BZNW	*Beiheft zur Zeitschrift für die neutestamentliche Wissenschaft*
CBQ	*Catholic Biblical Quarterly*
CBSC	Cambridge Bible for Schools and Colleges
CD	Damascus Document(s), also called the Zadokite Work
CentB	Century Bible (Nelson)
CGT	Cambridge Greek Testament
CIG	*Corpus Inscriptionum Graecarum*
I Clem.	First Epistle of Clement
Clem. Hom.	*Clementine Homilies*
Clem. Recog.	*Clementine Recognitions*
CNT	Commentaire du Nouveau Testament (Delachaux et Niestlé)
EB	Études Bibliques (Gabalda, Paris)
EGT	Expositor's Greek Testament
Eng. tr.	English translation
Ep. Barn.	*Epistle of Barnabas*
EQ	*Evangelical Quarterly*
ERV	English Revised Version (1881)
Ev Th	*Evangelische Theologie*
Exp.	*The Expositor*
Exp.B	Expositor's Bible
ExT	*Expository Times*
FS	*Festschrift*
HAT	Handbuch zum Alten Testament (Tübingen)
HCNT	Handcommentar zum Neuen Testament (ed. H. J. Holtzmann)
HDB	Dictionary of the Bible, ed. J. Hastings (Edinburgh, 1898–1904)
HE *(Hist. Eccl.)*	*Ecclesiastical History*
HNT	Handbuch zum Neuen Testament (Tübingen)
HThR	*Harvard Theological Review*
HUCA	*Hebrew Union College Annual*
IB	*Interpreter's Bible* (New York, 1952–57)

ICC	International Critical Commentary (Edinburgh)
IEJ	*Israel Exploration Journal*
INT	*Introduction to the New Testament*
JBL	*Journal of Biblical Literature*
JE	*Jewish Encyclopaedia* (New York)
JJS	*Journal of Jewish Studies*
JNES	*Journal of Near Eastern Studies*
JRS	*Journal of Roman Studies*
JThS	*Journal of Theological Studies*
Jub.	Jubilees
KHC	Kurzer Handcommentar zum Alten Testament
Leg. Alleg.	*On the Allegorical Interpretation of the Laws* (Philo)
LSJ	*Greek-English Lexicon*, by H. G. Liddell and R. Scott, revised by H. S. Jones (Oxford, 1940)
Luc.	Lucian
LXX	Septuagint version
MK	Meyer Kommentar (Kritisch-exegetischer Kommentar über das Neue Testament, begründet von H. A. W. Meyer)
MM	*The Vocabulary of the Greek Testament*, by J. H. Moulton and G. Milligan (London, 1930)
MNTC	Moffatt New Testament Commentary
Mor.	*Moralia* (of Plutarch)
MT	Massoretic Text (of the Hebrew Bible)
NBD	*New Bible Dictionary* (London and Grand Rapids, 1962)
NEB	New English Bible (1961)
NICNT	New International Commentary on the New Testament (Grand Rapids)
NovT	*Novum Testamentum*
N.S.	new series
NT	New Testament
NTS	*New Testament Studies*
OT	Old Testament
PEQ	*Palestine Exploration Quarterly*
Preliminary Studies	Philo's *On Mating with the Preliminary Studies (De Congressu Quaerendae Eruditionis Gratia)*
Ps. Sol.	Psalm(s) of Solomon
PThR	*Princeton Theological Review*
1Q	Qumran Cave 1
1QH	Scroll of Hymns *(hodayoth)* from Qumran Cave 1
1QM	*Rule of War (milḥamah)* from Qumran Cave 1
1QpHab.	Commentary *(pesher)* on Habakkuk from Qumran Cave 1
1QS	*Rule of the Community (serekh hayyaḥad)* from Qumran Cave 1
1QSa	*Rule of the Congregation (serekh ha'edah)* from Qumran Cave 1
4Q	Qumran Cave 4
4QpPs. 37	Commentary *(pesher)* on Psalm 37 from Qumran Cave 4
RB	*Revue Biblique*
RÉJ	*Revue des Études Juives*
RHPR	*Revue d'Histoire et de Philosophie Religieuses*
RSV	Revised Standard Version (1952)

RThR	*Reformed Theological Review* (Australia)
SJTh	*Scottish Journal of Theology*
TB	Babylonian Talmud
Test. Levi, etc.	*Testament of Levi* (and other *Testaments of the Twelve Patriarchs*)
ThZ	*Theologische Zeitschrift*
TJ	Jerusalem (Palestinian) Talmud
TNTC	Tyndale New Testament Commentary
TR	"Received Text" (of the Greek New Testament)
TU	*Texte und Untersuchungen*
TWNT	*Theologisches Wörterbuch zum Neuen Testament* (ed. G. Kittel and G. Friedrich)
Vg (Vulg)	Latin Vulgate version
VH	*Vera Historia* (Lucian)
VT	*Vetus Testamentum*
WC	Westminster Commentaries
ZAW	*Zeitschrift für die alttestamentliche Wissenschaft*
ZK	Zahn Kommentar (Kommentar zum NT herausgegeben von Theodor Zahn)
ZNW	*Zeitschrift für die neutestamentliche Wissenschaft*
ZThK	*Zeitschrift für Theologie und Kirche*

ARGUMENT OF THE EPISTLE TO THE HEBREWS

I

God spoke in various ways to our fathers through the prophets, but now He has spoken His final word to us in His Son, His perfect representative. The Son of God is greater than any prophet; He is greater even than the angels, as the ancient scriptures abundantly testify. It was through angels that Moses' law was communicated, and its sanctions were severe enough; how much more perilous must it be to ignore the saving message brought by no angel, but by Jesus, the Son of God!

Jesus, the Son of God, is the One to whom the dominion of the world has been committed for all time to come. As the eighth psalm teaches us, God has put everything under the dominion of man, and it was the nature of man—*our* nature—that the Son of God took upon Himself in order to win back this dominion. To do this He had to conquer the devil who had usurped it, and rescue those whom he held in bondage; and He conquered the devil when in death He invaded the realm of death, which the devil had controlled until then. It is because Jesus is truly Man, moreover, that He is qualified to serve as high priest on His people's behalf; He knows all their trials from His own experiences and therefore can give them the timely help they need.

II

But let us beware: those who rebelled against God in the days of the wilderness wanderings were excluded from His rest in the promised land. There is, however, a better rest than that which the Israelites found in Canaan; it is the rest which awaits the people of God. We must take care not to forfeit that rest by rebelling against God, when He speaks to us no longer through His servant Moses, as He did in those days, but through His Son, a greater than Moses.

III

As has already been said, Jesus is our great high priest, able to sympathize with His people and help them. We may safely look for understanding and delivering grace to the One who endured the agony of Gethsemane. He has been called to His high-priestly office by God Himself, as an inspired oracle makes clear: "The LORD has sworn and will not change his mind, Thou art a priest for ever, after the order of Melchizedek."

(I should like to enlarge on this subject, but really I do not know if I can; you are so spiritually immature. I must warn you solemnly that those who have once been baptized and tasted the blessings of the new age can never repeat the experience of repentance and conversion if they commit apostasy. Not that I think you actually mean to be apostates; I have better hopes of you than that. I want you rather to press on from the point you have reached, so as to attain full maturity, instead of sticking there, or slipping back.)

IV

Christ, then, is by divine appointment a high priest of Melchizedek's order. You remember the story of Melchizedek, priest of God Most High. He appears suddenly in the sacred record, without antecedents, and nothing is said of his subsequent career. Yet he was a very great man; our father Abraham paid him tithes and received his blessing. You might even say that Levi, ancestor of the priestly families of Israel, paid Melchizedek tithes in the person of his great-grandfather Abraham. This implies that Melchizedek is greater than Levi, and Melchizedek's priesthood better than Aaron's. And indeed that is obvious, for if perfect access to God had been attainable under the Aaronic priesthood, why should God have acclaimed the Messiah as priest of a different order?

In many ways Jesus' priesthood after Melchizedek's order is superior to Aaron's priesthood. Jesus, unlike Aaron and his successors, was confirmed in office by the oath of God. Jesus is immortal, whereas the priests of Aaron's line die one by one. Jesus is sinless, whereas the priests of Aaron's line have to present a sin-offering for their own cleansing before they can present one for the people. *Their* sacrificial service must constantly be repeated, because it is never truly effective; Jesus, by the single sacrifice of Himself, put away His people's sin for ever.

V

The Aaronic priests minister under the old covenant instituted at Mount Sinai; Jesus is the Mediator of the new covenant—the covenant whose inauguration Jeremiah foretold. The introduction of a new covenant means that the former one is obsolete. The old covenant made provision for the removal of external pollution by means of animal sacrifices and similar rites, but these things could never remove *sin*; under the new covenant Jesus, by yielding up His life to God as an acceptable and efficacious sacrifice, cleanses the *conscience* from guilt and thus abolishes the barrier between His people and God. The Aaronic priests minister in an earthly sanctuary belonging to the old order, where access to the divine presence is barred by a curtain; Jesus exercises *His* high priesthood in the heavenly sanctuary, where there is no such barrier between the worshippers and God. And this heavenly sanctuary in which direct access to God is accorded through Jesus is that spiritual and eternal order of which the earthly sanctuary is only a temporary and inadequate copy. For the new order into which Christ brings His people is to the old Levitical order as substance to shadow.

VI

Let us, then, abandon the old obsolescent order and approach God along this new and living way which Jesus by His death has opened up for us. Let us maintain steadfast hope and faith in Him. Thus we shall have a firm assurance of those eternal realities which are invisible to the outward eye; we shall be able to look forward with eager expectation to the sure advent of the Coming One. It was by such forward-looking faith that the saints of earlier days won the approval of God; they lived in the good of those promises whose fulfilment has come in our day. Let us follow their example; better still, let us follow the example of Jesus. He ran the race of faith from first to last, for all the disgrace of the cross, and is now enthroned at God's right hand.

Let us not grow faint-hearted because of our trials: these trials are the proof that we are indeed the trueborn sons of God. And think of the glory which is our heritage in this age of fulfilment— something far surpassing what men and women of faith experienced in days gone by. How could we ever think of going back to the old ways?

VII

So maintain your Christian confession in patience and hope; live as Christians should; and may God, who raised Jesus from the dead, help you to do His will in all things.

INTRODUCTION

The Epistle to the Hebrews differs from most of the New Testament epistles in that, while it ends like a letter, it does not begin like one; it lacks the customary opening salutation containing the names of the writer and of the people addressed.[1] Yet, not only in the personal notes at the end[2] but throughout its length, it is clearly addressed to a particular community in which the writer takes a lively interest. Since, however, neither that community nor the writer is expressly identified in the text as it has been preserved to us, the document presents us at the outset with a number of critical problems to which no agreed solution has been found.

(a) The people addressed

The document was known and quoted before the end of the first century,[3] but not under its traditional title "To (the) Hebrews." This title goes back to the last quarter of the second century,[4] if not earlier, and from that time on it is the regular designation for the work in New Testament manuscripts and Christian writers.

---

[1] The one other exceptional document in this respect among the New Testament epistles is I John, which neither begins nor ends like a letter, but is from first to last, like the greater part of Hebrews, a "word of exhortation" (cf. pp. xlviii, 413).

[2] Cf. Ch.13:1 (p. 386 with nn. 2–4); Ch. 13:22ff.(pp. 413f. with nn.126–128).

[3] It was certainly known to Clement of Rome c. A.D. 96 (see p. xxxiv with n. 53), and almost as certainly to Hermas, also of Rome, not long afterwards (cf. in the light of Heb. 3:12 his warnings against "apostasy from the living God" in *Shepherd*, Vision ii.3.2; iii.7.2; see also p. 66, n. 61; p. 118, n. 35; p. 123, n. 55; p. 125, n. 58; pp. 260f., nn. 142–146).

[4] The earliest occurrence of Πρὸς Ἑβραίους seems to be at the head of the copy of the epistle on folio 21r of P^{46}, the oldest extant codex of the *corpus Paulinum*. Clement of Alexandria (c. A.D. 180), in the extract from his *Hypotyposes* quoted by Eusebius, does not use the precise phrase Πρὸς Ἑβραίους, but evidently knew the epistle under this title, since he speaks of it as written "for Hebrews" (Ἑβραίοις, Euseb. *Hist. Eccl.* vi.14.3, 4). Tertullian, in his treatise *On Modesty* (20), written c. A.D. 220, knows it under the corresponding Latin title *ad Hebraeos* (cf. pp. xxxvii, 123).

How it originated is not known; it may very well be that when, in the course of the second century, the work was included in the Pauline corpus, the editor gave it this title by analogy with "To (the) Romans", etc.[5] But what precisely was understood by the term "Hebrews" we cannot say; the title may simply have reflected the editor's impression (shared, no doubt, with other readers) that the people addressed were Jews or, more probably, Jewish Christians.[6] There are a few places in the New Testament where the term "Hebrews" is used of a distinct class of Jews or Jewish Christians, as opposed to those who are called Hellenists;[7] but it is unlikely that this distinctive usage is reflected in the traditional title of our epistle.[8] Indeed, if we think in terms of the Hebrew-Hellenist division, we should naturally classify this epistle as a Hellenistic document.

If the title "To (the) Hebrews"[9] is an editorial label attached to the work for convenient reference, and not an original designation, we should not be greatly influenced by it in endeavoring to establish the identity of the addressees. This must be established, in so far as it is possible, on the basis of internal evidence.

---

[5] It is difficult to accept the suggestion of F. C. Synge that the title means "Against (the) Hebrews" (*Hebrews and the Scriptures* [London, 1959], p. 44).

[6] For the general use of Ἐβραῖοι to designate Jewish Christians *cf.* M. Black, *The Scrolls and Christian Origins* (London, 1961), p. 78; it appears in this sense in the title of the *Gospel according to the Hebrews* and in the Paris magical papyrus 574, ll. 3018f., "I adjure thee by Jesus the God of the Hebrews".

[7] *Cf.* Acts 6:1; II Cor. 11:22; Phil. 3:5. See *Acts*, NICNT, pp. 127f.

[8] W. Manson, *The Epistle to the Hebrews* (London, 1951), p. 162, suggests that the epistle was intended for a minority of "Hebrews" in this distinctive sense, who formed "a section of the Jewish-Christian Church at Rome". On p. 44 he states that this minority, "in reaction from the larger freedom of the world-mission gospel were asserting principles and counter-claims akin to those of the original 'Hebrew' section in the Jerusalem Church". But we have only the scantiest means of knowing what principles and counter-claims were made by the "Hebrews" in the early Jerusalem church; and we do know that Stephen, who was presumably a Hellenist, and Paul, who was born and bred a "Hebrew", found equally bitter hostility among the non-Christian Hellenists of Jerusalem (Acts 6:9; 9:29). In general, however, I am in very great sympathy with W. Manson's thesis (see p. xxxv).

[9] C. Spicq suggests that "To the Hebrews" means "To the pilgrims"—those "passing through" this world; he appeals to the probable kinship between Heb. '*ibrī* ("Hebrew") and '*ābar* ("pass through or over"); *cf.* the LXX translation of "Abram the Hebrew" (Gen. 14:13) as Ἀβρὰμ ὁ περάτης (see also p. 130 with n. 80; pp. 304f., nn. 114–123). He points out how this sense of "Hebrew" is

No doubt it was natural for second-century readers, like many others since their day, to think of the addressees as Jews or Jewish Christians. The whole argument is conducted against a background of Old Testament allusion; considerable familiarity with the Levitical ritual, and interest in it, are presupposed. Yet all this in itself does not require either the author or the people addressed to be Jewish; we have known at the present time Gentile Christians who were thoroughly familiar with the Old Testament, accepted it as sacred and authoritative scripture, and manifested a lively interest in the details of the Mosaic tabernacle and the Levitical offerings, in which they found a remarkably full adumbration of the gospel. So, it has been pointed out, our author's knowledge of the Levitical ritual, like the knowledge which he presupposes in his readers, is a literary knowledge—that is to say, it is drawn from the Old Testament writings (with the aid, possibly, of some midrashic tradition)[10] and not from any first-hand acquaintance with procedure in the Jerusalem temple in the closing years of the Second Jewish Commonwealth. A number of scholars in the past generation or two, among whom the commentators Moffatt and Windisch are outstanding,[11] have maintained that the epistle was addressed to Gentile Christians, who were in danger of committing apostasy and thus renouncing true religion altogether—"falling away from the living God", as our author puts it

---

exploited by Philo (*L'Épître aux Hébreux* i [Paris, 1952], pp. 243ff.). In his later article, "L'Épître aux Hébreux: Apollos, Jean-Baptiste, les Hellénistes et Qumrân", *Revue de Qumran* i (1958–59), pp. 365ff., he repeats this suggestion (quoting from Jerome, *On Jeremiah* i.14: "Hebrew: that is περάτης, pilgrim and passer through"); he also points out that the designation μέτοχοι found in this epistle (*e.g.* in Ch. 3:1) may reflect the Hithpaʿel of the verb ʿārab (occurring in the sense "associate with" in OT and the Qumran texts). This might suggest a play on the metathesis ʿābar/ʿārab, but μέτοχοι might also reflect Heb. ḥabērîm ("associates" in a religious society or ḥabūrāh); the thought of this as the word lying behind Ἑβραῖοι in the title of our epistle may commend itself to some (not to me).

[10] *Cf.* p. xlix, n. 116; p. 215, n. 137 (on Ch. 9:19).

[11] ʿ *Cf.* J. Moffatt, *The Epistle to the Hebrews*, ICC (Edinburgh, 1924), p. xvi *et passim*; H. Windisch, *Der Hebräerbrief*, HNT (Tübingen, 1931), p. 31 (on Ch. 3:12) *et passim*; also A. C. McGiffert, *A History of Christianity in the Apostolic Age* (Edinburgh, 1897), pp. 463ff. (with bibliography on p. 468, n. 3); E. F. Scott, *The Epistle to the Hebrews* (Edinburgh, 1922); E. Käsemann, *Das wandernde Gottesvolk* (Göttingen, 1938); G. Vos, *The Teaching of the Epistle to the Hebrews* (Grand Rapids, 1956).

(Ch. 3:12). If Jewish Christians relapsed into Judaism, it is implied, this would not involve a renunciation of "the living God"; relapsing into Judaism would at least mean that they continued to worship the God of Israel. And, further, is it not a pagan past that is indicated in the repeated phrase "dead works"—when the readers are reminded of the "foundation of repentance from dead works" which, once laid, cannot be laid again (Ch. 6:1), and of the efficacy of the blood of Christ to "cleanse your conscience from dead works to serve the living God" (Ch. 9:14)?[12]

From our author's point of view deliberate disobedience to the living God was practical apostasy against Him, whether those guilty of it were Jewish or Gentile by birth. When he warns his readers against "falling away from the living God", he adduces the example of the Israelites in the wilderness under Moses who disobeyed God, rejected Moses' leadership and failed to enter the promised land. What was possible for Israelites then was equally possible for Israelites now. And the "dead works" are things which call for repentance and cleansing, on the part of Jews and Gentiles without discrimination. More particularly, the whole "foundation" of Ch. 6:1ff. implies the Jewish antecedents of the readers, as does also the description of Christ's death in Ch. 9:15 as procuring "redemption of the transgressions that were under the first covenant".

Moreover, his insistence that the old covenant has been antiquated is expressed with a moral earnestness and driven home repeatedly in a manner which would be pointless if his readers were not specially disposed to live under that covenant, but which would be very much to the point if they were still trying to live under it, or imagined that, having passed beyond it, they could revert to it.[13]

---

[12] The argument that προσεληλύθατε in Ch. 12:18, 22, implies that the readers were "proselytes" from paganism is not sufficiently strong to bear much weight; at most it identifies them as converts to Christianity (cf. pp. 372f. with nn. 142–144).

[13] There is nothing in the argument to suggest that the readers were Gentile Christians exposed to judaizing propaganda like those to whom the Epistle to the Galatians was addressed. The non-mention of circumcision is not surprising in a letter to a Jewish-Christian community, where this would not be the issue that it was among Gentile converts in the churches of Galatia or the Lycus valley.

Again, his appeals to the Old Testament scriptures reflect his confidence that his readers, even if their loyalty to the gospel is wearing thin, will recognize their authority. This they would indeed do, if they were Jews; they had recognized the authority of those scriptures before they became Christians, and if they relapsed from Christianity into Judaism they would continue to recognize their authority. Converts to Christianity from paganism, on the other hand, adopted the Old Testament as their sacred book along with the Christian faith; if they were tempted to give up their Christian faith, the Old Testament would go with it. Not only so, but the very terms in which our author assumes on their part an acknowledgement of Old Testament authority imply that they accepted Jewish premises; for example, commenting on the announcement in Ps. 110:4 of a priesthood after the order of Melchizedek, he asks: "Now if there was perfection through the Levitical priesthood ..., what further need was there that another priest should arise after the order of Melchizedek, and not be reckoned after the order of Aaron?" (Ch. 7:11). This argument suggests that the people addressed took it for granted (rightly) that the Levitical priesthood was instituted by divine authority, and also might be inclined to take it for granted (wrongly) that it represented the final stage in this aspect of God's provision for them. Converts from paganism would not be so assured of the divine institution of the Levitical priesthood, and to the author's argument "if there was perfection through the Levitical priesthood ..." their answer would naturally be: "We never thought there was!" And while, if we were compelled to regard the addressees as Gentiles, we might give some sort of meaning to the exhortation in Ch. 13:13 to go forth to Christ "outside the camp", such language is much more intelligible if addressed to Jews.

Some students of the epistle, concluding that the people addressed were Jews, have gone farther and tried to identify them with a particular class of Jews. Karl Bornhäuser, for example, inferred from such a passage as Ch. 5:12 (where the readers are told that by this time they should have been able to teach others) that they were not rank-and-file Jewish Christians, but more probably converts from the Jewish priesthood—some of the "great company of the priests" who "were obedient to the faith" in the period before the expulsion of Hellenistic believers from Jerusalem

(Acts 6:7).[14] Besides, priests would have a natural interest in the ritual details of our author's argument. Further points in support of this view are adduced by C. Spicq in his great commentary on the epistle.[15] Seven years after the publication of his commentary, Spicq elaborated this part of his thesis by arguing that these converted priests were "Esseno-Christians", including former members of the Qumran sect, whose "doctrinal and biblical formation, intellectual preoccupations and religious presuppositions" were well known to our author.[16]

Since the discovery of the Qumran documents in 1947 and the following years, repeated attempts have been made to bring their evidence into some kind of relation with the Epistle to the Hebrews. In 1955 F. M. Braun expressed the view that "of all the New Testament writings, the Epistle to the Hebrews is the one which gives the fullest answer to the basic tendencies of the [Qumran] sect".[17] Since then a number of other writers have elaborated this statement, none so fully as H. Kosmala in his work *Hebräer-Essener-Christen*, published in 1959, in which it is argued that the people addressed in the epistle were not Christians, but Jews who had come so far on the way to Christianity, but had stopped short of the goal—that they were, in fact, people holding views very similar to those of the Qumran sect and other Essenes. In his introduction to Hebrews in the "Layman's Bible Commentaries" J. W. Bowman maintains that the recipients of the epistle were members of the Hellenistic-Jewish Christian community of Palestine who had come under the influence of the Qumran sect. There were serious defects in their understanding of the gospel, and these the author set himself to correct. The particular group of Hellenists addressed Professor Bowman locates at Sychar, where John the Baptist and

[14] K. Bornhäuser, *Empfänger und Verfasser des Briefes an die Hebräer* (Gütersloh, 1932), condensed by C. Sandegren, "The Addressees of the Epistle to the Hebrews", *EQ* xxvii (1955), pp. 221ff.

[15] *L'Épître aux Hébreux* i (Paris, 1952), pp. 226ff.

[16] *Revue de Qumran* i (1958–59), p. 390 (*cf.* p. xxiv, n. 9).

[17] *Revue Biblique* lxii (1955), p. 37 (in an article "L'arrière-fond judaïque du quatrième Évangile et la Communauté de l'Alliance", pp. 5ff.). *Cf.* also Y. Yadin, "The Dead Sea Scrolls and the Epistle to the Hebrews", *Scripta Hierosolymitana* iv (1958), pp. 36ff.; D. Flusser, "The Dead Sea Sect and Pre-Pauline Christianity", *ibid.*, pp. 215ff.; J. Daniélou, *The Dead Sea Scrolls and Primitive Christianity* (Eng. tr., Baltimore, 1958), pp. 111ff.; H. Kosmala, *Hebräer-Essener-Christen* (Leiden, 1959).

Jesus, and later Philip, had preached. But since Philip's evangelistic campaign in those parts, "the centre of Christian evangelistic effort had passed from Jerusalem to Syrian Antioch, bypassing Samaria and its Hellenistic-Jewish community on the way!"[18] The most that can be said on this score, however, is that the recipients of the epistle were probably Jewish believers in Jesus whose background was not so much the normative Judaism represented by rabbinical tradition as the nonconformist Judaism of which the Essenes and the Qumran community are outstanding representatives, but not the only representatives.[19]

One prominent feature of this nonconformist Judaism was its practice of ceremonial washings beyond those prescribed in the law.[20] Josephus, for example, tells us that the Essenes were distinguished from other Jews when they performed their sacrificial duties "by the superiority of the purifications which they habitually practised".[21] But the Essenes were not the only Jewish groups of which this could be said. There is evidence, indeed, that such "baptist" groups were found in the Diaspora as well as in Judaea. Philo does not speak of ceremonial washings when he describes the settlement of the Therapeutae near Lake Mareotis in Egypt[22]—he does not speak of them either in his descriptions of the Essenes—but the Therapeutae are certainly to be reckoned as an Egyptian offshoot of the Palestinian nonconformist tradition. As for the Jewish community in Rome, it appears to have preserved nonconformist features, especially in the matter of ceremonial washings, which in due course were taken over into Roman Christianity, as the *Apostolic Tradition* of Hippolytus testifies at the beginning of the third century A.D.[23] If the Epistle to the Hebrews was addressed to a group of Jewish Christians which retained such features, certain points which the author makes, such as his

[18] J. W. Bowman, *Hebrews, James, I & II Peter* (London, 1962), pp. 13–16. For a critique of all such views see J. Coppens, *Les affinités qumrâniennes de l'Épître aux Hébreux* (Bruges-Paris and Louvain, 1962).

[19] *Cf.* F. F. Bruce, " 'To the Hebrews' or 'To the Essenes'?", *NTS* ix (1962–63), pp. 217ff.

[20] *Cf.* J. Thomas, *Le mouvement baptiste en Palestine et Syrie* (Gembloux, 1935); M. Black, *The Scrolls and Christian Origins* (London, 1961), pp. 91ff.; J. A. T. Robinson, *Twelve New Testament Studies* (London, 1962), pp. 11ff.

[21] *Antiquities* xviii.19.

[22] *The Contemplative Life*, 21ff.

[23] See pp. 115f. with nn. 20–25 (on Heb. 6:2).

reference to "instruction about ablutions" in Ch. 6:2, could have had a more immediate relevance to their situation than might be readily apparent to twentieth-century readers.

The addressees appear, then, to have been a group of Jewish Christians who had never seen or heard Jesus in person, but learned of Him (as the writer of the epistle also did) from some who had themselves listened to Him.[24] Since their conversion they had been exposed to persecution—particularly at one stage shortly after the beginning of their Christian career[25]—but while they had had to endure public abuse, imprisonment and the looting of their property, they had not yet been called upon to die for their faith.[26] They had given practical evidence of their faith by serving their fellow-Christians and especially by caring for those of their number who suffered most in the time of persecution.[27] Yet their Christian development had been arrested; instead of pressing ahead they were inclined to come to a full stop in their spiritual progress, if not indeed to slip back to a stage which they had left.[28] Very probably they were reluctant to sever their last ties with a religion which enjoyed the protection of Roman law and face the risks of irrevocable commitment to the Christian way. The writer, who has known them, or known about them, for a considerable time, and feels a pastoral concern for their welfare, warns them against falling back, for this may result in falling away from their Christian faith altogether; he encourages them with the assurance that they have everything to lose if they fall back, but everything to gain if they press on.[29]

We may infer from the epistle that they were Hellenists; they knew the Old Testament in the Greek version. It is implied, too, that their knowledge of the ancient sacrificial ritual of Israel was derived from the reading of the Old Testament and not from firsthand contact with the temple services in Jerusalem. Perhaps they formed a "house-church" within the wider fellowship of a city church, and were tending to neglect the bonds of fellowship that bound them to other Christians outside their own inner circle.

---

[24] *Cf.* Heb. 2:3f.
[25] Ch. 10:32ff.
[26] Ch. 12:4 (*cf.* pp. xlii f., 266ff., 357).
[27] Chs. 6:10; 10:34.
[28] Ch. 5:11ff.
[29] Chs. 2:1ff.; 3:12ff.; 6:4ff.; 10:26ff.; 12:15ff.

(b) Destination

Where did they live? We do not know. Opinions have ranged between Judaea in the east and Spain[30] in the west.

If their knowledge of the Jewish ritual was not derived from firsthand contact with the temple services, then Jerusalem seems to be excluded. They may, of course, have had an earlier association with the Jerusalem church; we recall the large exodus of Hellenistic believers from Jerusalem in the persecution that followed the death of Stephen. Those Hellenists scattered in many directions, carrying the gospel wherever they went;[31] one can easily think of the readers of this epistle as one of the communities of new believers founded at that time.

Even so, Jerusalem has not been without its advocates as the place to which the epistle was sent.[32] Sir William Ramsay, for example, hazarded the guess that it written to the Jerusalem church from Caesarea during Paul's imprisonment in that city (A.D. 57–59) by one of his companions, Philip the evangelist perhaps.[33] C. H. Turner argued that it was sent to the Jerusalem church shortly before the outbreak of the war against Rome in A.D. 66, when they "had to face the issue squarely between the abandonment of their Christianity and the abandonment of their city. Criticism [he added] which shuts its eyes to such patent historical probabilities stands self-condemned".[34]

But the religious situation in Jerusalem was dominated by the temple, to which no explicit reference is made by our author. When an earlier leader of his school, Stephen, addressed himself to the situation in Jerusalem, the temple occupied a prominent place in his polemic—the temple, moreover, in express distinction from the movable tabernacle of earlier days.[35] Our author has

---

[30] So Nicolas of Lyra (cf. C. Spicq, L'Épître aux Hébreux i, p. 234, n. 4).

[31] Cf. Acts 8:4; 11:19.

[32] Cf. G. Salmon, INT (London, 1889), pp. 468ff.; B. F. Westcott, The Epistle to the Hebrews (London, 1903), p. xl ("in Jerusalem, or in the neighbourhood of Jerusalem"); W. Leonard, The Authorship of the Epistle to the Hebrews (London, 1939), and many others listed by Spicq, op. cit., i, p. 239, n. 1.

[33] Luke the Physician (London, 1908), pp. 301ff.

[34] Catholic and Apostolic (London, 1931), pp. 81f. Cf. p. lviii, n. 139.

[35] Acts 6:13f.; 7:44–50 (see Acts, NICNT [Grand Rapids, 1954], pp. 134ff., 141ff., 156ff.).

much to say about the tabernacle, but not about the temple. The priesthood and ritual associated with the tabernacle, of course, were in principle those associated with the temple too; but what we find in the epistle is literary allusion to the former and not, as might have been expected in an exhortation addressed to Jerusalem, contemporary allusion to the latter. Even at the latest reasonable date for the epistle, there would still have been a few members of the Jerusalem church who had seen and heard Jesus for themselves and did not have to depend on the testimony of others. And when the writer refers to his readers' long-standing and continued ministering "to the saints" (Ch. 6:10), we may reflect that throughout the apostolic age the Jerusalem church is more prominent as a recipient than as a giver of such ministry.[36]

Other places in Palestine have been suggested: J. W. Bowman, as we have seen, thinks of Samaria (preferably Sychar); C. Spicq thinks of Caesarea,[37] but regards Syrian Antioch as more probable.[38] T. W. Manson, leaving the beaten track, suggested Colossae or some neighboring place in the Lycus valley; he detected in the epistle references to the "Colossian heresy" at an earlier stage than that which it had reached by the time Paul wrote the Epistle to the Colossians.[39] W. F. Howard thought of Ephesus; he envisaged the people addressed as a group of wealthy and cultivated Jews who had been converted during Paul's Ephesian ministry, but whose faith waned after Paul's imprisonment and subsequent execution in Rome.[40] They had little sympathy with their fellow-Christians of Gentile birth, whom they despised as low-born and too much influenced by the lax morality of their pagan days.

---

[36]   *Cf.* Acts 11:29f.; Rom. 15:25ff.; I Cor. 16:1ff.; II Cor. 8:1ff.; Gal. 2:10.

[37]   *Op. cit.*, i, pp. 247ff. The experiences of Ch. 10:32ff. could be placed in the context of the tension between the Jewish and Gentile populations of Caesarea in the decade preceding A.D. 66 (Josephus, *War* ii.266ff.; *Antiquities* xx.173ff.).

[38]   *Op. cit.*, i, pp. 250ff. *Cf.* V. Burch, *The Epistle to the Hebrews* (London, 1936), p. 137, for the argument that the allusions to the Maccabaean martyr-cult in Ch. 11:35bff. "are met by a Syrian notice of the cult which is markedly Antiochian in detail".

[39]   *Studies in the Gospels and Epistles* (Manchester, 1962), pp. 242ff. (article "The Problem of the Epistle to the Hebrews" reprinted from *BJRL* xxxii [1949], pp. 3ff.).

[40]   "The Epistle to the Hebrews", *Interpretation* v (1951), pp. 80ff. So, in his later days, J. V. Bartlet ("The Epistle to the Hebrews once more", *ExT* xxxiv [1922–23], pp. 58ff.).

Cyprus has commended itself to Antony Snell;[41] this hangs together with his ascription of the authorship to Barnabas, whose close association with Cyprus is well attested. A number of scholars have thought of Alexandria in Egypt as the city where the readers lived.[42] Some Alexandrian association is evident throughout the epistle; the author is evidently acquainted with the literature of Alexandrian Judaism, like Wisdom and IV Maccabees, and especially the writings of Philo. But this speaks more for his association with the city than for theirs. The Muratorian Canon, which makes no mention of Hebrews, does refer to an epistle "to the Alexandrines"; but as this is described as forged in Paul's name to support Marcion's heresy, it takes a powerful stretch of the imagination to identify it with our epistle. In the nineteenth century J. E. C. Schmidt,[43] A. Hilgenfeld[44] and S. Davidson[45] argued for Alexandria; they were followed in the twentieth century by G. Hoennicke,[46] C. J. Cadoux[47] and (most recently) S. G. F. Brandon.[48] Alexandria indeed has much that could be urged in its favor;[49] but there is one great obstacle in the way of thinking that the epistle was sent there. That is that precisely in Alexandria the belief in its Pauline authorship first arose, and it is difficult to suppose that the Christians of the city to which the epistle was sent so quickly forgot who sent it to them and ascribed it to another. Clement of Alexandria refers to some-

---

[41] *New and Living Way* (London, 1959), p. 19. Cyprus had previously been suggested by E. Riggenbach, *Der Brief an die Hebräer*, ZK (Leipzig, 1913), pp. xlviff.—a work which Snell characterizes as "much the best commentary on the Epistle known to me" (*op. cit.*, p. 22).

[42] *Cf.* Spicq, *op. cit.*, i, p. 237, n. 2, for a list.

[43] *Einleitung in das Neue Testament*, i (Giessen, 1804), pp. 284, 293.

[44] *Historisch-kritische Einleitung in das Neue Testament* (Leipzig, 1875), pp. 385ff.

[45] *INT*, i (London, 1882), pp. 223ff.

[46] *Das Judenchristentum im ersten und zweiten Jahrhundert* (Berlin, 1908), pp. 93ff.

[47] "The Early Christian Church in Egypt", *ExT* xxxiii (1921–22), pp. 536ff.

[48] *The Fall of Jerusalem and the Christian Church* (London, 1951), pp. 239f.

[49] Not, however, the fact that the Jewish temple of Leontopolis was not far away. K. Wieseler argued that deviations in the description of the cultus in Hebrews from that prescribed in the Old Testament and followed in Jerusalem (*e.g.* the daily ministration of the high priest, Ch. 7:27) reflected the practice at Leontopolis ("Die Leser des Hebräerbriefs und der Tempel zu Leontopolis," *Theologische Studien und Kritiken* xl [1867], pp. 665ff.).

one called "the blessed elder"—possibly his teacher Pantaenus—as saying that Paul, being the apostle of the Gentiles, wrote for the Hebrews anonymously since he recognized our Lord as Apostle to the Hebrews.[50] Thus, about a century after the epistle was written, it was being ascribed to Paul at Alexandria—perhaps because it was at Alexandria that the Epistle to the Hebrews was for the first time copied into a codex as part of the *corpus Paulinum*.[51] But could this ascription have been made so soon in a place where the true authorship was most likely to have been remembered?

The first place where, according to our extant literature, the Epistle to the Hebrews appears to have been known is Rome.[52] For Clement of Rome shows clear evidence of his acquaintance with it in the letter which he wrote on behalf of the Roman church to the Corinthian church *c*. A.D. 96.[53] Unfortunately he drops no hint about its authorship; he was writing for his contemporaries, not for us. But the Roman church, and the west in general, took a long time before they consented to regard it as one of the Pauline letters; their resistance to the belief in its Pauline authorship springs in all probability from an original positive knowledge that it was not written by Paul.

No certain inference in this regard can be drawn from the greetings which the writer sends his readers from those "of Italy" (Ch. 13:24).[54] "They of Italy" may have lived in Italy or outside Italy, so far as the language is concerned; and while the message could easily be construed in agreement with a Roman destination for the letter, it would agree equally well with Rome (or some other place in Italy) as the place where it was written.

What has been said above of the presence of "nonconformist" Jewish elements in the Christian community of Rome would chime in well with a Roman destination. There were many other places in the Diaspora as well as in Palestine where such elements were

---

[50] *Hypotyposes*, quoted by Eusebius, *Hist. Eccl.* vi. 14.1–4.

[51] *Cf.* G. Zuntz, *The Text of the Epistles* (London, 1953), pp. 14ff., 276ff.

[52] Some (*e.g.* E. Nestle, *ExT* x [1898–99], p. 422; G. Milligan, *The Theology of the Epistle to the Hebrews* [Edinburgh, 1899], p. 50) have linked a Roman destination for the epistle with the presence in Rome of a "synagogue of the Hebrews" (συναγωγὴ Αἰβρέων, *CIG* 9909); this is a very doubtful link.

[53] This is particularly evident in the précis of Heb. 1:3–7 interwoven into the language of I Clem. 36:1–5.

[54] See p. 415 with n. 133.

to be found, but it is at Rome that we have the best attestation of their survival for several generations in *Christian* practice.

One of the best known statements of the case for the Roman destination of the epistle was an article by Adolf Harnack in the first issue of the *Zeitschrift für die neutestamentliche Wissenschaft*, in which he related it to the early history of Christianity at Rome and envisaged it as sent to a "house-church" in that city by someone well acquainted with the addressees.[55] More recently a persuasive case has been presented by William Manson, in the Baird Lecture delivered in New College, Edinburgh, in 1950.[56] The Roman church, he infers from Rom. 11:13, 18, had a Jewish-Christian base. As a whole it had accepted the implications of the Gentile world-mission, but a small conservative enclave within it clung to the more conservative principles of traditional Judaism, and to this enclave in particular Hebrews is addressed. Professor Manson found a straight line running from the ministry of Stephen (the record of which in Acts forms the prelude to the rise of the Gentile world-mission) to the argument of the Epistle to the Hebrews. His thesis will be found to influence the present commentary at many points; but certainty on the destination of the epistle is unattainable in the present state of our knowledge, and fortunately its exegesis is for the most part independent of this question.

(c) Authorship

If we do not know for certain to whom the epistle was sent, neither do we know by whom it was sent. If Clement of Rome had any inkling of the author's identity, he gives us no indication of it. But we can be quite sure that he himself was not the author, although it has been suggested at various times that he was. In spite of Clement's familiarity with the epistle, he "turns his back

---

[55] 'Probabilia über die Adresse und den Verfasser des Hebräerbriefes", *ZNW* i (1900), pp. 16ff. Harnack's thesis is elaborated (but not strengthened) by M. A. R. Tuker: "The Roman origin of the Epistle indeed is enshrined in the Roman liturgy. In that liturgy, and in no other, the priesthood of Melchizedek is invoked, and the words are those of the Epistle to the Hebrews—*summus sacerdos Melchisedech*. Moreover, they are recorded in the oldest reference to the Roman Canon, and must take their place by the side of the 'Amen' of Justin as root-words of the Liturgy" (from "The Gospel according to Prisca", *Nineteenth Century*, January 1913, pp. 81f., quoted by A. Nairne, *The Epistle of Priesthood* [Edinburgh, 1913], p. 6, n. 1).

[56] *The Epistle to the Hebrews* (London, 1951).

on its central argument in order to buttress his own arguments about the Church's Ministry by an appeal to the ceremonial laws of the Old Testament".[57]

The Alexandrian belief that Paul was the author influenced the judgment of eastern Christianity, and ultimately, towards the end of the fourth century, of western Christianity too. But even at Alexandria, the sense of literary criticism possessed by the leaders of the catechetical school made it plain that Pauline authorship could not be predicated *simpliciter* of this epistle as it could of Romans or Galatians. Attempts were therefore made to reconcile the Pauline ascription with the linguistic data. Clement of Alexandria in his *Hypotyposes*[58] said that it was written by Paul for Hebrews in the Hebrew language, but that Luke translated it and published it for the Greeks; thus he endeavored to account for the similarity in style between Hebrews and the Lucan writings. (As for the absence of the Pauline superscription, he accounted for that by saying that "in writing for Hebrews who had conceived a prejudice against him and suspected him, he very prudently did not put them off at the outset by setting down his name".)[59] Origen, a generation later, knowing as he did Hebrew in addition to Greek, probably realized that the Greek of the epistle bore no sign of having been translated from Hebrew.[60] His account of its authorship is as follows:

> The character of the diction of the epistle superscribed to the Hebrews lacks the apostle's rudeness of expression (a rudeness of expression or style which he himself acknowledged); the epistle is more idiomatically Greek in the composition of its diction. This will be acknowledged by anyone who is

---

[57] T. W. Manson, *The Church's Ministry* (London, 1948), pp. 13f.; he describes Clement's procedure in this regard as "a retrogression of the worst kind".

[58] Quoted by Eusebius, *Hist. Eccl.* vi.14.2.

[59] Eusebius, *Hist. Eccl.* vi.14.3. Clement's account is followed in a fourth-century preface to the epistle included in most manuscripts of the Vulgate.

[60] Against its being a translation from Hebrew (apart from the general consideration that it is not written in translation-Greek) certain specific points tell: thus, not only is the Old Testament quoted in the LXX, but the author argues on the basis of a LXX deviation from the Hebrew text (*cf.* the use made of Ps. 40:6, "a body hast thou prepared me", in Heb. 10:5ff.); again, the argument of Ch. 9:15–20 depends on the double sense "covenant" and "testament" of Gk. διαθήκη and could not have been used with Heb. berīth (*cf.* Calvin, *ad loc.*).

skilled to discern differences of style. But on the other hand the thoughts of the epistle are admirable and in no way inferior to those of the acknowledged writings of the apostle. The truth of this will be admitted by any one who pays attention to the reading of the apostle .... For my own part, if I may state my opinion, I should say that the thoughts are the apostle's, but that the style and composition are the work of someone who called to mind the apostle's teaching and wrote short notes, as it were, on what his master said. If any church, then, regards this epistle as Paul's, let it be commended on this score; for it was not for nothing that the men of old have handed it down to us as Paul's. But as to who actually wrote the epistle, God knows the truth of the matter. According to the account which has reached us, some say that the epistle was written by Clement, who became bishop of the Romans; others, that it was written by Luke, the writer of the Gospel and the Acts.[61]

Although the Pauline authorship was resisted in the west until late in the fourth century, the only positive ascription of authorship to come down to us from the west during that period is Tertullian's; he appeals to the epistle as having greater authority than the *Shepherd* of Hermas because of the eminence of its author, Barnabas, and he names Barnabas as the author of the epistle not as though he were expressing a private judgment of his own but as though this were a commonly agreed ascription in his circle.[62] The

---

[61] Quoted by Eusebius, *Hist. Eccl.* vi.25.11–14.

[62] *On Modesty* 20 (*cf.* p. 123 with n. 55). Whether this tradition was well founded or based, *e.g.*, on a collocation of the λόγος παρακλήσεως of Heb. 13:22 with the υἱὸς παρακλήσεως of Acts 4:36, cannot be ascertained. It has been objected that a man who appears so early in Christian history as Barnabas could not have written in terms of Heb. 2:3b; but he may not have heard Jesus teach. Barnabas was regarded as the author in the later part of the fourth century by Gregory of Elvira (*cf.* Spicq, *op. cit.*, i, p. 199 with n. 7), and by a host of modern writers (*cf.* Spicq, *ibid.*, n. 8), including B. Weiss (MK, Göttingen, 1897), G. Salmon (*INT* [London, 1889], pp. 466ff.), F. Blass (*Der Brief an die Hebräer* [Halle, 1903]), J. V. Bartlet (in *Exp.* VI.v [1902], pp. 409ff., vi [1902], pp. 28ff., viii [1903], pp. 381ff., xi [1905], pp. 431ff., VIII.v [1913], pp. 548ff.; he later gave up this view in favor of Apollos's authorship), C. R. Gregory (*Canon and Text of the NT* [Edinburgh, 1907], pp. 223f.), E. Riggenbach (ZK, Leipzig, 1913), C. J. Cadoux (*ExT* xxxiii [1921–22], pp. 536ff.), K. Bornhäuser (*Empfänger und Verfasser des Hebräerbriefs* [Gütersloh, 1932], pp. 75ff.), H. Strathmann (*Der Brief an die Hebräer* [Göttingen, 1937], pp. 64f.), A. Snell (*New and Living Way* [London, 1959], pp. 17ff.). According to F. J.

Muratorian Canon,[63] Irenaeus,[64] Hippolytus[65] and Gaius of Rome[66] did not regard the epistle as Pauline. Eusebius (c. A.D. 325) remarks that even in his day some among the Romans did not consider it to be the apostle's.[67] Half a century later the writer whom we call Ambrosiaster did not include Hebrews in the Pauline epistles on which he wrote commentaries; to him it is always an anonymous work.[68]

It was Jerome and Augustine who swayed opinion in the west towards accepting Hebrews as a Pauline epistle—not that they were convinced that it was so on grounds of literary criticism but because as a practical issue its canonicity was bound up with the belief in its apostolic authorship. "I am moved rather," wrote Augustine, "by the prestige of the eastern churches which include this epistle too among the canonical writings."[69] Even so, the earliest synodical promulgations of the Canon in the west preserved for some time a distinction between this epistle and the others

Badcock, "the voice is the voice of Barnabas the Levite, but the hand is the hand of Luke" (*The Pauline Epistles and the Epistle to the Hebrews in their Historical Setting* [London, 1937], p. 198); *cf.* p. 386, n. 3. (The Barnabas ascription is not affected one way or the other by the existence or content of the later work called the *Epistle of Barnabas.*)

[63] It lists Paul's letters as addressed to seven named churches and three named individuals, thus clearly excluding Hebrews. *Cf.* also Victorinus of Pettau (d. 303), commenting on Rev. 1:11.

[64] *Cf.* C. H. Turner in *Novum Testamentum Sancti Irenaei*, ed. W. Sanday and C. H. Turner (Oxford, 1923), pp. 226f.

[65] According to Photius, *Bibliotheca* 121; *cf.* R. H. Connolly, "New Attributions to Hippolytus", *JThS* xlvi (1945), pp. 199f.

[66] According to Eusebius, *Hist. Eccl.* vi.20.3.

[67] *Hist. Eccl.*, ibid.

[68] A. Souter, *A Study of Ambrosiaster* (Cambridge, 1905), pp. 171f.; *The Earliest Latin Commentaries on the Epistles of St. Paul* (Oxford, 1927), pp. 53f. The commentary on Hebrews included in some manuscripts among Ambrosiaster's Pauline commentaries is actually by Alcuin of York (E. Riggenbach, *Die ältesten lateinischen Kommentare zum Hebräerbrief* [Leipzig, 1907], pp. 18ff.). Pelagius regards Hebrews as Pauline, perhaps not in the same sense as the thirteen epistles which bear Paul's name; he wrote commentaries on them, but not on Hebrews.

[69] *Forgiveness of Sins*, i.50. Jerome on balance accepts it as Pauline, along (he says) with all the Greek-speaking churches, although he knows that many of the Latins have doubts on its authorship; "and it does not matter whose it is, since it is the work of a churchman *(ecclesiastici uiri)* and honored daily by being read in the churches" (*Epistle* 129.3).

ascribed to Paul: both the Synod of Hippo in 393 and the Third
Synod of Carthage in 397 enumerate "Of Paul the apostle, thirteen
epistles; of the same to the Hebrews, one". Not until the Sixth
Synod of Carthage (A.D. 419) do we find "fourteen epistles" in so
many words ascribed to Paul, in terms which Athanasius of
Alexandria had used in his Festal Letter of A.D. 367. From then
on the Pauline ascription became traditional in the west as in the
east, although commentators of critical judgment continued to
speak of Clement of Rome or Luke as translator or editor of the
epistle. Thus Thomas Aquinas says that "Luke, who was an
excellent advocate, translated it from Hebrew into that elegant
Greek".[70]

But with the reopening of traditional questions in the age of the
Reformation, fresh attention was directed to the authorship of
Hebrews. Calvin[71] thought of Luke or Clement of Rome as the
author, not merely translator or editor; while Luther[72] was apparently the first to make the brilliant guess that the author was
Apollos—a guess which has commended itself to many since his
day,[73] including (in our own time) T. W. Manson,[74] W. F. Howard[75]
and C. Spicq.[76] The Alexandrian characteristics of the thought,
style and vocabulary of the epistle have been thought to speak in
favor of Apollos's authorship; William Manson, however, while
conceding that "Apollos would admirably suit the part in point of
his Jewish-Alexandrian origin and training", finds it "difficult to
think that the Alexandrian Church would not have preserved
some knowledge of the fact in view of the distinguished rôle of this

[70] *Preface to the Epistle to the Hebrews* (quoted by Spicq, *op. cit.*, i, p. 198, n. 1).
[71] On Heb. 13:23.
[72] Luther speaks as though others had suggested Apollos before him. In his *Lectures on Hebrews*, 1517–18, he still ascribes the epistle conventionally to Paul; but in his *Preface to Hebrews*, 1522 (Weimar edition vii, p. 344), he describes the author as "an excellent man of learning, who had been a disciple of the apostles and learned much from them, and who was very well versed in Scrip-ture". In a sermon on I Cor. 3:4ff., in 1537 (Weimar edition xlv, p. 389), he says that Hebrews was certainly the work of Apollos, and expresses the same view in his *Commentary on Genesis*, 1545 (Weimar edition xliv, p. 709).
[73] Including (in his later days) J. V. Bartlet ("The Epistle to the Hebrews once more", *ExT* xxxiv [1922–23], pp. 58ff.). *Cf.* the list in Spicq, *op. cit.*, i, p. 210, n. 2.
[74] *Studies in the Gospels and Epistles*, pp. 254ff.
[75] *Interpretation* v (1951), pp. 80ff.
[76] *L'Épître aux Hébreux* i, pp. 207ff.

son of Alexandria in the world-mission, and that Clement would not have mentioned him in writing to the Corinthians in whose history Apollos had played a notable part". He adds that "other attempts to discover the writer's identity have no greater interest than a parlour-game".[77]

Among those other attempts, mention should certainly be made of Harnack's, who argued that the epistle was written by Priscilla and Aquila, with Priscilla as the dominant partner.[78] Their quality as teachers is attested by the instruction which they gave to Apollos;[79] they were closely associated with Timothy;[80] they were host and hostess to a house-church in Rome[81] (if the salutations in Rom. 16:3–16 are intended for Rome); the transition back and forth between "we" and "I" would be suitable to a married couple;[82] the disappearance of the author's name from the memory of the Church could be explained by the same anti-feminist tendency as the Western text (more particularly Codex D)

---

[77] *The Epistle to the Hebrews*, pp. 171f. Especially when a name like Peter is suggested, as by A. Welch, *The Authorship of the Epistle to the Hebrews* (Edinburgh and London, 1898).

[78] *ZNW* i (1900), pp. 16ff. (*cf.* p. xxxv, n. 55). *Cf.* J. R. Harris, *Side-lights on New Testament Research* (London, 1908), pp. 148ff. (see below, p. 299, n. 92). The one place in the epistle where the requirements of Greek grammatical gender indicate the author's sex uses the masculine: in Ch. 11:32 the author says "the time will fail me telling (διηγούμενον)...". Harnack (*loc. cit.*, pp. 26f.) calls this "an indifferent phrase" (meaning, no doubt, that the masculine is purely formal); Harris (*op. cit.*, p. 175) treats it more seriously: "this masculine participle is the real rock in the track, if we want to refer the Epistle to the Hebrews (or even the eleventh chapter) to Priscilla.... And... it is only fair to say that the adverse evidence at this point to the Priscilla hypothesis is very strong: and it would not be proper to cure the text of its difficulty by a conjectural emendation unless the case were already settled by other considerations." For Harris to resist the temptation to emend the text conjecturally argues uncommon self-restraint. (*Cf.* also p. xxxv, n. 55, for article by M. A. R. Tuker.)

[79] Acts 18:26.

[80] Who, like them, was in Paul's company in Corinth and in Ephesus (Acts 18:5; 19:22; I Cor. 16:10, 19).

[81] Rom. 16:5 (similarly they accommodated a church in their house at Ephesus during their stay there; *cf.* I Cor. 16:19).

[82] "We" much more frequently than "I" (*cf.* Harnack, *loc. cit.*, p. 24). One may recall Sidney and Beatrice Webb; when they said "Our thought is..." those who knew them realized that it was Beatrice's thought that was being expressed.

displays in toning down the relatively prominent part which Priscilla plays in Acts.[83]

A case can be made out for several of the suggested names because they have left no other writings by which we could judge whether Hebrews is written in their style or not.[84] Paul is in the opposite case; it is because we have other indubitable writings from his pen that we can say confidently with Calvin: "The manner of teaching and the style sufficiently show that Paul was not the author, and the writer himself confesses in the second chapter that he was one of the disciples of the apostles, which is wholly different from the way in which Paul spoke of himself."[85] What Paul and the author of Hebrews have in common is the basic apostolic teaching; but when we come to distinctive features we may say with certainty that the thought of the epistle is not Paul's, the language is not Paul's, and the technique of Old Testament quotation is not Paul's. In brief, "I can adduce no reason to show that Paul was its author".[86] So Calvin wisely sums up.[87]

---

[83] For the Western text of Acts 18:26 see *Acts*, NICNT, p. 380, n. 50.

[84] With the exception of Luke, to whom some part in the composition of the epistle has been ascribed since Clement of Alexandria. He has been regarded as author (not simply editor or translator) by Calvin (with Clement of Rome as an alternative), F. Delitzsch (*Commentary on the Epistle to the Hebrews* [Eng. tr., Edinburgh, 1872], ii, pp. 409ff.) and others. Stylistically Hebrews is closer to the writings of Luke than to anything else in the New Testament; but this may be because our author and Luke approximate more closely than other New Testament writers to the models of literary Hellenistic—our author even more so than Luke. "Hebrews may be more typical of the cultured speech of the educated classes than any of the other documents in the New Testament" (M. E. Thrall, *Greek Particles in the New Testament* [Leiden, 1962], p. 9). *Cf.* C. P. M. Jones, "The Epistle to the Hebrews and the Lucan Writings", in *Studies in the Gospels*, ed. D.E. Nineham (Oxford, 1955), pp. 113ff.

[85] Translated by W. B. Johnston: *Calvin's Commentaries: The Epistle... to the Hebrews and the First and Second Epistles of Peter* (Edinburgh, 1963), p. 1.

[86] *Ibid.*

[87] The latest substantial defence of Pauline authorship is by W. Leonard, *The Authorship of the Epistle to the Hebrews* (London, 1939). No weight can be attached to the argument that Hebrews is the Pauline letter referred to in II Pet. 3:15, written "to the same Hebrew Christians" (A. Saphir, *Expository Lectures on the Epistle to the Hebrews* i [London, 1874], p. 2); II Peter was not written specially to "Hebrew Christians", and the reference in II Pet. 3:15 is surely to Rom. 2:4. As for the argument that Hebrews must be Pauline because then the number of Pauline epistles is a multiple of seven (*cf.* E. W. Bullinger, *Number in Scripture* [London, 1913], p. 26, also pp. 37ff.), that is a curiosity which has no place in serious Bible study. And to say, as another expositor

xli

The author was a second-generation Christian, well versed in the study of the Septuagint, which he interpreted according to a creative exegetical principle. He had a copious vocabulary and was master of a fine rhetorical style, completely different from Paul's; we might well describe him as "a learned man, ... mighty in the scriptures".[88] He was a Hellenist who inherited the outlook of those Hellenists described in Acts 6–8; 11:19ff., the associates of Stephen and Philip, pioneers in the Gentile mission.

"But as to who actually wrote the epistle, God knows the truth of the matter." Even today we have not got far beyond Origen's confession of ignorance. "It may be some compensation for our ignorance, however, to have it brought home to us that Early Christianity was even richer in creative minds and personalities than the exiguous surviving evidence of tradition gives us to understand."[89]

(d) Date

When was it written? In the absence of any clear evidence for the identity of the recipients or the author, the date of the epistle is also uncertain. A first-century date is required by the external evidence (the near-quotation of the epistle by Clement of Rome c. A.D. 96) and by the internal evidence, according to which the author and, probably, his readers came to know the gospel from people who themselves had listened to the teaching of Jesus (Ch. 2:3). If Timothy, whose release is announced in Ch. 13:23, is (as seems likely) Paul's junior colleague of that name, a date within his active lifetime is indicated, but as we do not know when Timothy was born (he was considerably younger than Paul, and may not have been out of his teens when Paul co-opted him as a fellow-missionary in A.D. 49) or when he died, this does not help us much.

If the words in Ch. 12:4, "Ye have not yet resisted unto blood,

---

does, that "the apostolic under-current is apparent to a spiritual mind" (J. N. Darby, *Collected Writings* [London, 1867-83], xxvii, p. 615), is simply to say that the expositor feels that the apostle was the author.

[88] The description of Apollos in Acts 18:24, ERV. Whether λόγιος means "learned" (ERV, ARV mg., NEB mg.) or "eloquent" (AV, ARV, RSV, NEB) is uncertain; it may mean either, and Apollos may have been both.

[89] W. Manson, *The Epistle to the Hebrews*, p. 172. *Cf.* B. F. Westcott, *The Epistle to the Hebrews*, p. lxxix.

striving against sin",[90] are to be taken literally, they would mean that the community addressed had not yet been called upon to suffer death for the faith, whatever lesser forms of persecution it had endured. This would seem to rule out the Jerusalem church; and if the epistle was sent to Rome, it would have to be dated before the persecution of A.D. 64 (the minor persecution of Ch. 10:32ff. could be placed in Rome about A.D. 49).[91] If, however, the language of Ch. 12:4 is figurative (in the sense that "unto blood" does not imply the actual shedding of their blood)—and this seems a less natural way to take it—then the field is much more widely open. The addressees could then be Christians in Rome (or elsewhere) of the age of Domitian (A.D. 81–96), and the events of Ch. 10:32ff. might be those of A.D. 64.[92] The view tentatively adopted in this commentary is that the epistle was written before, but not long before, the outbreak of persecution in Rome in A.D. 64.

Another line of approach to its dating is to ask how it stands in relation to the destruction of the Jerusalem temple and the cessation of the cultus in A.D. 70. True, there is no overt reference to the temple; the ritual details which figure in the epistle are mostly taken from the Old Testament account of the tabernacle. Yet in principle the tabernacle and the temple were one; the ritual of the former was the ritual of the latter. And our author writes as if the ritual were still going on. "The priests go in continually into the first tabernacle, accomplishing the services; but into the second the high priest alone, once in the year, not without blood, which he offereth for himself, and for the errors of the people: the Holy Spirit this signifying, that the way into the holy place hath not yet been made manifest, while the first tabernacle is yet standing; which is a figure for the time present; according to which are offered both gifts and sacrifices that cannot, as touching the conscience, make the worshipper perfect" (Heb. 9:6–9). The recurring present tense in this passage would be more pointed if this state of affairs were still going on; but it could be explained

---

[90] See p. 357 with n. 64.

[91] See pp. 267ff. with nn. 176–183.

[92] *Cf.* T. Zahn, *INT* ii (Edinburgh, 1909), p. 347; to the contrary (and rightly) E. Riggenbach, ZK, pp. 332f.: "In Heb. 10:32–34 there is not the slightest hint of martyr deaths".

as a literary present, setting forth rather vividly the state of affairs portrayed in the Old Testament record. Again, when our author quotes Jeremiah's prophecy of the new covenant,[93] he remarks that the very mention of a new covenant implies the supersession of the old one, and adds: "But that which is becoming old and waxeth aged is nigh unto vanishing away" (Ch. 8:13). This would be specially apt in the period immediately preceding A.D. 70; on the other hand, it could be said that he is simply stating a general truth and applying it to the situation in hand with the implication that Jeremiah's prophecy in itself involved the impending dissolution of the old covenant and all that went with it.

Later, in mentioning the endless repetition of the sacrifices offered under the law, he says that they could never bring the offerers to perfection (that is, to immediate and permanent access to God)—"else would they not then have ceased to be offered?" (Ch. 10:1f.). This could mean that the Old Testament legislation made no provision for the end of the sacrificial order, but envisaged its indefinite continuation; but if in fact the sacrificial order had come to a full stop by the time our author wrote (as it did in the summer of A.D. 70),[94] the knowledge of this fact would surely have modified his wording here. In short, there are several passages which, while they do not demand a date before A.D. 70, would have special point if in fact the Jerusalem temple was still standing and the cultus still going on; while there is no passage which suggests that sanctuary and cultus were by now things of the past.

There is also the quotation in Ch. 3:7ff. of Ps. 95:7ff., with its emphasis on the forty years of probation and provocation in the wilderness. The period of forty years is not explicitly related to the contemporary situation; but here too the language would be the more pointed if in fact the fortieth year from the crucial events of A.D. 30 were approaching.[95]

(e) Canonicity

Canonicity and authorship are in principle quite distinct, but in the early Christian centuries, as a practical issue, the canonicity

---

[93] Jer. 31:31ff. (see pp. 168ff.).

[94] Josephus (*War* vi.94) records the cessation of the daily sacrifice on August 5, A.D. 70, with a solemnity which suggests that he saw in this the fulfilment of Dan. 9:27.

[95] See p. 65 with n. 57.

of New Testament books and their apostolic authorship were frequently involved the one with the other, and nowhere more so than in relation to this epistle. Augustine and Jerome, as we have seen, followed Alexandrian precedent in recognizing Hebrews as one of Paul's epistles not so much because they were convinced on internal evidence that it was by him (in point of fact they entertained private doubts on the matter), as because the ascription of apostolic authorship safeguarded its canonical status.[96]

Hebrews may be said to have first received some sort of canonical status when it was incorporated by a second-century editor (at Alexandria, in all probability) into the *corpus Paulinum*.[97] From that time forth its canonicity was not questioned in Alexandria.[98] Origen did not doubt its canonical merit, whatever reservations he might cherish about its authorship. The example of Alexandria was followed by Syria; Eusebius of Caesarea includes Hebrews among the "acknowledged" books, although he knows of the doubts about it in the west;[99] and the Syriac fathers, from Ephrem (*c.* 300–373) onwards, make it clear that its canonicity and apostolicity were undisputed in their part of the world. The Peshitta New Testament included it from the first.

It was otherwise in the west. Some histories of the New Testament Canon have not made it sufficiently plain that for a book to be known and quoted is not tantamount to its being received as canonical. This distinction is well illustrated by the history of the Epistle to the Hebrews in the west. So far as extant records go, it was known and quoted in the west some decades

---

[96] See p. xxxviii with n. 69.

[97] See p. xxxiv with n. 51. It occupied various positions in relation to the Pauline epistles. In P[46] (the oldest manuscript of the *corpus Paulinum*) and originally in Syria it comes second, after Romans. It follows II Corinthians in the Sahidic Coptic; it followed Galatians in the archetype of B. In the great uncials and at Alexandria generally it comes between Paul's letters to churches and those to individuals. In the west and later in Syria it occupied the position with which we are most familiar, after the thirteen epistles which bear Paul's name; this position reflects the long western hesitation to reckon it as a Pauline epistle. See W. H. P. Hatch, "The Position of Hebrews in the Canon of the NT", *HThR* xxix (1936), pp. 133ff.

[98] Pantaenus, Clement, Origen, Dionysius, Theognostus, Peter Martyr, Alexander and Athanasius of Alexandria all attest the unanimous tradition of their church.

[99] *Hist. Eccl.* iii.3.5 ("the fourteen letters of Paul are obvious and plain").

before it was known in the east, but the west was slow in according it canonical status. Clement of Rome knows it so well that he weaves its language into his own,[100] but there is no suggestion in his letter that Hebrews is regarded as canonical or apostolic. Hermas almost certainly knows it.[101] Valentinus appears to know it and echoes its language;[102] there are possible, though not certain, allusions to it in Justin Martyr.[103] Gaius of Rome evidently did not treat it as apostolic or canonical; neither did Irenaeus nor Hippolytus. Irenaeus's position is noteworthy in view of his Asian provenance. [104] The Muratorian Canon (c. A.D. 190) does not mention it (according to this list, Paul wrote letters to seven churches, which excludes Hebrews). Tertullian, as we have seen, thought highly of it and was disposed to accord it near-apostolic authority, although he accepted Barnabas as its author. Ultimately, however, the Alexandrian position on canonicity and authorship alike triumphed in the west, and we have seen that the epistle was included in the Canon by the Synod of Hippo (393) and by the Third (397) and Sixth (419) Synods of Carthage.

"O felix culpa!" says W. F. Howard, suggesting that we owe the presence of Hebrews in the New Testament to "the mistaken critical judgement of the ancient Church".[105] But one may wonder whether, in fact, the intrinsic merit of the epistle would not ultimately have won a place in the canon for it even had the name of Paul never been associated with it. At least, when the question was reopened at the Reformation, the uncertainty about its authorship did not affect its canonical recognition. Luther, indeed, gave

---

100 See p. xxxiv, n. 53.

101 See p. 66, n. 61; p. 260 with n. 142.

102 See p. 52, n. 86 (with reference there).

103 Justin's calling Christ ἀπόστολος (First Apology 12:9; 63:5, 10, 14; cf. Heb. 3:1) and ἀρχιερεύς (Dialogue with Trypho 116:1) might denote dependence on Hebrews, as might also His designation as ἀρχιερεύς by Ignatius (Philadelphians 9:1, "the high priest who has been entrusted with the holy of holies") and probably by Polycarp (Epistle 12:2, "the eternal high priest").

104 See p. xxxviii, n. 64. Eusebius ascribed to Irenaeus "a little book of various discourses in which he makes mention of the Epistle to the Hebrews and the so-called Wisdom of Solomon, setting alongside each other certain quotations from them" (Hist. Eccl. v.26). Marcion, who also came from Asia Minor, did not include Hebrews in his Apostolikon; quite apart from the question of authorship, the whole content of the epistle would have precluded his accepting it.

105 In The Bible in its Ancient and English Versions, ed. H. W. Robinson (Oxford, 1940), p. 68.

it what might be called deuterocanonical status, but this was not on account of its non-Pauline authorship but rather because of his personal estimate of his quality, for he reckoned that some "wood, straw or hay" might be found mingled with the "gold, silver and precious stones" which were built into its fabric.[106] Calvin, on the other hand, while he was perfectly sure that Paul was in no sense its author, set a high value on its authority. "I class it without hesitation among the apostolical[107] writings", he said; "I do not doubt that it has been through the craft of Satan that any have been led to dispute its authority. There is, indeed, no book in Holy Scripture which speaks so clearly of the priesthood of Christ, which so highly exalts the virtue and dignity of that only true sacrifice which He offered by His death, which so abundantly deals with the use of ceremonies as well as their abrogation, and, in a word, so fully explains that Christ is the end of the Law. Let us therefore not allow the Church of God or ourselves to be deprived of so great a benefit, but firmly defend the possession of it."[108]

The canonical quality of the epistle, having thus been so clearly and properly distinguished from the question of authorship, continues, as is most justly due, to be acknowledged by the Church.

(f) Hebrews and the Old Testament

Apart from the personal notes at the end the Epistle to the Hebrews is not an epistle or letter in the strict sense of the term. Its literary character is defined for us by the author himself: it is

---

[106] *Preface to Hebrews* (Weimar edition, vii, pp. 344f.). "One must not place it in all things on a level with the apostolic epistles," although it contains much good instruction which is to be received "with all honor". Indeed, in commenting on Gen. 14:18–20, he calls Heb. 7:1ff. "the most trustworthy testimony of the Holy Spirit" (Weimar edition, xlii, p. 545). In the list of books in his New Testament Luther numbers the first twenty-three, "the right certain capital books", in serial order, but separates the remaining four—Hebrews, James, Jude and Revelation—from them by a space and gives no serial number to these. Tyndale's Cologne edition does the same (and indeed this order was followed in successive editions of the English Bible until the Great Bible of 1539 reverted to the familiar order). But there is no particular reason to think that Tyndale shared Luther's deuterocanonical evaluation of Hebrews and the other three books; indeed, in *his* preface to Hebrews he retains Luther's reference to the "gold, silver and precious stones" but says nothing of "wood, straw or hay".

[107] "Apostolical" in authority rather than in authorship.

[108] Eng. tr. by W. B. Johnston (*cf.* p. xli, n. 85), p. 1.

a "word of exhortation", as he puts it in Ch. 13:22.[109] A "word of exhortation" is a form of sermon or homily, as is made plain in Acts 13:15, where the rulers of the synagogue in Pisidian Antioch invite Paul and Barnabas to speak if they have "any word of exhortation for the people". The sermon by Paul, which is summarized in the following verses, is a good example of a "word of exhortation".[110] The main difference between such a sermon and the Epistle to the Hebrews is that the former was spoken, the latter written. "It is a midrash in rhetorical Greek prose—it is a homily."[111]

A synagogue homily would be based on one or more biblical texts, drawn by preference from the lessons for the day. Professor Aileen Guilding points out that the early chapters of Hebrews appear to be based on the readings for Pentecost in the three successive years of the triennial lectionary—Gen. 14:18–15:21 (the Melchizedek story and the covenant with Abram), Ex. 19 (the arrival at Sinai) and Num. 18 (the account of Aaron's budding rod)[112]—and on Ps. 110, which was reached at Pentecost in the third year of the triennial reciting of the Psalter.[113] She further suggests that the season between Pentecost and New Year formed the background of a piece of Christian *didachē*, possibly called "The Way", and points out that the theme of the "new and living way" is prominent in Hebrews, while Pentecostal and New Year readings

---

[109] Gk. λόγος (τῆς) παρακλήσεως. See p. 413.

[110] G. Vermes classes Hebrews and the Zadokite *Admonition* in the same literary genre (*The Dead Sea Scrolls in English* [Harmondsworth, 1962], pp. 96f.).

[111] G. Zuntz, *The Text of the Epistles*, p. 286. As an outstanding reason for so describing it Professor Zuntz mentions its repeated use of *synkrisis*—"a traditional device of encomiastic Greek and Latin rhetoric: the person or object to be praised is placed beside outstanding specimens of a comparable kind and his, or its, superiority (ὑπεροχή) urged.... And so does Hebrews, in contrasting Jesus, and his Church, with angels, Moses, Melchizedek, high-priests, the synagogue, the 'heroes of faith', etc." This *a fortiori* argument is substantially that used by the rabbis under the designation *qal wā-ḥōmer* ("light and heavy"); *cf.* Chs. 1:4; 3:3; 12:4; also p. 2, n. 6; p. 29, n. 4; p. 359, n. 74.

[112] *JThS*, N.S. iii (1952), p. 53; *The Fourth Gospel and Jewish Worship* (Oxford, 1960), p. 72. If we include the readings for the following sabbaths, we have the inauguration of the "old covenant" (Ex. 24) and the ritual of the red heifer (Num. 19); *cf.* Ch. 9:19 (pp. 215f.). This whole question has also been examined by C. H. Cave, *The Influences of the Lectionary of the Synagogue on the Formation of the Epistle to the Hebrews* (unpublished M. A. thesis, University of Nottingham, 1960).

[113] *The Fourth Gospel and Jewish Worship*, p. 100.

are telescoped in Ch. 12:18ff. (the enrolment in heaven and divine judgment being New Year themes).[114]

The form in which the Old Testament is quoted throughout the epistle is regularly that of the Septuagint version. In so far as we can distinguish two Septuagint recensions, corresponding in the main to the texts exhibited by the Codices A (Alexandrinus) and B (Vaticanus), about two-thirds of the quotations in Hebrews agree with the A-text and about one-third with the B-text. The natural inference is that our author used a type of text earlier than either the A-text or the B-text as we know these from extant witnesses. Where his text deviates from both A and B, he appears to have selected his variants for interpretational purposes. These variants were sometimes borrowed from other parts of the Greek Bible or from Philo, but appear for the most part to have been introduced on his own responsibility. It has been argued on the basis of his use of certain Old Testament quotations that he was familiar with the interpretations of Philo and used some quotations in such a way as to counter these interpretations.[115]

The variations which he introduced into the Septuagint text have to some extent influenced the form in which the Septuagint is quoted by early Christian writers, and even the text of some manuscripts of the Septuagint, but in extremely few instances (not more than two) do they appear to have influenced the A-text or B-text.

From time to time, especially in details of sacrificial ritual and sanctuary installations, the epistle gives some evidence of a strictly limited use of an oral midrash on the Pentateuch.[116]

To our author the Old Testament is a divine oracle from first to last; not only passages which in their original setting are the direct utterance of God (such as Ps. 110:4, "Thou art a priest for ever ...") but others are treated as spoken by God—like the words

---

[114] Op. cit., p. 72.

[115] This has been worked out in detail by K. J. Thomas, The Use of the Septuagint in the Epistle to the Hebrews (unpublished Ph.D. thesis, University of Manchester, 1959).

[116] Cf. Chs. 7:5, on the receiving of tithes; 7:27, on the high priest's daily sacrificial duties; 9:4, on the position of the incense-altar and contents of the ark; 9:19, on the institution of the first covenant; 9:21, on the purifying of all the sanctuary vessels with blood; 12:21, on the Sinai theophany (with exposition and notes ad loc.).

of Moses in Deut. 32:43 (Heb. 1:6) and the words of psalmists concerning the messengers of God (Ps. 104:4, quoted in Heb. 1:7), addressed to a royal bridegroom (Ps. 45:6f., quoted in Heb. 1:8f.), or addressed to God (Ps. 102:25-27, quoted in Heb. 1:10-12). Ch. 3:7 introduces a quotation from Ps. 95:7-11 with the words "even as the Holy Spirit saith"—words which apply not only to the divine utterance quoted in Ps. 95:8ff., but to the psalmist's cry which precedes them: "O that you would hear his voice today!" (Ps. 95:7b). In the details of the Old Testament sanctuary the Holy Spirit signifies spiritual truths for the present time (Ch. 9:8). The psalmist's words of consecration and obedience in Ps. 40:6-8 are spoken by the Messiah "when he cometh into the world" (Heb. 10:5-7).[117]

The Old Testament writings are treated by our author as a *mashal*, a parable or mystery which awaits its explanation,[118] and the explanation given in the pages of the epistle takes the form of messianic typology. "We never find in our author the least trace of that allegorical exegesis which was to remain, alas, the specialty of the Alexandrian school"[119] and which is illustrated so abundantly in the works of Philo, a generation or so earlier than our epistle. This contrast is the more marked because of the affinities in thought and language which can otherwise be traced between our author and Philo.[120] But Philo treats the Old Testament characters and incidents as allegories setting forth eternal principles of ethics and

---

[117] *Cf.* B. F. Westcott, *The Epistle to the Hebrews*, pp. 471ff.; J. van der Ploeg, "L'exégèse de l'Ancien Testament dans l'Épître aux Hébreux", *RB* liv (1947), pp. 187ff.; R. A. Stewart, *The Old Testament Usage in Philo, Rabbinic Writings and Hebrews* (unpublished M. Litt. thesis, University of Cambridge, 1947); C. Spicq, *L'Épître aux Hébreux* i, pp. 330ff.; R. M. Grant, *The Letter and the Spirit* (London, 1957); F. C. Synge, *Hebrews and the Scriptures* (London, 1959); M. Barth, "The Old Testament in Hebrews", in *Current Issues in NT Interpretation*, ed. W. Klassen and G. F. Snyder (New York, 1962), pp. 53ff. From our author's point of view the identity of the human writer of an OT passage is a matter of minor importance; this appears, *e.g.*, from the introduction of a quotation from Ps. 8:4-6 in Heb. 2:6 with the words "someone has testified somewhere". (*Cf.* also the treatment of the narrative statement of Gen. 2:2 as a divine utterance in Heb. 4:4.)

[118] *Cf.* the *rāz-pesher* ("mystery-interpretation") pattern in biblical apocalyptic and in Qumran exegesis, also in Mark 4:11f. See F. F. Bruce, *Biblical Exegesis in the Qumran Texts* (London, 1960), pp. 7ff., 75ff.

[119] C. Spicq, *op. cit.*, p. 61.

[120] *Cf.* especially C. Spicq, *op. cit.*, pp. 39ff.; see also p. lvii, n. 135.

1

metaphysics, while our author treats them as types of Christ and the gospel, temporary foreshadowings of the fulfilment which has now taken place once for all. By Philo, for example, Melchizedek is allegorized as Reason;[121] by our author he is interpreted as a type of Christ, "made like unto the Son of God" (Ch. 7:3). There is much in common between the two writers' detailed exegetical procedures—both, for example, emphasize that Melchizedek, king of Salem, is "king of righteousness" and "king of peace"[122]—but their basic hermeneutical principles are quite distinct. The historical perspective of the Old Testament is well preserved in Hebrews because our author thinks of the age of anticipation as foreshadowing the age of fulfilment; he finds it necessary to look before and after. In Chs. 3 and 4 he distinguishes between the wilderness period, when the Israelites looked forward to a "rest" which in fact they did not fully experience when they entered Canaan under Joshua; the age of David, "so long a time afterward" (Ch. 4:7), when the same "rest" was still spoken of; and the present time, when there still remains "a sabbath rest for the people of God" (Ch. 4:9). And in Ch. 11 he shows a clear appreciation of the historical sequence of the Old Testament, as men and women of faith drew ever nearer to the time when God would fulfil the promises which they themselves greeted "from afar" (Ch. 11:13).

The framework of much of our author's argument is supplied by quotations from the Psalter. Apart from the quotations from Pss. 2, 104, 45, 102 and 110 in Ch. 1, we may think of the use made of Ps. 8:4–6 in Ch. 2, of Ps. 95:7–11 in Chs. 3 and 4, of Ps. 110:4 in Chs. 5:6ff.; 6:20ff., and of Ps. 40:6–8 in Ch. 10. First a section of the Psalter is quoted more or less verbatim, and then words and phrases from the quotation are incorporated into the following exposition, somewhat in the manner now familiar to us from the *pesher* texts at Qumran.[123] Again, more than once he starts a phase of his argument with a psalm quotation and then turns to other Old Testament passages dealing with the same theme for material to elaborate his argument.[124] Thus he elaborates his

---

[121] *Leg. Alleg.* iii.82; see p. 135, n. 14.

[122] Philo, *Leg. Alleg.* iii.79; Heb. 7:2.

[123] *Cf.* S. Kistemaker, *The Psalm Citations in the Epistle to the Hebrews* (Amsterdam, 1961).

[124] *Cf.* R. Rendall, "The Method of the Writer to the Hebrews in Using Old Testament Quotations", *EQ* xxvii (1955), pp. 214ff.

exegesis of Ps. 95:7–11 with references to the Pentateuchal narrative of the wilderness wanderings (Ch. 3:12ff.); and his exegesis of Ps. 110:4 by reference to the narrative of Melchizedek in Gen. 14 (Ch. 7:1ff.).

(g) Hebrews and the Gospel

The purpose of our author's exegesis of Old Testament scripture, as of his general argument, is to establish the finality of the gospel by contrast with all that went before it (more particularly, by contrast with the Levitical cultus), as the way of perfection, the way which alone leads men to God without any barrier or interruption of access. He establishes the finality of Christianity by establishing the supremacy of Christ, in His person and in His work.[125]

As regards His person, Christ is greater than all the servants and spokesmen of God who have gone before—not only greater than other human servants and spokesmen (even Moses) but greater than angels. For He is the Son of God, His agent in creating and maintaining the universe, who yet became the Son of Man and submitted to humiliation and death. He is now exalted above all heavens, enthroned at God's right hand, and He lives for ever there as His people's representative.

The special aspect of the person and ministry of Christ which is emphasized in this epistle is His priesthood. This epistle, in fact, is the only New Testament document which expressly calls Him a priest, although His priesthood is implied in others.[126] One source of our author's priestly Christology is the Old Testament: if the ruler addressed in Ps. 110 is the Davidic Messiah, as was believed by Jews and Christians alike, then it is the Messiah who is acclaimed in verse 4 of that psalm as "a priest for ever after the order of Melchizedek"—the perfect priest-king.[127] But the mere

[125] *Cf.* E. Riehm, *Der Lehrbegriff des Hebräerbriefs* (Basel, 1867); E. Ménégoz, *La Théologie de l'Épître aux Hébreux* (Paris, 1894); G. Milligan, *The Theology of the Epistle to the Hebrews* (Edinburgh, 1899); H. A. A. Kennedy, *The Theology of the Epistles* (London, 1919), pp. 182ff.; R. V. G. Tasker, *The Gospel in the Epistle to the Hebrews* (London, 1950).
[126] Especially in Revelation, where the garment reaching to the feet and the golden sash around his breast (1:13) are high-priestly vestments. See p. liii, n. 128.
[127] *Cf.* A. J. B. Higgins, "Priest and Messiah", *VT* iii (1953), pp. 324ff.; O. Cullmann, *The Christology of the New Testament* (Eng. tr., London, 1959),

citation of an Old Testament text would have been pointless if in fact the character and work of Christ had not had a recognizably priestly quality. And our author stresses repeatedly Jesus' qualifications to be His people's effective high priest—not only was He personally "holy, guileless, undefiled" (Ch. 7:26) but having been "in all points tempted" as His people are, He can sympathize with them and supply the help they need in the hour of trial (Chs. 4:15f.; 2:18). This presentation of Jesus agrees with the testimony of the Gospels. In Luke 22:32 He prays for Peter, lest his faith should fail; in John 17 we hear Him pray His prayer of consecration as He offers up His life to God on His followers' behalf, and His prayer of intercession for them that they may fulfil their witness in the world as He has fulfilled His.[128] Nor is this kind of activity confined to the earthly phase; we have His assurance in Luke 12:8: "Every one who shall confess me before men, him shall the Son of Man also confess before the angels of God."[129]

All this was appreciated in the early Church. Stephen, condemned by the Sanhedrin, makes his confident appeal to the heavenly court, where he sees as his advocate "the Son of man standing on the right hand of God" (Acts 7:56).[130] To the same effect Paul challenges any one to bring a charge against God's elect, since "it is Christ Jesus that died, yea rather, that was raised from the dead, who is at the right hand of God, who also maketh

---

pp. 83ff. The inference from v. 1 to v. 4 of Ps. 110 is not made explicitly (and perhaps not even implied) in the Synoptic Gospels or anywhere else in NT outside this epistle; our author may well have been the first Christian to make it.

[128] C. Spicq finds a Johannine origin for the priestly portrayal of Christ elaborated in Hebrews; cf. his article "L'origine johannique de la conception du Christ-prêtre dans l'Épître aux Hébreux", in Aux sources de la tradition chrétienne, M. Goguel FS (Paris, 1950), pp. 258ff.; in addition to the "high-priestly" prayer of John 17 he points to the seamless robe of John 19:23 as a high-priestly garment (cf. p. lii, n. 126). See Cullmann, op. cit., p. 105, for comments and further bibliography.

[129] Cf. Matt. 10:32. In the Gospels the Son of Man acts both as παράκλητος ("advocate") and as κατήγορος ("prosecutor") in the heavenly court; for the latter rôle see Luke 12:9; Matt. 10:33; Mark 8:38. See on this general subject A. J. B. Higgins, "The OT and some aspects of NT Christology", in Promise and Fulfilment, S. H. Hooke FS (Edinburgh, 1963), pp. 128ff.

[130] Cf. C. F. D. Moule, "From Defendant to Judge—and Deliverer", Studiorum Novi Testamenti Societas Bulletin iii (Oxford, 1952), pp. 40ff.

intercession for us" (Rom. 8:34).[131] And John, while he writes to his "little children" to guard against their sinning, reminds them that nevertheless, "if any man sin, we have an Advocate with the Father, Jesus Christ the righteous: and he is the propitiation for our sins ..." (I John 2:1f.). Here the reference to propitiation implies a priestly element in the advocacy and intercession of the risen Christ.[132] Our author then was not a complete innovator in presenting Christ as His people's high priest, but he elaborates the priesthood of Christ in quite a distinctive manner, and does so in order to establish that in Christ and the gospel God has spoken His final and perfect word to mankind.

Arguments of various kinds are adduced to show that the priesthood of Christ is not only superior to that of the Aaronic succession, but belongs to an entirely different order from theirs. It belongs to the new covenant foretold by Jeremiah—a new covenant marked by better promises and a better hope than the old covenant of Sinai, under which the Aaronic priests ministered. In particular, the priesthood of Christ is associated with a better sacrifice than any that went before, and is discharged in a better sanctuary than that prescribed in the Levitical cultus.

Priesthood and sacrifice are inseparable entities. The Aaronic priests offered up sacrifices repeatedly, and our author pays particular attention to the annual sin-offering presented on the nation's behalf by the high priest on the Day of Atonement. But these animal sacrifices could not meet the real need of men and women. A sin-stained conscience is a barrier to communion with God, and the cleansing of the conscience could not be effected by such sacrifices as the Levitical cultus provided. But Christ exercises His priestly ministry on the basis of a real and efficacious sacrifice—"the sacrifice of himself" (Heb. 9:26). The nature of this sacrifice our author finds expressed in the language of Ps. 40:6-8, where someone who knows the uselessness of animal sacrifices dedicates his life to God for the obedient accomplishment of His will. This language is recognized as the language of Christ

---

[131] Behind the last two clauses lies a unified exegesis of Ps. 110:1 and Isa. 53:12.

[132] T. W. Manson (*Ministry and Priesthood* [London, 1958], p. 48, n. 16) expresses the view that in this respect the writer of Hebrews was anticipated by Paul in Rom. 3:21-26, and refers to his article "$I\Lambda A\Sigma THPION$" in *JThS* xlvi (1945), pp. 1ff.

"when he cometh into the world" (Heb. 10:5). In the body which
God prepared for Him He fulfilled the will of God, and at the end
it was that consecrated body, that obedient life, that He offered
up to God in death. Such a sacrifice must necessarily be acceptable
to God, but it is not only acceptable to God in itself; it effectually
cleanses in heart and conscience those who embrace Christ as their
high priest with God. By the will of God, fulfilled in death as in
life by Christ, His people "have been sanctified by the offering
of the body of Jesus Christ once for all" (Ch. 10:10) and have
"boldness to enter into the holy place by the blood of Jesus"
(Ch. 10:19). It is His life, offered up to God, that is alternatively
spoken of as His "body" or His "blood". And it is thanks to the
efficacy of His sacrifice in the lives of His people that the new
covenant comes into being, in which God undertakes to implant
His law in their hearts (as it was implanted in the heart of Christ)
and to remember their sins no more.[133]

This efficacy of the sacrifice of Christ on behalf of others could
be readily inferred neither from Ps. 110 nor from Ps. 40. It was,
of course, already a matter of vital experience for a whole generation of believers when our author wrote; they knew (however
they expressed it) that through the Christ who died and rose again
they had been inwardly purified from the defilement of sin and

---

[133] T. F. Torrance ("Doctrinal Consensus on Holy Communion", *SJTh* xv
[1962], pp. 4ff.) distinguishes three aspects of the redemption or atonement
wrought by Christ which he relates respectively to three Hebrew verbs—*pādāh*,
the "dramatic" (*i.e.* the "Christus Victor") aspect; *kipper*, the "cultic-forensic"
aspect; *gā'al*, the "incarnational" aspect. In different Protestant traditions one
or another of these aspects is emphasized to a point where insufficient justice
is done to the rest. "A new and deeper biblical wholeness" could help to bring
them together "through a more adequate doctrine of atonement. It has long
been my conviction [he adds] that joint study of the *Epistle to the Hebrews* would
have an immense part to play in such a rapprochement" (p. 9). A few items
from the vast literature on priesthood and sacrifice with special relation to this
epistle are A. Nairne, *The Epistle of Priesthood* (Edinburgh, 1913); D. K. Burns,
"The Epistle to the Hebrews", *ExT* xlvii (1935–36), pp. 184ff.; V. Taylor, *The
Atonement in New Testament Teaching* (London, 1940), pp. 147ff.; A. M. Stibbs,
The Meaning of the Word "Blood" in Scripture (London, 1947), and *The Finished
Work of Christ* (London, 1952); G. J. C. Marchant, "Sacrifice in the Epistle to
the Hebrews", *EQ* xx (1948), pp. 196ff.; J. Denney, *The Death of Christ* (London,
1951 reissue), pp. 119ff.; L. Morris, *The Apostolic Preaching of the Cross* (London,
1955); C. F. D. Moule, *The Sacrifice of Christ* (London, 1956); S. S. Smalley,
"The Atonement in the Epistle to the Hebrews", *EQ* xxxiii (1961), pp. 34ff.

emancipated from its domination. Our author expresses this in terms of sacrifice and priesthood, but it was no new thing that he thus expressed.

He who offers up His life to God in unreserved consecration is both priest and sacrifice at once. This is true of the speaker in Ps. 40:6ff.; it is even more explicitly true of the Isaianic Servant of the Lord, whose willing self-offering "to bear the sins of many" is interpreted of the work of Christ in Heb. 9:28. The Servant is introduced as a priest, destined to "sprinkle many nations" (Isa. 52:15), and he is equally a sacrifice, yielding himself up as "an offering for sin" (Isa. 53:10). His portrayal was fulfilled in history when "the Son of man also came not to be ministered unto, but to minister, and to give his life a ransom for many" (Mark 10:45). In this spirit Jesus accepted death, and the redemptive and cleansing efficacy of His death in the lives of His followers has been a matter of plain experience for over nineteen centuries. Our author is not airily theorizing when he speaks of priesthood and sacrifice, but expressing basic realities. Such a sacrifice as Christ's needs no repetition; its "once-for-all" character involves the finality of the gospel.

It is because of his concentration on the priestly aspect of Christ's work that our author has so much to say of His death and exaltation, but so little of His resurrection.[134] The two principal moments in the great sin-offering of Old Testament times were the shedding of the victim's blood in the court of the sanctuary and the presentation of its blood inside the sanctuary. In the antitype these two moments were seen to correspond to the death of Christ on the cross and His appearance at the right hand of God. In this pattern the resurrection, as generally proclaimed in the apostolic preaching, finds no separate place.

The presence of God, the heavenly sanctuary, where Christ now ministers as His people's high priest, is naturally superior to any holy place on earth, and the priesthood which is exercised in the former is naturally superior to any priesthood which is exercised in one of the latter sanctuaries. The earthly sanctuary, where the Aaronic priests ministered, is but a material copy of "the true tabernacle, which the Lord pitched, not man" (Ch. 8:2). Here it is natural to recognize the influence of Platonic idealism in our

---

[134] *Cf.* Ch. 13:20 (p. 411). But see p. 50f. (on Ch. 2:15).

author's thought and language, mediated through Philo and Alexandrian culture in general; and such influence need not be ruled out.[135] For Plato and his followers material and sensible objects are not the ultimate realities; they are but copies of archetypes or "ideas" laid up in heaven, which can be discerned only by the intellect.[136] But the idea of the earthly sanctuary as a copy of the heavenly dwelling-place of God goes back far beyond Plato's day. To Israel's neighbors in Old Testament times this idea was commonplace; and our author finds Old Testament authority for his view of the earthly sanctuary as a copy of the heavenly in the direction given to Moses to construct the tabernacle in all respects according to the model shown him by God on Mount Sinai.[137] This view of the relation of the earthly and heavenly sanctuaries finds frequent expression in apocalyptic literature, not least in the New Testament book of Revelation.

In the heavenly and eternal sanctuary where Christ ministers, His people inevitably enjoy more direct and permanent access to God through Him than would be possible in any earthly and material shrine. But just how is this heavenly and eternal sanctuary envisaged? We must not think that because our author speaks of Jesus as having "passed through the heavens" and having "sat down at the right hand of the throne of God" he thought of the heavenly sanctuary as being, in reverse, a glorified replica of the sanctuary on earth, established in perpetuity on some higher plane.

---

[135] It is going too far, however, to say with H. von Soden that "the Philonic logology is the armory for the Christology of the Epistle" (*Der Brief an die Hebräer* [HCNT, Freiburg, 1899], p. 6). He regards our author as the epoch-making man who brought Alexandrianism into the service of Christianity. *Cf.* J. B. Carpzov, *Sacrae exercitationes in ep. ad Hebraeos ex Philone Alexandrino* (Amsterdam, 1750); E. Ménégoz, *op. cit.*, pp. 197ff.; J. Cabantous, *Philon et l'Épître aux Hébreux* (Montauban, 1895); J. Moffatt, *The Epistle to the Hebrews*, ICC (Edinburgh, 1924), pp. xxxiff.; L. O. Bristol, *The Logos Doctrine of Philo and its Influence on the Epistle to the Hebrews* (Th.D. thesis, Victoria University, 1947); C. Spicq, *L'Épître aux Hébreux*, i, pp. 39ff.; J. Héring, "Eschatologie biblique et idéalisme platonicien", in *The Background of the NT and its Eschatology*, ed. W. D. Davies and D. Daube, C. H. Dodd *FS* (Cambridge, 1956), pp. 444ff.

[136] With this is associated the Platonic theory of knowledge as remembrance (ἀνάμνησις); the soul remembers the perfect archetypes which it saw in its earlier existence in the supracelestial realm and recognizes things in this world as imperfect copies of these. *Cf.* p. 167 with nn. 33–35.

[137] Ch. 8:5 (pp. 165f. with nn. 29, 30).

He uses pictorial language indeed, but uses it to denote realities of the spiritual order, where men and women, inwardly purified from a polluting conscience, draw near to God to worship Him in spirit and in truth. This "perfection" is the inauguration of the eschatology which is soon to be consummated.[138] The sanctuary in which they worship God through Christ is the fellowship of the new covenant; it consists in the communion of saints. The house of God, over which Christ, as His Son, is Lord, comprises His people, "if we hold fast our boldness and the glorying of our hope" (Ch. 3:6). Our author in his own terms communicates the truth expressed by Paul when he speaks of Jewish and Gentile believers, made one in Christ, as having "access in one Spirit unto the Father ... builded together for a habitation of God in the Spirit" (Eph. 2:18, 22), or by Peter when he describes how those who have come to Christ "are built up a spiritual house, to be a holy priesthood, to offer up spiritual sacrifices, acceptable to God through Jesus Christ" (I Pet. 2:5). It is the same truth which John sees consummated in the Apocalypse, when he describes the appearance of the glorified Church on earth and hears a voice proclaiming that now the blessings of the new covenant are world-wide in their scope: "Behold, the tabernacle of God is with men, and he shall dwell with them, and they shall be his peoples, and God himself shall be with them, and be their God" (Rev. 21:3).

The Epistle to the Hebrews is no intruder into the New Testament, but makes its proper and indispensable contribution to the canonical literature of the Christian Church.[139]

---

[138] *Cf.* Chs. 4:9; 9:27f.; 10:25, 36ff.; 12:26f.; 13:14. See C. K. Barrett, "The Eschatology of the Epistle to the Hebrews", in *The Background of the NT and its Eschatology*, ed. W. D. Davies and D. Daube, pp. 363ff.

[139] *(Addition to* p. xxxi, *nn.* 32–34.*)* A. Ehrhardt has newly revived the view of F. Overbeck *(Zur Geschichte des Kanons:* i. *Die Tradition der alten Kirche über den Hebräerbrief* [Chemnitz, 1880], pp. 3ff.) that Hebrews "was a message of consolation from the Church at Rome to Christians in the Holy Land after the fall of Jerusalem" *The Framework of the NT Stories* [Manchester, 1964], p. 109).

SELECT BIBLIOGRAPHY

1. Editions, Commentaries and Expository Studies*

*ALFORD, H. *The Greek Testament*, Vol. IV, Part I (Cambridge, 1870), pp. 1–87 (Prolegomena), 1–273 (Text and Commentary).

ANDERSON, R. *The Hebrews Epistle* (London, 1911).

ANDREWS, H. T. "Hebrews" in *The Abingdon Bible Commentary* (New York, 1929), pp. 1295–1326.

BARCLAY, W. *The Letter to the Hebrews*. The Daily Study Bible (Edinburgh, 1955).

*BENGEL, J. A. *Gnomon of the New Testament*, Eng. tr., Vol. IV (Edinburgh, 1877), pp. 333–502.

*BLASS, F. *(Barnabas) Brief an die Hebräer: Text mit Angabe der Rhythmen* (Halle, 1903).

*BLEEK, F. *Der Brief an die Hebräer*, I–III (Berlin, 1828, 1836, 1840).

*BLEEK, F. *Der Hebräerbrief*. Abridged by K. Windrath (Elberfeld, 1868).

BONSIRVEN, J. *Épître aux Hébreux*. Verbum Salutis (Paris, 1943).

BOWMAN, J. W. *Hebrews, James, I & II Peter*. Layman's Bible Commentaries (London, 1962).

BROWN, J. *An Exposition of Hebrews* (Edinburgh, 1862; reprinted, London, 1961).

BRUCE, A. B. *The Epistle to the Hebrews: The First Apology for Christianity* (Edinburgh, 1899).

CALVIN, J. *Commentary on the Epistle to the Hebrews*, first edition, Latin (Geneva, 1549); Eng. tr. by W. B. Johnston in *The Epistle of Paul the Apostle to the Hebrews and the First and Second Epistles of St. Peter* (Edinburgh, 1963), pp. ix–xiv, 1–216.

DARBY, J. N. *Brief Analysis of the Epistle to the Hebrews*. Collected Writings (London, 1867–83), XV, pp. 308–366.

DARBY, J. N. *Notes from Lectures on the Epistle to the Hebrews*. Collected Writings XXVII, pp. 497–615.

DARBY, J. N. *Notes on the Epistle to the Hebrews*. Collected Writings XXVIII, p. 1–51.

DAVIDSON, A. B. *The Epistle to the Hebrews*. Handbooks for Bible Classes (Edinburgh, 1882).

DELITZSCH, F. *Commentary on the Epistle to the Hebrews*, Eng. tr., 2 volumes (Edinburgh, 1872).

*DODS, M. "The Epistle to the Hebrews", *EGT* iv (London, 1910), pp. 219–381.

EDWARDS, T. C. *The Epistle to the Hebrews*, ExpB (London, 1888).

GAYFORD, S. C. "The Epistle to the Hebrews" in *A New Commentary on Holy Scripture*, ed. C. Gore (London, 1928), NT, pp. 596–627.

GRANT, F. C. *The Epistle to the Hebrews*, Harper's Annotated Bible Series (New York, 1956).

---

* Those marked with an asterisk are based on the Greek text.

*GROSHEIDE, F. W. *De Brief aan de Hebreeën* in *De Brief aan de Hebreeën en de Brief van Jakobus.* Commentaar op het Nieuwe Testament (Kampen, 1955), pp. 5–322.

HALDANE, J. A. *Notes on Exposition of Hebrews* (London, 1860).

*HÉRING, J. *L'Épître aux Hébreux*, CNT (Paris & Neuchatel, 1955).

HEWITT, T. *The Epistle to the Hebrews*, TNTC (London, 1960).

HOLMES, W. H. G. *The Epistle to the Hebrews.* Indian Church Commentaries (London, 1919).

ISAACS, W. H. *The Epistle to the Hebrews* (Oxford, 1933).

KELLY, W. *The Epistle to the Hebrews* (London, 1905).

LANG, G. H. *The Epistle to the Hebrews* (London, 1951).

LINCOLN, W. *Lectures on the Epistle to the Hebrews* (London, 1873).

LINDSAY, W. *Lectures on Hebrews*, 2 volumes (Edinburgh, 1867).

LUTHER, M. *Lectures on the Epistle to the Hebrews*, delivered in 1517–18 (Weimar edition, lvii, 1939, Part 3, pp. 1–238), Eng. tr. by J. Atkinson in *Luther: Early Theological Works*, Library of Christian Classics XVI (London, 1962), pp. 19–250.

McCAUL, J. B. *The Epistle to the Hebrews: A Paraphrastic Commentary, with Illustrations from Philo, the Targums, the Mishna and Gemara*, etc. (London, 1871).

*MICHEL, O. *Der Brief an die Hebräer*, MK (Göttingen, 1949).

*MOFFATT, J. *The Epistle to the Hebrews*, ICC (Edinburgh, 1924).

MORGAN, G. C. *God's Last Word to Man* (London, 1936).

NAIRNE, A. *The Epistle of Priesthood* (Edinburgh, 1913).

NAIRNE, A. *The Alexandrine Gospel* (London, 1917).

*NAIRNE, A. *The Epistle to the Hebrews*, CGT (Cambridge, 1917).

NAIRNE, A. *The Epistle to the Hebrews*, CBSC (Cambridge, 1921).

NARBOROUGH, F. D. V. *The Epistle to the Hebrews*, Clarendon Bible (Oxford, 1930).

NEIL, W. *The Epistle to the Hebrews.* Torch Commentaries (London, 1955).

*OLSHAUSEN, H., and EBRARD, J. H. A. *Biblical Commentary on the Epistle to the Hebrews* (Eng. tr., Edinburgh, 1853).

OWEN, J. *Exposition of Hebrews*, 4 volumes (London, 1668–74). Frequently reprinted.

OWEN, J. *Hebrews: The Epistle of Warning.* Abridgement of the foregoing (Grand Rapids, 1953).

PEAKE, A. S. *The Epistle to the Hebrews*, CentB (Edinburgh, 1914).

PINK, A. W. *An Exposition of Hebrews* (Grand Rapids, 1954).

PURDY, A. C. "The Epistle to the Hebrews" in *IB* xi (New York, 1955), pp. 575–763.

*RENDALL, F. *The Epistle to the Hebrews* (London, 1883).

*RIGGENBACH, E. *Der Brief an die Hebräer*, ZK (Leipzig, 1913).

ROBINSON, T. H. *The Epistle to the Hebrews*, MNTC (London, 1933).

SAPHIR, A. *Expository Lectures on the Epistle to the Hebrews*, 2 vols. (London, 1874–75).

SCHLATTER, A. "Der Brief an die Hebräer" in *Erläuterungen zum Neuen Testament* 9 (⁵Stuttgart, 1950), pp. 220–436.

SCHNEIDER, J. *The Letter to the Hebrews* (Eng. tr., Grand Rapids, 1957).

SCOTT, E. F. "Hebrews" in *A Commentary on the Bible*, ed. A. S. Peake (Edinburgh, 1920), pp. 889–900.

SNELL, A. *New and Living Way* (London, 1959).
*SODEN, H. VON "Der Brief an die Hebräer" in *HCNT*, ed. H. J. Holtzmann (³Freiburg, 1899).
*SPICQ, C. *L'Épître aux Hébreux*, EB. 2 vols. (Paris, 1952).
STRACK, H. L., and BILLERBECK, P. *Kommentar zum Neuen Testament aus Talmud und Midrasch*, III (Munich, 1926), pp. 671–750.
STRATHMANN, H. *Der Brief an die Hebräer.* Das NT Deutsch (Göttingen, 1937).
STUART, M. *A Commentary on the Epistle to the Hebrews* (London, 1937).
THOMAS, W. H. G. *Let us go on* (London, 1923).
*VAUGHAN, C. J. *The Epistle to the Hebrews* (London, 1890).
VINE, W. E. *The Epistle to the Hebrews* (London, 1952).
*WEISS, B. *Der Brief an die Hebräer*, MK (Göttingen, 1897).
*WESTCOTT, B. F. *The Epistle to the Hebrews*² (London, 1892).
*WETTSTEIN, J. J. *Hē Kainē Diathēkē* (Amsterdam, 1752), II, pp. 383–446.
WICKHAM, E. C. *The Epistle to the Hebrews*², WC (London, 1922).
*WINDISCH, H. *Der Hebräerbrief*, HNT (Tübingen, 1931).
WUEST, K. S. *Hebrews in the Greek NT for the English Reader* (Grand Rapids, 1947).

2. OTHER WORKS

BARRETT, C. K. "The Eschatology of the Epistle to the Hebrews" in *The Background of the NT and its Eschatology* [C. H. Dodd *FS*], ed. W. D. Davies and D. Daube (Cambridge, 1956), pp. 383ff.
BEARE, F. W. "The Text of the Epistle to the Hebrews in P⁴⁶", *JBL* lxiii (1944), pp. 379ff.
BORNHÄUSER, K. *Empfänger und Verfasser des Briefes an die Hebräer* (Gütersloh, 1932).
BÜCHSEL, F. *Die Christologie des Hebräerbriefs* (Gütersloh, 1923).
BURCH, V. *The Epistle to the Hebrews: Its Sources and Message* (London, 1936).
CABANTOUS, J. *Philon et l'Épître aux Hébreux* (Montauban, 1895).
CARPZOV, J. B. *Sacrae exercitationes in S. Pauli epistolam ad Hebraeos ex Philone Alexandrino* (Amsterdam, 1750).
COPPENS, J. *Les affinités qumrâniennes de l'Épître aux Hébreux* (Bruges, Paris, Louvain, 1962).
DALE, R. W. *The Jewish Temple and the Christian Church*² (London, 1870).
DICKIE, J. "The Literary Riddle of the Epistle to the Hebrews", *Exp.* VIII.v (1913), pp. 371ff.
DU BOSE, W. P. *High Priesthood and Sacrifice* (New York, 1908).
GAYFORD, S. C. *Sacrifice and Priesthood* (London, 1924).
HARNACK, A. "Probabilia über die Adresse und den Verfasser des Hebräerbriefs", *ZNW* i (1900), pp. 16ff.
HARRIS, J. R. *Testimonies*, II (Cambridge, 1920), pp. 43ff.
HATCH, W. H. P. "The Position of Hebrews in the Canon of the NT", *HThR* xxix (1936), pp. 133ff.
HICKS, F. C. N. *The Fullness of Sacrifice* (London, 1930).
KÄSEMANN, E. *Das wandernde Gottesvolk* (Göttingen, 1938).
KENNEDY, H. A. A. *The Theology of the Epistles* (London, 1919), pp. 182ff.
KISTEMAKER, S. *The Psalm Citations in the Epistle to the Hebrews* (Amsterdam, 1961).
KÖGEL, J. *Der Sohn und die Söhne: Eine exegetische Studie zu Hebr. 2, 5–18* (Gütersloh, 1904).

Kosmala, H. *Hebräer-Essener-Christen* (Leiden, 1959).
Lidgett, J. S. *Sonship and Salvation: A Study of the Epistle to the Hebrews* (London, 1921).
Loane, M. L. *Key-Texts in the Epistle to the Hebrews* (London, 1961).
Manson, T. W. "The Problem of the Epistle to the Hebrews" (1949), reprinted in *Studies in the Gospels and Epistles* (Manchester, 1962), pp. 242ff.
Manson, W. *The Epistle to the Hebrews: An Historical and Theological Reconsideration* (London, 1951).
Maurice, F. D. *The Epistle to the Hebrews*. Warburton Lectures (London, 1846).
Ménégoz, E. *La Théologie de l'Épître aux Hébreux* (Paris, 1894).
Milligan, W. *The Ascension and Heavenly Priesthood of our Lord²* (London, 1894).
Milligan, G. *The Theology of the Epistle to the Hebrews* (Edinburgh, 1899).
Milligan, G. "The Roman Destination of the Epistle to the Hebrews", *Exp.* VI.iv (1901), pp. 437ff.
Murray, A. *The Holiest of All* (London, 1895).
Nauck, W. "Zum Aufbau des Hebräerbriefes", in *Judentum, Urchristentum, Kirche, FS* für J. Jeremias, *BZNW* xxvi (1960), pp. 199ff.
Peake, A. S. *The Heroes and Martyrs of Faith. Studies in the Eleventh Chapter of Hebrews* (London, 1910)
Purdy, A. C. "The Epistle to the Hebrews in the Light of Recent Studies in Judaism" in *Amicitiae Corolla* [J. R. Harris *FS*], ed. H. G. Wood (London, 1933), pp. 253ff.
Quell, G., and Behm, J. Article διαθήκη in *TWNT* ii (Stuttgart, 1935), pp. 105ff.
Riehm, E. *Der Lehrbegriff des Hebräerbriefs* (Basel, 1867).
Riggenbach, E. *Die ältesten lateinischen Kommentare zum Hebräerbrief.* Forschungen zur Geschichte des neutestamentlichen Kanons, ed. T. Zahn, VIII, 1 (Leipzig, 1907).
Sauer, E. *In the Arena of Faith* [Exposition of Hebrews 12] (Eng. tr., London, 1955).
Scott, E. F. *The Epistle to the Hebrews: Its Doctrine and Significance* (Edinburgh, 1922).
Synge, F. C. *Hebrews and the Scriptures* (London, 1959).
Tasker, R. V. G. *The Gospel in the Epistle to the Hebrews* (London, 1950).
Vanhoye, A. *La structure littéraire de l'Épître aux Hébreux* (Paris-Bruges, 1963).
Vos, G. "The Priesthood of Christ in the Epistle to the Hebrews", *PThR* v (1907), pp. 423ff., 579ff.
Vos, G. "Hebrews, the Epistle of the Diatheke", *PThR* xiii (1915), pp. 587ff., xiv (1916), pp. 1ff.
Vos, G. *The Teaching of the Epistle to the Hebrews* (Grand Rapids, 1956).
Weiss, B. *Der Hebräerbrief in zeitgeschichtlicher Beleuchtung* = *TU* xxxv, Heft 3 (Leipzig, 1910).
Williams, R. R. *Reading through Hebrews* (London, 1960).
Wrede, W. *Das literarische Rätsel des Hebräerbriefs* (Göttingen, 1906).
Zuntz, G. *The Text of the Epistles*. British Academy Schweich Lectures, 1946 (London, 1953).

Other relevant literature, especially articles in periodicals, will be found cited in the notes.

ANALYSIS OF THE EPISTLE TO THE HEBREWS

CHAPTER I

I. THE FINALITY OF CHRISTIANITY

Chs. 1:1–2:18

1. GOD'S FINAL REVELATION IN HIS SON

Ch. 1:1–4

1 God, having of old time spoken unto the fathers in the
prophets by divers portions and in divers manners[1],
2 hath at the end of these days spoken unto us in *his* Son[2],
whom he appointed heir of all things, through whom also
he made the worlds;
3 who being the effulgence of his glory, and the very image
of his substance, and upholding[3] all things by the word of
his power[4], when he had made purification of sins, sat
down on the right hand of the Majesty on high;
4 having become by so much better than the[5] angels, as[6] he
hath inherited a more excellent name than they.

1–2a *"God has spoken"*. This initial affirmation is basic to the
whole argument of this epistle, as indeed it is basic to Christian
faith. Had God remained silent, enshrouded in thick darkness,
the plight of mankind would have been desperate indeed; but now
He has spoken His revealing, redeeming and life-giving word, and

---

[1] Gk. πολυμερῶς καὶ πολυτρόπως, lit. "in many parts and in many ways"
(NEB "in fragmentary and varied fashion"). The alliteration with initial π is
a familiar literary figure.
[2] Gk. ἐν υἱῷ ("in [one who is] Son," "Son-wise").
[3] Gk. φέρων, "upholding" or "carrying along"; for the latter rendering *cf.*
A. H. McNeile, *ExT* xix (1907–8), p. 19. The first hand in B (*cf.* also the fourth-
century Ps.-Serapion) has the scribal error φανερῶν ("manifesting"). A
corrector deleted the superfluous letters αν, but a later reader (*c.* 13th cent.)
replaced them and added a note rebuking the corrector: "Most ignorant and
wicked man, leave the original (reading) alone; do not change it!"
[4] In place of αὐτοῦ, "his" (the reading of א A B D^b H* 6 33 etc.), P[46] and
1739 (with M =0121 and 424**) have δι᾽ αὐτοῦ or δι᾽ ἑαυτοῦ, "through himself",
which must be construed with the following clause. D* K L with the bulk of
later manuscripts and TR exhibit both readings, αὐτοῦ δι᾽ ἑαυτοῦ (hence AV,
"upholding all things by the word of his power, when he had by himself purged
our sins"). G. Zuntz (*The Text of the Epistles* [London, 1953], pp. 43ff.) submits

1

in His light we see light. Our author is not thinking of that general revelation of Himself which God has given in creation, providence and conscience—

"Lo, these are but the outskirts of his ways:
and how small a whisper do we hear of him!"[7]—

but of that special revelation which He has given in two stages: first, to the fathers through the prophets, and finally in His Son. These two stages of divine revelation correspond to the Old and New Testaments respectively. Divine revelation is thus seen to be progressive—but the progression is not from the less true to the more true, from the less worthy to the more worthy, or from the less mature to the more mature. How could it be so, when it is one and the same God who is revealed throughout? Men's conceptions of God may change, but the evolution of the idea of God is quite a different thing from the progress of divine revelation. The progression is one from promise to fulfilment,[8] as is made abundantly clear in the course of this epistle: the men of faith in Old Testament days did not in their lifetime experience the fulfilment of the divine promise in which they had trusted, "because, with us in mind, God had made a better plan, that only in company with us should they reach their perfection" (Ch. 11:40, NEB). The earlier stage of the revelation was given in a variety of ways:

that δι' ἑαυτοῦ is the original reading, αὐτοῦ being an easy corruption and αὐτοῦ δι' ἑαυτοῦ the conflation of the other two; the text would then mean: "Jesus supports the universe by the word of power; through Himself He has effected the purification of sins". A further pointer to the original absence of the genitive αὐτοῦ after τῷ ῥήματι τῆς δυνάμεως he finds in the fact that without it the participial phrase ends in the fourth paeonic foot δυνάμεως, the one metre which Aristotle (Rhetoric iii. 8) commends as a clausula in rhetorical prose, and one which is found elsewhere in this epistle (op. cit., p. 285, where he cites W. B. Sedgwick).

[5] Gk. τῶν ἀγγέλων. From the fact that τῶν is omitted by P[46] B and Clement of Rome, G. Zuntz infers that the anarthrous ἀγγέλων is the true reading (op. cit., p. 218).

[6] Gk. τοσούτῳ κρείττων ... ὅσῳ ("by so much better ... as") is an example of the rhetorical figure called synkrisis (cf. p. xlviii, n. 111). See G. Zuntz, op. cit., p. 286; he refers to F. Focke, "Synkrisis", Hermes viii (1923), pp. 327ff., especially 335ff. Cf. Chs. 3:3; 12:4, and the special uses of the a fortiori argument mentioned on p. 29, n. 4; p. 359, n. 74.

[7] Job 26:14.

[8] Cf. J. K. S. Reid, The Authority of Scripture (London, 1957), pp. 182ff.

God spoke in His mighty works of mercy and judgment, and made known through His servants the prophets the meaning and purpose of these works; they were admitted into His secret council and learned His plans in advance.[9] He spoke in storm and thunder to Moses,[10] in a still small voice to Elijah.[11] To those who would not heed the gently flowing stream of Shiloah He spoke by means of the Euphratean flood.[12] Priest and prophet, sage and singer were in their several ways His spokesmen; yet all the successive acts and varying modes of revelation in the ages before Christ came did not add up to the fulness of what God had to say. His word was not completely uttered until Christ came; but when Christ came, the word spoken in Him was indeed God's final word. In Him all the promises of God meet with the answering "Yes!" which seals their fulfilment to His people and evokes from them an answering "Amen!"[13] The story of divine revelation is a story of progression up to Christ, but there is no progression beyond Him. It is "at the end of these days" that God has spoken in Him, and by this phrase our author means much more than "recently"; it is a literal rendering of the Hebrew phrase which is used in the Old Testament to denote the epoch when the words of the prophets will be fulfilled,[14] and its use here means that the appearance of Christ "once for all at the end of the age" (Ch. 9:26, RSV) has inaugurated that time of fulfilment. God's previous spokesmen were His servants, but for the proclamation of His last word to man He has chosen His Son.

2b-3 Seven facts are stated about the Son of God which bring out His greatness and show why the revelation given in Him is the highest that God can give.

(a) God has appointed Him "heir of all things". These words

---

9 *Cf.* Jer. 23:18, 22; Amos 3:7.
10 Ex. 19:19; Deut. 5:22ff.
11 I Kings 19:12.
12 Isa. 8:6ff.
13 *Cf.* II Cor. 1:20.
14 Gk. ἐπ' ἐσχάτου τῶν ἡμερῶν τούτων, a Septuagintalism, reflecting Heb. *be'aḥarîth hayyāmîm* ("in the latter end of the days"), which according to the context may mean "hereafter", "ultimately" or "in the end-time". *Cf.* Gen. 49:1; Num. 24:14; Deut. 4:30; 31:29; Isa. 2:2; Jer. 23:20; 30:24; 48:27; 49:39; Ezek. 38:16; Dan. 10:14; Hos. 3:5; Mic. 4:1. The use of the phrase here implies an inaugurated eschatology. See pp. 221f. with nn. 160-163 (on Ch. 9:26).

no doubt echo the oracle of Ps. 2:8, addressed to one who is both the Lord's Anointed and acclaimed by God as His Son:

"Ask of me, and I will give thee the nations for thine inheritance,
And the uttermost parts of the earth for thy possession."

Our author applies the preceding words of this oracle to Christ in verse 5 below. But in his mind the inheritance of the Son of God is not limited to earth;[15] it embraces the universe, and particularly the world to come.[16] This is restated in fuller detail in Ch. 2:5-9, where Jesus, as the last Adam, has all things put under His feet.

(b) It was through Him that God "made the worlds". The Greek word here rendered "worlds" is *aiōnes*, which primarily means "ages"; but its meaning cannot be restricted to "ages" either here or in Ch. 11:3, where it reappears in a similar context.[17] The whole created universe of space and time is meant, and the affirmation that God brought this universe into being by the agency of His Son is in line with the statements of other New Testament writers that "all things were made through him; and without him was not anything made that hath been made" (John 1:3) and that "all things have been created through him, and unto him" (Col. 1:16).[18] In these and other statements to the same effect we may trace the language of a primitive Christian hymn or confession of faith in which Christ, as the Word or Wisdom of God, is acknowledged as the Father's agent in the work of creation.[19] This conception of Christ is based (i) on such Old

---

15 *Cf.* the extension of Abraham's promised inheritance in Ch. 11:9f., 14–16.

16 *Cf.* Ch. 2:5, τὴν οἰκουμένην τὴν μέλλουσαν.

17 There is ample evidence for this later use of αἰών, in singular and plural alike, to denote the world of space; *cf.* Ex. 15:18 LXX ("The Lord reigns over the world [βασιλεύων τὸν αἰῶνα] for ever and ever"); Wisdom 13:9; 14:6; 18:4, etc. The rabbis used Heb. *'ōlām*, Aram. *'ālam*, in the same sense after the beginning of the Christian era. See H. Sasse in *TWNT* i (Stuttgart, 1933), pp. 197ff., *s.v.* αἰών.

18 See E. K. Simpson and F. F. Bruce, *The Epistles to the Ephesians and to the Colossians*, NICNT (Grand Rapids, 1957), pp. 192ff. According to Philo, "the image (εἰκών) of God is the Word (λόγος) through whom the whole world was constructed" (*Special Laws* i. 81; *cf. Sacrifices of Abel and Cain*, 8; *Migration of Abraham*, 6; *Immutability of God*, 57).

19 The piling up of participial clauses embodying predications about God was characteristic of the liturgical style of the synagogue. *Cf.* E. Percy, *Probleme der Kolosser- und Epheserbriefe* (Lund, 1946), pp. 38f.

Testament passages as Prov. 8:22ff., where Divine Wisdom is personified and pictured as being the companion and assessor of the Almighty in the beginning, when He created heaven and earth,[20] and (ii) on a very early Christian identification of Christ with Divine Wisdom incarnate—an identification arising in all probability from the fact that Christ on occasion actually spoke in the rôle of Divine Wisdom.[21]

(c) He is the "effulgence" of God's glory. This statement, like the last, is involved in the identification of Christ with the Wisdom of God. In the Alexandrian Book of Wisdom, a work with which our author may well have been acquainted, Wisdom is said to be:

"... a breath of the power of God,
And a clear effluence of the glory of the Almighty;
... an effulgence from everlasting light,
And an unspotted mirror of the working of God,
And an image of His goodness" (Wisdom 7:25f., ERV).

The word "effulgence" (Gk. *apaugasma*) used both there and here denotes the radiance shining forth from the source of light;[22] and Philo similarly uses it of the Logos in relation to God.[23] But while our author's language is that of Philo and the Book of Wisdom, his meaning goes beyond theirs. For them the Logos or Wisdom is the personification of a divine attribute; for him the language is descriptive of a man who had lived and died in Palestine a few decades previously, but who nonetheless was the eternal Son and supreme revelation of God. Just as the radiance of the sun reaches this earth, so in Christ the glorious light of God shines into the hearts of men.

(d) He is the very image of the substance of God—the impress

---

[20] *Cf.* also Rev. 3:14, where the exalted Christ speaks as "the beginning of the creation of God" (another echo of Prov. 8:22).

[21] *Cf.* J. R. Harris, *The Origin of the Prologue to St. John's Gospel* (Cambridge, 1917), pp. 57ff.

[22] Both an active sense ("effulgence", "radiance") and a passive sense ("reflection") are attested for ἀπαύγασμα. The active sense is more appropriate here; in later credal language, the Son of God is "light of light" (φῶς ἐκ φωτός), the effulgent light being "of the same substance" (ὁμοούσιος) as the source of light.

[23] *The Making of the World*, 146; *Noah's Planting*, 50; *cf. Special Laws* iv. 123, where he says that what God breathed into the first man (Gen. 2:7) was "an effulgence (ἀπαύγασμα) of His blessed, thrice-blessed nature".

of His being. Just as the image and superscription on a coin exactly correspond to the device on the die, so the Son of God "bears the very stamp of his nature" (RSV).[24] The Greek word *charaktēr*, occurring here only in the New Testament, expresses this truth even more emphatically than *eikōn*, which is used elsewhere to denote Christ as the "image" of God (II Cor. 4:4; Col. 1:15).[25] Just as the glory is really in the effulgence, so the substance (Gk. *hypostasis*)[26] of God is really in Christ, who is its impress, its exact representation and embodiment.[27] What God essentially is, is made manifest in Christ. To see Christ is to see what the Father is like.

(e) He upholds all things "by the word of his power".[28] This last expression is probably an instance of the Hebraic adjectival genitive: "the word of his power" may mean "His mighty word" or "His enabling word."[29] The creative utterance which called the universe into being[30] requires as its complement that sustaining utterance by which it is maintained in being. So Paul can write to the Colossians of Christ as the One in whom all things were created and also as the One in whom "all things hold together" (Col. 1:17, RSV). He upholds the universe not like Atlas supporting a dead weight on his shoulders, but as One who carries all things forward on their appointed course.

(f) He has "made purification of sins".[31] Here we pass from

[24] Gk. χαρακτήρ (from the verb χαράσσω in the sense "engrave") is used especially of the impression or stamp on coins and seals. Philo uses it repeatedly of the image of God in man, stamped by the Logos as by the divine seal (*e.g. Noah's Planting*, 18).

[25] It is εἰκών that is rendered "image" in Wisdom 7:26, quoted above ("an image of his goodness"). See *Ephesians and Colossians*, NICNT, pp. 193f.; *cf.* also Heb. 10:1 (pp. 225ff.).

[26] Gk. ὑπόστασις occurs five times in NT (the other four being II Cor. 9:4; 11:17; Heb. 3:14; 11:1); here it has the meaning "substance" or "real essence" (in contrast to what merely appears to be). See p. 67 with n. 67; *cf.* T. B. Strong, *JThS* ii (1901), pp. 224ff.; iii (1902), pp. 22ff.

[27] *Cf.* A. E. Garvie, *ExT* xxviii (1916–17), p. 398.

[28] Gk. τῷ ῥήματι τῆς δυνάμεως. *Cf.* Zuntz, *op. cit.*, p. 45, for the view that "the powerful word" is here an expression denoting the Logos.

[29] *Cf.* R. A. Knox's translation: "all creation depends, for its support, on his enabling word".

[30] *Cf.* Heb. 11:3, "the worlds have been framed by the word of God"; there as here the Greek noun translated "word" is ῥῆμα.

[31] Gk. καθαρισμὸν τῶν ἁμαρτιῶν ποιησάμενος. The absence of a perfect participle active in Latin (except for deponent verbs) has led to the use of the

the cosmic functions of the Son of God to His personal relations with mankind, to His work as His people's high priest, which is elaborated throughout the epistle. The reference here, as appears from its fuller development later, is to the cleansing efficacy of "his one oblation of himself once offered".[32] The wisdom which created the worlds and maintains them in their due order may well beget in us a sense of wondering awe; but the grace which has provided a remedy for the defilement of sin by a life freely offered up to God on our behalf calls forth a sense of personal indebtedness which the contemplation of divine activity on the cosmic scale could never evoke. The underlying emphasis here, however, is that by making purification for sins the Son of God has accomplished something incapable of achievement by anyone else. And this accomplishment has as its proper sequel the seventh in the present series of facts which bring out the unequalled greatness of the Son of God.

(g) He "sat down on the right hand of the majesty on high". "The majesty on high" is a periphrasis for God.[33] That Jesus is enthroned at the right hand of God is one of the earliest affirmations of Christian faith; it goes back to Jesus' own application to Himself of the opening words of the divine oracle in Ps. 110: "Sit thou at my right hand".[34] That no literal location is intended was as well understood by Christians in the apostolic age as it is by us: they knew that God has no physical right hand or material throne where the ascended Christ sits beside Him; to them the language denoted the exaltation and supremacy of Christ as it does to us.

---

present participle here in the Vulgate as the equivalent of the Greek aorist participle ποιησάμενος (*purgationem peccatorum faciens*); this rendering, reflected in most translations based on the Vulgate (*e.g.* R. A. Knox, "making atonement for our sins"), has facilitated the view that during His present heavenly session Christ continues to make purification for sin. *Cf.* Ch. 10:12 (p. 239, n. 67).

[32] From the Prayer of Consecration, *Book of Common Prayer*. If we retain the reading δι' ἑαυτοῦ, "by himself" (*cf.* p. 1, n. 4), the meaning may be not only that Christ made this purification by His own act, without assistance from others, but also that He made it by means of His own person—*i.e.* that He presented Himself as the purificatory offering (which is, of course, repeatedly emphasized in this epistle). *Cf.* Zuntz, *op. cit.*, p. 44.

[33] Gk. τῆς μεγαλωσύνης ἐν ὑψηλοῖς (*cf.* Ch. 8:1 for a similar periphrasis with μεγαλωσύνη). *Cf.* the use of "The Power" (Gk. ἡ δύναμις) as a surrogate for the divine name in Mark 14:62.

[34] "From henceforth shall the Son of man be seated at the right hand of the power of God" (Luke 22:69). See p. 24 below.

Paul can express the same thought in different language by saying that Christ has "ascended far above all heavens, that he might fill all things" (Eph. 4:10), that "God highly exalted him, and gave unto him the name which is above every name" (Phil. 2:9). Ps. 110 is the key text of this epistle, and the significance of Christ's being a *seated* high priest is explicitly set forth in the following chapters, especially in Ch. 10:11ff., where He is contrasted with the Aaronic priests who remained standing because their sacrificial service never came to an end. It may also be observed that the oracle of Ps. 110 is addressed to a prince of the house of David, and it was evidently a prerogative of the house of David to be seated in the divine presence, like David himself when he "went in, and sat before Jehovah" (II Sam. 7:18).[35]

Thus the greatness of the Son of God receives sevenfold confirmation, and it appears, without being expressly emphasized, that He possesses in Himself all the qualifications to be the mediator between God and men. He is the Prophet through whom God has spoken His final word to men; He is the Priest who has accomplished a perfect work of cleansing for His people's sins; He is the King who sits enthroned in the place of chief honor alongside the Majesty on high.

4 His exaltation to the right hand of God in itself marks Him out as being superior to the angels—a superiority which is further shown by the title which He bears. His name which is more excellent than theirs may be inferred from the context to be the title "Son".[36] If He is said to have "inherited" the name of Son, this does not mean that the name was not His before His exaltation. It was clearly His in the days of His humiliation: "Son though He was, He learned obedience by the things which he suffered" (Ch. 5:8). It was His, indeed, ages before His incarnation: this is the plain implication of the statement in Ch. 1:2 that God has spoken to us "in his Son, ... through whom also he made the worlds". He inherits the title "Son", as He inherits all things (verse 2), by the Father's eternal appointment.

---

[35]   In Ezekiel's vision of the new commonwealth the Davidic prince has the privilege of sitting in the temple "as prince" (*i.e.* only as prince, not as priest) "to eat bread before Jehovah" (Ezek. 44:3).

[36]   *Cf.* v. 5. On the other hand, "the name which is above every name" in Phil. 2:9 is probably "LORD" (in the LXX sense of κύριος as equivalent of Heb. *Yahweh*).

8

The comparative adjective "better"[37] is used thirteen times[38] in Hebrews to contrast Christ and His new order with what went before Him. Here His superiority to angels is asserted, and elaborated by the following chain of Old Testament quotations, for two specific reasons—to show (i) that the final message of God, communicated by the Son, is safeguarded by even more majestic sanctions than those which attended the law, communicated by angels (Ch. 2:2f.), and (ii) that the new world over which the Son is to reign as Mediator far surpasses the old world in which various nations were assigned to angels for administration (Ch. 2:5). It may be that there was also a general reason for emphasizing the Son's superiority to angels, if the "divers and strange teachings" against which these Hebrews are warned (Ch. 13:9) included a doctrine of angel-worship such as had been introduced among the Colossian Christians;[39] but this must remain uncertain.

2. CHRIST BETTER THAN ANGELS

Ch. 1:5-14

5 For unto which of the angels said he at any time,
    Thou art my Son,
    This day have I begotten thee?[40]
and again,
    I will be to him a Father,
    And he shall be to me a Son?[41]

6 And when he again bringeth in the firstborn into the
   world he saith,
    And let all the angels of God worship him.[42]

7 And of the angels he saith,
    Who maketh his angels winds,
    And his ministers a flame of fire:[43]

---

[37] Gk. κρείττων.

[38] Cf. Chs. 6:9; 7:7, 19, 22; 8:6 (bis); 9:23; 10:34; 11:16, 35, 40; 12:24.

[39] Cf. T. W. Manson, "The Problem of the Epistle to the Hebrews", *Studies in the Gospels and Epistles* (Manchester, 1962), pp. 242ff.

[40] Ps. 2:7.

[41] II Sam. 7:14; I Chron. 17:13.

[42] Deut. 32:43 LXX.

[43] Ps. 104:4 (LXX 103:4).

9

8 but of the Son *he saith*,
> Thy throne, O God, is forever and ever;[44]
> And the sceptre of uprightness is the sceptre of
> thy kingdom.[45]

9   Thou hast loved righteousness, and hated iniquity;[46]
> Therefore God, thy God, hath anointed thee
> With the oil of gladness above thy fellows.[47]

10 And,
> Thou, Lord, in the beginning didst lay the foundation
> of the earth,
> And the heavens are the works of thy hands:

11   They shall perish; but thou continuest:
> And they all shall wax old as doth a garment;

12   And as a mantle shalt thou roll them up,[48]
> As a garment,[49] and they shall be changed:
> But thou art the same,
> And thy years shall not fail.[50]

13 But of which of the angels hath he said at any time,
> Sit thou on my right hand,
> Till I make thine enemies the footstool of thy feet?[51]

14   Are they not all ministering spirits, sent forth to do service
> for the sake of them that shall inherit salvation?

---

[44] Gk. εἰς τὸν αἰῶνα τοῦ αἰῶνος. A few authorities (B 33 t) omit τοῦ αἰῶνος.

[45] Gk. τῆς βασιλείας σου (so LXX); but P⁴⁶ ℵ B have αὐτοῦ instead of σου ("his kingdom" instead of "thy kingdom"), and this is probably the true text here, the majority reading being the result of a very natural assimilation to the LXX.

[46] Gk. ἀνομίαν, for which ℵ A 33 and a few other authorities have ἀδικίαν (a variant reading found also in some LXX authorities).

[47] Ps. 45:6f. (LXX 44:7f.).

[48] Gk. ἑλίξεις, for which ℵ* D* and the Latin Vulgate have "thou shalt change" (ἀλλάξεις). Both variants are attested for LXX, but ἀλλάξεις has the weight of authority there (*cf.* MT), whereas ἑλίξεις has it here.

[49] Gk. ὡς ἱμάτιον. These words are absent from LXX, but are well attested for the present passage (P⁴⁶ ℵ A B D* 1739); as a result of assimilation to LXX they are omitted from K L P with the majority of later manuscripts and TR; hence they do not appear in AV.

[50] Ps. 102:25–27 (LXX 101:26–28).

[51] Ps. 110:1 (LXX 109:1).

In these ten verses our author adduces seven Old Testament passages to corroborate his argument that the Son of God is superior to the angels. His use of them introduces us to his distinctive principles of biblical exegesis, which receive further copious illustration throughout the epistle. The general New Testament use of the Old Testament is a highly important and interesting study,[52] but the use of the Old Testament in the Epistle to the Hebrews, while it has its place within that more general study, exhibits a number of features of its own. Among these is the prominence given to the Psalter;[53] more than once the writer interprets a passage from the other Old Testament books by way of exegesis of a passage from the Psalms.[54] Of the seven quotations here, five are taken from the Psalter; of the other two, one is taken from the Former Prophets and one from the Torah.

5 *(a)*   The first quotation is from Ps. 2:7. The words "Thou art my Son, this day have I begotten thee" were never addressed by God to any angel. The angels may be called collectively "the sons of God",[55] but no one of them is ever called the son of God in terms like these, which single out the person addressed and give him a status apart.[56] The divine decree of Ps. 2:7b–9, which opens with these words, may, as has been suggested, "have preserved the text of a coronation liturgy used by the Davidic dynasty".[57]

---

[52] For recent work on this subject *cf.* C. H. Dodd, *According to the Scriptures* (London, 1952), and *The Old Testament in the New* (London, 1952); R. V. G. Tasker, *The Old Testament in the New Testament* (London, 1954); B. Lindars, *New Testament Apologetic* (London, 1961); M. Barth, "The Old Testament in Hebrews," in *Current Issues in NT Interpretation*, ed. W. Klassen and G. F. Snyder (New York, 1962), pp. 53ff. See Introduction, p. 1, n. 117.

[53] *Cf.* S. Kistemaker, *The Psalm Citations in the Epistle to the Hebrews* (Amsterdam, 1961).

[54] *Cf.* R. Rendall, "The Method of the Writer to the Hebrews in Using Old Testament Quotations", *EQ* xxvii (1955), pp. 214ff.

[55] *Cf.* Gen. 6:2, 4; Job 1:6; 2:1; 38:7 (in most of the places LXX calls the "sons of God" angels).

[56] Dan. 3:25 is not an exception, despite AV "the Son of God"; ARV and RSV rightly render the Aramaic phrase "a son of the gods" (*i.e.* a divine being or an angel).

[57] E. Voegelin, *Order and History*, i (Oxford, 1956), p. 306. *Cf.* A. Bentzen, *King and Messiah* (London, 1955), pp. 16ff.; S. Mowinckel, *He That Cometh* (Oxford, 1956), pp. 11, 64, *et passim*. So far as the form is concerned, we recognize here the language which was widely used in enthronement ceremonies throughout the Ancient Near East. Thus Voegelin (*op. cit.*, p. 305) quotes parallels from the Pyramid texts: "This is my son, my firstborn ... This is my

At any rate, they are cited in the psalm by the Lord's Anointed as the ground of his confidence in the face of the plottings of his enemies. But, like much else that was said with regard to the Davidic dynasty in its early days, it was believed in later days that these words would be most fully realized in the Messiah of David's line who would rise up in the time of fulfilment.[58] About the middle of the first century B.C., for example, they are quoted in the *Psalms of Solomon* with reference to the Davidic Messiah whose advent is ardently prayed for.[59] An allusion to them, too, may be found in Gabriel's annunciation to Mary about her coming child: "He shall be great, and shall be called the Son of the Most High: and the Lord God shall give unto him the throne of his father David" (Luke 1:32). More important still is the fact that the heavenly voice which greeted Jesus at His baptism hailed Him in the opening words of the decree of Ps. 2:7, "Thou art my Son" (Mark 1:11).[60] Indeed, the "Western" text of Luke 3:22 represents the heavenly voice as addressing to Jesus the fuller wording from Ps. 2:7 which is quoted here by the author of Hebrews: "Thou art my Son, this day have I begotten thee". The words were evidently in widespread use as a *testimonium* in the apostolic age, as Acts 13:33 bears witness;[61] and not only these words but the other parts of the psalm were given a messianic interpretation, as may be seen from the quotation and explanation of its first two verses in Acts 4:25ff.[62]

beloved with whom I have been satisfied" (1a-b), and "This is my beloved, my son; I have given the horizons to him, that he may be powerful over them like Harachte" (4a-b).

[58] A. R. Johnson (*Sacral Kingship in Ancient Israel* [Cardiff, 1955], pp. 118ff.) finds in the original intention of the second psalm "the thought of the eventual fulfilment of this promise [that David would be made supreme over the kings of the earth] in the person of his descendant and ideal successor upon the throne, the true Messiah of the House of David".

[59] Ps. Sol. 17:26.

[60] The following words spoken by the heavenly voice ("my beloved, in whom I am well pleased") echo the language in which the Servant of the Lord is introduced in Isa. 42:1. Jesus plainly understood that His mission as the Messiah and Divine Son of Ps. 2:7 was to be fulfilled in terms of the obedient, humble, suffering and triumphant Servant of the Lord introduced in Isa. 42:1; and His understanding was in conformity with the original intention of the Servant Songs. See pp. 158ff., 205, 223, 233f.

[61] See F. F. Bruce, *The Book of the Acts*, NICNT (Grand Rapids, 1954), pp. 275f.

[62] See *Acts*, NICNT, pp. 105f. *Cf.* the application of the "rod of iron" of Ps. 2:9 to the Messiah in Rev. 12:5; 19:15, and to the Messiah's associates in Rev. 2:27.

What did our author understand by the phrase "this day" in this quotation? In view of the emphasis laid throughout the epistle on the occasion of Christ's exaltation and enthronement, it is probable that he thought of this occasion as the day when He was vested with His royal dignity as Son of God.[63] It is certainly to this occasion that our author refers the divine acclamation of Christ as high priest in Ps. 110:4,[64] and the collocation of that acclamation with the present one in Ch. 5:5f.[65] suggests strongly that both are associated with the same occasion. The eternity of Christ's divine Sonship is not brought into question by this view; the suggestion rather is that He who was the Son of God from everlasting entered into the full exercise of all the prerogatives implied by His Sonship when, after His suffering had proved the completeness of His obedience, He was raised to the Father's right hand.

(b) The second quotation comes from II Sam. 7:14. There the prophet Nathan conveys the divine response to David's desire to build a house for the ark of God. God desires no house of cedar, but promises to establish David's house in perpetuity. Yet after David's death his son and successor will build a house for God, and his royal throne will endure for ever. "I will be his father," says God, "and he shall be my son" (II Sam. 7:14).[66]

---

[63] *Cf.* Rom. 1:4, where Paul's words "declared to be the Son of God with power ... by the resurrection from the dead" have reference to that "particular event in the history of the Son of God incarnate by which he was *instated* in a position of sovereignty and invested with power, an event which in respect of investiture with power surpassed everything that could previously be ascribed to him in his incarnate state" (J. Murray, *The Epistle to the Romans*, NICNT, i [Grand Rapids, 1959], p. 10). We might also compare the comment on Ps. 2:7 in Midrash *Tehillim* (so also Midrash *Samuel*, Ch. 19, with the readings of *Yalquṭ Shim'oni* ii. 620): "Rabbi Huna says in the name of Rabbi Acha: The sufferings are divided into three parts: one for David and the fathers, one for our own generation, and one for King Messiah, as it is written, 'He was wounded for our transgressions ...' And when the hour comes, the Holy One—blessed be He!—says to them, I must create him a new creation, as it is said, 'This day have I begotten thee'." The implication here seems to be that Ps. 2:7 refers to the time when Messiah, after suffering and death, is brought back to the realm of the living.

[64] *Cf.* v. 13 below (pp. 23f.).

[65] See pp. 94f.

[66] See also p. 57, n. 15. With this prose narrative are closely associated the poetic oracles of Pss. 89:19-37 (LXX 88:20-38) and 132:11-18 (LXX 131:11-18) as well as 2:7-9.

Although David's immediate successor, Solomon, did build a temple for the God of Jacob, the event proved that the divine promises made to David regarding his son and heir were not exhausted in Solomon.[67] The later prophets looked forward to a greater son of David in coming days in whom "the sure mercies of David" would be adequately realized. This son of David is the peaceful ruler of Mic. 5:2ff., the prince of the four names of Isa. 9:6f., the "leader and commander to the peoples" of Isa. 55:4, the one "whose right it is" of Ezek. 21:27, Zion's king of Zech. 9:9. On the eve of Christ's coming the *Psalms of Solomon* and the Qumran texts alike attest the eagerness with which the son of David was expected. In a document from Cave 4 at Qumran, provisionally entitled 4Q *Florilegium*,[68] a few biblical passages are brought together as describing the imminent restoration of David's house, including an abridged form of II Sam. 7:11-14, "The LORD declares to you that he will build you a house; and I will raise up your seed after you, and I will establish the throne of his kingdom for ever. I will be his father, and he shall be my son." This quotation is immediately followed by the comment: "He is the shoot of David, who is to arise with the Expounder of the Law ... in Zi[on in the l]ast days."[69] The "shoot[70] of David" is, of course, the "righteous Branch" to be raised up for David in Jer. 23:5; 33:15—the Davidic Messiah. The fulfilment of the ancient promise made through Nathan is clearly celebrated in Gabriel's words of annunciation to Mary (Luke 1:32f.) and in Zechariah's thanksgiving (Luke 1:68f.):

> "Blessed be the Lord, the God of Israel;
> For he hath visited and wrought redemption for his people,
> And hath raised up a horn of salvation for us
> In the house of his servant David."

The general testimony of the New Testament to the bringing near of God's salvation in "his Son, who was born of the seed of David

---

[67] *Cf. Acts*, NICNT, pp. 157ff., 273f. (on Acts 7:46f.; 13:22f.).

[68] *Cf.* J. M. Allegro, "Further Messianic References in Qumran Literature", *JBL* lxxv (1956), pp. 174ff., especially pp. 176f.; "Fragments of a Qumran Scroll of Eschatological Midrashim", *JBL* lxxvii (1958), pp. 350ff.

[69] These words are immediately followed by the quotation and messianic application of Amos 9:11a (*cf.* Acts 15:16).

[70] Heb. *ṣemaḥ*, the word translated "Branch" in Jer. 23:5; 33:15 (ARV).

according to the flesh" (Rom. 1:3), provides sufficient justification for our author's referring to Jesus the language of II Sam. 7:14.

6 *(c)* The third quotation ("And let all the angels of God worship him") is preceded by words which, especially as rendered in ARV, have been thought to refer to the second advent of Christ. If "again" is taken closely with "bringeth in", the meaning appears to be: "And when he brings the firstborn into the world a second time." For this interpretation Westcott argues strongly. But the word order is not so conclusive as he maintains.[71] The RSV and NEB have rightly reverted to the construction of AV; a slight alteration would suffice to bring ARV into line: "And when, again, he bringeth in the firstborn into the world." The adverb "again" marks this as a further quotation setting forth the preeminence of Christ.[72] The two previous quotations have marked Him out as the Son of God; this one marks Him out as One who is worshipped by angels. He is called "the firstborn" because He exists before all creation and because all creation is His heritage. The title may be traced back to Ps. 89:27, where God says of David (and in general of the Davidic king):

"I also will make him my firstborn,
The highest of the kings of the earth."[73]

The quotation "And let all the angels of God worship him" bears a general resemblance to Ps. 97:7, "Worship him, all ye gods" (more especially in the Septuagint, "Worship him, all his angels"). But it bears an even closer resemblance to words from the longer Septuagint form of Deut. 32:43, the concluding words of the Song of Moses:

---

[71] Indeed, as soon as he has said that "such a transposition of πάλιν [as is involved in the view that it simply introduces a fresh quotation] is without parallel" he adds a parenthesis calling attention to Wisdom 14:1 where just such a transposition is found (πλοῦν τις πάλιν στελλόμενος does not mean "one preparing to sail again" but, as ERV and RSV rightly render, "Again, one preparing to sail").

[72] Following upon the πάλιν of verse 5b (*cf.* Chs. 2:13; 4:5; 10:30; John 19:37; Rom. 15:10f.; I Cor. 3:20). We need not think that δέ (in ὅταν δὲ πάλιν) is strongly adversative; the theme of this quotation is the same as that of the two preceding ones, the supremacy of Christ, but it is carried farther in this quotation by being set over against the inferior rôle of angels.

[73] Quoted of Christ in Rev. 1:5; He is called the "firstborn" also in Rom. 8:29; Col. 1:15, 18 (see *Ephesians and Colossians*, NICNT, pp. 194ff., 205f.).

"Rejoice, ye heavens, along with him,
    And let the sons of God worship him;[74]
Rejoice, O ye nations, with his people,[75]
    And let all the angels of God ascribe strength to him;
For he avenges the blood of his sons, and will avenge it,
    And will recompense punishment to his adversaries;
Even to those who hate him will he recompense it,
    And the Lord will cleanse His people's land."[76]

Two questions arise with regard to the use of this quotation. Since in its original setting it is Yahweh, the God of Israel, whom all angels are to worship, why is their worship here said to be paid to the Son? And why is it paid to Him when God brings Him into the world?

There is a rabbinic tradition to the effect that when Adam (who in one sense was God's "firstborn") was created (or "introduced into the world"), God invited the angels to worship him, but at Satan's instigation they refused. According to *The Life of Adam and Eve* (13f.), "God the Lord spoke: 'Here is Adam. I have made him in our image and likeness'. And Michael went out and called all the angels, saying: 'Worship the image of God as the Lord God has commanded'. And Michael himself worshipped first."[77] Here, however, it is not the first Adam but the last who is the object of angelic homage; our author was possibly acquainted with an interpretation of the words he quotes which represented the angels as called upon to pay allegiance to the heavenly Son of Man at

---

[74] The text of Deut. 32:43 known to our author may have varied somewhat from this. But his quotation, as it stands, conforms to line 2 of this passage, except that the expression "the sons of God" has been replaced by "all the angels of God" from line 4; we can well understand that such a substitution could have been deliberate in this context.

[75] This line is quoted by Paul in Rom. 15:10 as fulfilled in the extension of the gospel of Christ to the Gentiles.

[76] A Hebrew manuscript with the longer text of Deut. 32:43 (previously known only from LXX) has been identified in the material from Qumran Cave 4; *cf*. P. W. Skehan, "A Fragment of the 'Song of Moses' (Deut. 32) from Qumran", *BASOR* 136 (December, 1954), pp. 12ff.; F. M. Cross, *The Ancient Library of Qumran and Modern Biblical Studies* (New York, 1958), pp. 135f.

[77] Allusions to this story have been traced in TB *Sanhedrin* 59b; II Enoch 31:3; *cf. Ascension of Isaiah* 11:23ff., which may be influenced by our present passage. See W. Bousset, *Hauptprobleme der Gnosis* (Göttingen, 1907) pp. 198f.; C. H. Dodd, *The Bible and the Greeks* (London, 1935), pp. 156f.; W. D. Davies, *Paul and Rabbinic Judaism* (London, 1948), p. 42.

16

more probable that he was a prince of the house of David.[84] That he should be addressed as God "has seemed too daring to many commentators who seek to evade it or explain it away".[85] The marginal alternative "Thy throne is God"[86] is quite unconvincing, and whatever may be said in support of the RSV rendering of Ps. 45:6, "Your divine throne endures for ever and ever",[87] still more can be said in support of the Septuagint rendering reproduced by our author here. Indeed, our author may well have understood "God" in the vocative twice over in this quotation; the last clause could easily be construed "Therefore, O God, thy God has anointed thee with the oil of gladness above thy fellows".[88] This is not the only place in the Old Testament where a king, especially of the Davidic line, is addressed in language which could only be described as the characteristic hyperbole of oriental court style if interpreted solely of the individual so addressed. But to Hebrew poets and prophets a prince of the house of David was the vicegerent of Israel's God; he belonged to a dynasty to which God had made special promises bound up with the accomplishment of His purpose

---

[84]   It was certainly on the ground of its attachment to the Davidic monarchy that it was included in the temple collection of the "sons of Korah". In the *Testament of Judah* 24:5f. the language of Ps. 45:6 (along with that of Isa. 11:1 and Zech. 9:9) is used with reference to the coming Messiah of Judah's tribe. The Targum on Ps. 45:2 paraphrases: "Thou, O King Messiah, art fairer than the children of men". And no doubt the application of this psalm to the Davidic Messiah underlies our author's present use of it.

[85]   J. Paterson, *The Praises of Israel* (New York, 1950), pp. 26f.

[86]   Suggested as a variant rendering in ARV and RSV, but such an expression would not "be consistent with the religion of the psalmists" (T. K. Cheyne, *The Book of Psalms* [London, 1888], p. 127).

[87]   "Your divine throne" is a free rendering of *kissekhā 'elōhīm*, construed as meaning "your throne (is like that) of God", after the analogy of Cant. 1:15; 4:1, where *'ēnayikh yōnīm* is to be construed as "your eyes (are like those) of doves". (*Cf.* A. R. Johnson, *op. cit.*, p. 27; he refers to earlier treatments of the passage by G. R. Driver in *The Psalmists*, ed. D. C. Simpson [Oxford, 1926], p. 124, and C. R. North, "The Religious Aspects of Hebrew Kingship", *ZAW* 1 [1932], pp. 29ff.) The analogy with the construction in Cant. 1:15; 4:1, is criticized by Cheyne (*op. cit.*, p. 127) as "very harsh"—"would a Hebrew reader", he asks, "have understood the phrase thus? A dove has really eyes, but God has only metaphorically a throne: would the reader have naturally thought of 'God's throne'?"

[88]   *Cf.* NEB: "Therefore, O God, thy God has set thee above thy fellows, / By anointing with the oil of exultation" (with the alternative rendering in a footnote: "Therefore God who is thy God ...").

in the world. Besides, what was only partially true of any of the historic rulers of David's line, or even of David himself, would be realized in its fulness when that son of David appeared in whom all the promises and ideals associated with that dynasty would be embodied. And now at length the Messiah had appeared. In a fuller sense than was possible for David or any of his successors in ancient days, this Messiah can be addressed not merely as God's Son (verse 5) but actually as God,[89] for He is both the Messiah of David's line and also the effulgence of God's glory and the very image of His substance.

All things created, even the angels, are subject to time and tide, change and decay, but the throne of God's Son endures for ever; His is the kingdom that is to know no end. His, too, is the only kingdom characterized by perfect righteousness. The righteousness and justice which are the foundation of God's throne[90] are equally the foundation of Messiah's throne:[91] "righteousness shall be the girdle of his waist, and faithfulness the girdle of his loins" (Isa. 11:5).[92] That is to say, the Messiah is personally devoted to those principles of equity and uprightness which it is His royal prerogative to maintain. His anointing with "the oil of gladness" refers not so much to His official inauguration as Messiah[93]—when "God anointed Jesus of Nazareth with the Holy Spirit and with power" (Acts 10:38)[94]—as to the joy with which God has blessed Him in acknowledgment of His vindication of divine justice, "the joy that was set before him" mentioned in Ch. 12:3.[95]

But who are Messiah's "fellows"—His peers or companions—whose joy is thus surpassed by His? In reference to a king of

---

[89]   Cf. "Mighty God" as a title of the coming king in Isa. 9:6. The analogy with similar compound expressions whose first element is 'Ēl makes it unlikely that 'Ēl gibbōr here is simply to be construed as "a god of a hero." See further B. B. Warfield, "The Divine Messiah in the Old Testament", Biblical and Theological Studies (Philadelphia, 1952), pp. 79ff.

[90]   Ps. 89:14 (LXX 88:15).

[91]   Messiah's throne, in fact, is God's throne (cf. the variant reading αὐτοῦ mentioned on p. 10, n. 45).

[92]   Cf. also Isa. 9:7; 32:1.

[93]   "An official anointing (89:21) is not meant here; the phrase is symbolic for 'gladdened thee with prosperity'" (Cheyne, op. cit., p. 127).

[94]   That is to say at His baptism (Mark 1:10; cf. Luke 4:18, quoting Isa. 61:1); see Acts, NICNT, pp. 226f.

[95]   Cf. the expression "the oil of joy" in Isa. 61:3; the Hebrew is the same as in Ps. 45:7 (shemen sāsōn).

David's line they might be kings of neighbouring nations, or members of his own family and court. In the present context, however, the term must have a special meaning—unless we say that our author has simply allowed the quotation to run on without attaching any particular significance to its closing words, which is improbable. The angels cannot be intended; their inferiority to the Son is so insisted on here that they could scarcely be described as His "fellows". It is most likely that the reference is to the "many sons" of Ch. 2:10, whom the firstborn Son is not ashamed to call His "brethren" (Ch. 2:11), and who are designated in Ch. 3:14 as the Messiah's *metochoi*—the same Greek word as is here translated "fellows".[96] Their joy is great, because of their companionship with Him, but His is greater still.

10–12 *(f)* The sixth quotation is taken from Ps. 102:25–27. The psalm, which begins "Hear my prayer, O Jehovah", is truly described in its superscription as "a prayer of the afflicted, when he is overwhelmed, and poureth out his complaint before Jehovah". Both he and Zion, his city, have experienced the judgment of God, but he makes confident supplication for mercy and restoration for himself and Zion, that men may assemble to give praise to God. He is oppressed by a sense of the brevity of his personal span of life, with which he contrasts the eternal being of God. In comparison with his own short life, heaven and earth are long-lived; yet heaven and earth must pass away. They had their beginning when God created them, and they will grow old and disappear one day; but the God who created them existed before they did, and He will survive their disappearance. As one man in his lifetime outlives many successive suits of clothes, so God has seen and will yet see many successive material universes, but He Himself is eternal and unchanging.

The words in which the psalmist addresses God, however, are here applied to the Son, as clearly as the words of Ps. 45:6f. were in verses 8 and 9. What justification can be pleaded for our author's applying them thus? First, as he has already said in verse 2, it was through the Son that the worlds were made. The angels were but worshipping spectators when the earth was founded,[97] but the Son was the Father's agent in the work. He

---

96 See p. 68, n. 68.
97 Job 38:7.

21

therefore can be understood as the one who is addressed in the words:

"Of old didst thou lay the foundation of the earth;
And the heavens are the work of thy hands."

Moreover, in the Septuagint text the person to whom these words are spoken is addressed explicitly as "Lord"[98] ("Thou, Lord, in the beginning didst lay the foundation of the earth"); and it is God who addresses him thus. Whereas in the Hebrew text the suppliant is the speaker from beginning to end of the psalm, in the Greek text his prayer comes to an end with verse 22;[99] and the next words read as follows:

"He answered[100] him in the way of his strength:
'Declare to me[101] the shortness of my days:
Bring me not up in the midst of my days.
Thy years are throughout all generations.
Thou, Lord, in the beginning didst lay the foundation
of the earth ...' ".

This is God's answer to the suppliant; He bids him acknowledge the shortness of God's set time (for the restoration of Jerusalem, as in verse 13) and not summon Him to act when that set time has only half expired, while He assures him that he and his servants' children will be preserved for ever.[102] But to whom (a Christian reader of the Septuagint might well ask) could God speak in words like these? And whom would God Himself address as "Lord", as the maker of earth and heaven?[103] Our author knows of one

---

[98] Gk. κύριε (omitted by ℵ* in LXX text, but restored by ℵc.a).

[99] Verse 23 in MT and LXX.

[100] LXX has treated Heb. 'innāh ("he afflicted", "he humbled") as 'ānāh ("he answered"); the difference is purely one of vocalization.

[101] LXX has treated Heb. 'ōmar 'ēlī ("I say, 'My God'") as 'emōr 'ēlai ("say to me"); again, the difference is purely one of vocalization.

[102] Cf. B. W. Bacon, "Heb. 1:10-12 and the Septuagint Rendering of Ps. 102:23", ZNW iii (1902), pp. 280ff. Bacon suggested that the Hebrew, as well as the Greek, text of this psalm formed a basis for messianic eschatology, especially its reference to the "shortness" of God's days, i.e. of the period destined to elapse before the consummation of His purpose; he found here the OT background of Mark 13:20, Matt. 24:22 and Ep. Barn. 4:3 ("as Enoch says, 'For to this end the Master has cut short the times and the days, that His Beloved should make haste and come to his inheritance'").

[103] It is unlikely that this passage is primarily responsible for our author's description of the Son in v. 2 as the one through whom God made the worlds—a

person only to whom such terms could be appropriate, and that is the Son of God.

That our author understood this quotation from Ps. 102 as an utterance of God seems plain from the way in which it is linked by the simple conjunction "and" to the preceding quotation from Ps. 45. Both quotations fall under the same rubric: "But unto[104] the Son he [God] saith". If in the preceding quotation the Son is addressed by God as "God", in this one he is addressed by God as "Lord". And we need not doubt that to our author the title "Lord" conveys the highest sense of all, "the name which is above every name". No wonder that the Son has ascribed to Him a dignity which surpasses all the names that angels bear. Nor is our author the only New Testament writer to ascribe to Christ the highest of divine names, or to apply to him Old Testament scriptures which in their primary context refer to Yahweh.[105]

13 *(g)* The seventh quotation, which clinches the argument, consists of the opening words of Ps. 110, "Yahweh's oracle unto my Lord".[106] The language of the oracle, "Sit at my right hand", has already been reflected in the wording of verse 3, where the Son of God is said to have "sat down on the right hand of the Majesty on high"; now it is expressly quoted. Like the first of these seven quotations ("Thou art my Son, this day have I begotten thee"), it refers to the king's enthronement, and carries with it the promise of victory over all his enemies. Whether Ps. 110 was composed against the background of some particular event in the history of the Hebrew monarchy,[107] such as Solomon's installation as king, or had its place in the national cult[108], the New Testament

---

description which probably owes more to Prov. 8:22ff. than to any other OT passage—but it could be taken as corroborative testimony for the identification of Wisdom in Prov. 8:22ff. with the Messiah.

[104] So AV, rendering Gk. πρός. While πρὸς τοὺς ἀγγέλους in v. 7 must be rendered "of (concerning) the angels", that is no reason for not rendering πρὸς τὸν υἱόν in v. 8 "to the Son". *Cf.* p. 149, n. 64.

[105] *Cf.* the application to Christ of Isa. 45:23 in Phil. 2:10f. (see p. 8, n. 36), and of Isa. 8:13 ("Jehovah of hosts, him shall ye sanctify") in I Pet. 3:15 ("sanctify in your hearts Christ as Lord").

[106] Heb. *ne'um yhwh la'dōnī* (ARV "Jehovah saith unto my Lord").

[107] The installation of Simon as "leader and high priest for ever" in 140 B.C. (I Macc. 14:41) is certainly not the occasion which stimulated the composition of the psalm (*cf.* p. 96, n. 35).

[108] *Cf.* A. R. Johnson, *op. cit.*, pp. 120ff.; H. Ringgren, *The Messiah in the OT* (London, 1956), pp. 13ff.

uniformly interprets it as messianic, and applies it to Jesus. When Jesus asked how the scribes of His day could say that the Messiah was David's son, whereas the opening words of Ps. 110 acclaimed Him as David's Lord, the messianic interpretation of the psalm was evidently common ground to Him and them.[109] Its general messianic interpretation forms the background to its use in the apostolic preaching: the words "Sit at my right hand", which by common consent were addressed to the Messiah, must be regarded as addressed to Jesus, the apostles claimed, since His death and resurrection had shown that He was the Messiah.[110] Indeed, Jesus Himself at His trial claimed to be the one addressed in these words when He told His judges that they would from then on see the Son of man seated at the right hand of the Almighty.[111] This claim, condemned as blasphemy by the Sanhedrin, was held by the apostles to have been vindicated by the subsequent act of God; and the heavenly session of Christ has, from the earliest days of the Church's existence, formed part of the language of Christian confession.[112] It remained for the writer to the Hebrews, however, to bring out further implications of the ascription of this psalm to Jesus, by taking along with the divine utterance of verse 1 ("Sit thou on my right hand ...") the further divine utterance of verse 4 ("Thou art a priest for ever after the order of Melchizedek").[113]

14 The most exalted angels are those whose privilege it is to "stand in the presence of God" like Gabriel (Luke 1:19),[114] but none of them has ever been invited to sit before Him, still less to sit in the place of unique honor at His right hand. Their standing

---

[109] Mark 12:35ff.

[110] *Cf.* Acts 2:33ff., with *Acts*, NICNT, pp. 72f.

[111] See p. 7, n. 34; in Mark 14:62 ("you shall see the Son of Man sitting at the right hand of The Power, and coming with the clouds of heaven") there is a combined allusion to Ps. 110:1 and Dan. 7:13. For the figure of the Son of Man see below, pp. 34ff. (on Ch. 2:6ff.).

[112] *Cf.* Acts 7:55f.; Rom. 8:34; Eph. 1:20; Col. 3:1; I Pet. 3:22; Rev. 3:21. See J. Daniélou, "La session à la droite du Père" in *The Gospels Reconsidered* (Oxford, 1960), pp. 68ff.

[113] See Chs. 5:6, 10; 6:20; 7:1ff.; 10:12f. (pp. 94ff., 105ff., 132ff., 238ff.).

[114] *Cf.* "the seven angels that stand before God" (Rev. 8:2). In Tobit 12:15 Tobias's fellow-traveller introduces himself as "Raphael, one of the seven holy angels who present the prayers of the saints and enter into the presence of the glory of the Holy One". In Daniel's vision of the Ancient of Days, however, "ten thousand times ten thousand stood before him" (Dan. 7:10).

posture betokens their promptness to execute His commands, or simply to abide His pleasure.

> "Thousands at his bidding speed
> And post o'er land and ocean without rest:
> They also serve who only stand and wait."[115]

All of them, the highest angels as well as the lowest, are but servants of God, "ministering spirits" (a phrase which echoes the language of Ps. 104:4 as quoted above in verse 7),[116] and not to be compared with the Son. More remarkable still, their service is performed for the benefit of a favored class of human beings, the heirs of salvation. That these should be the beneficiaries of angelic ministry may well be due to their close association with the Son of God, by whom they are being brought to glory (Ch. 2:10).[117] These angels are clearly different beings from the world-rulers and elemental spirits mentioned in Paul's epistles, whose influence has been broken over the lives of those who have died with Christ.[118]

The salvation here spoken of lies in the future; it is yet to be inherited, even if its blessings can already be enjoyed in anticipation. That is to say, it is that eschatological salvation which, in Paul's words, is now "nearer to us than when we first believed" (Rom. 13:11) or, in Peter's words, is "ready to be revealed in the last time" (I Pet. 1:5).[119] Our author does not need to explain

---

[115]   John Milton, *Sonnet on his Blindness.*

[116]   Gk. λειτουργικὰ πνεύματα (*cf.* v. 7, ὁ ποιῶν τοὺς ἀγγέλους αὐτοῦ πνεύματα, καὶ τοὺς λειτουργοὺς αὐτοῦ πυρὸς φλόγα). *Cf.* Philo's reference to "ministering angels" (ἄγγελοι λειτουργοί) in *Virtues,* 73. In the *Testament of Levi* 3:5 the "archangels"—or "angels of the presence (πρόσωπον) of God"—are described as "those who minister (λειτουργοῦντες) and make propitiation before the Lord for all the sins of ignorance (ἄγνοιαι) of the righteous" (*cf.* below, Chs. 5:2; 9:7). There is no good reason to suppose that the "ministering spirits" here are the vanquished enemies of Ps. 110:1 (*cf.* I Cor. 15:24ff.), as does O. Cullmann (*Christ and Time* [Eng. tr., London, 1951], p. 196; *cf.* C. D. Morrison, *The Powers that be* [London, 1960], pp. 33f.).

[117]   In the light of Ch. 11, we need not exclude from these heirs of salvation several persons in the Old Testament record who received angelic ministry (*cf.* also Ch. 13:2). The fact that angels, though higher than men in the order of creation, render service to the heirs of salvation shows how the relation between the two is reversed in the order of grace.

[118]   *Cf.* Eph. 6:12; Col. 2:8, 15, 20 (also Rom. 8:38; I Cor. 2:8).

[119]   *Cf.* Ch. 9:28, where Christ's second appearing is "unto salvation" (p. 224).

to his readers what he means by this salvation; the term and its meaning are familiar to them already. What they do need to understand is the fearful danger to which they will be exposed if they treat this salvation lightly.

The Son of God's ascendancy over angels has thus been asserted and confirmed by the testimony of Old Testament scripture. Some of the Old Testament passages adduced, and especially the first and the last (Pss. 2:7; 110:1), were already well established in the Church as messianic testimonies, and were acknowledged as having met their fulfilment in Jesus. In them Jesus was addressed by God in terms that surpassed the honors enjoyed by the mightiest of archangels, who indeed are called upon to pay Him homage in recognition of His sovereignty over them. And the authority of the gospel which the readers of this epistle had embraced was the authority of Jesus, the Son of God, supremely exalted by His Father. As God had no greater messenger than His Son, He had no further message beyond the gospel.

CHAPTER II

3. FIRST ADMONITION: THE GOSPEL AND THE LAW

Ch. 2:1-4

1 Therefore we ought to give the more earnest heed to the things that were heard, lest haply we drift away *from them.*

2 For if the word spoken through angels proved stedfast, and every transgression and disobedience received a just recompense of reward;

3 How shall we escape, if we neglect so great a salvation? which having at the first been spoken through the Lord, was confirmed unto us by them that heard;

4 God also bearing witness with them, both by signs and wonders, and by manifold powers, and by gifts of the Holy Spirit, according to his own will.

1 The main reason for which the Son's superiority to angels has been so emphasized now begins to appear. The older revelation, the law of Sinai, was communicated by angelic intermediaries, but God's final revelation was given in His Son, and therefore demands correspondingly serious attention. The truths and teachings of the gospel must not be held lightly; they are of supreme moment, they are matters of life and death, and must be cherished and obeyed at all costs. The danger of drifting away from them, and so losing them, cannot be treated too gravely. ARV "lest haply we drift away from them" contemplates Christians as in peril of being carried downstream past a fixed landing place and so failing to gain its security. AV "lest at any time we should let them slip" reflects another use of the same verb, of allowing a ring to slip off the finger and so losing it.[1] Whatever be the precise metaphorical force of the verb here, our author is warning Christian readers, who have heard and accepted the gospel, that if they yield to the temptation to abandon their profession their plight is hopeless.

---

[1] Gk. μήποτε παραρρυῶμεν. For various meanings of παραρρέω (literally "flow past") *cf.* LSJ, MM, AG.

2 The sanctions which attended the law given at Sinai were severe and inescapable. Every commandment had the appropriate penalty prescribed for its infringement, and for those who deliberately and of set policy defied or disregarded the law of God there was no reprieve—for such behavior the death sentence was fixed in advance.[2] Yet the law was not imparted by such august mediation as the gospel; the law was "the word spoken through angels".

The angelic mediation of the law is not recorded in the Old Testament. The nearest thing to it is the description of the Sinai theophany at the beginning of the Blessing of Moses (Deut. 33:2):

> "Jehovah came from Sinai,
> And rose from Seir unto them;
> He shined forth from mount Paran,
> And he came from the ten thousands of holy ones:
> At his right hand was a fiery law for them."

In the Septuagint this last clause is rendered: "At his right hand were angels with him". This associates the angels more closely with the law-giving, but does not make them mediators. Their mediatorship finds clearer expression in the intertestamental and early Christian age, and is mentioned as a matter of general knowledge in two other places in the New Testament. In Gal. 3:19 the fact that the law "was ordained through angels by the hand of a mediator" is adduced by Paul to prove its inferiority to God's unmediated promise to Abraham; and in Acts 7:53 Stephen charges the Jewish nation with having repudiated the law from earliest days, even though it was conveyed to them "as it was ordained by angels".[3] For our author the mediation of the law by angels is not bound up (as it was for Paul) with the tension between angels and their world order on the one hand and Christ and His salvation on the other. In this epistle, moreover, the law is not a principle set in opposition to the grace manifested in

---

[2] *Cf.* Num. 15:30, "But the soul that doeth aught with a high hand, ... the same blasphemeth Jehovah; and that soul shall be cut off from among his people".

[3] *Cf.* Calvin *ad* Deut. 33:2; *Acts*, NICNT, p. 163, n. 84. There are further allusions to this angelic mediation in Jubilees 1:29; *Sifre* Num. 102 (on Num. 12:5); *Mekhilta* Ex. 20:18; *Pesiqta rabbati* 21. See also Ch. 12:22 (p. 375 with n. 155).

Christ's saving work, but rather an anticipatory sketch of that saving work. Here we find a concern with the sacrificial cultus rather than with the "tradition of the elders", with the ritual law as a means of access to God rather than with the moral law as a way of life.

3 But the great salvation proclaimed in the gospel was brought to earth by no angel, but by the Son of God Himself. To treat it lightly, therefore, must expose one to sanctions even more awful than those which safeguarded the law. Here we have the first of many warnings which recur throughout the epistle, which make it plain that our author was afraid that his readers, succumbing to more or less subtle pressures, might become liable to these sanctions—if not by an overt renunciation of the gospel, then possibly by detaching themselves increasingly from its public profession until it ceased to have any influence upon their lives. Hence his urgent monition: "what escape can there be for us if we ignore a deliverance so great?" (NEB). This is the first of several places in the epistle where an inference is drawn *a fortiori* from law to gospel.[4]

The great salvation of which the gospel speaks was, to begin with, "spoken through the Lord". It had, of course, been proclaimed in advance by the prophets; but not until the coming of Christ, when promise gave place to fulfilment, could it be effectively brought near. The note of fulfilment was heard when Jesus came into Galilee after John the Baptist's imprisonment, "preaching the gospel of God, and saying, The time is fulfilled, and the kingdom of God is at hand: repent ye, and believe in the gospel" (Mark 1:14f.), and when, as in the synagogue at Nazareth, He read the words of Isa. 61:1f. which announce "good tidings to the poor" and "release to the captives", and proclaim "the acceptable year of the Lord", and followed them with the declaration: "Today hath this scripture been fulfilled in your ears" (Luke 4:18ff.).[5] Neither our author nor his readers had heard the liberating message direct from the lips of the Lord, but depended on the sure testimony of those who had listened to Him. Our author, unlike

---

⁴ See Chs. 7:21f.; 9:14; 10:28f. C. Spicq (*L'Épître aux Hébreux* [Paris, 1952], i, p. 53) adduces parallels from Philo. It is essentially the *a minori ad maius* argument which the rabbis described as *qal wā-ḥōmer* ("light and heavy"). See p. 2, n. 6; p. 359, n. 74.

⁵ *Cf.* N. B. Stonehouse, *The Witness of Luke to Christ* (London, 1951), pp. 68ff.

Paul, does not claim any direct revelation from Christ for himself or assert his independence of the apostles; in this respect he puts himself on the same level as his fellow-Christians who heard the gospel from those "who from the beginning were eyewitnesses and ministers of the word" (Luke 1:2).

4 The witness of their informants, however, was confirmed by the signs and wonders and mighty works which attended their proclamation of the message; these were tokens granted by God to attest the truth of what was proclaimed. The testimony of the New Testament writings to the regularity with which these phenomena accompanied the preaching and receiving of the gospel in the early apostolic age is impressive in its range. The "mighty works and wonders and signs"[6] which marked the ministry of Jesus (Acts 2:22) continued to mark the ministry of the apostles from Pentecost onwards (Acts 2:43). They were associated particularly with the bestowal of the Spirit, as indeed they are here: God's "distributions of the Holy Spirit"[7] to believers in His sovereign pleasure[8] formed the most conclusive demonstration and seal of the truth of the gospel. When Paul tries to recall the Galatian Christians to the simplicity of Christ, he reminds them that it was the message of faith and not the imposition of legal requirements that was confirmed among them in the beginning by God's supplying the Spirit to them and performing mighty works in their midst (Gal. 3:5). Similarly the recipients of Peter's first epistle are reminded how the gospel was first preached to them in the power of "the Holy Spirit sent forth from heaven" (I Pet. 1:12).[9] The New Testament writers (including our author at this point) would not have appealed to the evidence of these miraculous manifestations if there was any possibility that their readers would reply

---

[6] Gk. δυνάμεσι καὶ τέρασι καὶ σημείοις. The same three nouns are used in Acts 2:22 as here, in a different order (cf. Acts, NICNT, pp. 69f., 80).

[7] Gk. πνεύματος ἁγίου μερισμοῖς. The question arises whether πνεύματος ἁγίου is here subjective genitive, in which case I Cor. 12:11 would be a ready parallel ("all these worketh the one and the same Spirit, dividing to each one severally even as he will"), or objective genitive, in which case we might compare Gal. 3:5 ("He therefore that supplieth to you the Spirit, and worketh miracles [δυνάμεις] among you ..."). The latter construction is probably the more natural in the present context; the reference then is to God's distribution of spiritual gifts to His people.

[8] Gk. θέλησις, not found elsewhere in NT.

[9] Cf. also Acts 8:7ff.; 10:44ff.; 19:6; I Cor. 14:1ff.

that they had never seen or heard of such things.[10] They were matters of common knowledge and widespread Christian experience, and the reference to them here is calculated to restore the readers' faith in the gospel as God's authoritative message.

4. THE HUMILIATION AND GLORY OF THE SON OF MAN

Ch. 2:5-9

5   For not unto angels did he subject the world to come, whereof we speak.

6   But one hath somewhere testified, saying,[11]
       What[12] is man, that thou art mindful of him?
       Or the son of man, that thou visitest him?

7   Thou madest him a little lower than the angels;
       Thou crownedst him with glory and honor,
       And didst set him over the works of thy hands:[13]

---

[10] *Cf.* W. L. Knox, *The Acts of the Apostles* (Cambridge, 1948), pp. 62, 89.

[11] Ps. 8:4-6 (LXX 8:5-7).

[12] Gk. τί ἐστιν ἄνθρωπος. In P^{46} and a few less important authorities (C* P 104 917 1288 1319 1891 2127 *d* Vg^tol boh) τίς ("who?") is read in place of τί ("what?"). G. Zuntz (*The Text of the Epistles* [London, 1953], pp. 48f.) argues that τίς is the original reading here, and that it has been assimilated to LXX τί in the majority of our authorities. He would then translate: "Who is the man (ἄνθρωπος with rough breathing, by crasis for ὁ ἄνθρωπος) whom thou mindest? Truly (ἦ with circumflex accent in place of ἤ, 'or') the Son of Man, for him thou visitest." Our author, he thinks, has deliberately altered the LXX for his purpose, which is to show that God placed the coming world under the rule not of angels but of the Son of Man, the Messiah. For a little while, indeed, He made Him lower than the angels (in His suffering and death), but even so He crowned Him with glory and honor. Professor Zuntz finds that this construction, with the reading τίς, "alone permits a coherent interpretation of this passage", and points out that incidentally it "makes an end of that chapter of New Testament theology which is headed 'The anthropology of Hebrews'." See, however, the critique by R. V. G. Tasker in *NTS* i (1954-5), p. 185: "It is true that the *auctor ad Hebraeos* more than once makes deliberate changes in the text of the Septuagint, but that he should have played havoc with the parallelism of the psalmist in this way in the interests of a Son of Man Christology seems to me unlikely."

[13] This clause is missing from P^{46} and B and possibly from Tertullian's biblical text; it is omitted in a number of Peshitta codices and asterisked by the Harclean Syriac; it is marked for deletion by a corrector in D and is lacking in a very large proportion of later Greek MSS. This shorter text is probably the original; the longer text represents a natural assimilation to LXX. It is unlikely

8   Thou didst put all things in subjection under his feet.
For in that he subjected all things unto him,[14] he left
nothing that is not subject to him. But now we see not yet
all things subjected to him.

9   But we behold him who hath been made a little lower than
the angels, *even* Jesus, because of the suffering of death
crowned with glory and honor, that by the grace of God[15]
he should taste of death for every *man*.

5 A further reason for emphasizing the superiority of Christ
to the angels now appears. To angelic beings the present world
has been entrusted for administration, but not so the world to
come. The biblical evidence for the angelic government of the
world is early: it goes back to the Song of Moses in Deut. 32. The

---

that the omission of the clause has any theological significance, although G.
Zuntz (*op. cit.*, p. 172) suggests that its retention would have been in conflict
with our author's argument that "we see not yet all things subjected to him"
(v. 8b). But this consideration would have dictated even more imperiously the
omission of the following clause of the quotation.

[14] In P[46] B and a few other authorities "unto him" (αὐτῷ) is omitted,
probably rightly. *Cf.* G. Zuntz, *op. cit.*, pp. 32f.

[15] Gk. χάριτι θεοῦ. But the minuscule 1739 (followed by M = 0121 and
424**), one Vulgate codex (G) and several Peshitta codices, and many of the
Fathers (Origen, Eusebius, Theodore of Mopsuestia, Theodoret, Jerome,
Ambrose and others) attest the reading χωρὶς θεοῦ ("apart from God"), which
is so obviously *lectio ardua* as to call for consideration. It is easy to see how χωρὶς
would be changed to χάριτι here; it is difficult to see how χάριτι could ever have
been changed to χωρίς. But if χωρὶς θεοῦ is earlier than χάριτι θεοῦ, how can it
be accounted for? The best explanation is that a scribe or annotator, reading
the words of v. 8, "he left nothing that is not subject to him", remembered
Paul's remark on the same words in I Cor. 15:27b, "But when he saith, All
things are put in subjection, it is evident that he is excepted who did subject all
things unto him", and added at this place in Hebrews a marginal note to the
same effect: "[nothing, that is to say,] apart from God". The marginal note
was later written into the text of v. 9, and subsequently changed to the unexceptionable χάριτι θεοῦ. If this was what happened, it must have happened
early enough for P[46] (*c.* A.D. 200) to exhibit the reading χάριτι θεοῦ. J. A.
Bengel (*Gnomon, ad loc.*) accepts "apart from God" but construes it in its context
with ὑπὲρ παντός, "for all apart from God". G. Zuntz, *op. cit.*, p. 34, regards
χωρὶς θεοῦ as having the same meaning as δι' ἑαυτοῦ in Ch. 1:3; he agrees with
A. Harnack (*Studien zur Geschichte des NT* i [Berlin and Leipzig, 1931], p. 236)
that the change to χάριτι θεοῦ was made on dogmatic grounds. See R. V. G.
Tasker, *NTS* i (1954–5), p. 184; he follows Tischendorf in thinking χωρὶς θεοῦ
to be a correction "made in the light of I Cor. 15:27 to exclude God from the
inclusiveness implied in ὑπὲρ παντός".

Septuagint reading of Deut. 32:8 (which has claims to represent the original text) runs thus:

"When the Most High gave to the nations their inheritance,
When he separated the children of men,
He set the bounds of the peoples
According to the number of the angels of God."[16]

(The following verse goes on to say that Yahweh has nevertheless reserved Israel as His own heritage.)   This reading implies that the administration of the various nations has been parcelled out among a corresponding number of angelic powers. At a later time this implication becomes explicit: in Daniel, for example, we meet the angelic "prince of Persia" and "prince of Greece" (Dan. 10:20), while Michael is "the great prince" who champions the people of Israel (Dan. 10:21; 12:1). In a number of places some at least of these angelic governors are portrayed as hostile principalities and powers—the "world-rulers of this darkness" of Eph. 6:12.[17] In Hebrews nothing is said about their possible hostility; all that matters in the argument of this epistle is the fact that they are angels. "The world to come, which is our theme" (NEB) is the new world-order inaugurated by the enthronement of Christ at the right hand of God,[18] the world-order over which He reigns from that place of exaltation, the world of reality which replaces the preceding world of shadows.[19]   It has been *inaugurated* by Christ's enthronement, although it is not yet present in its fulness; its consummation awaits the time when Christ appears to bring His people into the final blessings of the salvation which He has procured for them;[20] but here and now "the powers of the age

---

[16]   LXX ἀγγέλων θεοῦ at the end of the verse presupposes Heb. *benē 'ēl* or *benē 'elōhīm*, lit. "sons of God", in place of MT *benē Yisrā'ēl* ("sons of Israel"). *Cf.* RSV. Since the publication of RSV a Hebrew witness to this reading has been identified among the biblical texts from Cave 4 at Qumran; see P. W. Skehan. "A Fragment of the 'Song of Moses' (Deut. 32) from Qumran", *BASOR* 136 (December, 1954), p. 12; "Qumran and the Present State of Old Testament Text Studies: The Masoretic Text", *JBL* lxxviii (1959), p. 21.

[17]   *Cf.* G. B. Caird, *Principalities and Powers* (London, 1956), pp. ix, 81, etc.

[18]   *Cf.* Ch. 1:6 (see p. 17 with n. 78). Here as there οἰκουμένη (literally "inhabited world") is used; here ἡ οἰκουμένη ἡ μέλλουσα is practically synonymous with the μέλλων αἰών of Ch. 6:5 (*cf.* p. 122 with n. 49).

[19]   *Cf.* Chs. 8:5; 10:1 (pp. 165ff., 225f.).

[20]   *Cf.* Ch. 9:28 (pp. 223f.).

to come" (Ch. 6:5), some of which have just been referred to in verse 4, are experienced by them. If then this world to come has not been entrusted to angels for its administration, to whom has it been placed in subjection? To the Son of God, whom His Father has "appointed heir of all things" (Ch. 1:2). It is not in the rôle of the Son of God that He now appears, however, but as the Son of Man, in accordance with the words which our author quotes from the eighth psalm.

6–8a The writer to the Hebrews is not careful to name the particular author of any scripture that he may quote. All the Old Testament is to him a divine oracle, the voice of the Holy Spirit; but as for the human author, the vaguest allusion will suffice: "one hath somewhere testified". With these words he introduces Psalm 8: 4–6 according to the Septuagint, with the omission of one clause.[21] The one significant difference between the Septuagint and Hebrew texts comes in the first line of Ps. 8:5; whereas the Hebrew is most naturally translated "thou hast made him but little lower than God" (ARV), the Septuagint says "thou madest him a little (*or* for a little while[22]) lower than the angels".[23]

The psalmist is overcome with wonder as he thinks of the glory and honor that God has bestowed on mankind, in making them but little lower than Himself and giving them dominion over all the lesser creation.[24] The language of the psalm is plainly based on the words of the Creator in Gen. 1:26: "Let us make man in our image, after our likeness: and let them have dominion over the fish of the sea, and over the birds of the heavens, and over

---

[21] For "somewhere" (Gk. πον) *cf.* Ch. 4:4 (p. 75, n. 22). For the omitted clause "Thou makest him to have dominion over the works of thy hands" (Ps. 8:6a) see p. 31, n. 13.

[22] Gk. βραχύ τι might have temporal force.

[23] LXX here translates Heb. *mē'elōhīm* by παρ' ἀγγέλους. The question is whether Heb. *'elōhīm* here denotes God in the usual OT sense, or is a plural in sense as well as in form, meaning "divine beings" or "angels" (as in Ps. 82:1b, "He judgeth among the gods"). Despite the rendering of Ps. 8:5 in ARV and RSV, the LXX may well be right.

[24] "At first sight", says H. Ringgren (*The Messiah in the Old Testament* [London, 1956], p. 20), "these words seem to refer to man in general or to Adam, but there is reason to believe that they were originally said about the king." The truth of the matter is, as H. L. Ellison has put it: "The real prototype of the king was Adam, God's viceregent, with his dominion over the world" (*The Centrality of the Messianic Idea for the Old Testament* [London, 1953], p. 14).

every living thing that moveth upon the earth".[25]   Our author, however, applies these words not to the first Adam but to Christ as the last Adam, the head of the new creation and ruler of the world to come.   Here is probably a tacit identification of "the son of man" in Ps. 8:4 with the "one like unto a son of man" in Dan. 7:13, who receives from the Ancient of Days "an everlasting dominion, which shall not pass away".   It is true that in the psalm "the son of man" stands in a relation of synonymous parallelism with "man" in the preceding line;[26] but then it is equally true that "one like unto a son of man"[27] in Dan. 7:13 simply means "one like a human being".   The fact remains that, ever since Jesus spoke of Himself as the Son of Man, this expression has had for Christians a connotation beyond its etymological force, and it had this connotation for the writer to the Hebrews.

The conception of Christ as the last Adam is certainly no innovation on our author's part, and it may not even be original with Paul[28]—especially if we can recognize in Phil. 2:6-11 a pre-Pauline hymn in which the faithfulness of the second man is contrasted with the fall of the first man.[29] God's man as the fulfiller of God's purpose meets us in the Old Testament;[30] he is "the man of thy right hand, ... the son of man whom thou madest strong for thyself" for whose triumph another psalmist prays to God (Ps. 80:17).   When one man fails in the accomplishment of the divine purpose (as, in some degree, all did in Old Testament times), God raises up another to take his place.   But who could take the place of Adam?   Only one who was capable of undoing the effects of Adam's fall and thus ushering in a new world order.   It is unnecessary to look for the origins of this conception in the idea of a Heavenly Man belonging, perhaps, to the Zoroastrian realm of thought.[31]   The New Testament portrayal of Christ as the last

---

[25]   Cf. Wisdom 9:2, "by thy wisdom [thou] hast formed man, to have dominion over the creatures thou hast made".

[26]   Heb. 'enōsh ... ben-'ādām.

[27]   Aram. kebar 'enāsh.

[28]   It may be implicit in the temptation narrative of Mark 1:13; cf. W. D. Davies, Paul and Rabbinic Judaism (London, 1948), pp. 42f.

[29]   Cf. E. Lohmeyer, Der Brief an die Philipper[11], MK (Göttingen, 1956), pp. 90ff.; A. M. Hunter, Paul and his Predecessors[2] (London, 1961), pp. 39ff.; R. P. Martin, An Early Christian Confession (London, 1960).

[30]   Cf. H. L. Ellison, op. cit., pp. 7ff.

[31]   Cf. discussions in J. M. Creed, "The Heavenly Man", JThS xxvi (1925),

Adam can be accounted for adequately on the basis of the Old Testament, interpreted in the light of the character and achievement of Christ. By His character and achievement He is immediately recognizable by His people as

"the Proper Man,
Whom God Himself hath bidden."[32]

The quotation from Psalm 8 is linked with what has gone before in that the clause with which the quotation ends—"Thou didst put all things in subjection under his feet"—echoes the earlier quotation from Ps. 110:1, "Till I make thine enemies the footstool of thy feet".[33] Not His enemies only, but the whole creation, will ultimately be brought into manifest subjection to Him.

It is as the true representative of humanity that Christ is viewed as fulfilling the language of the psalm, and as fulfilling therewith the declared purpose of the Creator when He brought man into being. As mankind's true representative, accordingly, He must share in the conditions inseparable from man's estate; only so could He blaze the trail of salvation for mankind and act effectively as His people's high priest in the presence of God. This means that He is not only the one in whom the sovereignty destined for man is realized, but also the one who, because of man's sin, must realize that sovereignty by way of suffering and death. Therefore He who has already been introduced as "so much better than the angels" had to be "made a little lower than the angels", as the psalmist said. Why this should be our author proceeds to show.

8b The psalmist's words, "Thou didst put all things in subjection under his feet", had reference to things on earth so far as Adam was concerned; but the dominion of Christ knows no such limitation. "For in subjecting all things to him, he left nothing

---

pp. 113ff.; C. H. Dodd, *The Bible and the Greeks* (London, 1935), pp. 145ff.; W. Manson, *Jesus the Messiah* (London, 1943), pp. 174ff.; S. Mowinckel, *He That Cometh* (Oxford, 1956), pp. 346ff.; further bibliography will be found in these publications.

[32] From T. Carlyle's translation of Luther's *Ein' feste Burg*; Luther's wording is: "der rechte Mann/Den Gott selbst hat erkoren".

[33] These two OT passages are similarly conjoined by Paul in I Cor. 15:25ff. *Cf.* Ch. 10:13 (p. 240).

that is not subject" (NEB). Our author does not add, as Paul did, "it is evident that he is excepted who did subject all things unto him" (I Cor. 15:27); but this exception is, of course, implied. (A very early copyist or reader perhaps added a marginal note here to make explicit what our author left implicit.)[34] As things are, however, the subjection of the created world to man, declared by the psalmist to be God's ordinance, is not yet fully realized, and even the Man of God's right hand does not yet command the willing allegiance of all.[35]   But the sovereignty which man has proved unable to exercise thus far is already wielded on man's behalf by the true Son of Man; His suffering and triumph constitute the pledge of His eternal kingdom.

9 For there at God's right hand He sits enthroned, and "crowned with glory and honor". Jesus, who became man; Jesus, who was made "a little lower than the angels"; Jesus, who endured death—this Jesus has been raised to the place of highest exaltation, and reigns there until all opposition to His sovereignty comes to

---

[34]   See p. 32, n. 15.

[35]   There is a minor *crux interpretum* here: when our author says that "now we see not yet all things subjected to him", does "to him" (Gk. αὐτῷ) mean "to man" or "to Christ"? The *crux* is only a minor one, because in any case Christ is in view as the representative Man. But in the first instance the reference is probably to man (so Westcott, Moffatt; *cf*. NEB: "But in fact we do not yet see all things in subjection to man"). We do not see man exercising his God-given right as lord of creation, but we do see God's Man invested with universal sovereignty. The writer confesses that it is not easy to recognize in man the being whom the psalmist describes as "crowned with glory and honor" and enjoying dominion over all the works of the Creator's hands. "Man's un-fulfilled promise, however, he sees fulfilled in Christ, and for mankind fulfilled through Christ" (A. E. Garvie, "Shadow and Substance," *ExT* xxviii [1916–17], p. 461). For the view that αὐτῷ means "to Christ" *cf*. Spicq, *ad loc.*: "Jesus is still far from having been accepted and acclaimed as king by all the universe: 'unbelieving sinners and demons are not yet subject to him' (St. Thomas). The author must here be expressing the anguish, if not the discouragement, of the despised and persecuted Christians, vainly awaiting God's kingdom on earth (II Pet. 3:4). The truth is that Christ's militant kingdom is progressive; he must put down his enemies (Ch. 1:13) before its plenary and triumphant realization." Our author recognizes that, even in exaltation and enthronement, Christ is waiting "till his enemies be made the footstool of his feet" (Ch. 10:13); this implies that while He is the rightful ruler of all, all do not yet acknowledge His sovereignty. So, while man is primarily indicated by αὐτῷ, the Son of Man cannot be totally excluded from its scope.

an end. Then indeed in the fullest degree will be seen "all things subjected to him".[36]

Moreover, it is precisely because of His humiliation, suffering and death that He has been invested with heavenly glory. This interpretation of our author's argument at this point brings it into line with Paul's "Wherefore also God highly exalted him" in Phil. 2:9. But very many commentators on Hebrews have found themselves obliged by the construction here to think of the crowning with glory and honor as something preceding the suffering of death, as a solemn preparation for it.[37] The transfiguration of Christ has been thought of as the occasion referred to;[38] it was then that "he received from God the Father honor and glory" (II Pet. 1:17), and it was immediately thereafter that He set out upon the last journey to Jerusalem.[39] "The crowning", says Alexander Nairne, "marks the victim, or the hero going gallantly to his contest, not the victorious king."[40] Yet it is difficult to fit this interpretation into the context of the general argument of this epistle, in which the glory is consistently presented as the

[36] Our author does not add, as Paul does, that then the whole creation, which "groaneth and travaileth in pain together until now", will be "delivered from the bondage of corruption into the liberty of the glory of the children of God" (Rom. 8:19ff.); this cosmic aspect of the redemptive work of Christ falls outside his theme.

[37] "The crowning with glory and honour must, on any natural rendering of the Greek, precede the death" (A. Nairne, *The Epistle of Priesthood* [Edinburgh, 1913], p. 70). *Cf.* A. B. Bruce, *The Epistle to the Hebrews* (Edinburgh, 1899), pp. 79ff. The clause ὅπως ... ὑπὲρ παντὸς γεύσηται θανάτου need not, however, be closely dependent on ἐστεφανωμένον, but rather epexegetic of διὰ τὸ πάθημα τοῦ θανάτου. See p. 39, n. 43.

[38] *Cf.* A. E. Garvie, *ExT* xxvi (1914–15), p. 549: "He had this foretaste of heaven, however, only to confirm Him in and equip Him for the purpose to surrender the glory and honour He might have claimed as His right, to put Himself in man's place, and to share with man the doom of death, which in no way was His due."

[39] *Cf.* Luke 9:31 (Moses and Elijah conversed with Jesus about His "exodus" which He was to accomplish at Jersualem), followed by v. 51: "when the days of his being received up were now reaching their fulfilment, he set his face steadfastly to go to Jerusalem". At the moment of His transfiguration He was "ripe for glory" (A. E. Garvie, *loc. cit.* in n. 38), but instead of ascending from the holy mount to heaven He came down to the plain and set out for Jerusalem.

[40] *Op. cit.*, p. 313. Nairne saw a reference to the crown of thorns.

sequel to the passion.[41] The phrase "because of the suffering of death" more naturally suggests that the crowning followed the suffering as its divinely appointed end than that the crowning took place *with a view to* the suffering of death.[42] As for the clause "that ... he should taste death for every man", it does indeed express purpose—not, however, the purpose of the crowning by itself, but rather the purpose of the whole sequence of preceding events, the humiliation, passion and glory combined.[43] Because the Son of Man suffered, because His suffering has been crowned by His exaltation, therefore His death avails for all.[44] Chrysostom's comment on Christ's tasting death for every man has been frequently quoted: "As a physician, though not needing to taste the food prepared for the sick man, yet in his care for him tastes first himself, that he may persuade the sick man with confidence to venture on the food; so, since all men were afraid of death, in persuading them to take courage against death, He tasted it also Himself though He had no need so to do."[45] But the point of our author's argument is that Christ did have need so to do, if the purpose of His incarnation was to be accomplished; Chrysostom has been over-influenced by the verb "taste".[46] Calvin's comment is more penetrating than Chrysostom's: "By saying 'for every man', he means not only that Christ might be an example to others, as Chrysostom says, when he adduces the example of a physician taking the first taste of a bitter draught, that the patient may

---

[41] *Cf.* Ch. 12:2 (pp. 353f.).

[42] *Cf.* Westcott *ad loc.* for the point that διά with the accusative in NT expresses "the *ground* and not the *object*: *because* something is, and not *in order that* something may be realized".

[43] "Thus ὅπως ... θανάτου explains and expounds the idea of διὰ τὸ πάθημα (which consists in) τοῦ θανάτου, gathering up the full object and purpose of the experience which has just been predicated of Jesus" (Moffatt, ICC, *ad loc.*). *Cf.* also the comments *ad loc.* of Westcott, Spicq and Michel.

[44] It is because Christ has been exalted as supreme over all that His death is now seen to be effective ὑπὲρ παντός. So far as the form goes, παντός might be masculine ("everyone") or neuter ("everything"); but since our author's concern is with Christ's work for humanity, and not with the cosmic implications of His work (*cf.* p. 38, n. 36), it is more probably to be taken as masculine. *Cf.* NEB: "so that ... in tasting death he should stand for us all".

[45] *Homilies on Hebrews*, iv. 12.

[46] *Cf.* Chrysostom's further refinement on the use of the verb "taste": "Moreover he rightly said '*taste* death for every man'; he did not say 'die'. For as if He were only *tasting* it [instead of swallowing the bitter draught, so to speak], when He had spent but a little time therein, He immediately arose."

consent to drink it; he means rather that Christ died for us, and that by taking on Himself what was due to us, He redeemed us from the curse of death."[47]

Whatever may be said of the textual warrant for the phrase "by the grace of God",[48] it is entirely appropriate in the context and makes for a smooth transition to the words which follow.

5. THE SON OF MAN THE SAVIOR AND HIGH PRIEST OF HIS PEOPLE

Ch. 2:10–18

10 For it became him, for whom are all things, and through whom are all things, in bringing[49] many sons unto glory, to make the author[50] of their salvation perfect through sufferings.

11 For both he that sanctifieth and they that are sanctified are all of one: for which cause he is not ashamed to call them brethren,

12 saying,
I will declare thy name unto my brethren,
In the midst of the congregation will I sing thy praise.[51]

13 And again, I will put my trust in him.[52] And again,
Behold, I and the children whom God hath given me.[53]

---

[47] *Commentary on Hebrews, ad loc.*

[48] *Cf.* p. 32, n. 15.

[49] Gk. ἀγαγόντα, to be construed as a simultaneous aorist participle, which moreover, despite its accusative case, is to be taken in sense with αὐτῷ ("him") and not with ἀρχηγόν ("author"). *Cf.* Westcott, *ad loc.*

[50] Gk. τὸν ἀρχηγὸν τῆς σωτηρίας αὐτῶν (RSV "the pioneer of their salvation"; NEB "the leader who delivers them"). *Cf.* Acts 3:15 for the similar title τὸν ... ἀρχηγὸν τῆς ζωῆς (with *Acts*, NICNT, p. 89, n. 32, and E. K. Simpson, *EQ* xviii [1946], pp. 35f., in article "The Vocabulary of the Epistle to the Hebrews").

[51] Ps. 22:22 (LXX 21:23). LXX is followed except that ἀπαγγελῶ takes the place of διηγήσομαι as the rendering of Heb. 'asapperāh, "I will declare".

[52] Isa. 8:17, last clause (LXX); *cf.* also Isa. 12:2; II Sam. 22:3 // Ps. 18:2 (LXX 17:3).

[53] Isa. 8:18a (LXX).

14 Since then the children are sharers in flesh and blood,[54] he also himself in like manner partook[55] of the same; that through death he might bring to nought him that had the power of death, that is, the devil;

15 and might deliver all them who through fear of death were all their lifetime subject to bondage.

16 For verily not to angels doth he give help,[56] but he giveth help to the seed of Abraham.

17 Wherefore it behooved him in all things to be made like unto his brethren, that he might become a merciful and faithful high priest in things pertaining to God, to make propitiation[57] for the sins of the people.

18 For in that he himself hath suffered being tempted, he is able to succor them that are tempted.

---

[54] Literally "blood and flesh" (αἵματος καὶ σαρκός); for this order cf. Eph. 6:12.

[55] Gk. μετέσχεν, whereas "are sharers in" in the previous clause renders Gk. κεκοινώνηκεν. To press a distinction in meaning between the two verbs would be highly precarious here, where our author insists that Christ partook of flesh and blood "in like manner" with "the children", so that His humanity was as genuine as theirs (cf. also v. 17: "it behooved him in all things to be made like unto his brethren"). Such significant distinction as there is between the two forms lies in the tenses: "the children are sharers in (κεκοινώνηκεν, perfect) flesh and blood" in the sense that that is their original and natural state; human beings are per se creatures of flesh and blood. Our Lord, however, existed before His incarnation; "flesh and blood" form no essential part of His eternal being; but at a fixed point in time, by His own choice, "he also himself in like manner partook (μετέσχεν, aorist) of the same" and so began to share fully the nature of those whom He willed thus to redeem.

[56] Gk. ἐπιλαμβάνεται, "takes hold". So ERV: "For verily not of angels doth he take hold, but he taketh hold of the seed of Abraham." Cf. NEB: "It is not angels, mark you, that he takes to himself, but the sons of Abraham." E. K. Simpson (Words Worth Weighing in the Greek New Testament [London, 1946], pp. 27ff.) protests against weakening the meaning of the verb here to "help" (a rendering for which Sir. 4:11 is invoked, but that, he says rightly, "can be otherwise construed"). He adduces good Hellenistic evidence for the sense "take hold". Cf. its use in Ch. 8:9 (also Matt. 14:31).

[57] Gk. εἰς τὸ ἱλάσκεσθαι. The renderings of RSV ("to make expiation for") and NEB ("to expiate") might be justified here because the direct object of the verb is "sins" (ἁμαρτίας). But if sins require to be expiated, it is because they are sins committed against someone who ought to be propitiated. The NT meaning of ἱλάσκομαι and cognate words has been studied intensively in recent years; among NT occurrences the verb is found here and in Luke 18:13 (lit.

41

10 The One "for whom are all things, and through whom are all things",[58] must here be God the Father, of whose perfecting work the Son is object. There are many who are ready to tell us confidently what would and what would not be worthy of God; but in fact the only way to discover what is a worthy thing for God to do is to consider what God has actually done. The man who says, "I could not have a high opinion of a God who would (or would not) do this or that", is not adding anything to our knowledge of God; he is simply telling us something about himself. We may be sure that all that God does is worthy of Himself, but

---

"be thou propitiated", ARV margin), the substantive ἱλαστήριον ("place or means of propitiation") in Ch. 9:5 (see p. 190) and in Rom. 3:25 (unless in the latter place it is accusative singular masculine of the adjective ἱλαστήριος), and the substantive ἱλασμός ("propitiation") in I John 2:2; 4:10. The NT use of these words follows the precedent of LXX, where (together with other cognates, especially the intensive verb ἐξιλάσκομαι) they are chiefly used as equivalents of the Piʻel conjugation of Heb. k-p-r and its derivatives. Whether the etymological force of this Piʻel conjugation is "cover completely" or "wipe out", its cultic use denotes the restoration of a relationship between God and man which has been broken by man's sin, the mediator in this work being normally the priest. That this propitiatory work is far from resembling the placating of a vengeful or capricious power is evident from the way in which OT and NT alike represent God as taking the initiative in providing the means for restoring the broken relationship between Himself and His people: cf. Lev. 17:11, "I have given it (the sacrificial blood) to you upon the altar to make atonement (le-kappēr) for your souls"; Rom. 3:25, "whom (i.e. Christ) God set forth to be a propitiation (ἱλαστήριον), through faith, in his blood". See S. R. Driver, "Propitiation", HDB iv (Edinburgh, 1902), pp. 128ff.; J. Herrmann and F. Büchsel, TWNT iv (Stuttgart, 1942), pp. 300ff. (s.v. λούω); C. H. Dodd, The Bible and the Greeks (London, 1935), pp. 82ff.; The Epistle to the Romans, MNTC (London, 1932), pp. 54f.; The Johannine Epistles, MNTC (London, 1945), pp. 25ff.; R. R. Nicole, "C. H. Dodd and the Doctrine of Propitiation", WThJ xvii (1954–5), pp. 117ff.; L. Morris, The Apostolic Doctrine of the Cross (London, 1955), pp. 125ff.; "Propitiation", NBD (London, 1962), pp. 1046f.; E. K. Simpson, Words Worth Weighing in the Greek New Testament (London, 1946), pp. 10ff. W. M. Ramsay (ExT x [1898–99], p. 158) and A. Deissmann (Bible Studies [Edinburgh, 1909], p. 224f.) quote as a parallel to the present use of ἱλάσκομαι with the direct object ἁμαρτίας the inscription of the Lycian Xanthus relating to the sanctuary which he founded for Mēn Tyrannos, where he says of a certain type of offender against this deity: "let him incur a debt of sin (ἁμαρτίαν ὀφειλέτω) against Mēn Tyrannos, which he will by no means be able to expiate (ἐξιλάσασθαι)."

[58] The preposition διά is used first with the accusative and then with the genitive, denoting God as "the final Cause and the efficient Cause of all things" (Westcott, ad loc.).

here our author singles out one of God's actions and tells us that "it became him"[59]—that it was a fitting thing for Him to do. And what was that? It was His making Jesus, through His sufferings, perfectly qualified to be the Savior of His people. It is in the passion of our Lord that we see the very heart of God laid bare; nowhere is God more fully or more worthily revealed as God than when we see Him "in Christ reconciling the world unto himself" (II Cor. 5:19).

For the great salvation which the gospel proclaims was not only "spoken through the Lord", as we have been told above, but was procured for us by Him through His passion. He is the Pathfinder, the Pioneer of our salvation; this is the meaning of the word *archēgos*, rendered "author" here in ARV and "captain" in AV.[60] He is the Savior who blazed the trail of salvation along which alone God's "many sons" could be brought to glory. Man, created by God for His glory, was prevented by sin from attaining that glory until the Son of Man came and opened up by His death a new way by which man might reach the goal for which he was made. As His people's representative and forerunner He has now entered into the presence of God to secure *their* entry there.

But what is meant by His being made "perfect" through His sufferings? If the Son of God is the effulgence of His Father's glory and the very impress of His being, how can He be thought of as falling short of perfection? The answer is this: the perfect Son of God has become His people's perfect Savior, opening up their way to God; and in order to become that, He must endure suffering and death. The pathway of perfection which His people must tread must first be trodden by the Pathfinder;[61] only so could He be their adequate representative and high priest in the presence of God. There is much in this epistle about the attain-

---

[59] Gk. ἔπρεπεν γὰρ αὐτῷ. *Cf.* Ch. 7:26, "such a high priest became(ἔπρεπεν) us". Spicq (*op. cit.*, i, p. 53) notes that the argument about what befits God is otherwise unknown in the Bible, but appears in Greek literature, and in Philo (*Leg. Alleg.* i. 48; *Age of the World*, 41, etc.) and Josephus (*Apion* ii. 168).

[60] The word ἀρχηγός appears four times in NT, the other three being in Ch. 12:2 (see pp. 351f.); Acts 3:15; 5:31. *Cf.* p. 40, n. 50.

[61] "The many sons in being brought to glory are perfected through suffering; and so it is in accord with the divine method of dealing that the pioneer of salvation should pass through the same experience" (A. E. Garvie, *ExT* xxvi [1914–15], p. 504).

ment of perfection[62] in the sense of unimpeded access to God and unbroken communion with Him, but in this as in other things it is He who leads the way.

In order to be a perfect high priest, a man must sympathize with those on whose behalf he acts, and he cannot sympathize with them unless he can enter into their experiences and share them for himself. Jesus did just this. Moreover, in order to be a perfect high priest, a man must learn the lesson of obedience to God; if he failed in this, he would really need a priest for himself, to enter into God's presence for him with the assurance of being admitted there. Of Jesus' obedience there could be no question.[63] But a high priest had one specially solemn service to perform; he had to present an atonement for men to God. And an atonement efficacious in itself could be presented only by a high priest whose sympathetic self-identification with his people was unreserved, and at the same time by a high priest whose obedience to God was unmarred by any reluctance—not to say refusal—to obey. There is only one who fulfils these conditions perfectly—the one whose obedience and death fitted Him completely to be His people's representative. He suffered not only with them but for them; His suffering was both voluntary and vicarious. He who suffered was the Son of God, and the "many" for whom He suffered are thus led to glory as sons of God in their turn.

11 "For a consecrating priest and those whom he consecrates are all of one stock" (NEB). That is a general truth, and in this supreme instance it is exemplified by the fact that He who consecrates or sanctifies is the Son of God and those who are sanctified are the sons of God.[64] It is by His sacrifice of Himself in obedience to God's will that they are sanctified, as appears more fully later in the epistle—"sanctified through the offering of the body of

---

[62] See Chs. 5:9, 14; 6:1; 7:11, 19, 28; 9:9, 11; 10:1, 14; 11:40; 12:2, 23, with exposition and notes below. *Cf.* Westcott, pp. 66ff.; Spicq, i. pp. 64f. (where Philonic parallels are adduced); P. J. du Plessis, *ΤΕΛΕΙΟΣ: The Idea of Perfection in the New Testament* (Kampen, 1959), pp. 206ff.; A. Wikgren, "Patterns of Perfection in the Epistle to the Hebrews", *NTS* vi (1959–60), pp. 159ff.

[63] See Ch. 5:7f. (pp. 97ff.).

[64] The argument here requires the "one" from whom the sanctifier and the sanctified alike have their being to be God—not Abraham (in the sense of v. 16 below) and still less Adam (*cf.* O. Procksch in *TWNT* i, p. 113, *s.v.* ἁγιάζω, although it is to Adam that the same phrase ἐξ ἑνός refers in Acts 17:26).

Jesus Christ once for all" (Ch. 10:10).[65] By His death they are consecrated to God for His worship and service and set apart for God as His holy people, destined to enter into His glory. For sanctification is glory begun, and glory is sanctification completed. And since those who are sanctified to God through His death are sons of God, the Son of God is not ashamed to acknowledge them as His brothers—not only as those whose nature He took upon Himself, but those whose trials He endured, for whose sins He made atonement, that they might follow Him to glory on the path of salvation which He Himself cut.

12–13 Three Old Testament quotations are introduced here, in which His solidarity with His people is set forth.[66]

(a) The first quotation (Ps. 22:22) is taken from a psalm in which no Christian of the first century would have failed to recognize Christ as the speaker. It is the psalm whose opening words Jesus took upon His lips as the expression of His own experience in the hour of dereliction on the cross: "My God, my God, why hast thou forsaken me?"[67] Practically the whole of the lament to which the first part of the psalm is devoted was used in the Church from very early times as a *testimonium* of the crucifixion of Christ; not only is it expressly quoted, but its language has been worked into the very fabric of the New Testament passion narratives, especially in the First and Fourth Gospels.[68] It is most natural, then, that when the psalmist's lament gives way to the public thanksgiving of which the second part of the psalm consists, the same speaker should be recognized, and the once crucified, now exalted Christ should be heard saying: "I will declare thy name unto my brethren; in the midst of the congregation will I sing thy praise."[69] Following the Septuagint, our

---

[65] *Cf.* also Chs. 9:13f.; 10:14, 29; 13:12; see p. 241, n. 73.

[66] The exegesis of these three quotations in their present context is greatly indebted to G. Vos, *The Teaching of the Epistle to the Hebrews* (Grand Rapids, 1956), pp. 60f.

[67] Mark 15:34; Matt. 27:46.

[68] The parting of our Lord's garments among the soldiers appears to have been recognized from the first as a fulfilment of Ps. 22:18 (*cf.* Mark 15:24); in John 19:24 that passage is explicitly quoted as a *testimonium* of the incident. *Cf.* C. H. Dodd, *According to the Scriptures* (London, 1952), pp. 97f.; B. Lindars, *New Testament Apologetic* (London, 1961), pp. 88ff.

[69] *Cf.* the adaptation of Ps. 22:22 in *Odes of Solomon* 31:3f.:
"He [our Lord] opened his mouth and spake grace and joy;

author uses the word *ekklēsia* for "congregation" (the Hebrew of Ps. 22:22 has *qāhāl*). The employment of this word in synonymous parallelism with "brethren" in a Christian context indicates that those whom the Son of God is pleased to call His brethren are the members of His church. By virtue of His suffering He has now become "the representative Head of a new mankind".[70]

(b) If it is easy to see the relevance of the quotation of Ps. 22:22 here, it is less easy to see the relevance of the quotation which follows it. "I will put my trust in him" is taken from the Septuagint of Isa. 8:17b (ARV "I will look for him"). This is a good example of C. H. Dodd's thesis that the principal Old Testament quotations in the New Testament are not isolated proof–texts, but carry their contexts with them by implication.[71] In the context of this quotation, Isaiah, finding that his oracles of salvation and judgment meet with no response from either king or people, seals them up and hands them over to his disciples for safe keeping, in order that, when their fulfilment comes, it may be made apparent that what he had spoken was the true word of God. Meanwhile, he says, "I will wait for Jehovah, that hideth his face from the house of Jacob, and I will look for him." God's hiding of His face from the house of Jacob provides the link with Psalm 22, where His face is hidden from the righteous sufferer who (in the Christian interpretation) is the representative of the whole house of Jacob, enduring the dereliction which was due to them. If Isaiah, one of the prophets through whom God of old time spoke to the fathers, was rejected by those to whom he came, so was the Son in whom God more recently spoke His final word; if Isaiah nonetheless maintained his trust in God and waited for vindication from Him, so did the Son of God. "Commit thyself unto Jehovah", the righteous

---

And He spake a new (song of) praise to His name.
And He lifted up His voice to the Most High,
And offered to Him the sons that were in His hands."
(See notes in J. R. Harris and A. Mingana, *The Odes and Psalms of Solomon*, ii [Manchester, 1920], pp. 371f.)

[70] C. H. Dodd, *According to the Scriptures*, p. 20. See also E. Schweizer, *Lordship and Discipleship* (London, 1960), pp. 71ff., 88ff.

[71] *According to the Scriptures*, p. 126 *et passim*. In accordance with this insight, we may recall Calvin's interpretation of the two Isaiah quotations here in association with the "rock" of Isa. 8:14 (a notable *testimonium* in NT), and link it with II Sam. 22:3, "God, my rock, in him will I take refuge" (LXX ... πεποιθὼς ἔσομαι ἐπ᾽ αὐτῷ), and its parallel in Ps. 18:2.

sufferer is exhorted in mockery in Psalm 22;[72] but when the suffering is past he gratefully bears witness to the faithfulness of the God in whom he trusted:

> "For he hath not despised nor abhorred the affliction of the afflicted;
> Neither hath he hid his face from him;
> But when he cried unto him, he heard."[73]

This recurring pattern of men's trust in God in days of darkness and their glad acknowledgement of God's faithfulness when He acts for their vindication is found in the lives of many biblical characters; but there is something quite outstanding in the case of Isaiah. For it is with him that we begin to see the historical emergence of the righteous remnant, the faithful Israel within the empirical Israel, the group in whose survival the hope of the future was assured, one might almost say the *ekklēsia* of the Messiah. Certainly, in Isaiah's prophetic ministry the coming King and the remnant are closely associated—or, to use the language of Hebrews, the Son of God and His brethren. Moreover, there is reason to believe that Isaiah himself took steps to give a conscious corporate existence to the embryonic remnant of his own day, partly in the circle of his disciples of whom he speaks in Isa. 8:16 and partly in his own family.

(c) Isaiah's family is referred to directly in the third quotation, which comes from Isa. 8:18a, and in the Old Testament text follows immediately upon the second quotation. One may wonder, then, why the two quotations are separated by "And again", but the reason no doubt is that two separate points are being made. In the Septuagint the words quoted from Isa. 8:18a form a separate sentence, as they do here: "Here am I, and the children God has given me" (RSV). But in the Hebrew text they form the first part of a longer sentence: "Behold, I and the children whom Jehovah hath given me are for signs and for wonders in Israel from Jehovah of hosts, who dwelleth in mount Zion."[74] The people might pay no heed to Isaiah's oracles, but so long as Isaiah himself

---

[72] Verse 8 (practically quoted in Matt. 27:43a).
[73] Ps. 22:24 (LXX 21:24), echoed in Ch. 5:7 (see pp. 100f.).
[74] LXX starts a new sentence after "whom God hath given me": "And there shall be signs and wonders in the house of Israel from the Lord of hosts ..."

went about in Jerusalem, he was an abiding witness to the message of God which had been conveyed through him. Not only so, but his own significant name ("Yahweh is salvation") and the equally significant names of his two sons—Shearjashub ("Remnant will return") and Mahershalalhashbaz ("Hasten booty, speed spoil")[75] —reminded the people of the dominant themes of his message. Indeed, his sons' names were the expression of his own obedient trust in God, his confidence that what God had said would surely come to pass.

That the Son of God's confidence in His Father had been vindicated by His exaltation was not yet a matter of public manifestation; it had been revealed to believers and was proclaimed by them as part of their witness. But the life and witness of these believers—members of the family of Christ—was a token to men that they had not seen or heard the last of Jesus of Nazareth. If He represented His people at the right hand of God, they represented Him on earth. Isaiah's words about his children might therefore be understood in an extended sense as the words of Christ about His people. Once again His solidarity with them is affirmed, not now by means of the term "brethren", as in verses 11 and 12, but by means of the term "children". The description of Christians as the "children" or "sons" of Christ is peculiar to this epistle among the New Testament writings; yet Old Testament precedent for it might be found not only in the words of Isa. 8:18 but in a statement about the Suffering Servant in Isa. 53:10: "when he makes himself an offering for sin, he shall see his offspring" (RSV). As for the thought of their being given by God to His Son, a close parallel appears in our Lord's prayer in John 17, where He repeatedly speaks of His disciples as "the men whom thou gavest me out of the world" (verse 6, etc.).[76]

14 Who are those "children" whom God has given to Christ? Men and women, creatures of flesh and blood. But if His solidarity with them is to be real, He also must be a true human being, a genuine partaker of flesh and blood. Moreover, He must partake of flesh and blood "in like manner" with them—that is to say, by the gateway of birth. No docetic or Apollinarian Christ will satisfy men's need of a Savior or God's determination to supply

---

75 Isa. 7:3; 8:3.
76 Cf. John 6:37, 39.

that need. And if His fellow-men, entering this earthly life by birth, leave it in due course by death, it was divinely fitting that He too should die. Indeed, this is stated here as the purpose of His incarnation—that He should die, and in the very act of dying draw the sting of death.

It calls for an exceptional effort of mind on our part to appreciate how paradoxical was the attitude of those early Christians to the death of Christ. If ever death had appeared to be triumphant, it was when Jesus of Nazareth, disowned by His nation, abandoned by His disciples, executed by the might of imperial Rome, breathed His last on the cross. Why, some had actually recognized in His cry of pain and desolation the complaint that even God had forsaken Him. His faithful followers had confidently expected that He was the destined liberator of Israel; but He had died—not, like Judas of Galilee or Judas Maccabaeus, in the forefront of the struggle against the Gentile oppressors of Israel, but in evident weakness and disgrace—and their hopes died with Him. If ever a cause was lost, it was His; if ever the powers of evil were victorious, it was then. And yet—within a generation His followers were exultingly proclaiming the crucified Jesus to be the conqueror of death and asserting, like our author here, that by dying He had reduced the erstwhile lord of death to impotence. The keys of death and Hades were henceforth held firmly in Jesus' powerful hand, for He, in the language of His own parable, had invaded the strong man's fortress, disarmed him, bound him fast and robbed him of his spoil.[77] This is the unanimous witness of the New Testament writers; this was the assurance which nerved martyrs to face death boldly in His name. This sudden change from disillusionment to triumph can only be explained by the account which the apostles gave—that their Master rose from the dead and imparted to them the power of His risen life.

The prince or angel of death is here identified with the devil— that is, Satan. It is not easy to parallel this outright identification, but it is not inconsonant with the general teaching of the New Testament. "To this end was the Son of God manifested," says another New Testament writer, "that he might destroy the works

---

[77] Luke 11:21f. While the release of demon-possessed persons is primarily in view there, the release of those held fast in death cannot be excluded.

of the devil" (I John 3:8),[78] and while the particular work of the devil most prominent in that context is sin, the association between sin and death is close enough for the destruction of death to be included in the purpose of the Son of God's appearance.[79] Our author in all probability belonged to the circle from which the Book of Wisdom came at an earlier date, and shared the sentiments on this subject which find expression there:

"God did not make death,
and he does not delight in the death of the living.
For he created all things that they might exist, ...
and the dominion of Hades is not on earth" (Wisdom 1:13f.).

"God created man for incorruption,
and made him in the image of his own eternity,
but through the devil's envy death entered the world,
and those who belong to his party experience it" (Wisdom 2:23f.).

These quotations do not amount to a statement that the devil "had the power of death," but they come very near to it.[80] Jesus broke the devil's grip on His people when in death He became the death of death, when (in S.W. Gandy's words)—

"He hell in hell laid low,
Made sin, He sin o'erthrew,
Bowed to the grave, destroyed it so,
And death, by dying, slew."

15 Only by becoming man could the Son of God conquer death, which man without Him could never have done; until His conquest of death, death seemed to have the last word. The resurrection faith was cherished before He came, but His resurrection "brought life and immortality to light"[81] and gave that faith a firmer basis. His resurrection is not expressly mentioned here (or anywhere else in the epistle, for that matter, outside the doxology

---

[78] Cf. Rev. 12:5ff., where the downfall of the dragon is the sequel to the birth and exaltation of the "man child".

[79] Cf. I Cor. 15:26, where death is the last of the enemies destined to be brought low by Christ, in ultimate fulfilment of Ps. 110:1.

[80] Since Satan is chief prosecutor in the heavenly court, there is no difficulty in regarding him also as executioner-in-chief. Cf. I Cor. 5:5, "deliver such a one unto Satan for the destruction of the flesh".

[81] II Tim. 1:10, where Christ is said already to have "abolished ($\varkappa\alpha\tau\alpha\varrho\gamma\acute{e}\omega$) death".

of Ch. 13:20f.), but it is implied none the less. If death had had the last word with Him too, how would anyone have supposed that through death He had disabled the prince of death? The fear of death is a most potent fear. Through fear of death many men will consent to do things that nothing else could compel them to do. Some braver souls, it is true, will accept death sooner than dishonor; but for the majority the fear of death can be a tyrannous instrument of coercion. And death is indeed the king of terrors to those who recognize in it the penalty of sin. But by the death of their Sanctifier, the brethren of Christ are sanctified; His death has transformed the meaning of death for them. To them His death means not judgment, but blessing; not bondage, but liberation. And their own death, when it comes, takes its character from His death. If, then, death itself cannot separate the people of Christ from God's love which has been revealed in Him, it can no longer be held over their heads by the devil or any other malign power as a means of intimidation.

16 He became man, then, in order to help men. When the Son of God, the Creator and Lord of angels, humbled Himself, He passed by angelic estate and stooped lower still, becoming man for men's salvation. Not of angels but of men does He take hold; the verb is the same as that used in Ch. 8:9, where God recalls how He "took hold" of His people Israel by the hand to bring them out of Egypt, and in both places the "taking hold" carries with it the idea of help and deliverance. It is unduly weakening the force of the word to translate with RSV, "it is not with angels that he is concerned but with the descendants of Abraham".[82]

No one, moreover, can become a man without thereby becoming a member of some particular human group or family. So when the Son of God took our nature upon Himself, He became "the son of Abraham" (Matt. 1:1). In doing that, however, He became the helper and liberator of all the sons of Abraham, and here quite certainly we are not to confine the scope of "the seed of Abraham" to his natural descendants; we are rather to understand the whole family of faith.[83] Our author was in hearty agreement with Paul:

---

[82] *Cf.* p. 41, n. 56.

[83] OT believers, who could not attain perfection except in company with believers of NT times (Ch. 11:40), are included in this family (*cf.* B. W. Newton, *The Old Testament Saints not to be Excluded from the Church in Glory* [London, 1887], pp. 12f.).

"they that are of faith, the same are sons of Abraham" (Gal. 3:7).
They are, in other words, the "many sons" whom God is bringing
to glory through His first-begotten Son (verse 10).[84]

17 Having thus emphasized our Lord's solidarity with His
brethren, our author now introduces that particular aspect of His
solidarity with them which he is specially concerned to expound—
His high-priestly ministry on their behalf. Any priest must be one
with those whom he represents before God, and this is equally so
with Christ as His people's high priest.[85] In order to serve them
in this capacity, He was obliged to become completely like His
brethren—apart from sin, of course, as is pointed out below (Ch.
4:15). He suffered with them and for them, and through His
sufferings was made perfect—qualified in every way to be their
high priest. He is merciful, because through His own sufferings
and trials He can sympathize with theirs; He is faithful, because
He endured to the end without faltering.[86] It is difficult to decide
whether His faithfulness here is His steadfast loyalty to God (as in
Ch. 3:2) or His utter trustworthiness so far as His people are
concerned. Since in fact both aspects are essential in a perfect
high priest, and are true of Christ, it may not be necessary to
decide too narrowly between them.

His high priesthood is exercised "in matters for which they are
responsible to God".[87] And most crucial among these matters is

---

[84] Christ's passing by angels in order that men might be saved may provide
a further reason why the inferiority of angels is so much stressed in Ch. 1;
human beings who inherit salvation are actually served by angels (Ch. 1:14).

[85] Christ is called a "high priest", and not merely a "priest" (as in Ps.
110:4), because our author views His redemptive work as the antitypical fulfilment of the sacrificial ritual of the day of atonement, where the high priest in
person was required to officiate (Ch. 9:7, 11f.).

[86] An echo of the words ἐλεήμων ... καὶ πιστός appears in the Valentinian
Gospel of Truth (Jung Codex 20:10): "This is why the merciful one, the faithful
one, Jesus, was patient to endure the sufferings until he took that book, for he
knows that this death of his means life for many" (*cf.* W. C. van Unnik in *The
Jung Codex*, ed. F. L. Cross [London, 1955], pp. 108, 110; K. Grobel, *The
Gospel of Truth* [London, 1960], pp. 62f.). See p. 210, n. 118.

[87] So τὰ πρὸς τὸν θεόν (*cf.* Ch. 5:1) is translated by T. W. Manson, *Ministry
and Priesthood: Christ's and Ours* (London, 1958), p. 57; he illustrates this issue of
πρός from the Eumeneian formula ἔσται αὐτῷ πρὸς τὸν θεόν, "he will be answerable to God", and refers to W. M. Calder in *Anatolian Studies presented to W. H.
Buckler* (London, 1939), pp. 15ff. A.Nairne renders the phrase "on the Godward
side" (*op. cit.*, p. 45; in the Preface he acknowledges indebtedness for this translation to a Cambridge sermon by G. H. Whitaker).

the matter of sin. How can sinners approach the holiness of God, either personally or through a representative? They can come to Him with confidence only if their sin has been dealt with. And this above all else makes Jesus so incomparable a high priest and representative of His people; not only is He sinless Himself, and therefore entitled to enter the presence of God on His own account, but He has dealt effectively with His people's sins, and can therefore enter the presence of God on their account too. The purpose of His incarnation was that through His death He might "make propitiation for the sins of the people"—do in effective reality what the sacrificial ritual of Old Testament times could do only in a token form. A high priest who has actually, and not merely in symbolism, removed His people's sins, and therewith the barrier which their sins erected between themselves and God, is a high priest worth having.

18 He endured keen trials and temptations Himself, not only the trials incidental to our human lot, but those subtle temptations which attended His messianic calling. Time and again the temptation came to Him from many directions to choose some less costly way of fulfilling that calling than the way of suffering and death,[88] but He resisted it to the end and set His face steadfastly to accomplish the purpose for which He had come into the world. Now His people were not only enduring those trials which are common to mankind, but were being tempted in their turn to be disloyal to God and give up their Christian profession.[89] What a source of strength it was to them to be assured that in the presence of God they had as their champion and intercessor one who had known similar and even sorer temptations, and had withstood them victoriously!

---

[88] *Cf.* His friends' attempts to restrain Him (Mark 3:21 [and 31?]) and Peter's well-meant remonstrance (Mark 8:32), in which He recognized another form of the temptation which He faced earlier in the wilderness and later in Gethsemane; hence His rebuke to Peter (Mark 8:33) took the same form as His reply to the tempter in the wilderness (Matt. 4:10).

[89] On the general subject see K. G. Kuhn, "Temptation, Sin and Flesh", in *The Scrolls and the New Testament*, ed. K. Stendahl (London, 1958), pp. 94ff., especially pp. 96, 112.

CHAPTER III

II. THE TRUE HOME OF THE PEOPLE OF GOD
Chs. 3:1–4:13

1. JESUS GREATER THAN MOSES

Ch. 3:1–6

1 Wherefore, holy brethren, partakers of a heavenly calling, consider the Apostle and High Priest of our confession, *even* Jesus;

2 who was faithful to him that appointed him, as also was Moses in all[1] his house.

3 For he hath been counted worthy of more glory than Moses, by so much as he that built the house hath more honor than the house.

4 For every house is builded by some one; but he that built all things is God.

5 And Moses indeed was faithful in all his house as a servant,[2] for a testimony of those things which were afterward to be spoken;

6 but Christ as a son, over his house; whose house[3] are we, if we hold fast our boldness and the glorying of our hope firm unto the end.[4]

---

[1] Gk. ἐν[ὅλῳ]τῷ οἴκῳ αὐτοῦ. The omission of ὅλῳ in P¹³ P⁴⁶ B and the Coptic versions with Cyril and Ambrose may well be original; in that case it has been supplied here in our other authorities on the basis of v. 5 (following LXX).

[2] Cf. Num. 12:7.

[3] Gk. οὗ οἶκος. A few texts (P⁴⁶ D* M 1739 and the Latin and Coptic versions) have ὅς οἶκος, "which house"; this reading is preferred by G. Zuntz as being "logically correct" (*The Text of the Epistles* [London, 1953], p. 93).

[4] The closing words "firm unto the end" (Gk. μέχρι τέλους βεβαίαν) are omitted in P¹³ P⁴⁶ B and the Sahidic (Coptic) and Ethiopic versions with Lucifer and Ambrose (μέχρι τέλους is omitted in 1022). In the rest of our authorities they probably represent an insertion from the end of v. 14, as has been held by Mill, Bentley, Riggenbach, Windisch, Moffatt and Zuntz (*op. cit.*, p. 33); cf. RSV, NEB.

1 To Jesus, then, the attention of the readers is directed. The terms in which they are addressed—"brothers in the family of God, who share a heavenly calling" (NEB)—are calculated to remind them of the dignity with which God has invested them, a dignity which it would be insulting to God for them to treat lightly. Two common New Testament designations of Christians are joined together in the phrase "holy brethren",[5] while the insistence on the heavenly character of their calling[6] marks them out as citizens of a realm not circumscribed by the conditions of earthly life. They are set apart by God for Himself, made members of His family, and called to share in His eternal rest. The practical implications of all this become clear as the present phase of our author's argument proceeds.

When Jesus is designated as "the Apostle and High Priest of our confession",[7] He is marked out as being both God's representative among men and men's representative in the presence of God. The Old Testament writings tell the story of God's self-revelation to man and man's response to that revelation; in both respects these writings find their fulfilment in Jesus. For He is not only, as has been emphasized already, the one in whom God has revealed Himself finally and completely, but also the perfect embodiment of man's obedient response to God.

2 In both respects Jesus has proved Himself faithful—a faithful high priest (*cf.* Ch. 2:17) and a faithful envoy. The faithfulness of an envoy consists in his loyal discharging of the commission with which he has been entrusted; and such faithfulness was manifested

---

[5] Gk. ἀδελφοὶ ἅγιοι. *Cf.* Col. 1:2, ἁγίοις καὶ πιστοῖς ἀδελφοῖς (*Ephesians-Colossians*, NICNT, p. 178). *Cf.* Ch. 6:10 (p. 126, n. 65).

[6] Elsewhere in NT it is called a "holy calling" (II Tim. 1:9) and an "upward calling" (Phil. 3:14, ARV margin); *cf.* also Rom. 1:7; 8:28, 30; I Pet. 1:15, etc. The church is the community of those whom God has called (Ch. 9:15; Eph. 4:4; Col. 3:15, etc.).

[7] Gk. τὸν ἀπόστολον καὶ ἀρχιερέα τῆς ὁμολογίας ἡμῶν. Philo (*Life of Moses* ii. 2ff.) describes Moses as filling the rôles of prophet and high priest, and also of king and legislator. The two possible ways of understanding ὁμολογία ("confession" either as "that which is confessed" or as "the act of confessing") are indicated respectively by NEB text ("the Apostle and High Priest of the religion we profess") and margin ("him whom we confess as God's Envoy and High Priest"). The former is preferable; *cf.* AG ("the high priest of whom our confession speaks"). On "apostle and high priest" see also K. H. Rengstorf in *TWNT*i (Stuttgart, 1933), *s.v.* ἀπόστολος, pp. 416, 419, 423f. Justin calls Jesus "apostle" in his *First Apology*, 12:9; 63:5.

preeminently in the Sent One of God, who glorified His Father on earth by finishing the work which He had given Him to do.[8]

The combining of the two rôles of divine envoy and priest in one person is not common in the Old Testament; it appears only in a few outstanding characters, among whom Moses occupies a special place. That Moses was an apostle of God to his people does not call for demonstration; it is equally true that he was his people's most effective intercessor with God. It was his brother Aaron, and not he, who was high priest of Israel so far as title and investiture were concerned; but it was Moses, and not Aaron, who was Israel's true advocate with God. After the idolatrous festival in honor of the golden calf, in which Aaron himself was implicated, it was Moses whose prevailing plea procured pardon for his guilty people (Ex. 32:11ff., 31f.), as it did on a later occasion when the unfavorable report of the spies caused a rebellion in the camp and a resolution to return to Egypt (Num. 14:13ff.). When Moses' unique position as the spokesman of God was challenged even by members of his own family, his faithfulness was vindicated by God. Other spokesmen of God might receive communications from Him by vision or dream, but Moses enjoyed more direct revelation than they: "My servant Moses is not so; he is faithful in all my house: with him will I speak mouth to mouth, even manifestly, and not in dark speeches; and the form of Jehovah shall he behold" (Num. 12:7f.).[9] Moses was acknowledged by God as chief steward[10] over His household,[11] and if "it is required in stewards, that a man be found faithful" (I Cor. 4:2), Moses certainly met this requirement. The "house" of Num. 12:7 in

---

[8] Cf. John 17:4.

[9] Quoted by Philo (Leg. Alleg. iii. 103) to emphasize Moses' greatness. Cf. E. J. Young, My Servants the Prophets (Grand Rapids, 1952), pp. 38ff. On Moses as advocate and intercessor, see N. Johansson, Parakletoi (Lund, 1940), pp. 5, 67, 161, quoted by C. K. Barrett, From First Adam to Last (London, 1962), p. 61 n.

[10] His position was that denoted by the Hebrew phrase 'al ha-bayith (lit. "over the house", used, e.g., of Shebna in Isa. 22:15), although this phrase is not used in Num. 12:7.

[11] Gk. οἶκος (like Heb. bayith) can mean both "house" ("dwelling") and "household" ("family"); it is the latter sense that is uppermost in the present passage (as in Num. 12:7). It must be further noted that "his house" in vv. 2, 5 and 6 means "God's house(hold)".

which Moses served so faithfully is not the tent of meeting but the people of Israel, the family of God.[12]

3-4 Yet, great as Moses was, his status was inferior to Christ's. The implication for the recipients of this epistle is plain: the old economy, inaugurated by Moses, is inferior to the new order introduced by Christ. Moses was a household servant[13] exalted by virtue of his outstanding faithfulness to the post of chief administrator of God's household; but Christ, the Son of God, through whom the universe was made and to whom it has been given by His Father as His heritage, is founder and inheritor of the household. No distinction can be made between the Father and the Son in this regard: God the Father, the Maker of all things,[14] is inevitably the founder of His own household, and it was through His Son that He brought into being all things in general and His own household in particular.

5-6a Moses' relation to God's household, then, was that of a servant; Christ's relation to it is that of the Son and heir. Moses served *in* the household as one who was himself part of the household; Christ rules *over* the household[15] as the Son whom His

---

[12] So the Targum of Onqelos at Num. 12:7 paraphrases *bēthī* ("my house") as *'ammī* ("my people"). *Cf.* n. 15 below. In a comment on Gen. 28:17, Philo (*Migration of Abraham*, 5) equates God's house with the Logos.

[13] Gk. θεράπων (v. 5) as in Num. 12:7 (LXX); Wisdom 10:16 (*cf.* p. 316, n. 169). As a household servant Moses was a member of the household, and therefore lower in rank than the founder and master of the household. Justin Martyr (*First Apology* 20:5) refers to Menander and other writers for the sentiment that the builder (δημιουργός) is greater than what he builds.

[14] It is just possible to take the second clause of v. 4 to mean that "he who founded everything" (*i.e.* Christ, according to Ch. 1:2) is God (ὁ δὲ πάντα κατασκευάσας θεός)—in other words, to take it as an assertion of the deity of Christ. But it is simpler to regard the clause as an affirmation that God is the Creator of everything.

[15] In a higher sense than that implied by Heb. *'al ha-bayith* (see p. 56, n. 10). S. Aalen ("'Reign' and 'House' in the Kingdom of God in the Gospels", *NTS* viii [1961–62], pp. 215ff.) points out that the Targum on I Chron. 17:14 (*cf.* II Sam. 7:16) reads: "I will maintain him [the son of David] faithful in my people and in my holy house for ever". He suggests that this interpretation, as well as Num. 12:7, stands behind our present passage, and finds here the explanation of our author's making both Christ and God builder of the house (vv. 3–4). "The motif of the faithful son who is the builder of God's house and is in God's house is exactly that which we find" in the Targum. *Cf.* vv. 6, 14 for the identification of the house and people of God; *cf.* also Ch. 1:5b for the application to Christ of II Sam. 7:14//I Chron. 17:13.

Father, the owner of the household, has appointed to exercise this rule. The Son's authority is greater than the servant's; Moses was not the *author* of the old economy as Christ is the author of the new. Yet God issued a solemn warning to any who might venture "to speak against my servant, against Moses" (Num. 12:8); more solemn still is the implicit warning against denying or ignoring the claims of Christ and the gospel. The claims of Christ and the gospel, indeed, are foreshadowed in the ministry which was committed to Moses: Moses' ministry was designed as "a testimony of those things which were afterward to be spoken"[16]—or, in the language used later in this epistle, it was designed as "a shadow of the good things to come" (Ch. 10:1), the good things which now have indeed come in Christ. In some sections of Jewish Christianity Christ's rôle was envisaged as primarily that of a second Moses; here He is presented as being much more than that.[17]

6b If the household of God in which Moses served Him so loyally was the people of Israel, what is the household of God today, over which the Son of God bears rule? That household comprises all believers:[18] "we are that household of his, if only we

---

[16] In the word "testimony" (μαρτύριον) there may be an echo of the repeated references to the σκηνὴ τοῦ μαρτυρίου ("tent of testimony") in Num. 12:4f., 10 (*cf.* Acts 7:44); the typology of the tent is elaborated later in Ch. 9:1ff. Yet, if there is such an echo, it is no more than an echo; it is the prophetic and anticipatory character of Moses' rôle and ministry that is referred to, with the implication that the fulfilment which has now come in Christ surpasses the work of Moses. This work embraces not only the tent of testimony with its furniture and ritual but everything that was bound up with the wilderness covenant (Ch. 8:6ff.), including the Levitical priesthood (Ch. 7:11ff.).

[17] E. L. Allen ("Jesus and Moses in the New Testament", *ExT* lxvii [1955–56], pp. 104ff.) suggests that our author is here refuting a "new Moses Christology", as he elsewhere refutes an "angel-Christology". It is principally among the Ebionites that a "Moses Christology" is attested (*cf. Clem. Recog.* i. 36ff., iv. 5; *Clem. Hom.* iii. 47ff., viii. 5ff.; H. J. Schoeps, *Theologie und Geschichte des Judenchristentums* [Tübingen, 1949], pp. 87ff.); it goes back to the prophecy about the Prophet like Moses in Deut. 18:15ff. This prophecy, which played an important part in the eschatological thinking of the Samaritans and of the Qumran community, is applied to Christ in several places in NT (*cf.* Mark 9:7; John 6:14; 7:20; Acts 3:22f.; 7:37), but does not occupy a central place in NT Christology (*cf.* O. Cullmann, *The Christology of the New Testament* [London, 1959], pp. 13ff.; F. F. Bruce, *Biblical Exegesis in the Qumran Texts* [London, 1960], pp. 46ff.).

[18] Under Christ, as in the time of Moses, there is but one continuous household of God; it goes back beyond Moses and even Abraham to embrace Abel

are fearless and keep our hope high" (NEB). The conditional sentences of this epistle are worthy of special attention.[19] Nowhere in the New Testament more than here do we find such repeated insistence on the fact that continuance in the Christian life is the test of reality. The doctrine of the final perseverance of the saints has as its corollary the salutary teaching that the saints are the people who persevere to the end. In the parable of the sower the seed sown on rocky ground made a fair showing at first, but could not withstand the heat of the sun "because it had no root"; and in the interpretation of the parable this is said to refer to people "who, when they have heard the word, straightway receive it with joy; and they have no root in themselves, but endure for a while; then, when tribulation or persecution ariseth because of the word, straightway they stumble" (Mark 4:5f., 16f.). This is precisely what our author fears may happen with his readers; hence his constant emphasis on the necessity of their maintaining fearless confession[20] and joyful hope.[21] Christians live by faith and not by sight; but while their hope is in things unseen, it is something to exult in, not to be ashamed of. The waning of the first expectant enthusiasm of these "Hebrews",[22] the apparent postponement of their hope, and various kinds of pressure brought to bear upon them, all combined to threaten the steadfastness of their faith.

---

and Enoch and Noah (Ch. 11:4ff., 40). So, in Eph. 2:19 Gentile Christians are called "fellow-citizens with the saints [*i.e.* with Israel, God's holy people], and of the household of God". The conception of the faithful community as the house of God is paralleled at Qumran; *e.g.* the inner council or nucleus of the Qumran community is described as "a holy house for Israel, a most holy assembly for Aaron, ... a most holy dwelling for Aaron, ... a house of perfection and truth in Israel" (1QS viii. 5ff.; *cf.* p. 177). See F. F. Bruce, "'To the Hebrews' or 'To the Essenes'?", *NTS* ix (1962–63), pp. 217ff.

[19] *Cf.* v. 14; Ch. 10:26.

[20] On "boldness" (Gk. παρρησία, recurring in Chs. 4:16; 10:19, 35) *cf.* W. C. van Unnik, "De semitische Achtergrond van *ΠΑΡΡΗΣΙΑ* in het Nieuwe Testament", *Mededelingen der koninklijke Nederlandse Akademie van Wetenschappen* (*Afd. Letterkunde*), Nieuwe Reeks, Deel 25 (Amsterdam, 1962); "The Christian's Freedom of Speech in the New Testament", *BJRL* xliv (1961–62), pp. 466ff.

[21] *Cf.* Rom. 5:2; 8:24f.; Eph. 1:18; Col. 1:23; I Pet. 1:13 for the relation between the maintenance of Christian hope and the attainment of final salvation. Rom. 5:2 (καυχώμεθα ἐπ᾽ ἐλπίδι ...) bears a special resemblance to the wording here (τὸ καύχημα τῆς ἐλπίδος).

[22] *Cf.* A. Pott, *Das Hoffen im Neuen Testament* (Leipzig, 1915), pp. 84ff., 87, for the view that the language here reflects a time when the first enthusiasm was in danger of being quenched. *Cf.* also Chs. 6:11; 10:23.

Hence our author, in deep concern, urges upon them that they have everything to gain by standing fast, and everything to lose by slipping back. He reinforces his warning by appealing to a familiar Old Testament precedent.

2. SECOND ADMONITION:

THE REJECTION OF JESUS MORE SERIOUS THAN
THE REJECTION OF MOSES

Ch. 3:7–19

7   Wherefore, even as the Holy Spirit saith,[23]
     To-day if ye shall hear his voice,[24]

8   Harden not your hearts, as in the provocation,
     Like as in the day of the trial in the wilderness,

9   Where your fathers tried[25] *me* by proving[26] *me*,
     And saw my works forty years.[27]

10   Wherefore I was displeased with this[28] generation,
     And said, They do always err in their heart:
     But they did not know my ways;

---

[23] The Holy Spirit is viewed as the author of the Old Testament revelation not only in its words, as here (*cf.* Ch. 10:15), but also in its material content such as the plan for the construction of the wilderness tabernacle (Ch. 9:8).

[24] Better, as the OT passage itself is rendered in ARV, "oh that ye would hear his voice!" (Ps. 95:7). Heb. *'im* ("if") expresses a wish here as certainly as it expresses a strong negative in v. 11.

[25] M P 1739 with the bulk of later MSS, the Latin, Syriac and Bohairic (Coptic) versions, add με after ἐπείρασαν.

[26] Gk. ἐν δοκιμασίᾳ ("by way of proving"). LXX has ἐδοκίμασαν, which is the reading probably represented in Heb. 3:9 by the Latin and Peshitta (Syriac) versions. K L and the bulk of later MSS have ἐδοκίμασάν με here.

[27] In MT and LXX "forty years" belongs to the following clause ("Forty years long was I grieved with that generation"); but our author clearly attaches it to the words that precede by inserting διό ("Wherefore") before προσώχθισα ("I was displeased").

[28] Gk. ταύτῃ, in place of LXX ἐκείνῃ (there is no pronoun here in MT). Our author perhaps replaced "that" by "this" in order to point the moral more tellingly for the generation which he himself was addressing. *Cf.* our Lord's repeated references to "this generation" (Matt. 11:16; 12:41f., 45; 23:36; 24:34 and parallels; *cf.* also Acts 2:40).

11   As I sware in my wrath,
      They shall not enter[29] into my rest.[30]

12   Take heed, brethren, lest haply there shall be in any one
      of you an evil heart of unbelief, in falling away from the
      living God:

13   but exhort one another day by day, so long as it is called
      To-day; lest any one of you be hardened by the deceit-
      fulness of sin:

14   for we are become partakers of Christ, if we hold fast the
      beginning of our confidence firm unto the end:

15   while it is said,[31]
      To-day if ye shall hear his voice,
      Harden not your hearts, as in the provocation.

16   For who, when they heard, did provoke? nay, did not
      all they that came out of Egypt by Moses?

17   And with whom was he displeased forty years?[32] was it
      not with them that sinned, whose bodies fell in the
      wilderness?[33]

18   And to whom sware he that they should not enter into
      his rest, but to them that were disobedient?[34]

19   And we see that they were not able to enter in because of
      unbelief.

---

[29]   Gk. εἰ εἰσελεύσονται, following LXX, represents an over-literal rendering
of the Hebrew idiom 'im yebō'ūn, rightly translated"They shall not enter". AV
gives the right rendering here, but in Ch. 4:3, 5, follows the Geneva and Bishops'
Bibles with the misleading literalism, "if they shall enter into my rest"—the
more surprisingly, since Tyndale and Coverdale had already given the true
idiomatic sense throughout.
[30]   Ps. 95 (LXX 94):7b-11, quoted according to LXX apart from variations
mentioned in nn. 26, 27, 28 above.
[31]   "While it is said" (ἐν τῷ λέγεσθαι) should perhaps be taken as the beginning of a new sentence, as in NEB: "When Scripture says, 'Today if you hear
his voice, do not grow stubborn as in those days of rebellion', who, I ask, were
those who heard and rebelled?" Here γάρ in τίνες γάρ (ARV "For who ...?") is
taken as a particle of emphasis.
[32]   Here the construction of MT and LXX is presupposed (cf. n. 27 above).
[33]   Cf. Num. 12:29, 32.
[34]   Gk. ἀπειθήσασιν, for which P[46] has ἀπιστήσασιν ("that did not believe"),
probably under the influence of ἀπιστία ("unbelief") in v. 19.   Cf. similar
variants in Chs. 4:6, 11; 11:31.

61

7-11 The New Testament bears witness, in a number of places, to a primitive and widespread Christian interpretation of the redemptive work of Christ in terms of a new Exodus.[35] In some of its features this interpretation may have originated during the Galilaean ministry of Jesus;[36] but after His resurrection it comes to present a reasonably fixed form. The death of Christ is itself called an "exodus";[37] He is the true passover, sacrificed for His people,[38] "a lamb without blemish and without spot".[39] They, like Israel in early days, are "the church in the wilderness";[40] their baptism into Christ is the antitype of Israel's passage through the Red Sea;[41] their sacramental feeding on Him by faith is the antitype of Israel's nourishment with manna and the water from the rock.[42] Christ, the living Rock, is their guide through the wilderness;[43] the heavenly rest which lies before them is the counterpart to the earthly Canaan which was the goal of the Israelites.[44] The moral implications of this typology are pressed upon Christian readers by more than one New Testament writer: Paul tells the Corinthians that the record of Israel's rebellion and punishment in the wilderness has been preserved "for our admonition", lest we should imitate their disobedience and be overtaken by comparable judgment;[45] Jude similarly draws practical lessons for his

---

[35] *Cf.* J. R. Harris, "Jesus and the Exodus", in *Testimonies* ii (Cambridge, 1920), pp. 51ff.; E. Käsemann, *Das wandernde Gottesvolk* (Göttingen, 1938); H. Sahlin, "The New Exodus of Salvation according to S. Paul", in A. Fridrichsen etc., *The Root of the Vine* (London, 1953), pp. 81ff.; J. Daniélou, *From Shadow to Reality* (London, 1960); R.E. Nixon, *The Exodus in the NT* (London, 1963). At an earlier time the return of Israel from the Babylonian exile had been portrayed in terms of a new Exodus (*cf.* Isa. 41:17f.; 42:9; 43:16-21; 52:12).

[36] *Cf.* H. W. Montefiore, "Revolt in the Desert?" *NTS* viii (1961-62), pp. 135ff.

[37] Luke 9:31 (Gk. ἔξοδος, ARV "decease").

[38] I Cor. 5:7b (the same idea underlies the passion narrative of the Fourth Gospel).

[39] I Pet. 1:19. The paschal symbolism is unmistakable, although it has been exaggerated by F. L. Cross, *I Peter: A Paschal Liturgy* (London, 1954).

[40] Acts 7:38 (see *Acts*, NICNT, p. 152); *cf.* also L. Cerfaux, *The Church in the Theology of St. Paul* (London, 1959), pp. 100ff.

[41] I Cor. 10:1f.

[42] I Cor. 10:3f.

[43] I Cor. 10:4b.

[44] This is the point of our author's argument in Chs. 3:7-4:11; it emerges clearly in Ch. 4:1ff.

[45] I Cor. 10:6ff.

fellow-believers from the fact that "Jesus, having saved a people out of the land of Egypt, afterward destroyed them that believed not".[46]

This typology was familiar to our author, and quite probably to his readers as well; he uses it, therefore, to warn them against giving up their faith and hope. After his fashion, he bases his argument on a passage from the Psalter, which he expounds in the light of the historical record.

Psalm 95 falls into two parts: the first (verses 1–7a) consists of a call to worship God, while the second (verses 7b–11), reproduced by our author here, is a warning against disobeying Him, reinforced by a reminder of what happened to Israel in the wilderness for disobedience. The liturgical use of the psalm at this day by Jews (for whom it is one of the special psalms appointed for the inauguration of the sabbath[47]) and Christians (for whom it has been from very early times an integral part of the service of morning prayer[48]) no doubt perpetuates earlier practice, in which it was sung as part of the temple service for the sabbath day.[49] The two parts should not be dissociated from each other:[50] it is a good thing to worship God, but acts and words of worship are acceptable only if they proceed from sincere and obedient hearts.

---

[46]   Jude 5. For "Jesus" AV, ARV, NEB have "the Lord" ($\varkappa \acute{\upsilon} \varrho \iota o \varsigma$), which is the reading of ℵ C*; but the textual evidence strongly supports the view that the original reading was "Jesus" (so A B and the Latin and Coptic versions). It is unlikely that "Jesus" in this place "might be understood as Joshua" (NEB margin); Joshua played a minor rôle in the wilderness and became Israel's leader only on the eve of the entry into Canaan (see Ch. 4:8). It is much more probable that Jude's language reflects an identification of Jesus (the pre-incarnate Son of God) with the Rock which supplied Israel's need in the wilderness (so Paul in I Cor. 10:4b) or with the Angel of the Divine Presence who guarded and guided them from Egypt to the promised land—the one of whom God said, "My name is in him" (Ex. 23:21) and who was commissioned both to provide protection and to mete out judgment (Ex. 14:19; 23:20ff.; Isa. 63:9; cf. Acts 7:38).

[47]   Cf. S. Singer, The Authorised Daily Prayer Book of the United Hebrew Congregations of the British Empire (London, 1939), p. 108a.

[48]   Cf. "The Order for Morning Prayer" in the Anglican Book of Common Prayer, where Psalm 95 forms the Invitatory.

[49]   Cf. W. E. Barnes. The Psalms, WC (London, 1931), pp. 456ff.

[50]   As is done, e.g., by T. K. Cheyne, The Book of Psalms (London, 1888), pp. 265f. In the Deposited Prayer Book of 1928 the Invitatory consists of vv. 1–7a only (ending with "Let us kneel before the Lord our Maker").

"O that you would listen to His voice today!" says the psalmist, and then he introduces God Himself as addressing His people: "Harden not your hearts, as at Meribah ...". "The provocation" (so the Septuagint,[51] followed by our author) is the equivalent of "Meribah" in the Hebrew text, as "the trial"[52] is the equivalent of "Massah". When the Israelites threatened revolt against Moses at Rephidim, because there was no water there, he asked them: "Why strive[53] ye with me? wherefore do ye tempt[54] Jehovah?" (Ex. 17:2)—and called the place Massah ("tempting") and Meribah ("striving") because of their behaviour (Ex. 17:7). But it was not on that occasion only, but repeatedly throughout the forty years of wandering, that they "tempted" God, in the sense of trying to see how long His patience would hold out in face of their stubbornness of heart.

Of these other occasions the one which is uppermost in the psalmist's mind is that recorded in Num. 14:20ff. When the majority of the spies brought back to Kadesh-barnea an unfavorable report of the land of Canaan, the people revolted against the leadership of Moses and Aaron, and were on the point of choosing a new leader who would take them back to Egypt. In response to Moses' intercession on their behalf, God refrained from wiping the whole nation out by plague, but, said He, "all those men that have seen my glory, and my signs, which I wrought in Egypt and in the wilderness, yet have tempted me these ten times, and have not hearkened to my voice; surely they shall not see the land which I sware unto their fathers, neither shall any of them that despised me see it" (Num. 14:22f.).[55] Therefore, instead of invading the promised land at once and taking possession of it, the people remained in the neighborhood of Kadesh-barnea thirty-eight years, "until all the generation of the men of war were consumed from the midst of the camp, as Jehovah sware unto them" (Deut. 2:14). Of those who were already full-grown men when they came

---

[51] Gk. παραπικρασμός (cf. the verb παραπικραίνω in v. 16, with p. 68, n. 71).

[52] Gk. πειρασμός.

[53] Heb. rīb, the root of "Meribah". So again in Num. 20:13.

[54] Heb. nāsāh (Pi'el conjugation), the root of "Massah". The same verb is used in Deut. 8:2 where God speaks of leading Israel forty years in the wilderness to "prove" them.

[55] See p. 56. Cf. also Deut. 1:26, 34ff.

out of Egypt, none except Caleb and Joshua survived to enter Canaan, the "rest" or home which God had prepared for them.[56]

A later generation of Israelites was warned by the psalmist not to follow the bad example of their ancestors' refusal to listen to God, lest disaster should overtake them in turn; and now a still later generation has the same warning impressed upon it by the writer to the Hebrews. Although the writer does not say so in so many words, it may well be that he saw a special significance in the "forty years" of Ps. 95:10. We have evidence of a belief that God's dealings with Israel, which began with a probationary period of forty years, would be rounded off at the end-time by a probationary period of like duration;[57] and (if this epistle was written shortly before A.D. 70), it was nearly forty years now since Jesus had accomplished His "exodus" at Jerusalem. Hence the urgency of the present appeal to the readers to take heed "so long as it is called To-day" (verse 13).[58]

12 The judgment of the wilderness days befell the Israelites who rejected Moses. But just as Christ is greater in glory than Moses (verse 3), so the loss incurred in rejecting Christ is greater even than that incurred in rejecting Moses. The rebels in Moses' day missed the promised blessing of entry into an earthly Canaan, but latter-day rebellion would forfeit the greater blessings of the

---

[56] In Deut. 12:9 Canaan is called "the rest (Heb. *menūḥāh*, as in Ps. 95:11) and the inheritance, which Jehovah thy God giveth thee". The domestic sense of the word appears in Ruth 1:9, "Jehovah grant you that ye may find rest (Heb. *menūḥāh*), each of you in the house of her husband" (similarly in Ruth 3:1, Heb. *mānōaḥ*).

[57] Especially in the Qumran literature; *cf.* the interval of forty years between the death of the Teacher of Righteousness and "the consuming of all the men of war who returned with the Man of Falsehood" (CD xx. 14f., echoing Deut. 2:14-16); the forty years after which the wicked are to be no more (4Q p Ps. 37, fragment A, i. 6ff.); the forty years' warfare of 1QM (further documentation in Y. Yadin, *The Scroll of the War* ... [Oxford, 1962], p. 37, n. 1). In TB *Sanhedrin* 99a Eliezer ben Hyrcanus infers from Ps. 95:10 that the days of the Messiah will last forty years.

[58] In this connection it is interesting to notice a messianic interpretation of the "Today" of Ps. 95:7b in TB *Sanhedrin* 98a: when Elijah sends a rabbi to interview the Messiah at the gates of Rome, the rabbi asks the Messiah, "Lord, when comest thou?" and receives the answer "Today". Elijah explains to him that this means "Today if ye will hear his voice".

new age.[59] It was "an evil heart of unbelief"[60] that prevented the generation that witnessed the Exodus from enjoying the "rest" which they had hoped to attain in Canaan; our author urges his readers to take heed lest such a heart be found in any of them. "Falling away from the living God" is a more positive activity than the English words themselves might suggest; it denotes rebellion against Him.[61] When the Israelites at Kadesh-barnea repudiated the leadership of Moses and Aaron, they revolted in effect against God, who had appointed these two men to be their leaders. And for Christians to repudiate the apostle and high priest of their confession, similarly appointed by God, would be if possible an even more outrageous revolt against the living God. It has indeed been questioned whether a relapse from Christianity into Judaism could be described in such words; do they not denote a complete abandonment of faith in God in any form, whereas in Judaism the living God was acknowledged and worshipped? But a relapse from Christianity into Judaism would be comparable to the action of the Israelites when they "turned back in their hearts unto Egypt";[62] it would not be a mere return to a position previously occupied, but a gesture of outright apostasy, a complete break with God. For those who had never been illuminated by God's final revelation of Himself in Christ, Judaism provided a means of access to God—shadowy and imperfect as it might be.[63] But for those who had received the illumination of the gospel to renounce it in favor of the old order which the gospel had super-seded was the irretrievable sin—the sin against light.[64]

---

[59] So in TB *Sanhedrin* 110*b* Rabbi Aqiba deduces from Ps. 95:11 (and Num. 14:35) that the generation of Israelites that perished in the wilderness will have no part in the age to come.

[60] Their "unbelief" (ἀπιστία) involved disloyalty as well as the passive failure to believe. The whole expression (καρδία πονηρὰ ἀπιστίας) bears at least a verbal resemblance to one or two source-passages for the rabbinical doctrine of the "evil inclination" (yēṣer hā-rā‘); cf. the "evil heart" and "evil root" of IV Ezra (II Esdras) 3:20–22 (with the "evil root" cf. Heb. 12:15, p. 366), the "grain of evil seed ... sown in Adam's heart from the beginning" of IV Ezra 4:30, and the "evil thought" of IV Ezra 7:92.

[61] Gk. ἀποστῆναι (whence ἀποστασία, "apostasy"). Hermas has an echo of this passage in *Shepherd*, Vision ii. 3.2: "you are saved by not having fallen away (ἀποστῆναι) from the living God".

[62] Cf. Acts 7:39 (echoing Num. 14:3).

[63] Cf. Ch. 10:1.

[64] Cf. Ch. 6:4ff.

13 Let them be vigilant therefore, and encourage one another with might and main to be steadfast in their faith, during the present time of probation. While this time lasts, each succeeding day is a fresh "To-day" in which they may heed the psalmist's warning to hear the voice of God and render Him heart-obedience. The exhortation to mutual encouragement was wise: in isolation from his fellow-believers each individual among them was more liable to succumb to the subtle temptations that pressed in upon him from so many sides, but if they came together regularly for mutual encouragement the devotion of all would be kept warm and their common hope would be in less danger of flickering and dying.[65] In isolation each was prone to be impressed by the specious arguments which underlined the worldly wisdom of a certain measure of compromise of their Christian faith and witness; in the healthy atmosphere of the Christian fellowship these arguments would be the more readily appraised at their true worth, and recognized as being so many manifestations of "the deceitfulness of sin".[66] Where the right path lies clear before the eyes, a disinclination to follow it can be reinforced in the mind by many beguiling lines of rationalization; but to surrender to them results in a hardening of the heart, a reduced sensitivity of conscience, which makes it more difficult to recognize the right path on a subsequent occasion. But in a fellowship which exercised a watchful and unremitting care for its members the temptation to prefer the easy course to the right one would be greatly weakened, and the united resolution to stand firm would be correspondingly strengthened.

14 Again the paramount necessity of perseverance is stressed: only if they kept their original confidence[67] firm to the end could they be truly called partners of Christ. The word rendered "partners" in NEB (ARV "partakers") is the word used at the end of the quotation from Psalm 45:6f. in Ch. 1:8f.—"God ...

---

[65] *Cf.* Ch. 10:24f. (pp. 252ff.).

[66] Gk. τῇ ἀπάτῃ τῆς ἁμαρτίας (*cf.* Gen. 3:13; II Cor. 11:3).

[67] Gk. ὑπόστασις, as in Ch. 11:1 (a different meaning from that in Ch. 1:3). This sense of "confidence", "assurance", "conviction", is readily derivable from the primary sense of "that which underlies" ("ground", "basis"); this confidence rests upon a stable foundation. *Cf.* H. Dörrie, "ΥΠΟΣΤΑΣΙΣ: Wort- und Bedeutungsgeschichte", *Nachrichten der Akademie der Wissenschaften in Göttingen, philologisch-historische Klasse*, 1955, No. 3, pp. 35–92. See pp. 277f., with nn. 4–8.

hath anointed thee with the oil of gladness above thy fellows".[68] The meaning of the phrase "partners of Christ" is probably not that of participation in Him (as in the Pauline expression "in Christ"), but rather that of participation with Him in His heavenly kingdom—the unshakable kingdom of Ch. 12:28.[69] To begin well is good, but it is not enough; it is only those who stay the course and finish the race that have any hope of gaining the prize.[70] The Israelites made a good beginning when they crossed the Sea of Reeds and praised God for their deliverance; but the good beginning was not matched by their later behavior.

15-18 When the scripture already quoted says, "Harden not your hearts, as in the provocation", to whom is God speaking? Who were the people who turned a deaf ear to His voice and so provoked[71] Him to anger? It was those[72] who came out of Egypt under the leadership of Moses, those who had experienced the redeeming power of God. When He says, "Forty years long was I grieved with that generation",[73] to which generation does He refer? To that generation which witnessed His mighty works, and nevertheless rebelled against Him—that "evil congregation" against which sentence was passed: "As I live, saith Jehovah, surely as ye have spoken in mine ears, so will I do to you: your dead bodies shall fall in this wilderness" (Num. 14:27ff.). And

---

[68] Gk. μέτοχοι. Apart from Luke 5:7, where the sons of Zebedee are "partners" in fishing with Simon Peter and his brother (note the alternative use of κοινωνοί in the same sense in Luke 5:10), μέτοχοι in NT is used only in Hebrews, its occurrences being (in addition to the present passage and Ch. 1:9) Chs. 3:1 ("partakers of a heavenly calling"), 6:4 ("partakers of the Holy Spirit"), and 12:8 ("partakers" of chastening).

[69] This involves taking the genitive τοῦ χριστοῦ here in a different way from the genitive πνεύματος ἁγίου in Ch. 6:4, but the context in either place must determine the precise force of the genitive. For the general idea here cf. Paul's words of encouragement and warning about inheriting the kingdom (e.g. I Cor. 6:9f.; Gal. 5:19-21; Eph. 5:5; cf. Rom. 8:17; II Tim. 2:12).

[70] Cf. Ch. 12:1f.

[71] Gk. παρεπίκραναν (for the cognate noun παραπικρασμός cf. vv. 8, 15); this verb παραπικραίνω, perhaps a Septuagintal coinage (cf. Moffatt, ICC, ad loc.), is used of Israel's wilderness behavior in Deut. 31:27; 32:16; Pss. 78 (LXX 77):8, 17; 105 (LXX 104):28; cf. Ps. 107 (LXX 106):11, etc.

[72] "All they that came out (πάντες οἱ ἐξελθόντες) of Egypt," says our author, leaving out of view for the moment the two exceptions, Caleb and Joshua; contrast Paul in I Cor. 10:5, "with most of them (ἐν τοῖς πλείοσιν αὐτῶν) God was not well pleased."

[73] The construction of MT and LXX is implied in v. 17; cf. p. 60, n. 27.

who were the people to whom He swore in His wrath: "They shall not enter into my rest"? Those who, having covenanted to obey Him, proved repeatedly disobedient, and showed themselves to be "a very perverse generation, children in whom is no faithfulness" (Deut. 32:20).

19 It was unbelief,[74] faithlessness, then, that kept them out of the promised land. They had enjoyed God's delivering mercy in the Exodus, and had heard Him speak when He gave the law at Sinai; but those initial experiences did not keep them from dying in the wilderness, or guarantee their safe arrival in Canaan. The moral must have been plain enough to the recipients of the epistle. For they too had experienced the redeeming power of God; they too had the promise of the homeland of the faithful to look forward to; but one thing could prevent them from realizing that promise, just as it had prevented the mass of the Israelites who left Egypt from entering Canaan—and that one thing was unbelief.

---

[74] The juxtaposition of δι' ἀπιστίαν ("because of unbelief") in v. 19 and τοῖς ἀπειθήσασιν ("to them that were disobedient") in v. 18 (*cf.* p. 61, n. 34 for textual variant) emphasizes the close relation in NT between ἀπιστία and ἀπείθεια (*cf.* ὁ πιστεύων over against ὁ δὲ ἀπειθῶν in John 3:36).

CHAPTER IV

3. THE TRUE REST OF GOD MAY BE FORFEITED

Ch. 4:1-10

1 Let us fear therefore, lest haply, a promise being left[1] of entering into his rest, any one of you should seem[2] to have come short of it.

2 For indeed we have had good tidings preached unto us, even as also they: but the word of hearing[3] did not profit them, because it was not united by faith with them that heard.[4]

---

[1] Gk. καταλειπομένης, here in the sense of being "left open". The promise (ἐπαγγελία) is implied in the warning.

[2] Gk. δοκῇ, "might be deemed". *Cf.* NEB: "one or another among you should be found to have missed his chance".

[3] Gk. ὁ λόγος τῆς ἀκοῆς. *Cf.* Rom. 10:16f. for the use of ἀκοή in the sense of the gospel message (based on the meaning of the word in Isa. 53:1; so NEB renders the passage: "For Isaiah says, 'Lord, who has believed our message?' We conclude that faith is awakened by the message, and the message that awakens it comes through the word of Christ").

[4] Gk. μὴ συνκεκερασμένος τῇ πίστει τοῖς ἀκούσασιν. There is a bewildering diversity of readings here: for the masculine singular συνκεκερασμένος, agreeing with λόγος (א d, the Sixto-Clementine Vulgate, Peshitta, some Sahidic texts, Lucifer, TR), a preponderant weight of authorities has the accusative plural συνκεκερασμένους, agreeing with ἐκείνους (P[13] P[46] ABCD* M and the majority of later MSS, Vulgate MSS, Harclean Syriac, the Bohairic, Armenian and Ethiopic versions, Chrysostom, Theodore of Mopsuestia, etc.). The latter reading is adopted by ERV (as against ARV): "because they were not united by faith with them that heard". On a possible interpretation of this reading see p. 255, n. 119; failure to understand it probably gave rise to the replacement of the active participle ἀκούσασιν by the passive ἀκουσθεῖσιν (1912, Theodore of Mopsuestia), which gives the smoother rendering "because they were not united by faith with the things that they heard". The replacement of the dative by the genitive ἀκουσάντων (D* 104 1611 2005 d, Harclean margin, Lucifer, etc.) yields the sense: "... united with the faith of the hearers"; this is intelligible only with the nominative συνκεκερασμένος. We are confronted here, in all probability, with "a variety of ancient conjectures vainly striving to heal a primitive corruption" (G. Zuntz, *The Text of the Epistles* [London, 1953], p. 16; *cf.* Westcott, pp. 94f., 112f.). But the sense is plain enough; the good news had to be appropriated or assimilated by faith if it was to bring any benefit to the hearers.

3   For[5] we who have believed do enter into that rest;[6] even
    as he hath said,
        As I sware in my wrath,
        They shall not enter into my rest:[7]
    although the works were finished from the foundation of
    the world.[8]

4   For he hath said somewhere of the seventh *day* on this
    wise, And God rested on the seventh day from all his
    works;[9]

5   and in this *place* again,
        They shall not enter into my rest.

6   Seeing therefore it remaineth that some should enter
    thereinto, and they to whom the good tidings were before
    preached failed to enter in because of disobedience,[10]

7   he again defineth a certain day, To-day, saying in David
    so long a time afterward (even as hath been said before),[11]
        To-day if ye shall hear his voice,
        Harden not your hearts.[12]

---

[5] In place of γάρ ("for"), οὖν (probably in a resumptive sense, "well then")
is read by ℵ A C 1739 with a few minuscules and the Bohairic version.

[6] Gk. εἰς τὴν κατάπαυσιν, but τήν is omitted by P[13] P[46] B D* (and this may
well be the original reading).

[7] Ps. 95:11 (LXX 94:11).

[8] Gk. ἀπὸ καταβολῆς κόσμου. For the καταβολὴ κόσμου cf. Ch. 9:26; also
Matt. 13:35; 25:34; Luke 11:50; John 17:24; Eph. 1:4; I Pet. 1:20; Rev.
13:8; 17:8. The attempt to render it "downfall of the world" and link it with
the "catastrophic" interpretation of Gen. 1:2 cannot be sustained. For another
usage of καταβολή see Ch. 11:11.

[9] Gen. 2:2. LXX simply has καὶ κατέπαυσεν τῇ ἡμέρᾳ τῇ ἑβδόμῃ ... ; here
our author has inserted ὁ θεὸς ἐν after κατέπαυσεν (Moffatt, ICC, *ad loc.*, points
out that the present form of the quotation corresponds to Philo's in *Cain's
Posterity*, 64). The LXX choice of καταπαύω here to render Heb. *shābath* eases
our author's interpretation of the κατάπαυσις of Ps. 95:11 in terms of God's
cessation from His works of creation. Philo (*Leg. Alleg.* i. 6, 16) takes κατέπαυσεν
in Gen. 2:2 as transitive, "he caused to rest"; similarly Heb.4:4 could be rendered
"God caused (His people) to rest on the seventh day" and the κατάπαυσις of
Ps. 95:11 would be the rest that God gives; but this is an awkward construction,
and does not suit the context.

[10] Gk. δι' ἀπείθειαν (so A B D with the majority of MSS. and the Syriac
version); P[46] ℵ* and the Latin, Coptic and Armenian versions read δι' ἀπιστίαν
("because of unbelief"); cf. Ch. 3:18f. (p. 61, n. 34; p. 69, n. 74).

[11] Gk. προείρηται (B 1739 read the active προείρηκεν, "he hath said before").

[12] Ps. 95 (LXX 94): 7b–8a.

8 For if Joshua had given them rest, he would not have spoken afterward of another day.

9 There remaineth therefore a sabbath rest[13] for the people of God.

10 For he that is entered into his rest hath himself also rested from his works, as God did from his.

1 The promise of entering the "rest" of God remains open. The meaning of that "rest" was not exhausted by the earthly Canaan which was entered by the Israelites of the generation that had grown up to manhood in the wilderness; the spiritual counterpart of the earthly Canaan is the goal of the people of God today. Our author therefore urges his readers again to press on and attain that goal. It will not be reached automatically; they will do well to fear[14] the possibility of missing it,[15] just as the generation of Israelites that died in the wilderness missed the earthly Canaan, although that was the goal which they had before them when they set out from Egypt.

2 The parallel between those Israelites and the people of God in the new age is impressive enough for the disaster that befell the former to serve as a warning to the latter. The Israelites of those earlier days had good news proclaimed to them, just as the readers of this epistle had good news proclaimed to *them*[16] (*cf.* Ch. 2:3f.). But the hearing of the good news brought no lasting benefit to

---

[13] Gk. σαββατισμός, "sabbath-keeping"; this is the earliest attested occurrence of the word in extant Greek literature (it appears some decades later in Plutarch, *Moralia* 166a, in a list of superstitious practices). The verb σαββατίζω, from which it is formed, is used in LXX with the meaning "keep sabbath"—usually as the rendering of Heb. *shābath* (Ex. 16:30; Lev. 23:32; 26:35 *ter*; II Chron. 36:21 *bis*; I Esdras 1:58; II Macc. 6:6).

[14] Fear of the consequences of apostasy is a recurrent note in this epistle (*cf.* especially Ch. 10:27, 31), but those who have a proper fear of God (Ch. 12:28f.) need fear none else (Ch. 13:6).

[15] Gk. ὑστερηκέναι, "to have fallen short". W. M. Ramsay, in *ExT* x (1898–99), pp. 57f., draws attention to the same form in a Greek inscription from Asia Minor (*Cities and Bishoprics of Phrygia* i [Oxford, 1895], No. 42), where a man has failed in his duty of attendance at a temple of Apollo (διὰ τὸ ὑσ[τερηκέν]ε καὶ μὴ παραγεγον[ένε]).

[16] Gk. ἐσμεν εὐηγγελισμένοι, "we have been evangelized" (*cf.* v. 6, οἱ πρότερον εὐαγγελισθέντες, "those who had formerly been evangelized"). The noun εὐαγγέλιον is not used in this epistle.

those earlier Israelites; it did not ensure their attainment of the goal for which they set out. Why? Because they did not appropriate the good news by faith when they heard it. The good news which was proclaimed to them, summarized in such Old Testament passages as Ex. 19:3-6; 23:20-33, told them how the God of their fathers, who had delivered them from Egypt, would bring them safely to the promised land and give them possession of it, and would make them "a kingdom of priests, and a holy nation" to Himself, if only they would obey His voice and keep His covenant. The reason why this message did not do them as much good as it was designed to do was that, in spite of their serious undertaking, they did not obey His voice or keep His covenant: "they brought no admixture of faith to the hearing of it" (NEB). The practical implication is clear: it is not the hearing of the gospel by itself that brings final salvation, but its appropriation by faith; and if that faith is a genuine faith, it will be a persistent faith.

3-5 It is for those who have accepted the saving message by faith, then, that entry into the "rest" of God is intended[17]—that rest which, in Ps. 95:11, He refers to as "my rest". But in what sense does God speak of "my rest"? Does it simply mean "the rest which I bestow" or does it also mean "the rest which I myself enjoy"? It means the latter: the "rest" which God promises to His people is a share in that rest which He Himself enjoys. Here, then, our author proceeds to bring out the underlying meaning of the reference to God's "rest" in Ps. 95:11 by relating it to Gen. 2:2f., where God is said to have "rested on the seventh day from all his work which he had made" in the course of the preceding six days. The Septuagint uses the same Greek word for God's "resting" or "desisting" on the sabbath day from His creative work (Gen. 2:2f.; Ex. 20:11) as for the "rest" of God in Ps. 95:11 (in the former case, the verb *katapauō;* in the latter, the substantive *katapausis*), although the Hebrew words are different (in the former case, the verb *shābath*, explaining the sense of *shabbāth*, "sabbath"; in the latter, the substantive *menūhāh*).

---

[17] AV, ERV, ARV give a somewhat misleading impression by rendering εἰσερχόμεθα by "do enter"; the auxiliary "do" may suggest that the entrance is here and now, whereas it lies ahead as something to be attained. The present tense is used in a generalizing sense: entry into (that) rest is for us who have believed.

It was not because the "rest" of God was not yet available that the wilderness generation of Israelites failed to enter into it; it had been available ever since creation's work was ended. When we read that God "rested on the seventh day from all his work which he had made" (Gen. 2:2), we are to understand that He *began* to rest then; the fact that He is never said to have completed His rest and resumed His work of creation implies that His rest continues still, and may be shared by those who respond to His overtures with faith and obedience. This interpretation which views the divine sabbath as beginning from the moment when creation's work came to an end and going on to the present time is paralleled in Philo[18] and is implied by our Lord's words in John 5:17, "My Father worketh even until now, and I work".[19] It differs from another interpretation which was widespread in the early Church, according to which the seventh day of Gen. 2:2f. is a type of the seventh age of righteousness which is to follow six ages of sin's domination.[20] The identification of the rest of God in the Epistle to the Hebrews with a coming millennium on earth

---

[18] Moffatt (ICC, p. 53) refers to Philo, *On the Cherubim* 26, and *On the Sacrifices of Abel and Cain* 8, for his treatment of the sabbath as the rest of God, but points out rightly that all such speculations as we find in Philo "are remote from our author". On the biblical basis of our author's thought see G. von Rad, "Es ist noch eine Ruhe vorhanden dem Volke Gottes" in *Gesammelte Studien zum Alten Testament* (Munich, 1958), pp. 101ff.

[19] The point of this reply to the charge that Jesus had broken the sabbath by performing an act of healing on that day is this: "You charge me with breaking the sabbath by working on it. But although God's sabbath began after the work of creation was finished, and is still going on, He continues to work—and therefore so do I."

[20] Cf. the *Epistle of Barnabas* 15:4f., 8: "Pay attention, children, to the meaning of the words: 'He finished it in six days'. It means that in 6,000 years the Lord will bring everything to completion. For the 'day' with Him is a thousand years, of which He Himself bears me witness when He says: 'Behold, the day of the Lord shall be as a thousand years'. Therefore, children, in six days—that is in 6,000 years—everything will be brought to completion. 'And He rested the seventh day'. This means: when His Son comes and brings to nought the period of the Lawless One and judges the ungodly and changes the sun and moon and stars, then He will rest properly on the seventh day ... Finally He says to them: 'Your new moons and your sabbaths I cannot endure'. See what He means: it is not your present sabbaths that are acceptable, but the sabbath that I have made, in which, when I have put everything to rest, I will make a beginning of the eighth day, that is, the beginning of a new world." The sabbath of God is here the seventh millennium of the present creation, which is to be followed

has, indeed, been ably defended;[21] but it involves the importation into the epistle of a concept which in fact is alien to it.

The vagueness of the terms with which the quotation from Gen. 2:2 is introduced is characteristic of our author: "he hath said somewhere[22] of the seventh day on this wise" (where "he" is probably "God", the subject of the preceding "hath said" of verse 3; otherwise one might use the pronoun "it", referring to "Scripture"; cf. NEB: "does not Scripture somewhere speak thus of the seventh day ... ?"). The repetition of the warning words of Ps. 95:11b after the Genesis quotation emphasizes the identification of the one rest with the other: God's rest has remained open to His people since the work of creation was finished, but it will be forfeited by disobedience.

6-7 It was disobedience, as we have seen, that kept the generation of the Exodus out of God's promised rest, in spite of the good news which was announced to them. But that same promised rest was still open for the people of God centuries after the wilderness period, for the writer of Psalm 95 urges his contemporaries to listen to the voice of God "to-day", instead of hardening their hearts in obstinacy like their ancestors and being debarred from entering into the rest of God as they had been. Psalm 95 is anonymous in the Massoretic text, but the Septuagint assigns it to David.[23] Our author's phrase "in David" (verse 7)[24] may mean simply "in the Psalter"; whether he thought of David as the composer of this particular psalm or not is immaterial to his argument, which is that the wording of the psalm implies that entry into the "rest" of God is still available "so long a time"[25] after the age of the Exodus and wilderness wanderings. Whether

---

by the eternal age of the new creation. (Barnabas has confused the issue by superimposing on the Jewish schema of the millennial sabbath or seventh "day" the Christian concept of an eighth millennium corresponding to the resurrection day.)

[21] Notably in more recent times by G. H. Lang, *The Epistle to the Hebrews* (London, 1951), pp. 73ff. See p. 368, n. 121.

[22] Gk. που, as in Ch. 2:6 (perhaps to be translated not "somewhere" but more generally "as we know" or "to quote familiar words"; cf. Westcott, *ad loc.*).

[23] The LXX title to this psalm is Αἶνος ᾠδῆς τῷ Δαυείδ.

[24] Cf. Rom. 11:2, ἐν 'Ηλείᾳ (where authorship is not implied); 9:25, ἐν τῷ 'Ωσηέ.

[25] Gk. μετὰ τοσοῦτον χρόνον. Our author takes historical perspective into account.

the psalm is the composition of David or not, the point of paramount importance is that it was God who spoke "in David" (*cf.* Ch. 3:7) and His word remains in effective vitality long after it was uttered, addressing the heart and conscience of hearers in the Christian era with the same convicting relevance as characterized it when first it was spoken. By dint of repetition our author endeavors to bring home to his readers the fact that the divine warning is as applicable to them as it was in the days of Moses or David. If they treat the saving message lightly, if they "tempt" God by trying to see how far they can presume upon His patience, they in their turn will forfeit His "rest". Therefore to them, as to the psalmist's contemporaries, the urgent appeal goes forth:

"While it is called To-day, repent
And harden not your heart."

8 It is plain (our author implies) that the "rest" spoken of in Ps. 95:11 is not the earthly Canaan. For that land of rest was occupied by the Israelites of the second generation, who entered it under the command of Joshua. The people addressed in the ninety-fifth psalm were already living in the land of Canaan, as their ancestors had been for generations now. Likewise, the "rest" which they were in danger of forfeiting through stubbornness of heart must have been something different from the "rest ... from all their enemies round about" which God had given to Israel in Joshua's day (Josh. 23:1; *cf.* 21:44).[26]

We have, of course, to use the personal name "Joshua" here instead of "Jesus" which appears in AV (the revisers of 1611 would have done better to follow the precedent of Tyndale, Coverdale and Whittingham, all of whom had used "Joshua").[27] Yet it must be recognized that the ordinary reader of the Greek Bible had (and still has, where he exists) an advantage over the reader of the English Bible because to him "Joshua" and "Jesus" are not two

---

[26] In both these places LXX uses καταπαύω, rendering the Hiph'il of Heb. *nūaḥ* (the root whence *menūḥāh* of Ps. 95:11 is derived).

[27] The Geneva and Bishops' versions have "Jesus". In LXX Joshua the son of Nun appears as Ἰησοῦς Ναυῆ. *Cf.* Acts 7:45 (ARV rightly "Joshua"; AV "Jesus"). Because Greek-speaking Christians saw a divinely designed coincidence between the names of the great Old Testament "Jesus" and of their own Savior, Aquila in his second-century Greek version of the Old Testament avoided the use of Ἰησοῦς for "Joshua", preferring the more exact transliteration Ἰωσουα.

names but one; he could distinguish between our Lord and his most illustrious namesake of Old Testament days, and at the same time appreciate some of the implications of the fact that they *are* namesakes. The parallel between the Old Testament "Jesus", who led his followers into the earthly Canaan, and Jesus the Son of God, who leads the heirs of the new covenant into their heavenly inheritance, is a prominent theme of early Christian typology,[28] and could scarcely have been absent from our author's mind. Yet he does not dwell on it here; he is more concerned to point the contrast between the temporal "rest" which Israel entered under Joshua and the true rest which is still reserved for the people of God.

9-10 This rest which is reserved for the people of God is properly called a "sabbath rest"—a *sabbatismos* or "sabbath keeping"[29]—because it is their participation in God's own rest. When God completed His work of creation, He "rested"; so His people, having completed their service on earth, will enter into His rest.[30] Verse 10, with its initial conjunction "for", explains the description of the believers' coming rest as a "sabbath keeping" in verse 9. Some ambiguity is occasioned by the threefold "his" in verse 10;[31] the meaning is brought out clearly in the NEB rendering: "Therefore, a sabbath rest still awaits the people of

---

[28] *Cf.* the *Epistle of Barnabas* 6:8f.; Justin, *Dialogue with Trypho* 113, 132. J. R. Harris (*Testimonies* ii [Cambridge, 1920], pp. 51ff.) shows how in early Christian apologetic Jesus is regarded as the antitype not only of the earlier Joshua but also of the later Joshua (or Jeshua), the first post-exilic high priest (Ezra 3:20; Hag. 1:1; Zech. 3:1; 6.11ff., etc.; *cf.* p. 86, n. 68; pp. 91f.; p. 96, n. 33; p. 249, n. 97); he traces a threefold typological pattern: "Jesus the Guide to the Land of Rest; Jesus the new Circumciser (*cf.* p. 81, n. 51); Jesus the great High-Priest" (p. 55). Harris went so far as to deprecate the alteration of AV "Jesus" to "Joshua" in ERV and ARV as obscuring the typology and altering the proper emphasis of the conditional clause with which v. 8 begins; he argued that the sense was "If it was *to them* that Jesus gave rest"—our author's point being, in his judgment, that Jesus gave rest, not to the Israelites of wilderness days, but to believers of the Christian age. But this is to read into our author's argument the more far-fetched typology of later *testimonia*. (*Cf.* the reference to Jude 5 on p. 63, n. 46.)

[29] See p. 72, n. 13.

[30] Compare the remarkable parallel in Rev. 14:13, where the Spirit confirms the blessedness of "the dead who die in the Lord" with the words, "yea, ... that they may rest (ἀναπαύομαι, 'have relief') from their labors; for their works (ἔργα, as here) follow with them".

[31] The first two occurrences of "his" represent Gk. αὐτοῦ, the third represents Gk. ἴδιος (ἀπὸ τῶν ἰδίων, "from His own").

God; for anyone who enters God's rest, rests from his own work as God did from his."[32] In other words, he has completed his appointed work in accordance with God's will.

What then is this sabbath rest which awaits them? It is evidently an experience which they do not enjoy in their present mortal life, although it belongs to them as a heritage, and by faith they may live in the good of it here and now.[33] How they may do so is illustrated with a wealth of biographical detail in Ch. 11. And in that chapter we have further references to the eternal homeland which is the heritage of believers—the "better country, that is, a heavenly" which they desire, the "city" which God has prepared for them (Ch. 11:16), "the city which hath the foundations, whose builder and maker is God" (Ch. 11:10). Of this city of God men and women of faith are citizens already, although the full exercise of their civic privileges in it is reserved for the future. Do they, then, receive these privileges and enter into the rest of God at death or at resurrection? Our author gives us no explicit answer to this question. So far as believers of Old Testament days are concerned, however, it appears that they did not attain their heavenly homeland immediately at death. When we are told that "they did not enter upon the promised inheritance, because, with us in mind, God had made a better plan, that only in company with us should they reach their perfection" (Ch. 11:39f., NEB),[34] the meaning must be that they had to wait until the time of fulfilment was introduced by Christ before they could realize completely those promised blessings whose prospect enabled them to live as they did. It may be, then, that in resurrection they, "in company with us", are to attain this perfection and enter into God's rest; but in the absence of an express statement to this effect (there is but little reference to resurrection throughout this epistle), we cannot be certain that this was our author's understanding of the matter. It is, indeed, perfectly conceivable that in his view the

---

[32] So E. Nestle in *ExT* ix (1897–98), pp. 47f.: "Here there can be no doubt that the first αὐτοῦ refers to God, the second αὐτοῦ and αὐτός [ARV "himself"] to man."

[33] *Cf.* C. K. Barrett, "New Testament Eschatology", *SJTh* vi (1953), pp. 136ff., 225ff.; "The Eschatology of the Epistle to the Hebrews" in *The Background of the New Testament and its Eschatology*, ed. W. D. Davies and D. Daube (Cambridge, 1956), pp. 363ff.

[34] See pp. 343f.; *cf.* also p. 378 (on Ch. 12:23).

Old Testament believers entered into the rest of God as soon as Christ had accomplished His redemptive work, while believers of the New Testament age enter it at death. One way or the other, this blissful rest in unbroken fellowship with God is the goal to which His people are urged to press forward; this is the final perfection which has been prepared for them by the sacrifice of their heavenly high priest. "It is for you", our author might well have told them (in the words of a younger contemporary of his),[35] "that paradise is opened, the tree of life is planted, the age to come is prepared, plenty is provided, a city is built, rest is appointed, goodness is established and wisdom perfected beforehand" (IV Ezra 8:52).

4. EXHORTATION TO ATTAIN GOD'S REST

Ch. 4:11–13

11 Let us therefore give diligence to enter into that rest, that no man fall after the same example of disobedience.[36]

12 For the word of God is living, and active,[37] and sharper than any two-edged sword, and piercing even to the dividing of soul and spirit, of both joints and marrow, and quick to discern the thoughts and intents[38] of the heart.

13 And there is no creature that is not manifest in his sight: but all things are naked and laid open before the eyes of him with whom we have to do.

11 In view of all the glory that is accessible to faith, in view of the disaster that follows upon unbelief, our author urges his readers once more to make it their earnest endeavor[39] to attain the

---

35 IV Ezra (II Esdras) is probably to be dated somewhere within the last thirty years of the first century A.D.

36 Gk. ἀπειθείας, for which ἀπιστίας ("of unbelief") is read by P⁴⁶ 1611 2005 with the Latin, Sahidic Coptic and Armenian versions. *Cf.* Chs. 3:8; 4:6; 11:31 (p. 61, n. 34; p. 71, n. 10; p. 325, n. 212).

37 Gk. ἐνεργής, for which B reads ἐναργής ("manifest", "clear-shining")—a reading known to Jerome. *Cf.* Mangey's conjectural but certain emendation ἐνάργειαν for ἐνέργειαν in Philo, *Migration of Abraham* 35, ἐνάργειαν τῶν πραγμάτων ἀριδηλοτάτην ("the most distinct clarity of things").

38 Gk. ἐνθυμήσεων καὶ ἐννοιῶν, for which D* reads ἐνθυμήσεως ἐννοιῶν τε and C* I (and possibly Origen in one out of two instances) ἐνθυμήσεως καὶ ἐννοιῶν.

39 Gk. σπουδάσωμεν ("Let us then make every effort", NEB; "Let us therefore strive", RSV).

eternal home of the people of God, and not miss it through disobedience like that of the Israelites in the wilderness. Zeal and perseverance are called for; no one can

"be carried to the skies
On flowery beds of ease."[40]

God is not to be trifled with; His word cannot be ignored with impunity, but must be received in faith and obeyed in daily life. God's "To-day" has arrived; let us take His word seriously and make haste to enter His rest.[41]

12 For God's word—that word which fell on disobedient ears in the wilderness and which has been sounded out again in these days of fulfilment—is not like the word of man; it is living, effective and self-fulfilling; it diagnoses the condition of the human heart, saying "Thou ailest here, and here"; it brings blessing to those who receive it in faith and pronounces judgment on those who disregard it.

All that our author says here about the word *(logos)* of God is in line with the Old Testament witness. There are verbal links with Philo, who can, for example, speak of the Logos as the "cutter"[42]; but Moffatt rightly says that "our author is using Philonic language rather than Philonic ideas". With the "living" word we may compare Stephen's reference to the "living oracles" received by Moses at Sinai (Acts 7:38), and Peter's description of "the word of God, which liveth and abideth" (I Pet. 1:23). The word is "active" in the sense that it speeds to fulfil the purpose for which it has been uttered: this self-fulfilling character which it possesses is well summed up in Isa. 55:11 where the God of Israel says of "my word ... that goeth forth out of my mouth": "it shall not return unto me void, but it shall accomplish that which I please, and it shall prosper in the thing whereto I sent it".[43]

If the word of God is personified here, the personification is slight—slighter, for instance, than in Wisdom 18:15f., where the

<hr>

[40] I. Watts.

[41] *Cf.* C. H. Dodd, *According to the Scriptures* (London, 1952), pp. 20f.

[42] He explains the dividing of the covenant victims in Gen. 15:10 as performed by God "by means of His word, the cutter of everything (τῷ τομεῖ τῶν συμπάντων ἑαυτοῦ λόγῳ)" *(Who is the heir of divine things?* 130).

[43] *Cf.* Jer. 23:29, "Is not my word (LXX οἱ λόγοι μου) like fire? ... and like a hammer that breaketh the rock in pieces?"

Logos is not simply compared to a sharp sword, but is portrayed as the personal wielder of the sword:

> "Thy all-powerful word leaped from heaven, from the royal throne,
> into the midst of the land that was doomed,
> a stern[44] warrior carrying the sharp sword of thy authentic command,
> and stood and filled all things with death,
> and touched heaven while standing on the earth."

The "word of God" in this Hebrews passage is parallel not so much to "thy all-powerful word"[45] as to "thy authentic command"[46] in the Wisdom passage, for it is God's "authentic command" that is described as a sharp sword.[47]

Here, however, the divine word is not merely described as a sharp sword, but as sharper than the sharpest sword. The expression "a two-edged sword"[48] occurs a few times in the Old Testament,[49] but there is no particular reference here to any one of its Old Testament occurrences, nor yet (in all probability) to other Old Testament passages which have been suggested as being in our author's mind here, such as the dividing of the carcasses in Gen. 15:10[50] or the circumcising of the Israelites with flint knives in Josh. 5:2ff.[51] The words which follow—"piercing even to the

---

[44]   Gk. ἀπότομος (cf. here τομώτερος, "sharper").

[45]   Gk. ὁ παντοδύναμός σου λόγος. See p. 324, n. 206.

[46]   Gk. τὴν ἀνυπόκριτον ἐπιταγήν σου.

[47]   Gk. ξίφος ὀξύ (as against τομώτερος ὑπὲρ πᾶσαν μάχαιραν here); cf. Isa. 49:2, where God makes the Servant's mouth "like a sharp sword". (See p. 324, n. 206.)

[48]   Gk. δί-στομος (lit. "two-mouthed"), not δισ-τόμος ("twice-cutting"). The word is classical; cf. Euripides Helena 983, δίστομον ξίφος ("two-edged sword").

[49]   Judg. 3:16; Ps. 149:6; Prov. 5:4; Sir. 21:3. Its other NT occurrences are in Revelation (1:16; 2:12, and in some authorities 19:15), of the "sword" (Gk. ῥομφαία) proceeding from the mouth of the glorified Christ. In the Valentinian Gospel of Truth (Jung Codex 26:2) the judgment (κρίσις) that comes from heaven is described as "a drawn sword of two edges cutting this way and that". There may be an allusion there to the sword at the east of Eden (Gen. 3:24), which Philo (On the Cherubim, 28) interprets as the Logos.

[50]   Cf. Philo's treatment of this narrative (p. 80, n. 42 above).

[51]   Justin Martyr, drawing out the parallel between Joshua and Jesus (see p. 77, n. 28 above), says: "Jesus Christ circumcises all who will with knives of stone" (Dialogue with Trypho, 24). This becomes a commonplace interpretation

dividing of soul and spirit, of both joints and marrow"—are to be understood as a "rhetorical accumulation of terms to express the whole mental nature of man on all its sides"; so A. B. Davidson, who further points out that since "the idea of dividing the soul and spirit suggests the division of a body into its members, hence joints and marrow are attributed to them, expressing the subtle articulations of the spiritual being and the innermost nature and substance of it".[52] It would indeed be precarious to draw any conclusions from these words about our author's psychology, nor is it necessary to understand them in the sense of the Pauline distinction between soul and spirit.[53] That the word of God probes the inmost recesses of our spiritual being and brings the sub-conscious motives to light is what is meant; we may compare Paul's language about the coming day when the Lord "will both bring to light the hidden things of darkness, and make manifest the counsels of the hearts" (I Cor. 4:5). It is not surprising, accordingly, that a judicial function is here attributed to the word of God.[54] It is "discriminative of the heart's thoughts and intents"; this is the rendering of E. K. Simpson who, in a survey of the use

---

of Josh. 5:2 in early Christian literature; the Syriac father Aphrahat in his treatise *On Circumcision* puts it thus: "Jesus our Saviour circumcised a second time, with the circumcision of the heart, the people who had been baptized by baptism, and they were circumcised *with the scimitar which is sharper than a sword with two edges*" (J. R. Harris, *Testimonies* ii [Cambridge, 1920], pp. 55f.). Aphrahat evidently thinks of the "word of God" (as described in this passage of Hebrews) as the means by which our Lord effects the circumcision of the heart. But it is going too far to suppose with Rendel Harris (*loc. cit.*) that Aphrahat's language reflects a use of the *testimonium* (Josh. 5:2) which was already accessible to the author of Hebrews, and that accordingly the heart-discerning power of the Logos in our present passage is another way of expressing the circumcision of the heart.

[52] A. B. Davidson, *The Epistle to the Hebrews* (Edinburgh, 1882), p. 96.

[53] C. Spicq, however, following A. J. Festugière (*L'idéal religieux des Grecs et l'Évangile* [Paris, 1932], pp. 212ff.), sees here the Philonic dichotomy between ψυχή and πνεῦμα, the latter being the higher part which apprehends divine philosophy (*L'Épître aux Hébreux*, i [Paris, 1952], pp. 52f.). *Cf.* G. H. Lang, *op. cit.*, pp. 82f.: "It is of the highest importance to recognize these two types of life, the soulish and the spiritual".

[54] With the application to the word of God of the epithet κριτικός here may be compared Philo's comment on Gen. 14:7, where the same place is called En-mishpat ("the spring of judgment", LXX τὴν πηγὴν τῆς κρίσεως) and Kadesh ("holy place"): "The wisdom of God is both holy ... and the judgment (κρίσις) of all things, by which all opposites are disjoined" (*On Flight*, 196).

of the adjective *kritikos* (ARV "quick to discern")[55] by Aristotle and others, says: "In all these examples it is a sifting process that is at work; and what winnowing-fan can vie with the gales of the Spirit blowing through the Word?" With the function here ascribed to the word of God we may compare the epithet "heart-knowing" applied to God Himself in Acts 1:24; 15:8.[56]

13 We may conceal our inner being from our neighbors, and we can even deceive ourselves; but nothing escapes the scrutiny of God; before Him everything lies exposed and powerless.[57] And it is with Him, not with our fellow-men or with our own conscience, that our final reckoning[58] has to be made. Stripped of all disguise and protection we are utterly at the mercy of God, the Judge of all. Therefore, "let us give diligence ...!"

With these words, the second admonition of the epistle is concluded.

---

[55] *EQ* xviii (1946), pp. 37f.

[56] Gk. καρδιογνώστης.

[57] Gk. τετραχηλισμένος, perfect participle passive of τραχηλίζω, which appears to denote bending back the neck (τράχηλος) or seizing by the throat. The former sense is quoted from Theophrastus (bending back the sacrificial victim's neck for the fatal stroke). E. K. Simpson quotes examples from Philo and Josephus in support of the rendering "exhausted": "in the wrestler's art τραχηλισμός was a grip of the antagonist's throat akin to the bandit's *garrote*, rendering him limp and powerless ... This characteristic figure then may be held to represent either the denuded or helpless plight of all created persons or forces when brought face to face with their Creator and Lord" (*EQ* xviii [1946], p. 38, at the end of an article on "The Vocabulary of the Epistle to the Hebrews").

[58] Gk. λόγος, in a different sense from that in which it is used at the beginning of v. 12. *Cf.* Ch. 13:17 (p. 407 with n. 99). The idiom is classical.

III. THE HIGH PRIESTHOOD OF CHRIST

Chs. 4:14–6:20

1. CHRIST'S HIGH PRIESTHOOD AN ENCOURAGEMENT
TO HIS PEOPLE

Ch. 4:14–16

14 Having[59] then a great high priest, who hath passed
through the heavens, Jesus the Son of God, let us hold
fast our confession.

15 For we have not a high priest that cannot be touched
with the feeling of our infirmities; but one that hath been
in all points tempted like as *we are, yet* without sin.

16 Let us therefore draw near with boldness unto the throne
of grace, that we may receive mercy, and may find[60]
grace to help *us* in time of need.

14 With admonition is coupled positive encouragement.
Jesus has already been presented to the readers as "a merciful and
faithful high priest" (Ch. 2:17), and they are now shown how He
is the one from whom they can receive all the strength they need to
maintain their confession and resist the temptation to let go and
fall back. "Jesus the Son of God" is not disqualified by His divine
origin from sharing in His people's troubles and sympathizing with
their weakness. He Himself endured every trial that they are
likely to undergo, but remained steadfast throughout, and has
now "passed through the heavens" to the very throne of God. In
Him, then, His people have a powerful incentive to perseverance
in faith and obedience.

"The heavens" through which Jesus passed are the heavenly
regions in general; we need not try to enumerate the successive
"heavens" involved and determine whether He is envisaged as

---

[59] In the versions of Tyndale and Coverdale (following Luther) Ch. 4:14
appears as Ch. 5:1.

[60] Gk. $\varepsilon\ddot{v}\varrho\omega\mu\varepsilon\nu$, omitted from B; according to Zuntz (*op. cit.*, p. 41) its
omission means that we have as the object of the remaining verb $\lambda\dot{\alpha}\beta\omega\mu\varepsilon\nu$ the
typical LXX expression $\ddot{\varepsilon}\lambda\varepsilon o\varsigma$ $\varkappa\alpha\dot{\iota}$ $\chi\dot{\alpha}\varrho\iota\nu$ ("mercy and grace").

passing through three or seven of them.[61] The plural "heavens", as regularly in the New Testament and Septuagint, reflects the Hebrew word used in the Old Testament, which is always plural. What is emphasized here is His transcendence; He is "made higher than the heavens", as we are told later in the epistle (Ch. 7:26), or, as it is put in Eph. 4:10, He "ascended far above all the heavens, that he might fill all things".[62] It is because He has been so highly exalted that He is such a "great" high priest;[63] there is already the implied contrast here (which is brought out in explicit detail later) between Him and the earthly high priests of Aaron's line, whose highest privilege was to pass once a year through the inner veil into the holy of holies in a material and temporary sanctuary, there to appear for a few moments before God on behalf of their people. With Him as their helper, the people of Christ might well hold fast the "confession"[64] in which He played a central part.

15 His transcendence, however, has made no difference to His humanity. Our author has already stated that, in order to "become a merciful and faithful and high priest", the Son of God had "in all things to be made like unto his brethren"; and that "he is able to succor them that are tempted" because "he himself hath suffered being tempted" (Ch. 2:17f.). So here he repeats that Christians have in heaven a high priest with an unequalled capacity for sympathizing with them in all the dangers and sorrows and trials which come their way in life, because He Himself, by virtue of His likeness to them,[65] was exposed to all these experiences. Yet He endured triumphantly every form of testing that man could endure,

---

[61] For the enumeration of heavens (three or seven) *cf.* II Cor. 12:2; *Test. Levi* 2:7ff.; *Ascension of Isaiah* 6:13; 7:13ff.; TB *Hagigah* 12*b* (see p. 374, n. 150). For the view that "the heavens" through which Christ has passed are symbolized by the outer compartment of the earthly sanctuary see p. 194, n. 57.

[62] *Cf.* Eph. 1:21.

[63] In OT "high priest" is literally (for the most part) "great priest" (Heb. *kōhēn gādōl*); so in Ch. 10:21 (p. 249 with n. 97). The unusually full expression here (Gk. ἀρχιερεὺς μέγας) probably marks Jesus out as greater than the Aaronic high priests; it is used in I Macc. 13:42 (of Simon Maccabaeus) and in Philo, *On Dreams* i. 214, 219; ii. 183 (of the Logos).

[64] Gk. ὁμολογία, as in Ch. 3:1.

[65] Gk. καθ' ὁμοιότητα, lit. "according to likeness" (rendered "like as *we are*" in ARV, following AV). NEB brings out the meaning well: "one who, because of his likeness to us, has been tested every way, only without sin".

85

without any weakening of His faith in God or any relaxation of His obedience to Him. Such endurance involves more, not less, than ordinary human suffering: "sympathy with the sinner in his trial does not depend on the experience of sin but on the experience of the strength of the temptation to sin which only the sinless can know in its full intensity. He who falls yields before the last strain".[66] The phrase "apart from sin"[67] does not mean that our Lord experienced every kind of human temptation except temptation to sin; like the Israelites in Moses' day, He too had His day of trial in the wilderness, and any compromise with the tempter's suggestions, any inclination to put God to the test, would have been as certainly sin as His refusal to countenance these suggestions or abate one iota of His confidence in His Father meant spiritual victory—victory for Himself and also for His people.[68]

16 Therefore, says our author, let us come with full confidence[69] to the throne of grace. This throne of grace is the throne of God, where Jesus, as His people's high priest, sits exalted at the Father's right hand. It is the antitype, in our author's mind, to the "mercy-seat" in the earthly sanctuary, of which he speaks below in Ch. 9:5; in Tyndale's New Testament and the Great Bible (1539) the same rendering, "the seat of grace", is used both there and here. It was before the earthly mercy-seat that the work of propitiation was completed in token on the day of atonement and the grace of God extended to His people; the presence of the Christians' high priest on the heavenly throne of grace bespeaks a work of propitiation completed not in token but in fact, and the constant availa-

---

[66] B. F. Westcott, *ad loc.*

[67] Gk. χωρὶς ἁμαρτίας. *Cf.* B. F. C. Atkinson, *The Theology of Prepositions* (London, 1944), p. 5 ("His sinless nature contained nothing that responded to temptation, as does ours"); J. Moffatt, ICC, *ad loc.* ("The special reference is to temptations leading to apostasy or disobedience to the will of God. It is true that χωρὶς ἁμαρτίας does exclude some temptations ... a number of our worst temptations arise out of sin previously committed").

[68] J. R. Harris (*ExT* xxxiii [1921–22], pp. 217f.) sees an allusion here to the typological parallel between Jesus and Joshua the high priest of Zech 3:1ff. (p. 77, n. 28; p. 249, n. 97); the parallel is incomplete in that Joshua required to be cleansed from his own sins (*cf.* Ch. 7:27), whereas Jesus was χωρὶς ἁμαρτίας. On the general subject which our author treats here *cf.* J. K. S. Reid, "Tempted, yet without sin", *EQ* xxi (1949), pp. 161ff.; A. H. Curtis, *The Vision and Mission of Jesus* (Edinburgh, 1954), pp. 131ff.

[69] Gk. παρρησία (*cf.* p. 244 with n. 82, on Ch. 10:19).

bility of divine aid in all their need. Thanks to Him, the throne of God is a mercy-seat to which they have free access and from which they may receive all the grace and power required "for timely help"[70] in the hour of trial and crisis.

---

[70]   Gk. $εἰς$ $εὔκαιρον$ $βοήθειαν$. *TWNT* i, p. 629, cites a close parallel from a Greek inscription: $βοηθεῖτο$ $κατὰ$ $τὸ$ $εὔκαιρον$ ("received timely help").

CHAPTER V

2. QUALIFICATIONS FOR HIGH PRIESTHOOD

Ch. 5:1–4

1 For every high priest, being taken from among men, is appointed[1] for men in things pertaining to God, that he may offer both[2] gifts and sacrifices for sins:[3]

2 who can bear gently with the ignorant and erring, for that he himself also is compassed with infirmity;

3 and by reason thereof is bound, as for the people, so also for himself, to offer for sins.[4]

4 And no man taketh the honor unto himself, but when he is called of God, even as was Aaron.

Our author makes two points about the general qualifications which any high priest must satisfy, before he goes on to speak more particularly of Christ's qualifications to be His people's high priest. A high priest must be *(a)* able to sympathize with those whom he represents, and *(b)* divinely appointed to his office. How these two conditions apply to the Aaronic high priesthood is briefly set out.

1 *(a)* A high priest represents men "in matters for which they are responsible to God";[5] it is necessary therefore that he should be a man himself. Aaron and his successors, who represented the

---

[1] Gk. καθίσταται. That it is to be construed here (and in Ch. 8:3) as a passive is confirmed by the corresponding use of the active καθίστησιν in Ch. 7:28 ("the law appointeth men high priests"). It might be parsed as middle and transitive, and is so interpreted by Calvin (*ad loc.*), its object being regarded as τὰ πρὸς τὸν θεόν ("every high priest ordains the things which pertain to God"); but τὰ πρὸς τὸν θεόν is an adverbial phrase (*cf.* Ch. 2:17, p. 52, n. 87).

[2] Gk. τε ("both") is omitted by P⁴⁶ B Dᶜ; for its retention *cf.* G. Zuntz, *The Text of the Epistles* (London, 1953), p. 62.

[3] Gk. ὑπὲρ ἁμαρτιῶν, for which P⁴⁶ 1739 read περὶ ἁμαρτιῶν (probably under the influence of v. 3). For περὶ ἁμαρτιῶν *cf.* I Pet. 3:18. This is not precisely the idiomatic LXX use of περὶ ἁμαρτίας as the equivalent of Heb. ḥaṭṭā'th, for which see Ch. 10:6 (p. 234, n. 42).

[4] Gk. περὶ ἁμαρτιῶν, for which the Byzantine text has ὑπὲρ ἁμαρτιῶν (*cf.* v. 1, and n. 3 above).

[5] *Cf.* p. 52, n. 87.

nation of Israel in the presence of God, were Israelites themselves, conversant with the conditions under which their people lived, exposed to the same pressures and trials.

The high priest's duties are here said to be the presenting of his people's gifts and sin-offerings to God.[6] "Gifts" is the more comprehensive term; it would normally include "sacrifices" but not be coextensive with them. But "gifts and sacrifices" appears to be used by our author as a general expression in the sense of "offerings"; here the particular class of offerings intended is indicated by the added words "for sins".[7] And it emerges clearly in the course of his later argument that the particular sin-offerings which he has in mind are those presented annually on the day of atonement; that was the occasion above all others on which the high priest in person was required to discharge the sacrificial functions.[8]

2 In order to fulfil these duties worthily, a high priest needs not only to pay heed to the precise performance of the several ritual details, but also to have inward feelings which are in keeping with his sacred work. This is something which commands our instant approval. No one can read the history of the Second Temple without being conscious of the preposterous situation which made a man like Alexander Jannaeus[9] his subjects' representative before God in the most solemn moments of national worship. Even if his ritual acts had been more punctiliously correct than many of the worshippers thought them to be,[10] the

---

[6] The linking of "gifts" (Gk. $\delta\tilde{\omega}\varrho\alpha$) and "sacrifices" (Gk. $\theta\upsilon\sigma\iota\alpha\varsigma$) by "both ... and" (Gk. $\tau\varepsilon\;\varkappa\alpha\iota$) suggests that the two terms are not sharply disjoined, as though the sense were: "that he may offer (a) gifts and (b) sacrifices for sins"; $\upsilon\pi\grave{\varepsilon}\varrho\;\dot{\alpha}\mu\alpha\varrho\tau\iota\tilde{\omega}\nu$ probably qualifies $\delta\tilde{\omega}\varrho\dot\alpha\;\tau\varepsilon\;\varkappa\alpha\iota\;\theta\upsilon\sigma\iota\alpha\varsigma$ and not $\theta\upsilon\sigma\iota\alpha\varsigma$ alone. The phrase "gifts and sacrifices" may be a generic term current in Alexandrian Judaism; cf. Epistle of Aristeas 234: "to honor God, not with gifts or sacrifices ($o\upsilon\;\delta\dot\omega\varrho\iota\varsigma\;o\upsilon\delta\grave{\varepsilon}\;\theta\upsilon\sigma\iota\alpha\iota\varsigma$), but with purity of soul ..." (cf. Chs. 8:3; 9:9).

[7] Cf. the very different tone of Philo's summary of the high priest's functions: since his vestments symbolize the cosmos, "he who has been consecrated to the Father of the cosmos must needs have that Father's son [the cosmos] with all his fulness of excellence to plead his cause, that sins may be remembered no more and good things be supplied in most lavish abundance" (Life of Moses ii. 134).

[8] Cf. Ch. 9:7 (pp. 192ff.).

[9] Hasmonaean king and high priest, 103-76 B.C.

[10] By combining the indications from Josephus, Ant. xiii. 372ff., and TB Sukkah, 48b, we learn that once, at the Feast of Tabernacles, the populace pelted him with citrons because he insisted on performing the ceremony of

character of the man made him hopelessly unsuitable for the high priesthood. No man in Israel was less disposed to "bear gently with the ignorant and erring"—or with anyone else. And indeed, from the fall of the house of Zadok[11] to the destruction of the temple two hundred and forty years later there were very few high priests in Israel who manifested the personal qualities so indispensable for their sacred office. Our author, however, in all that he has to say about Israel's priesthood and sacrificial worship has the literary data of the Pentateuch in mind and not the facts of more recent history.

The Greek verb translated "bear gently"[12] denotes in general "the golden mean between indifference and mawkish sentimentality"; here it indicates more particularly forbearance and magnanimity on the part of people who are subject to great

---

water-pouring in a way which did not commend itself to them as proper (pouring the water on the ground beside the altar, after the Sadducean manner, and not on the altar itself, in the Pharisaic manner).

[11] When Onias III was assassinated (171 B.C.); cf. II Macc. 3:34.

[12] Gk. μετριοπαθεῖν. "This striking expression," says E. K. Simpson (EQ xviii [1946], pp. 36f.), "traces its genesis to the Peripatetic philosophy, in contradistinction from the Stoic's affectation of a marble apathy of demeanour. Within the bounds of self-respect it advocates a tolerant or sympathetic posture of mind in respect of provocations from others or misfortunes that may have overtaken them. The term μετριοπάθεια is accordingly coupled with πραότης and ἐπιείκεια, especially by Plutarch, with whom it is a favourite locution. The noble portrait of Achilles limned by Euripides in the Iphigeneia in Aulis (920f.) presents its prototype:

ἐπίσταμαι δὲ τοῖς κακοῖσί τ᾿ ἀσχαλᾶν
μετρίως τε χαίρειν τοῖσιν ἐξωγκωμένοις.

Such a blend of forbearance and condolence was ideally requisite in God's high priest under the old dispensation, both in his sacerdotal and judicial functions. But human infirmity marred the fair vision, till the Eternal Priest, Perfection's real Counterpart, trod the scene. For (and this renders the word almost untranslatable) μετριοπάθεια is the golden mean between indifference and mawkish sentimentality. Aaron's fond compliance with Israel's masked idolatry and Eli's lax indulgence of his profligate sons were gross abuses of their lofty office. The true high-priest's long-suffering will be duly measured, proportionate to the case in hand and the ignorance or waywardness he has to deal with; it will be adjusted to an equitable standard and free from extravagance no less than insensibility; not gushing, yet unfeignedly gracious (cf. Aristeas, 256: τὰ πρὸς τὸν καιρὸν πράσσειν δεόντως μετριοπαθῆ καθεστῶτα) ... To treat considerately is an inadequate rendering, yet we can devise no better." Cf. also C. Spicq, L'Épître aux Hebreux i (Paris, 1952), p. 43; he mentions several occurrences in Philo.

provocation and who could, if they wished, give way to un-moderated anger and meet the provocation with the utmost severity. A high priest could not make fitting expiation for sins which filled him, at that very time, with feelings of indignation and exasperation against those who were guilty of them. Aaron is credited with exemplary forbearance in face of the repeated provocation and envy of those on whose behalf he served as high priest[13]—although in this respect, as in most others, he falls far behind his brother Moses.[14]

The objects of his gentle forbearance are those who are ignorant and astray—probably we should understand a hendiadys here and take the phrase to mean "those who go astray through ignorance".[15] It was for such people—for those who succumbed to the moral infirmities that are common to mankind—that sin-offerings were prescribed in the law: "and the priest shall make atonement for the soul that erreth, when he sinneth unwittingly, before Jehovah, to make atonement for him; and he shall be forgiven" (Num. 15:28).[16] No such provision was made for the deliberate and defiant lawbreaker.[17]

But with those who erred through ignorance the high priest might well sympathize, for he was prone to the same weaknesses himself. This was manifest from the records of several priests of Old Testament times (not to speak of those of the Hellenistic and Roman eras). Outstanding examples of high priests "compassed with infirmity" were Joshua the son of Jehozadak, whose unfitness for the office had to be removed by the cleansing pronouncement

---

[13] Cf. Num. 14:5; 16:22, 47f.; Ps. 106:16.

[14] Cf. Num. 12:3 (see also p. 56).

[15] Gk. τοῖς ἀγνοοῦσιν καὶ πλανωμένοις.

[16] Cf. Lev. 4:2 et passim; 5:17. The guilt-offering of Lev. 6:1ff., making provision for cases of fraud in civil negotiations which involve "a breach of faith against the LORD" (RSV), implies less inadvertence than does the sin-offering of Lev. 4; the case of Lev. 5:17 "appears when someone feels an obscure sense of guilt weighing upon him through the unintentional transgression of a divine commandment, without being able to give a more exact account of the matter; in this case too he is to bring a guilt-offering, because the transgression might conceivably consist of a 'breach of faith' or 'trespass' [of the kind mention-ed in Lev. 5:15]; but as the extent of the trespass cannot be gauged, there can naturally be no question of making restitution in the proportion of six parts to five" (A. Dillmann, in A. Dillmann and V. Ryssel, Die Bücher Exodus und Leviticus[3] [Leipzig, 1897], p. 478, on Lev. 5:17).

[17] Cf. Num. 15:30 (p. 28, n. 2).

of God (Zech. 3:3ff.), and Aaron himself, whose feeble yielding to the people's demand for a visible symbol of deity is matched only by the ineptitude of his excuse to Moses: "I said unto them, Whosoever hath any gold, let them break it off: so they gave it me; and I cast it into the fire, and there came out this calf" (Ex. 32:24). Aaron was in no condition to make priestly intercession to God for the people on whom he had brought this great sin; it was Moses who went into the presence of God to make atonement for their sin and procure His pardon for them.[18]

3 No wonder, then, that the high priest had to present a sin-offering for himself as well as for his people. This is specifically provided for in the directions for the day of atonement. Only after Aaron had presented a bullock as a sin offering to make atonement for himself and his family, in accordance with prescription of Lev. 16:6, could he proceed with the atoning ritual on the people's behalf. As our author points out later in the epistle (Ch. 7:27), this is one of the features which distinguish the Christians' high priest from those of the Aaronic succession: Jesus, being "holy, guileless, undefiled", had no need to offer a preliminary sacrifice for Himself. It is by enduring the common weaknesses and temptations of man's lot, not by yielding to them, that He has established His power not only to sympathize with His people but to bring them help, deliverance and victory.

4 *(b)* If one qualification in a high priest is his ability to sympathize, another is his being called by God to this honorable service. No man can of his own accord set himself up as high priest, nor can he hold office validly by the gift of any earthly authority. (Had our author been minded to review the history of the Jewish high priesthood during the last two centuries or so of its existence, he could have illustrated this last point very effectively!)[19] Aaron,

---

[18]   Ex. 32:11ff., 31f.

[19]   After the deposition of Onias III in 174 B.C., Jason and later Menelaus were appointed to the high priesthood by Antiochus IV; Alcimus was appointed by Demetrius I in 162 B.C.; the Hasmonaean Jonathan was appointed by Alexander Balas, putative son of Antiochus IV, in 152 B.C.; his brother Simon and his successors were appointed by decree of the Jewish people in 140 B.C. (I Macc. 14:41). With the fall of the Hasmonaean house the high priests were appointed successively by Herod the Great (37–4 B.C.), Archelaus (4 B.C.–A.D. 6), Roman governors (A.D. 6–41), and members of the Herod family (A.D. 41–66). The last high priest, Phanni, son of Samuel, was appointed by popular ballot during the war against Rome (*c*. A.D. 67).

the first of Israel's high priests, occupied his office by divine
appointment (Ex. 28:1ff.; Lev. 8:1ff.; Num. 16:5; 17:5; 18:1ff.;
Ps. 105:26), and so did his heirs and successors (Num. 20:23ff.;
25:10ff.). And others who were not of Aaronic descent, but in a
time of emergency exercised an intercessory and sacrificial ministry
like that of the Aaronic priests, did so by a direct and special call
from God, as did Samuel (I Sam. 6:3ff.).[20] If our author is to
sustain his thesis that Jesus is His people's great high priest, he
must produce comparable evidence of a divine call in His case.

3. CHRIST'S QUALIFICATIONS FOR HIGH PRIESTHOOD

Ch. 5:5-10

5 So Christ also glorified not himself to be made a high
priest, but he that spake unto him,
> Thou art my Son,
> This day have I begotten thee:[21]

6 as he saith also in another *place*,
> Thou art a priest for ever
> After the order of Melchizedek.[22]

7 Who in the days of his flesh, having offered up prayers
and supplications[23] with strong crying and tears unto him
that was able to save him from death, and having been
heard for his godly fear,

8 though he was a Son,[24] yet learned obedience by the
things which he suffered;

---

[20] Note the collocation of Samuel with Moses in Jer. 15:1; *cf.* Ps. 99:6
(LXX 98:6). See pp. 333f. (on Ch. 11:32).

[21] Ps. 2:7 (*cf.* Ch. 1:5a, pp. 11ff.).

[22] Ps. 110:4 (LXX 109:4). The verb εἶ ("art"), present in LXX, is left
to be understood here.

[23] Gk. δεήσεις τε καὶ ἱκετηρίας. The collocation of the two words is quoted
from Isocrates, Polybius and Philo (*cf.* AG, *s.v.* ἱκετηρία; Spicq, *op. cit.*, i, p. 45;
ii, p. 112f.). Whereas δέησις is common in NT, ἱκετηρία occurs here only (it
occurs in LXX in Job 40:22 [conjoined with δέησις]; II Macc. 9:18); it is
originally the feminine of the adjective ἱκετήριος, and such a substantive as ἐλαία
or ῥάβδος is implied along with it, the olive branch being the regular token of
supplication.

[24] Gk. καίπερ ὢν υἱός, "Son though he was". See pp. 102f.

9   and having been made perfect, he became unto all them
     that obey him the author of eternal salvation;

10   named of God a high priest after the order of Melchizedek.

The same two qualifications as are requisite in any high priest
are present in Christ; in His case, however, our author presents
them in the reverse order: *(a)* His divine appointment and *(b)* His
ability to sympathize with His people.

5 *(a)*   Even Christ, the Son of God, did not assume the high-
priestly dignity by His own initiative; He was called to it by God,
who acclaimed Him as His Son in the words of Ps. 2:7. The words
"Thou art my Son, this day have I begotten thee", have already
been quoted in Ch. 1:5. It was suggested in the exposition of
that verse (largely on the basis of the present context of the
quotation) that "this day" in our author's mind is the day of
Christ's enthronement—the day when the Most High gave public
notice that He had exalted the crucified Jesus as "both Lord and
Christ" (Acts 2:36). And, says our author, the same God who
acclaimed Jesus as His Son has also acclaimed Him as perpetual
high priest.

6   The opening words of Ps. 110, as we have seen already in
our study of their quotation in Ch. 1:13, form one of the earliest
Christian *testimonia* to the Messiahship of Jesus.[25] But our author
takes up verse 4 of that psalm and applies it to Jesus in a way
which, so far as we can tell, was unprecedented in the early Church.
In some strands of Jewish expectation, a distinction was made
between the lay Messiah (the "Messiah of Israel" or prince of the
house of David) and the priestly Messiah (the "Messiah of
Aaron").[26] It has indeed been argued that the people to whom
this epistle was addressed were related to those groups which held
a twofold messianic hope of this kind.[27] But here they are assured

---

[25]   See pp. 7f., 23f.

[26]   This distinction appears most clearly in the Qumran literature (*e.g.*,
1QS ix. 11); *cf.* A. S. van der Woude, *Die messianischen Vorstellungen der Gemeinde
von Qumran* (Assen, 1957), *passim*; K. G. Kuhn, "The Two Messiahs of Aaron
and Israel", *The Scrolls and the New Testament*, ed. K. Stendahl (London, 1958),
pp. 54ff.; F. F. Bruce, *Biblical Exegesis in the Qumran Texts* (London, 1960),
pp. 41ff.

[27]   *Cf.* Y. Yadin, "The Dead Sea Scrolls and the Epistle to the Hebrews",
Scripta Hierosolymitana iv (1958), pp. 36ff.; H. Kosmala, *Hebräer-Essener-Christen*
(Leiden, 1959). See pp. xxviii f.

that Jesus, who was acclaimed by God as the Davidic Messiah in Ps. 2:7, was also acclaimed by God as high priest in Ps. 110:4. Christians acknowledge not two Messiahs, but one, and that one is both king and priest.[28] But if the Messiah of David's line is high priest as well as king, he cannot be a "Messiah of Aaron"; Aaron belonged to the tribe of Levi, whereas David and his house belonged to the tribe of Judah, "as to which tribe Moses spake nothing concerning priests" (Ch. 7:14). No appeal can be made to those scriptures which establish the Levitical and Aaronic priesthood to support the claim that Jesus the son of David exercises a high-priestly ministry on His people's behalf.[29] But there is no need to appeal to those scriptures, for here is another scripture which speaks of another priestly order, and designates the Davidic king as priest of this order.

Melchizedek makes his appearance in Gen. 14:18 as king of Salem (traditionally, and in all probability rightly, identified with Jerusalem[30]) and priest of God Most High *('Ēl 'Elyōn)*.[31] When, centuries later, Jerusalem fell into David's hands and became his capital city (II Sam. 5:6ff.), he and his heirs became successors to Melchizedek's kingship, and probably also (in a titular capacity

---

[28] *Cf.* B. Lindars, *New Testament Apologetic* (London, 1961), p. 142.

[29] The attempt to establish a Levitical relationship for Jesus through His mother's kinswoman Elizabeth, who was "of the daughters of Aaron" (Luke 1:5), cannot be traced earlier than Hippolytus. According to Hippolytus (on Gen. 49:8) Jesus was descended from Levi as well as from Judah (an inference apparently drawn from *Testament of Simeon* 7:2); he also interprets Moses' blessing of Levi (Deut. 33:8ff.) with reference to Jesus (*cf.* M. Brière, L. Mariès and B. C. Mercier, *Hippolyte de Rome sur les Bénédictions d'Isaac, de Jacob et de Moïse* in *Patrologia Orientalis* xxvii [1954], pp. 72, 144ff.; also L. Mariès, "Le messie issu de Lévi chez Hippolyte de Rome", *Recherches de science religieuse* xxxix–xl [1951–52], *Mélanges Lebreton*, pp. 381ff.). For a recent attempt to establish a similar argument *cf.* J. L. Teicher in *Journal of Jewish Studies* ii (1950), pp. 134ff.

[30] *Cf.* Ps. 76:2, where "Salem" stands in synonymous parallelism with "Zion"; also the interpretation of Salem as Jerusalem in 1Q *Genesis Apocryphon* xxii. 13 (1st cent. B.C.) and in Josephus, *Antiquities* i. 180. Others would identify Melchizedek's Salem with Shalem near Shechem (Gen. 33:18, AV, ARV mg.; *cf.* John 3:23). See p. 136, n. 16.

[31] *'Ēl 'Elyōn* is identified with *Yahweh* in Gen. 14:22 (MT); *'Elyōn* and *Yahweh* also appear repeatedly as synonyms in poetic parallelism in the Psalms and elsewhere (*e.g.* Ps. 18:13). According to Philo of Byblus, *Elioun* ("Most High") was the chief deity among the Phoenicians.

at least) to the priesthood of God Most High.[32] But in the Hebrew monarchy "fundamentally, the union of religious and civil leadership seen in the 'divine kingship' of the fertile crescent was dissolved".[33] The chief priesthood in the Jerusalem temple was exercised throughout the period of the monarchy, and for long afterwards, by the family of Zadok—a family quite distinct from the Davidic line, and one that laid no claim to the succession of "the order of Melchizedek".[34] Under the Hasmonaeans, from Jonathan Maccabaeus onwards, the chief priesthood and the chief civil power in Israel were combined in one person; but even if some justification for this unwonted combination was sought in the tradition of Melchizedek's royal priesthood,[35] the justification was empty, for the Hasmonaeans had nothing to do with Melchizedek. Indeed the most pious groups in Israel strongly disapproved of the

---

[32] Cf. A. R. Johnson, Sacral Kingship in Ancient Israel (Cardiff, 1955), pp. 29ff., 42ff.; H. Ringgren, The Messiah in the Old Testament (London, 1956), p. 15.

[33] H. L. Ellison, The Centrality of the Messianic Idea for the Old Testament (London, 1953), p. 11. He continues: "In Ps. 110:4 we see the union recreated". Even if the oracle of Ps. 110:4 was repeated regularly in the coronation ritual of the southern monarchy, it expressed a future ideal rather than a present fact. Zech. 6:13 has frequently been regarded as portraying a Davidic priest-king (so AV, ARV, "he ['the man whose name is the Branch'] shall be a priest upon his throne"), but RSV is preferable: "there shall be a priest by his throne" (cf. LXX, "there shall be a priest at his right hand"). The recognition of two separate persons, a royal governor and a priest, is required by the following clause ("and the counsel of peace shall be between them both"); the reference would be to Zerubbabel and Joshua, "the two anointed ones" of Zech. 4:14.

[34] See, however, H. H. Rowley, "Zadok and Nehushtan", JBL lviii (1939), pp. 113ff.; "Melchizedek and Zadok", in Festschrift für A. Bertholet, ed. W. Baumgartner (Tübingen, 1950), pp. 461ff.

[35] The language of the decree of the Jewish people in I Macc. 14:41, "that Simon should be their leader and high priest for ever", is probably based on Ps. 110:4 ("high priest for ever" here denoting an hereditary high priesthood). The view that Ps. 110 was actually composed in honor of Simon has now been generally abandoned, together with the attempt to find an acrostic of his name in its opening verses (so G. Margoliouth in Academy, Feb. 20, 1892; G. W. H. Bickell, ibid., April 9, 1892; R. H. Charles, "The Christ of the NT", Exp. VI. v [1902], pp. 252f.; B. Duhm, Die Psalmen, KHC [Tübingen, 1922], pp. 254ff.; R. H. Pfeiffer, Introduction to the Old Testament [New York, 1941], p. 630). "The contention held by some that the psalm belongs to the Maccabaean age because the letters composing the name of Simon, the Maccabaean leader, are the initial ones of the first four lines, can only be described as fantastic; for the fact is that these letters are not the initial ones of the lines in question, and can be made

Hasmonaeans' assumption of the high priesthood,[36] and some of them—in particular, the community of Qumran—refused to recognize their usurpation of the sacred office, preferring to cherish the hope of a day when the legitimate line of Zadok would again be invested with the high-priestly dignity in a purified temple in a new Jerusalem.[37] But even so, this hope did not envisage the union of priesthood and kingship; it maintained a distinction, as has just been said, between the anointed priest and the anointed king of the new age.[38] For aught we know to the contrary, the writer to the Hebrews was the first to identify these two eschatological personages in such a way as to provide the fulfilment of the divine oracle in Ps. 110:4.[39] The promised prince of the house of David is, by the same divine right, perpetual priest of Melchizedek's order. The implications of this are unfolded in detail in Ch. 7; but for the present our author, having established Jesus' qualification to be His people's high priest in terms of His divine appointment, turns to speak of a second qualification.

7 *(b)* His second qualification is His ability to sympathize with those whose cause He maintains. We have already been assured that Jesus is faithful and merciful as His people's high priest because He was made like His brothers in every respect—that He sympathizes with His people's weaknesses because He was

---

so only by arbitrary manipulation" (W. O. E. Oesterley, *The Psalms* [London, 1953], p. 461). *Cf* H. Gunkel, *Die Psalmen* (Göttingen, 1926), p. 485. If the Hasmonaeans used this psalm to support their own high-priestly claims, that in itself might account for its non-appearance among the Qumran *testimonia*.

[36] For the Pharisees' attitude *cf.* Josephus, *Ant.* xiii. 288ff.; TB *Qiddushin*, 66a.

[37] CD iv. 1ff.; in the Qumran commentaries the holder of the Hasmonaean high-priesthood is referred to as "the wicked priest".

[38] So later, during the war of liberation led by the messianic claimant Simeon Ben-Kosebah (A.D. 132–135), the otherwise unknown "Eleazar the priest" is named on the national coinage alongside "Simeon, prince of Israel".

[39] Whatever may be said about the provenience of the *Testaments of the Twelve Patriarchs*, there can be little doubt about the Christian origin of such a passage as that in *Test. Levi* 8:14: "a king shall arise out of Judah and shall establish a new priesthood ... for all Gentiles". This is dependent on the Epistle to the Hebrews, and not *vice versa* (*cf.* also Ch. 7:14, pp. 144ff., with nn. 46, 50). The converse prediction in *Testament of Reuben* 6:7ff., where kingship as well as priesthood is granted to the tribe of Levi, suggests a very different provenience. Elsewhere in the *Testaments* the kingship of Judah and the priesthood of Levi are kept distinct, the kingship being subordinate to the priesthood (as at Qumran).

exposed to all the tests and trials that they have to endure.[40] Now these statements are elaborated. These tests and trials befell Him "in the days of his flesh"[41]—an expression which emphasizes the conditions of human weakness of which He partook during His earthly life and which does not imply that His incarnate state was terminated with His exaltation to the right hand of God. If the expression did have this meaning, it would seriously weaken our author's argument that Christians have right now a high priest who feels for them and with them in all their temptations and sorrows.

It would be a matter of great interest to discover something about the form in which our author knew the gospel story. He certainly does not dismiss the details of our Lord's earthly life or His inward experiences up to and including His passion as possessing no relevance for the "post-Easter" faith of the Church.[42] On the contrary, he draws from those details and experiences lessons of great practical import for his readers' Christian life. He probably knew of a number of incidents in the life of Jesus when He "offered up[43] prayers and supplications with strong crying and tears unto him that was able to save him from death"; but for us, restricted as we are to the Gospel narratives, "Gethsemane seems to offer the most telling illustration"[44] of these words. Mark tells

---

[40] Cf. Chs. 2:17f.; 4:15f.

[41] Gk. ἐν ταῖς ἡμέραις τῆς σαρκὸς αὐτοῦ (NEB, "in the days of his earthly life").

[42] And, for that matter, neither does Paul, whose words about not knowing Christ "after the flesh" in II Cor. 5:16 have been misinterpreted in this way (his meaning is excellently reproduced in NEB: "With us therefore worldly standards have ceased to count in our estimate of any man; even if once they counted in our understanding of Christ, they do so now no longer"). It is unfortunate that the ministry of Christ is given so little place in early Christian confessions of faith: H. B. Swete speaks of the words "and lived among men" in the Creed of Caesarea (Socrates, HE i. 8) as standing alone in such documents as a reference to our Lord's career between His incarnation and passion (The Ascended Christ [London, 1912], p. xv n.). See also A. M. Ramsey, "The Gospel and the Gospels", in Studia Evangelica = TU lxxiii (Berlin, 1959), pp. 39f.

[43] Gk. προσενέγκας, from προσφέρω, rendered "offer" also in vv. 2, 3. But it has no such sacrificial sense here, as though Christ's Gethsemane experience were somehow the counterpart to the Aaronic high priest's offering for himself in v. 3 (so, e.g., A. B. Bruce, The Humiliation of Christ⁴ [Edinburgh, 1895], p. 277).

[44] A. E. Garvie, ExT xxvi (1914–15), p. 549 (in an article "The Pioneer of Faith and of Salvation"). "While we must not limit the reference to Gethsemane," he says, "yet there this element in the passion is most clearly and fully presented to us."

us how "horror and dismay came over him" there, and He said
to the three disciples who accompanied Him: " 'My heart is ready
to break with grief; stop here, and stay awake'. Then he went
forward a little, threw himself on the ground, and prayed that, if
it were possible, this hour might pass him by. 'Abba, Father', he
said, 'all things are possible to thee; take this cup away from me.
Yet not what I will, but what thou wilt' " (Mark 14:33b–36, NEB).

Some curious interpretations of the Gethsemane agony and
prayer have been offered, with the well-meant intention of doing
justice to our author's words. It has been suggested that what
our Lord prayed for in Gethsemane was that He might be saved
from dying there and then, either through physical exhaustion or
by satanic assault.[45] But the reader of the Gospel accounts knows
already what our Lord means by "this cup"; it cannot be anything
other than "the cup which I drink" which He warned James and
John that they also would have to drink if they desired to share
His glory (Mark 10:38f.). For Him, indeed, the cup was more
bitter than for them, or for any of His other followers who have
drunk it since; they have known that He shared it with them, but
He drank it alone.[46] Our author's words here are further illustrated
by the Johannine counterparts to the Gethsemane narrative of
the Synoptic records. According to John, a day or two before His
arrest in the garden Jesus said: "Now is my soul troubled; and
what shall I say? Father, save me from this hour.[47] But for this
cause came I unto this hour. Father, glorify thy name." The
response came immediately from heaven: "I have both glorified
it, and will glorify it again" (John 12:27f.).[48] Later in the same

---

[45]   In *ExT* vi (1894–95), p. 433, A. F. Schauffler is quoted for the view that
"the 'cup' from which He prayed to be delivered was not the death on the Cross,
but death in Gethsemane itself. He was praying for strength to reach the Cross,
not for grace to escape it". Similarly T. Hewitt in *The Epistle to the Hebrews*,
TNTC (London, 1960), pp. 97ff.: "If Christ had died in the Garden, no greater
calamity could possibly have fallen on mankind" (p. 100). But why? Once He
had said "Not my will, but thine, be done", the offering up of His life at any
subsequent moment must have constituted "a ransom for many", as He had
said it would (Mark. 10:45).

[46]   Not to mention the taking away of the sin of the world (John 1:29) which
His drinking of the cup involved, as no one else's could have done.

[47]   The construing of this prayer as a question ("Shall I say, 'Father, save
me from this hour'?") may be felt to import a slightly histrionic element out of
keeping with the spiritual intensity of the moment.

[48]   *Cf.* also John 13:31f.; 17:1, 4f.

Gospel, Jesus at the moment of His arrest rebukes Peter's impetuous attempt to defend Him: "Put up the sword into the sheath: the cup which the Father hath given me to drink, shall I not drink it?" (John 18:11). The Father's name was glorified by the Son's willing acceptance of the cup of suffering from His hand. "The point to be emphasised is, not so much that the prayer of Jesus was heard, as that it *needed* to be heard: that He needed heavenly aid to drink the appointed cup."[49]

A difficulty has sometimes been felt in referring our author's words here to Jesus' Gethsemane experience, since He was not delivered from death[50]—the cup was not removed from Him. Attempts to relieve the difficulty by insisting that the prepositional phrase here is not "from death" but "out of death"[51] do not touch the heart of the matter. But while Gethsemane provides "the most telling illustration" of our author's words, they have a more general reference to the whole course of our Lord's humiliation and passion. More than that: they have been influenced by the language of the twenty-second psalm, a psalm whose currency as a primitive Christian *testimonium* we have already noted.[52] "Strong crying and tears" might well describe the supplication and complaint of the first part of the psalm, while the statement that Christ was "heard[53] for his godly fear" echoes Ps. 22:24: "when he cried

---

[49] A. B. Bruce, *The Epistle to the Hebrews* (Edinburgh, 1899), p. 186.

[50] It certainly does less than justice to our author's language to regard "him that was able to save him from death" as little more than a circumlocution for "God"—in the sense of I Sam. 2:6 ("Jehovah killeth, and maketh alive: He bringeth down to Sheol, and bringeth up").

[51] A. E. Garvie (*loc. cit.*, p. 549), G. H. Lang (*The Epistle to the Hebrews* [London, 1951], pp. 91f.), K. S. Wuest (*Hebrews in the Greek New Testament* [Grand Rapids, 1947], p. 99) and others emphasize that our Lord prayed to be delivered ἐκ θανάτου, "out of the midst of the death state" (after having entered into it), and not ἀπὸ θανάτου, "from death" (in the sense that He prayed that He might not die). But in fact no such clearcut distinction can be made between the two prepositional phrases; Westcott (*ad loc.*) makes it quite clear that ἐκ θανάτου can cover both these distinct ideas; the prayer was not answered in the one sense, that it might be answered in the other. It is possible that ἐκ θανάτου here is an echo of Hos. 13:14 (LXX), ἐκ χειρὸς ᾅδου ῥύσομαι, καὶ ἐκ θανάτου λυτρώσομαι αὐτούς ("from the power of Hades I will rescue, and from death I will redeem them").

[52] *Cf.* Ch. 2:12 with exposition and notes (pp. 45f.).

[53] Gk. εἰσακουσθείς, with which *cf.* also Ps. 22:2 (LXX), οὐκ εἰσακούσῃ ("thou wilt not hear"). A. Harnack emended the text here by inserting οὐκ before εἰσακουσθείς ("Zwei alte dogmatische Korrekturen im Hebräerbrief",

unto him, he heard".[54]   In the detailed Christological interpretation of the psalm, these words were understood as a reference to the resurrection of Christ;[55] our author may well have understood them thus, but he does not go into this question, which would have taken him beyond his present intention. His present intention is to insist that Jesus has been qualified for His high-priestly service by His agony and tears, His supplication and suffering, throughout which His trust in God never failed.[56]

That He was "heard for his godly fear"[57] is the best interpretation of a phrase which has been understood in a variety of ways;[58] other interpretations are that He was "heard (and delivered) from the fear (of death)"[59] or that He was "heard by (the Object of) his godly fear".[60] The general New Testament usage of the word here rendered "godly fear" and of its cognates (and not least the usage in this epistle itself)[61] makes it improbable that fear of death

---

in *Studien zur Geschichte des NT und der alten Kirche* [Berlin and Leipzig, 1931], pp. 245ff., reprinted from *Sitzungsberichte der preussischen Akademie der Wissenschaften*, phil.-hist. Klasse, 1929, pp. 62ff.); the emendation has been adopted by R. Bultmann in *TWNT* ii (Stuttgart, 1935), p. 751 (*s.v. εὐλαβής*, etc.); *cf.* H. Windisch, *Der Hebräerbrief*, HNT (Tübingen, 1931), *ad loc.*, pp. 43f.

[54]   Gk. εἰσήκουσέ μου (LXX 21:25). *Cf.* also the occurrence of δέησις (*cf.* p. 93, n. 23) earlier in this verse of the psalm (LXX). Other passages in the Psalter which may have influenced our author here are Pss. 31:22 (LXX 30:23); 39:12f. (LXX 38:13f.); 69:1-3 (LXX 68:2-4), and especially Ps. 116 (LXX 114 and 115), *passim* (for parallels in the last-named psalm *cf.* A. Strobel, "Die Psalmengrundlage der Gethsemane-Parallele, Hbr. 5, 7ff.", *ZNW* xlv [1954], pp. 252ff.).

[55]   *Cf.* Justin Martyr, *Dialogue with Trypho*, 106 (in section 99 Justin has interpreted Ps. 22:2 [LXX 21:3] of the agony in Gethsemane).

[56]   "What gives the reality to the priesthood is that it is no external office, inherited, usurped, or granted by favour, but it is an inward vocation and qualification in experience and character" (A. E. Garvie, *ExT* xxviii [1916-17], p. 463, in an article "Shadow and Substance").

[57]   Gk. ἀπὸ τῆς εὐλαβείας.

[58]   *Cf.* Spicq, *ad loc.*; O. Michel, MK, *ad loc.*

[59]   So Calvin, Beza, and many commentators since. R. Bultmann (*TWNT* ii, p. 751) regards this ("er ist erhört worden aus seiner Angst") as the best interpretation of the text as it stands, but he prefers Harnack's emendation (see p. 100, n. 53).

[60]   *Cf.* the OT designation of God as "the Fear of Isaac" (Gen. 31:42). MM (*s.v. εὐλάβεια*) cite a papyrus of A.D. 505 for the use of the word in the sense of "Your reverence" as a courtesy title.

[61]   The substantive εὐλάβεια appears in Ch. 12:28 (see p. 381, n. 190) and the verb εὐλαβέομαι in Ch. 11:7; the consistent meaning is reverence towards God. The substantive and the verb do not appear in NT outside this epistle; the

is in view here; what is in view is rather our Lord's devotion and submission to the will of God. The fact that the cup was not removed qualifies Him all the more to sympathize with His people; when they are faced with the mystery and trial of unanswered prayer they know that their high priest was tested in the same way and did not seek a way of escape by supernatural means of a kind that they do not have at their disposal.[62] At no point can the objection be voiced that because He was the Son of God it was different, or easier, for Him.[63] He who would not have recourse to miraculous means to relieve His hunger in the wilderness refused to summon angelic forces to rescue Him from His enemies.[64] He recognized the path of the Father's will, and followed it to the end; herein lay His "godly fear"—His "humble submission", as NEB renders it.

8 "Though he was a Son", the rendering of ARV (following AV and followed by RSV), fails to bring out the force of the clause. The absence of the definite article before the substantive "Son" in the Greek text here[65] should not be expressed by the indefinite

---

adjective εὐλαβής appears in the Lukan writings only, and always of devout Jews (Luke 2:25; Acts 2:5; 8:2; 22:12). "Trench has rescued this noun [εὐλάβεια] from detraction by showing that the Stoics reckoned it a positive virtue, the golden mean between rashness and poltroonery. According to Diogenes Laertius it is the very antithesis of fearfulness. In Luke's diction εὐλαβής is the devout, god-fearing soul, and later on in this Epistle the cognate verb is predicated in commendation of Noah's watchfulness. It corresponds with Cicero's *cautio*, defined in his *Tusculans* (iv. 6) as *a malis declinatio, si cum ratione fit*, and is summed up by Plutarch in the dictum: τὸ εὐλαβεῖσθαι σοφῶν ἴδιον (*Mor.* 1038). Philo uses the term of Eve's initial scruple to eat of the forbidden tree. It stands then for *circumspection, heedfulness*, the German *Behutsamkeit*. Πρὸς τὸ θεῖον εὐλάβεια is Plutarch's standing phrase for religious punctiliousness, and γεροντικὴ εὐλάβεια (*Brut.* 12) a praiseworthy feature of old age, namely *wariness*" (E. K. Simpson, *Words Worth Weighing in the Greek New Testament* [London, 1946], p. 19). See also Westcott, *ad loc.* The sense of the phrase ἀπὸ τῆς εὐλαβείας is exactly conveyed by the Vulgate rendering *pro sua reuerentia*.

[62] *Cf.* M. Rissi, "Die Menschlichkeit Jesu nach Hebr. 5, 7 und 8", *ThZ* xi (1955), pp. 28ff.

[63] This was precisely what He refused at His first temptation in the wilderness; having been so recently hailed by the heavenly voice as the Son of God, He was invited to exploit His divine Sonship for His personal advantage in a way that was not open to His people, but would not entertain the suggestion for a moment (Matt. 4:2–4; Luke 4:2b–4).

[64] *Cf.* Matt. 26:53.

[65] As in Ch. 1:2.

article in English. It is the most natural thing in the world for a son to learn obedience by suffering; indeed, our author makes this very point in Ch. 12:5ff. But it is not any ordinary son that he is speaking about here, but the Son of God: "Son though He was"[66] —that is to say, Son of God though He was—even He was granted no exemption from the common law that learning comes by suffering.[67] The construction of the clauses and participial phrases in the ARV of verses 7 and 8 suggests that the clause "though he was a Son" goes more closely with what precedes than with what follows. This would be in keeping with classical purity, so far as the laws governing concessive clauses of this type are concerned;[68] but in Hellenistic Greek there is ample precedent for placing such a clause before the principal clause to which it belongs,[69] and this certainly gives better rhythm and sense here.

In what sense, then, did the Son of God learn obedience "by the things which he suffered"? We know the sense in which the words are true of us; we learn to be obedient because of the unpleasant consequences which follow disobedience. It was not so with Him: He set out from the start on the path of obedience to God, and learned by the sufferings which came His way in consequence just what obedience to God involved in practice in the conditions of human life on earth. Perhaps the obedient Servant of the Lord in Isa. 50:4ff. was in our author's mind. The Servant's eagerness to pay heed to the voice of God exposes him to ridicule

---

[66]   Gk. καίπερ ὢν υἱός. NEB "son though he was" would be the perfect translation if only "son" were given an initial capital.

[67]   Gk. ἔμαθεν ἀφ᾽ ὧν ἔπαθεν. The rhyming relation of παθεῖν-μαθεῖν (πάθος-μάθος) gave rise to many epigrams in Greek literature to the effect that learning comes by suffering; so, e.g., in Aeschylus, Agamemnon, 176ff., Zeus is described as the one "who has marked out the path of wisdom for mortals, and decreed as a sure law that learning comes by suffering (πάθει μάθος)". Cf. H. Dörrie, Leid und Erfahrung: Die Wort- und Sinn-Verbindung παθεῖν-μαθεῖν im griechischen Denken (Wiesbaden, 1956). Spicq (op. cit., i, pp. 46f.) lists some Philonic parallels.

[68]   This is the main reason for Harnack's emendation (p. 100, n. 53), which yields the sense: "He was not heard, for all His godly fear, Son though He was". Blass-Debrunner (Greek Grammar of the NT, § 211) take ἀπὸ τῆς εὐλαβείας with the following clause: "because of His godly fear, Son though He was, (and) because of the things which He suffered, He learned obedience ..." (even though He was Son, He had to exercise godly fear)—a construction which weights v. 8 too heavily.

[69]   Especially in LXX; cf. J. Jeremias, "Hbr. 5, 7–10", ZNW xliv (1952–53), pp. 107ff.

and ill-treatment, but he accepts this as something inseparable from his obedience: "The Lord Jehovah hath opened my ear, and I was not rebellious, neither turned away backward. I gave my back to the smiters, and my cheeks to them that plucked out the hair; I hid not my face from shame and spitting" (Isa. 50:5f.). So the sufferings which Jesus endured were the necessary price of His obedience—more than that, they were part and parcel of His obedience, the very means by which He fulfilled the will of God. At the threshold of His public ministry, He silenced the Baptist's objections to baptizing Him with the words "thus it becometh us to fulfil all righteousness"—or, as NEB puts it, "we do well to conform in this way with all that God requires" (Matt. 3:15). Unlike those others who were baptized by John in Jordan, confessing their sins, it was with no consciousness of sin that He accepted baptism, but with the resolution to place Himself unreservedly at God's disposal for the accomplishment of His saving purpose—and if, in doing so, He associated Himself publicly with sinners, that was something which He was going to do throughout His ministry, until He was "numbered with the transgressors" on the cross. It is not by accident that He spoke of His impending passion not only as the cup which He was going to drink but also as the baptism with which He was going to be baptized (Mark 10:38f.; Luke 12:50); the career of public obedience which was inaugurated in the earlier baptism was crowned by the second baptism—the fulfilment of "all righteousness" by the utmost endurance of trial and suffering as the first baptism had been by anticipation.

The Christians for whom this letter was intended found that the maintenance of their faith and loyalty exposed them to trial and suffering which they could escape by renouncing their confession— or possibly even by drawing less public attention to it. But the question for them to face was: were they to fall back and lose everything or press on to perfection? Our author urges them to press on, in spite of all the suffering it may involve, and he sets before them the example of Jesus, who set His face "like a flint", refusing to turn back, and was thus made "perfect through sufferings". His example and His present aid might well encourage them too to persevere; no hardship could befall them in which He did not sympathize with them.

9–10 As we have already been told in Ch. 2:10, it was through sufferings that He was made perfect—fully qualified to be the Savior and High Priest of His people. To suffer death for God's sake is itself described as the attainment of perfection,[70] and the death of Christ is of course bound up with His being "made perfect" here; but the essence of the perfection which our author has in mind consists in the fact that by His suffering and death Christ (a) "became unto all them that obey him the author of eternal salvation"[71] and (b) was "named of God a high priest after the order of Melchizedek". We can clearly recognize the motif of humiliation and suffering followed by exaltation in glory which pervades the primitive *kerygma*.

The expression "the author (or 'cause') of salvation" is found in classical Greek;[72] Philo also uses it—with regard to Noah, for example, and to the brazen serpent of wilderness days.[73] Here it has practically the same meaning as "the pioneer of their salvation" in Ch. 2:10 (RSV). The salvation which Jesus has procured is an "eternal" one. The phrase "eternal salvation" appears in the Old Testament: "Israel shall be saved by Jehovah with an everlasting salvation" (Isa. 45:17). Here, however, the Christian salvation is eternal, like the "eternal redemption" of Ch. 9:12, the "eternal inheritance" of Ch. 9:15, and the "eternal covenant" of Ch. 13:20, because it is based on the sacrifice of Christ, once for all accomplished, never to be repeated, and permanently valid. The salvation which Jesus has procured, moreover, is granted "unto all them that obey him". There is something appropriate in the fact that the salvation which was procured by the obedience of the Redeemer should be made available to the obedience of the redeemed. Once again the

---

[70] So Eusebius says of the martyr Marinus, "having been led off to death, he was perfected (τελειοῦται)" (*HE* vii. 15.5). *Cf.* Ch. 12:23; Luke 13:32.

[71] Gk. αἴτιος σωτηρίας αἰωνίου.

[72] *E.g.* in Aeschines, *Against Ctesiphon*, 57: "the gods have become the authors of salvation (τῆς μὲν σωτηρίας ... αἰτίους) for the city". *Cf.* Josephus, *Ant.* xiv. 136: "Antipater was the author of their victory and also of their safety (ἅμα καὶ τῆς σωτηρίας αἴτιον)".

[73] Noah's son Ham is reproached for his unfilial conduct towards his father, "the author of his salvation (τὸν αἴτιον τῆς σωτηρίας)" (*On the Virtues*, 202); the brazen serpent was "the author of complete deliverance" (αἴτιος σωτηρίας ... παντελοῦς) to those who beheld it (*Agriculture*, 96); so also the Red Sea was a means of preservation (σωτηρίας αἴτιον) to the Israelites but of destruction to the Egyptians (*Contemplative Life*, 86), and God Himself is the Author of His people's salvation (τῆς σωτηρίας αἴτιον) (*Special Laws* i. 252).

readers are encouraged to persevere in their loyalty to Christ, in whom alone eternal salvation is to be found—in whom also they have a high priest designated for them by God Himself, "after the order of Melchizedek". Our author reverts to Melchizedek at the end of this section of his argument, because he intends to go on now and elaborate the significance of his high-priestly order.

4. THIRD ADMONITION: SPIRITUAL IMMATURITY

Ch. 5:11–14

11 Of whom we have many things to say,[74] and hard of interpretation, seeing ye are become dull of hearing.

12 For when by reason of the time ye ought to be teachers, ye have need again that someone teach you[75] the rudiments of the first principles of the oracles of God and are become such as have need of milk, and not of solid food.

13 For every one that partaketh of milk is without experience of the word of righteousness; for he is[76] a babe.

14 But solid food is for fullgrown men, *even* those who by reason of use have their senses exercised to discern good and evil.

11 With the repeated reference to Ps. 110:4 in verse 10, the logical sequence of our author's argument would have led him on to expound the significance of Christ's being a priest "after the order of Melchizedek". This he does in Ch. 7:1ff., but first he turns aside (as he has done before[77]) to address some words of

---

[74] Gk. πολὺς ἡμῖν ὁ λόγος ... λέγειν, but ὁ is omitted in P⁴⁶* D* P 1319. Zuntz (*op. cit.*, p. 118) prefers the anarthrous reading, and takes the sense to be: "on this subject there is much to say but it would be obscure".

[75] Gk. τοῦ διδάσκειν ὑμᾶς τινα. For διδάσκειν ὑμᾶς some authorities (462 1912 with the Latin versions and margin of the Harclean Syriac) have διδάσκεσθαι (ὑμᾶς), "you have need to be taught"; this may have been a change consequential upon the reading of τινα ("someone") as τίνα ("what [are the rudiments]"), a reading found in Bᶜ Dᶜ L and many other MSS, with the Latin and Coptic versions (it is the reading of TR, whence AV "which be the first principles of the oracles of God"). (In 424** 1739 τινα in either form is absent; *cf.* Zuntz, *op. cit.*, p. 75.)

[76] D* has the amplified reading "for he is still (ἀκμήν) a babe"—a reading attested also by Origen.

[77] *E.g.* in Ch. 3:7ff. (pp. 60ff.).

practical admonition to his readers' spiritual condition. Melchizedek's person and office are subjects of deep import,[78] he says, but his readers may not be in a position to grasp what he has to say in this regard because their minds are so sluggish.[79]

12 You have been Christians for such a long time now, he goes on, that you ought to be able to teach others;[80] but as it is, you yourselves need to be taught—not only do you need to learn mysteries of deep import like the priestly order of Melchizedek, but the very ABC[81] of divine revelation. In view of the time that

[78] Gk. δυσερμήνευτος. Melchizedek was a subject of much speculation among Jews, as later among Christians. One line of Jewish tradition identified him with Shem (whose life, according to the Massoretic chronology, overlapped Abraham's by more than a century); this removed the difficulty of supposing that outside the line of the holy seed there should be one whom Abraham treated with such veneration. Another line thought of him as the prototype of the great priest of the age to come, but in a way which distinguished him from the Messiah of Ps. 110:1. As a result of polemic with the Christians, however, Judaism tended to take a less favorable view of Melchizedek. His blessing Abraham before he blessed God (Gen. 14:19f.) was reprobated, and it was held that on this account his priesthood was taken away from him and conferred on Abraham. See Justin, *Dialogue with Trypho*, 19; M. R. James, *The Lost Apocrypha of the OT* (London, 1920), pp. 17ff.; Strack-Billerbeck iv (Munich, 1928), pp. 452ff.; M. Friedlaender, "La secte de Melchisédeq et l'Épître aux Hébreux", *RÉJ* v (1882), pp. 1ff., 188ff., vi (1882), pp. 187ff.; M. Simon, "Melchisédech dans la polémique entre juifs et chrétiens et dans la légende", *RHPR* xvii (1937), pp. 58ff.; J. Klausner, *The Messianic Idea in Israel* (London, 1956), pp. 456, 515; J. J. Petuchowski, "The Controversial Figure of Melchizedek", *HUCA* xxviii (1957), pp. 127ff.; O. Cullmann, *The Christology of the New Testament* (London, 1959), pp. 83–85 (with a useful bibliographical apparatus in the footnotes); R. A. Stewart, *Rabbinical Theology* (Edinburgh, 1961), pp. 112ff.; J. Fitzmyer, "Now this Melchizedek… (Heb. 7:1)," *CBQ* xxv (1963), pp. 305ff.

[79] Gk. νωθρός, here and in Ch. 6:12 only in NT; in LXX, Prov. 22:29 (of "slothful men"); Sir. 4:29; 11:12.

[80] The statement that the recipients of this letter ought by now to have qualified as teachers of others has been made to bear an excessive weight of exegesis; K. Bornhäuser used it as one of his arguments for identifying the recipients with the converted priests of Acts 6:7 (*Empfänger und Verfasser des Briefes an die Hebräer* [Gütersloh, 1932], pp. 16ff.). The idea that ordinary Christians would not be expected to become teachers is quite unwarranted; the word διδάσκαλος is used here in quite an informal sense, and not of trained catechists or anything like that. It was an axiom of Stoicism that anyone who had mastered true learning was in a position to impart it to others; and it is equally a Christian axiom.

[81] *Cf.* NEB; Gk. στοιχεῖα (ARV "rudiments"). In addition to this primary sense of the letters of the alphabet, στοιχεῖα is used in NT of the "elements" which make up the material universe (II Pet. 3:10, 12) and of the "elemental

has elapsed since your conversion to Christianity, you ought to be taking solid food, like grown-up men and women; in fact, however, you are still unable to digest anything stronger than milk, the food of infants.

The contrast between milk and solid food in this spiritual sense appears to have been commonplace in the early Church, as it was in Greek moral philosophy.[82] Paul makes it in I Cor. 3:1ff., where he tells the Corinthian Christians that, for all their claim to be "spiritual" men, they cannot be treated as such, since their fostering of party spirit in the church shows them to be still "carnal". They must therefore be treated as spiritual infants, and fed on the "milk" of elementary Christian ethics. There is indeed further wisdom to be imparted to those who have attained spiritual maturity—the hidden wisdom "which God foreordained before the worlds unto our glory" (I Cor. 2:7)—but the Corinthians will not be able to assimilate this "meat" until they have grown up more, not in knowledge but in charity. (Was our author influenced here by that passage in I Corinthians? It would be interesting if he was, in view of Apollos's association with Corinth and Paul's mention of him in that same context.) The "milk" figure is used, without the contrast between it and strong meat, in I Pet. 2:2, where Peter exhorts his readers to acquire an appetite for pure spiritual milk, "so that you may thrive upon it to your souls' health" (NEB). But Peter is writing to "newborn babes", that is to say, to people who have only recently been converted to Christianity.

13-14 The immaturity of the people addressed by our author, which caused him to doubt whether they were able to appreciate his teaching about the Melchizedek priesthood of Christ, was due to a disinclination to press on in the Christian way. Their sluggishness showed itself in a disposition to settle down at the point which they had reached, since to go farther would have meant too complete a severing of old ties. To such people the exposition of the high-priestly service of Christ, with the corollary that the old order of priesthood and sacrifice had been abolished

---

spirits" of the world which seek to bring men into bondage and from which the gospel delivers them (Gal. 4:3, 9; Col. 2:8, 20). *Cf.* H. N. Ridderbos, *Galatians*, NICNT (Grand Rapids, 1953), p. 153, n. 5; F. F. Bruce, *Colossians*, NICNT (Grand Rapids, 1957), p. 231.

[82] For details *cf.* Moffatt, Michel and Spicq *ad loc.*; also Spicq, i, pp. 53ff.

once for all, might well have been unacceptable; the intellect is not over-ready to entertain an idea that the heart finds unpalatable.

The "milk" corresponds to the ABC of the divine oracles; some of the "first principles"[83] of which the ABC consists are mentioned in Ch. 6:1f. Those who have not proceeded beyond this stage are still infants, "without experience of the word of righteousness"—or, as it may be rendered, "a principle of righteousness".[84] It is ethically mature men, those "who by reason of use[85] have their senses exercised to discern good and evil", who have built up in the course of experience a principle or standard of righteousness by which they can pass discriminating judgment on moral situations as they arise. The general idea is widespread among contemporary writers on ethics, although our author uses it for a purpose of his own.

---

[83] Gk. ἀρχή, here and in Ch. 6:1. In the phrase τὰ στοιχεῖα τῆς ἀρχῆς here, τῆς ἀρχῆς may be taken as a genitive of definition; one cannot well press a distinction between the στοιχεῖα and the ἀρχή.

[84] Gk. λόγος δικαιοσύνης (cf. the ὀρθὸς λόγος of Philo and Marcus Aurelius). The rendering "a principle of righteousness" is suggested by H. P. Owen, "The 'Stages of Ascent' in Hebrews v. 11–vi. 3", NTS iii (1956–57), pp. 243ff. He distinguishes two phases in the stage of full growth: (a) the phase of ethical maturity, in which a "principle of righteousness" is acquired through experience; (b) the phase in which those who have thus had "their senses exercised to discern good and evil" are supplied with solid food such as the doctrine of Christ's high-priesthood (this latter phase being the "perfection" of Ch. 6:1). This threefold ascent (infancy, moral maturity, spiritual illumination) he finds paralleled in Philo and the Stoics (but not Epictetus, who makes no room for the last phase). Cf. E. Percy, Probleme der Kolosser- und Epheserbriefe (Lund, 1946), p. 323. See further on Ch. 6:1 (p. 111). G. Delling (TWNT i [Stuttgart, 1933] p. 188, s.v. αἰσθάνομαι) takes the meaning to be that only to Christians of developed moral character can the doctrine of justification by faith (λόγος δικαιοσύνης) be imparted; νήπιοι so easily misunderstand it. This does not suit the context.

[85] Gk. διὰ τὴν ἕξιν. The ἕξις is the habitus, experience or skill acquired through practice.

CHAPTER VI

5. NO SECOND BEGINNING POSSIBLE

Ch. 6:1–8

1 Wherefore leaving the doctrine of the first principles of Christ,[1] let us press on[2] unto perfection; not laying again a foundation of repentance from dead works, and of faith toward God,

2 of the teaching of baptisms,[3] and of laying on of hands, and of resurrection of the dead, and of eternal judgment.

3 And this will we do,[4] if God permit.

4 For as touching those who were once enlightened, and tasted of the heavenly gift, and were made partakers of the Holy Spirit,

5 and tasted the good word of God,[5] and the powers of the age to come,[6]

---

[1] Literally "the word of the beginning of Christ" (ARV margin).

[2] Gk. φερώμεθα, of swift and energetic movement.

[3] Gk. βαπτισμῶν διδαχῆς. For the genitive διδαχῆς a few authorities (P⁴⁶ B d (e)) read the accusative διδαχήν. This is the reading underlying ARV margin: "*even* the teaching of baptisms". It is more likely that an original accusative was assimilated to the adjacent genitives than that an original genitive was altered to an accusative. If the accusative be preferred (so G. Zuntz, *The Text of the Epistles* [London, 1953], p. 93), it is parallel, and probably in apposition, to θεμέλιον ("foundation"); and the following genitives ἐπιθέσεως ("imposition"), ἀναστάσεως ("resurrection") and κρίματος ("judgment") are probably, like βαπτισμῶν ("baptisms"), dependent on διδαχήν. Cf. F. W. Beare, *JBL* lxiii (1944), p. 394; R. V. G. Tasker, *The Gospel in the Epistle to the Hebrews* (London, 1950), p. 25.

[4] Gk. ποιήσομεν, for which a handful of authorities (notably A C D) have ποιήσωμεν ("let us do").

[5] Better, as in ARV margin, "tasted the word of God that it is good" (*cf.* RSV: "tasted the goodness of the word of God").

[6] Gk. δυνάμεις τε μέλλοντος αἰῶνος. A Greek text having δύνοντος in place of μέλλοντος seems to be implied by Tertullian's quotation of this passage in *On Modesty*, 20: "For it is impossible that those who ... have tasted the word of God and found it sweet, when—their age already setting (*occidente iam aeuo*)—they have fallen away, should be recalled again unto repentance"; but this reading probably arose through the accidental omission of letters in δυν(άμεις τε μέλλ)οντος.

6 and *then* fell away, it is impossible to renew them again unto repentance; seeing they crucify to themselves the Son of God afresh,[7] and put him to an open shame.

7 For the land which hath drunk the rain that cometh oft upon it, and bringeth forth herbs meet for them for whose sake it is also tilled, receiveth blessing from God:

8 but if it beareth thorns and thistles, it is rejected and nigh unto a curse; whose end is to be burned.

1 The opening words of this section are surprising. Our author has just told his readers that they are not really able to assimilate the solid food which he would like to give them—the teaching about the priestly order of Melchizedek—because they are immature. We might have expected him to say, as Paul says to the Corinthians[8] in a similar situation: "Therefore I must continue to feed you with milk". But he does not say this; he says: "let us press on". He judged that no good purpose would be served by going over the first principles again. That being so, we might have expected him to say: "You are not ready for solid food yet, you still need milk; *nevertheless* I am going to press on with the provision of solid food". But he does not say "nevertheless"; he says "therefore". "*Therefore* let us leave the elementary doctrines of Christ and press forward to maturity." Why "therefore"? Probably because their particular condition of immaturity is such that only an appreciation of what is involved in Christ's high priesthood will cure it. Their minds require to be stretched, and this will stretch them as nothing else can. They have remained immature too long; *therefore* he will give them something calculated to take them out of their immaturity.[9]

---

[7] The adverb "afresh" is intended to convey the force of the prefix ἀνα- in ἀνασταυροῦντας, but it is more probable that ἀνασταυρόω (not found elsewhere in biblical Greek) has the meaning "crucify" here which it has in non-biblical writers (ἀνα- denoting "up", not "again"). So RSV ("they crucify the Son of God on their own account") and NEB ("with their own hands they are crucifying the Son of God"). The dative ἑαυτοῖς ("to themselves") may, mean "to their own hurt" (*cf.* p. 345, n. 5, on Ch. 12:3). But the sense "crucify again" was accepted here by the Greek fathers and ancient versions (*cf.* Vulgate, *rursum crucifigentes*), possibly because of a feeling that this sense was specially appropriate to *Jewish* Christians (see also p. 124, n. 57).

[8] I Cor. 3:2.

[9] *Cf.* H. P. Owen, "The 'Stages of Ascent' in Hebrews v. 11–vi. 3", *NTS* iii (1956–57), pp. 243ff.

"So", he says, "let us stop discussing the rudiments; do not let us start laying our foundations all over again." The rudiments ("the elementary doctrines of Christ", RSV) and the foundation are the same thing described in two different figures. Before he goes on, however, he lists some of the rudiments, quoting perhaps from a catechesis familiar to himself and his readers.[10] Six matters are listed, which fall naturally into three pairs: (a) "repentance from dead works" goes closely with (b) "faith toward God"; (c) "the teaching of baptisms"—or better, "instruction about ablutions" (RSV)—goes with (d) "laying on of hands"; while there is a patent association between (e) "resurrection of the dead" and (f) "eternal judgment". But the connection between these six subjects is more complicated than that. On the most probable reading of the text, "teaching" or "instruction" in verse 2 appears to be in apposition to "foundation" in verse 1;[11] this suggests that the laying of a "foundation of repentance ... and of faith" consists in instruction about (i) ablutions, (ii) laying on of hands, (iii) resurrection and (iv) judgment.[12]

We are thus given some insight into what was regarded as a suitable foundation of Christian teaching in a non-Pauline church, and one which had a Jewish basis. When we consider the "rudiments" one by one, it is remarkable how little in the list is distinctive of Christianity, for practically every item could have its place in a fairly orthodox Jewish community. Each of them, indeed, acquires a new significance in a Christian context; but the impression we get is that existing Jewish beliefs and practices were used as a foundation on which to build Christian truth. "It is significant," wrote Alexander Nairne, "that the points taken as

---

[10] Cf. O. Michel, MK, ad loc.

[11] See p. 110, n. 3.

[12] "This renouncing of a past way of life, whether it be a Jewish or a pagan way, and this turning to God in faith to receive new power from Him were symbolized, in early Christian practice, in the initiation ceremonies of 'baptism and the laying-on-of-hands'; and the outstanding characteristics of the new life that a Christian sought to live were the new sense of purpose and the increased sense of seriousness which were imparted to it by the certainty that, because Christ had been raised from the dead, there would be 'a resurrection of the dead' followed by a 'judgment' which would have eternal consequences" (R. V. G. Tasker, loc. cit.). According to G. Zuntz (op. cit., p. 93), "διδαχήν is defined by the genitives βαπτισμῶν and ἐπιθέσεως, just as θεμέλιον is defined by μετανοίας and πίστεως. The two concluding genitives, 'resurrection' and 'judgement', denote the main objects of the teaching."

representing the foundation of penitence and faith are all consistent with Judaism. 'Doctrines of washings'—how unnatural are the attempts to explain this plural as referring to Christian Baptism; 'imposition of hands, resurrection of dead, eternal judgement'—all this belonged to the creed of a Pharisaic Jew who accepted the whole of the Old Testament."[13] Very true; but it belonged equally to the creed of a nonconformist Jew of Essene or comparable outlook.

(a) *Repentance from dead works.* "Dead works" are works which must be repented of; in Ch. 9:14 they are works from which the conscience requires to be cleansed. Therefore they are probably not the works of the law, not even the sacrificial ceremonies prescribed by the cultic law,[14] although our author does regard these as obsolete and moribund. They are works which issue in death because they are evil; they belong to the way of death and not the way of life. One could well believe that the catechesis on which the readers of this epistle had been trained included a version of the "Two Ways" teaching incorporated in the *Didache* and the *Epistle of Barnabas*, but certainly earlier in date than either of these documents.[15] The *Didache* begins its account of the way of death (which, it says, is "evil and fraught with a curse") with a catalogue of the sins which belong to it: "murders, adulteries, lusts, fornications, thefts, idolatries, magic arts, sorceries, robberies, false depositions, hypocrisies, a double heart, fraud, arrogance, malice, obstinacy, covetousness, filthy language, envy, audacity, haughtiness, boastfulness ..."[16] It was with regard to precisely

---

[13] *The Epistle of Priesthood* (Edinburgh, 1913), p. 15. *Cf.* G. H. Lang, *The Epistle to the Hebrews* (London, 1951), pp. 95f.

[14] They have been taken in this sense, however, by able expositors, such as A. B. Bruce, *The Training of the Twelve* (Edinburgh, 1883), p. 81; *cf.* also R. V. G. Tasker, *op. cit.*, p. 25 (where he describes this repentance as "an abandonment of the attempt to obtain righteousness by seeking to obey the precepts of a lifeless moral code").

[15] *Didache* 1:1–5:2; *Ep. Barn.* 18:1–20:2. As it appears in these documents, the ethical treatise of the "Two Ways"—the Way of Life and the Way of Death (or the Way of Light and the Way of Darkness)—is a slightly Christianized edition of an originally Jewish manual, going back to the pre-Christian era. Traces of it appear in the *Testaments of the Twelve Patriarchs* (*Judah* 20:1–5; *Asher* 1:3–6:6) and in the Qumran literature (1QS iii. 18–iv. 26). On the use of the "Two Ways" in early Judaeo-Christian baptismal instruction see J. V. Bartlet, *The Apostolic Age* (Edinburgh, 1929), pp. 250ff., 313.

[16] *Didache* 5:1.

such vices that Paul told the Roman Christians that "the end of those things is death" (Rom. 6:21); very appropriately, therefore, might they be called dead works. Repentance from such things was insisted upon in the Old Testament, and in all the strains o-Jewish thought and life which were derived from the Old Testas ment. The sectaries of Qumran, for example, described themselvef as "the repentant of Israel";[17] and they were by no means the only Jews to think and speak in such terms. The keynote of John the Baptist's preaching was a call to repentance;[18] and when Jesus began to proclaim the kingdom of God in Galilee, He called upon His hearers to "repent, and believe in the gospel" (Mark 1:15). So too Paul could remind the elders of the Ephesian church how he had spent over two years in their city "testifying both to Jews and to Greeks repentance toward God, and faith in our Lord Jesus Christ" (Acts 20:21).

(b) Faith toward God. The last two quotations illustrate the close association between repentance and faith. The foundation of faith in God was, of course, well and truly laid in the Old Testament. Throughout the volume faith is marked out as essential to true religion, from the statement that Abraham "believed in Jehovah; and he reckoned it to him for righteousness" (Gen. 15:6) to Habakkuk's testimony that "the righteous shall live by his faith" (Hab. 2:4).[19] The readers of this epistle had already been reminded that it was unbelief that kept the generation of the Exodus from entering the promised land, and they were urged to apply this lesson to their own situation. Faith in God must include faith in His messengers, and in the gospel faith in God included—or indeed became tantamount to—faith in Christ. These "Hebrews" had certainly been taught the way of faith in Christ, but this way had been prepared for them in advance by the Old Testament insistence on faith in God: "if ye will not believe, surely ye shall not be established" (Isa. 7:9).

2 *(c) The teaching of baptisms.* This has commonly been regarded as a reference to Christian baptism, but it is very doubtful whether Christian baptism is directly in view here at all. Apart from the fact that the word is in the plural, it may be significant that our author does not use *baptisma*, the Greek noun regularly

---

[17] CD iv. 2.
[18] Matt. 3:2; Mark 1:4; Luke 3:8.
[19] Quoted in Ch. 10:38 (see pp. 272ff.).

employed in the New Testament to denote Christian baptism (and the baptism of John), but *baptismos*, which in its two other indubitable New Testament occurrences refers to Jewish ceremonial washings.[20] "Instruction about ablutions" (RSV) or "instruction about cleansing rites" (NEB) expresses the sense more adequately. There is no lack of instruction about these things in the Old Testament, and this provided a further foundation on which the Christian truths could be erected. Later in the epistle (Ch. 9:13) the ritual of the red heifer in Num. 19, one of the most important of the ceremonial purifications prescribed in the Old Testament, is treated as a counterpart in the temporal order of the cleansing efficacy of the sacrifice of Christ in the spiritual order. The prophet Ezekiel in earlier days had used the terminology of the old ceremonial ablutions to describe God's inward cleansing of His people in the age of restoration: "I will sprinkle clean water upon you, and ye shall be clean: from all your filthiness, and from all your idols, will I cleanse you" (Ezek. 36:25). In language like this the baptist groups that flourished in Judaism at the beginning of the Christian era found scriptural authority for their ceremonial washings which went beyond what the letter of the law required.[21] Formerly our knowledge about these groups was derived from ancient writings which described them from the outside; but the discovery and decipherment of the Qumran texts have introduced us to one such group from the inside. The members of the Qumran community practised ceremonial ablution in terms of Num. 19 and Ezek. 36; but they did not regard such ablution as a means of removing iniquity from a man's heart. Only by submission to the commandments of God, they believed, could a man be inwardly purified, and not until then would ceremonial washings have any value for him.[22] There is evidence that such baptist groups of Jews

---

[20] In Ch. 9:10 βαπτισμός is used of "divers washings" associated with the sacrificial cultus of the Old Testament; in Mark 7:4 of the Jewish purification "of cups, and pots, and brasen vessels". In Col. 2:12 there is weighty textual support for βαπτισμῷ (P⁴⁶ B D* G) as against βαπτίσματι, in the sense of Christian baptism. But the plural is against a straightforward interpretation in terms of Christian baptism here. (Βάπτισμα is peculiar to Christian writers.)

[21] *Cf.* also Zech. 13:1. See W. Brandt, *Die jüdischen Baptismen* (*BZAW* xviii, Giessen, 1910); J. Thomas, *Le mouvement baptiste en Palestine et Syrie* (Gembloux, 1935).

[22] 1QS iii. 4–9; v. 13f. Josephus's acount of the baptism of John is evidently colored by the historian's knowledge of Essene doctrine and practice: according

were found in the lands of the Dispersion as well in their homeland; the Jewish community in Rome, in particular, probably preserved some characteristic features of this nonconformist Judaism—features which were carried over into Roman Christianity, if the Hippolytan *Apostolic Tradition* may be trusted. According to Hippolytus, for example, baptism, as the central act of Christian initiation, took place on a Sunday, but on the preceding Thursday the candidate was required to have a ritual bath for the removal of impurity.[23] This pre-baptismal bath has no warrant in the New Testament, but it may well have been a legacy from Roman Judaism.[24] If this epistle was sent to a group of believing Jews in Rome, the reference to "instruction about ablutions" may have had a more direct significance than meets the eye of the twentieth-century reader.[25]

(d) Laying on of hands. The imposition of hands (Heb. *semīkhāh*) was an early Christian practice,[26] associated especially with the impartation of the Holy Spirit,[27] and that is most probably its significance here.[28] But it too was inherited from the Old Testa-

to him, John "taught that baptism would be regarded as acceptable by God provided that people underwent it not to procure pardon for certain sins but for the purification of the body when once the soul had been purified by righteousness" (*Ant.* xviii. 117). *Cf.* p. 197, n. 65; p. 203, n. 88.

[23] "And let those who are to be baptized be instructed to wash and cleanse themselves on the fifth day of the week" (*The Apostolic Tradition of St. Hippolytus*, ed. G. Dix [London, 1937], p. 31). *Cf.* R. J. Zwi Werblowsky, "On the Baptismal Rite according to St. Hippolytus", *Studia Patristica* ii = *TU* lxiv (Berlin, 1957), pp. 93ff.

[24] *Cf.* J. Daniélou, "La communauté de Qumrân et l'organisation de l'Église ancienne", *RHPR* xxxv (1955), pp. 104ff.; M. Black, *The Scrolls and Christian Origins* (London, 1961), pp. 99ff., 114f.

[25] D. Daube, *The New Testament and Rabbinic Judaism* (London, 1956), p. 109, points to the high importance attached to baptism among leading first-century members of the school of Hillel, some of whom were prepared to say that baptism alone (not as a ceremonial purification but as a rite with a deep moral and spiritual meaning) was sufficient to make a Gentile (whether male or female) a Jewish proselyte. M. Black (*op. cit.*, p. 51) compares Justin Martyr's "baptizing Pharisees" (*Dialogue with Trypho*, 80).

[26] *Cf.* Acts 6:6; 8:17; 9:12, 17; 19:6, with accompanying exposition and notes in NICNT.

[27] *Cf.* G. W. H. Lampe, *The Seal of the Spirit* (London, 1951), pp. 70ff.; T. W. Manson, "Entry into Membership of the Early Church", *JThS* xlviii (1947), pp. 25ff.; R. E. O. White, *The Biblical Doctrine of Initiation* (London, 1960), pp. 195ff.

[28] *Cf.* references to the Holy Spirit in verse 4; Chs. 2:4; 10:29.

ment, where it is used especially in commissioning someone for public office,[29] or as part of the sacrificial ritual.[30] In rabbinical Judaism the term appears regularly in the sense of ordination (of elders).[31]

(e) Resurrection of the dead. The resurrection of Jesus gave special importance to this doctrine in the Church, but the doctrine as such was no innovation in New Testament times. It was held, as we know, by the Pharisees,[32] who found in it the guarantee that Israel's ancestral hope would be realized in perpetuity; it was taught expressly in the Old Testament (*cf.* Isa. 26:19; Dan. 12:2), and, as Jesus pointed out, it was taught implicitly at an earlier stage, when God, who is the God of the living, not of the dead, proclaimed Himself to be the God of Abraham, Isaac and Jacob (Ex. 3:6; *cf.* Mark 12:26f.).

(f) Eternal judgment. The Jewish belief in resurrection was closely associated with the expectation of judgment to come. That the God of Israel is Judge of all the earth and of His people in particular is an essential part of the Old Testament revelation (Gen. 18:25; Isa. 33:22); His recurring judgments in history will be summed up in the eschatological judgment of Dan. 7:9ff.[33] In Christian belief the "one like unto a son of man" through whom the eschatological judgment is carried out is identified with Jesus (Matt. 25:31ff.; John 5:22, 27; Acts 17:31, etc.).

3 It was on a foundation already laid in the Old Testament, then, and one on which their way of life was already based, that these people had received the gospel. All these things were now given a fresh and fuller significance because of the coming of Christ into the world. But the "Hebrews" were exposed to a subtle danger which could not be experienced by converts from paganism. If a convert from paganism gave up Christianity and reverted to paganism, there was a clean break between the faith which he renounced and the paganism to which he returned. But it was possible for the recipients of this letter, yielding gradually to

---

[29] *Cf.* Num. 27:18, 23; Deut. 34:9.
[30] *Cf.* Lev. 1:4; 3:2; 4:4; 8:14; 16:21, etc. See also p. 193, n. 56.
[31] *Cf.* Mishnah, *Sanhedrin* iv. 4.
[32] *Cf.* Acts 23:8, with exposition and notes *ad loc.* in NICNT.
[33] It is here called "eternal judgment" (κρίμα αἰώνιον) because it is the judgment which is valid for the whole age (αἰών) to come, as distinct from the temporal judgments of the present age.

pressures from various quarters, to give up more and more those features of faith and practice which were distinctive of Christianity, and yet to feel that they had not abandoned the basic principles of repentance and faith, the realities denoted by religious ablutions and the laying on of hands, the expectation of resurrection and the judgment of the age to come. To go on insisting on these things, therefore, would not really help them; it would be better to press on to those teachings which belonged to spiritual maturity, in the hope that the maturity would come with the teachings. "And this will we do, if God permit"[34]—that is to say, not merely will our author go on to give his mature teaching about the Melchizedek priesthood, but he and his readers together will advance to full growth in Christ, God permitting.

4-6 The reason why there is no point in laying the foundation over again is now stated: apostasy is irremediable. Once more our author emphasizes that continuance is the test of reality. In these verses he is not questioning the perseverance of the saints; we might say that rather he is insisting that those who persevere are the true saints. But in fact he is stating a practical truth that has verified itself repeatedly in the experience of the visible Church. Those who have shared the covenant privileges of the people of God, and then deliberately renounce them, are the most difficult persons of all to reclaim for the faith. It is indeed impossible to reclaim them, says our author. We know, of course, that nothing of this sort is ultimately impossible for the grace of God, but as a matter of human experience the reclamation of such people is, practically speaking, impossible.[35] People are frequently immunized against a disease by being inoculated with a mild form of it, or with a related but milder disease. And in the spiritual realm experience suggests that it is possible to be "immunized" against

---

[34] Gk. ἐάνπερ ἐπιτρέπῃ ὁ θεός, in which we should see more than a conventional expression of piety.

[35] According to C. Spicq, ἀδύνατον in Philo, "when understood of man and in relation to the moral plane, should be translated by 'incapable'; the impossibility in question is subjective and relative, due reservation being made with regard to divine intervention, and it is in this sense that *Hebrews* conceives the impossibility, not of the apostate's pardon, but of his turning" (*L'Épître aux Hébreux* [Paris, 1952], i, pp. 57f.). There is a closer parallel in Hermas, *Shepherd*, Similitude ix. 26. 6 ("it is impossible [ἀδύνατον] for him who will now deny his Lord to be saved"); but this is probably dependent on our present passage in Hebrews.

Christianity by being inoculated with something which, for the time being, looks so like the real thing that it is generally mistaken for it. This is not a question of those who are attached in a formal way to the profession of true religion without ever having experienced its power; it is blessedly possible for such people to have an experience of God's grace which changes what was once a matter of formal attachment into a matter of inward reality. It is a question of people who see clearly where the truth lies, and perhaps for a period conform to it, but then, for one reason or another, renounce it.[36]

In our Lord's parable of the sower, the seed which fell on rocky ground, where there was no depth of earth, sprouted quickly, and for a time the passer-by might have seen no difference between what was growing there and what was growing in the good ground. It was only when a time of testing came that the difference became evident.[37]   It was a time of testing now for the recipients of the epistle, and our author is anxious that they should respond triumphantly to the test and prove that in their case the seed had fallen into good ground.

From his description of the experiences of those who may nevertheless fall away, it would certainly be difficult to distinguish them at the outset from those who are going to stay the course. For they have (a) been enlightened, (b) tasted the heavenly gift, (c) partaken of the Holy Spirit, (d) tasted the goodness of the word of God and the mighty works of the age to come. Just as the Hebrew spies who returned from their expedition carrying visible tokens of the good land of Canaan nevertheless failed to enter the

---

[36] Comparisons have been drawn with our Lord's words about the unpardonable sin against the Holy Spirit (Mark 3:29) and John's words about a "sin unto death" for which prayer should not be offered (I John 5:16). The sin spoken of by our Lord cannot be apostasy in the ordinary sense; it was rather a deliberate closing of eyes to the light, refusing to accept the evidence of God's visitation and ascribing the work of the Spirit of God to the power of Beelzebul. The sin of I John 5:16 could well be apostasy; cf. C. H. Dodd, The Johannine Epistles, MNTC (London, 1946), pp. 135ff., for the view that John, like the writer to the Hebrews, "is thinking of apostasy or denial of Christ as the sin that places a man beyond the pale. We know that he traced the presence and power of Antichrist in the denial of the Incarnation (4:2-5), and if a man had become identified with Antichrist it was perhaps natural to feel that he was past praying for."

[37] Mark 4:3ff. and parallels. See p. 59 above.

land because of their unbelief, so those who had come to know the blessings of the new covenant might nevertheless in a spiritual sense turn back in heart to Egypt and so forfeit the saints' everlasting rest.[38]

(a) *They were enlightened.* It is tempting to understand the verb here in the sense of baptism—a sense which it bore among Christians in Rome in the middle of the second century.[39] The use of "enlightenment" in the sense of baptism need not be a borrowing from the language of the mysteries; it is quite in line with New Testament teaching.[40] At any rate, the enlightenment here is something which has taken place once for all—like baptism itself, which is unrepeatable for the simple reason that its repetition would contradict its whole significance.[41] The light of the gospel has broken in upon these people's darkness, and life can never be the same again; to give up the gospel would be to sin against the light, the one sin which by its very nature is incurable.

(b) *They had tasted the heavenly gift.* As enlightenment suggests baptism, so the tasting[42] of the heavenly gift may suggest the

---

[38] *Cf.* the lessons drawn from the Israelites' day of temptation in the wilderness in Ch. 3:7ff. It may be that the wilderness narrative is still in our author's mind. The Israelites who failed to enter Canaan failed in spite of the fact that they had been baptized in the Red Sea and had their camp illuminated by heavenly light, in spite of the provision of bread from heaven and water from the rock, and God's "good Spirit to instruct them" (*cf.* Neh. 9:20), in spite of their hearing the oracles of God and seeing His mighty works in their midst (*cf.* G. H. Lang, *op. cit.*, pp. 98ff.).

[39] It is so translated in the Syriac Peshitta here and in Ch. 10:32. Justin (*First Apology*, 61:12f.; 65:1) uses the verb φωτίζω and the noun φωτισμός to describe baptism, and does so in a way which indicates that this was a current usage among the Christians of his acquaintance.

[40] Especially with Johannine teaching about Christ as the Light. *Cf.* the quotation in Eph. 5:14, frequently taken to be a snatch of a baptismal hymn, in which the convert is invited to wake up from the darkness of spiritual death into the light of Christ. The rhythm of the words was the characteristic rhythm of initiation chants in the Greek world (*cf.* A. M. Hunter, *Paul and his Predecessors* [London, 1961], pp. 38f.). The Greek text of Ps. 34:5a (LXX 33:6a), "Come to him and be enlightened (φωτίσθητε)", was early used in the Christian baptismal liturgy (it is probably reflected in I Pet. 2:4).

[41] *Cf.* Origen, *On Martyrdom*, 30, for the point that one cannot be baptized a second time. See also J. A. T. Robinson, *Twelve New Testament Studies* (London, 1962), p. 172.

[42] For γεύομαι ("taste") in a eucharistic context *cf.* Acts 20:11. But a closer parallel is I Pet. 2:3, echoing Ps. 34:8 (LXX 33:9), in a *baptismal* context (*cf.* n. 40 above). C. Spicq (*op. cit.*, p. 57) adduces examples to show that "to taste

Eucharist; certainly the people in question have communicated in addition to being baptized.[43] And certainly it is possible for people who have had experience of both the gospel sacraments to commit apostasy nonetheless. But the "heavenly gift" need not be restricted to the Eucharist; it may indicate the whole sum of spiritual blessings which are sacramentally sealed and signified in the Eucharist.[44]

(c) They had become partakers of the Holy Spirit. It is precarious to argue that the personal Holy Spirit is not intended here, but rather His gifts or operations, seeing that the definite article is lacking in the Greek. The presence or absence of the article is not in itself sufficient to decide whether the Giver or His gifts are in question. Whether it is possible for one who has been in any real sense a partaker of the Holy Spirit[45] to commit apostasy has been questioned, but our author has no doubt that it is possible in this way to do "despite unto the Spirit of grace" (Ch. 10:29). The people whom he has in mind had not only been baptized and received the Eucharist, but had experienced the laying on of hands. Early apostolic history has a record of one outstanding character who believed when he heard the gospel, was baptized, attached himself to the evangelist whose preaching had convinced him, and presumably received the Spirit when apostolic hands were laid upon him—yet Simon Magus was pronounced by Peter to be still "in the gall of bitterness and in the bond of iniquity" (Acts 8:9ff., 18ff.), and showed himself in the following decades

---

the heavenly gift (Heb. 6:4) is an Alexandrinism, and to taste the word of God (Heb. 6:5) is a Philonism". On the former point he refers to Wisdom 16:3, where the quails of Num. 11:31ff. are described as ξενὴ γεῦσις, "an unaccustomed delicacy". This is not a very impressive parallel, but it might be added to the wilderness parallels mentioned on p. 120, n. 38.

[43] Moffatt (*ad loc.*) draws attention to Philo, *On Flight and Finding*, 139, for the food-metaphor following upon the light-metaphor (as here): "The divine ordinance both enlightens and sweetens the soul that has vision, flashing forth the beam of truth, and with persuasion, that sweet virtue, imparting sweetness to those who hunger and thirst after nobility of character". Philo has immediately before (*ibid.*, 137) explained the manna as being the "utterance of God and divine Word" (ῥῆμα θεοῦ καὶ λόγον θεῖον).

[44] *Cf.* Paul's application of the spiritual food and drink of the wilderness wanderings in I Cor. 10:3ff.

[45] "Partakers" represents Gk. μέτοχοι (*cf.* Ch. 3:1, 14). *Cf.* the "distributions of the Holy Spirit" in Ch. 2:4.

to be the most determined opponent of apostolic Christianity.[46] If we ask in what sense a man like that could have partaken of the Holy Spirit, the words that follow here may point the way to an answer.

(d) They had tasted the good word of God[47] *and the powers of the age to come.* Simon Magus realized how good the word of God was when he heard it from Philip's lips, and he was amazed at the signs and great "powers"[48] that accompanied the proclamation and reception of the gospel. Those "powers" or mighty works were "signs" that the age to come had already broken in upon the present age; the words of Jesus about the mighty works of His ministry continued to be true of the mighty works performed in His name in the apostolic age: "if I by the Spirit of God cast out demons, then is the kingdom of God come upon you" (Matt. 12:28).[49] But Jesus also spoke of a day when many would say to Him: "Lord, lord, did we not prophesy by thy name, and by thy name cast out demons, and by thy name do many mighty works?"[50]—only to be told: "I never knew you: depart from me, ye that work iniquity" (Matt. 7:22f.). The Scriptures contain encouragement enough and to spare for the feeblest believer, but are full of solemn warnings to those who think they stand to beware lest they fall. A credible profession of faith must be accepted as genuine, but ultimately it is only the Lord who knows those who are His.

For it is possible for people who can be described in the language of verses 4 and 5 to "fall away" irretrievably. This warning has been both unduly minimized and unduly exaggerated. It has been unduly minimized as when K. S. Wuest assures us that "having

---

[46] *Cf.* exposition and notes in *Acts*, NICNT, pp. 178ff.; A. Ehrhardt, "Christianity before the Apostles' Creed", *HThR* lv (1962), pp. 73ff., esp. pp. 85f.

[47] *Cf.* Philo's interpretation of the manna, quoted on p. 121, n. 43.

[48] Gk. δυνάμεις, used in this sense here as in Acts 8:13; *cf.* Ch. 2:4 (p. 30), from which it is evident that these "Hebrews" all had experience of such δυνάμεις in the days when the gospel was first brought to them.

[49] The parallel passage in Luke 11:20 has "finger of God" where Matthew has "Spirit of God". In the apostolic age such δυνάμεις continue to be ministered by the Spirit (Gal. 3:5), who is the firstfruits of the coming age (Rom. 8:23). *Cf.* p. 35, n. 18 (on Ch. 2:5).

[50] Gk. δυνάμεις.

fallen away"[51] is "a conditional participle here presenting a hypothetical case, a straw man" and that the sin in question "cannot be committed today since no temple and no sacrifices are in existence, and no transition period obtains".[52] It does not require temple and sacrifices, or a transitional period of the kind implied in this epistle, for men and women who have taken Christ's name upon themselves to commit apostasy; and biblical writers (the writer to the Hebrews being no exception) are not given to the setting up of men of straw. The warning of this passage was a real warning against a real danger, a danger which is still present so long as "an evil heart of unbelief" can result in "falling away from the living God" (Ch. 3:12).

On the other hand, our author's meaning can be exaggerated to the point of distortion when he is understood to say that for sins committed after baptism there can be no repentance. "The author of Hebrews," wrote F. C. Burkitt, "will allow no forgiveness for Christian sinners."[53] In this he was following the rigorist interpretation of Tertullian,[54] who quotes the opening verses of Heb. 6 to prove that there can be no pardon or restoration to communion for post-baptismal sin. Tertullian had one particular kind of sin in mind, and one which actually does not enter into our author's argument here: according to Tertullian, the writer of this warning passage (identified by him with Barnabas), "who learnt this *from* apostles, and taught it *with* apostles, never knew of any second repentance promised by apostles to the adulterer and fornicator."[55]

---

[51] Gk. παραπεσόντας. The verb παραπίπτω, found here only in NT (by contrast with the cognate noun παράπτωμα, which is frequent in the sense of "trespass"), means "fall aside" or "go astray"; it is not its root meaning but its context which indicates that its reference here is to apostasy—the same sin as is expressed by ἀποστῆναι in Ch. 3:12. *Cf.* I. H. Marshall, *Perseverance, Falling Away and Apostasy* (unpublished Ph.D. thesis, University of Aberdeen, 1963).

[52] "Hebrews Six in the Greek New Testament", *Bibliotheca Sacra* cxix (1962), pp. 45ff. (quotation on p. 52); *cf.* his *Hebrews in the Greek New Testament* (Grand Rapids, 1947), pp. 113ff.

[53] In a review of A. E. Brooke's commentary on *The Johannine Epistles* (ICC) in the *Cambridge Review*, November 14, 1912, quoted with disapproval by A. Nairne, *op. cit.*, p. 130.

[54] Burkitt, of course, unlike Tertullian, did not adopt as his own viewpoint what he believed the writer to the Hebrews to mean.

[55] *On Modesty*, 20. Tertullian is here criticizing the *Shepherd* of Hermas (the "*Shepherd* of the adulterers", as he scathingly calls it), which conceded one (but

But the writer to the Hebrews himself distinguishes (as did the Old Testament law) between inadvertent sin and wilful sin,[56] and the context here shows plainly that the wilful sin which he has in mind is deliberate apostasy. People who commit this sin, he says, cannot be brought back to repentance; by renouncing Christ they put themselves in the position of those who, deliberately refusing His claim to be the Son of God, had Him crucified and exposed to public shame.[57] Those who repudiate the salvation procured by Christ will find none anywhere else.

The margin of ARV suggests an alternative rendering which may appear to moderate the gravity of our author's words: "it is impossible to renew them again unto repentance, *the while* they crucify to themselves the Son of God ..." By suggesting that these people cannot be brought back to repentance so long as they repudiate Christ, this rendering might be thought to imply that when they cease to repudiate Him repentance will be possible. But this is certainly not what is meant. To say that they cannot be brought to repentance so long as they persist in their renunciation of Christ would be a truism hardly worth putting into words. The participle "crucifying" is much more appropriately taken as causal than as temporal in force; it indicates *why* it is impossible for such people to repent and make a new beginning. God has pledged Himself to pardon all who truly repent, but Scripture and experience alike suggest that it is possible for human beings to arrive at a state of heart and life where they can no longer repent.

7–8 Such people are compared to land which, in spite of all the care expended in its cultivation, refuses to produce a good crop. The figure here is to much the same effect as Isaiah's vineyard song (Isa. 5:1ff.). That vineyard received all the attention that any

---

only one) opportunity of repentance and forgiveness for post-baptismal sin. See the exposition of Ch. 10:26ff. on pp. 260f., with nn. 144–146.

[56] Cf. Chs. 2:2; 5:2 (with exposition and notes).

[57] Cf. E. Ménégoz, *La théologie de l'Épître aux Hébreux* (Paris, 1894), pp. 21f. On the question whether ἀνασταυρόω here means "crucify" or "crucify again" see p. 111, n. 7. Taking it to mean "crucify again", J. A. T. Robinson (*op. cit.*, p. 172) says: "Baptism means being put on the Cross once with Christ: it is absurd to think of renewing it for those who for their own ends are actually crucifying the Son of God again (*cf.* 10:29)". Among the LXX occurrences of παραδειγματίζω ("put to an open shame") is Num. 25:4, where it is used of the leaders of the Baal-peor apostasy who were hung up "unto Jehovah before the sun".

vineyard could have received, but when the time came for it to produce grapes, it produced nothing but wild grapes.[58]   It was clearly reprobate[59] land, which would never respond to cultivation; it must simply be allowed thenceforth to lie untended and become derelict.   So our author compares those believers who persevere in faith to fertile land which produces fruit, while those in whose lives the fruits of righteousness do not appear are compared to land which will never produce anything but thorns and thistles,[60] to be kept down by burning, "for our God is a consuming fire" (Ch. 12:29).

6. ENCOURAGEMENT TO PERSEVERANCE

Ch. 6:9-12

9   But, beloved, we are persuaded better things of you, and things that accompany salvation,[61] though we thus speak:

10   for God is not unrighteous to forget your work and the love[62] which ye showed toward his name, in that ye ministered unto the saints, and still do minister.

---

[58]   *Cf.* Hermas, *Shepherd* (Mandate x. 1. 5): "Even as good vineyards when they are neglected become unfruitful because of the thorns and various kinds of weeds, so men who have believed and fall into the many aforementioned preoccupations [secular business, moneymaking, pagan friendships, etc.], wander from a right mind and have absolutely no understanding of righteousness."

[59]   Gk. ἀδόκιμος ("rejected" in ARV here). *Cf.* those people who are described in Tit. 1:16 as "unto every good work reprobate" (*cf.* also occurrences of the same word in I Cor. 9:27; II Cor. 13:5). E. K. Simpson, discussing the meaning of ἀδόκιμος in I Cor. 9:27, says: "Paul is thinking of spurious pretensions ... we might construe: 'lest, after preaching to others, I myself should prove *base metal*'" (*Words Worth Weighing in the Greek New Testament* [London, 1946], pp. 17f.).

[60]   And therefore "nigh unto a curse" (Gk. κατάρας ἐγγύς), for in Gen. 3:17f. thorns and thistles are a consequence of the cursing of the land for man's sake. So in the "Two Ways" the way of death is κατάρας μεστή, "fraught with a curse" (*Didache* 5:1; *Ep. Barn.* 20:1). *Cf.* Luke 13:6ff.; John 15:6.

[61]   Gk. ἐχόμενα σωτηρίας, "things that belong to salvation" (ARV margin; RSV); the presence of those things in the readers' lives was a token of the presence of salvation too, since they were so closely and invariably bound up with salvation.

[62]   AV "your work and labour of love" represents an assimilation to the text of I Thess. 1:3, found in K L with several minuscules and TR.

11 And we desire that each one of you may show the same diligence unto the fulness of hope even to the end:[63]

12 that ye be not sluggish, but imitators of them who through faith and patience inherit the promises.

9 Our author makes haste to reassure his readers, after his words of solemn warning: he does not believe that there are apostates, or even potential apostates, among them. He was encouraged to believe and hope the best of them because the fruits of righteousness had beyond all question manifested themselves in their lives. Those fruits, being the natural concomitants of salvation, bore witness that the people in whom they appeared were genuine heirs of salvation. His desire to reassure them, his concern that what he has just said should not discourage them, may have prompted his affectionate language here: this is the only place in the epistle where he calls them "beloved"—"my dear friends".

10 The fruits of righteousness which have shown themselves in their lives are the acts of service performed for their fellow-Christians. Further details of the circumstances in which these acts of service were rendered are given later, in Ch. 10:32–34. If the recipients of the letter were resident in Rome, then the behavior for which our author commends them was a precedent for the reputation for Christian charity which the Roman church enjoyed in later times. We may think of Ignatius's description of that church as "having the presidency of love";[64] or the words of Dionysius, bishop of Corinth, in his letter to Soter, bishop of Rome (c. A.D. 170): "This has been your custom from the beginning, to do good in manifold ways to all the brethren, and to send contributions to the many churches in every city, in some places relieving the poverty of the needy, and ministering to the brethren in the mines".[65] The point here, however, is that deeds of kindness done to the people of God are reckoned by God as done to Himself, and will surely receive their reward from Him.

---

[63] Gk. ἄχρι τέλους, with which cf. Ch. 3:14, μέχρι τέλους.

[64] Ign., *Ep. ad Rom.*, preface.

[65] Eusebius, *Hist. Eccl.* iv. 23. 10. There is no particular reason to confine "the saints" to Jerusalem because of the similar language of Rom. 15:25; I Cor. 16:1; II Cor. 9:1; in the latter passages the context makes it clear that Jerusalem believers are intended. *Cf.* Ch. 3:1 (p. 55, n. 5).

11-12 But let them go on as they have begun. Our author's insistence on the grace of continuance appears again as he assures them of his affectionate longing[66] that they should go on exhibiting the same zeal as marked them in the beginning, until the final and full realization of their hope. "Don't become sluggish,"[67] he urges them; "follow the example of those who have gone before, those who are now entering into the enjoyment of things which God promised them long ago, because they believed His word and persevered in hope." This exhortation to imitate the faith of the men of old anticipates the argument of Ch. 11; that the reference is to men of God in Old Testament times is clear from the words that follow.

7. THE STEADFASTNESS OF GOD'S PROMISE

Ch. 6:13-20

13 For when God made promise to Abraham, since he could swear by none greater, he sware by himself,

14 saying, Surely blessing I will bless thee, and multiplying I will multiply thee.[68]

15 And thus, having patiently endured, he obtained the promise.

16 For men swear by the greater: and in every dispute of theirs the oath is final for confirmation.

17 Wherein God, being minded to show more abundantly unto the heirs of the promise the immutability of his counsel, interposed[69] with an oath;

---

[66] Chrysostom (*Homilies on Hebrews*, x. 5) draws attention to the writer's "fatherly affection" here.

[67] Gk. νωθρός (*cf*. Ch. 5:11). The warning here is against the deadly sin of *accidie* (ἀκήδεια), described in Dante's *Purgatorio* xvii. 76ff. Dorothy L. Sayers, in her edition of Dante, mentions such modern forms of it as false tolerance, "disillusionment", and escapism. *Cf.* Sir John C. Hawkins, "The Use of Dante as an Illustrator of Scripture", *ExT* xvi (1904-5), pp. 548f.

[68] Gen. 22:16f.

[69] Gk. ἐμεσίτευσεν, literally "mediated" (this is the only NT occurrence of the verb; for the noun μεσίτης from which it is derived *cf*. Chs. 8:6; 9:15; 12:24).

18 that by[70] two immutable things, in which it is impossible for God[71] to lie, we may have a strong encouragement, who have fled for refuge to lay hold of the hope set before us:

19 which we have[72] as an anchor of the soul, *a hope* both sure and stedfast and entering into that which is within the veil;

20 whither as a forerunner Jesus[73] entered for us, having become a high priest for ever after the order of Melchizedek.

13–15 The example of Abraham, as father of all who have faith in God, was invoked in many strands of primitive Christianity. Even before the Christian message began to be proclaimed, John the Baptist pointed out that something more than biological descent from Abraham was necessary for acceptance with God; God did indeed desire "children of Abraham", but if need be He could bring them into being by His own creative act (Matt. 3:9; Luke 3:8). Paul justifies his claim that the way of righteousness opened up in the gospel is attested by the law and the prophets by pointing to the testimony of Scripture about Abraham, who "believed in Jehovah; and he reckoned it to him for righteousness" (Gen. 15:6; quoted in Rom. 4:3; Gal. 3:6). James quotes the same testimony, but relates it to Abraham's offering up of Isaac in support of his insistence that "faith apart from works is dead" (Jas. 2:21ff.). Our author here, and more fully in Ch. 11:8ff., presents Abraham as the supreme example of a man who received promises from God, and lived in the good of these promises, persevering to the end in faith and hope.

---

[70] Gk. διά, for which P[46] and D have μετά, probably under the influence of μετά in the following ἀμεταθέτων, and possibly independently in the two MSS (*cf.* Zuntz, *op. cit.*, p. 41).

[71] Gk. θεόν, according to B D and the majority of later authorities, but P[46] ℵ* A 1739 and a few other minuscules, with citations in Eusebius (²/₄), Didymus (²/₂), Chrysostom, Cyril and Theodoret (¹/₄), have the articulated τὸν θεόν. According to Zuntz (*op. cit.*, p. 130), the addition of the article is an early Alexandrian corruption from which, however, B is free; the force of the anarthrous reading is that "it is impossible for one who is God to lie".

[72] Gk. ἔχομεν, for which D (Gk., not Lat.) and a few other authorities have the subjunctive ἔχωμεν, probably under the influence of the subjunctive after ἵνα in the previous verse.

[73] D* adds "Christ".

To our author Abraham was a significant figure, not only because of his faith in the promise of God, but also because of the
part he plays in the story of Melchizedek. God's faithfulness to
His promise to Abraham is a token of His faithfulness in regard
to another of His promises, that concerning the Melchizedek
priesthood. These two promises "hang together, and as Paul
worked out the one in Galatians so our author will work out the
other".[74]

The particular promise in view here is that made by God to
Abraham after his offering up of Isaac: "By myself have I sworn ...
that in blessing I will bless thee, and in multiplying I will multiply
thy seed" (Gen. 22:16f.).[75] But this was a recapitulation and
elaboration of God's earlier promise to Abraham that He would
bless him and make of him a great nation (Gen. 12:2f.). At the
time when that earlier promise was made, Abraham was childless.
As time went on, however, it was made clear to him that the
promise would be fulfilled through the birth of a son to Sarah and
himself when, by all natural reckoning, such a prospect would
have been dismissed as impossible. Yet Abraham believed God,
and in due course the promised child was born. On Isaac now
hung every hope that the further promises of God regarding
Abraham's descendants would be fulfilled; yet it was Isaac whom
Abraham was commanded to offer up to God. When Abraham's
faith and obedience were shown in his readiness to do even this,
he received Isaac back from the dead "in a figure" (Ch. 11:19),
and received at the same time a reaffirmation of the promises of
God, reinforced on this occasion by the divine oath: "and thus,
having patiently endured, he obtained the promise". There was
much in God's promise to Abraham whose fulfilment lay in the
distant future, but in the restoration to Abraham of the son upon
whose survival the promise depended Abraham did, in a very
substantial sense, "obtain the promise".[76]

---

[74] T. W. Manson, *Studies in the Gospels and Epistles* (Manchester, 1962),
p. 249.

[75] The constructions "in blessing" and "in multiplying" are intended as
equivalents of the Hebrew absolute infinitive, which intensifies the force of the
accompanying finite verb; *cf.* the present passage in NEB ("I vow that I will
bless you abundantly and multiply your descendants") and Gen. 22:17, RSV
("I will indeed bless you, and I will multiply your descendants ...").

[76] With "he obtained the promise" (Gk. ἐπέτυχεν τῆς ἐπαγγελίας [*cf.* Ch.
11:33]) here may be contrasted "not having received the promises" (Gk.

16–17 Our author emphasizes the fact that when God repeated His promise to Abraham after the offering up of Isaac, He confirmed it with an oath. When men swear an oath in order to underline the certainty and solemnity of their words, they swear by someone or something greater than themselves. "As the LORD liveth" was the supreme oath in Israel. Abraham himself swore by God and made others do the same (Gen. 14:22; 21:23f.; 24:3). But, says our author, God has none greater than Himself by whom to swear,[77] so when He wishes to confirm His promise in this way, He swears by Himself (we may compare the recurring "as I live" in divine oracles throughout the Old Testament). This insistence on the divine oath in God's promise to Abraham prepares the readers for the significance of the fact that God's promise regarding the Melchizedek priesthood was similarly confirmed by an oath: "Jehovah hath sworn, and will not repent" (Ps. 110:4).[78]

The bare word of God is guarantee enough in all conscience, but by confirming it thus He "makes assurance double sure". On this same passage from Genesis Philo remarks: "There is nothing amiss in God's bearing witness to Himself. For who else would be capable of bearing witness to Him? ... He alone shall make any affirmation regarding Himself, since He alone has unerringly exact knowledge of His own nature. God alone therefore is the strongest security first for Himself, and in the next place for His deeds also, so that He naturally swore by Himself when giving assurance regarding Himself, a thing impossible for anyone else."[79]

Who are "the heirs of the promise" to whom God wished in this way "to show more abundantly ... the immutability of his counsel"? Not so much Abraham and the other patriarchs,[80] who

---

μὴ λαβόντες τὰς ἐπαγγελίας) in Ch. 11:13 (cf. "these all ... received not [οὐκ ἐκομίσαντο] the promise" in Ch. 11:39); but in Ch. 11:13 the reference is to the full realization of the promise of which the birth and, later, the restoration of Isaac were initial pledges. Cf. also Ch. 11:17 (pp. 310f.).

[77] Cf. Philo, Leg. Alleg. iii. 203: "Well did He confirm His promise by an oath [Gk. ὅρκῳ βεβαιῶσαι, with which cf. πέρας εἰς βεβαίωσιν ὁ ὅρκος, "the oath is final for confirmation," v. 16], and by an oath worthy of God; for, you see, God does not swear by another, for there is nothing greater than He, but by Himself, who is the best of all" (in reference to the oath of Gen. 22:16f.).

[78] Cf. Ch. 7:20ff. (pp. 149f.)

[79] Leg. Alleg. iii. 205f.; cf. also On Abraham 273ff.; On the Sacrifices of Abel and Cain 91ff.

[80] As in Ch. 11:9, where Abraham is described as a tent-dweller "with Isaac and Jacob, the heirs with him of the same promise"; they are so called because

for all their faith did not live to see it vindicated and in this sense "received not the promise" (Ch. 11:39); but those, like the writer and his readers, who experienced in the gospel the fulfilment of the oath which God swore to Abraham.

18-20 It is *we*, says our author, for whom this "strong encouragement" is intended. The "two immutable things" from which this encouragement is derived are *(a)* the promise of God (for "it is impossible for God to lie"), and *(b)* the oath by which His promise is confirmed. We are refugees from the sinking ship of this present world-order, so soon to disappear; our hope is fixed in the eternal order, where the promises of God are made good to His people in perpetuity. Our hope, based upon His promises, is our spiritual anchor. The figure of the anchor is not pressed; all that is meant is that "we are moored to an immoveable object"[81]— and that immovable object is the throne of God Himself. "That which is within the veil" is the heavenly holy of holies (as is made clear in Ch. 9); it is the counterpart in the eternal order to the material holy of holies in the wilderness tabernacle, shut off from the outer sanctuary by the heavy curtain behind which dwelt the invisible presence of the God of Israel. And our hope is fixed there because Jesus is there, seated, as we have already been told, at "the right hand of the Majesty on high" (Ch. 1:3). His presence there is a powerful corroboration of our hope. Abraham rested his hope in the promise and oath of God; but we have more than that to rest our hope upon: we have the fulfilment of His promise in the exaltation of Christ. No wonder that our hope is "both sure and stedfast".[82]

For Jesus has entered into the eternal world not only on His own behalf but on His people's too. He is there as our "forerunner", a word in which the conception of precedency prevails

---

they came next to Abraham in the line of promise, but here those who have inherited the fulfilment of the promise are meant. See p. 129, n. 76. *Cf.* also the reference in Ch. 9:15 to "the promise of the eternal inheritance" realized under the new covenant.

[81]   A. B. Davidson, *ad loc.*; his comment on the anchor simile is a model of sanity. For the "veil" (καταπέτασμα) see p. 184, n. 14; p. 246, n. 87.

[82]   The adjectives "sure and stedfast" might grammatically refer either to "hope" or to "anchor"; the construction slightly favors the latter (so probably AV, and certainly RSV and NEB, as against ARV). But since our hope is our "anchor", it is in reality our hope that is "both sure and stedfast".

over that of speed, as E. K. Simpson tells us.[83] "As applied to the Saviour," he continues, "it recalls His own care-quelling utterance: 'I go to prepare a place for you'. But the errand of this Forerunner embraces far wider ends than that of preparation. It proclaims an accomplished work of redemption and signalizes the first fruits of a mighty aftercrop. *Precursor* is a relative term implying a sequence. With their glorified Head, the members of His body must in due time be conjoined; and the sublime office of intercession above vested in the Eternal Priest constitutes the indispensable medium of its accomplishment. His advocacy is the safeguard of His Church and the earnest of *her* glorification."

He is there as His people's forerunner, the surety of their admission to the dwelling-place of God; He is there, too, as their perpetual high priest, "after the order of Melchizedek". With these words our author comes back to the point from which he digressed in Ch. 5:11; now he will go on and say what he has to say about the Melchizedek priesthood, "hard of interpretation" though it may be, in order that his readers may be educated to maturity of faith and life.

---

[83] *EQ* xviii (1946), p. 187; he adduces instances from Arrian, Aristophanes, Euripides, Plutarch, Theophrastus and the elder Pliny; and compares "Julius Caesar's *antecursores*, one of whose chief functions was that of selecting and staking out stations for encampment".

CHAPTER VII

IV. THE ORDER OF MELCHIZEDEK
Ch. 7:1–28

1. MELCHIZEDEK THE PRIEST-KING
Ch. 7:1–3

1 For this Melchizedek, king of Salem, priest of God Most High,[1] who met[2] Abraham returning from the slaughter of the kings[3] and blessed him,[4]

2 to whom also Abraham divided a tenth part of all[5] (being first, by interpretation, King of righteousness, and then also[6] King of Salem, which is, King of peace;

3 without father, without mother, without genealogy, having neither beginning of days nor end of life, but made like unto the Son of God), abideth a priest continually.[7]

1–2 In order to draw out the significance of Christ's being acclaimed as perpetual high priest "after the order of Melchizedek", our author goes back from his text, Ps. 110:4, to the only other place in the Bible where Melchizedek appears, the story of

---

[1] Gk. τοῦ θεοῦ τοῦ ὑψίστου, the LXX rendering of Heb. 'ēl 'elyōn (cf. p. 95, n. 31). Since (θεὸς) ὕψιστος was current as a divine title among Jews and Greeks alike (among the latter it was a designation of Zeus), it provided them with a common denominator in referring to the supreme God. Cf. Acts 7:48; 16:17; see also C. H. Dodd, *The Bible and the Greeks* (London, 1935), pp. 11ff.

[2] Gk. ὁ συναντήσας (P⁴⁶ C* Byz); the authority for the dittographic variant ὃς συναντήσας, however, is so weighty (ℵ A B D and a few others) that the former (grammatical) reading was regarded as secondary, or as a successful Byzantine conjecture, until it was found in P⁴⁶.

[3] The minuscules 456 and 460 add "because he pursued the foreigners and rescued Lot with all the captivity" (ὅτι ἐδίωξεν τοὺς ἀλλοφύλους καὶ ἐξείλατο Λὼτ μετὰ πάσης αἰχμαλωσίας).

[4] D* 330 440 823 continue "and Abraham having been blessed by him ..." (καὶ Ἀβραὰμ εὐλογηθεὶς ὑπ' αὐτοῦ ....)

[5] Gk. πάντων (for which P⁴⁶ B read the singular παντός).

[6] Gk. ἔπειτα δὲ καί (P⁴⁶ and a few other authorities omit δὲ καί).

[7] Gk. εἰς τὸ διηνεκές (in the Greek Bible only in this epistle, the other occurrences being in Ch. 10:1, 12, 14), here synonymous with εἰς τὸν αἰῶνα of Ps. 110:4 (LXX 109:4, for Heb. le-'ōlām). The adjective διηνεκής is classical from Homer onwards.

133

Abraham's rout of the four invading kings from the east (Gen. 14). From the part played by Melchizedek in that narrative, it will be shown how aptly he prefigures the high priesthood of Christ.

According to that narrative (which belongs, as archaeological evidence indicates, to the Middle Bronze Age), Chedorlaomer, an Elamite king, with three allied rulers, raided Transjordan and the Negeb, defeated the city-states of the "circuit of Jordan"— Sodom and her neighbors—and carried off a large number of captives, including Lot, Abraham's nephew. When news of this came to Abraham at Mamre, near Hebron, he armed his own retainers, enlisted the aid of his neighbors, and set off in pursuit of the invaders. He overtook them near Damascus, launched a surprise attack on them, put them to flight, and recovered the captives and the plunder. On his homeward progress he was met by the grateful king of Sodom, who proposed that Abraham should return the captives to him but retain the material plunder as his proper spoils of war. Abraham declined to retain anything because of an oath he had just sworn to "God Most High, possessor of heaven and earth".[8] For, immediately before the king of Sodom made his proposal to Abraham, Abraham had been greeted by another local ruler, Melchizedek.

> "And Melchizedek king of Salem brought forth bread and wine: and he was priest of God Most High. And he blessed him, and said, Blessed be Abraham of God Most High, possessor of heaven and earth: and blessed be God Most High, who hath delivered thine enemies into thy hand. And he gave him a tenth of all"[9] (Gen. 14:18–20).

This is all that the Genesis narrative has to say about Melchizedek, but it is enough for our author; more would have been superfluous. He finds as much significance in what is not said about Melchizedek as he does in what is said about him. It is indeed noteworthy that

---

[8] Heb. *'ēl 'elyōn qōneh shāmayim wā-'āreṣ* (where *qōneh* probably means "creator" or "maker"; so LXX, RSV). A similar divine designation appears on a bilingual Hittite-Phoenician inscription (discovered by H. T. Bossert in 1946) of Azitawandas, king of Danuna (Karatepe) in the Taurus foothills (9th cent. B.C.): *b'l shmm w'l qwn 'rṣ* ("the lord [*ba'al*] of heaven and god ['*ēl*] creator [*or* possessor] of earth"). *Cf.* R. Marcus and I. J. Gelb, *JNES* viii (1949), pp. 111f.; A. M. Honeyman, *PEQ* lxxxi (1949), pp. 25ff.

[9] This last clause is ambiguous as it stands—who gave whom a tenth of all?—but in the context, as our author has no difficulty in seeing, it must be Abraham who gives a tenth to Melchizedek. See p. 140, n. 27.

one of the things that is said about Melchizedek in the Genesis narrative is passed over by our author without mention—his bringing forth bread and wine for Abraham's refreshment.[10] Few typologists of early Christian or more recent days could have resisted so obvious an opportunity of drawing a eucharistic inference from these words![11]

Philo's treatment of the Melchizedek story presents points of comparison, but even more markedly points of contrast, with the treatment here. He contrasts Melchizedek's provision of bread and wine with the refusal of the Ammonites and Moabites (the descendants of Lot) to supply Israel in the wilderness with bread and *water*:[12] "but let Melchizedek bring forth wine instead of water, let him give souls unmixed wine to drink, that they may be seized by a divine intoxication which is more sober than sobriety itself; for he is a priest, even Reason *(logos)*, and has as his portion the Existing One".[13]

The difference between Philo's allegorization and our author's typological exegesis is plain. The only substantial coincidence between their accounts of Melchizedek lies in their both pointing out the etymological sense of his name and title: "God has made him king of peace," says Philo, "for that is how 'Salem' is to be interpreted, and His own priest. He did not fashion any work of his beforehand, but made him from the first a king of this character, both peaceful and worthy of His own priesthood, for he is called 'righteous king'."[14] Both authors, that is to say, connect *zedek*, the

---

[10] This is a more probable explanation, in the circumstances, of the bread and wine than that they constituted a sacrificial offering, being the food of the gods (so Spicq, *ad loc.*, citing A. Vincent, *La religion des judéo-araméens d'Éléphantine* [Paris, 1937], p. 129). In *Test. Levi* 8:5 a meal of bread and wine forms part of the consecration of the priest (*cf.* G. Widengren, "Royal Ideology and the Testaments of the Twelve Patriarchs", in *Promise and Fulfilment* [S. H. Hooke *FS*, Edinburgh, 1963], pp. 207f.). See p. 401 (on Ch. 13:10).

[11] *Cf.* Cyprian, *Epistle* 62:4: "For who is more a priest of God Most High than our Lord Jesus Christ, who offered a sacrifice to God the Father, and offered that same thing which Melchizedek had offered, namely bread and wine—that is, His body and blood?"

[12] Deut. 23:4.

[13] *Leg. Alleg.* iii. 82. "The Existing One" as in Ex. 3:14, LXX (ὁ ὤν).

[14] *Leg. Alleg.* iii. 79 (*cf.* Josephus, *Ant.* i. 180). Here Philo goes on to say that Melchizedek (i.e. Reason) is a king, not a tyrant, the author of laws, not of lawlessness. Elsewhere he interprets the five "kings" of the circuit of Jordan as

second element in Melchizedek's name, with the Hebrew word commonly translated "righteousness";[15] and both relate the name of his city to Hebrew *shālōm*, "peace".[16] There is a fitness in this collocation of righteousness and peace both in the natural order and preeminently in our author's explanation of Melchizedek in terms of the gospel, where peace with God is based upon the righteousness of God.[17]

3 The words which follow present an outstanding example of the argument from silence in a typological setting.[18] When Melchizedek is described as being "without father, without

---

denoting the five senses and the four kings who conquered them as the four passions: pleasure, desire, fear and grief (*On Abraham*, 236ff.).

[15] Heb. *ṣedeq*. *Cf.* the name of Adonizedek, king of Jerusalem (Josh. 10:1ff.). It is debated whether in these names the first element ("my king is righteous"; "my lord is righteous") or the second ("Zedek is my king"; "Zedek is my lord") should be regarded as the divine title (*cf.* the Phoenician deity *Sydyk* mentioned by Philo of Byblus); see A. R. Johnson, *Sacral Kingship in Ancient Israel* (Cardiff, 1955), pp. 31ff., where the words of another king of Jerusalem, Abdi-hiba, are quoted from Tell el-Amarna Tablet No. 287, lines 32f.: "Behold, my lord the king, I am in the right (*ṣaddūq*) with regard to the Kashi people".

[16] The etymology of "Jerusalem" (MT *yerushālaim*; Akkadian *Uru-salim*) is "foundation of Shalem" or "city of Shalem"; to the Jebusites Shalem may have been a divine name (attested as such at Ugarit; *cf.* A. R. Johnson, *op. cit.*, p. 46), but even so it is to be associated with Heb. *shālōm* ("peace") and its cognates, and our author's etymology is well founded. A later etymology, connecting the first element in Jerusalem with Heb. *rā'āh* ("see"), explains the name as "vision of peace"; compare the hymn *urbs beata uera pacis uisio Ierusalem* ("Blessed city, vision bright/Of true peace, Jerusalem!"). W. F. Albright has recently suggested that we should read in Gen. 14:18 not *melekh shālēm* ("king of Salem") but *melekh shelōmōh* ("king of his peace", *i.e.* "a king allied to him"); the emendation, even if it be, as he says, "the simplest possible haplography", seems quite unnecessary (*BASOR* 163 [October, 1961], p. 52). *Cf.* p. 95, n. 30.

[17] *Cf.* Isa. 32:17 ("the work of righteousness shall be peace"); Rom. 5:1 ("Being therefore justified by faith, we have peace with God").

[18] The argument from silence plays an important part in rabbinical interpretation of Scripture where (for exegetical purposes) nothing must be regarded as having existed before the time of its first biblical mention (*cf.* Strack-Billerbeck, *Kommentar zum NT aus Talmud und Midrasch*, iii [Munich, 1926], pp. 694f.). The argument is used extensively by Philo for allegorical purposes; thus Sarah is "without mother" (ἀμήτωρ, the word here used of Melchizedek) because her mother is nowhere mentioned (*cf.* Gen. 20:12, where Abraham says: "she is ... not the daughter of my mother"); this means that Sarah, "the virtue-loving mind", was not born "from perceptible matter which is always in a state of formation and dissolution, ... but from the Author (αἴτιος) and Father of all" (*On Drunkenness*, 59ff.).

mother,[19] without genealogy, having neither beginning of days nor end of life", it is not suggested that he was a biological anomaly, or an angel in human guise.[20] Historically Melchizedek appears to have belonged to a dynasty of priest-kings in which he had both predecessors and successors. If this point had been put to our author, he would have agreed at once, no doubt; but this consideration was foreign to his purpose. The important consideration was the account given of Melchizedek in holy writ; to him the silences of Scripture were as much due to divine inspiration as were its statements. In the only record which Scripture provides of Melchizedek—Gen. 14:18-20—nothing is said of his parentage, nothing is said of his ancestry[21] or progeny, nothing is said of his birth, nothing is said of his death. He appears as a living man,

---

[19] Attempts have been made to link this description of Melchizedek with the words used of himself by Abdi-hiba, king of Jerusalem (14th cent. B.C.), in Amarna Tablet No. 288, lines 14f. (*cf.* p. 136, n. 15): "Neither my father nor my mother but the mighty arm of the king [of Egypt] set me in the house of my father" (*cf.* C. Marston, *The Bible is True* [London, 1934], p. 127). There is no connection at all between the two documents. Abdi-hiba means that his sacral kingship was not so much hereditary as conferred by his overlord. There is not even any real connection between this passage and Philo's statement that "the high priest is not a human being but a divine *logos*, having no part in any unrighteousness whether intentional or otherwise; for Moses says that he cannot be defiled either for his father, the mind, or for his mother, sense-perception [Lev. 21:11], because, to my mind, he has parents most pure and incorruptible, his Father being God, who is also the Father of all, and his mother Wisdom, through whom the universe came into being" (*On Flight and Finding*, 108f.). There is a contact in these words of Philo with Melchizedek, whom he elsewhere (see p. 135) explains as being Reason (*logos*); but our author attaches to the fatherless and motherless condition of Melchizedek quite another significance, which appears plainly from the course of his argument.

[20] *Cf.* J. B. McCaul: "Cunaeus ... believes, as Ewald does, and I do, that Melchizedek was the second person in the Ever Blessed Trinity, the Divine *angel of the Lord*, who continually appeared to the Fathers under the Old Testament dispensation ... if Melchizedek was 'without beginning of days or end of life', but 'abideth a priest continually', how can it be believed of him that he was a mere mortal? ... Melchizedek, as the Divine *Logos*, existed from eternity" (*The Epistle to the Hebrews* [London, 1871], pp. 75, 80).

[21] For the Aaronic priest, on the other hand, the establishment of proper parentage was an essential qualification; as late as the Hasmonaean dynasty any uncertainty on this score could invalidate a man's claim to the office (Lev. 21:13f.; Ezra 2:62; Neh. 7:64; Josephus, *Ant.* xiii. 292; TB *Qiddushin*, 66*a*). It was therefore necessary that the identity of an Aaronic priest's father and mother should be publicly known. This contrast between the two orders of priesthood may have been present to our author's mind.

king of Salem and priest of God Most High; and as such he disappears. In all this—in the silences as well as in the statements—he is a fitting type of Christ; in fact, the record by the things it says of him and by the things it does not say has assimilated him to the Son of God. It is the eternal being of the Son of God that is here in view; not His human life. Our author has no docetic view of Christ; he knows that "our Lord hath sprung out of Judah" (verse 14). But in His eternal being the Son of God has really, as Melchizedek has typically, "neither beginning of days nor end of life"; and more especially now, exalted at the right hand of God, He "abideth a priest continually". Melchizedek remains a priest continually for the duration of his appearance in the biblical narrative; but in the antitype Christ remains a priest continually without qualification. And it is not the type that determines the antitype, but the antitype that determines the type; Jesus is not portrayed after the pattern of Melchizedek, but Melchizedek is "made like unto the Son of God".[22]

2. THE GREATNESS OF MELCHIZEDEK

Ch. 7:4-10

4 Now consider how great[23] this man was, unto whom[24] Abraham, the patriarch, gave a tenth out of the chief spoils.

5 And they indeed of the sons of Levi that receive the priest's office have commandment to take tithes of the people according to the law, that is, of their brethren, though these have come out of the loins of Abraham:

---

[22] Similarly the earthly sanctuary is a "copy" of the heavenly sanctuary in which Christ discharges His high-priestly ministry, and not *vice versa* (Ch. 8:2, 5).

[23] Gk. οὗτος, omitted by D* 1739 424** (perhaps by the independent operation of homoeoteleuton; *cf.* G. Zuntz, *The Text of the Epistles* [London, 1953], p. 87). This shorter text is perhaps implied in RSV "See how great he is!" and NEB "Consider how great he must be ..."

[24] Gk. ᾧ, to which ℵ A with the Latin versions, the Harclean Syriac, the bulk of the later MSS and TR add καί ("to whom indeed"), influenced perhaps by ᾧ καί at the beginning of v. 2.

6   But he whose genealogy is not counted from them hath taken tithes of Abraham, and hath blessed him that hath the promises.

7   But without any dispute the less is blessed of the better.

8   And here men that die receive tithes; but there one, of whom it is witnessed that he liveth.

9   And, so to say,[25] through Abraham even Levi, who receiveth tithes, hath paid tithes;

10   for he was yet in the loins of his father, when Melchizedek met him.

4   The surpassing dignity of Melchizedek's priestly order will be appreciated the more if one considers the tokens of Melchizedek's greatness.   Abraham was a great man indeed—"a prince of God" to his neighbors, called "my friend" by God Himself—but in the account of his interview with Melchizedek, it is Melchizedek who appears as the greater of the two.[26]   And if Melchizedek was

---

[25]   Gk. ὡς ἔπος εἰπεῖν, a classical phrase qualifying what might otherwise be an exaggeration (RSV "one might even say").   Not elsewhere in the Greek Bible, but common in Philo.

[26]   That Melchizedek should be greater than Abraham, as Gen. 14 so clearly indicates, constituted a problem for Jewish exegetes.   Some of them identified him with Shem, whose life, according to MT, overlapped Abraham's—he survived the Flood by some 500 years (Gen. 11:11), and may even have been reckoned to have outlived Abraham.   If Abraham paid respect to such a venerable ancestor by giving him tithes and accepting his blessing, no offence would be caused to any reader, however great Abraham might appear in his eyes.   But later it was felt necessary to modify the honor thus implicitly ascribed to Shem. So Rabbi Zechariah said in the name of Rabbi Ishmael: "God wanted to derive the priestly line from Shem, as it is said, 'He was priest of God Most High.' But God derived it [the priestly line] from Abraham, when Shem placed the blessing of Abraham before the praise of God, as it is said, 'Blessed be Abram ... and blessed be God Most High ...' (Gen. 14:19).   Abraham said to him: 'Does one place the blessing of a servant before that of his master?' Straightway it [the priesthood] was given to Abraham, as it is said, 'The LORD saith unto my Lord, Sit thou at my right hand, until I make thine enemies thy footstool' (Ps. 110:1). And after this it is written, 'The LORD hath sworn, and will not repent: Thou art a priest for ever after the order of Melchizedek' (Ps. 110:4).   This means: 'on account of what Melchizedek had said'.   And hence it is written, '*he* was priest of God Most High'—he was priest, but his descendants were not priests" (TB *Nedarim*, 32*b*).   This remarkable exegesis, which takes "Thou art a priest for ever" as addressed to Abraham, and regards Melchizedek's priesthood as

greater than Abraham, his priesthood (our author argues) must be greater than a priesthood which traces its descent from Abraham. The superior greatness of Melchizedek appears in two important respects: he accepted tithes from Abraham and bestowed his blessing on Abraham.

5–6a The tithes which he received from Abraham evidently amounted to one tenth of all the spoils of war[27] that Abraham had recovered from the invading kings. The dedication of one tenth of the spoils of war to a deity (on whose behalf his priest acted) was practised among the Greeks and other nations,[28] but is not attested for Israel. So far as the institution of the "holy war" in Israel was concerned, it was not one tenth only, but all that was captured, that was devoted to God according to the law of the *ḥērem* or "ban".[29] In Israel agricultural produce was tithed year by year and the tithe was allocated to the tribe of Levi "for an inheritance" (Lev. 18:21, the "commandment" of verse 5), and one tenth of that tithe was further ear-marked for the priesthood (Num. 18:26ff.).[30] In Nehemiah's time the Levites received the tithes under the supervision of the priests and brought the "tithe of the tithes" to the temple to be handed over to the priests (Neh. 10:38f.). By the first century A.D., however, there is reason

---

superseded by Abraham's (and consequently by that of Levi, who "was yet in the loins of his father, when Melchizedek met him"), might almost have been designed as a deliberate rebuttal of the argument in Heb. 7:4ff. See p. 107, n. 78, with bibliography at the end of that note.

[27] Gk. ἀϰϱοθίνια. That the "tenth of all" which Abraham gave Melchizedek (Gen. 14:19) was the tenth part of the spoils is implied, but not stated, in the Old Testament narrative. According to the *Genesis Apocryphon* from Qumran Cave 1, Abraham "gave him a tithe of all the goods of the king of Elam and his companions" (col. 22, line 17). Philo says that Abraham, "being declared the winner of the trophies by God, the giver of victory, dedicated the tithes to Him as a thank-offering for his victory" (*Preliminary Studies*, 93), and that "when the great priest of the all-great God saw him approaching, bearing his trophies ... he honored him with prayers and offered up sacrifices in celebration of the victory (ἐπινίϰια)" (*On Abraham*, 235). So too Josephus says that Abraham offered Melchizedek "the tithe of the plunder" (*Ant.* i. 181).

[28] See Herodotus, *History* i. 89; Xenophon, *Anabasis* v. 3; *Hellenica* iv. 3 (for Greek practice); Livy, *History* v. 21 (for Roman practice); *cf.* also Pindar, *Olympian Odes* xi. 51; Xenophon, *Cyropaedia* vii. 5.

[29] *Cf.* Deut. 20:16–18; Josh. 6:21, 24. See G. von Rad, *Der heilige Krieg im alten Israel* (Zürich, 1951), pp. 13f.; C. H. W. Brekelmans, *De Ḥerem in het Oude Testament* (Nijmegen, 1959); R. de Vaux, *Ancient Israel* (London, 1961), pp. 260f.

[30] *Cf.* R. de Vaux, *op. cit.*, pp. 140f., 360, 380ff., 403ff.

to think that the administration of the tithes was carried out by the priests.[31] It may have been knowledge of the actual practice at that time that led our author to say that it was those "of the sons of Levi that receive the priest's office" who tithed the people in accordance with the commandment—although in general his description of the laws relating to the priesthood and sanctuary is based on the Pentateuch and not on contemporary custom.

Our author's argument, however, does not rest upon the details of the administration of the tithe according to the Old Testament law, but on the fact that whereas the members of the tribe of Levi received tithes from their fellow-Israelites, who were children of Abraham like themselves, Abraham—ancestor alike of the Levites and of their brethren who paid them tithes—recognized the superiority of Melchizedek by paying tithes to *him*. The priesthood of Melchizedek's order is thus shown to enjoy higher status than the Levitical priesthood;[32] Melchizedek, like Christ, who has been acclaimed high priest after his order, does not have his genealogy reckoned among the sons of Levi.

6b-7 Moreover, great as Abraham's privileges were by virtue of the promises which he received from God, he recognized the superiority of Melchizedek by accepting a blessing at his hands— "and beyond all dispute the lesser is always blessed by the greater" (NEB).

8 Another token of Melchizedek's superiority to the Levitical priesthood is this: nowhere is it related that Melchizedek lost his priestly office by death, whereas we have the record, generation after generation, of Levitical priests who died and had to hand on their dignity and duty to their heirs. The tithe prescribed by Israelite law is paid to mortal men; the tithe which Abraham gave Melchizedek was received by one who, so far as the record goes, has no "end of life". So far as the record goes, for our author is not interested in anything that might be known or inferred about Melchizedek outside the biblical narrative. But what was true of Melchizedek in this limited and "literary" sense is true absolutely of Him who serves His people as high priest in the presence

---

[31] So E. Schürer, *History of the Jewish People in the Time of Christ* (Edinburgh, 1892-1901), II. i. p. 248, infers from Josephus, *Life*, 80; *Ant.* xx. 181, 206f.

[32] That this higher status is permanent may be indicated by the two perfect tenses of v. 6: Melchizedek "hath taken tithes" (δεδεκάτωκεν) and "hath blessed" (εὐλόγηκεν).

141

of God. Of Melchizedek "it is witnessed that he liveth" in the sense that we never read of him otherwise than as a living man; of Christ it can be said that He lives in the sense that, having died once for all and risen from the dead, He is alive for evermore.[33] The practical implications of this are drawn out more fully in verses 23–25 of the present chapter.

9–10 Reverting for a moment to the tithe-receiving tribe of Levi, our author points out that Levi, the ancestor of that priestly tribe and the embodiment of its corporate personality, may be said himself to have paid tithes to Melchizedek (thus conceding the superiority of the Melchizedek priesthood) in the person of his ancestor Abraham. Levi was Abraham's great-grandson, and was yet unborn when Abraham met Melchizedek; but an ancestor is regarded in biblical thought as containing within himself all his descendants.[34] That Levi may be thought of thus as paying tithes to Melchizedek is an afterthought to what has already been said about the significance of this particular payment of tithes; lest it should be criticized as far-fetched, our author qualifies it with the phrase "so to say" ("it might even be said", NEB).

3. IMPERFECTION OF THE AARONIC PRIESTHOOD

Ch. 7:11–14

11 Now if there was perfection through the Levitical priesthood[35] (for[36] under it hath the people received the law),[37] what further need *was there* that another priest should arise after the order of Melchizedek, and not be reckoned after the order of Aaron?

---

[33] *Cf.* Rev. 1:18; Rom. 6:9; with v. 16 of this chapter.

[34] *Cf.* Jacob and Esau (Gen. 25:23; Mal. 1:2f.; Rom. 9:11ff.), and preeminently Adam (Rom. 5:12, where "all sinned" is a way of indicating what happened when Adam sinned).

[35] Gk. διὰ τῆς Λευιτικῆς ἱερωσύνης. The adjective occurs in LXX only in the title of the book of Leviticus; it is used by Philo (*e.g.* he refers to "the Levitical tribe" in *On Flight and Finding*, 93). Here and in vv. 12, 24, ἱερωσύνη is used for "priesthood"; in v. 5 ἱερατεία was used (there only in this epistle; *cf.* Luke 1:9). Both words are used in LXX, ἱερατεία being the commoner. *Cf.* p. 151, n. 71.

[36] P[46] omits γάρ.

[37] Gk. νενομοθέτηται (so also in Ch. 8:6), for which K L have the pluperfect ἐνενομοθέτητο. Since νομοθετέω means "legislate", its passive use with ὁ λαός as

12 For the priesthood being changed, there is made of necessity[38] a change[39] also of the law.

13 For he of whom these things are said belongeth to[40] another tribe, from which no man hath given attendance at[41] the altar.

14 For it is evident that our Lord hath sprung[42] out of Judah; as to which tribe Moses spake nothing concerning priests.[43]

11 It could not be argued that the later priesthood (of Aaron) superseded the earlier (of Melchizedek);[44] for when the priesthood of Aaron was well established the divine oracle was uttered which hailed the Messiah of David's line as "a priest for ever after the order of Melchizedek". So, our author argues, the order of Aaron did not exhaust the mediatorial functions which, in the divine purpose, were to be discharged between man and God. If God had intended the Aaronic priesthood to introduce the age of perfection, the time when man would enjoy unfettered access to Him, why should He have conferred on the Messiah a

---

the subject is curious; AG can cite only one instance of the active verb with a personal object, and that from Pseudo-Galen.

[38] Gk. ἐξ ἀνάγκης καί, a Philonic formula (cf. Spicq, i, p. 42).

[39] Gk. μετάθεσις, which here (as in Ch. 12:27) implies not merely change but abrogation (cf. ἀθέτησις in v. 18).

[40] Gk. μετέσχηκεν, "has partaken of"; cf. Ch. 2:14 for the aorist μετέσχεν, which is read here in P[46]. (See p. 41, n. 55.)

[41] Gk. προσέσχηκεν ("has attended to"), so אֵ B D and the majority of MSS, as against προσέσχεν, the reading of P[46] 1739 A C 33 1288 2004 (the "minor Alexandrians"). G. Zuntz prefers the aorist here after the perfect μετέσχηκεν in the preceding clause: "the differentiation is excellent; it intimates that no one of the tribe of Judah *had ever attended* to the altar (προσέσχε) and that Jesus *'has permanently a share in'* (μετέσχηκε, 'belongs to') that tribe" (*op. cit.*, p. 79).

[42] Gk. ἀνατέταλκεν, here a synonym of ἀνίστασθαι in v. 11, but chosen perhaps because it echoes the rising of the star out of Jacob in Num. 24:17 (where, interestingly enough, LXX ἀνατελεῖ appears in parallelism to ἀναστήσεται in the following clause); cf. also the messianic associations of ἀνατολή in Zech. 6:12 (for Heb. ṣemaḥ, ARV "branch"), identified with the Logos by Philo (*Confusion of Tongues*, 62f.); Matt. 2:2. Cf. the reproduction of ἀνατέλλω from Num. 24:17 in *Test. Judah* 24:1 (cf. *Test. Dan* 5:10; *Test. Gad* 8:1).

[43] D[c] K L with TR "priesthood" (ἱερωσύνης); cf. AV.

[44] For such an argument cf. p. 140, n. 26.

priestly dignity of His own—different[45] from Aaron's and by implication superior to Aaron's? In fact, as is argued below in manifold
detail, the Aaronic priesthood was neither designed nor competent
to inaugurate the age of fulfilment; that age must be marked by
the rise of another priest, whose priesthood was of a different
order and character from Aaron's. Some phases of Jewish expectation did look forward to a new age—the age of restoration—when
a worthy priest would preside over the state;[46] but this coming
priest of the tribe of Levi could at best be actually what the
Aaronic high priest was ideally and could not bring in perfection
in the sense intended by our author. For that, another priest of a
different kind was called for.

The words "Now if there was perfection through the Levitical
priesthood" have a bearing on the class of readers at whom our
author's argument was aimed. If they were Gentile converts, in
danger of abandoning their Christian faith, their only response to
these words would have been: "We never thought there *was*
perfection through the Levitical priesthood"—they certainly never
thought so in their pagan days and they would have received no
encouragement to think so in their Christian days. But if they
were Jews by birth, now in danger of giving up the distinctive

---

[45]   The new priest is designated in v. 11 ἕτερον ... ἱερέα ("a different priest")
and not merely ἄλλον ("another"), if one may press the distinction between
ἕτερος and ἄλλος.

[46]   Such an expectation finds expression in the Qumran literature; influenced
probably by the description of the new commonwealth in Ezek. 40–48, where
the priesthood takes practical precedence over "the prince", the Qumran
community evidently envisaged the high priest (the "Messiah of Aaron") as
head of state in the coming age of restoration, taking precedence over the Davidic prince (the "Messiah of Israel"). Thus in 1Q Sa, col. 2, line 12, precedence
over "the Messiah of Israel" is accorded to "the priest who is head of the whole
congregation of Israel". But he is a Levitical (probably Zadokite) priest, and
fulfils Moses' blessing of Levi in Deut. 33:8ff. (*cf.* 4Q *Testimonia*, lines 14ff.).
We might compare the "new priest" of the *Testament of Levi* 18:2ff., but the
recensions in which the *Testaments of the Twelve Patriarchs* have come down to
us (apart from the recently discovered Qumran fragments) have been so
thoroughly worked over in a Christian sense that it is highly precarious to draw
firm conclusions from them about Jewish expectations. M. de Jonge has good
reason for concluding that the purport of the *Testament of Levi* 18:2ff., and of
other passages which describe the priest of the new age (see p. 146, n. 50), in
their present form, is to "glorify Jesus Christ" (*The Testaments of the Twelve
Patriarchs* [Assen, 1953], p. 90). *Cf.* M. Black, "The Messiah in the Testament
of Levi xviii", *ExT* lx (1948–49), pp. 321f., lxi (1949–50), pp. 157f.

features of their Christian confession and merging once more in their former Jewish environment, the situation was quite different. Before their conversion they had envisaged no priesthood beyond the Levitical priesthood; even if they looked for a new priest to arise in the age to come, he was still a Levitical priest. Their Christian teachers would have encouraged them to think of the Levitical priesthood as something belonging to the age of preparation, which had now given way to the age of fulfilment; but they were in danger of concluding that, after all, the old order (including the Levitical priesthood and everything else that went with it) had still much to be said in its favor. To such people our author's assurance that the supersession of the Levitical priesthood by another had been decreed by God long before would have had practical relevance.

12 Nor is it only the Aaronic priesthood which must be superseded. That priesthood was instituted under the Mosaic law, and was so integral to it that a change in the priesthood carries with it inevitably a change in the law. If the Aaronic priesthood was instituted for a temporary purpose, to be brought to an end when the age of fulfilment dawned, the same must be true of the law under which that priesthood was introduced. So by his own independent line of argument our author reaches the same conclusion as Paul: the law was a temporary provision, "our tutor to bring us unto Christ ... but now that faith is come, we are no longer under a tutor" (Gal. 3:24f.). Paul, indeed, thinks of the law as an institution designed to promote men's awareness of sin and not (as he had once believed) to procure their justification before God, whereas our author thinks rather of the sacrificial cultus as something which could never effectively remove sin.[47] If we like, we may say that Paul has the moral law mainly in mind, whereas the author of Hebrews is concerned more with the ceremonial law—although the distinction between the moral and ceremonial law is one drawn by Christian theologians, not by those who accepted the whole law as the will of God, nor yet by the New Testament writers.[48] But in principle Paul and our

---

[47] *Cf.* H. Windisch: Hebrews views the law "not as a prescription for the behavior of the individual, but as the sum of sacrificial regulations for the ancient cultic community" (*Der Hebräerbrief*, HNT [Tübingen, 1931], p. 66).

[48] This does not mean that the distinction is not a valid one, but it does not come to the fore in either OT or NT.

author are agreed that the law was a temporary dispensation of God, valid only until Christ came to inaugurate the age of perfection. Its supersession is here seen to be implied in the acclamation of Messiah as a priest after the order of Melchizedek.

13–14 How radical is the change in the law which is involved in the announcement of a priesthood after Melchizedek's order may be appreciated when it is considered that the person to whom this announcement refers has nothing to do with the tribe of Levi, to which the priesthood was restricted by the law. It is a matter of common knowledge that our Lord belonged to the tribe of Judah. This, it may be remarked, could be a matter of common knowledge only if it was generally accepted that He was born of the royal line of David—that He was so born was a commonplace of primitive Christian preaching and confession.[49] But whatever hopes and promises were attached in the Pentateuch to the tribe of Judah, priestly service found no place among them.[50] No member of the tribe of Judah was appointed to officiate at the altar.[51] The attempts which were made at a later date to justify the doctrine of the priesthood of Christ by providing Him with a Levitical lineage[52] would have been dismissed by our author (had he known anything about them) not only as irrelevant but as perverse, because they blunted the point of his argument—the calculated supersession of the Levitical priesthood by one of a different kind. Nor would he have looked with any greater favor on attempts to establish a new *earthly* priesthood to be exercised

---

[49] *Cf.* Acts 2:29ff.; 13:23; Rom. 1:3; II Tim. 2:8; Rev. 22:16 (not to mention the Matthaean and Lukan nativity narratives).

[50] If the *Testaments of the Twelve Patriarchs* speak of a priest of the tribe of Judah (*Testament of Levi* 8:14), that is one of the clearest signs of Christian influence in the extant recensions (*cf.* p. 144, n. 46). The normal arrangement is that expressed by Judah when he says of himself and Levi: "To me the Lord gave the kingdom, and to him the priesthood, and he set the kingdom beneath the priesthood" (*Test. Judah* 21:2). *Cf.* p. 97, n. 39.

[51] So far as the Pentateuchal legislation is concerned, at least. David and Solomon are said to have offered sacrifice on various occasions (*cf.* II Sam. 6:13, 17f.; 24:25; I Kings 3:4; 8:62ff.).

[52] *Cf.* p. 95, n. 29. Our author's position is much more satisfactory, and could have been established on historical grounds as well as by the arguments he uses, had he been minded to appeal to the former (Jesus, the Son of David, is the true heir to Melchizedek's office).

by members of the holy family,[53] although the holy family undoubtedly belonged to the tribe of Judah. The priesthood in which he is interested is different not only because it is exercised by one who came from another tribe than Levi, but also because it is not exercised on earth: it belongs to the eternal order, not to the material world.

4. SUPERIORITY OF THE NEW PRIESTHOOD

Ch. 7:15-19

15 And *what we say* is yet more abundantly evident, if after the likeness of Melchizedek there ariseth another priest,

16 who hath been made, not after the law of a carnal commandment, but after the power of an endless[54] life:

17 for it is witnessed *of him*,
    Thou art a priest for ever,
    After the order of Melchizedek.[55]

18 For there is a disannulling[56] of a foregoing commandment because of its weakness and unprofitableness

19 (for the law made nothing perfect), and a bringing in[57] of a better hope, through which we draw nigh unto God.

---

[53] In some Jewish Christian circles James the Just and his successors appear to have been regarded as constituting a new priestly line by virtue of their relation κατὰ σάρκα to Jesus. It is this situation that probably underlies the curious statement of Hegesippus that James the Just "alone was accustomed to enter the sanctuary (ναός) and be found kneeling and praying for the people's forgiveness" (Eusebius, *Hist. Eccl.* ii. 23. 6). He certainly did not have the entrée into the literal sanctuary. See A. Ehrhardt, *The Apostolic Succession in the First Two Centuries of the Church* (London, 1953), pp. 1 *et passim*.

[54] Gk. ἀκατάλυτος (ARV margin "indissoluble"; RSV "indestructible"; NEB "that cannot be destroyed").

[55] Ps. 110:4 (LXX 109:4).

[56] Gk. ἀθέτησις, a stronger word than μετάθεσις in v. 12. "The earlier rules are cancelled" (NEB). The noun occurs once again in NT, in Ch. 9:26, of the cancellation of sin by the self-oblation of Christ (see p. 222 with n. 165); the verb ἀθετέω appears about a dozen times (*cf.* Ch. 10:28), being used, for example, in Mark 7:9 of those who "set aside the commandment of God" (NEB) in order to maintain their own tradition. E. K. Simpson points out that its Hellenistic sense of "an act of supersession or setting aside" appears in its technical use by "the Alexandrian grammarians to signify the obelizing of a suspected passage

15–17 A further token of the imperfection of the old priesthood and the superiority of the new lies on the face of our author's Old Testament text, "Thou art a priest *for ever*". These words are quite inapplicable to the old order; no priest of Aaron's line could have been described as "a priest for ever",[58] for the simple reason that each one of them died in due course. But the Christians' high priest is immortal; having died once for all and risen from the dead, He discharges His ministry on His people's behalf in the power of a life that can never be destroyed. The law which established the Aaronic priesthood is called a "carnal commandment" because it is "a system of earth-bound rules" (NEB); it is concerned with the externalities of religion—the physical descent of the priests,[59] a material shrine, animal sacrifices and so forth. Like everything else in the Levitical régime, the Aaronic order of priesthood was marked by transience; it stands thus in contrast to the permanence and effectiveness of the priestly office of Christ.

18–19 The declaration "Thou art a priest for ever after the order of Melchizedek" thus announces the abrogation of the earlier law which instituted the Aaronic order. It was inevitable that the earlier law should be abrogated sooner or later; for all the impressive solemnity of the sacrificial ritual and the sacerdotal ministry, no real peace of conscience was procured thereby, no

---

counted spurious (Luc. *V.H.* ii. 20) and therefore to be expunged from an author's text. In this sense of deletion we find it in the papyri with reference to annulled decrees and even paid-off loans. The Palestinian writer Philodemus (*Rhet.* i. 43) writes of certain locutions 'not easily to be discarded' (οὐκ ἂν ῥᾳδίως ἀθετῆσαι); and there are passages such as Gal. 2:21; 3:15, in the New Testament where this translation would be plausible" (*EQ* xviii [1946], p. 190).

[57] Gk. ἐπεισαγωγή, where the prefix ἐπί may retain something of its classical force "in addition", "over and above" (Moffatt, ICC, *ad loc.* quotes its use by Josephus in *Ant.* xi. 196 for the "replacement" of Vashti by another wife in the Persian king's affections).

[58] The Aaronic priesthood itself is described as "an everlasting priesthood" (Ex. 40:15; *cf.* Jer. 33:18), but no individual member of the priesthood is described as an everlasting priest. When the language of Ps. 110:4 was applied to Simon the Hasmonaean (I Macc. 14:41), "a priest for ever" was probably understood in the weaker sense of "founder of an hereditary priesthood". See p. 96, n. 35; *cf.* also p. 152.

[59] *Cf.* the RSV rendering of v. 16: "not according to a legal requirement concerning bodily descent".

immediate access to God. That is not to say that faithful men and women in Old Testament times did not enjoy peace of conscience and a sense of nearness to God; the Psalter provides evidence enough that they did. The psalmist who cried "Blessed is he whose transgression is forgiven, whose sin is covered; blessed is the man unto whom the LORD imputeth not iniquity" (Ps. 32:1f.) knew the blessedness of a peaceful conscience; and his colleague who said, "it is good for me to draw near unto God" (Ps. 73:28), knew that access to the divine presence was always available to the man of faith. But these experiences had nothing to do with the Levitical ritual or the Aaronic priesthood. The whole apparatus of worship associated with that ritual and priesthood was calculated rather to keep men at a distance from God than to bring them near. But the "hope set before us" in the gospel is better because it accomplishes this very thing which was impossible under the old ceremonial; it enables Christians to "draw nigh unto God". How it enables them to so is explained in greater detail later on;[60] but the fact that the gospel, unlike the law, has opened up a way of free access to God is our author's ground for claiming that the gospel has achieved that perfection which the law could never bring about.

5. SUPERIOR BECAUSE OF THE DIVINE OATH

Ch. 7:20-22

20 And inasmuch as *it is* not without the taking of an oath[61]
21 (for they indeed have been made[62] priests without an oath; but he with an oath by[63] him that saith of[64] him,
The Lord sware and will not repent himself,
Thou art a priest for ever);[65]

---

[60] *Cf.* Ch. 10:19-22 (pp. 243ff.).

[61] Gk. ὁρκωμοσία (rendered "oath" twice in v. 21); this word was a neuter plural in classical Greek (with proparoxytone accent) but appears as a feminine singular in the Hellenistic idiom (three instances are quoted from LXX).

[62] Our author uses the elegant periphrasis εἰσὶν ... γεγονότες (*cf.* v. 23).

[63] Gk. διά with the genitive (ARV margin "through"), but nevertheless it is the agent, not the intermediary (God, not the psalmist), that is intended.

[64] Or "unto him" (margin), a more appropriate rendering here of Gk. πρὸς αὐτόν. *Cf.* p. 23, n. 104.

[65] The Western and Byzantine texts complete the quotation from Ps. 110:4 by adding "after the order of Melchizedek" (*cf.* AV).

22   by so much also hath Jesus become the surety of a better covenant.

20–21   Our author continues to examine his text, so as to extract from it its last degree of significance for the character of the new priesthood. He now draws his readers' attention to the fact that the acclamation of Messiah as a perpetual priest was confirmed by a divine oath: "The LORD has sworn, and will not change His mind: 'Thou art a priest for ever'." What he has said about God's oath to Abraham in Ch. 6:13ff.[66] is equally true about God's oath here. The bare word of God is assurance enough, but God, "desiring to show even more clearly ... how unchanging was his purpose, guaranteed it by oath" (Ch. 6:17, NEB). The inauguration of the Aaronic priesthood rested on a divine command: "bring thou near unto thee Aaron thy brother", said God to Moses, "and his sons with him, from among the children of Israel, that he may minister unto me in the priest's office" (Ex. 28:1). But there is no mention of a divine oath in the record of their appointment as there is in Ps. 110:4, where a new priest "after the order of Melchizedek" is introduced. This suggests the superior dignity of the Melchizedek priesthood.[67]

22   And since it is Jesus who is acclaimed as priest after the order of Melchizedek, it is Jesus whose superior dignity is thus confirmed. Our author emphasizes this by arranging the construction of this long sentence,[68] verses 20–22, so that the weight of the argument falls on its last word, "Jesus". And when he does so, he introduces a further aspect of the priesthood of Jesus which will be developed in the following chapters—Jesus' rôle as guarantor and mediator of a covenant which is as much superior to the covenant of the *ancien régime* as His priesthood is superior to that

---

[66]   *Cf.* p. 130, with n. 77.

[67]   Moffatt points out (*ad loc.*) that "Roman readers could understand from their former religion how oaths were needful in such a matter", quoting Suetonius (*Life of Claudius*, 22) to the effect that the Emperor Claudius nominated no one to membership of the priestly colleges without swearing (*nisi iuratus*) that he was suitable. The parallel is worth recording, but the present commentary (unlike Moffatt's) is not written in the belief that the "former religion" of the addressees of this epistle was the old Roman religion.

[68]   The construction of this long sentence, with the parenthesis and inserted quotation of v. 21, is characteristically Philonic. For the *a fortiori* argument *cf.* Ch. 2:1–3 (p. 29, n. 4).

of Aaron. This is the first occurrence of the term "covenant" in this epistle, but the term is about to play such a central part in the argument to follow that the whole epistle has been described as "The Epistle of the *Diatheke*".[69] For the moment, however, the designation of Jesus as "the surety[70] of a better covenant" prepares the reader for what is to come; there are still two further tokens of the superiority of the Melchizedek priesthood which must be mentioned.

6. SUPERIOR BECAUSE OF ITS PERMANENCE

Ch. 7:23–25

23 And they indeed have been made[71] priests many in number, because that by death they are hindered from continuing:

24 but he, because he abideth for ever, hath his priesthood[72] unchangeable.[73]

---

[69]   Gk. διαθήκη ("settlement"). *Cf.* the title of articles by G. Vos, "Hebrews, the Epistle of the Diatheke", *PThR* xiii (1915), pp. 587–632, xiv (1916), pp. 1–61.

[70]   Gk. ἔγγυος, here only in NT; it occurs three times in LXX (Sir. 29:15f.; II Macc. 10:28). In common Greek it is found frequently in legal and other documents in the sense of a surety or guarantor. The ἔγγυος undertakes a weightier responsibility than the μεσίτης or mediator (*cf.* Chs. 8:6; 9:15; 12:24); he is answerable for the fulfilment of the obligation which he guarantees. Moffatt (ICC, *ad loc.*) draws attention to the close association between the rôles of surety and savior in Sir. 29:15f.:

"Do not forget all the kindness of your surety,
    for he has given his life for you.
A sinner will overthrow the prosperity of his surety,
    and one who does not feel grateful will abandon his rescuer."

The old covenant had a mediator (*cf.* Gal. 3:19) but no surety; there was no one to guarantee the fulfilment of the people's undertaking: "All that Jehovah hath spoken will we do, and be obedient" (Ex. 24:7). But Jesus guarantees the perpetual fulfilment of the covenant which He mediates, on the manward side as well as on the Godward side. As the Son of God, He confirms God's eternal covenant with His people; as His people's representative, He satisfies its terms with perfect acceptance in God's sight.

[71]   Gk. εἰσιν γεγονότες, as in v. 21.

[72]   Gk. ἱερωσύνην (ἱερατείαν in D*); *cf.* p. 142, n. 35.

[73]   ARV margin: "hath a priesthood that doth not pass to another". The Greek adjective is ἀπαράβατος (see p. 153, n. 76).

25   Wherefore also he is able to save to the uttermost them
that draw near unto God through him, seeing he ever
liveth to make intercession for them.

23 It has already been pointed out (verses 16f.) that our
Lord's indissoluble life makes it possible for Him to fulfil to the
letter the words "Thou art a priest *for ever*". If these words were
applied to a dynasty of priests, "for ever" could be understood only
of a hereditary succession of indefinite duration.[74] The Aaronic
priests were indeed appointed on the hereditary principle (not, of
course, on the basis of Ps. 110:4); but none of them could enjoy
the priestly dignity in perpetuity. Aaron, the first of the line, served
his people in the high priesthood throughout the wilderness
wanderings; but the day came when Aaron and his son Eleazar
were taken by Moses to the summit of Mount Hor. There "Moses
stripped Aaron of his garments, and put them upon Eleazar his
son; and Aaron died there on the top of the mount: and Moses
and Eleazar came down from the mount" (Num. 20:28). Later,
after the settlement in the land of Canaan, Eleazar died in his turn
(Josh. 24:33) and was succeeded by his son Phinehas; and so the
tale went on. In generation after generation the high priest died
and his office passed to another, until in all (so Josephus reckons[75])
eighty-three high priests officiated from Aaron to the fall of the
Second Temple in A.D.70. Our author has good reason for what
he here says of them: "Those other priests are appointed in
numerous succession, because they are prevented by death from
continuing in office" (NEB).
24 "But the priesthood which Jesus holds is perpetual, because
he remains for ever" (NEB). Our author, says E. K. Simpson,
"has already dwelt on the perpetuity of Christ's priesthood as in
keeping with the unprocessionate type of Melchizedek, and stressed
its intransmissibility in the ascription of 'an indissoluble life' to the
ideal Priest he is setting forth. But he now affirms that it is in its
very nature unsupersedable, that finality inheres in it. The high-
priestly Son, in contrast with mortal intermediaries, is described
at the close of the chapter as 'perfected for evermore'. Perhaps
indefectible would be a suitable translation. ... In the one flawless
Mediator we descry priesthood at its summit-level. His unique

[74]   As in Ex. 40:15; Num. 25:13. *Cf.* p. 96, n. 35.
[75]   *Ant.* xx. 227.

endowments exhaust the requisites of the office and invest it with ineffaceable validity."[76]

Here no high allegorical interpretation of the mortality of Old Testament priests is offered such as we find in Philo. According to him, the death of the high priest means the departure of "the most sacred Logos" from the soul of man, in consequence of which all kinds of inadvertent errors find an entrance there.[77] But to our author the death of the high priest (or of any other priest) means that he is no longer available to those who counted upon him to intercede for them with God. Of course, so long as the old order endured, a new priest was always at hand to step into the place of his predecessor, but people might feel that because of certain personal qualities which he possessed over and above the sacredness of his office, the late priest was a more effective intercessor with God than his successor could ever be. No such misgivings could be entertained with regard to the high priesthood of Christ, however. He would never have to hand it over to someone less well qualified to discharge its mediatorial functions. Those who entrusted their cause to Him knew therefore that it was permanently secure in His hands.

25 Those who have Christ as their high priest and mediator with God have in Him a Savior whose saving power is available without end,[78] not liable to the mischances of mortal life. He lives eternally, eternally engaged to bless and protect those who have committed themselves to Him. The way of approach to God through Him is a way that is always open, because in the presence of God He represents His people as "a priest for ever". He is no mediator in the ordinary sense, a go-between who places his good offices at the disposal of two parties in the hope of bringing them to agreement. He is the unique Mediator between God and man because He combines Godhead and manhood perfectly in His

---

[76] *EQ* xviii (1946), pp. 187f., on the word ἀπαράβατος (see p. 151, n. 73). Simpson points out that "Epictetus (*Enchir.* 51) urges his pupil to let all that is best be to him a νόμος ἀπαράβατος and Josephus (*Contra Ap.* ii. 41) asks what is a fairer spectacle than εὐσέβεια ἀπαράβατος; moreover, the adverb equals *without fail* in Vettius Valens" (*loc. cit.*, p. 188).

[77] *On Flight and Finding*, 116f., in a discussion of Num. 35:25, where the unintentional homicide stays in the city of refuge until the death of the high priest.

[78] Gk. εἰς τὸ παντελές (ARV margin "completely"; NEB "absolutely"); the phrase appears in one other place in NT (Luke 13:11).

own person; in Him God draws near to men and in Him men may draw near to God, with the assurance of constant and immediate access.

What is our Lord's special function as His people's high priest with God, apart from ensuring their never-failing acceptance before God? In Ch. 2:17f. we have been told that He became high priest to make propitiation for His people's sins and strengthen them in temptation; in Ch. 4:15f. we have been told that He sympathizes with their weakness and supplies the mercy and grace to help them in time of need. Here His high-priestly function is summed up in terms of intercession: "he is always living to plead on their behalf". The intercessory work of Christ at the right hand of God is not a doctrine peculiar to our author; it appears in one of Paul's great lyric outbursts:

> "Who shall lay anything to the charge of God's elect?
> It is God that justifieth; who is he that condemneth?
> It is Christ Jesus that died,
> yea rather, that was raised from the dead,
> who is at the right hand of God,
> who also maketh intercession for us" (Rom. 8:33f.).

In these words we may trace the echo of an early Christian confession of faith, which in addition to acknowledging the death, resurrection and enthronement of Christ made mention also of His intercessory ministry. We may also trace the echo of the fourth Servant Song, where the Servant of the LORD, once humbled and put to shame but now highly exalted, is said to have made, or to be making, "intercession for the transgressors".[79] This is one of the statements about the Servant which indicate that this ministry is priestly, as well as prophetic and royal.

But the teaching and action of Jesus on earth must have encouraged His disciples to recognize in Him their all-prevailing intercessor. "I have prayed for you," He said to Simon Peter at the Last Supper, "that your faith may not fail; and when you have turned again, strengthen your brethren" (Luke 22:32, RSV). If it be asked what form His heavenly intercession takes, what

---

[79] Isa. 53:12. An intercessory ministry is implied in Acts 7:56, where Stephen sees the Son of Man standing at God's right hand as his witness or advocate (cf. Acts, NICNT, p. 168 with n. 98). Cf. Luke 12:8, where the Son of Man confesses in heaven those who confess him on earth. Cf. p. liii.

better answer can be given than that He still does for His people at the right hand of God what He did for Peter on earth? And the prayer recorded in John 17, also belonging to the same night in which He was betrayed, is well called (after David Chytraeus) His high-priestly prayer, and (such is the affinity of mind between the Fourth Evangelist and our present author) a careful study of John 17 will help us considerably to understand what is intended here when our Lord is described as making intercession for those who come to God through Him.

It is important to emphasize this, for the character of our Lord's intercession has at times been grotesquely misrepresented in popular Christian thought. He is not to be thought of "as an orante, *standing* ever before the Father with outstretched arms, like the figures in the mosaics of the catacombs, and with strong crying and tears pleading our cause in the presence of a reluctant God; but as a *throned* Priest-King, asking what He will from a Father who always hears and grants His request. Our Lord's life in heaven is His prayer."[80] His once-completed self-offering is utterly acceptable and efficacious; His contact with the Father is immediate and unbroken; His priestly ministry on His people's behalf is never-ending, and therefore the salvation which He secures to them is absolute.

7. SUPERIOR BECAUSE OF THE CHARACTER OF JESUS

Ch. 7:26-28

26 For such a high priest became us, holy, guileless, undefiled, separated from sinners, and made higher than the heavens;[81]

27 who needeth not daily, like those high priests, to offer up sacrifices, first for his own sins, and then for the *sins* of

---

[80] H. B. Swete, *The Ascended Christ* (London, 1912), p. 95.

[81] These words have the solemn style of a cultic hymn; O. Michel suggests that in "such a high priest became us, / holy, guileless, undefiled, / separated from sinners, / made higher than the heavens" we have a quatrain from an early hymn in praise of Christ (MK, p. 177; *cf.* H. Windisch in HNT, p. 67). With the last phrase A. Ehrhardt compares an Orphic fragment on the Logos: αὐτὸς ἐπουράνιος καὶ ἐπὶ χθονὶ πάντα τελευτᾷ, "he himself being above the heavens also accomplishes all upon earth" (*Ev. Th.* xxx [1960], pp. 572ff.).

the people: for this he did once for all,[82] when he offered up himself.

28 For the law appointeth men high priests,[83] having infirmity; but the word of the oath, which was after the law, *appointeth* a Son, perfected for evermore.

26 But whatever other reasons may be adduced to demonstrate the superiority of the new priesthood, there is one final argument. The new priesthood is better because the new priest is Jesus. Jesus, who endured sore temptations on earth; Jesus, who poured out His heart in earnest prayer to God; Jesus, who learned by suffering how hard the way of obedience could be; Jesus, who interceded for His disciples that their faith might not fail when the hour of testing came; Jesus, who offered up His life to God as a sin-offering on their behalf—this same Jesus is the unchanging high priest and helper of all who come to God through Him. "Such a high priest does indeed fit our condition" (NEB). He has the unique qualification of having experienced the full force of temptation without once yielding to it. There is no question of His fitness to appear in the presence of God; He is the Holy[84] One of God, free from all guile[85] and defilement. Philo can speak of the Logos as the ideal high priest, free from all defilement;[86] but Christians have as their high priest one who does not

---

[82] Gk. ἐφάπαξ (*cf.* Chs. 9:12; 10:10), a more emphatic form of ἅπαξ (Chs. 6:4; 9:7, 26, 27, 28; 10:2; 12:26, 27), "once (for all)"—used repeatedly in this epistle to convey the finality and perfection of the self-offering of Christ.

[83] A few authorities, including P[46] (apparently) and D, read "priests" instead of "high priests".

[84] Gk. ὅσιος, used of Christ also in Acts 2:27; 13:35. In both these places the words of Ps. 16:10 (LXX, 15:10), "Neither wilt thou suffer thy holy one to see corruption", are viewed as fulfilled in the resurrection of Christ. In LXX ὅσιος most often represents Heb. ḥāsîd, a word which can be used both of the godly man (as in Ps. 16:10) and of God Himself (as in Ps. 145 [LXX 144]:17; *cf.* ὅσιος in Rev. 15:4; 16:5). The Hebrew word is cognate with ḥesed ("lovingkindness", "steadfast love") and has the basic sense of "loyal to covenant obligations".

[85] Gk. ἄκακος (*cf.* Rom. 16:18, where it has the sense, not present here, of being so guileless as to be unsuspecting and easily led astray).

[86] Gk. ἀμίαντος, the same word as our author uses here (*cf.* Philo, *Special Laws* i. 113; similarly *On Flight and Finding* 108ff.). But Philo is concerned to present the undefiled character of the Logos as the truth denoted allegorically by the law forbidding the high priest to touch a corpse or mourn for the dead (Lev. 21:10f.).

remain in the realm of ideas but is the incarnate Logos, one who preserved His purity while treading the common ways of this world and sharing our human lot. Although He came to earth "in the likeness of sinful flesh",[87] lived among sinners, received sinners, ate with sinners, was known as the friend of sinners, yet He is set apart from sinners,[88] "in a different class from sinful men";[89] and is now exalted above all the heavens to share the throne of God.

27 Aaron and his successors, before they presented a sin-offering on behalf of the people, had to present one for themselves. This was preeminently true on the annual day of atonement: before the ritual of the two goats was enacted, to cleanse the nation from the accumulated sin of the past twelve months, the direction ran: "Aaron shall present the bullock of the sin-offering, which is for himself, and make atonement for himself, and for his house" (Lev. 16:6).[90] But there were other occasions on which a similar atonement had to be made: "if the anointed priest shall sin so as to bring guilt on the people, then let him offer for his sin, which he hath sinned, a young bullock without blemish unto Jehovah for a sin-offering" (Lev. 4:3). This occasional sin-offering may have been in our author's mind when he used the expression "daily" in this connection. There is indeed no explicit command for a daily sin-offering to be presented by the high priest on his own account; but inadvertent sinning, of the kind provided for in Lev. 4:1ff., could well have been a daily hazard. And the high priest occupied a special position; an inadvertent sin on his part brought guilt on the people. It was wise therefore to take precautions against the very possibility of his having committed an inadvertent sin. According to Philo, "the high priest ... day by day offers prayers and sacrifices and asks for blessings ... that every age and every part of the nation, as of a single body, may be joined

---

[87] Rom. 8:3 (cf. exposition and notes ad loc. by J. Murray in NICNT and F. F. Bruce in TNTC).

[88] Gk. κεχωρισμένος ἀπὸ τῶν ἁμαρτωλῶν. The high priest of Israel, while not personally free from sin, was ceremonially set apart from his fellows for the proper discharge of his sacred functions. But Jesus has no need to be set apart in any such ceremonial manner; His separation is, on the one hand, inward and moral, and, on the other hand, the consequence of His being now exalted to the right hand of God, withdrawn from the midst of a sinful world.

[89] W. Manson, *The Epistle to the Hebrews* (London, 1951), pp. 116f.

[90] Cf. Ch. 9:7 (p. 193).

harmoniously into one and same fellowship, having peace and good order as their aim".[91] But these daily or occasional sacrifices, whether offered for his own sins or for those of the people, were summed up and "raised, so to speak, to a higher power"[92] by the special ceremonies of the day of atonement.

But Jesus has no need to present a daily sacrifice—or, for that matter, a yearly sacrifice—for His people's sins. He presented a permanently valid sin-offering on their behalf when He offered up His own life—an offering so perfect and efficacious that it needs no repetition. Still less has He any need to present such a sacrifice for Himself; He is "holy, guileless, undefiled". For all the completeness of His identification with His people and His sympathetic entering into their trials and sufferings, He is personally free from the guilt and tyranny of sin, and for that very reason is the more able to be their effective high priest. We have already been told that He "made purification of sins" (Ch. 1:3), that He was appointed "to make propitiation for the sins of the people" (Ch. 2:17), since it is the function of every high priest to "offer both gifts and sacrifices for sins" (Ch. 5:1). But now we are told expressly the nature of the sacrifice which our Lord offered: "he offered up himself". There is an Old Testament adumbration of such a self-offering in the portrayal of the Suffering Servant who "makes himself an offering for sin" (Isa. 53:10, RSV).[93] The

---

[91]   *Special Laws* iii. 131; *cf.* his reference in *Who is the heir of divine things?* (174) to "the permanent sacrifices, both the oblation of flour which the priests offer for themselves and the oblation of two lambs which they are directed to offer on behalf of the nation". The oblation of flour which the priests were directed to offer for themselves (Lev. 6:19ff.) was not a *pro forma* sin-offering, and indeed it might be inferred from the terms of the prescription that it was presented only on the day of their anointing (in that case "perpetually" in Lev. 6.20 would mean "when each new priest is anointed in his turn"). But quite clearly it came to be observed as a daily ceremony, whatever its original intention was; *cf.* Sir. 45.14, concerning Aaron: "His sacrifices (θυσίαι) shall be wholly burned twice every day continually" (καθ' ἡμέραν ἐνδελεχῶς δίς).

[92]   A. B. Davidson, *The Epistle to the Hebrews* (Edinburgh, 1882), p. 144. It is doing violence to the natural sense of the Greek to interpret it, with Westcott (*ad loc.*), as meaning: "The characteristic High-priestly office of the Lord is fulfilled 'daily', 'for ever', and not only, as that of the Levitical High-priest, on one day in the year." That is true, but it is not what our author says here. *Cf.* "daily" (καθ' ἡμέραν, as here) in Ch. 10.11.

[93]   See further on Ch. 9:28 (p. 223 with nn. 169–172). The word translated "offering for sin" in Isa. 53:10 is Heb. 'āshām, the "trespass-offering" (ARV) or "guilt offering" (RSV) of Lev. 5:6ff.; 7:1ff. This passage may form the OT

158

martyrs of Maccabaean days yielded up their lives with the confidence that they would be accepted as an atonement on their fellow-Israelites' behalf (II Macc. 7:37f.; IV Macc. 6:27ff.; 17:22; 18:4);[94] and it was similarly the belief of the Qumran sectaries that their piety and privations would make propitiation for the land of Israel.[95] But there is no need for our author to look for precedents to enable him to interpret the death of Jesus in terms of a voluntary sin-offering; this was how Jesus Himself envisaged His death. When He said that the Son of Man had come "to give his life a ransom for many" (Mark 10:45) and spoke of His covenant blood as about to be "poured out for many" (Mark 14:24), He indicated clearly that He was presenting Himself to God as a sacrifice for others. And when the hour came and He was stretched upon the cross, instead of having His heart filled with bitter resentment against His executioners or with feelings

---

background for Paul's statements that Jesus was sent "as an offering for sin" (Rom. 8:3, ARV margin) and that He was "made to be sin on our behalf" (II Cor. 5:21); perhaps also for our Lord's own words about giving His life "a ransom for many" (Mark 10:45). On the relation of the Isaianic Servant of the Lord to Jesus see Acts, NICNT, p. 189, n. 49; p. 191, n. 56; to the bibliography in these notes add W. Zimmerli and J. Jeremias, *The Servant of God* (London, 1957); M. D. Hooker, *Jesus and the Servant* (London, 1959).

[94] In his article "The Background of Mark 10:45" in *New Testament Essays: Studies in Memory of T. W. Manson*, ed. A. J. B. Higgins (Manchester, 1959), pp. 1ff., C. K. Barrett quotes these passages from II and IV Maccabees as containing the doctrine of *kappārāh*, and suggests that a creative mind working upon such a background as these passages provide could produce a saying like that recorded in Mark 10:45. He concludes also "that the connection between Mark 10:45 and Isa. 53 is much less definite and more tenuous than is often supposed" (p. 15). It is indeed an exaggeration of that connection to speak and write, as some have done, as though Mark 10:45 were practically a quotation from Isa. 53. But Jesus and the Evangelists certainly knew and were influenced by the book of Isaiah; there is little if any evidence for their acquaintance with II and IV Maccabees. Moreover, that the Son of Man "should suffer many things and be set at nought" is something that is *written* (Mark 9:12; *cf.* 14:21). This expression implies canonical scripture; Isa. 52:13–53:12 will satisfy the terms of reference, but scarcely the martyrologies of Maccabees. True, when Jesus spoke of His life as being λυτρὸν ἀντὶ πολλῶν He did not say so simply because this was written "in the volume of the book" but because it was His own fixed purpose and ardent desire in accordance with what He knew to be God's will. Yet, I believe, not only did He by His acceptance of the death of the cross fulfil the prophecy of Isa. 52:13–53:12 but He knew that He was fulfilling it.

[95] *Cf.* 1QS iii. 6–12; iv. 20f.; v. 6f.; ix. 3–5; see F. F. Bruce, *Biblical Exegesis in the Qumran Texts* (London, 1960), pp. 57ff. *Cf.* p. 177 with n. 66; p. 196, n. 63.

of reproach against God for allowing this to happen to Him, He offered up His life to God as a sin-offering in His people's stead. How acceptable to God this sacrifice was, or how effective in the purifying of heart and life, let those bear witness who have found through faith in Him that peace with God and release from sin which nothing else could have brought about.[96]

28 Under the ancient law, as we have already been told, the high priest "is compassed with infirmity; and by reason thereof is bound, as for the people, so also for himself, to offer for sins" (Ch. 5:2f.). But the divine acclamation, given under oath, of a new and perpetual priesthood after Melchizedek's order, was designed to supersede the earlier priesthood established by the law. This supersession came into effect when the Messiah appeared and vindicated his high-priestly title on the basis of a perfect sacrifice. Fully equipped to discharge an intercessory ministry at the right hand of God, this is no high priest subject to all the conditions of earthly frailty; this is the one whom God addresses as Son, whose high priesthood is absolutely efficacious[97] and eternally suited to meet His people's need.[98]

---

[96] The self-offering of Christ, as Priest and Sacrifice, Victor and Victim, in one, is further elaborated in Chs. 9:11ff.; 10:5ff.

[97] This is the sense of His being "perfected" ($\tau\epsilon\tau\epsilon\lambda\epsilon\iota\omega\mu\acute{\epsilon}\nu\upsilon\nu$); cf. Chs. 2:10; 5:9.

[98] As in Ch. 5:5f. our author brings together Ps. 2:7 and 110:4 (LXX 109:4) in the collocation of the words "Son ... for evermore" (Gk. $\upsilon\acute{\iota}\grave{\upsilon}\nu$ $\epsilon\grave{\iota}\varsigma$ $\tau\grave{\upsilon}\nu$ $\alpha\grave{\iota}\tilde{\omega}\nu\alpha$). For the anarthrous "Son" cf. Chs. 1:2; 5:8.

CHAPTER VIII

V. COVENANT, SANCTUARY AND SACRIFICE
Chs. 8:1–10:18

1. PRIESTHOOD AND PROMISE
Ch. 8:1–7

1 Now in the things which we are saying the chief point *is
   this:*[1] We have such a high priest, who sat down on the
   right hand of the throne of the Majesty in the heavens,[2]

2 a minister of the sanctuary,[3] and of the true tabernacle,
   which the Lord pitched,[4] not man.

---

[1] Or, "Now to sum up what we are saying" (ARV margin). Moffatt (*ad
loc.*) aptly refers to Coverdale's rendering: "Of the thinges which we haue
spoken, this is the pyth." The question is whether κεφάλαιον should be understood here as meaning "chief point" (so in the classical writers and Philo) or
"sum", "summary" (Coverdale's "pith"). The former rendering is preferred
by RSV and NEB. But our author may feel that his argument about the superiority of the Melchizedek priesthood has been too involved for some of his
readers to follow, so he sums it up by saying: "What all this amounts to, what
it all leads up to, is this: it is a high priest of this superior order and quality that
we have." See, however, p. 163, n. 16.

[2] "The Majesty in the heavens" (Gk. ἡ μεγαλωσύνη ἐν τοῖς οὐρανοῖς) is a
reverential periphrasis for the name of God, like "the Majesty on high" in
Ch. 1:3. (See p. 7, n. 33.) The expression used here is fuller than that in
Ch. 1:3 because of the addition of "the throne" between "right hand" and the
surrogate for the divine name; for the fuller expression *cf.* also Ch. 12:2 ("the
right hand of the throne of God").

[3] Gk. τῶν ἁγίων λειτουργός, which might equally well be rendered "a
minister of the holy things"; the principal reason for preferring the rendering
"sanctuary" is that this is the regular sense of the neuter plural (τὰ) ἅγια in this
epistle (*cf.* Chs. 9:2, 8, 12, 24, 25; 10:19; 13:11). The substantive λειτουργός
(which refers to angels in Ch. 1:7) is used in Rom. 13:6 of civil rulers as servants
of God, in Rom. 15:16 of Paul in his apostleship to the Gentiles, in Phil. 2:25
of Epaphroditus ministering to Paul's need as the Philippian church's representative; in LXX the verb λειτουργέω and the *nomen actionis* λειτουργία (*cf.* v. 6)
are frequently used in the Pentateuch of the ministration of the priests and
Levites in the wilderness tabernacle.

[4] Gk. ἣν ἔπηξεν ὁ κύριος, an echo of Num. 24:6, LXX, where Balaam describes the Israelite encampment as being "like tents which the Lord pitched"
(ὡσεὶ σκηναὶ ἃς ἔπηξεν κύριος).

3 For every high priest is appointed[5] to offer both gifts and sacrifices:[6] wherefore it is necessary that this *high priest* also have somewhat to offer.

4 Now if[7] he were on earth, he would not be a priest at all, seeing there are those who offer[8] the gifts according to the law;

5 who serve *that which is* a copy and shadow of the heavenly things, even as Moses is warned *of God*[9] when he is about to make[10] the tabernacle: for, See, saith he, that thou make all things according to the pattern that was showed thee in the mount.[11]

6 But now hath he obtained[12] a ministry[13] the more excellent, by so much as he is also the mediator of a better covenant, which hath been enacted[14] upon better promises.

7 For if that first *covenant* had been faultless, then would no place have been sought for a second.[15]

---

[5] Gk. καθίσταται, as in Ch. 5:1 (*cf.* p. 88, n. 1).

[6] The "gifts and sacrifices" (δῶρά τε καὶ θυσίαι) are not distinguished here any more than they are in Ch. 5:1 (see p. 89).

[7] Gk. εἰ μὲν οὖν, for which K L with the majority of later MSS and TR have εἰ μὲν γάρ (whence AV "For if ...").

[8] Gk. ὄντων τῶν προσφερόντων. K L with the majority of later MSS, the Peshitta, and TR, add ἱερέων after ὄντων (whence AV "seeing that there are priests that offer ...").

[9] Gk. κεχρημάτισται. *Cf.* Chs. 11:7; 12:25; Matt. 2:12, 22; Luke 2:26; Acts 10:22 for χρηματίζω meaning "give a divine oracle" (*cf.* also χρηματισμός in Rom. 11:4).

[10] Gk. ἐπιτελεῖν (ARV margin, "complete").

[11] Ex. 25:40, LXX. Here πάντα, "all things", is added to the LXX text (as in Philo, *Leg. Alleg.* iii. 102); LXX Cod. F (Ambrosianus), which includes πάντα, is probably influenced by the text of our present passage. This quotation has the aorist participle δειχθέντα as against the perfect δεδειγμένον of LXX.

[12] Gk. τέτυχεν (P⁴⁶ ℵ* A D* K L and 9 minuscules), for which B and many Byzantine witnesses have τέτευχεν, and P Ψ 33 1739 and many other minuscules τετύχηκεν (see G. Zuntz, *The Text of the Epistles* [London, 1953], pp. 119f.).

[13] Gk. λειτουργία. *Cf.* p. 161, n. 3.

[14] Gk. νενομοθέτηται. *Cf.* Ch. 7:11 (p. 142, n. 37), where the subject of the verb (in the passive, as here) is "the people".

[15] Gk. δευτέρας, for which B* reads ἑτέρας ("another"), a reading "unbelievable in the context", according to Zuntz (*op. cit.*, p. 41).

1–2 Having established the superiority of the high priesthood of Christ, our author now proceeds to relate His high priesthood to the themes of covenant, sanctuary and sacrifice, with which the Aaronic priesthood was closely bound up. As the Aaronic priesthood gives place to the priesthood after the order of Melchizedek, so the old covenant gives place to the new, the earthly sanctuary gives place to the heavenly, and sacrifices which were but temporary tokens give place to one that is effective and of eternal validity. "To crown the argument",[16] then, the great high priest whom Christians have is one who is enthroned at the right hand of God, who discharges his ministry in no earthly shrine but in the heavenly dwelling-place of God, a tabernacle pitched by no human hands. By contrast with all material sanctuaries, this one is called the true or "real[17] sanctuary" (N.E.B.), the only one which is not an imitation of something better than itself, the only one whose durability comes anywhere near to matching the eternity of the living and true God whose dwelling-place it is. This "real sanctuary" belongs to the same order of being as the saints' everlasting rest of Chs. 3 and 4, the better country and well-founded city of Ch. 11:10, 16, the unshakable kingdom of Ch. 12:28. What its essential character is will appear more clearly in the course of our exposition.[18]

3 But if Jesus ministers as high priest in this authentic sanctuary, what is the nature of His ministry? A high priest, as has been said before (Ch. 5:1), is appointed to present "gifts and sacrifices for sins";[19] therefore this high priest must also have something to

---

[16]   This is W. Manson's paraphrase of κεφάλαιον (*The Epistle to the Hebrews* [London, 1951], p. 123). To render the word "point", or even "sum" or "gist", he thinks, "throws us too much back on the past course of the argument, and fails to bring out the transcendent character of the vista which here opens to our eyes".

[17]   Gk. ἀληθινός. *Cf.* Ch. 9:24 (and 10:22, which is not such an apt parallel). While the classical distinction is that ἀληθής means "true" as opposed to "false", and ἀληθινός "real" as opposed to merely "apparent", it would be precarious to press this distinction in NT, as a comparison of the two adjectives in John's Gospel will show. In this epistle ἀληθινός is not found. As God Himself is real—τὸν μόνον ἀληθινὸν θεόν of John 17:3 (*cf.* Paul's solitary use of ἀληθινός, in relation to God, in I Thess. 1:9)—so other entities are real in so far as they are associated with His reality.

[18]   *Cf.* especially Chs. 10:19ff. (pp. 244ff.); 12:22ff. (pp. 372ff.).

[19]   The additional phrase "for sins" (*cf.* p. 88, n. 3) is missing here; but it is our Lord's presenting of Himself as a sin-offering that our author has principally in mind (*cf.* Chs. 1:3; 7:27).

offer. The nature of His offering, however, is not stated until Ch. 9:14 (although it has been mentioned already in Ch. 7:27), because in the meantime there are further points of contrast between the old order of worship and the new which have to be elucidated. In passing we may note that it is not implied that Jesus is continually or repeatedly presenting His offering; this is excluded by Ch. 7:27, which contrasts the daily sacrifices of the Aaronic high priests with the offering which the Christians' high priest has already presented once for all. The tense and mood of the Greek verb "to offer" in this clause also exclude the idea of a continual offering;[20] indeed, N.E.B. suggests in a footnote a rendering which would make the situation completely unambiguous: "this one too must have had something to offer".[21] It is a pity that the nuance of meaning here should be obscured in a well-known and generally admirable private version which renders the passage: "It follows, therefore, that in these holy places this man has something that he is offering".[22]

4 That Jesus' high-priestly ministry must be exercised in the heavenly sanctuary is further shown by the fact that there would be no room for Him to exercise it in the earthly sanctuary. In the earthly sanctuary, whether we think of the earlier tent-shrine or the later temple in Jerusalem, the high priesthood was confined to one family; and far from belonging to that family, Jesus did not even belong to the tribe from which it came.[23] On earth Jesus was a layman, excluded by the law from all priestly functions. The founder of the Qumran community was a priest,[24] even if for

---

[20] The infinitive "to offer" at the end of v. 3 (unlike the identical phrase in the first clause of the verse, which represents Gk. εἰς τὸ προσφέρειν), renders the adjective clause ὃ προσενέγκῃ with its antecedent τι ("somewhat"). The fact that προσενέγκῃ is aorist (subjunctive) is consistent with our author's repeated emphasis on the singularity of the sacrifice which Christ offered (cf. Chs. 7:27; 10:12).

[21] The verb "to be" is not expressed here with the adjective "necessary" (Gk. ἀναγκαῖον); this is indicated in AV (but not in ARV) by the italicization of "it is". One may therefore understand the past tense "it was" as readily as the present "it is".

[22] J. B. Phillips, *Letters to Young Churches* (London, 1947), p. 170; *The New Testament in Modern English* (London, 1958), *ad loc*. But Prebendary Phillips cannot be charged with any ulterior motive in so translating!

[23] Cf. Ch. 7:14.

[24] Cf. 1Qp Hab. ii. 6–10, where "the priest into whose heart God has put wisdom to interpret all the words of His servants the prophets" is probably the Teacher of Righteousness.

one reason or another he was excluded from performing priestly functions in the Jerusalem temple; but the founder of Christianity was not, and the Essenes would no more have looked upon Him as a priest than the Jerusalem hierarchy did. But to our author, this simply emphasizes the dignity of Jesus' high priesthood; for a high priesthood exercised in any earthly shrine is far inferior to that heavenly high priesthood which depends for its exercise on a perfect sacrifice offered once for all and consequent admission to the sanctuary above.

5 For the earthly sanctuary from the outset was designed to be nothing more than a "copy[25] and shadow"[26] of the heavenly reality. This is how our author understands the divine injunction to Moses, regarding the details of the tabernacle in the wilderness: "And see that thou make them after their pattern,[27] which hath been shewed thee in the mount" (Ex. 25:40). This "pattern" (referred to also in Ex. 25:9; 26:30; 27:8) was something visible;[28] it did not consist merely of the verbal directions of Ex. 25-30. It may have been a model for which the verbal directions served as a commentary; it may have been the heavenly dwelling-place of God which Moses was permitted to see.[29] The tabernacle was intended to serve as a dwelling-place for God in the midst of His

---

[25] Gk. ὑπόδειγμα, used in Ch. 9:23 in a similar sense to this, and in Ch. 4:11 in the sense of a moral example (so also in all its other NT occurrences, John 13:15; Jas. 5:10; II Pet. 2:6). In Ezek. 42:15 (LXX) the prophet's angel-guide is said to have "measured the plan (ὑπόδειγμα) of the house [the temple of the new commonwealth] round about in order". In Attic Greek παράδειγμα was preferred to ὑπόδειγμα, but whereas here it is the earthly copies of the heavenly realities that are the ὑποδείγματα, in Attic Greek the heavenly exemplars themselves are called the παραδείγματα (cf. p. 166, n. 32). Cf. T. F. Torrance, Royal Priesthood (Edinburgh, 1955), pp. 20f.

[26] Gk. σκιά (cf. Ch. 10:1 and see p. 166, n. 32).

[27] Gk. τύπος, rendering Heb. tabnīth ("building", "construction"); the implication is that Moses was shown something like a scale model of the sanctuary which was to be erected.

[28] In the Hebrew text of Ex. 25:40 the phrase "which hath been shewed thee" means literally "which thou art caused to see" (’asher ’attāh mor’eh).

[29] Cf. F. M. Cross, Jr.: "Probably the conception of the tabnīth, the 'model' (Exodus 25:9), also goes back ultimately to the idea that the earthly sanctuary is the counterpart of the heavenly dwelling of a deity" ("The Tabernacle", BA x [1947], pp. 45ff., more particularly p. 62). In Wisdom 9:8 Solomon's temple is "a copy (μίμημα) of the holy tent which thou didst prepare from the beginning." (Cf. I Chron. 28:19.) See also G. E. Wright, "The Temple in Palestine and Syria", BA vii (1944), pp. 66ff.

people on earth, and it would be completely in keeping with current practice that such an earthly dwelling-place should be a replica of God's heavenly dwelling-place.[30] This, of course, is how our author understands the situation. The high priests of Aaron's line ministered[31] in the earthly sanctuary; Jesus exercises His high-priestly ministry in the heavenly sanctuary, of which the earthly one was but a replica. There is indeed some affinity with Platonic idealism here, but it is our author's language, and not his essential thought, that exhibits such affinity. For him, the relation between the two sanctuaries is basically a temporal one. If the earthly sanctuary is a "shadow" of the heavenly, it is because the whole Levitical order *foreshadowed* the spiritual order of the new age. Here as in Ch. 10:1 the old order has "a shadow of the good things to come".[32]

How the pattern which Moses saw on Mount Sinai could be

---

[30] As early as the Babylonian *Enuma elish* there is a heavenly *ubshukkinaku* or "court of assembly" corresponding to the earthly temple (iii. 61, 119, 131). *Cf.* W. F. Albright, *Archaeology and the Religion of Israel*[3] (Baltimore, 1953), pp. 142ff. (where cosmic significance is attached to the pillars, sea, altar-base, etc., of the temples of Solomon and Ezekiel); also p. 88, for the point that in Phoenician "it would seem that the words *bêtu*, 'house', and *hêkalu*, 'temple', refer both to a residence in heaven and to temples on earth". The antiquity of the cosmic interpretation of the tabernacle and temple is illustrated by its appearance in Josephus (*Ant.* iii. 123; *War* v. 212f.); *cf.* II Baruch 4:2ff.; *Ascension of Isaiah* 7:10. See also E. Burrows, "Some Cosmological Patterns in Babylonian Religion", in *The Labyrinth*, ed. S. H. Hooke (London, 1935), pp. 45ff., especially 59ff.; R. E. Clements, *The Dwelling Place of God in the Old Testament* (unpublished Ph.D. thesis, University of Sheffield, 1961). On the other hand, R. de Vaux expresses considerable scepticism with regard to the cosmic symbolism of the sanctuary in Israel (*Ancient Israel* [London, 1961], pp. 328f.). See Ch. 12:22 (pp. 372ff.).

[31] Gk. λατρεύω, preeminently of worship or priestly service (*cf.* Chs. 9:9, 14; 10:2; 12:28; 13:10, with the related substantive λατρεία in Ch. 9:1, 6).

[32] *Cf.* Paul's description of the Jewish laws regarding food and festivals as "only a shadow of what is to come; but the substance belongs to Christ" (Col. 2:17, RSV). This is a different use of the "shadow" concept from Philo's: he interprets the name Bezaleel as "in the shadow of God" and explains that Bezaleel constructed the copies (μιμήματα) whereas Moses constructed the exemplars (παραδείγματα); "therefore the one drew an outline as it were of shadows (οἷα σκιὰς ὑπεγράφετο), whereas the other fashioned no shadows, but the archetypal entities themselves" (*On Dreams*, i. 206; *cf. Leg. Alleg.* iii. 101ff.). (*Cf.* Plotinus, *Enneads* i. 6. 8.) For the conception of the earthly sanctuary as a copy of the sanctuary in heaven *cf.* also Rev. 11:19; 14:17; 15:5f. (in Rev.

handled by a thorough-going Platonist is seen in Philo's treatment of the Exodus passage: Moses "saw with the soul's eye the immaterial forms ('ideas') of the material objects which were about to be made, and in accordance with these forms copies perceptible to the senses had to be reproduced, as from an archetypal drawing and patterns conceived in the mind".[33] Moses, in other words, was enabled to grasp with his mind the invisible "ideas" laid up eternally in the "place above the heavens"[34] (much as Plato envisaged a pattern of his republic laid up in heaven, so that it was a matter of minor importance whether an earthly copy of it ever came into existence or not),[35] and commanded to give material expression to these "ideas" in a tabernacle on earth.

6 It is, then, in no earthly replica of the heavenly dwelling-place of God that Jesus ministers as His people's high priest, but in the heavenly dwelling-place itself; His ministry accordingly is far superior to any earthly ministry. And it is superior besides because of the superiority of the covenant in the power of which it is exercised—the covenant of which Jesus is Himself the Mediator. He has already been called, in passing, "the surety of a better covenant" (Ch. 7:22); the present description of Him as "the mediator of a better covenant" (repeated with variations in Chs. 9:15; 12:24) "presents an instance", as E. K. Simpson says,[36] "of the profound enhancement conferred on expressions already in vogue by the Christian revelation". For, he continues, the Greek word translated "mediator"[37] is shown by the papyri to have been a common business term "in the sense of *arbitrator* or *go-between*.... The somewhat wider usage for any *internuntius* occasionally met with prepared the way for its loftiest connotation. Thus Moses is styled in Philo as well as by St. Paul *mesitēs*, the 'middleman' of the old covenant. But Christ is the Mediator *par excellence*, not with that merely metaphysical application by which Plutarch (*Mor.* 369) alludes to Mithras as the *mesitēs* between Ormuzd and

---

4–7 heaven itself is the temple of God). The conception, while much earlier than Plato, lends itself to a Platonic interpretation. *Cf.* O. Procksch in *TWNT* i, pp. 96f. (*s.v.* ἅγιος).

[33] *Life of Moses* ii. 74.

[34] Gk. ὑπερουράνιος τόπος (Plato, *Phaedrus* 247c). See p. lvii with n. 136.

[35] Plato, *Republic* ix. 592b.

[36] *EQ* xviii (1946), p. 188.

[37] Gk. μεσίτης (once in LXX, in Job 9:33, where Job wishes that there were such an intermediary between himself and God). See p. 127, n. 69.

Ahriman in Persian theosophy, but in its supreme ethical significance, typified in the 'reconciling rainbow' encircling the throne,
or in the ladder of Jacob's vision conjoining sundered heaven and
earth—one, to borrow a fine coinage of Tyndale, who is the perfect
Atonemaker, conserving the interests of both parties for whom He
acts. Intensely zealous that God's honour should contract no
stain, this ideal Mediator, having secured that supreme end, will
with equal zeal seek the offender's rescue and reclamation. Such
an unique Intermediary evangelical faith recognizes in her beloved
Lord."[38]

What the better promises are on which this better covenant is
established will appear in the quotation from Jer. 31:31ff. which
follows in verses 8–12. For the better covenant of which our Lord
is Mediator is the new covenant foretold by Jeremiah. From the
words of the quotation, too, it will be possible to gather something
of the meaning which the term "covenant" has in this epistle.

7 But indeed, the covenant of which Jesus is Mediator may
be inferred to be a better covenant from the simple fact that it is
a *new* covenant. If the old covenant had been perfect, it would not
have required to be superseded by a new one. And the new one
must be better, for there would have been no point in replacing
the old covenant by another no better than itself.

2. THE OLD COVENANT SUPERSEDED

Ch. 8:8–13

8 For finding fault with them, he saith,[39]
   Behold, the days come, saith the Lord,
   That I will make[40] a new covenant with the house of
      Israel and with the house of Judah;

9   Not according to the covenant that I made with their
      fathers

---

[38] *Cf.* pp. 153ff. (on Ch. 7:25).

[39] Jer. 31:31–34 (LXX 38:31–34).

[40] LXX διαθήσομαι ("I will covenant") is replaced here by συντελέσω ("I
will accomplish"); in verse 10 below (as in Ch. 10:16) it is retained. In Jer.
34:8, 15 (LXX 41:8, 15) συντελεῖν διαθήκην is used of a covenant made under
Zedekiah, by which Hebrew slaves were to be set free. In all these places,
whatever the Greek rendering may be, the Hebrew idiom *kārath berīth* (literally
"to cut a covenant") is used (*cf.* p. 211, n. 124).

In the day that I took them by the hand to lead them
    forth out of the land of Egypt;
For they continued not in my covenant,
And I regarded them not,[41] saith the Lord.

10   For this is the covenant[42] that I will make with the
        house of Israel
After those days, saith the Lord;
I will put my laws into their mind,
And on their heart also will I write[43] them:
And I will be to them a God,
And they shall be to me a people:

11   And they shall not teach every man his fellow-citizen,[44]
And every man his brother, saying, Know the Lord:
For all shall know me,
From the least to the greatest of them.

12   For I will be merciful[45] to their iniquities,
And their sins[46] will I remember no more.

13 In that he saith, A new *covenant*, he hath made the first
old. But that which is becoming old and waxeth aged is
nigh unto vanishing away.

8-12 The speaker in this oracle of the new covenant is God:
it is to Him that the repeated pronouns of the first person singular—
I, me, my—refer. The oracle itself is punctuated by the phrase
"oracle of Yahweh" (here rendered "saith the Lord"). So our
author, as is his custom, ignores the fact that it was delivered
through Jeremiah; the divine authorship is all that he is concerned
with. "He saith" in the sentence which introduces the quotation

---

[41] LXX κἀγὼ ἠμέλησα αὐτῶν as against Heb. *we'ānōkhî bā'altî bām* ("although
I was a husband unto them"), perhaps reading *gā'altî* for *bā'altî*. (Peshitta
follows LXX; Vulgate follows MT.)

[42] Codd. A and D have "this is my covenant".

[43] Gk. ἐπιγράψω ("I will inscribe"), for which P^{46} B Ψ have the simple
verb γράψω ("I will write").

[44] Gk. ἵλεως ἔσομαι, translating Heb. *'eslaḥ*, "I will forgive".

[45] Gk. πολίτην, for which P 1912 with the Latin versions, the margin of the
Harclean Syriac and TR have πλησίον (AV "neighbour"), by way of assimilation
to the sense of the Hebrew text.

[46] A D and the bulk of later manuscripts, followed by TR, insert καὶ τῶν
ἀνομιῶν αὐτῶν after τῶν ἁμαρτιῶν αὐτῶν (*cf.* AV: "their sins and their iniquities
will I remember no more"), following the homiletic expansion of Ch. 10:17.

169

means "God says" (*cf.* Ch. 10:15, where the same oracle is introduced as the Holy Spirit's witness); "finding fault with them" refers to the terms in which the oracle itself charges the Israelites with breaking God's earlier covenant.

The new covenant foretold by Jeremiah is set in contrast with the covenant which Yahweh made with the people of Israel when He delivered them from the land of Egypt. The ratification of that earlier covenant is recorded in Ex. 24:1–8, a passage to which specific reference is made below in Ch. 9:18–20.[47] At that time, as Jeremiah on a previous occasion reminded his hearers, the essence of God's covenant with Israel was: "Hearken unto my voice, and I will be your God, and ye shall be my people; and walk ye in all the way that I command you, that it may be well with you" (Jer. 7:23). But His commandment was disregarded; His charge against His people, reiterated in Jeremiah's day, was: "But they hearkened not, nor inclined their ear, but walked in their own counsels and in the stubbornness of their evil heart,[48] and went backward, and not forward. Since the day that your fathers came forth out of the land of Egypt unto this day, I have sent unto you all my servants the prophets, daily rising up early and sending them: yet they hearkened not unto me, nor inclined their ear, but made their neck stiff: they did worse than their fathers" (Jer. 7:24–26).

Prophet after prophet came to Israel and Judah, recalling the people to their covenant loyalty; Jeremiah himself was no exception. "Hear ye the words of this covenant, and do them", was his call (Jer. 11:6); and with that call went the assurance that the blessings attached to the keeping of the covenant would still be theirs if they were obedient, while persistent disobedience to it would bring a curse upon them as it had done upon their fathers.

The covenant theme was all the more topical in Jeremiah's day because of the solemn covenant that had been made by the king and the leaders of the nation in the eighteenth year of Josiah. The discovery by Hilkiah the priest of "the book of the law"—probably

---

[47] See pp. 214ff.

[48] Heb. *sherīrūth libbām* (*hārā'*), a characteristic Jeremianic phrase (elsewhere in OT only in Deut. 29:19 and Ps. 81:12), used of those who disregard the divine covenant; found also repeatedly in the Qumran texts, *e.g.* C D iii. 5, etc., in the context of the new covenant established "in the land of Damascus". *Cf.* p. 366, n. 107.

the law of Deuteronomy[49]—in the temple in that year (621 B.C.) was followed by a solemn act of national repentance and rededication. The newly discovered law-book was read at a great gathering in the temple, "and the king stood by the pillar, and made a covenant before Jehovah, to walk after Jehovah, and to keep his commandments, and his testimonies, and his statutes, with all his heart, and all his soul, to confirm the words of this covenant that were written in this book: and all the people stood to the covenant" (II Kings 23:3).

The king's repentance and covenant were genuine enough; but the others who took part in this ceremony and in the accompanying reformation of national religion did so largely by way of conforming to the royal will. Jeremiah was quick to perceive this, and to recognize that there was no ground for expecting this covenant to be kept any more than the covenant of Deut. 29:1 of which it was essentially a reaffirmation. Jeremiah's attitude and relation to King Josiah's covenant and reformation have often been discussed;[50] but there is very little in his recorded words that can be interpreted as a direct reference to these events, apart from the damning indictment of Jer. 3:10, where a divine oracle, explicitly uttered "in the days of Josiah the king", reprobates the kingdom of Judah for not taking warning from the fate of its sister-nation Israel: "for all this her false sister Judah did not return to me with her whole heart, but in pretence, says the LORD" (RSV). "I do not doubt," says H. L. Ellison, "that the first impulse of Jeremiah's heart was to leap with joy, when the news of a clean sweep of all heathenism was first received. But as a prophet, viewing it from God's standpoint, he could see that it never had any chance of success. It was not that it stayed superficial; there never was any question of its being anything else."[51] No reaffirmation of the Deuteronomic covenant, or even of that earlier covenant made on the morrow of the Israelites' escape from Egypt, could meet the situation. A new covenant, new in character as well as in time,

---

[49]   A view expressed as early as Jerome (*Commentary on Ezekiel* 1:1).

[50]   *Cf.* J. Skinner, *Prophecy and Religion* (Cambridge, 1922), pp. 89ff.; G. A. Smith, *Jeremiah* (4th edn., London, 1929), pp. 134ff.; H. H. Rowley, "The Prophet Jeremiah and the Book of Deuteronomy", in *Studies in Old Testament Prophecy presented to T. H. Robinson* (Edinburgh, 1950), pp. 157ff.; W. Rudolph, *Jeremia²*, HAT (Tübingen, 1958), p. 73.

[51]   *EQ* xxxiv (1962), p. 162.

was called for, and such a new covenant Jeremiah proclaimed.

We do not stay to argue that the oracle of the new covenant is an authentic utterance of Jeremiah[52]—although, to sure, the identity of the prophet through whom these words of God were spoken would probably have been a matter of small importance to the author of this epistle. It is precisely in Jeremiah's prophetic ministry that the oracle finds its proper life-setting. The days were dark; national life was in collapse; it was "the time of Jacob's trouble" (Jer. 30:7).[53] But the people's life would be reconstituted on a new basis, and a new relationship between them and their God would be brought into being. This new relationship would involve three things in particular: *(a)* the implanting of God's law[54] in their hearts; *(b)* the knowledge of God as a matter of personal experience; *(c)* the blotting out of their sins.

(a) The implanting of God's law in their hearts means much more than their committing of it to memory. Ample provision for memorizing it had already been made in the prescriptions of Deuteronomy: "these words, which I command thee this day, shall be upon thy heart: and thou shalt teach them diligently unto thy children, and shalt talk of them when thou sittest in thy house, and when thou walkest by the way, and when thou liest down, and when thou risest up. And thou shalt bind them for a sign upon thy hand, and they shall be for frontlets between thine eyes. And thou shalt write them upon the door-posts of thy house, and upon thy gates" (Deut. 6:6–9). Even the memorizing of the law of God does not guarantee the performance of what has been memorized.

---

[52] Its authenticity was denied by B. Duhm, on the ground that there is nothing here worthy of Jeremiah—that this "new covenant" does not go beyond that of Deuteronomy, and that even the promise that Israel and Judah would know it by heart does not add anything to the provision for memorizing the ancient law laid down in Deut. 6:6ff. (*Das Buch Jeremia Erklärt* [Tübingen/ Leipzig, 1901], pp. 36ff.); for its authenticity *cf.* J. Skinner, *op. cit.*, pp. 325ff.; G. A. Smith, *op. cit.*, pp. 374ff.; J. A. Bewer, *The Prophets* (New York and London, 1955), p. 260 ("Its Jeremian authorship has been validated over against critical doubts").

[53] G. A. Smith may be right in dating the oracle in the brief period of Gedaliah's governorship at Mizpah (*op. cit.*, pp. 292f.).

[54] The original wording of Jer. 31:33 is: "I will put my *tōrāh* within them." Heb. *tōrāh* means more than statutory law; it embraces the ideas of guidance, direction and instruction. The New Testament fulfilment of this promise is nowhere better expressed than in Paul's words in Rom. 8:1ff. of the work of the indwelling Spirit of God in the believer.

Jeremiah's words imply the receiving of a new heart by the people —as is expressly promised in the parallel prophecy of his younger contemporary Ezekiel: "I will give them one heart, and put a new spirit within them; I will take the stony heart out of their flesh and give them a heart of flesh, that they may walk in my statutes and keep my ordinances and obey them; and they shall be my people, and I will be their God" (Ezek. 11:19f., RSV; cf. 36:26ff.). When first they heard the covenant-law they said: "All that Jehovah hath spoken will we do, and be obedient" (Ex. 24:7). But they did not have the moral power to match their good intention. Hence the necessity arose of repeatedly returning to their God and His covenant, only to turn aside to their own ways once again. The defect did not lie in the covenant-law; it was good in itself but, to borrow Paul's language, "it was weak through the flesh" (Rom. 8:3)—because of the inadequacy of the human material which it had to work upon. What was needed was a new nature, a heart liberated from its bondage to sin, a heart which not only spontaneously knew and loved the will of God but had the power to do it.

The new covenant was a new one because it could impart this new heart. It was not new in regard to its own substance: "I will be to them a God, and they shall be to me a people", quoted here from Jer. 31:33, was the substance of the covenant of Moses' day. "I will take you to me for a people, and I will be to you a God" was God's promise to the Israelites while they were still in Egypt (Ex. 6:7); "I ... will be your God, and ye shall be my people" was His promise to them when He had given them His law in the wilderness (Lev. 26:12), a promise taken up and applied in apostolic days to the people of the new covenant (II Cor. 6:16).[55] And in the New Testament Apocalypse, when a new heaven and earth come into being, and God's dwelling-place is established with men, the ancient covenant-promise is repeated: "they shall be his peoples,[56] and God himself shall be with them, and be their God" (Rev. 21:3). But while the "formula" of the covenant remains the same from age to age, it is capable of being filled with

---

[55]   Cf. Ex. 29:45; Jer. 7:23; 30:22; Ezek. 11:20; Hos. 2:23; Zech. 8:8; 13:9.

[56]   Note the plural (Gk. λαοί); for in the event the new covenant is not restricted to Israel and Judah.

fresh meaning to a point where it can be described as a *new* covenant. "I will be your God" acquires fuller meaning with every further revelation of the character of God; "you shall be my people" acquires deeper significance as the will of God for His people is more completely known.

(b) The knowledge of God as a matter of personal experience is evidently regarded in Jeremiah's oracle as something beyond what the old covenant provided. There was a sense in which the people of Israel knew their God, because He had revealed Himself to them, by contrast with the nations that did not know Him; but even Israel tended to forget Him.[57] Thus, when the generation that entered Canaan under Joshua died out, "there arose another generation after them, that knew not Jehovah, nor yet the work which he had wrought for Israel" (Judg. 2:10). At a later date, the prophet Hosea lamented the fact that there was no "knowledge of God in the land" of Israel and that disaster was fast overtaking the people on this account (Hos. 4:1, 6); "knowledge of God", which was closely coupled with covenant-loyalty, was the one thing needful, more desirable in God's sight than the costliest burnt-offerings (Hos. 6:6). Jeremiah himself, in his tribute to King Josiah as one who did "justice and righteousness" and "judged the cause of the poor and needy", equates such behavior with the knowledge of God (Jer. 22:15f.); Josiah was a king, that is to say, who was mindful of his covenanted obligations. But now it is not simply a national acknowledgement of God and His covenant that is envisaged, nor yet such acknowledgment on the part of those in positions of high responsibility. It is a personal knowledge of God such as marked Jeremiah himself, a personal knowledge of God to be possessed by each individual member of the covenant community, because of the new heart received by each. Such knowledge of Him by whom they are known,[58] increasing until it attains its consummation in knowing even as

---

[57] In the Old Testament knowledge of God frequently connotes acknowledgment of His holiness and obedience to His will. When it is said (I Sam. 3:7) that "Samuel did not yet know Jehovah", the reason simply is that He had not revealed Himself to Samuel; but when it is said (I Sam. 2:12) that the sons of Eli "knew not Jehovah", it is a reflection on their character and conduct.

[58] *Cf.* Gal. 4:9 ("now that ye have come to know God, or rather to be known by God"); I Cor. 8:3 ("but if any man loveth God, the same is known by him").

they are known,[59] is of the essence of that "perfection" to which our author invites his readers to press forward.

(c)   The blotting out of His people's sins is essential to this new relationship into which God calls them with Himself.[60]   This indeed was not a novel idea when Jeremiah proclaimed it: the God of Israel was incomparably a pardoning God, passing over transgression, unwilling to retain His anger, delighting in loving-kindness, treading His people's iniquities underfoot, casting all their sins into the depths of the sea.[61]   These are the words of Micah, a century and more before the time of Jeremiah; but the idea was not original with Micah.   When the God of Israel proclaimed His "name" in the ears of Moses, this note of forgiveness was emphasized, alongside the note of retribution for the impenitent: "Jehovah, a God merciful and gracious, slow to anger, and abundant in lovingkindness and truth; keeping lovingkindness for thousands, forgiving iniquity and transgression and sin; and that will by no means clear the guilty, visiting the iniquity of the fathers upon the children, and upon the children's children, upon the third and upon the fourth generation" (Ex. 34:6f.).   But now the assurance of forgiveness of sins is written into the very terms of the covenant in the most unqualified fashion: "I will forgive their iniquity, and their sin will I remember no more."   For the Hebrew, "remembering" was more than a mental effort; it carried with it the thought of doing something to the advantage, or disadvantage, of the person remembered.   When Cornelius's prayers and alms ascended as a memorial before God, God took action to Cornelius's advantage and sent His servant to him with a message which brought salvation to him and his household (Acts 10:4, 31; 11:13f.).   When, on the other hand, "Babylon the great was remembered in the sight of God", it was "to give unto her the cup of the wine of the fierceness of his wrath" (Rev. 16:19).   If men's sins are remembered by God, His holiness must take action against them; if they are not remembered, it is because His grace has determined to forgive them—not in spite of His holiness, but in harmony with it.   Under the old sacrificial system, there was "a remembrance made of sins year by year" (Ch. 10:3); if no such

---

[59]   *Cf.* I Cor. 13:12.
[60]   *Cf.* Isa. 43:25; 44:22.
[61]   Mic. 7:18f.

remembrance of sins is made under the new covenant, it is because of a sacrifice offered up once for all (Ch. 7:27).

Here, then, are the "better promises" on which the new covenant is established: *(a)* "I will put my laws into their mind"; *(b)* "all shall know me"; *(c)* "their sins will I remember no more". The covenant at Sinai involved divine promises, but not promises like these. The fulfilment of such promises gives a new meaning to the ancient covenant-words: "I will be to them a God, and they shall be to me a people." It has, indeed, been maintained more than once that the covenant concept, with its suggestion of a contractual obligation, is inadequate to convey the religious relationship subsisting between God and His people.[62] This, however, is to concentrate on the form to the exclusion of the substance. It is true, no doubt, that so far as its form is concerned the early biblical covenant has closest affinities with the treaties which bound vassal-states to their imperial overlords in the second millennium B.C. But it makes all the difference in the world to the substance of the covenant when it is God who takes the initiative in His grace, bestowing His promises freely on those whom He has called to be His people, and binding them to Himself with bands of love. When analogies are drawn from human life to illustrate God's covenant with men, it is from the family circle and not from the field of international politics that they are drawn —from the relation between husband and wife, or that between a father and his children.[63]

We know of at least one community of Israelites which, in the second century B.C., endeavored to realize the promise of the new covenant. The members of the Qumran community are described as "entering the new covenant in the land of Damas-

---

[62]   The fact is, Jeremiah's prophecy and the New Testament fulfilment give a new depth of meaning to the old term "covenant". In any case, the biblical covenant is much more than "a compact between God and man" (Skinner, *op. cit.*, p. 333); it is not a συνθήκη, an agreement between parties who are more or less equal in status, but a διαθήκη, a settlement by a superior on inferiors, "tendered on the one hand for acceptance on the other" (E. K. Simpson, *EQ* xviii [1946], p. 189). See further on Ch. 9:15ff. (pp. 210ff. with nn. 114–133).

[63]   Perhaps both these analogies are present in Jer. 31:32 (MT); "in the day that I took them by the hand" may suggest a father leading his children (*cf.* Hos. 11:1, 3f.); "although I was a husband unto them" suggests the marriage relationship (*cf.* Jer. 2:2; Hos. 2:7, 14ff.).

cus"[64]—the "land of Damascus" being probably their wilderness retreat on the shores of the Dead Sea.[65] They were to constitute "a holy house for Israel, a most holy assembly for Aaron ... the foundation of a holy spirit according to eternal truth, to make atonement for the guilt of rebellion and for sinful disloyalty, and to obtain favor for the land apart from the flesh of burnt-offerings and the fat of sacrifice".[66] But our author would not have recognized in this community the fulfilment of Jeremiah's oracle. The men of Qumran might regard their obedience and endurance as an acceptable substitute for the sacrificial ritual while the temple and its services were polluted by an unworthy priesthood; but they looked forward to a new age which would revive the highest ideals of the old age; they looked forward to a renovated temple which would still be a temple made with hands, to a pure sacrificial worship which would still involve the slaughter of bulls and goats, to a worthy priesthood which would still be confined to the sons of Aaron. To our author, the new covenant involves the abolition[67] of the old sacrificial order because of a perfect and unrepeatable sacrifice, and a high-priestly ministry discharged in the heavenly, no longer in an earthly, sanctuary on the basis of that sacrifice by a priest of a different line from Aaron's. True worship, "in spirit and in truth",[68] is thus released from dependence on the externalities of religion.

When Jesus, on the night in which He was betrayed, gave His disciples the cup and said, "This is my blood of the covenant, shed for many"[69] (Mark 14:24, NEB), the paschal context of the

---

[64]   C D vi. 19, viii. 21; *cf.* xx. 12.

[65]   *Cf.* R. North, "The Damascus of Qumran Geography", *PEQ* lxxxvii (1955), pp. 34ff.

[66]   1QS viii. 5f., ix. 3f. (for the former context see also p. 58, n. 18; for the latter context see also pp. 405ff.).

[67]   This is the plain force of the words παλαιόω and ἀφανισμός in verse 13. Tyndale does not go beyond the due sense of the former word in his rendering: "In that he sayth a new testament he hath abrogat the olde." The latter word (with the verb ἀφανίζω) is used in classical Greek of legislation which becomes inoperative because it is no longer relevant to the changed circumstances.

[68]   John 4:23f., another passage where worship is liberated from external restrictions of time and place.

[69]   Matt. 26:28 adds "unto remission of sins". Neither Matthew nor Mark (according to the most probable reading) records the adjective "new" before "covenant" in this word of institution, as is done by Paul (I Cor. 11:25) and the longer text of Luke (Luke 22:20); but the new covenant is intended, whether

incident would surely have made them link His words with "the blood of the covenant" which God established with His people Israel in the days of Moses on the basis of the Ten Commandments (Ex. 24:8). Nor can we doubt that His intention was to announce that now at length that earlier covenant was to be replaced by the "new covenant" foretold by Jeremiah midway between Moses' day and His own.[70] Whether, in fact, the sacrifice of Jesus has had the effect which Jeremiah said the new covenant would have, let those tell who have proved its saving power. Or let one tell for all: "What the law could never do, because our lower nature robbed it of all potency, God has done: by sending his own Son in a form like that of our own sinful nature, and as a sacrifice for sin, he has passed judgment against sin within that very nature, so that the commandment of the law may find fulfilment in us, whose conduct, no longer under the control of our lower nature, is directed by the Spirit" (Rom. 8:3f., NEB).[71]

In Jeremiah's oracle the new covenant is to be made "with the house of Israel and with the house of Judah". In the New Testament fulfilment it is not confined to them, but extends to all believers of every nation—and indeed, in the Old Testament itself indications are not lacking that it was to have this all-embracing character.[72] Whether Jeremiah consciously envisaged the wider extension of the new covenant or not, its wider extension is really implicit in his prophecy: national origin and racial descent must also be included among those externalities from whose control

---

"new" is expressed or only implied. The phrase "for many" may echo Isa. 53:11f. (cf. the phrase "a covenant of the people" in association with the first and second Servant Songs, Isa. 42:6; 49:8); J. Jeremias (*The Eucharistic Words of Jesus* [Oxford, 1955], p. 151) interprets the phrase as meaning "for the whole world", Gentiles as well as the house of Israel (cf. John 6:51; I John 2:2). Cf. also H. Kosmala, *Hebräer-Essener-Christen* (Leiden, 1959), pp. 174ff.

[70] Cf. G. A. Smith, *op. cit.*, p. 380.

[71] On this passage see J. Murray, *The Epistle to the Romans*, NICNT, i (Grand Rapids, 1959), pp. 277ff.

[72] Thus in Isa. 42:6 the Servant is given not only "for a covenant of the people" but also "for a light of the Gentiles" (cf. Isa. 49:6). See also the catena of Old Testament passages in Rom. 15:9ff. in which Paul finds the Gentile mission adumbrated; and, perhaps most impressive of all, Isa. 19:24f.: "In that day shall Israel be the third with Egypt and with Assyria, a blessing in the midst of the earth; for that Jehovah of hosts hath blessed them, saying, Blessed be Egypt my people, and Assyria the work of my hands, and Israel mine inheritance."

true religion is released by the new covenant. "It is one thing to say that Jeremiah was not given to see what the new covenant would mean for the world, it is entirely another to say that by Israel and Judah he really meant the Church.... On the other hand, we must not fall into the opposite error of supposing that the new covenant will mean something else for 'all Israel' than it does for the Church, that saved Israel will be saved in some other way than is the Church. God does not abolish physical Israel, but in saving it transcends it, just as He does not scrap this earth but renews it."[73]

13 The very words "a new covenant" antiquate the previous one. In saying this our author does not go beyond Jeremiah, who explicitly contrasts the new covenant of the future with the covenant made at the time of Exodus, and implies that when it comes, the new covenant will supersede that earlier one. The moral of the situation had been appreciated already by Paul, who speaks of himself and his colleagues as "ministers of a new covenant; not of the letter, but of the spirit"; and by contrast with this new covenant refers to that associated with Moses as "the old covenant" (II Cor. 3:6, 14).[74] And if the covenant of Moses' day is antiquated, our author further implies, so must be the Aaronic priesthood, the earthly sanctuary, and the Levitical sacrifices, which were all established under that covenant. The age of the law and the prophets is past; the age of the Son is here, and here to stay.

But, our author goes on, if the earlier covenant, with all that accompanied it, is antiquated, it is ready to vanish away: "anything that is growing old and ageing will shortly disappear" (NEB). It cannot be proved from these words that the Jerusalem temple was still standing and its sacrificial ritual still being carried on. They could simply mean that by predicting the inauguration of a new covenant Jeremiah in effect announced the impending dissolution of the old order. They do indeed have that meaning. But if in fact the Jerusalem temple was still standing, if the priests of Aaron's line were still discharging their sacrificial duties there, then our author's words would be all the more telling. Jesus,[75] and

---

[73]   H. L. Ellison, *Men Spake from God* (London, 1958), p. 92.
[74]   See P. E. Hughes, *Paul's Second Epistle to the Corinthians*, NICNT (Grand Rapids, 1962), pp. 93ff.
[75]   *Cf.* Mark 13:2; John 2:19.

shortly after Him Stephen,[76] had foretold the downfall of the temple. Thirty years, more or less, had elapsed since then, and it might have been thought that the event had belied their prediction. But now that prediction is taken up by another Christian, who in many respects stands within the tradition of Stephen,[77] and shown to be logically involved in Old Testament prophecy. If the end of the temple and its ministry had been imminent thirty years before, it was the more imminent now that the forty years of probation[78] were more than three-quarters of the way towards their end.

---

[76] *Cf.* Acts 6:14.

[77] *Cf.* W. Manson, *op. cit.*, pp. 25ff.

[78] See p. 65 (on Ch. 3:9). [On the two covenants see most recently J. de Vuyst, *Oud en Nieuw Verbond in de Brief aan de Hebreeën* (Kampen, 1964).]

CHAPTER IX

3. THE SANCTUARY UNDER THE OLD COVENANT

Ch. 9:1–5

1 Now even the first *covenant* had ordinances[1] of divine service,[2] and its sanctuary, *a sanctuary* of this world.[3]

2 For there was a tabernacle prepared, the first, wherein *were* the candlestick,[4] and the table, and the showbread;[5] which is called the Holy place.[6]

3 And after the second veil, the tabernacle which is called the Holy of holies;[7]

4 having a golden altar of incense, and the ark of the covenant overlaid round about with gold, wherein *was* a golden pot holding the manna, and Aaron's rod that budded, and the tables of the covenant;

---

[1] Gk. δικαιώματα (*cf.* v. 10), "regulations".

[2] "Divine service" represents the single Greek word λατρεία (*cf.* the cognate verb λατρεύω in Ch. 8:5).

[3] Gk. τό τε ἅγιον κοσμικόν, where κοσμικός means "mundane" or "material" (the temptation to render it "cosmic" and relate it to the cosmological symbolism referred to on p. 166, n. 30, should be resisted). The only other NT occurrence of κοσμικός is in Tit. 2:12, of "worldly lusts". Both ἅγιον and κοσμικόν are adjectives in the neuter gender, but here one of them must be taken as filling the rôle of a substantive qualified by the other. By general agreement ἅγιον is taken as the substantive here, qualified by κοσμικόν, although elsewhere in this epistle it is not the neuter singular ἅγιον but the neuter plural ἅγια that is used in the sense of "sanctuary" or "holy place". In a letter dated March 19, 1959, Dr. B. F. C. Atkinson makes the interesting suggestion that τό τε ἅγιον κοσμικόν might mean "and the holy ritual". "It seems to me," he writes, "(i) to fit the immediate context much better, (ii) to agree better with the order of words, (iii) that κοσμικόν is not the right word to use for *earthly*."

[4] Gk. λυχνία, "lampstand" (so LXX for Heb. *menōrāh*).

[5] Cod. B and the Sahidic Coptic version insert here "and the golden incense-altar" (transposing it from v. 4).

[6] Gk. ἅγια (neuter plural, as is plain from the reading of B, τὰ ἅγια). Elsewhere in the epistle the simple ἅγια is used for the holy of holies on earth and for its heavenly prototype.

[7] Gk. ἅγια ἁγίων (both neuter plural). אᶜBDᶜKL read τὰ ἅγια τῶν ἁγίων. P⁴⁶ has ἅγια here and ἅγια ἁγίων in v. 2! This points to some primitive disturbance of the text.

5   and above it cherubim[8] of glory overshadowing the mercy-seat; of which things we cannot now speak severally.[9]

1 The inadequacy of the old order as compared with the new is now set forth with reference first to the arrangements of the sanctuary under the old covenant and then to the sacrificial ritual associated with that sanctuary. Provision was made under the old covenant for the people of God to worship Him, but the sanctuary erected for this worship was a material one. The particular sanctuary which our author has in mind is plainly the wilderness tent described in detail in the book of Exodus. The fact that he makes the tent the basis of his argument here and not the Jerusalem temple may suggest that neither he nor his readers belonged to Jerusalem, but it cannot be treated as proof of this. Neither can it be treated as proof that the temple was no longer standing, nor yet that the readers were not Jews at all. What it does prove is that our author's argument is biblical through and through. Even Solomon's temple is not so apposite to his purpose as the Mosaic tabernacle, which is introduced (in Ex. 25:1ff.) immediately after the inauguration of the covenant (Ex. 24). It is not suggested here, as it is in Stephen's speech (Acts 7:44ff.), that the mobile tabernacle of the wilderness wanderings was a more suitable shrine for a pilgrim people than the permanent house which Solomon built.[10] Our author's point is different: the sanctuary of the old covenant, in its very furnishings and sacrificial arrangements, proclaimed its own temporary character; and while this is shown with more special reference to the tabernacle, the principle holds good equally for the temple, whether Solomon's or Herod's.

2 The wilderness tent-shrine consisted of the court, the outer compartment, and the inner compartment. Although the successive temples which superseded it were much more elaborate, they preserved the same ground plan; the courts might be multiplied in number, but the holy house itself, standing towards the west side of the inmost court, consisted of the two essential compartments—the outer ("the holy place") and the inner ("the holy of holies"). Here each of the compartments of the wilderness

---

[8]   The Hebrew plural -*īm* is preserved in the Greek transliteration χερουβειν.
[9]   Gk. κατὰ μέρος (RSV "in detail").
[10] *Cf. Acts*, NICNT (Grand Rapids, 1954), pp. 156ff.

sanctuary is called a "tent" or "tabernacle". The outer compartment was twenty cubits long, (approximately) ten cubits wide, and ten cubits high; here it is described simply in terms of its furniture. The "candlestick" (AV, ARV) or, better, the "lampstand" (RSV, NEB) was placed at the south side of the holy place; it was made of gold, with three branches springing from either side of the main stem; the main stem and all six branches each supported a flower-shaped lamp-holder (Ex. 25:31ff.; 37:17ff.). The seven-branched lampstands of the later sanctuaries appear to have been more elaborate than that prescribed for the wilderness tabernacle; some idea of their appearance may be obtained from representations on Hasmonaean coins and in a well-known relief on the Arch of Titus in Rome.[11] "The table, and the showbread" (a hendiadys for "the table of showbread") stood on the north side of the holy place. The table was made of acacia wood overlaid with gold; it was two cubits long, one cubit broad, and one and a half cubits high, and was equipped with golden plates, spoons, flagons and bowls (Ex. 25:23ff.; 37:10ff.). The "showbread" (literally, "the setting forth of the loaves")[12] consisted of twelve cakes, baked of choice flour, placed fresh upon the table every sabbath day (Lev. 24:5-8); the old cakes, which were removed when the new cakes were placed on the table, became the perquisite of the priests, who ate them in the holy place; no layman might eat them, because they were "most holy" (Lev. 24:9).[13]

3 At the west end of the holy place hung a curtain of em-

[11] The seven-branched *menorah* on the Arch of Titus has been adopted as the coat of arms of the modern State of Israel. The appearance of non-Jewish figures in relief on the base of this *menorah* has occasioned some doubt as to its identity with the lampstand that stood in the temple; see, however, M. Kon, "The Menorah of the Arch of Titus", *PEQ* lxxxii (1950), pp. 25ff. *Cf.* also E. R. Goodenough, "The Menorah among Jews in the Roman World", *HUCA* xxiii. 2 (1950–51), pp. 449ff. See p. 224, n. 175.

[12] Gk. ἡ πρόθεσις τῶν ἄρτων, a transposition of the LXX οἱ ἄρτοι τῆς προθέσεως ("the loaves of proposition", in the literal rendering of the Douay Bible in Ex. 25:30, etc.). The Hebrew expression is *leḥem happānim*, "bread of the face", *i.e.* bread set before the face or presence of God (Ex. 25:30; 35:13; 39:36, etc.), or *leḥem hammaʿarekheth*, literally "bread of setting in order" (I Chron. 9:32, etc.).

[13] *Cf.* I Sam. 21:1-6, where the priest of Nob gave David and his companions "holy bread" to eat; "for there was no bread there but the showbread, that was taken from before Jehovah, to put hot bread in the day when it was taken away" (with our Lord's reference to this incident in Mark 2:25f.).

broidered linen, suspended under the clasps which coupled together the two sets of linen curtains draped over the tabernacle framework (Ex. 26:31ff.; 36:35f.). This curtain (Hebrew *pārōkheth*) is here called "the second veil"[14] to distinguish it from the linen screen through which one entered from the court into the holy place (Ex. 26:36f.; 36:37f.). Beyond "the second veil" lay the inner compartment, the "holy of holies", which formed a cube on a side of 10 cubits.

4 Two pieces of furniture are mentioned in connection with the holy of holies: the golden incense-altar and the ark of the covenant.

The mention of the incense-altar raises two questions: *(a)* whether the reference actually is to the incense-altar and not rather to a "censer" (AV) or incense-shovel; *(b)* if the incense-altar is meant, how this statement relates to the Old Testament indications that the incense-altar stood in the holy place, not in the holy of holies.

(a) The Greek word *thymiatērion*, which our author employs here, is used in the Septuagint with the meaning "censer" but never with the meaning "incense-altar".[15] This fact, however, is not decisive for its meaning here. The word in itself simply means "a place where incense is put" or "a vessel for burning incense" and was used not only in the sense of "censer", but also in the

---

[14] Gk. τὸ δεύτερον καταπέτασμα. In LXX καταπέτασμα is also used for the screen at the entrance into the holy place (Ex. 26:37; 37:5 [corresponding to 36:37 of MT and ARV], etc., although in Ex. 26:36 another Greek word, ἐπίσπαστρον, is used); hence our author distinguishes the curtain at the entrance into the holy of holies as "the second veil". Two distinct words are used in Hebrew; whereas "the second veil" is the *pārōkheth*, the screen at the outer entrance is a *māsākh*. Philo distinguishes the two by reserving καταπέτασμα for the inner veil and calling the outer screen a κάλυμμα (*Life of Moses*, ii. 101). The Mishnah tractate *Yoma* (v. 1) records a dispute between rabbis on the nature of the inner veil in the Second Temple: whereas one school of thought held that it was a single curtain (which is in agreement with such historical evidence as we have), another held that it was double, the two curtains of which it was composed being a cubit apart. *Cf.* the excursus by H. Laible in Strack-Billerbeck iii (Munich, 1926), pp. 733ff. See also p. 246, n. 87.

[15] It appears three times in LXX: in II Chron. 26:19 and Ezek. 8:11 it represents Heb. *miqṭereth* ("censer"); and in IV Macc. 7:11, where Aaron is described as being "equipped with a θυμιατήριον", the word plainly has the same sense. But Theodotion and Symmachus use it in Ex. 30:1 of the incense-altar (Heb. *mizbēaḥ miqṭar qeṭōreth*).

general sense of "incense-altar"[16] and more particularly, by Philo[17] and Josephus,[18] of the incense-altar in the Israelite tabernacle or temple. We should expect some reference to the incense-altar here, along with the references to other articles of tabernacle furniture; there is no reason to expect a reference to a censer, since there is no mention of such an instrument in all the prescriptions for the construction and furnishing of the tabernacle in Ex. 25:1–31:11 or 35:1–40:33.[19] There was only one incense-altar, but there were several censers; and though it might be argued that the special reference here is to Aaron's censer, which he used on the Day of Atonement (Lev. 16:12; *cf.* Num. 16:46), this censer was scarcely distinctive enough to be mentioned separately; further, we are not told where it was kept, but since Aaron used it to carry fire into the holy of holies, to burn incense on it there, it is unlikely that it was kept in the holy of holies.[20] On the whole, it is more probable that ARV is right (with RSV and NEB) in preferring "altar of incense" as the rendering here to "censer" of AV and ERV text.[21]

(b) If that is so, the question of the location of the incense-altar arises. According to Ex. 30:6, it was to be put "before the veil that is by the ark of the testimony, before the mercy-seat that is over the testimony".[22] This does not make it altogether clear on which side of the veil dividing the holy place from the holy of

---

[16] *Cf.* Herodotus, *Hist.* ii. 162; Aelian, *Varia Historia* xii. 51.

[17] *Who is Heir of Divine Things?* 226f.; *Life of Moses* ii. 94, 101 (in reference each time to the incense-altar in the Mosaic tabernacle).

[18] *War* v. 218; *Ant.* iii. 147, 198 (the former reference being to the incense-altar in the temple that fell in A.D. 70, the two latter references to the one in the Mosaic tabernacle).

[19] The "firepans" of Ex. 27:3; 38:3, while designated by a Hebrew word (*maḥtāh*, LXX πυρεῖον) which can also denote a censer (as in Lev. 10:1; 16:12), were not censers but utensils belonging to the altar of burnt-offering in the tabernacle court.

[20] According to TB *Yoma* 47a, the "censer heaped with incense" (*maḥtāh gedūshāh shel qeṭōreth*) was brought to the high priest on the Day of Atonement "out of the chamber in the house of Abtinas (Euthinos)".

[21] Its interpretation as "altar of incense" certainly underlies its transposition in Cod. B and the Sahidic version to verse 2, among the furnishings of the holy place. In the one place in NT where a "censer" is unambiguously mentioned (Rev. 8:3–5) the Greek term used is λιβανωτός.

[22] The words "before the mercy-seat that is over the testimony" are absent from LXX and the Samaritan Bible. In the Samaritan Bible, indeed, the whole section dealing with the incense-altar, Ex. 30:1–10, comes between verses 35

holies the incense-altar stood, but the phrase "before the veil" does rather suggest that it stood in the holy place, not in the holy of holies.[23] This is confirmed by Lev. 16:18, where Aaron on the Day of Atonement is directed, after discharging his ministry in the holy of holies, to "go out unto the altar that is before Jehovah[24] [*i.e.* the incense-altar], and make atonement for it". On the other hand, the incense-altar in Solomon's temple is described as "the whole altar that belonged to the inner sanctuary" (I Kings 6:22, RSV).[25] It smacks of special pleading to argue that our author does not say that the incense-altar was situated *in* the holy of holies, but only speaks of the holy of holies as "*having* a golden altar of incense".[26] The participle "having" should naturally mean the same thing with reference to the incense-altar as with reference to the ark of the covenant. There was, however, a special connection between the incense-altar and the holy of holies, no matter on which side of the veil the altar stood; on the

---

and 36 of Ex. 26. P. E. Kahle has suggested that our author used a text of LXX which had the same order as the Samaritan Bible, and that this explains his assigning the incense-altar to the holy of holies (*The Cairo Geniza*[1] [London, 1947], pp. 146f.). It is true that in this order the incense-altar is brought into closer association with the inner veil and the ark (for which directions are given in Ex. 26:31–34), but even so it is separated from them by Ex. 26:35, in which directions are given for the placing of the table and lampstand in the outer sanctuary.

[23] On the other hand, it does suggest that the incense-altar stood near the veil, whereas in the Second Temple it apparently was nearer the outer screen, since we are told that it was the first piece of furniture on which the priest came when he entered the holy place, before he came to the lampstand (TB *Yoma*, 33*a*). Josephus, in his description of the Mosaic tabernacle, says that the incense-altar stood between the lampstand and the table of showbread (*Ant.* iii. 147); both in this description and in his description of the Second Temple (*War* v. 216) he makes it clear that the incense-altar stood in the holy place.

[24] The Samaritan Bible adds "before Jehovah" in Ex. 40:27, where incense is burned on this altar for the first time.

[25] This verse is absent from LXX. In II Baruch 6:7 the incense-altar is included among the objects removed by an angel from the *holy of holies* before the destruction of Solomon's temple by the Chaldaeans. In a Canaanite temple of the Mosaic period excavated at Hazor the incense-altar was in the *debīr* or "holy of holies". In Rev. 8:3 the golden altar from which the prayers of the saints ascend as incense is "before the throne"; but there is no inner veil separating two compartments in the heavenly sanctuary as portrayed in Revelation.

[26] *Cf.* A. S. Peake, *The Epistle to the Hebrews*, Century Bible (Edinburgh and London, 1902), p. 175.

one day in the year when the holy of holies was entered the incense-altar played a significant part; not only was the holy of holies never entered without incense from the incense-altar (Lev. 16:12f.), but the blood of the sin-offering on the Day of Atonement was sprinkled on the horns of the incense-altar as well as on the mercy-seat (Ex. 30:10; Lev. 16:15).[27]

In any case, our author does not stay to answer the questions which his passing reference to the incense-altar may raise in his readers' minds; this is not the feature of the tabernacle to which he wishes to draw their attention more particularly, any more than the contents of the ark of the covenant, which he also passes over quickly.

The ark of the covenant was the principal, if not the only, article of furniture in the holy of holies in the tabernacle and in Solomon's temple. No more is heard of it after the destruction of the first temple by the Chaldaeans in 587 B.C. (although legend is more than willing to supply the lack of historical evidence);[28] it was not replaced in the post-exilic temple, in which the holy of

---

[27] Speculations on whether the directions about the incense-altar may have been a later addition to the description of the tabernacle in Exodus are irrelevant to the exegesis of this epistle, together with all other questions concerning the composition of the Pentateuch. The Pentateuch as our author knew it had the same contents as the Pentateuch known to us, although it was probably arranged in the LXX order (which in Ex. 35-40 particularly differs from the order of MT). See D. W. Gooding, *The Account of the Tabernacle: Translation and Textual Problems of the Greek Exodus* (Cambridge, 1959); also the same writer's article "Tabernacle" in *NBD*.

[28] *Cf.* the passage from II Baruch referred to in n. 25 above, where the ark and the veil, with other objects belonging to the holy of holies, are removed by an angel. According to Tosefta *Yoma* iii. 7 (*cf.* TB *Yoma* 52b; TJ *Soṭa* iii. 22c, 6), the ark and the objects which accompanied it in the holy of holies (*cf.* p. 189, n. 37) were hidden at that time (since the pot of manna was one of these objects, the "hidden manna" of Rev. 2:17 may be recalled here); according to *Mekhilta* 59b (on Ex. 16:33), Elijah will bring them to light when he comes. In II Macc. 2:4-8 Jeremiah is said to have hidden "the tent and the ark and the altar of incense" in a cave in "the mountain where Moses had gone up and had seen the inheritance of God"; they will be revealed again by God when He "gathers his people together again and shows his mercy". In Samaritan tradition the ark and the holy vessels of the tabernacle were hidden on Mount Gerizim at the beginning of the epoch of divine displeasure (*fanuta*); they will be restored by the Taheb, the Prophet like Moses (Deut. 18:15ff.), when he comes to inaugurate the new epoch of divine favor (*rahuta*). This belief was held by them in NT times, as is clear from the incident recorded in Josephus, *Ant.* xviii. 85-87.

holies was completely empty, as Pompey found to his surprise when he insisted on forcing his way into it in 63 B.C.[29] The ark was a box of acacia wood plated with gold; it was called "the ark of the covenant" or "the ark of the testimony" (Ex. 25:22, etc.) because the covenant-terms, engraved on two stone tablets, were placed inside it (Ex. 25:16, 21).[30] When, at a later time, it was placed in the holy of holies in Solomon's temple, "there was nothing in the ark save the two tables of stone which Moses put there at Horeb, when Jehovah made a covenant with the children of Israel, when they came out of the land of Egypt" (I Kings 8:9). "The very terms of this statement," according to Franz Delitzsch, "may almost seem to imply that other things had been there formerly."[31] By the "other things" he means more particularly the pot of manna and Aaron's rod, which the Old Testament does not place inside the ark. According to Ex. 16:33f. Moses commanded Aaron to put an omer of manna (about four pints, one-tenth of an ephah) in a pot,[32] "and lay it up before Jehovah, to be kept throughout your generations"; and Aaron accordingly "laid it up before the Testimony, to be kept". Similarly, when twelve rods or sceptres, one for each tribe of Israel, had been laid up "in the tent of meeting before the testimony", Aaron's rod, the rod of the tribe of Levi, was found next day to have put forth buds, blossoms and ripe almonds—a token that Aaron was the man whom God had chosen for the priesthood (Num. 17:1ff.). Moses was then directed to "put back the rod of Aaron before the testimony, to be kept for a token against the children of rebellion" (Num. 17:10).[33] Does the phrase "before the testimony" imply

[29] Cf. Josephus, War i. 152f.; Ant. xiv. 71f.; Tacitus, Hist. v. 9; Ps. Sol. 2:1ff., 30f. In the post-exilic holy of holies the position of the ark was marked by a slab called "the stone of foundation" (Heb. 'eben shattiyyāh).

[30] Cf. Deut. 10:1–5; these tablets were the two which replaced those previously broken by Moses at the foot of Mount Sinai (Ex. 32:19). Cf. M. G. Kline, Treaty of the Great King (Grand Rapids, 1963), pp. 13ff.

[31] Commentary on the Epistle to the Hebrews ii (Eng. trans., Edinburgh, 1862), p. 57.

[32] Heb. ṣinṣeneth ("receptacle"), Gk. στάμνος ("jar", especially for racking off wine). This jar or "urn" (RSV) is said to have been of gold in LXX (followed by Philo, Preliminary Studies, 100), but not in MT.

[33] This incident belongs to the sequence of lessons prescribed for the season of Pentecost in the third year of the triennial synagogue lectionary (cf. A. E. Guilding, The Fourth Gospel and Jewish Worship [Oxford, 1960], p. 224; see p. xlviii above).

that these objects were placed inside the ark, or simply that they were laid in front of it? Delitzsch thinks that the former "is a natural conclusion" from the phrases "before Jehovah" and "before the testimony";[34] this is by no means clear, especially as regards the phrase "before Jehovah", for this phrase is used of other installations in the tabernacle, which were certainly not inside the ark.[35] On the other hand, it will not do to say that the antecedent of "wherein" is not "the ark" but "the tabernacle which is called the Holy of holies" (verse 3);[36] this puts an intolerable strain on the natural construction of the sentence by the distance which it places between the relative and its antecedent. It is not to be doubted that our author represents the pot of manna and the rod as having been inside the ark along with the tables of the law. Since the Old Testament has nothing to say of the pot of manna outside Ex. 16:33f., and nothing to say of Aaron's rod after it was used to strike the rock in Kadesh (Num. 20:8–11), it is open to anyone to surmise that, even if they were not originally in the ark, they were put there subsequently for safe keeping, and to surmise further that they were lost when the ark was captured by the Philistines (I Sam. 4:11ff.).[37] But this would simply be calling upon imagination to take the place of evidence, and on a par with rabbinical speculation about the disappearance of the ark and the objects which accompanied it when the first temple fell.

5 The lid of the ark was a golden slab called the mercy-seat

---

[34] *Op. cit.*, p. 57.

[35] For example, it is used of the incense-altar in Lev. 16:18 (see p. 186).

[36] *Cf.* G. H. Lang, *The Epistle to the Hebrews* (London, 1951), p. 144.

[37] *Cf.* J. O. Boyd, "What was in the Ark?" *EQ* xi (1939), pp. 165ff. Rabbinical tradition placed *in* the ark (in addition to the two tablets of stone) two silver columns belonging to the tablets of stone, the fragments of the original tablets of stone which Moses broke at the foot of Sinai, a copy of the Torah, and the names of God (TB *Baba Bathra* 14a). (The tradition about the copy of the Torah probably goes back to Deut. 31:26, where the Levites are commanded by Moses to "take this book of the law, and put it by the side of the ark of the covenant of Jehovah". *Cf.* CD v. 2, which speaks of "the sealed book of the law" as being "in the ark".) But in rabbinical tradition the pot of manna and Aaron's rod were not *in* the ark but stood beside it, along with the coffer of golden jewels which (according to I Sam. 6:4, 8, 11, 15) the Philistines sent as a guilt-offering along with the ark when they returned it to Israel (Tosefta *Yoma* iii. 7). On the general biblical significance of ark and sanctuary see G. von Rad, "Zelt und Lade", in *Gesammelte Studien zum Alten Testament* (Munich, 1958), pp. 109ff.

or place of propitiation,[38] viewed by our author as the earthly counterpart of the "throne of grace" to which he has already exhorted his readers to draw near for help in the hour of need (Ch. 4:16). It was given this name because of the part it played in the sacrificial ritual of the Day of Atonement; the blood both of the bullock which was offered to make atonement for the high priest and his family, and of the goat which was killed as a sin-offering for the whole nation, was sprinkled on the mercy-seat and in front of it, while the God of Israel undertook to "appear in the cloud upon the mercy-seat" (Lev. 16:2; *cf.* verses 14f.). The "cherubim of glory" were two gold figures of composite creatures which overshadowed the mercy-seat (Ex. 25:18–22; 37:7–9) and served to support the invisible presence of Israel's God, who accordingly is repeatedly described as the One "who sitteth above the cherubim" (I Sam. 4:4, etc.). It was because of this function that they were called "cherubim of glory"; the glory is the *shekhīnāh*, the radiant presence of God dwelling in the midst of His people.[39] Originally the cherubim appear to have symbolized the storm-winds,[40] on which the God of Israel was pictured as riding through the sky; thus in the theophany of Ps. 18:10 "he rode upon a cherub, and did fly; yea, he soared upon the wings of the wind" (*cf.* Deut. 33:26). Some idea of their composite character may be gained from Ezek. 10:10–14 (supplemented by 1:5–13), where they are portrayed as the supporters of the chariot-throne of God, which is not tied to His earthly shrine, but is capable of moving in any direction at will.[41] If it be asked why the golden

---

[38] Gk. ἱλαστήριον, so LXX for Heb. *kappōreth*. That Heb. *kappōreth* means more than "lid" or "cover", and is akin in sense to the Piʻel conjugation *kipper*, "make atonement", is suggested by the emphasis which is placed upon it (in its own right) in the ritual for the Day of Atonement (Lev. 16:2, 13ff.). *Cf.* Ch. 2:17 (p. 41, n. 57); Ch. 4:16 (pp. 86f.).

[39] *Cf.* Rom. 9:4 ("who are Israelites, whose is ... the glory").

[40] Later they appear to have symbolized, more generally, the powers of creation. According to Philo the two cherubim "are allegorical representations of the two most august and highest potencies of Him Who Is, the creative and the kingly" (*Life of Moses*, ii. 99; *cf. Questions and Answers on Exodus*, no. 62). In his treatise *On the Cherubim* (which deals mainly with the cherubim of Gen. 3:24) he suggests alternatively that the two cherubim represent "the outermost sphere of the fixed stars" and "the inner contained sphere" in which are set the seven planetary zones; or the two hemispheres (23–26).

[41] *Cf.* Ben Sira's encomium on Ezekiel (Sir. 49:8f.):
"It was Ezekiel who saw the vision of glory

cherubim did not come under the ban imposed by the Second Commandment on the making of images (as contrasted, for example, with the golden bull-calves of Dan and Bethel), the answer may lie in their symbolic nature;[42] they were not the "likeness of any thing that is in heaven above, or that is in the earth beneath, or that is in the water under the earth" (Ex. 20:4; cf. Deut. 5:8).[43]

What our author would have had to say about the parabolic significance of the cherubim and the other installations which he mentions we can only imagine; when he says that of these things "we cannot now speak severally" he leaves us with the impression that he could have enlarged at some length on their symbolism had he chosen so to do.[44] What he does proceed to enlarge upon is the use which was made of the ancient sanctuary on the annual Day of Atonement.

4. A TEMPORARY RITUAL

Ch. 9:6–10

6 Now these things having been thus prepared, the priests go in continually into the first tabernacle, accomplishing the services;[45]

7 but into the second the high priest alone, once in the year, not without blood, which he offereth for himself, and for the errors[46] of the people:

---

which God showed him above the chariot of the cherubim;
for God remembered his enemies with storm,
and did good to those who directed their ways aright."

[42] Moreover, the bull-calves were associated with the fertility cults of Israel's nearest neighbors.

[43] The much later golden cherubim from Herod's temple are said to have been exhibited on one of the gates of Antioch as trophies of the Roman triumph over Jerusalem; so John Malalas, *Chronographia*, book x. (*Cf.* W. L. Dulière, "Les Chérubins du troisième Temple à Antioche", *Zeitschrift für Religions- und Geistesgeschichte* xiii [1961], pp. 201ff.)

[44] Philo does enlarge on them in various places, and especially in his *Life of Moses*, ii. 71–108.

[45] Gk. λατρεία (as in v. 1, where the singular is translated "divine service"; cf. p. 181, n. 2).

[46] Gk. ἀγνοήματα, "sins of ignorance" (cf. Ch. 5:2, p. 91, nn. 15, 16). ARV margin compares Sir. 23:2, where Ben Sira prays not to be spared in his ἀγνοήματα, lest they be multiplied and be his undoing. At Qumran sins of inadvertence incurred penance, but deliberate sins excommunication (*cf.* 1QS ix. 1f.).

8 the Holy Spirit this signifying,[47] that the way into the holy place hath not yet been made manifest, while the first tabernacle is yet standing;[48]

9 which *is* a figure for the time present; according to which[49] are offered both gifts and sacrifices[50] that cannot, as touching the conscience, make the worshipper[51] perfect,

10 *being* only (with meats and drinks and divers washings) carnal ordinances,[52] imposed until a time of reformation.

6 In the tabernacle and in the temples which replaced it, the outer compartment, the holy place, was in continual use. Day by day, morning and evening, the appointed priests entered it to trim the lamps on the lampstand (Ex. 27:20f.) and at the same time to burn incense on the incense-altar (Ex. 30:7f.). The day on which the priest Zechariah was chosen by lot from among his fellow-priests of the course of Abijah to burn incense in the holy place (Luke 1:9ff.) would have been in any case the most outstanding day in the whole of his priestly career; but the angelic vision and annunciation granted to him beside the incense-altar made the occasion more notable still. Again, week by week the appointed priests entered the holy place to put fresh loaves on the table of showbread (Lev. 24:8f.). These were the principal "services" which were discharged in "the first tabernacle", and any member of the priesthood could discharge them.

7 But none except the high priest was permitted to enter "the second tabernacle", the holy of holies; and even he was permitted

---

[47] Gk. δηλοῦντος, "showing".

[48] Gk. ἐχούσης στάσιν, literally "having a standing", a literary phrase for "being in existence", or (more appropriately here) "retaining its status". It is not necessarily implied that the earthly sanctuary, as a material structure, no longer existed; what is implied is that, with Christ's passing "through the heavens" (Ch. 4:14) into the presence of God, the earthly structure has lost its sanctuary status.

[49] Gk. καθ' ἥν (the antecedent being σκηνῆς, "tabernacle"), for which later manuscripts (*e.g.* D^c K L P) and TR read καθ' ὅν, as though the antecedent were καιρόν, "time" (through failure to appreciate the parenthetical character of the clause "which is a figure for the time present").

[50] For this phrase *cf.* Chs. 5:1; 8:3 (see p. 89, n. 6).

[51] Gk. λατρεύω, as in Ch. 8:5 (see p. 166, n. 31); but there the subject is the priests, whereas here the ordinary worshipper is intended.

[52] Gk. δικαιώματα, as in v. 1.

to enter it only once a year, on the Day of Atonement, and the conditions of his entering it were strictly prescribed. These conditions are set out most fully in Lev. 16, where the holy of holies is called "the holy place within the veil" (verse 2). Aaron (and that means each successive high priest of Israel) might enter the holy of holies only on the tenth day of the seventh month (Tishri) in each year (around the time of the autumnal equinox). Attired not in his violet robe and its accessories,[53] but in vestments of white linen which were reserved for special sacrificial occasions,[54] he entered the holy of holies twice. On the first occasion he carried the blood of the bullock which had been sacrificed as a sin-offering for himself and his household,[55] and sprinkled it on the front of the mercy-seat and before the mercy-seat, which all the time was shrouded in the cloud arising from the incense which burned on the golden altar. Then, when a goat had been slaughtered as a sin-offering for the people at large, he brought its blood too into the holy of holies and sprinkled it on and before the mercy-seat. Having thus accomplished this part of the atoning ritual, he came out of the sanctuary and confessed the national sins over the head of the second goat, assigned by lot "to Azazel", which was then driven from the haunts of men into a "solitary land". In our author's typological application of the ritual of the Day of Atonement, however, no mention is made of this second goat;[56] he is concerned only with that part of the ritual which was associated with the sanctuary. And in this connection he emphasizes three

---

[53]   Ex. 28:31–35 (in the wider context of verses 2–38).

[54]   Ex. 28:39–43; Lev. 6:10; 16:4.

[55]   *Cf.* Chs. 5:3; 7:27.

[56]   And therefore it is no part of the exegesis of this epistle to investigate the origin and purpose of the setting aside of a "goat for Azazel" (AV "scapegoat", Lev. 16:8, 10, 26). In the *Epistle of Barnabas* (7:7–11) the scapegoat is treated as a type of Jesus bearing the curse and yet wearing the crown; Justin Martyr (*Dialogue with Trypho*, 40) regards the driving of the scapegoat into the wilderness as a type of the rejection of Jesus by the Jewish leaders. Some features of the scapegoat ceremony, especially the imposition of the high priest's hands on its head and the confession of the national sins over it, by which these sins were transferred to it (Lev. 16:21), have passed into the language of Christian devotion, as in Isaac Watts's lines:

"My faith would lay her hand
  On that dear head of Thine,
While like a penitent I stand
  And there confess my sin."

points: (i) except on this annual occasion, the way into the throne-room of God was barred for all Israelites, even for the high priest himself;[57] (ii) when the high priest did receive permission to enter, his entry was safeguarded by sacrificial blood; (iii) this sacrificial blood was not finally efficacious, for fresh blood had to be shed and a fresh entry made into the holy of holies year by year.

8 In the record of the tabernacle arrangements and the Levitical offerings the Holy Spirit has a lesson to teach, as in the other parts of Hebrew scripture. What lesson, then, does He teach in the prescriptions for the Day of Atonement? This, that throughout the age of the old covenant there was no direct access to God. "The way into the holy place" here means "the way into the holy of holies", which was barred by the inner veil. The use of "holy place" in the sense of "holy of holies" (recurring below in verses 12, 24, 25) is probably based on the similar usage of Lev. 16:2 (where ambiguity is excluded by the added words "within the veil, before the mercy-seat"), 3, 16, 17, 20, 23, 27.[58] It is further to be noted that, whereas hitherto our author has used "the first tabernacle" of the outer compartment of the sanctuary, here he uses it to mean

---

There is also the classic account of Charles Simeon's conversion in 1813, as told by himself, which has had such a profound influence ever since on the thought and language of Anglican evangelicalism: "But in Passion Week, as I was reading Bishop Wilson on the Lord's Supper, I met with an expression to this effect—'That the Jews knew what they did, when they transferred their sin to the head of their offering'. The thought came into my mind, What, may I transfer all my guilt to another? Has God provided an Offering for me, that I may lay my sins on His head? Then, God willing, I will not bear them on my own soul one moment longer. Accordingly I sought to lay my sins upon the sacred head of Jesus" (H. C. G. Moule, *Charles Simeon* [London, 1948], pp. 25f.). The relation of the scapegoat to the New Testament presentation of the atonement is discussed, among other questions of relevance to this section of Hebrews, by L. Morris in "The Day of Atonement and the Work of Christ", *RThR* xiv (1955), pp. 9ff. *Cf.* p. 397, n. 50.

[57] Josephus (*Ant.* iii. 123, 181) regards the holy of holies as symbolic of heaven, reserved for God alone, and the holy place (which in the tabernacle covered double the area of the holy of holies) as symbolic of earth and sea, which are accessible to men. So H. Koester (*HThR* lv [1962], p. 309) interprets the "tent" (*i.e.* the fore-tent) as "a symbol for the heavenly regions through which Christ was to pass to enter the heavenly sanctuary itself". This may well be our author's view. *Cf.* Ch. 4:14 (pp. 84f.).

[58] In Lev. 16 the outer compartment is called "the tent of meeting" in distinction from the inner compartment, which is there simply referred to as "the holy place" (verses 16f., 20, 23) "or the holy sanctuary" (verse 33).

the sanctuary of "the first covenant", comprising holy place and holy of holies together.[59] And by "the first tabernacle" here we are to understand not merely the Mosaic tabernacle, but the other structures which replaced it from time to time, down to and including Herod's temple. The phrase "while the first tabernacle is yet standing" sheds no light, however, on the question whether or not Herod's temple was still in being when the epistle was written (AV renders the genitive absolute by the past tense: "while as the first tabernacle was yet standing"). The phrase is part of a lengthy periodic sentence whose principal clause is "the priests go in continually into the first tabernacle ... but into the second the high priest alone, once in the year". The present tense in this principal clause is a historic present, indicating primarily the procedure laid down by the Levitical law rather than the procedure which was still being enacted at Jerusalem while the author was writing, although the latter is not excluded. What he means is that unimpeded access to the presence of God was not granted until Christ came to accomplish His sacrificial ministry.

9 This state of affairs—the prohibition of general entry into the holy of holies—is parenthetically described as "a figure for the time present".[60] There is an ambiguity in these words: is "the time present" to be understood as "the time then present" (AV) or "the time now present" (ERV; cf. RSV, NEB)? If the former, then our author's meaning is that the presence of the veil was an "outward and visible sign" of the spiritual conditions then prevailing: the way to God had not yet been opened up. If the latter, then the veil, together with its significance, constituted "a parable bearing on the present crisis",[61] emphasizing the contrast between the free access to God now guaranteed through Christ and the strictly limited access permitted by the structure and

---

[59] Moffatt (ICC, *ad loc.*, p. 118) takes "the first tabernacle" in v. 8 in the same sense as in vv. 2, 6; according to him, our author "calls the fore-tent a παραβολή". It is perhaps more likely, however, that the whole structure with its appropriate ritual is called a παραβολή.

[60] Gk. ἥτις παραβολὴ εἰς τὸν καιρὸν τὸν ἐνεστηκότα (the antecedent of ἥτις may be the whole situation of vv. 6-8, ἥτις being attracted to the gender and number of παραβολή).

[61] W. Manson, *The Epistle to the Hebrews* (London, 1951), p. 132. That is to say, the real meaning of the tabernacle can only now be understood, in the light of the work of Christ.

ceremonial of the earthly sanctuary. In the earthly sanctuary sacrifices were indeed offered, but their efficacy was sadly restricted; they could not bring "perfection" to the worshipper because they did not affect his conscience.[62] Now we see what our author wishes to teach his readers. The really effective barrier to a man's free access to God is an inward and not a material one; it exists in his conscience. It is only when the conscience is purified that a man is set free to approach God without reservation and offer Him acceptable service and worship. And the sacrificial blood of bulls and goats is useless in this regard.[63] Animal sacrifice and other material ordinances which accompanied it could effect at best a ceremonial and symbolical removal of pollution.

10 What had regulations concerning food and drink and a

---

[62] Cf. v. 14; Chs. 10:2, 22; 13:18. Gk. συνείδησις ("conscience") is not a classical word. It belonged to vernacular Greek and only a short time before the beginning of the Christian era did it attain literary status; even then it was not generally adopted by philosophic writers. It was probably Paul who baptized it into its deeper sense of "moral conscience"; the word appears several times in his letters and was taken over from him by later NT and other Christian writers. We may compare Philo's use of τὸ συνειδός to denote a faculty which examines and passes judgment on conduct, "established in the soul like a judge" (*On the Creation*, 128).

[63] This was appreciated by men of spiritual insight throughout Israel's history. That is plain enough from Ps. 51:16f., in the course of a prayer for forgiveness and restoration to fellowship with God. In later times the rabbis insisted that the repentance and confession which attended the Day of Atonement were the real means by which atonement was made: "though no sacrifices be offered, the day in itself effects atonement" (*Sifra, 'Emōr* 14). But this relates rather to the situation after A.D. 70, when it was perforce impossible to perform the ancient ritual; while the temple was standing, the absence of confession and heart-repentance would indeed have invalidated the ritual, but it is hardly suggested that confession and heart-repentance could in themselves have sufficed, apart from the ritual. The whole implication of the tractate *Yoma*, which deals with the celebration of the Day of Atonement under the Second Temple, is that the detailed prescriptions of Lev. 16 are binding commandments of God, not one of which may be neglected. In the Qumran texts it is taught that the members of the community by their devotion to the law of God can procure atonement for the land of Israel "without the flesh of holocausts and the fat of sacrifices" (1QS ix. 4); but they felt themselves conscientiously debarred from participation in the sacrificial services at Jerusalem because the temple was controlled by an unworthy and illegitimate priesthood; they looked forward to the day when acceptable sacrifices would be offered in a purified temple by a worthy priesthood. Their attitude was quite different from our author's; he regards the whole principle of an earthly sanctuary and animal sacrifices as a temporary expedient, now superseded for ever. Cf. p. 406 with n. 92.

variety of ritual washings to do with man's relation to God? The reference to "meats and drinks" probably has to do with the food-laws of Lev. 11.[64] There is much more said there about solid food than about drink; so far as drink goes, there is the direction that water may not be drunk from a vessel into which a dead animal has fallen (Lev. 11:34)—a sound hygienic direction, as no doubt were many of the food-laws, but having little enough to do with heart-religion. There were also the libations which accompanied several of the sacrificial offerings (cf. Num. 6:15, 17; 28:7f.). But for our author, as for Paul, these things were but "a shadow of the things to come" (Col. 2:17). As regards the "divers washings", not only had the high priest to "bathe his flesh in water" after performing the ritual of the Day of Atonement (Lev. 16:24), but similar purifications were prescribed for a great variety of actual or ceremonial defilements.[65] Again, these purifications undoubtedly had great hygienic value, but when they were given religious value there was always the danger that those who practised them might be tempted to think of religious duty exclusively, or at least excessively, in terms of externalities. But all these things were "outward ordinances" (NEB), "regulations for the body" (RSV), not for the conscience, with a temporary and limited validity until the "time of reformation". By the rendering "reformation"[66] we might understand "re-formation" in the sense of "reconstruction"; the coming of Christ involved a complete reshaping of the structure of Israel's religion. The old covenant was now to give way to the new, the shadow to the

---

[64] The expression "meats and drinks" denotes food-laws in general; we need not enquire too precisely which "drinks" our author had in mind. Moffatt (ICC, ad loc., p. 119) compares a few passages from the *Epistle of Aristeas*: "I suppose that most men feel some curiosity about the injunctions in the law with regard to meats and drinks and the animals which are considered unclean" (128); "our lawgiver ... fenced us around on every side with prescribed purifications with regard to meats and drinks ..." (142); "in the matter of meats and drinks he commands us first to offer a part as sacrifice, and only then to use the rest for ourselves" (158).

[65] We may think also of the Qumran purifications in water; these indeed were of no avail for the man who was defiled at heart, but none the less they were obligatory for members of the community. (*Cf.* 1QS iii. 4f., see p. 115 with n. 22, and p. 203, n. 88.)

[66] Gk. διόρθωσις, here only in NT; we might render it "the New Order".

substance,[67] the outward and earthly copy to the inward and heavenly reality.

5. CHRIST'S ETERNAL REDEMPTION

Ch. 9:11-14

11 But Christ having come a high priest of the good things to come,[68] through the greater and more perfect tabernacle, not made with hands, that is to say, not of this creation,

12 nor yet through the blood of goats and calves, but through his own blood, entered in once for all into the holy place, having obtained eternal redemption.

13 For if the blood of goats and bulls, and the ashes of a heifer sprinkling them that have been defiled, sanctify unto the cleanness of the flesh:

14 how much more shall the blood of Christ, who through the eternal Spirit[69] offered himself without blemish unto God, cleanse[70] your[71] conscience from dead works to serve the living[72] God?

---

[67] In Hebrews the law is a pattern or preliminary blueprint of the redemptive order introduced by Christ; cf. Col. 2:17 (with E. Percy, *Die Probleme der Kolosser- und Epheserbriefe* [Lund, 1946], pp. 287f.).

[68] Gk. τῶν μελλόντων ἀγαθῶν. This is the majority reading, but the weight of the evidence favors τῶν γενομένων ἀγαθῶν, the reading indicated in the ARV marginal variant, "the good things that are come" (so P⁴⁶ B D* 1611 1739 2005 d, with the Syriac versions, Chrysostom, and Cyril of Jerusalem). "The combination of the oldest Greek and Latin with the Syriac evidence is in itself almost irresistible" in support of γενομένων rather than μελλόντων (G. Zuntz, *The Text of the Epistles* [London, 1953], p. 119); the reading μελλόντων is probably due to the influence of Ch. 10:1. See p. 226.

[69] Gk. διὰ πνεύματος αἰωνίου (ARV suggests the alternative rendering "his eternal spirit"). A few witnesses (D* P, with the Latin and Coptic versions) have "holy spirit" (πνεύματος ἁγίου) for "eternal spirit".

[70] Codex B is not extant from this point onwards.

[71] The textual evidence is rather evenly divided between ὑμῶν ("your") and ἡμῶν ("our"); the latter is the reading of ARV margin, RSV margin and NEB.

[72] A few witnesses add καὶ ἀληθινῷ ("and true") after ζῶντι ("living"), under the influence of I Thess. 1:9.

11 But now the time of reformation has arrived; what used to be "the good things to come" (ARV) are now "the good things that have come" (RSV). For Christ has appeared, and in Him the shadows have given way to the perfect and abiding reality. And His appearance is properly announced with a triumphant trumpet-flourish; *His* entrance into the presence of God is not a day of soul-affliction and fasting,[73] like the Day of Atonement under the old legislation, but a day of gladness and song, the day when Christians celebrate the accession of their Priest-King.

The New Year, the Day of Atonement and the Feast of Tabernacles[74] originally belonged to one festal complex at which the kingship of the God of Israel was annually celebrated. What part was played in this celebration by the king of Israel, God's vicegerent over His people, is a debated question.[75] But in the New Testament antitype of this festal complex the divine Priest-King fills the central and decisive rôle; by virtue of His perfect self-sacrifice He has taken His seat at the right hand of the throne of God, and reigns for evermore from the heavenly Zion, high priest of the new and eternal order. The sanctuary in which He ministers is the true tabernacle of which the Mosaic shrine was but a material copy; it is a sanctuary not made with hands, not belonging to the earthly creation. The idea of a sanctuary not made with hands goes back to the earliest forms of Christian teaching.[76] Our Lord Himself spoke of the time when the Jerusalem temple would be replaced by a temple "made without hands"[77] (Mark 14:58; *cf.* John 2:19ff.), and Stephen and Paul insisted that no building "made with hands" could accommodate the Most High (Acts 7:48; 17:24).[78] What then is the nature of the spiritual temple in which God dwells? When Stephen maintained that "the Most High dwelleth not in houses made with hands", he confirmed his statement by quoting Isa. 66:1f. But in that same prophetic

---

[73] *Cf.* Lev. 16:29, 31; 23:26, 32.

[74] The first, tenth and fifteenth days of Tishri respectively.

[75] See, *e.g.*, S. Mowinckel, *He That Cometh* (Eng. tr., Oxford, 1956), pp. 21ff.; and for a contrary view N. H. Snaith, *The Jewish New Year Festival* (London, 1947), pp. 195ff., 205ff.

[76] *Cf.* A. Cole, *The New Temple* (London, 1950).

[77] While the words of Mark 14:58 are put into Jesus' mouth by "false witnesses", they are not a fabrication but a misrepresentation of something that He really said.

[78] *Cf. Acts*, NICNT, pp. 159ff., 356f.

context God declares that in preference to any material temple He chooses "him that is poor and of a contrite spirit, and that trembleth at my word". And this means that He prefers to make His dwelling with people of that character, as is shown by the similar words of Isa. 57:15: "For thus saith the high and lofty One that inhabiteth eternity, whose name is Holy: I dwell in the high and holy place, with him also that is of a contrite and humble spirit." Our author stands right in this prophetic tradition when he affirms that the people of God are the house of God: "whose house are we, if we hold fast our boldness and the glorying of our hope" (Ch. 3:6). But how can the Son of God, who has "passed through the heavens" (Ch. 4:14), be regarded as dwelling among His people? It takes Paul to answer this question effectively, when he speaks of the people of Christ as already raised up by God to share the throne of Christ in the heavenly realm (Eph. 2:6).

12 Whereas Aaron and his successors went into the earthly holy of holies on the Day of Atonement by virtue of animal-sacrifices—"through the blood of goats and calves"[79]—Christ has entered the heavenly sanctuary "through[80] his own blood". It is unfortunate that RSV says that He entered "taking not the blood of goats and calves but his own blood". Aaron certainly carried the sacrificial blood into the holy of holies,[81] but our author deliberately avoids saying that Christ carried His own blood into the heavenly sanctuary. Even as a symbolic expression this is open to objection. There have been expositors who, pressing the analogy of the Day of Atonement beyond the limits observed by our author, have argued that the expiatory work of Christ was not completed on the cross—not completed, indeed, until He ascended from earth and "made atonement 'for us' in the heavenly

---

[79] The plural is generalizing. "Calves" (Gk. μόσχος) is used here as a variation on "bulls" (Gk. ταῦρος, as in v. 13); the animal which Aaron was to sacrifice as a sin-offering for himself and his house was "a young bullock" (Lev. 16:3) and might therefore be designated in Greek either by μόσχος (so LXX in Lev. 16) or by ταῦρος.

[80] Gk. διά, as also in the previous clause.

[81] Cf. v. 7 ("not without blood"), v. 25 ("with [ἐν] blood not his own") —where ἐν is probably instrumental in force, as in Chs. 10:19; 13:20, implying that the sacrificial blood carried by the high priest was his title to enter the inner sanctuary).

holy of holies by the presentation of His efficacious blood".[82]   But while it was necessary under the old covenant for the sacrificial blood first to be shed in the court and then to be brought into the holy of holies, no such division of our Lord's sacrifice into two phases is envisaged under the new covenant.   When upon the cross He offered up His life to God as a sacrifice for His people's sin, He accomplished in reality what Aaron and his successors performed in type by the twofold act of slaying the victim and presenting its blood in the holy of holies. The title of the Anglican Article XXXI speaks rightly "of the one oblation of Christ finished upon the cross". And then "through his own blood"—that is, by virtue of the infinitely acceptable oblation of His life—He could appear before God, not on sufferance but by right, as His people's prevailing representative and high priest. The Aaronic high priests had to present themselves before God repeatedly, because such redemption as their ministry procured bore but a token and temporary character; but Christ entered in once for all,[83] to be enthroned there in perpetuity, because the redemption procured by Him is perfect in nature and eternal in effect.[84]

13   The blood of slaughtered animals under the old order did possess a certain efficacy, but it was an outward efficacy for the removal of ceremonial pollution. "The blood of goats and bulls" is a general term covering not only the sacrifices of the Day of Atonement but other sacrifices as well (we may compare the

---

[82]   K. M. Monroe, *EQ* v (1933), p. 404 (in an article "Time Element in the Atonement", pp. 397ff., which was answered by T. Houghton, "The Atonement", *EQ* vi [1934], pp. 137ff.).   Monroe argued that our Lord, after His resurrection, ascended immediately into heaven to sprinkle His blood on "the heavenly capporeth" and therefore could not allow Mary Magdalene to hinder Him (John 20:17) until He had completed this essential stage of His atoning work. The ascension of John 20:17 is thus quite distinct from the ascension of Acts 1:9. This thesis had been sustained nearly half a century earlier by C. E. Stuart in a number of papers, especially *Propitiation by Blood* (London, *c.* 1887) and *A Few Remarks as to Atonement, Propitiation, and the Priesthood of the Lord Jesus Christ* (London, 1888).   But it serves only to warn those who require such a warning against basing doctrines on types, instead of using types to illustrate· securely based doctrines.

[83]   Gk. ἐφάπαξ (as in Chs. 7:27; 10:10).

[84]   *Cf.* 5:9, where Christ is called "the author of eternal salvation". In the present verse "redemption" represents Gk. λύτρωσις, found elsewhere in NT only in Luke 1:68; 2:38. The word is derived from λύτρον, "ransom" (used of the Son of Man in Matt. 20:28 // Mark 10:45), whence also we have the derivatives λυτροῦσθαι, "to ransom" (Luke 24:21; Tit. 2:14; I Pet. 1:18),

ironical question of Ps. 50:13, "Will I eat the flesh of bulls, or drink the blood of goats?"). The sin-offerings presented on the Day of Atonement, or at any other time, had no effect on the consciences of those on whose behalf they were brought; they served merely in an external and symbolical manner to counteract the defilement of sin. Along with these offerings our author mentions "the ashes of a heifer[85] sprinkling them that have been defiled". This is a reference to a ritual prescribed in Numbers 19, for the removal of ceremonial impurity. A perfect red heifer, which had never borne the yoke, was to be slaughtered outside the camp of Israel in the presence of Eleazar the priest (representing his father Aaron, the high priest), who was then to sprinkle its blood seven times in front of the tabernacle. The body of the heifer was then to be completely incinerated; Eleazar was to throw cedar wood, hyssop (marjoram) and scarlet thread into the burning fire. When all was consumed, the ashes were to be gathered up and stored outside the camp to be used as occasion required for the preparation of *mē niddāh*, "water for (the removal of) impurity". Any one who contracted ceremonial defilement through touching or approaching a dead body was to be cleansed by being sprinkled with water containing some of the ashes of the heifer. Hence the allusion here to "the ashes of a heifer sprinkling them that have been defiled" so as to "sanctify[86] unto the cleanness of the flesh"[87]

λυτρωτής, "redeemer", "ransomer" (Acts 7:35), and ἀντίλυτρον, "counter-ransom" (I Tim. 2:6). The compound substantive ἀπολύτρωσις is commoner in NT than the simple λύτρωσις; it occurs in Chs. 9:15; 11:35, and in eight other NT passages, of which Rom. 3:24 is of outstanding importance for our understanding of the word as applied to the work of Christ. *Cf.* B. B. Warfield, "The New Testament Terminology of 'Redemption'", *Biblical Doctrines* (New York, 1929), pp. 327ff.; "'Redeemer' and 'Redemption'", *The Person and Work of Christ* (Philadelphia, 1950), pp. 325ff.; E. K. Simpson, *Words Worth Weighing in the Greek New Testament* (London, 1946), pp. 8f.

[85] Gk. δάμαλις, as in LXX of Num. 19, where the Hebrew word is simply *pārāh*, "cow". (The Targum of Pseudo-Jonathan has '*eglā*, "heifer".)

[86] Here "sanctify" (Gk. ἁγιάζειν) means little more than "purify"; the person who had been defiled was by this means restored to a state in which he was no longer religiously tabu but could take part once more in the prescribed ordinances of worship. According to R. Yohanan (*Num. Rabba* xix. 8), "neither does the dead body defile, nor does the water purify; but ... 'This is the statute of the law' [Num. 19:2]".

[87] "Flesh" in this epistle denotes the outer and physical element in man's make-up in contrast to his inner being, his conscience (vv. 9, 14). *Cf.* the "carnal ordinances" of v. 9, the "carnal commandment" of Ch. 7:16, and the contrast

(NEB, "to hallow those who have been defiled and restore their external purity"). The *mē niddāh* could be used for other purificatory purposes; according to Num. 31:21ff., metal vessels captured among the spoils of war could be cleansed from idolatrous contamination by being passed through fire and then sprinkled with this water. But while the water cleansed those who had incurred ceremonial defilement, it had the curious effect of rendering others who touched it (especially those who administered it) ceremonially unclean until sundown. The ritual of the red heifer is appropriately mentioned by our author at this point because, like the sacrifices on the Day of Atonement, "it is a sin-offering" (Num. 19:9).[88] In course of time a closer connection seems to have developed between the red heifer ceremony and the Day of Atonement than the written law prescribed: according

between "the fathers of our flesh" and "the Father of spirits" in Ch. 12:9. *Cf.* also I Pet. 3:21, where baptism is presented not as a means of removing outward defilement ("the filth of the flesh") but as the Godward appeal or response of "a good conscience".

[88] Heb. *ḥaṭṭā'th hī'*; hence the Mishnah repeatedly refers to the *mē niddāh* ("water for impurity") as *mē ḥaṭṭā'th* ("water of sin-offering" or "water for sin"), as in Num. 8:7 MT. The Mishnaic tractate *Parah* is devoted to this ritual. After A.D. 70 the slaying of the red heifer (which had previously taken place on the Mount of Olives, "outside the camp") was discontinued, and so the water for impurity could not be renewed once the existing stock of ashes was exhausted. According to Mishnah, *Parah* iii. 5, the last priest to kill the red heifer was Ishmael ben Phabi (high priest *c.* A.D. 58-60). Among the Samaritans it was held that all that was necessary for the ritual was a valid priesthood, not a temple or altar; accordingly the slaying and burning of the red heifer was continued by them until 1348, the ashes of this last burning being preserved until *c.* 1600 (*cf.* M. Gaster, *Samaritan Traditions and Oral Law* [London, 1932], pp. 195f.). It has been suggested that the Qumran community also continued to carry out the ritual in spite of their separation from the temple, since they possessed a legitimate priesthood (*cf.* J. Bowman, "Did the Qumran Sect burn the Red Heifer?", *Revue de Qumran* i [1958-59], pp. 73ff.). Whether they carried out the ritual or not, they certainly attached high importance to cleansing with *mē niddāh*, which nevertheless was of no avail to those whose heart remained impenitent (1QS iii. 4ff.). This probably explains Josephus's reference to the "purer lustrations" which the Essenes practised (*Ant.* xviii. 19). (*Cf.* the account of John's baptism in Josephus, *Ant.* xviii. 117, quoted on p. 115, n. 22; see also p. 197, n. 65.) The *Epistle of Barnabas* (8:1ff.) allegorizes the ritual of the red heifer, detail by detail, as a type of the cross and the gospel; *cf.* G. Allon, "Halakhah in the Epistle of Barnabas", *Tarbiz* xi (1939-40), pp. 23ff. (summarized by S. Lowy, *JJS* xi [1960], p. 247); R. A. Kraft, *The Epistle of Barnabas: Its Quotations and their Sources* (unpublished Ph.D. thesis, Harvard University, 1961), pp. 169ff. See also p. 251.

to Maimonides[89] (who presumably had some traditional basis for his information) the high priest was sprinkled with the ashes of a heifer twice during the seven days[90] for which he was kept isolated in the temple before the Day of Atonement, in case he had inadvertently contracted ceremonial defilement.

Just how the blood of sacrificed animals or the ashes of the red heifer effected a ceremonial cleansing our author does not explain; it was sufficient for him, and no doubt for his readers, that the Old Testament ascribed this efficacy to them.

14 But it is no mere ceremonial cleansing that is effected by the sacrifice of Christ. Here our author presents us with one of the most impressive instances of his favorite "how much more" argument. Those earlier rituals might effect external purification, but the blood of Christ[91]—His offering up of Himself to God— cleanses the conscience; it does the very thing that they could not do, since we have just been told that they could not, "as touching the conscience, make the worshipper perfect" (verse 9). They could restore him to formal communion with God and with his fellow-worshippers; but if it was an inward sense of guilt that kept him in heart at a distance from God, how could they possibly deal with that condition?

> "Not all the blood of beasts
>   On Jewish altars slain
> Could give the guilty conscience peace,
>   Or wash away the stain:

---

[89] *Yad ha-Ḥazaqah* i, *halakhah* 4 (quoted in full in F. Delitzsch, *Commentary on the Epistle to the Hebrews* ii [Edinburgh, 1872], p. 466). In his *Sepher Ṭohoroth* Maimonides expects that the burning of the red heifer will be resumed when Messiah comes, so that water for the removal of impurity can be prepared once more.

[90] The isolation of the high priest for seven days preceding the Day of Atonement is laid down in Mishnah *Yoma* i. 1. According to Maimonides it was on the third and seventh days of this period that he was to be sprinkled; it is a matter of interest in this connection that the Qaraites, having no ashes of a heifer at their disposal, substituted for the sprinkling with *mē niddāh* in the situation envisaged by Num. 19 a purificatory bath on the third and seventh days (P. S. Goldberg, *Karaite Liturgy* [Manchester, 1957], p. 40).

[91] "The blood of Christ" in v. 14 means His sacrificial death; "it is hard to envisage a reason for interpreting 'the blood' in a sense other than that given by the following 'a death having taken place'" (L. Morris, *JThS* N.S. iii [1952], p. 226, in an article "The Biblical Use of the Term 'Blood'", pp. 216ff.). *Cf.*

> But Christ, the heavenly Lamb,
> Takes all our sins away,
> A sacrifice of nobler name
> And richer blood than they."[92]

Those earlier sacrifices were but token sacrifices; the sacrifice of Christ was a real self-offering, accomplished on the moral and spiritual plane. It was "through the eternal Spirit" that He offered Himself to God. The phrase "through eternal spirit" (as it is literally, whether the substantive be spelt with a capital "S" or not) is extremely difficult to interpret with satisfactory precision. As regards the variant rendering of ARV margin, "through his eternal spirit", it may be said that if our author had meant this, he could have said so quite simply. That our Lord's self-sacrifice is described as being "a spiritual and eternal sacrifice" (NEB) is clear, but perhaps even more is intended. Behind our author's thinking lies the portrayal of the Isaianic Servant of the Lord, who yields up his life to God as a guilt-offering for many, bearing their sin and procuring their justification.[93] When this Servant is introduced for the first time, God says: "I have put my Spirit upon him" (Isa. 42:1). It is in the power of the Divine Spirit, accordingly, that the Servant accomplishes every phase of his ministry, including the crowning phase in which he accepts death for the transgression of his people, filling the twofold rôle of priest[94] and victim, as Christ does in this epistle. So, "in Christ's sacrifice we see the final revelation of what God is, that behind which there is nothing in God, so that the

---

J. Behm, *TWNT* i (Stuttgart, 1933), pp. 171ff. (*s.v.* αἷμα); A. M. Stibbs, *The Meaning of the Word "Blood" in Scripture* (London, 1947); F. J. Taylor, *A Theological Word Book of the Bible*, ed. A. Richardson (London, 1950), pp. 33f. (*s.v.* "Blood"). For the *a fortiori* argument cf. Ch. 2:1-3 (p. 29, n. 4).

[92] I. Watts. (His designation of Christ as "the heavenly Lamb" in this context is probably due simply to the New Testament designation of Him as the Lamb of God; *cf.* also I Pet. 1:19.)

[93] *Cf.* v. 28 (p. 223 with nn. 169-172).

[94] The Servant's priestly rôle appears especially in Isa. 52:15, "so shall he sprinkle many nations" (for a vindication of this rendering *cf.* E. J. Young, *Studies in Isaiah* [Grand Rapids, 1954], pp. 199ff.; H. L. Ellison, *The Servant of Jehovah* [London, 1953], pp. 29f.); the allusion may well be to the sprinkling of the water for the removal of impurity. *Cf.* the sprinkling of Chs. 10:22; 12:24.

religion which rests on that sacrifice rests on the ultimate truth of the divine nature, and can never be shaken".[95]

The animals used for sacrifice in earlier days were required to be physically unblemished; the life which Christ presented to God on the cross was a life free from inward blemish; like the Servant of the Lord, "he had done no violence, neither was any deceit in his mouth" (Isa. 53:9).[96] Our Lord's complete holiness, His "active obedience" to God, is essential to the efficacy of His sacrifice. "Only one who knew no sin could take any responsibility in regard to it which would create a new situation for sinners. ... Christ's offering of Himself without spot to God had an absolute or ideal character. It was something beyond which nothing could be, or could be conceived to be, as a response to God's mind and requirements in relation to sin. It was the final response, a spiritual response, to the divine necessities of the situation. ... His sacrifice was rational and voluntary,[97] an intelligent and loving response to the holy and gracious will of God, and to the terrible situation of man."[98] How this particular response, and nothing else, could satisfy both the divine will and the human predicament becomes clearer in Ch. 10:5-10, where our author interprets the work of Christ in terms of Ps. 40:6-8.

It is not contact with a dead body, or anything of a material and external nature, that conveys real defilement to men or interrupts true communion with God. Our Lord made it plain on a memorable occasion that no one is defiled by anything outside himself; "but the things which proceed out of the man are those which defile the man. ... For from within, out of the heart of men, evil thoughts proceed ... all these evil things proceed from within, and defile the man" (Mark 7:15, 21, 23). It is an inward and spiritual purification that is required if heart-communion with God is to be enjoyed. And therefore the "dead works" from which the conscience must be cleansed cannot be, as some commentators have held,[99] the unavailing ceremonial of Judaism; they must be

---

[95] J. Denney, *The Death of Christ* (London, 1951), p. 119. The πνεῦμα is eternal because divine.

[96] These actual words are applied to Christ in I Pet. 2:22.

[97] *Cf.* Mark 14:36 ("not what I will, but what thou wilt"); John 17:19 ("for their sakes I consecrate myself", ARV margin).

[98] J. Denney, *op. cit.*, pp. 129f.

[99] *Cf.* p. 113, n. 14.

things which convey inward and spiritual defilement. As in Ch. 6:1 (where "repentance from dead works" belongs to the rudiments of Christian teaching), they are those practices and attitudes which belong to the way of death, which pollute the soul and erect a barrier between it and God. But their pollution is removed from the conscience by the work of Christ, so that men and women, emancipated from inward bondage, can worship God in spirit and in truth. This is the "perfection" which the ancient ceremonial was unable to achieve.

6. THE MEDIATOR OF THE NEW COVENANT

Ch. 9:15-22

15 And for this cause he is the mediator of a new covenant, that a death having taken place for the redemption of the transgressions that were under the first covenant, they that have been called may receive the promise of the eternal inheritance.

16 For where a testament[100] is, there must of necessity be[101] the death of him that made it.

17 For a testament is of force where there hath been death:[102] for it doth never[103] avail while he that made it liveth.[104]

18 Wherefore even the first *covenant* hath not been dedicated[105] without blood.

---

100 "Testament" and "covenant" are variant renderings of the one Greek word διαθήκη.

101 Gk. φέρεσθαι, literally "be brought", here probably used in the technical sense "be registered" (so *P. Oxy.* ii [London, 1899], no. 244, line 12) or "be produced as evidence" (*cf.* J. J. Wettstein, *ad loc.*: "necesse est afferri testimonia de morte testatoris").

102 Gk. ἐπὶ νεκροῖς, literally "over dead people", *i.e.* "with reference to dead people"; not "over the dead bodies" of the covenant-victims, for they could not be classed as διαθέμενοι.

103 Gk. μήποτε, for which ℵ* D* have μὴ τότε ("not then").

104 In ERV this clause is treated as a question: "for doth it ever avail while he that made it liveth?" This construction does best justice to the negative μή, which is appropriate in a question expecting the answer "No".

105 Gk. ἐνκεκαίνισται (from ἐνκαινίζω, used in NT only here and in Ch. 10:20).

19 For when every commandment[106] had been spoken by Moses unto all the people according to the law,[107] he took the blood of the calves and the goats,[108] with water and scarlet wool and hyssop, and sprinkled both the book itself and all the people,

20 saying, This is the blood of the covenant which God commanded to you-ward.[109]

21 Moreover the tabernacle and all the vessels of the ministry he sprinkled in like manner with the blood.

22 And according to the law, I may almost say,[110] all things are cleansed with blood, and apart from shedding of blood there is no remission.

15 That Jesus is "the mediator of a better covenant"—the new covenant foretold by Jeremiah—has already been stated in Ch. 8:6. But now the basis of His mediatorship is made plain; that basis is His sacrificial death. By virtue of His death redemption has been provided for those who had broken the law of God; the life of Christ was the costly price paid to liberate them from their sins.[111] The first covenant provided a measure of atonement and remission for sins committed under it, but it was incapable of providing "eternal redemption"; this was a blessing which had to

---

106 Gk. πάσης ἐντολῆς, for which P46 D* and Chrysostom read πάσης τῆς ἐντολῆς ("all the commandment").

107 Gk. κατὰ τὸν νόμον, but the article is omitted by ℵ* with the bulk of later manuscripts and TR. Cf. Ch. 10:8 (p. 231, n. 29).

108 The phrase "and the goats" (Gk. καὶ τῶν τράγων) should probably be omitted with P46 ℵc K L Ψ 1739, about 30 Byzantine manuscripts, Chrysostom and the Syriac versions; the addition, if such it be, probably is due to the influence of v. 12 (cf. Zuntz, op. cit., p. 55). (If, on the other hand, the words are accepted as authentic, their omission from P46 and other authorities could be explained as due to harmonization with Ex. 24:5.)

109 Quoted from Ex. 24:8, where LXX, following the Hebrew, has ἰδού ("behold") for τοῦτο ("this [is]") and διέθετο ("covenanted") for ἐνετείλατο ("commanded"). The initial "this is" may be influenced by the words of institution of the *new* covenant (cf. Mark 14:24; I Cor. 11:25). On the absence of eucharistic reference from Hebrews see pp. 401f.

110 "I may almost say" (cf. NEB, "it might almost be said") represents one word in Greek, σχεδόν ("almost", used without elaboration in AV and RSV).

111 "The redemption of the transgressions that were under the first covenant" could have direct relevance only to readers of Israelite birth or adoption, since these transgressions were breaches of the Mosaic law, which was an

await the inauguration of the new covenant, which embodies God's promise to His people: "I will forgive their iniquity, and their sin will I remember no more" (Jer. 31:34). The basing of the new covenant on the death of Christ is a New Testament doctrine not peculiar to our author; it finds clearest expression in the words of institution spoken by our Lord over the cup: "This is my blood of the covenant, which is poured out for many" (Mark 14:24)[112] or, in their earliest recorded form, "This cup is the new covenant in my blood" (I Cor. 11:25). And now that this redemptive death has taken place, the "promise of the eternal inheritance" has been made good to those "that have been called"; the new covenant, and everything that the grace of God provides under it, is forever theirs. Christians have already been described in Ch. 6:17 as "the heirs of the promise"; the fulfilment of the promise is the "eternal inheritance" into which they have entered. "Eternal" is an adjective which our author associates especially with the new covenant; that covenant itself is eternal (Ch. 13:20), and so the redemption which it provides and the inheritance into which it brings the people of God are likewise eternal (verses 12, 15); the Mediator of this covenant, having offered Himself up to God as "a spiritual and eternal sacrifice" (verse 14, NEB), has become "unto all them that obey him the author of eternal salvation" (Ch. 5:9).[113] The eternal inheritance of grace and glory both here and hereafter is for those who "have been called"— for those who have already been designated "partakers of a heavenly calling" (Ch. 3:1). The close connection between God's effectual calling of His people and the heritage which is theirs as His sons and heirs, joint-heirs with Christ, is set out more fully by Paul in Rom. 8:14–30.

16–17 But why was the Mediator's death necessary for the ratification of the covenant? It is not easy to follow the argument

---

integral part of the "first covenant". This retrospective validity of the death of Christ is stated in more general terms, which cover Gentiles as well as Jews, in Rom. 3:25 ("whom God set forth to be a propitiation ... to show his righteousness because of the passing over of the sins done aforetime, in the forbearance of God"); cf. Acts 17:30. With "redemption" (ἀπολύτρωσις) cf. the uncompounded λύτρωσις in v. 12 (p. 201, n. 84).

[112] To the Markan wording Matt. 26:28 adds "unto remission of sins", making explicit what is in any case implied in the shorter form. See pp. 177f.

[113] This accounts for all the occurrences of αἰώνιος in the epistle with the exception of "eternal judgment" in Ch. 6:2 (see p. 117 with n. 33).

here in an English version, because we are almost bound to use two different English words[114] to represent two different aspects of the meaning of one Greek word, whereas our author's argument depends on his use of the same Greek word throughout. The Greek word is *diathēkē*, which has the comprehensive sense of "settlement".[115] As used elsewhere in the epistle, the particular kind of settlement which *diathēkē* denotes is a covenant graciously bestowed by God upon His people, by which He brings them into a special relationship wtih Himself;[116] in other words it is used, as it had been used by the Greek translators of the Old Testament, as the equivalent of the Hebrew *berīth*.[117] But in verses 16 and 17 of our present chapter it is used of another kind of settlement, a last will and testament, in which property is bequeathed by the owner to various other persons on the understanding that they have no title to it until he dies.[118] There are, in fact, some scholars

---

[114] This difficulty is eased in NEB by the rendering of the opening words of v. 15: "And therefore he is the mediator of a new covenant, or testament, under which ..." Moffatt's version makes similar use of two words at the beginning of v. 18; after using "covenant" twice in v. 15, and "will" in vv. 16f., it continues: "Hence even the first covenant of God's will was not inaugurated apart from blood".

[115] For διαθήκη consult MM, AG, and J. Behm and G. Quell in *TWNT* ii (Stuttgart, 1935), pp. 105ff.; they supply further documentation.

[116] "The covenant is a sovereign dispensation of God's grace. It is grace bestowed and a relation established" (J. Murray, *The Covenant of Grace* [London, 1954], p. 19).

[117] Heb. *berīth*, of course, is used in OT of covenants between men as well as of covenants between God and men; but even "when all the instances of merely human covenants are examined, it would definitely appear that the notion of sworn fidelity is thrust into prominence in these covenants rather than that of mutual contract" (J. Murray, *op. cit.*, p. 10). In this connection it is noteworthy that the aptest secular analogies to the divine statute-law in Israel (the law which takes the apodictic form "Thou shalt ..." rather than the casuistic form "If a man ...") are found not in ancient Near Eastern law-codes but in international treaties (*cf.* G. E. Mendenhall, *Law and Covenant in Israel and the Ancient Near East* [Philadelphia, 1955]). *Cf.* p. 213, n. 132.

[118] We may compare (and contrast) the use of the testamentary analogy made in the Valentinian *Gospel of Truth* (Jung Codex 20:15ff.), in a passage immediately following that quoted on p. 52, n. 86: "As the property of a deceased householder remains concealed so long as his testament has not been opened, so the All remained concealed so long as the Father of the All ... remained invisible. Therefore Jesus appeared and revealed this book; He was nailed to a tree; He affixed the testamentary disposition from the Father to the cross."

who have maintained that "testament" is the sense of *diathēkē* throughout this epistle,[119] if not indeed throughout the Greek Bible.[120] "Testament" is certainly the predominant sense of the word in Hellenistic Greek;[121] but in the Greek Bible it usually takes its meaning from the Old Testament Hebrew word *berīth*, which does not have the sense of "testament".[122] On the other hand, there have been exegetes who have endeavored to retain the meaning "covenant" even in Heb. 9:16f.; among these B. F. Westcott is outstanding.[123] But it simply is not true to say that "where a *covenant* is, there must of necessity be the death of him that made it"—nor of necessity the death of anyone else. Westcott takes "him that made it" to point to the covenant victim,[124] with

---

[119] So E. Riggenbach, "Der Begriff der *ΔΙΑΘΗΚΗ* im Hebräerbrief", in *Theologische Studien Theodor Zahn zum 10. Oktober 1908 dargebracht* (Leipzig, 1908), pp. 289ff.; *cf.* A. Deissmann, *Paul* (Eng. tr., London, 1926), p. 175 with n. 3.

[120] *Cf.* J. B. Payne, *The Theology of the Older Testament* (Grand Rapids, 1962), pp. 71ff., where "testament" is preferred as the translation of Heb. *berīth* as well as of Gk. διαθήκη.

[121] Occasionally it may have the sense of "contract" or "compact", a sense more naturally expressed by classical συνθήκη (a word not found in NT and but rarely in LXX). Aristophanes (*Birds* 439f.) provides a classical instance of διαθήκη used in more or less this sense.

[122] Another NT passage where a similar question arises regarding the precise sense of διαθήκη is Gal. 3:15, 17, where the principle that a man's διαθήκη, when once it has been validated, cannot be annulled or have a codicil added to it by any one else, is invoked to prove that God's covenant with Abraham could not be affected by the law, which came four centuries later. Although the question of death does not enter into the immediate argument here, it may be that Gal. 3:15 means that "the will (διαθήκη) of a human being is irrevocable when once duly executed" (W. M. Ramsay, *Historical Commentary on Galatians* [London, 1899], p. 349; Ramsay has an extended discussion of the meaning of διαθήκη both here and elsewhere in the Pauline letters, pp. 349–370). In that case there is the same oscillation between general and particular senses of διαθήκη as we have here in Hebrews. *Cf.* H. N. Ridderbos, *Galatians*, NICNT (Grand Rapids, 1953), pp. 130ff.

[123] B. F. Westcott, *The Epistle to the Hebrews* (London, 1903), pp. 300ff.; see the critique of his arguments by G. Vos, "Hebrews, the Epistle of the Diatheke", *PThR* xiii (1915), pp. 614ff. (*cf.* p. 151, n. 69). The rendering of "covenant" throughout the passage has been upheld also by E. Hatch, *Essays in Biblical Greek* (Oxford, 1889), p. 48; G. Milligan, *The Theology of the Epistle to the Hebrews* (Edinburgh, 1899), pp. 152f., 166ff. (Milligan later modified his position); A. Nairne, *The Epistle of Priesthood* (Edinburgh, 1913), pp. 140, 364f.

[124] The part played by the covenant-victim may be responsible for the idiom for covenant-making, found in various languages, which literally means

whom the maker of the covenant is representatively identified. But not only is this a straining of the natural force of the words here used; it is not always true that the maker of the covenant is identified with the covenant victim so that "in the death of the victim his death is presented symbolically".[125] In the covenant made with Abraham in Gen. 15:1-18, and in that made with Israel at the foot of Mount Sinai in Ex. 24:3-8, covenant-victims were slaughtered, but there is no suggestion that God, the covenant-maker on both occasions, was represented by them; neither did they represent Abraham and Israel, the respective recipients of those divine covenants. "The death of him that made it" is, as AV and NEB simply and rightly put it, "the death of the testator";[126] a testament is the only kind of *diathēkē* which depends for its ratification on the death of the person who makes it.

"J. H. Moulton,[127] after embracing Westcott's conclusion, felt himself obliged to 'capitulate', as he phrases it, to the dual version of the Authorized Version and Revised Version,[128] inconsistent as he deems it to be. But is that the case? If we revert to the teaching of the old theology (Turrettin, Witsius, Hodge), the covenant of redemption, viewed as the undertaking of the Son, will rank as the prior phase of the covenant of grace. By fulfilling that divine counsel of peace the heavenly Covenanter has met all the claims of outraged righteousness. His 'obedience unto death' fills up the breach with heaven as nothing else could do; and the covenant of grace in His hands at this stage assumes the aspect of a bequest

to "cut" or "strike" a covenant—Heb. *kārath berith* (*cf.* p. 168, n. 40), Gk. ὅρκια τέμνειν, Lat. *foedus ferire*. But the subject of these verbs (the διαθέμενος) is, in the nature of the case, never the covenant-victim.

[125] Westcott, *op. cit.*, p. 267.

[126] Gk. διαθέμενος. "Thus ὁ διαθέμενος (Heb. 9:17) signifies *the testator*, ἀδιάθετος became the technical term for *intestate*, and ἐπιδιαθήκη stands in Josephus for a codicil" (E. K. Simpson, *EQ* xviii [1946], p. 189). *Cf.* the present and aorist indicative of διατίθεσθαι (the verb of which διαθέμενος is the aorist participle) in Luke 22:29, "I appoint (διατίθεμαι) unto you a kingdom, even as my Father appointed (διέθετο) unto me".

[127] *Cf.* J. H. Moulton and G. Milligan in *Exp.* VIII. vi (1908), p. 563: "We may suppose the author of Heb. using the obsolete, Biblical word, and then dropping into the modern use of it for purposes of illustration" (in "Lexical Notes from the Papyri").

[128] AV renders διαθήκη by "testament" throughout Heb. 9:15-20 (as in Ch. 7:22), and by "covenant" elsewhere in the epistle; ARV and RSV have "covenant" throughout the epistle except in vv. 16 and 17 of this chapter.

accruing to His brethren through the death of the Testator, who in this unique transaction lives again to be the Administrator of His own mediatorial work" (E.K. Simpson).[129]

It is quite likely that the testamentary idea suggested itself to our author's mind because of his reference to the "eternal inheritance" at the end of verse 15. Nairne finds a difficulty in that "the mediator of a will would hardly be the testator, but what would now be called the executor, and his death would not come into the matter".[130] But all analogies from ordinary life must be defective when they are applied to Him who rose from the dead and is thus able personally to secure for his people the benefits which He died to procure for them. He is testator and executor in one, surety and mediator alike. "There is no more possibility or feasibility of interference with the effective application of the blessings of the covenant than there is of interfering with a testamentary disponement once the testator has died. This use of the testamentary provision of Roman law to illustrate the inviolable security accruing from the sacrificial death of Christ serves to underline the unilateral character of the new covenant" (J. Murray).[131] Christ, says our author, is the Mediator of the new *diathēkē*, and there is one kind of *diathēkē* that serves particularly well to illustrate this aspect of His ministry—namely, the testamentary *diathēkē* which does not come into effect before the death of the person who makes it.[132] It is well known that this kind of settlement cannot be ratified so long as its author lives. And so it

---

[129] *Loc. cit.* (*cf.* p. 212, n. 126).
[130] *The Epistle of Priesthood*, p. 365.
[131] *The Covenant of Grace*, p. 30.
[132] M. G. Kline (*Treaty of the Great King*, p. 41), referring to Heb. 9:16f., suggests that if "one might assume that the author's parenthetical allusion in these verses is to the dynastic-testamentary aspect of ancient suzerainty covenants and especially of the Old Covenant as exemplified by Deuteronomy, the way would be open to a satisfactory solution", since one of the recurrent themes of the epistle is "dynastic appointment and perpetuity (*cf.* 1:2ff., 8; 5:6ff.; 6:20ff.), the precise area of covenantal administration for which the merging of the covenantal and the testamentary is attested". In that case Jesus is presented here as "both dying Moses and succeeding Joshua". While the ancient Near Eastern principle of the dynastic covenant is of prime relevance to the Old Testament covenant, and not least to that of Deuteronomy, it is improbable that it would have readily occurred as an analogy to our author's mind in the first century A.D.

is with the new *diathēkē;* its validity depends upon the fact that its author has died.[133]

18 For the matter of that, he goes on, the earlier *diathēkē* also required death for its ratification—not, in that case, the death of the one who made it, but death none the less. And he recalls the incident of Ex. 24:3–8, the inauguration of the covenant of Moses' day at the foot of Mount Sinai.

19–20 According to Ex. 24:3–8, "Moses came and told the people all the words of Jehovah, and all the ordinances: and all the people answered with one voice, and said, All the words which Jehovah hath spoken will we do. And Moses wrote all the words of Jehovah, and rose up early in the morning, and builded an altar under the mount, and twelve pillars, according to the twelve tribes of Israel. And he sent young men of the children of Israel, who offered burnt-offerings, and sacrificed peace-offerings of oxen unto Jehovah. And Moses took half of the blood, and put it in basins; and half of the blood he sprinkled on the altar. And he took the book of the covenant, and read in the audience of the people: and they said, All that Jehovah hath spoken will we do, and be obedient. And Moses took the blood, and sprinkled it on the people, and said, Behold the blood of the covenant, which Jehovah hath made with you concerning all these words."

Verses 19 and 20 of Heb. 9 present what is for the most part a summary of these words from Exodus, but the summary includes certain features which do not appear in the Exodus narrative. The reference to goats in verse 19 is probably a later addition to the text of Hebrews;[134] in that case, this passage agrees with the Septuagint of Ex. 24:5 in specifying calves as the sacrificial animals used on this occasion.[135] But whereas in the Exodus

---

[133] *Cf.* J. S. Candlish, "The Notion of Divine Covenants in the Bible", *ExT* iv (1892–93), pp. 19ff., 65ff., especially the paragraph on p. 21 dealing with διαθήκη in the Epistle to the Hebrews. "The death of Christ fulfilled the condition necessary for the bestowal of the forgiveness and renewal promised by God, and so made His disposition of grace effectual and unchangeable."

[134] See p. 208, n. 108. Those commentators who take the reference to goats here as original commonly regard "bulls and goats" as a locution of our author's meaning "sacrificial animals" (as in Chs. 9:12f.; 10:4). Philo (*Questions and Answers on Exodus*, ii. 32) emphasizes the fact that calves, and not lambs or kids, were sacrificed on this occasion, "for these animals are weaker than calves, whereas he seems to make the sacrifice from more powerful animals".

[135] LXX has μοσχάρια ("young calves") for MT *pārīm* ("oxen"). The word used by our author here is μόσχοι ("calves").

narrative Moses sprinkles part of the sacrificial blood on the altar (as representing God, the Author of the covenant) and part on the people (who are thus brought into God's covenant), here he sprinkles it on the *book* and on the people.[136] The book indeed, containing the divine commandments which constituted the basis of the covenant, might represent God in this act as fittingly as would the altar. Again, whereas the Exodus narrative describes Moses as sprinkling nothing but blood, here the blood is accompanied by water, scarlet wool and hyssop. We have no evidence for the origin of these variations on the Exodus narrative; for them, as for some of the details of the tabernacle furniture in verse 4 (the position of the incense-altar and the contents of the ark) our author may well have drawn upon some source which is no longer extant.[137]

The hyssop, or marjoram, is probably envisaged as the means by which the blood was sprinkled on this occasion, just as hyssop was used to sprinkle the blood of the paschal lamb round the doorway of each Israelite house in Egypt (Ex. 12:22), to sprinkle blood (and water) on the cured leper or on the house which had been cleared of a "leprous" infection (Lev. 14:4ff., 49ff.), and (most significantly) to sprinkle *mē niddāh* on persons or objects that had become ceremonially defiled by contact with the dead (Num. 19:18).[138] The water and scarlet wool which our author mentions along with the sacrificial blood are also reminiscent of the ritual of the red heifer in Num. 19; it looks as if features of that ritual are here associated with the ratification of the ancient covenant. The two passages are linked by their common interest

---

[136] It is an undue straining of the language to take αὐτό τε τὸ βιβλίον as dependent on λαβών ("having taken") and coordinate with τὸ αἷμα ("the blood"); the participle τε links it with καὶ πάντα τὸν λαόν ("and all the people") as part of the object of ἐρράντισεν ("sprinkled").

[137] Possibly a halakhic and haggadic midrash such as G. Allon postulates as underlying the account of the red heifer in *Ep. Barn.* 7–8 (see p. 203, n. 88 *fin.*). Scarlet wool, which is mentioned here in connection with the ratification of the covenant and in Num. 19:6 in connection with the red heifer, was bound on the head of the scapegoat, according to Mishnah, *Yoma* iv. 2; vi. 6; Tertullian, *Against Marcion* iii. 7; *Against the Jews* 14.

[138] The language of Ps. 51:7, "Purify me with hyssop, and I shall be clean", represents a figurative use of this last ritual—figurative, because no literal sprinkling of *mē niddāh* with hyssop could have cleansed the penitent from blood-guiltiness (Ps. 51:14).

in ritual aspersion. A further link has been suggested in terms of the triennial synagogue lectionary, in which Ex. 24 and Num. 19 would have been read around the same season of the year in the second and third years respectively.[139]

21 Nor was the ratification of the covenant the only occasion on which similar purification by the sprinkling of blood was carried out under the old order. The tabernacle itself and the vessels of divine service were similarly sprinkled. In the Pentateuchal prescriptions the horns of the altar of burnt-offering were to be smeared with the blood of the bullock which was sacrificed as a sin-offering at the consecration of Aaron and his sons for their priestly service (Ex. 29:12; *cf.* Lev. 8:15); and on the Day of Atonement the mercy-seat and the horns of the altar of burnt-offering were to be sprinkled with the blood of the bullock presented as a sin-offering for Aaron and his house and of the goat which was killed as a sin-offering for the people (Lev. 16:14–19). That all the vessels of divine service were thus purified by the sprinkling of blood is not expressly stated in the Pentateuch; what is so stated is that the tabernacle and all its furnishings, inside and outside, were hallowed by being anointed with oil (Ex. 40:9–11; Lev. 8:10f.; Num. 7:1). But as Aaron and his sons were hallowed with the blood of the ram of consecration as well as with the oil of anointing when they were installed in their sacred office (Lev. 8:23f., 30), it might be inferred that the tabernacle and its furnishings, which were hallowed at the same time, were sprinkled with the blood in addition to being anointed with the oil. Josephus, to the same effect, says that Moses spent seven days[140] purifying the priests and their vestments, "as also the tabernacle and its vessels, both with oil ... and with the blood of bulls and rams".[141]

22 Indeed, our author goes on, "almost everything" (RSV) which requires to be ceremonially cleansed under the Old Testament law must be cleansed by means of blood. "Almost everything" but not absolutely everything; there are certain exceptions. For example, an impoverished Israelite might bring a tenth of an ephah (four pints) of fine flour to the priest as his sin-offering in-

---

[139] See p. xlviii, with n. 112.
[140] For the seven days *cf.* Ex. 29:35f.; Lev. 8:33, 35.
[141] *Ant.* iii. 206. Philo (*Life of Moses*, ii. 146ff.) also associates the consecration of the priests closely with the consecration of the tabernacle and its furniture, but restricts the application of blood to the priests.

stead of a lamb or even instead of two turtledoves or young pigeons (Lev. 5:11). In Num. 16:46 atonement was made for the congregation of Israel, after the destruction of Korah and his company, by means of incense; in Num. 31:22f. metal objects captured in war were to be purified by fire and *mē niddāh*;[142] in Num. 31:50 the Israelite commanders in the fighting against Midian brought the gold objects which they had captured "to make atonement for our souls before Jehovah". But such exceptions were rare; the general rule was that ceremonial cleansing or atonement had to be effected by means of blood: "apart from shedding of blood[143] there is no remission".[144]

7. THE PERFECT SACRIFICE

Ch. 9:23–28

23 It was necessary therefore that the copies of the things in the heavens should be cleansed with these; but the heavenly things themselves with better sacrifices than these.

24 For Christ entered not into a holy place made with hands, like in pattern to the true; but into heaven itself, now to appear before the face of God for us:

25 nor yet that he should offer himself often, as the high priest entereth into the holy place[145] year by year with blood not his own;

26 else must he often have suffered[146] since the foundation of the world: but now once at the end of the ages hath

---

[142] *Cf.* p. 203.

[143] Gk. αἱματεκχυσία, probably a coinage of our author's.

[144] This may have been a proverbial expression, to judge by instances in the rabbinical writings; *cf.* "Does not atonement come through the blood"? (TB *Yoma* 5a, twice); "Surely atonement can be made only with the blood" (TB *Zebaḥim* 6a). These aphorisms are regularly confirmed by the following quotation of Lev. 17:11 ("it is the blood that maketh atonement by reason of the life").

[145] Gk. τὰ ἅγια, to which a few minuscules (including 69 and 1912), with the Armenian and Sahidic Coptic versions, add τῶν ἁγίων (yielding the rendering "holy of holies" for "holy place"). See p. 194.

[146] Gk. παθεῖν, for which a few minuscules (including 241 and 1908) with the Sahidic version read ἀποθανεῖν ("have died"). *Cf.* p. 402, n. 77.

he been manifested to put away sin[147] by the sacrifice of himself.

27 And inasmuch as it is appointed unto men once to die, and after this *cometh* judgment;

28 so Christ also, having been once offered to bear the sins of many, shall appear a second time, apart from sin, to them that wait for him, unto salvation.[148]

23 With the blood of sacrificial animals, then, the material sanctuary and its accessories were cleansed from defilement and hallowed for the worship of God. Our author does not deny that such ritual cleansing was real and effective so far as it went. What he does deny is that cleansing of this kind could be of any use for the removal of inward and spiritual defilement. The various installations that were cleansed and fitted for the worship of God by the blood of animal sacrifices were but copies[149] of the spiritual realities; where the spiritual realities themselves are concerned, a superior sacrifice[150] and more effective cleansing must be forthcoming. It has frequently been asked in what sense "the heavenly things"[151] required to be cleansed; but our author has provided the answer in the context. What required to be cleansed was the defiled conscience of men and women; this is a cleansing which belongs to the spiritual sphere. The argument of verse 23 might be paraphrased by saying that while ritual purification is adequate for the material order, which is but an earthly copy of the spiritual order, a better kind of sacrifice is necessary to effect purification in

---

[147] Gk. εἰς ἀθέτησιν τῆς ἁμαρτίας (*cf.* p. 222, nn. 164, 165); τῆς is omitted by P⁴⁶ C and the Byzantine text (perhaps rightly, since our author has no objection to the use of ἁμαρτία without the article); D* (but not *d*) has the anarthrous plural ἁμαρτιῶν.

[148] A few authorities add the gloss διὰ πίστεως ("through faith") either before εἰς σωτηρίαν (*e.g.* 69) or after it (*e.g.* A P). *Cf.* I Pet. 1:15.

[149] Gk. ὑπόδειγμα, as in Ch. 8:5 (*cf.* p. 165, n. 25).

[150] Why the plural, "better sacrifices"? Our author probably uses the generic plural in stating the principle (purification in the heavenly order must be effected by better sacrifices than those required to effect purification in the earthly order); but when he comes to show how this principle was put into practice, he makes it plain that in fact only one such superior sacrifice was ever offered.

[151] Gk. τὰ ἐπουράνια, as in Ch. 8:5 (the same phrase is repeatedly rendered "the heavenly places" in Ephesians).

the spiritual order. If we envisage the heavenly dwelling-place of God in something like material terms (and, surrounded as we are by the material universe, it is difficult to avoid doing so), we shall find ourselves trying to explain the necessity for its cleansing in ways which are far from our author's intention.[152] But we have already had reason to emphasize that the people of God are the house of God, that His dwelling-place is in their midst.[153] It is they who require inward cleansing, not only that their approach to God may be free from defilement, but that they may be a fit habitation for Him. Just as the tabernacle in the wilderness, together with its furniture, had to be anointed and sanctified so that God might manifest His presence there among His people and they might serve Him there, so the people of God themselves require to be cleansed and hallowed in order to become "a habitation of God in the Spirit" (Eph. 2:22). The same essential teaching recurs in I Pet. 2:5, where believers in Christ are described as being "built up a spiritual house, to be a holy priesthood, to offer up spiritual sacrifices, acceptable to God through Jesus Christ". But in order to be a spiritual house of this kind they must have experienced regeneration and cleansing by "sprinkling of the blood of Jesus Christ" (I Pet. 1:2, 19, 22f.).

If more than this is felt to be involved in our author's language here, it may be supplied by the words of William Manson: "if we conceive our author to be writing to Jewish Christians who

---

[152] Thus it has been suggested that the cleansing was made necessary by the presence of Satan (Rev. 12:3ff.) or of other "spiritual hosts of wickedness" (Eph. 6:12) in the heavenly sphere (*cf.*, *e.g.*, O. Michel, *Der Brief an die Hebräer*, MK [Göttingen, 1949], pp. 213f. [following F. Bleek, *ad loc.*]; G. H. Lang, *The Epistle to the Hebrews* [London, 1951], pp. 153f.). This, however, imports into our author's argument something that is alien to it, whereas he states repeatedly what it is that actually has been cleansed by the sacrifice of Christ. By the removal of the defilement of sin from the hearts and consciences of the worshippers, the heavenly sphere in which they approach God to worship Him is itself cleansed from this defilement. The analogical use of language proper to the earthly sanctuary might give the impression that the heavenly sanctuary itself is envisaged as a locality; but we need not suppose that our author thought of it absolutely in local terms.

[153] See exposition of verse 11 (pp. 199f.), and *cf.* Ch. 12:22f. (pp. 372ff.). In 4Q *Florilegium*, line 12, God replaces the material sanctuary after its destruction by a "sanctuary of men" (*miqdash 'ādām*) who "will offer the works of the law like the smoke of incense" (*cf.* p. 406 with n. 91). In 1QS viii. 5f. the council of the Qumran community *is* the holy of holies (*cf.* p. 58, n. 18).

perhaps missed in the spiritual worship of Christianity the *many* holy sanctions and consecratory rites of the old religion, we shall not think it strange that he should, in effect, say to them that Christianity has its own sublime, though invisible, sanctions imparted by a greater Sacrifice. Following out this conception, we can well imagine him saying that the book of the New Covenant (the eternal gospel written in heaven ...), the Christian sanctuary (the heavenly Zion, *cf.* 12:18–24), and the New Israel (the Christian Church, including the company of the redeemed in heaven) have all been consecrated by the blood of Christ. The stamp of the Cross is on all of them. After all, the things in heaven represent realities which have a present existence for Christians through Christ."[154]

24 It is not into any material sanctuary that Christ has gone as His people's high priest, but into the presence of God in heaven. One who is personally "holy, guileless, undefiled" (Ch. 7:26) is at home and acceptable in the presence of God. But He appears now in the presence of God not only on His own behalf but on behalf of others, and those others are sinners. If sinners are to appear before God, even by proxy, through the representation of a sinless high priest, they must be cleansed from sin, or else the very presence of God would be polluted. And this cleansing Christ has effected, so that He can minister on His people's behalf in "the true tabernacle" which no human hands have erected.[155] The earthly sanctuary and the priestly ministry associated with it were but faint foreshadowings[156] of the spiritual and heavenly order in which Christ exercises His perpetual priesthood as His people's representative with God.

25 Moreover, when Christ entered into the heavenly sanctuary, He entered once for all. His entrance into the presence of God on

---

154 W. Manson, *The Epistle to the Hebrews* (London, 1951), pp. 140f.

155 As in Ch. 8:2 (see p. 163, n. 17) the heavenly tabernacle is ἀληθινός. With "made with hands" (χειροποίητος) *cf.* "not made with hands" (οὐ χειροποίητος) in verse 11 (p. 199 with notes 76–78).

156 The earthly sanctuary and its fittings are here described as ἀντίτυπα of the true heavenly sanctuary; ἀντίτυπος here has thus much the same meaning as τύπος ("pattern") in Ch. 8:5, and might be rendered "counter-pattern" or "corresponding pattern"; in other words, the earthly corresponds to the heavenly as a copy or symbol corresponds to the reality which is copied or symbolized. The only other occurrence of ἀντίτυπος in NT is in I Pet. 3:21, where it refers to

His people's behalf, by virtue of His own blood, in set in sharp contrast to the entrance of Israel's high priest into the material holy of holies on the Day of Atonement. Having entered in to present the sacrificial blood ("blood not his own"), Israel's high priest had to come out again immediately, to enter in and repeat the same ceremony the following year, and the year after that, and so on indefinitely. But the sacrifice of Christ, being a real sacrifice and not a token one, is perpetually effective and therefore calls for no repetition.

26 If His sacrifice did call for repetition, then He would have to endure suffering and death times without number throughout the ages of world history.[157] But that involves a patent absurdity; "it is appointed unto men once to die", and the Son of Man, who became "like unto his brethren" in all things, cannot and must not die more than once. To talk about His sacrifice as "the eternal sacrifice" can therefore be misleading. If it means that His sacrifice is the historical expression of the eternal mercy of God, or that its efficacy is eternal, no exception can be taken to the term; but if it means (as it does for many who use it) that He is eternally offering Himself in heaven (with the corollary that in the Eucharist His sacrifice is repeatedly re-enacted on earth), then it is in plain contradiction to the emphatic teaching of this epistle. He appears eternally in heaven for His people on the basis of "the sacrifice of Himself", presented and accepted once for all.

As it is,[158] Christ has been manifested once[159] on earth at the time of fulfilment in order to deal conclusively with sin. The phrase "the end of the ages" or "the consummation of the ages"[160] (as ARV margin has it) is not found in this precise form elsewhere in the New Testament, although it closely resembles the Matthaean

---

baptism as the Christian "counterpart" to Noah's salvation in the ark. Whereas in Hebrews it is the Old Testament symbol that is called the "antitype", in I Peter it is the New Testament reality. The usage in Hebrews is in line with Philo's use of the word (*cf.* C. Spicq, *L'Épître aux Hébreux* i [Paris, 1952], p. 75).

[157] For "since the foundation of the world" (ἀπὸ καταβολῆς κόσμου) *cf.* Ch. 4:3 (p. 71, n. 8).

[158] Gk. νυνὶ δέ, ARV "but now", where "now" (as in Ch. 8:6) is to be taken in a logical, not a temporal, sense.

[159] Here the simple adverb ἅπαξ is used, but it has much the same emphatic force as the compound ἐφάπαξ in verse 12.

[160] Gk. ἐπὶ συντελείᾳ τῶν αἰώνων.

"consummation of the age",[161] the Pauline "ends of the ages",[162] and the Petrine "end of the times",[163] being practically synonymous with the last two. It is not that Christ happened to come at the time of fulfilment but that His coming made that time the time of fulfilment. The purpose of His coming is stated to be the removal or cancellation of sin; the same substantive[164] is used here as in Ch. 7:18, where we are told that the announcement of the Melchizedek priesthood in Ps. 110:4 constitutes the "disannulling" or abrogation of the earlier law which set up the Aaronic priesthood. In the present context the word, says E. K. Simpson, "seems to imply *effacement*".[165] The statement of the purpose of the coming of Christ has a close parallel in I John 3:5: "ye know that he was manifested to take away[166] sins". "The sacrifice of himself", like "his own blood" in verse 12, is emphatic, marking once more the contrast between His priestly action and that of Aaron and his successors, who made expiation with the blood of others, namely of sacrificial animals. In what "the sacrifice of himself" consisted is shortly to be explained.[167]

27-28 Men die once, by divine appointment, and in their case death is followed by judgment.[168] Christ died once, by divine appointment, and His death is followed by salvation for all His

---

[161] *Cf.* Matt. 13:39f., 49; 24:3; 28:20 for (ἡ) συντέλεια (τοῦ) αἰῶνος.

[162] I Cor. 10:11 (τὰ τέλη τῶν αἰώνων); *cf.* also Gal. 4:4 (τὸ πλήρωμα τοῦ χρόνου).

[163] I Pet. 1:20, where Christ, "foreknown before the foundation of the world" (πρὸ καταβολῆς κόσμου), was manifested ἐπ' ἐσχάτου τῶν χρόνων. The Matthaean references are to the future; the present reference, like the Pauline and Petrine, is to the present order inaugurated by the advent and redemptive work of Christ. *Cf.* Ch. 1:2 ("at the end of these days"). The plural "ages" here and in I Cor. 10:11 may point to the intersection of the two ages when Christ appeared, or it may denote, more generally, "the climax of history" (W. Manson, *op. cit.*, p. 140). The phrase τῇ συντελείᾳ τῶν αἰώνων (*v.l.* τοῦ αἰῶνος) appears in *Test. Levi* 10:2.

[164] Gk. ἀθέτησις (see p. 147, n. 56).

[165] *EQ* xviii (1946), p. 190. "On the whole, then", he says, "the expression εἰς ἀθέτησιν ἁμαρτίας appears to be equivalent to Diodati's Italian version of it, *per annullare il peccato*, expressive of the *cancelling* or *elimination* of sin, a little more specific, that is to say, than our version, 'putting away'."

[166] Gk. αἴρειν (see p. 223, n. 169).

[167] In Ch. 10:5ff. (see pp. 231ff.).

[168] *Cf.* Ch. 10:27, 30; 12:23.

people. This is so because in His death He bore[169] "the sins of many", offering up His life to God as an atonement on their behalf. The language here is a plain echo of the fourth Servant Song—more especially of Isa. 53:12, "he bare the sin of many", but also of verses 10, "he makes himself an offering for sin"[170] (RSV), and 11, "by the knowledge of himself shall my righteous servant justify many, and he shall bear[171] their iniquities".[172] His bearing of sin implies the removing of sin from others, and the consequent liberation of those who enter into the benefits of His self-oblation.

The Israelites who watched their high priest enter the sanctuary for them waited expectantly for his reappearance; that was a welcome sign that he and the sacrifice which he presented had been accepted by God. His reappearance from the holy of holies on the Day of Atonement was a specially welcome sight. Ben Sira celebrates the joy with which the people saw the high priest Simon the Just emerge from the "house of the veil" after completing this sacred ministry:

"How glorious he was when the people gathered round him
    as he came out of the inner sanctuary!
Like the morning star among the clouds,
    like the moon when it is full;

---

[169] Gk. ἀνενεγκεῖν, aorist infinitive of ἀναφέρειν (which is used in the sense of "offering up" sacrifices in Chs. 7:27; 13:15); the same verb is used of Christ's sin-bearing in I Pet. 2:24, and in both places may be influenced by the LXX rendering of Isa. 53:12 (ἁμαρτίας πολλῶν ἀνήνεγκεν). The Hebrew verb there used is nāsā', which may mean not only "bear" but also "take away"; the latter sense is conveyed in NT in relation to Christ's redemptive work by Gk. αἴρειν, as in John 1:29; I John 3:5 (see p. 222, n. 166). On ἀνενεγκεῖν here as meaning "take upon oneself" see W. Bauer, *Griechisch-Deutsches Handwörterbuch zu den Schriften des NTs*⁵ (Berlin, 1958), s.v. ἀναφέρω (3).

[170] Heb. 'āshām, "a guilt-offering", LXX περὶ ἁμαρτίας, for which cf. Chs. 10:6, 18; 13:11. See p. 158, n. 93.

[171] The Hebrew verb in v. 11 is not nāsā' (as in v. 12) but sābal, but both are rendered in LXX by the same Gk. verb (see n. 169 above).

[172] On the influence of the fourth Servant Song on our author's thought and language about the sacrifice of Christ cf. V. Taylor, *The Atonement in New Testament Teaching* (London, 1940), pp. 149ff., 176, 182, 186f.; *The Life and Ministry of Jesus* (London, 1955), p. 144; W. Zimmerli and J. Jeremias, *The Servant of God* (Eng. tr., London, 1957), pp. 93, 96; A. Richardson, *An Introduction to the Theology of the New Testament* (London, 1958), pp. 220ff. See also pp. 158ff. above, pp. 233f. below, and, more generally, *Acts*, NICNT (Grand Rapids, 1954), pp. 88f., 187ff.

> like the sun shining upon the temple of the Most High,
>> and like the rainbow gleaming in glorious clouds;
> like roses in the days of the first fruits,
>> like lilies by a spring of water,
>> like a green shoot on Lebanon on a summer day;
> like fire and incense in the censer,
>> like a vessel of hammered gold
>> adorned with all kinds of precious stones;
> like an olive tree putting forth its fruit,
>> and like a cypress towering in the clouds" (Sir. 50:5–10).

So our author thinks of Jesus as going into the heavenly holy of holies, to reappear one day in order to confirm finally to His people the salvation[173] which His perfect offering has procured for them. Meanwhile they wait expectantly for His parousia. This presentation of the return of Christ in terms of the high priest's emergence from the sanctuary was in Frances Ridley Havergal's mind when she wrote:

> "Coming! In the opening east
> Herald brightness slowly swells;
> Coming! O my glorious Priest,
> Hear we not Thy golden bells?"[174]

But when He appears the second time to those who expect Him, it will not be to deal with sin once more. Sin was dealt with decisively at His first appearing. All the blessings which He won for His people at His first appearing will be theirs to enjoy in perpetual fulness at His second appearing. Therefore, let them not grow faint and weary but persevere in patience and faith.[175]

---

[173] For this future and final phase of salvation *cf.* Ch. 1:14 and other scriptures mentioned in exposition *ad loc.*

[174] Although on the Day of Atonement the high priest wore the "holy linen coat" (Lev. 16:4) and not the blue "robe of the ephod" (Ex. 28:31ff.) to which the bells and pomegranates were attached.

[175] *(Addition to p. 183, n. 11.)* According to Philo, *Who is the Heir of Divine Things?* 221, and Josephus, *Antiquities* iii. 146, the seven branches of the *menorah* represent the seven planets.

CHAPTER X

8. THE OLD ORDER A SHADOW OF THE REALITY

Ch. 10:1–4

1 For the law having a shadow of the good *things* to come, not the very image[1] of the things, can[2] never with the same sacrifices[3] year by year, which they offer continually, make perfect[4] them that draw nigh.

2 Else[5] would they not have ceased to be offered? because the worshippers, having been cleansed, would have had no more consciousness of sins.

3 But in those *sacrifices* there is a remembrance made of sins year by year.

4 For it is impossible that the blood of bulls and goats[6] should take away sins.

---

[1] P^{46} has the interesting reading $\varkappa a \grave{\iota} \ \tau \grave{\eta} \nu \ \varepsilon \grave{\iota} \varkappa \acute{o} \nu a$ ("and the image") for $o \grave{\upsilon} \varkappa \ a \grave{\upsilon} \tau \grave{\eta} \nu \ \tau \grave{\eta} \nu \ \varepsilon \grave{\iota} \varkappa \acute{o} \nu a$ ("not the very image"). This implies for $\varepsilon \grave{\iota} \varkappa \acute{\omega} \nu$ here the sense of a *mere* copy, something no better than a $\sigma \varkappa \iota \acute{a}$. But $\varepsilon \grave{\iota} \varkappa \acute{\omega} \nu$ normally has a more substantial meaning than this, and the construction of the sentence indicates that here it is contrasted with $\sigma \varkappa \iota \acute{a}$, not practically synonymous with it. *Cf.* G. Zuntz, *The Text of the Epistles* (London, 1953), pp. 20ff., where conclusive arguments are given against accepting the reading of P^{46}.

[2] Gk. $\delta \acute{\upsilon} \nu a \tau a \iota$, for which ℵ A C 33 with the Harclean Syriac and other authorities have the plural $\delta \acute{\upsilon} \nu a \nu \tau a \iota$, whence ERV "they can ..." (*cf.* ARV mg.). The plural reading makes our author guilty of a hanging nominative at the beginning of the sentence, whereas he is usually careful to observe grammatical accuracy. The singular is attested most notably by P^{46} and D*.

[3] ℵ P read "their same sacrifices" ($\tau a \tilde{\iota} \varsigma \ a \grave{\upsilon} \tau a \tilde{\iota} \varsigma \ \theta \upsilon \sigma \acute{\iota} a \iota \varsigma \ a \grave{\upsilon} \tau \tilde{\omega} \nu$).

[4] For $\tau \varepsilon \lambda \varepsilon \iota \tilde{\omega} \sigma a \iota$ ("make perfect") D reads $\varkappa a \theta a \varrho \acute{\iota} \sigma a \iota$ ("cleanse"), probably under the influence of v. 2. True inward cleansing is, of course, part of the perfecting (*cf. v.* 14).

[5] Gk. $\grave{\varepsilon} \pi \varepsilon \acute{\iota}$, in the *koiné* sense "for if it were otherwise" (German *da sonst*); the clause thus introduced is to be read as a question. Failure to recognize this led to early emendations: H* 1739 and some other authorities omit $o \grave{\upsilon} \varkappa$ ("not"), producing the unexceptionable statement "they would have ceased to be offered"; P^{46} 1518 improve the solecistic $\grave{\varepsilon} \pi \varepsilon \grave{\iota} \ \check{a} \nu$ which results from the omission of $o \grave{\upsilon} \varkappa$ by the elegant emendation $\grave{\varepsilon} \pi \varepsilon \grave{\iota} \ \varkappa \check{a} \nu$.

[6] The order is reversed to $\tau \varrho \acute{a} \gamma \omega \nu \ \varkappa a \grave{\iota} \ \tau a \acute{\upsilon} \varrho \omega \nu$ in P^{46} ℵ 69 and a few other authorities, in conformity with Ch. 9:13.

1 Both Paul and our author speak of the law as "a shadow"; but whereas Paul in Col. 2:17 has in mind the legal restrictions of Old Testament times (food-laws and regulations about special days),[7] our author is thinking more especially of the law prescribing matters of priesthood and sacrifice in relation to the wilderness tabernacle and the Jerusalem temple. In both places, however, "shadow" is used not so much in the Platonic sense of a copy of the heavenly and eternal "idea" as in the sense of foreshadowing. For Paul, the legal restrictions to which he refers are "a shadow of the things to come"; for our author, the sacrificial law of Israel provides "a shadow of the good things to come"; both writers think of Christ and His new order as the perfect reality to which the earlier ordinances pointed forward.

The "good things to come" (as in Ch. 9:11) embrace the un-repeatable sacrifice of Christ and His present high-priestly ministry, which carry with them eternal redemption and un-inhibited access to worship the living God. They are the only absolutely "good" things, because they comprise the "perfection" which the old order was incapable of supplying.

What now is the distinction which our author draws between "shadow" and "image"—unless we are to adopt the reading of our oldest manuscript which equates the two and says that the law had only the "shadow and image" of the coming reality?[8] The shadow is but a shadow; the "image" *(eikōn)*—especially "the very image"—is an exact replica, "not an imperfect, partial re-production, but a manifestation adequate to the reality itself".[9] The "image" is thus something superior to the "copies" or "patterns" of Ch. 9:23f. Platonic and Philonic antecedents for this use of *eikōn* can be readily adduced;[10] but within the New

---

[7] Cf. *Colossians*, NICNT (Grand Rapids, 1957), p. 245.

[8] See p. 225, n. 1.

[9] A. E. Garvie, *ExT* xxviii (1916–17), p. 398 (in an article "Shadow and Substance", pp. 397ff.). C. Spicq (*L'Épître aux Hébreux* i [Paris, 1952], p. 75) makes the point that an artist draws an outline (σκιά) before he produces the finished portrait (εἰκών), and that a similar relation exists in our author's mind between the Levitical ceremonial as the preliminary sketch and the high-priestly work of Christ as the completed masterpiece.

[10] J. Moffatt (*ad loc.*) quotes from Plato, *Cratylus* 306E, almost the same expression as our author uses here (εἰκόνα τῶν πραγμάτων). According to Philo (*Life of Moses* ii. 51), Moses regarded his laws as "an image most truly cor-responding to the constitution of the world" (ἐμφερεστάτην εἰκόνα τῆς τοῦ κόσμου

Testament itself we have Paul's repeated description of Christ as the *eikōn* of God (2 Cor. 4:4; Col. 1:15) and his statement of the divine purpose that believers should be conformed to the *eikōn* of the Son of God (Rom. 8:29; *cf.* 2 Cor. 3:18; Col. 3:10).

In any case, the old order could never bring those who worshipped under it to a state of perfection; this was plain enough from the fact that, as circling time moved round and year succeeded year, the same sacrifices had to be repeated over and over again. The sacrifice that is uppermost in our author's mind is still the annual sacrifice on the Day of Atonement.

2 If the old order had been able to bring "perfection"—access to God without the constant necessity of removing the barrier of freshly accumulated sin—then surely the sacrifices which belonged to it would have come to an end. The natural implication of the question "Else would they not have ceased to be offered?" is that the sacrificial ritual was still practised in the temple at Jerusalem.[11] It might be argued that our author, writing after A.D. 70, means that if perfection was attainable under the Levitical economy, its sacrificial system would have come to an end long before it did—even within the Old Testament period. But that is a much less natural interpretation of his words; it is simplest to regard them as an incidental pointer to the dating of the epistle before A.D. 70.[12]

If the old sacrificial order had possessed true cleansing efficacy —that is to say, if it had been able to cleanse the *conscience*—then the worshippers would have enjoyed unrestricted communion with God. It is the presence of sin in the conscience that hinders such communion; "if I regard iniquity in my heart", said the psalmist,

---

πολιτείας). *Cf.* Spicq, *loc. cit.*; H. Willms, *EIKΩN*: *Eine begriffsgeschichtliche Untersuchung zum Platonismus*, I: *Philon von Alexandria* (Münster, 1935).

[11] The similar ritual of the Jewish temple at Leontopolis in Egypt (founded by Onias IV *c.* 160 B.C.), which survived that at Jerusalem by a year or two (*cf.* Josephus, *BJ* vii. 420 ff.), hardly comes into the picture (see p. xxxiii, n. 49); whatever the Alexandrine affinities of this epistle may be, we may doubt whether the Leontopolis temple had much religious significance for the Alexandrine Jews (Philo, for example, speaks of going on pilgrimage "to our ancestral temple" [εἰς τὸ πατρῷον ἱερόν] in Jerusalem [*On Providence*, 64]).

[12] Had he been writing after A.D. 70 and had worded his argument precisely in these terms, it could have been said: "Well, they *have* ceased to be offered"—a superficial objection, no doubt, but even so one to which such a skilful disputant is not likely to have laid himself open.

227

"the Lord will not hear" (Ps. 66:18). The implication of our author's argument is that the true inward cleansing is permanently effective and therefore unrepeatable. When he speaks of the worshippers as "having been once cleansed" he means "once for all", and emphasizes this by his choice of the perfect tense. The sense is much the same as that of our Lord's words to Peter in John 13:10: "He that is bathed needeth not save to wash his feet, but is clean every whit".[13] The cleansing marks the beginning of the Christian life: Peter referred to it when he reminded the Council of Jerusalem that God, in giving the Holy Spirit to the Gentiles as He had done to the Jews, "made no distinction between us and them, cleansing their hearts by faith" (Acts 15:9).[14] But such a cleansing as this, which means that those who receive it are thenceforward "clean" without requiring any repetition of the cleansing, was unknown to the Levitical law.

3 As it is, the annually recurring ritual of the Day of Atonement involved a "remembrance"[15] of sins year by year. This remembrance (as regularly in biblical usage) is more than a calling to mind; it involves some appropriate form of action. The remembrance of sins may involve repentance for them,[16] or it may involve persistence in them.[17] But the remembrance of sins *in the sight of God* involves appropriate action on *His* part, either pardon or retribution.[18] A pardon that has to be bestowed repeatedly—so far at least as its ceremonial expression is concerned—cannot convey the same peace of conscience as a pardon bestowed once for all. And there is a manifest contrast, to our author's mind, between the old order in which "there is a remembrance made of

---

[13] Or, in the shorter reading reproduced in the text of NEB: "A man who has bathed needs no further washing; he is altogether clean."

[14] *Cf.* I Cor. 6:11, "ye were washed (Gk. ἀπελούσασθε) ..."

[15] Gk. ἀνάμνησις. *Cf.* Num. 5:15, where the ordeal of jealousy involves "a meal-offering of memorial, bringing iniquity to remembrance" (and Jub. 34:19, where the Day of Atonement is the anniversary of the day on which Joseph was sold by his brothers, and "has been ordained that they should grieve thereon for all their sins, and for all their errors, so that they might cleanse themselves on that day once a year"). On the biblical force of remembrance *cf.* p. 175 (on Ch. 8:12).

[16] *Cf.* Deut. 9:7.

[17] *Cf.* Ezek. 23:19.

[18] But mainly retribution (*cf.* I Kings 17:18; Rev. 16:19); pardon is regularly viewed in terms of God's ceasing to remember sins (*cf.* Ps. 25:7).

sins year by year"[19] and the new covenant which embodies God's promise to His people: "their sins will I remember no more" (Ch. 8:12).

It would not have occurred to an observant Jew under the Mosaic covenant to say that the Day of Atonement involved an annual "remembrance" of sins; he would have said, rather, that there was an annual *removal* of sins. Our author might have replied, truly enough, that the ritual designed to effect the removal of sins necessarily involves their remembrance; but he is influenced chiefly by the promise that under the new covenant God will remember His people's sins no more. Since the new covenant is contrasted with the old, the implication is that there was no such absolute wiping out of sins from the divine record under the sacrificial law.

It has been suggested that even in some forms of Christian liturgy a "remembrance" is made repeatedly of sins to a point where the Christian's sense of being constantly welcome in the presence of God for Christ's sake is seriously threatened.[20] There is a difference between the humble and contrite confession of sins to God and a morbid dwelling on sins already confessed and forgiven which might well call forth the Pauline reminder that "the Spirit you have received is not a spirit of slavery leading you back into a life of fear, but a Spirit that makes us sons, enabling us to cry 'Abba! Father!' " (Rom. 8:15, NEB).

4 But this condition of spiritual imperfection was inevitable so long as men's ideas of God and forgiveness were bound up with a sacrificial cultus like that of early Israel. "It is impossible that the blood of bulls and goats should take away sins." This impossibility has only to be stated plainly like this for its truth to be obvious. Moral defilement cannot be removed by material means.

---

[19] Philo (*Life of Moses* ii. 107) says that the sacrifices of the wicked "effect not a remission (λύσις) but a remembrance (ὑπόμνησις) of sins" (*cf. Planting* 108, where the sacrifices of the wicked "do but put God in remembrance of the sins, inadvertent and otherwise, of the various offerers"). Therefore let men eschew wickedness, "for it would be foolish to have the sacrifices effecting remembrance (ὑπόμνησις) rather than forgetting of sins" (*Special Laws* i. 215). But those who offer from a pure heart both seek (*Life of Moses* ii. 24) and obtain (*Special Laws* i. 242) ἀμνηστία of their sins on God's part. Our author, however, says that these sin-offerings involve a remembrance of sins irrespective of the character of the offerers.

[20] *Cf.* H. A. Williams, "Unchristian Liturgy", *Theology* lxi (1958), pp. 401ff.

Such spiritual value as the sacrificial ritual might have lay in its being a material foreshadowing or object-lesson of a moral and spiritual reality. The writer to the Hebrews was not the first man to appreciate this; the truth had been grasped centuries earlier, as by the penitent psalmist who prayed:

> "Create in me a clean heart, O God;
> And renew a right spirit within me. ...
> For thou delightest not in sacrifice; else would I give it:
> Thou hast no pleasure in burnt-offering.
> The sacrifices of God are a broken spirit:
> A broken and a contrite heart, O God, thou wilt not
> despise."[21]

And he was only one among other psalmists and prophets who made substantially the same affirmation. In the closing years of the Second Temple, there were many pious Jews who, while paying lip-service to the sacrificial cultus and indeed participating in it according to the law, yet realized that this was not the means by which sin could be removed.[22] The members of the Qumran community believed that when their strict interpretation of the divine commandments was carried out perfectly, "then the oblation of the lips according to right judgment shall be as a sweet savour of righteousness, and the perfectness of one's ways as an acceptable freewill offering".[23] A Pharisee might have criticized the un-compromising manner in which our author here dismisses animal sacrifice, "but there is no reason for thinking that he would have rejected a more guarded statement of the truth. The relatively easy adaptation of the Palestinian synagogue to the new conditions after the destruction of the Temple in 70 A.D. shows that the principle of the insufficiency of animal sacrifice had been widely grasped."[24] Yet the Pharisees took part in the sacrificial cultus so long as it endured, and when it disappeared they had to give

---

[21] Ps. 51:10, 16f. (LXX 50:12, 18f.); cf. I Sam. 15:22; Ps. 50:8ff. (LXX 49:8ff.); Isa. 1:11ff.; 66:1ff.; Jer. 7:21ff.; Hos. 6:6; 14:2; Amos 5:21ff.; Mic. 6:6ff.

[22] Cf. R. A. Stewart, *Rabbinical Theology* (Edinburgh, 1961), pp. 120ff.

[23] 1QS ix. 4f. There is an echo of Hos. 14:2 here; cf. Heb. 13:15 (p. 406 with n. 91).

[24] H. L. Ellison, *The Centrality of the Messianic Idea for the Old Testament* (London, 1953), p. 19.

serious thought to the question how sin was now to be expiated.[25]
The seriousness of this question must be appreciated by all who
understand the "exceeding sinfulness" of sin. Our author understood it well enough; but he could bid farewell to the sacrificial
cultus the more cheerfully because he knew of a sacrifice, presented
on quite another plane, which effectively dealt with sin as the old
cultus could not.

9. THE NEW ORDER THE REALITY

Ch. 10:5–10

5 Wherefore when he cometh into the world, he saith,
   Sacrifice and offering thou wouldest not,
   But a body didst thou prepare for me;

6 In whole burnt offerings[26] and *sacrifices* for sin thou
   hadst no pleasure:

7 Then said I, Lo, I am come
   (In the roll of the book it is written[27] of me)
   To do thy will, O God.[28]

8 Saying above, Sacrifices and offerings and whole burnt
   offerings and *sacrifices* for sin thou wouldest not, neither
   hadst pleasure therein (the which are offered according
   to the law),[29]

9 then hath he said, Lo, I am come to do thy will.[30] He
   taketh away the first, that he may establish the second.

10 By which will we have been sanctified through the offer-
    ing of the body[31] of Jesus Christ once for all.

---

[25] *Cf.* A. Büchler, *Studies in Sin and Atonement in the Rabbinic Literature of the First Century* (Oxford, 1928).

[26] Gk. ὁλοκαυτώματα (for which P⁴⁶ and D read the singular ὁλοκαύτωμα).

[27] P⁴⁶ and D* (but not d) add γάρ ("for").

[28] Quoted from Ps. 40:6–8 (MT 40:7–9; LXX 39:6–8).

[29] Gk. κατὰ νόμον (D P and some other MSS, with TR, read κατὰ τὸν νόμον).

[30] ℵᶜ L 1739 and TR, with the Latin and Syriac Peshitta, add "O God" (ὁ θεός) from v. 7.

[31] For σώματος ("body") D* reads αἵματος ("blood"), in conformity with v. 29.

5-7 For a biblical statement of the sacrifice which *could* take away sins our author goes back to the Psalter, and in Ps. 40:6–8 he finds a prophetic utterance which he recognizes as appropriate to the Son of God at the time of His incarnation. The title of this psalm marks it as Davidic (in Massoretic and Septuagint texts alike); he may have argued (as Peter did with regard to Ps. 16 on the Day of Pentecost)[32] that the words of the psalm could not refer to David *in propria persona* (since David did offer sacrifices), and that therefore they should be understood as referring to "great David's greater Son". However that may be, the appropriateness of his application of them is undeniable. He quotes them in the Septuagint version,[33] in which the Massoretic reading "ears hast thou digged for me" is replaced by the clause "a body didst thou prepare for me". The Greek version cannot well be explained as representing a variant or corrupted Hebrew reading;[34] it is rather an interpretative paraphrase of the Hebrew text. The Greek translator evidently regarded the Hebrew wording as an instance of *pars pro toto*; the "digging" or hollowing out of the ears is part of the total work of fashioning a human body.[35] Accordingly he rendered it in terms which express *totum pro parte*. The body which was "prepared" for the speaker by God is given back to God as a "living sacrifice", to be employed in obedient service to Him.

But if our author had preferred the Hebrew wording, it would have served his purpose almost as well, for in addition to reminding

[32] Acts 2:29ff. *Cf. Acts*, NICNT (Grand Rapids, 1954), pp. 71f.

[33] In a form approaching, as usual, the A text, except that he reads εὐδόκησας ("thou hadst ... pleasure") for ἐζήτησας (perhaps under the influence of Ps. 51:16 = 50:18, LXX), places the vocative ὁ θεός before τὸ θέλημά σου instead of after it (LXX has ὁ θεός μου, following MT, "O my God"), and omits ἠβουλήθην ("I have resolved") at the end of his quotation, thus making the infinitive clause τοῦ ποιῆσαι ("to do") a clause of purpose dependent on ἥκω ("I have come").

[34] Neither can σῶμα be satisfactorily explained as due to a corruption in the transmission of the LXX, as though it replaced an earlier ὠτία ("ears"), as has been suggested, *e.g.*, by F. Bleek, G. Lünemann and A. Kuyper. J. Moffatt says: "Whether ὠτία was corrupted into σῶμα, or whether the latter was an independent translation, is of no moment" (*ad loc.*); true enough, but that it is a corruption is, as F. Delitzsch rightly says (*ad loc.*), "highly improbable". (Aquila, Theodotion and Symmachus, with Origen's Quinta and Sexta, and some late LXX editions, read ὠτία, by way of conformity to MT.)

[35] There is no ground for relating Ps. 40:6 to the boring of the servant's ear in Ex. 21:6; Deut. 15:17.

him and his readers of the psalm from which it was taken, it might have reminded them also of the Isaianic Servant's language in the third Servant Song: "The Lord Jehovah ... wakeneth mine ear to hear as they that are taught. The Lord Jehovah hath opened mine ear, and I was not rebellious, neither turned away backward" (Isa. 50:4f.).

Wholehearted obedience is the sacrifice that God really desires, the sacrifice which He received in perfection from His Servant-Son when He came into the world. As for the other kinds of sacrifice enumerated in the psalm, they had religious worth only in so far as they were the tangible expression of a devoted and obedient heart; the prophets were never tired of insisting that God did not desire them for their own sake.[36]

It is probable that the four terms which the psalmist uses for sacrifice are intended to cover all the main types of offering prescribed in the Levitical ritual.[37] "Sacrifice" (Heb. *zebaḥ*), while capable of referring to any kind of animal sacrifice, is used in the Old Testament with more special reference to the peace-offering;[38] "offering" (Heb. *minḥāh*), while used in a general sense,[39] is restricted in the Levitical terminology to the "meal offering" or

---

[36] *Cf.* H. H. Rowley, "The Meaning of Sacrifice in the Old Testament", *BJRL* xxxiii (1950–51), pp. 74ff.

[37] "Every species of sacrifice had its own primary idea. The fundamental idea of the '*ōlāh* (burnt-offering) was *oblatio*, or the offering of worship; that of the *shelāmīm* (peace-offerings), *conciliatio*, or the knitting of fellowship; that of the *minḥāh* (meal-offering), *donatio*, or sanctifying consecration; that of the *ḥaṭṭā'th* (sin-offering), *expiatio*, or atonement; that of the '*āshām* (guilt-offering), *mulcta* (*satisfactio*), or a compensatory payment. The self-sacrifice of the Servant of Jehovah may be presented under all these points of view. It is the complete antitype, the truth, the object, and the end of all the sacrifices" (F. Delitzsch, *The Prophecies of Isaiah*, ii [Eng. tr., Edinburgh, 1867], pp. 333f., on '*āshām* in Isa. 53:10). (*Cf.* p. 234, n. 42.) In Ps. 40:6f. "sin-offering" may include the idea of "guilt-offering". *Cf.* also W. O. E. Oesterley, *The Psalms* (London, 1953), pp. 234f.; he suggests that the thank-offering (*tōdāh*) is not mentioned because it was included under the *zebaḥ* ("sacrifice"), which comes first of the four.

[38] Heb. *shelāmīm*. In the Levitical legislation *zebaḥ* (like its cognate verb *zābaḥ*, "to slaughter in sacrifice") is regularly restricted to peace-offerings (under which thank-offerings are subsumed).

[39] *E.g.* in its earliest biblical occurrence it is used of Cain's vegetable sacrifice and Abel's animal sacrifice alike (Gen. 4:3ff.). *Cf.* pp. 283ff. (on Ch. 11:4).

"cereal offering";[40] while the burnt offering (Heb. *'ōlāh*)[41] and sin offering (Heb. *ḥaṭṭā'āh*)[42] are specifically provided for by name in the Levitical legislation. The spiritual principles which underlay these various types of sacrifice are fulfilled and transcended in the perfect self-offering of Christ. Our author's contrast is not between sacrifice and obedience, but between the involuntary sacrifice of dumb animals and "sacrifice into which obedience enters, the sacrifice of a rational and spiritual being, which is not passive in death, but in dying makes the will of God its own".[43]

The Septuagint reading, "a body didst thou prepare for me", suggests to our author the incarnation of the Son of God, and the whole passage from Ps. 40 is understood as spoken by Him "when he cometh into the world". His incarnation itself is viewed as an act of submission to God's will and, as such, an anticipation of His supreme submission to that will in death. The psalmist's words, "Lo, I am come to do thy will, O God", sum up the whole tenor of our Lord's life and ministry, and express the essence of that true sacrifice which God desires. But what of the parenthetic clause: "In the roll of the book[44] it is written of me"? Its meaning is clarified by the clause which immediately follows the clauses which are quoted here: "Yea, thy law is within my heart."[45] The

---

40 Lev. 2:1ff.

41 In LXX ὁλοκαύτωμα (the word used here), "whole burnt-offering", "holocaust", is the commonest equivalent for Heb. *'ōlāh*.

42 Heb. *ḥaṭṭā'āh* is a variant of the commoner *ḥaṭṭā'th*. When this word is used in the sense of "sin-offering", its regular LXX equivalent is the phrase περὶ ἁμαρτίας (so here). This phrase (for which *cf.* vv. 8, 18; Ch. 13:11; Rom. 8:3), according to E. K. Simpson, "should be read as a single vocable, indeclinable, if you will, for a *sin-offering*. That is manifest from the LXX usage (Lev. 4:33; 14:19; Num. 8:8, and the ὁλοκαύτωμα καὶ περιαμαρτίας of Ps. 40:7). We even find the verb περιαμαρτίζειν in Aquila and Symmachus, and the latter employs the noun περιαμαρτισμός of Zechariah's fountain opened for uncleanness" (*Words Worth Weighing in the Greek New Testament* [London, 1946], p. 29). In Isa. 53:10, where the Servant gives his life as an *'āshām*, the LXX rendering is περὶ ἁμαρτίας (*cf.* pp. 158, n. 93; 233, n. 37).

43 J. Denney, *The Death of Christ* (London, 1951), p. 131.

44 Heb. *bimegillath sēpher* (*megillāh* is a "roll" or "scroll"); but LXX ἐν κεφαλίδι βιβλίου (so here) refers strictly to the κεφαλίς, the knob at the top of the stick round which the scroll was rolled, used here by metonymy for the scroll itself. The genitive βιβλίου may be regarded as genitive of definition, "the book in scroll-form" or "the scroll of writing". It would be going too far to press the etymological sense of βιβλίον and so render the phrase "the scroll of papyrus".

45 *Cf.* Jer. 31:33, quoted in Ch. 8:10.

"roll of the book" is the written *tōrāh* of God;[46] what was written there the speaker recognized to be written concerning *him*, to be God's prescription for *him*. His life would accordingly be the active counterpart of the written law; the will of God, which was set down in the "roll of the book", would be equally manifested in his obedience. It may be that for our author, as he applies these words to Jesus, the "roll of the book" was enlarged to include all that God had said in earlier days "unto the fathers in the prophets"; we recall how our Lord was led off to trial and death with the words on His lips: "Let the scriptures be fulfilled" (Mark 14:49). Yet it was not simply that He found His duty set down plainly in the written record and set Himself to carry it out: it was at the same time the dearest desire of His heart to fulfil that special service which was His Father's will for Him. While it was indeed His Father's will, it was also His own spontaneous choice. And therefore His undertaking and fulfilling it was a sacrifice utterly acceptable to God.

8–9 In these words of Ps. 40, then, interpreted as our Lord's declaration at His entry into the world, our author sees the abrogation of the old sacrificial cultus announced. The sacrifices in which God is said to take no pleasure are the sacrifices prescribed by the ancient cultic law of Israel; now that cultic law is to be superseded by a new order, inaugurated by Christ's perfect obedience to the will of God. The declaration falls into two parts: in the first part (which is said "above")[47] the old order is abolished; in the second the new is established.[48] The terms of the new covenant include the provision that God's law will henceforth be engraved in His people's hearts; and it was supremely fitting that this should be preeminently true of Him through whose obedience

---

[46] The suggestion that a heavenly book (*cf.* Ps. 139:16; Dan. 10:21, etc.) is meant here is unlikely (*cf.* W. E. Barnes, *The Psalms* i [London, 1931], p. 204: "The Psalmist's commission is written down in heaven in the book of God, which is pictured as a roll").

[47] Gk. ἀνώτερον, "higher up" in the passage quoted.

[48] The Gk. perfect εἴρηκεν at the beginning of v. 9 expresses completed action: what the speaker said stands henceforth on permanent record (*cf.* the use of γέγραπται or εἴρηται "it is written" or "it is said", to introduce a quotation of Scripture, as, *e.g.*, in Luke 4:4, 8, 12). The ordinal numerals "first" (πρῶτον) and "second" (δεύτερον) are neuter here; no particular substantive is understood with them. "The first" is the old sacrificial system; "the second" is our Lord's perfect self-dedication to do the will of God.

THE EPISTLE TO THE HEBREWS

and blood the new covenant has been ratified.[49] "I have come to do thy will" is written over the whole record of our Lord's life; this was His attitude from first to last.

10 And it is by His fulfilling the will of God[50] to the uttermost that He has "sanctified" His people and provided the "perfection" which was unattainable on the basis of the ancient sacrifices. His fulfilment of God's will to the uttermost involved the "offering" once for all of His body—that body prepared for Him at His incarnation. "It is the atonement which explains the incarnation: the incarnation takes place in order that the sin of the world may be put away by the offering of the body of Jesus Christ."[51] The offering of His body is simply the offering of Himself; if here sanctification and access to God are made available through His body, in verses 19 and 29 they are made available through His blood.[52] Whether our author speaks of His body or His blood, it is His incarnate life that is meant, yielded to God in an obedience which was maintained even to death. So perfect a sacrifice was our Lord's presentation of His life to God that no repetition of it is either necessary or possible: it was offered "once for all".[53] The sanctification which His people receive in consequence is their inward cleansing from sin and their being made fit for the presence of God, so that henceforth they can offer Him acceptable worship. It is a sanctification that has taken place once for all;[54] in this sense it is as unrepeatable as the sacrifice which effects it.

---

[49] See pp. 172ff.

[50] Gk. ἐν ᾧ θελήματι, "by which will", means "by the will of God thus fulfilled by Christ".

[51] J. Denney, op. cit., p. 131.

[52] Cf. our Lord's words about His "flesh" and His "blood" in John 6:51ff.; to "eat the flesh of the Son of man and drink his blood" are two expressions which equally denote His people's appropriation of, and participation in, Himself. Similarly in the Eucharist the "body" and the "blood" of Christ are not two complementary parts of His being; in the bread as in the cup it is His whole self that Christ communicates to His people.

[53] Gk. ἐφάπαξ, as in Chs. 7:27; 9:12 (see p. 156, n. 82); it receives special weight here from its emphatic position at the end of the sentence.

[54] It is expressed here in the perfect tense (ἡγιασμένοι ἐσμέν). Cf. the present ἁγιαζομένους in v. 14 (n. 58); perhaps we should contrast the use of the aorist in the case of the apostate in v. 29 (p. 257, n. 129).

Ch. 10:11–18

11 And every priest[55] indeed standeth day by day ministering and offering oftentimes the same sacrifices, the which can never take away sins:[56]

12 but he, when he had offered one sacrifice for sins for ever,[57] sat down on the right hand of God;

13 henceforth expecting till his enemies be made the footstool of his feet.

14 For by one offering he hath perfected for ever them that are sanctified.[58]

15 And the Holy Spirit also beareth witness to us; for after he hath said,

16   This[59] is the covenant that I will make[60] with them
         After those days, saith the Lord:
         I will put my laws on their heart,

---

55 Some authorities (cf. ARV margin) read "high priest" (ἀρχιερεύς): so A P 69 and many other codices, with the Sahidic Coptic.

56 P13 and the Coptic versions have the singular "sin" (ἁμαρτίαν).

57 Gk. εἰς τὸ διηνεκές (as in vv. 1, 14; Ch. 7:3; cf. p. 133, n. 7). Here a question of punctuation arises: should the phrase be constructed with the words that precede ("when he had offered ...") or with those that follow ("sat down ...")? It is equally appropriate with both. In favour of the former alternative it may be said that the phrase would then receive emphasis by coming at the end of a clause, like ἐφάπαξ in v. 10 (cf. n. 53 above); in favour of the latter we may recall the use of this phrase εἰς τὸ διηνεκές in Ch. 7:3 as a variant of εἰς τὸν αἰῶνα in Ps. 110:4 (LXX). The latter is preferred, e.g., by J. N. Darby (New Translation, ad loc.) and J. Moffatt (New Translation, ad loc.; cf. his note in ICC, p. 140); B. F. Westcott, however, rightly points out that the latter construction "is contrary to the usage of the Epistle; it obscures the idea of the perpetual efficacy of Christ's one sacrifice; it weakens the contrast with ἕστηκεν; and it imports a foreign idea into the image of the assumption (ἐκάθισεν) of royal dignity by Christ" (ad loc.).

58 Gk. ἁγιαζομένους (as in Ch. 2:11), for which P46 has the curious variant ἀνασωζομένους, "(them that are) being saved again"—probably due to the misreading of an indistinct exemplar.

59 Gk. αὕτη (P13 D* and the Vulgate read αὕτη δέ "But this").

60 Gk. διαθήσομαι, "I will covenant" (see p. 168, n. 40).

And upon their mind also will I write them;[61]
then saith he,[62]

17 And their sins and their iniquities will I remember no
more.[63]

18 Now where remission[64] of these is, there is no more offering for sin.

11–12 The unrepeatable character of the sacrifice of Christ,
by contrast with the sacrifices of the old order, is underlined by
an appeal to the language of Ps. 110. The introductory oracle of
this psalm, in which the Messiah is invited by God to sit at His
right hand, has already been quoted by our author (Ch. 1:13)
and has influenced his phraseology in Chs. 1:3; 8:1; but only
now does he draw out its full significance.[65] The Aaronic priests
never sat down in the sanctuary; they remained standing throughout the whole performance of their sacred duties. In this our
author sees a token of the fact that their sacred duties were never
done, that their sacrifices had always to be repeated. In verse 1
the repetition of the ritual of the Day of Atonement "year by
year" was mentioned; here, as in Ch. 7:27, the reference is to
those sacrifices which were offered "day by day".[66] But whether
the repetition was annual or daily, the main point is that repetition
was necessary; not one of these sacrifices could remove sin or
cleanse the conscience with permanent effect. The completion of
one sacrifice meant only that a similar one would have to be
offered in due course, and so on indefinitely; it was in keeping
with this that the priests of the old order never sat down in the
presence of God when a sacrifice had been presented to Him.

But it was equally in keeping with the perfection of Christ's
sacrifice of Himself that, when He had presented it to God, He
sat down. No further sacrificial service can be required of the

---

[61] Jer. 31:33a. The whole context is quoted in Ch. 8:8ff. (see pp. 168 ff.).

[62] These words, which in the authentic text are left to be understood, are
supplied by several later manuscripts and versions, in the form ὕστερον λέγει (69
1739 etc., with the Harclean Syriac, Armenian, and Sahidic Coptic), or in the
form τότε εἴρηκεν (1611).

[63] Jer. 31:34b, in a telescoped form (*cf.* Ch. 8:12).

[64] Gk. ἄφεσις, as in Ch. 9:22.

[65] See pp. 7f., 23f.

[66] See pp. 157f.

priest who appeared on earth in the fulness of time to put away sin and sanctify His people once for all. A seated priest is the guarantee of a finished work and an accepted sacrifice. The heavenly high priest has indeed a continual ministry to discharge on His people's behalf at the Father's right hand; but that is the ministry of intercession on the basis of the sacrifice presented and accepted once for all, it is not the constant or repeated offering of His sacrifice. This last misconception has no doubt been fostered in the Western Church by a defective Vulgate rendering which springs from a well-known inadequacy of the Latin verb.[67]

Translations and commentaries differ on the construction of the phrase "for ever" in verse 12; syntactically it might refer either to the preceding clause "when he had offered one sacrifice for sins" or to the following words "sat down ...", and so far as the sense is concerned, it would be equally appropriate either way. On the whole, however, it seems that the familiar English versions are right in taking it with the preceding clause.[68]

Christ, then, has taken His seat in token that His sacrificial work is finished; but more, the worth of His sacrifice and the dignity of His person are further indicated in that He has taken His seat not merely in the presence of God but at "the right hand of God".[69] From the shame of the cross He has been exalted to the place of highest glory. With the more confidence, therefore, may His people avail themselves of His high-priestly aid, assured that in Him they have access to all the grace and power of God. To all who are uncertain of their acceptance with God comes the

---

[67] The Greek aorist participle προσενέγκας ("having offered") in v. 12 is in sharp contrast to the present participle προσφέρων ("offering") in v. 11. But since Latin has no perfect participle active (except in deponent verbs), the Latin version uses the present participle *offerens* as the rendering of both these forms. The context here really rules out the implication of the Latin present participle; it is a contradiction in terms to say (as R. A. Knox's translation of the Vulgate puts it): "he sits for ever at the right hand of God, offering for our sins a sacrifice that is never repeated" (a footnote in Knox's version points out that the Greek means: "he has taken his seat at the right hand of God after offering a sacrifice"). (The Latin replacement of the Greek aorist indicative ἐκάθισεν by the present *sedet* does not materially affect the sense.) For a similar difficulty arising from the absence of a perfect participle active in the Latin verb *cf.* Ch. 1:3 (p. 6, n. 31).

[68] See p. 237, n. 57.

[69] This is the only place in the epistle where this expression appears without periphrasis (*cf.* its amplifications in Chs. 1:3; 8:1; 12:2).

voice that brought encouragement to the soul of John Bunyan: "Sinner, thou thinkest that because of thy sins and infirmities I cannot save thy soul, but behold my Son is by me, and upon him I look, and not on thee, and will deal with thee according as I am pleased with him."[70]

13 Our author continues to give the substance of Ps. 110:1 by adding the words: "henceforth expecting till his enemies be made the footstool of his feet". He offers no exegesis of these words, but if he had attached no significance to them in the present context he could easily have omitted them altogether, as he does in every other place (apart from the direct quotation of Ps. 110:1 in Ch. 1:13) where he speaks of Christ as enthroned at God's right hand. In the light of the solemn admonition which follows in verses 26–31, there may be an implied warning here to his readers not to let themselves be numbered among the enemies of the exalted Christ, but rather to be reckoned as His friends and companions by preserving their fidelity to the end (*cf.* Ch. 3:14). Paul has more to say about the eventual subjection of all the enemies of Christ beneath His feet in I Cor. 15:24–28, where he gives a combined exegesis of Ps. 110:1 and Ps. 8:6;[71] but Paul has in mind not the high-priestly ministry of Christ but His enthronement as mediatorial king: as such "he is destined to reign until God has put all enemies under his feet; and the last enemy to be abolished is death" (I Cor. 15:25f., NEB).

14 Christ, then, by His self-oblation has accomplished once for all what generations of Levitical sacrifices had never done. After hundreds of years those sacrifices were no nearer the attainment of their aim than they had been at the beginning. Nor can this contrast between them and the death of Christ be dismissed as an apt conceit of our author's, elaborated here for apologetic purposes. Its force was tacitly acknowledged in Christian practice. Many, probably most, of the early converts to Christianity had been accustomed to a form of worship in which animal sacrifices played a part; this was so whether they had previously been Jews or Gentiles. The fact that their new form of worship had no place for such sacrifices was in itself a recognition that they had been rendered for ever obsolete by the death of Christ. "Those who

---

[70] *Grace Abounding*, para. 258.
[71] *Cf.* Ch. 2:6ff. (pp. 34ff.).

looked upon this death as a sacrifice soon ceased to offer God any
blood-sacrifice at all."[72]   They might not all have used the
language of the Epistle to the Hebrews, but the logic of its argument
was implicit in their most elementary understanding of the gospel.
The sacrifice of Christ has purified His people from the moral
defilement of sin, and assured them of permanent maintenance
in a right relation with God. "For by one offering he has perfected
for all time those who are thus consecrated" (NEB).

In verse 10 the statement that "we have been sanctified" is
made in the perfect tense; here, as in Ch. 2:11, it is the present
participle passive that is used. In verse 10 the emphasis lay on the
unrepeatable nature of the death of Christ as the sacrifice by
which His people are set apart for the worship and service of God;
here their character as the people thus set apart is simply indicated
in timeless[73] terms, because emphasis is now laid on the fact that
by that same sacrifice Christ has eternally "perfected" His holy
people. Three outstanding effects are thus ascribed to the sacrifice
of Christ: by it His people have had their conscience cleansed
from guilt; by it they have been fitted to approach God as accepted
worshippers; by it they have experienced the fulfilment of what was
promised in earlier days, being brought into that perfect relation
to God which is involved in the new covenant.[74]

15–18   That the "perfection" of which our author speaks is
bound up with the new covenant is made plain by his repetition
of the words of Jer. 31:33f. and his application of them to the effect
of the sacrifice of Christ. These words, spoken by the prophet
under inspiration, are naturally quoted as the words of the Holy
Spirit,[75] and they are viewed as the Holy Spirit's confirmation of
the conclusion to which our author's argument has just led him.
The new covenant, according to Jeremiah's prophecy, not only
involved the implanting of God's laws, together with the will and
power to carry them out, in the hearts of His people; it also con-

---

[72]   A. Harnack, *What is Christianity?* (Eng. tr., London, 1904), p. 159.

[73]   As A. B. Davidson says of the present participles ἁγιάζων and
ἁγιαζόμενοι in Ch. 2:11, "the words are timeless designations of the two parties,
taken from the part characteristic of each" (*The Epistle to the Hebrews* [Edin-
burgh, 1882], p. 66). "He hath perfected" (v. 14) is perfect tense.

[74]   See A. B. Davidson, *op. cit.*, pp. 203–209 ("Note on the Words Purge,
Sanctify, Make Perfect").

[75]   *Cf.* "he saith" in Ch. 8:8 (pp. 169f.).

veyed the assurance that their past sins and iniquities would be
eternally blotted out from God's record, never to be brought up
in evidence against them. Here is something far beyond what the
sacrificial law of Old Testament times could provide: in that law
there was an annual "remembrance of sins",[76] whereas in the
new covenant there is no more remembrance of them. Repeated
remembrance of sins and repeated sin-offerings went inevitably
together; therefore, the irrevocable erasing of sins from the divine
record implies that no further sin-offering is called for. The finality
of the sacrifice of Christ is thus confirmed.

In Ch. 8 the oracle of Jer. 31:31–34 was quoted in order to
prove the obsolescence of the old economy; now it is quoted again
in order to establish the permanence of the era of "perfection"
inaugurated under the new covenant. "God has spoken in His
Son"; and He has no word to speak beyond Him.

---

[76] *Cf.* verse 3 (pp. 228f.).

VI. CALL TO WORSHIP, FAITH AND PERSEVERANCE
Chs. 10:19–12:29

1. ACCESS TO GOD THROUGH THE SACRIFICE OF CHRIST
Ch. 10:19–25

19 Having therefore, brethren, boldness to enter into the holy place by the blood of Jesus,

20 by the way which he dedicated for us, a new[77] and living way, through the veil, that is to say, his flesh;

21 and *having* a great priest over the house of God;

22 let us draw near[78] with a true heart in fulness of faith, having our hearts sprinkled from an evil conscience:[79] and having our body washed with pure water,

23 let us hold fast the confession of our[80] hope that it waver not; for he is faithful that promised:

24 and let us consider one another to provoke[81] unto love and good works;

---

[77] Gk. πρόσφατος, etymologically meaning "freshly killed"; the second element in the compound became otiose at an early stage, and the word simply means "new", "fresh", "recent" (*cf.* such LXX occurrences as Eccl. 1:9; Ps. 80:9 [Eng. 81:9]; and the adverb προσφάτως [ARV "lately"] in Acts 18:2).

[78] Gk. προσερχώμεθα, for which P⁴⁶* D K P and many other manuscripts have the indicative προσερχόμεθα ("we draw near"). In this hortatory context the subjunctive is required.

[79] This punctuation (which is that of TR) attaches ῥεραντισμένοι to the preceding clause and λελουσμένοι to the following. To disjoin the two parallel perfect participles in this way is a most unnatural proceeding; punctuate with AV: "having our hearts sprinkled from an evil conscience, and our bodies washed with pure water." The twofold participial phrase is thus appended rightly to "let us draw near ..." (so also in ARV margin, ERV, RSV, NEB). The participles are in the middle voice, as is appropriate for initiatory cleansing; *cf.* βάπτισαι ... ἀπόλουσαι in Acts 22:16 and ἀπελούσασθε in I Cor. 6:11.

[80] "Our" (ἡμῶν) is supplied in a few authorities (א* with the Latin Vulgate and Syriac Peshitta); in the others it is left to be understood.

[81] Gk. εἰς παροξυσμόν, literally "for provocation"; P⁴⁶ has ἐκ παροξυσμοῦ, which might be rendered "by way of provocation".

25   not forsaking our own assembling together, as the custom
of some is, but exhorting *one another*; and so much the
more, as ye see the day drawing nigh.

The practical implications of the foregoing argument are now
summed up in this sentence of sustained exhortation, which might
well have formed the conclusion of the homily, had not our author
judged it wise to expand and apply in greater detail the points
made here, for the further encouragement and strengthening of
his readers. In view of all that has been accomplished for us by
Christ, he says, let us confidently approach God in worship, let us
maintain our Christian confession and hope, let us help one
another by meeting together regularly for mutual encouragement,
because the day which we await will soon be here.

19   The "boldness" which believers in Christ have to enter the
heavenly sanctuary through Him is set in contrast with the restrictions which hedged about the privilege of symbolic entry into
the presence of God in Israel's earthly sanctuary. In it not all
the people could exercise this privilege, but the high priest only,
as their representative; and even he could not exercise the privilege
any time he chose, but at fixed times and under fixed conditions.
But those who have been cleansed within, consecrated and made
perfect by the sacrifice of Christ, have received a free right of
access into the holy presence; and our author urges his readers to
avail themselves fully of this free right. As regularly in the New
Testament, the *parrhēsia* enjoyed by Christians is "based on the
revelation of God in Jesus Christ who restored the relation between
God and man".[82] The invitation to "draw near with boldness
unto the throne of grace" has already been issued in this epistle
(Ch. 4:16); on that occasion the invitation was based on the
assurance that the high priest who has passed through the heavens
is one whose own experiences of temptation enable Him to sympathize with His people in their trials. Now a further assurance is
given: the way by which this high priest has entered into the
presence of God is a way which remains open for His people to
follow Him there.

---

[82]   W. C. van Unnik, "The Christian's Freedom of Speech in the New
Testament", *BJRL* xliv (1961–62), pp. 466ff. (quotation from p. 487). *Cf.*
pp. 59, n. 20; 271, n. 188.

The AV describes this free right of access as "boldness to enter into the holiest[83] by the blood of Jesus". The Greek text, indeed, does not use the superlative expression here which distinguishes the holy of holies from the holy place; but in Ch. 9:8 we have already seen the more general term "the holy place" used with reference to the earthly sanctuary where the inner compartment was actually meant. So here, as is indicated by the words "through the veil", it is to the very throne of God that believers in Christ have free entry—not to the material symbol of His throne where, as in the pre-exilic holy of holies, His invisible presence was upborne by the cherubim; but to His true and spiritual dwelling-place. "For thus saith the high and lofty One that inhabiteth eternity, whose name is Holy: I dwell in the high and holy place, with him also that is of a contrite and humble spirit" (Isa. 57:15). Believers have no need to ask "Who shall ascend into heaven?" when it is a question of their approaching God; here upon earth they may enter His heavenly abode and know direct communion with Him "by the blood of Jesus".[84] He who, "through his own blood, entered in once for all into the holy place" (Ch. 9:12) has procured for His people equal right of entry there by means of that same blood—that is, on the ground of His accepted sacrifice.

20 The way by which they enter the presence of God is a new way, which did not exist until He opened it up[85] and entered thereby Himself. It is thus a new way; it is also a "living way". For in effect the ever-living Christ Himself, as His people's sacrifice and priest, is the way to God; the present passage is our author's counterpart to the affirmation of John 14:6: "I am the way, and the truth, and the life: no one cometh unto the Father, but by

---

[83] Gk. παρρησίαν εἰς τὴν εἴσοδον τῶν ἁγίων (with the expression cf. Ch. 9:8, τὴν τῶν ἁγίων ὁδόν).

[84] Gk. ἐν τῷ αἵματι Ἰησοῦ, the instrumental use of ἐν (as in Ch. 13:20) being practically indistinguishable from that of διά in the similar phrase in Ch. 9:12.

[85] Gk. ἐνεκαίνισεν, "he consecrated or dedicated". "The death of Christ is seen as the new Encaenia or Dedication," says J. A. T. Robinson, adding that two ideas appear to be combined here, the Cross marking the dedication both of the new covenant—for "even the first covenant hath not been dedicated (ἐνκεκαίνισται) without blood" (Ch. 9:18)—and of the new temple (cf. the technical term ἐνκαίνια in John 10:22); "the whole argument of chapters 9 and 10 leads to the climax that Jesus has now 'opened' the new sanctuary in the temple of his body" (*Twelve New Testament Studies* [London, 1962], p. 172).

me."[86] It is a way which (to continue the symbolism of the tabernacle and temple) leads "through the veil" into the holy of holies.

It can scarcely be doubted that the "veil" of which our author is thinking is the inner veil which separated the holy place from the holy of holies, the "second veil" of Ch. 9:3,[87] through the heavenly archetype of which Jesus has already passed as His people's forerunner (Ch. 6:19f.). Here it is natural to ask whether these words contain an implicit allusion to the rending of the temple veil from top to bottom at the moment of Jesus's death (Mark 15:38; cf. Matt. 27:51; Luke 23:45). For the veil which was then rent in two was also probably the inner veil,[88] and its rending is recorded not as a natural portent[89] but as an event of theological significance: in the death of Jesus, we are to understand, God Himself is unveiled to us and the way of access to Him is thrown wide open. The teaching of the Synoptic passion narratives is thus to the same effect as that of our epistle; in both instances the teaching is given a cultic form, which is expressed realistically in the Gospels and symbolically by our author.[90] If our author knew about the rent veil, its significance was patent to him. But even if he did not know about it, his language here drives home the same lesson as the rending of the veil did.

---

[86]   Cf. Eph. 2:18; also Rom. 5:2; Eph. 3:12; I Pet. 2:4f.; 3:18.

[87]   With διὰ τοῦ καταπετάσματος here cf. τὸ δεύτερον καταπέτασμα in Ch. 9:3 (and the earlier instance of καταπέτασμα in the same sense in Ch. 6:19). In LXX καταπέτασμα is sometimes used for the outer screen (Ex. 26:37; 38:18; Num. 3:26), but regularly for the inner curtain or pārōkheth—"the inmost curtain" (τὸ ἐσωτάτω καταπέτασμα), as Philo calls it (Giants, 53). See p. 184, n. 14.

[88]   This is the majority view; however, it has been identified with the outer veil by Jerome and Thomas Aquinas and also by G. Dalman, E. Klostermann, A. H. McNeile, B. T. D. Smith, E. Lohmeyer, etc. (see list in V. Taylor, The Gospel according to St. Mark [London, 1952], p. 596).

[89]   Other portents associated with the temple are recorded for A.D. 30 and other occasions in the forty years preceding its destruction in A.D. 70 in Josephus (BJ vi. 288ff.), Tacitus (Hist. v. 13), The Gospel according to the Hebrews (quoted by Jerome, Epistle 120. 8. 1) and TJ (Yoma vi. 5. 3); it does not appear that the rending of the veil can be identified with any of these. But see H. W. Montefiore, "Josephus and the New Testament", NovT iv (1960), pp. 139ff. (especially pp. 148ff.).

[90]   Cf. C. H. Dodd, The Apostolic Preaching and its Developments (London, 1944), p. 51; G. Lindeskog, Coniectanea Neotestamentica xi (1947), pp. 132ff.; R. H. Lightfoot, The Gospel Message of St. Mark (Oxford, 1950), pp. 55f.

A still more important question is raised by the following clause, "that is to say, his flesh".[91] Do these words qualify "the veil" or the "new and living way"?[92] The Greek affords no more help in answering this question than the English does. ARV renders the passage in such a way as to preserve the ambiguity; AV probably, and RSV certainly ("through the curtain, that is, through his flesh"), identify "his flesh" with "the veil" ("the curtain"); NEB comes down unambiguously on the side of the other alternative—"the new, living way which he has opened for us through the curtain, the way of his flesh" (the variant rendering, "through the curtain of his flesh", is relegated to a footnote).

In favour of taking "that is to say, his flesh" as epexegetic of "the veil" one may appeal first to the word-order; it is rather awkward to relate the clause closely to the words "new and living way" in view of the intervention of the phrase "through the veil". Nor is there any difficulty in supposing that our author could explain the veil as being our Lord's "flesh"; like "the body of Jesus Christ" in verse 10 and "the blood of Jesus" in verse 19, "his flesh" here could mean His human life, offered up in sacrifice to God. It is by His sacrifice that the way of approach to God has been opened up.[93] The veil which, from one point of view, kept God and man apart, can be thought of, from another point of view, as bringing them together; for it was one and the same veil which on one side was in contact with the glory of God and on the other side with the need of men. So in our Lord Godhead and manhood were brought together; He is the true "daysman" or umpire who can lay His hand upon both because He shares the nature of both. And by His death, it could be added, the "veil" of His flesh was rent asunder and the new way consecrated through it by which man may come to God. "This beautiful allegorizing

---

[91] Unless, with K. Holsten, we treat this clause as a gloss added later, but for such a conjecture there is no textual evidence.

[92] If they qualify "the veil", the genitive τῆς σαρκός in τοῦτ᾽ ἔστιν τῆς σαρκὸς αὐτοῦ may be taken either as genitive in apposition with τοῦ καταπετάσματος ("the veil, that is his flesh") or as genitive in dependence on τοῦ καταπετάσματος ("the veil, that is [the veil] of his flesh"). If they qualify "new and living way", τῆς σαρκός can only be taken as genitive in dependence on ὁδόν ("new and living way, that is [the way] of his flesh").

[93] So J. Moffatt (ICC, ad loc.): "He allegorizes the veil here as the flesh of Christ; this had to be rent before the blood could be shed, which enabled him to enter and open God's presence for the people."

of the veil cannot, of course, be made part of a consistent and complete typology. It is not meant for this. But as the veil stood locally before the holiest in the Mosaic Tabernacle, the way into which lay through it, so Christ's life in the flesh stood between Him and His entrance before God, and His flesh had to be rent ere He could enter. This is the fact and the history which suggest the figure. But under this fact lie principles in the mind of God, and in the public law of the universe, and in the heart and mind of man, the object to be awakened and touched, which give to *through* a deeper sense, and in this sense for us also the way lies through His flesh" (A. B. Davidson).[94]

The protagonist for the interpretation "the way of his flesh" is B. F. Westcott. He found the equation of "veil" with "flesh" unsatisfactory because one would not expect to find the "flesh" of Christ "treated in any way as a veil, an obstacle, to the vision of God in a place where stress is laid on His humanity" and because one would expect a complete parallelism to be preserved "between the description of the approach of Christ to God and the approach of the believer to God".[95] On the former score, it should suffice to remember, in J. Moffatt's words, that the expression here "is a daring, poetical touch, and the parallelism is not to be prosaically pressed into any suggestion that the human nature in Jesus hid God from men 'in the days of his flesh', or that he ceased to be truly human when he sacrificed himself."[96] On the latter score, if our Lord's "flesh" and His "blood" alike denote His human life offered up in sacrifice, then He who entered into

---

[94]   *The Epistle to the Hebrews* (Edinburgh, 1882), pp. 211f. *Cf.* also O. Michel and C. Spicq *ad loc.*, and W. Manson, *The Epistle to the Hebrews* (London, 1951), p. 67.

[95]   *The Epistle to the Hebrews* (London, 1903), p. 322. A. Nairne finds that Westcott's interpretation "does make the whole sentence consistent and is probably right" (*The Epistle of Priesthood* [Edinburgh, 1913], p. 381). Westcott suggests that the construction favored by him is that followed by Tyndale ("by the newe and livynge waye, which he hath prepared for vs, through the vayle, that is to saye by his flesshe") and other earlier English versions (*cf.* Coverdale, Great Bible, Geneva Bible). But their use of "by" before "his flesh" may perhaps not be resumptive of "by" before "the new and living way" but intended rather to indicate that the preposition διά has a different sense in the phrase "through (*or* by) his flesh" from that which it has in "through the veil"; *cf.* A. B. Davidson's remark in the quotation above on the deepening of the meaning of "through".

[96]   ICC, *ad loc.*

248

the heavenly sanctuary "through his own blood" (Ch. 9:12) may equally well be thought of as entering there through His "flesh". Since Westcott's objections to the usual rendering and interpretation do not appear to carry as much weight as he assigned to them, it is better on the whole to take the line more naturally suggested by the word-order and conclude that our author looked upon the veil as symbolizing our Lord's human life, presented to God when He "suffered for sins once, the righteous for the unrighteous, that he might bring us to God" (I Peter 3:18).

21 Their confidence in entering the presence of God should be enhanced by the fact that there Jesus fulfils His ministry as "a great priest over the house of God". The expression "great priest" is the literal rendering of the commonest Hebrew title for the high priest; "great" has here superlative force, denoting "the priest that is great above his brethren" (according to the more literal rendering of Lev. 21:10).[97] The "house of God" over which He exercises His high priesthood is, of course, the community of God's people (cf. Ch. 3:6).[98]

22 "Let us draw near", our author repeats[99]—near to God, that is. No longer is the privilege of access to Him carefully fenced about by conditions like those laid down for the high priest when he made his annual entrance into the holy of holies on the Day of Atonement; the "better hope" of Ch. 7:19, "through which we draw nigh[100] unto God", has now been realized. Naturally such an approach can be made only with sincerity of heart—it is the pure in heart who will see God—and the "full assurance"[101] which faith in God's word begets. It is of faith like this that our author speaks a little later when he says that "he that cometh to God must believe that he is, and that he is a rewarder of them that seek after him" (Ch. 11:6). But those who have experienced the

---

[97] ARV "he that is the high priest among his brethren"; LXX ὁ ἱερεὺς ὁ μέγας ἀπὸ τῶν ἀδελφῶν αὐτοῦ. In Num. 35:25, 28, we have the simple phrase hakkōhēn haggādōl, LXX ὁ ἱερεὺς ὁ μέγας, lit. "the great priest", ARV "the high priest", as also in Zech. 3:1, 9; 6:11, where Joshua (LXX Jesus) is so designated (cf. p. 77, n. 28; p. 86, n. 68).

[98] See p. 58, n. 18.

[99] From Ch. 4:16.

[100] In Ch. 7:19 the verb is ἐγγίζω; here and elsewhere in the epistle προσέρχομαι is the verb used for approaching God.

[101] So AV, RSV, NEB rightly render πληροφορία here (the πληροφορία of faith here differs but little, if at all, from the πληροφορία of hope in Ch. 6:11).

inward cleansing that Christ's self-offering has effected may well be marked by sincerity of heart and "full assurance of faith"; this is what our author means when he speaks of himself and his readers as "having our hearts sprinkled from an evil conscience, and having our body washed with pure water". The punctuation of ARV, which makes a heavy stop between these two participial phrases, attaching the sprinkling of the hearts closely to the preceding exhortation "let us draw near" and the washing of the body closely to the following exhortation "let us hold fast ...",[102] may be due to the feeling that there is something incongruous in correlating the figurative sprinkling of the heart and the literal washing of the body. The same sense of incongruity has led some expositors to maintain that the washing of the body is as figurative as the sprinkling of the heart, and to deny that it refers to baptism.[103]

That the sprinkling of the heart denotes an inward and spiritual cleansing is obvious; it is equally obvious that our author has in mind the counterpart under the new order of the old ritual cleansing with the "water for impurity", the water prepared with the ashes of the red heifer.[104] He has made this plain by his rhetorical question in Ch. 9:13f.: "if ... the ashes of a heifer sprinkling them that have been defiled sanctify unto the cleanness of the flesh, how much more shall the blood of Christ, who ... offered himself without blemish unto God, cleanse your conscience from dead works to serve the living God?" Those who make bold to enter the heavenly sanctuary by the blood of Jesus are by that same blood purified and made fit for the divine presence; the cleansing of the conscience removes the barrier which prevented their free access. It is not so clear that the washing of the body with pure water is thought of as having a similar analogue in the Old Testament ceremonial, simply because our author does not stress an analogue to this as he does stress the ritual of the red heifer. He may, however, have thought of the requirement that the priest on the day of atonement should "bathe his flesh in water" (Lev. 16:4) before putting on the linen vestments in which he was to approach God in the holy of holies.[105] But the present

---

[102] See p. 243, n. 79.

[103] *Cf.* G. H. Lang, *The Epistle to the Hebrews* (London, 1951), p. 167.

[104] *Cf.* also the "water of expiation" (Heb. *mē ḥaṭṭā'th*) sprinkled on the Levites in Num. 8:7.

[105] *Cf.* also Ex. 29:4, where the priests at their hallowing are washed at

reality which he has in mind is surely Christian baptism—consisting, of course, not merely in the outward application of water, but in the outward application of water as the visible sign of the inward and spiritual cleansing wrought by God in those who come to Him through Christ. As we are told again in I Peter 3:21, the baptismal water is not intended to remove bodily impurity but to express "a pledge to God proceeding from a clear conscience".[106]

There is no impossible incongruity here in the collocation of the cleansing which is inward and spiritual ("having our hearts sprinkled from an evil conscience") with its outward and visible sign ("having our body washed with pure water").[107] A similar collocation of the outward and inward cleansing may be recognized in the Qumran texts. The Qumran community attached great importance to ritual bathing, and there are recurring references in their literature to the "water for impurity".[108] But a merely external sprinkling or cleansing with water will do a man no good if he cherishes an impenitent and apostate heart. Such a man "cannot be purified by atonement or cleansed with water for impurity. He cannot be sanctified in seas or rivers, or cleansed with any lustral water. ... It is through an upright and humble spirit that a man's sin will be expiated, and through his self-submission to all God's ordinances that his flesh will be cleansed, so that he may have water for impurity sprinkled on him and be sanctified by means of cleansing water."[109] Behind this passage from the Qumran *Rule of the Community*, as indeed behind the

the door of the tent of meeting; Num. 19:7f., where the priest who supervises the burning of the red heifer and the man who burns her must wash their bodies and their clothes. With the wording of this clause ("having our body washed with pure water") A. Nairne (*op. cit.*, p. 381) compares Aeschylus, fragment 32: καλοῖσι λουτροῖς ἐκλελουμένος δέμας εἰς ὑψίκρημνον Ἱμέραν ἀφικόμην.

[106] *Cf.* E. G. Selwyn, *The First Epistle of St. Peter* (London, 1946), pp. 204ff.

[107] The purificatory "sprinkling" of the heart and conscience "is put first, though the body had also its place and part in the cleansing experience. The καρδία and the σῶμα are a full, plastic expression for the entire personality, as the ancients conceived it" (J. Moffatt, *ad loc.*). The sprinkling (by the blood of Christ, according to Ch. 9:14; *cf.* 12:24) and the washing are both denoted here by means of perfect participles; they are once-for-all and unrepeatable acts with abiding effects.

[108] *Cf.* p. 203, n. 88.

[109] 1QS iii. 4ff. *Cf.* F. F. Bruce, "'To the Hebrews' or 'To the Essenes'?", *NTS* ix (1962–63), pp. 224ff.

thought of the writer to the Hebrews and other New Testament writers, we may discern such an Old Testament prophecy as that of Ezek. 36:25f., where the terminology of the ancient ritual ablutions is used to describe God's inward cleansing of His people in the age of restoration: "I will sprinkle clean water upon you, and ye shall be clean ... A new heart also will I give you, and a new spirit will I put within you."[110] Those who have received this inward cleansing from God may well enjoy that spiritual nearness to Him which is impossible for a polluted conscience.

23 The exhortation is threefold: "let us draw near ... let us hold fast ... let us consider one another". The importance of holding fast the Christian confession has already been emphasized: it is only "if we hold fast our boldness and the glorying of our hope" that we are the house of God (Ch. 3:6); it is only "if we hold fast the beginning of our confidence firm unto the end" that we are partakers or companions of Christ (Ch. 3:14). The powerful incentive which the knowledge of Christ's high-priesthood provides for firmly maintaining the confession of Him has also been stressed (Ch. 4:14);[111] here it is repeated together with the other incentives which are bound up with His high-priesthood, including above all the faithfulness of God whose promises, embodied and fulfilled in Christ, are set forth in the gospel for the encouragement and support of His people. "Let us hold fast the confession of our hope," says ARV, "that it waver not"—doing justice to the Greek construction in which the adjective "unwavering" agrees with "confession";[112] but if the confession wavers it is because the confessors waver, and this is brought out by RSV ("Let us hold fast the confession of our hope without wavering") and NEB ("Let us be firm and unswerving in the confession of our hope"). Our hope is based on the unfailing promise of God; why should we not cherish it confidently and confess it boldly?

24 The readers will be the more apt to confess their hope

---

[110] *Cf.* John 3:5, where the new birth ἐξ ὕδατος καὶ πνεύματος probably alludes to the water of Ezek. 36:25 and the spirit (wind or breath) of Ezek. 36:26f.; 37:9f. In Mark 1:8 the two are divided: John the Baptist applies the water; the Coming One will baptize with Holy Spirit.

[111] In Ch. 4:14 κρατέω is the verb used for "holding fast" the confession (as also in Ch. 6:18 for laying hold on the Christian hope as an anchor of the soul); here (as in Ch. 3:6, 14) the verb is κατέχω.

[112] Gk. κατέχωμεν τὴν ὁμολογίαν τῆς ἐλπίδος ἀκλινῆ.

courageously and unhesitatingly if they encourage one another. Christian faith and witness will flourish the more vigorously in an atmosphere of Christian fellowship. "We ought to see how each of us may best arouse others to love and active goodness" (NEB). The word which ARV renders "provoke" (RSV "stir up"; NEB "arouse") is a strong one;[113] it appears in one other place in the New Testament, and there in a very different way, of the "sharp contention" that broke out between Paul and Barnabas when they could not agree on taking Mark with them on a second apostolic visit to Cyprus and South Galatia (Acts 15:39). Perhaps this Greek word *paroxysmos*, like our English "provocation", is more commonly used in the unfavorable sense of irritation than in the more pleasant sense used here by our author. It is the former sense that Paul has in mind in 1 Cor. 13:5 when, using the cognate verb *paroxynō*, he says that love "is not provoked".[114] But here love *is* provoked in the sense of being stimulated in the lives of Christians by the considerateness and example of other members of their fellowship.

25 This will never happen, however, if they keep one another at a distance. Therefore, every opportunity of coming together and enjoying their fellowship in faith and hope must be welcomed and used for mutual encouragement. Our author exhorts his readers to continue meeting together the more earnestly because he knows of some who were withdrawing from the Christian fellowship. Paul had urged the Roman Christians to welcome one another for God's glory, as Christ had welcomed them (Rom. 15:7). But towards the end of the apostolic age we are made aware of a tendency in some quarters to withdraw from the Christian fellowship. "At first and indeed always," says Harnack, "there were naturally some people who imagined that one could secure the holy contents and blessings of Christianity as one did those of Isis and the Magna Mater, and then withdraw. Or, in cases where people were not so short-sighted, levity, laziness, or weariness were often enough to detach a person from the society. A vainglorious sense of superiority, and of being able to dispense with the spiritual aid of the society, was also the means of inducing

---

113 Gk. παροξυσμός, from the verb παροξύνω.

114 There is one further NT instance of παροξύνω in Acts 17:16, where "Paul's spirit was provoked within him" (NEB "exasperated") at the spectacle of so much idolatry in Athens.

many to withdraw from fellowship and from the common worship. Many, too, were actuated by fear of the authorities; they shunned attendance at public worship, to avoid being recognized as Christians."[115] What appears to have underlain the withdrawal which our author here describes as "the custom of some"?

We may find a clue in the word translated "assembling together". Basically this is the word which we know in its English form "synagogue", but here it carries the prefix *epi*, which in this place may conceivably have the force "in addition", as though the word were to be translated "episynagogue".[116] If this meaning were accepted, then we might think of a group of Jewish believers in Jesus who had not yet severed their connexion with the synagogue in which they had been brought up, but who in addition to their synagogue services had special meetings of their own in a "Christian appendage to the Jewish synagogue", as William Manson puts it.[117] In that case, our author fears that the discontinuance of their special Christian meetings will mean their complete merging in the life of the larger Jewish community with the loss of their distinctive Christian faith and outlook. What he would really like to see would be their decisive separation from the synagogue—this is what he means by "let us go forth" or "let us come out" in Ch. 13:13—but, if they are not ready for that, let them, as they value their lives, maintain their common meetings as believers in Jesus and so encourage one another in their common hope.

It may be pointed out, however, that there is no evidence elsewhere for the use of "episynagogue" in a different sense from

---

[115] A. Harnack, *Mission and Expansion of Christianity* (London, 1908), i. pp. 434f. On his last point he quotes in a footnote Tertullian, *On Flight in Persecution*, 3; on the general necessity of Christians' coming together and seeking one another's society he refers to Clement of Rome, *Epistle*, 48:1ff.; *Didache* 4:2; Hermas, Similitude ix. 20, 26; Barnabas 4:10; Ignatius, *Eph.* 13:1, *Polyc.* 4:2, *Magn.* 4; Justin, *First Apology* 67. In NT the tendency to withdrawal is specially manifest on the part of those who embraced forms of teaching deviating from what had been taught from the beginning (*cf.* I John 2:19, 24). *Cf.* Ch. 3:13 (p. 67).

[116] Gk. ἐπισυναγωγή, appearing once elsewhere in NT—"our gathering together unto him" (II Thess. 2:1), where, however, the prefix ἐπι- may have directive force, anticipating πρὸς αὐτόν.

[117] *The Epistle to the Hebrews* (London, 1951), p. 69.

"synagogue" or "meeting";[118] and our author may simply be urging his readers not to give up attending the general meeting of the church, as some were doing.[119] Under the various pressures which were being brought to bear upon them, to withdraw from the society of their fellow-believers was to court spiritual defeat; only by remaining united could they preserve their faith and witness.

Instead of growing slack in the practice of their Christian fellowship, they are bidden to encourage one another—"and so much the more, as ye see the day drawing nigh". It is plain from the closing verses of this chapter that the apparent postponement of the parousia was having its effect on their minds; at least the sense of tension created by the knowledge that they were living in the end-time was weakening.[120] Not only for them, but for their fellow-Christians in many other places, the necessity of coming to terms with the Church's continued existence in history as a community completely separated from Judaism involved an "agonizing reappraisal". The first generation of believers was passing away; a new generation was growing up. At this point in time other shocks were in store for them: the rather sudden hostility of the imperial power[121] (with which the Church had henceforth to live for two and a half centuries) and the destruction of the city and temple of Jerusalem.

---

[118] "Scarcely to be differentiated from συναγωγή" (AG, p. 301).

[119] W. Manson suggests that the ERV reading of Ch. 4:2, "they were not united by faith with them that heard" (see p. 70, n. 4), implies that "the Christian group at Rome whom the author addresses was separating itself off in the matter of 'faith' from the true believing body of the Church" (op. cit., p. 58). This reading of Ch. 4:2 might indeed be applicable to the people who are being addressed, but it would scarcely be applicable to Israel in the wilderness, of whom the words are explicitly spoken. Quite apart from that vexed textual crux, we could well visualize the community here addressed as members of a "house-church" in Rome which tended to detach itself from the wider fellowship of the city church.

[120] Cf. L. Goppelt, "The Existence of the Church in History according to Apostolic and Early Catholic Thought", Current Issues in NT Interpretation: Essays in Honor of Otto A. Piper, edited by W. Klassen and G. F. Snyder (New York, 1962), pp. 193ff.

[121] How sudden the overt hostility of the imperial power was may be gathered from the language of I Peter: in Ch. 3:13 "who is he that will harm you, if ye be zealous of that which is good?" implies that the situation of Rom. 13:3f., some six or seven years earlier, still continues; in Ch. 3:14 suffering for righteousness' sake is a remote possibility, as the use of the optative mood

THE EPISTLE TO THE HEBREWS

Before A.D.70 those Christians who remembered and took seriously Jesus' prophecy of the destruction of the temple were scarcely in a position to keep it distinct in their minds from the final coming of the Son of Man and the ingathering of His elect, which He also foretold. Only after the events of A.D.70 was it possible to appreciate clearly that two separate epochs were involved in the twofold question of the disciples in the form given to it in Matt. 24:3: "*(a)* When shall these things [the destruction of the temple] be? *(b)* and what shall be the sign of thy parousia, and of the consummation of the age?" It may be that our author, writing (as we think) before A.D.70, had the impending fall of Jerusalem and dissolution of the old order in mind when he spoke of "the day" as approaching.[122] The words "*ye see* the day drawing nigh" suggest that signs of the impending catastrophe in Judaea were already visible to men and women of discernment; and the fulfilment of that phase of Jesus' prediction pointed on to the fulfilment of the final phase. Yet for our author, as for the other New Testament writers, "the day" is primarily the final phase, the day of Christ's parousia. Whatever was implied by the Church's adaptation in her thought and life to the conditions of a second and further generations of Christian existence in the world, her teachers continued, long after A.D.70, to emphasize the certainty, and indeed the nearness, of the parousia. The period between the first advent of Christ and His parousia is the end-time, the "last days", the "last hour". Whatever the duration of the period may be, for faith "the time is at hand" (Rev. 1:3). Each successive Christian generation is called upon to live as the generation of the end-time, if it is to live as a *Christian* generation. This being so, "the question is: How can the tension between the eschatological and historical existence of faith be retained over a period of time?"[123] The most satisfactory answer is the Pauline answer which, while given in the first Christian generation, is equally applicable to every Christian generation: "If we live by the Spirit, by the Spirit let us also walk" (Gal. 5:25)—for the Spirit is the pledge and the firstfruits of the heritage of glory to be entered

---

shows ("even if ye should suffer ..."); but in Ch. 4:12ff. the fiery trial is imminent, and suffering as a Christian, enduring reproach for the name of Christ, is no longer a remote possibility but a matter of present and certain expectation.

[122] Gk. ἐγγίζουσαν (*cf.* p. 249, n. 100).

[123] L. Goppelt, *op. cit.*, p. 199.

by believers at the parousia of Christ (*cf.* Rom. 8:23; Eph. 1:13f.). In keeping with this answer, our author insists that since Christ appeared once for all, "at the end of the ages", to offer Himself to God as the perfect sacrifice for His people's sin, those who acknowledge Him as apostle and high priest have already experienced "the powers of the age to come" and receive the "kingdom which cannot be shaken" (Chs. 6:5; 12:27f.). Thus they anticipate here and now the consummation for which they hope; let them hold this hope fast by unswerving loyalty to Christ.

2. FOURTH ADMONITION: THE WILFUL SIN OF APOSTASY

Ch. 10:26–31

26 For if we sin wilfully after that we have received the knowledge of the truth, there remaineth no more a sacrifice for sins,[124]

27 but a certain fearful expectation of judgment, and a fierceness of fire[125] which shall devour the adversaries.

28 A man that hath set at nought Moses' law dieth without compassion[126] on *the word of* two or three witnesses:[127]

29 of how much sorer punishment, think ye, shall he be judged worthy, who hath trodden under foot the Son of God, and hath counted the blood of the covenant[128] wherewith he was sanctified[129] an unholy thing, and hath done despite unto the Spirit of grace?

---

[124] Gk. περὶ ἁμαρτιῶν (*cf.* Ch. 5:1, 3), for which P⁴⁶ D* 81 have περὶ ἁμαρτίας (*cf.* v. 6, p. 234, n. 42).

[125] Gk. πυρὸς ζῆλος, literally "zeal of fire"; the passage is an echo of Isa. 26:11 ("they shall see thy *zeal* for the people, ... yea, *fire shall devour thine adversaries*"; LXX "*zeal* shall take an uninstructed people, and *fire shall devour the adversaries*"). Isa. 26:11 occurs in a judgment context, from which a further quotation is taken in v. 37a (p. 273, n. 197). *Cf.* Ch. 12:29 (pp. 384f.).

[126] D* and the Harclean Syriac (Western authorities) add "and tears" (καὶ δακρύων), perhaps an echo of Ch. 12:17.

[127] Quotation from Deut. 17:6; 19:15 (*cf.* Matt. 18:16; II Cor. 13:1; I Tim. 5:19). *Cf.* H. van Vliet, *No Single Testimony* (Utrecht, 1958).

[128] *Cf.* Ch. 9:20 (quotation from Ex. 24:8). The African Old Latin MS. *r* adds "new" to "covenant".

[129] Gk. ἐν ᾧ ἡγιάσθη, omitted in A and some MSS of Chrysostom. See p. 236, n. 54.

30 For we know him that said, Vengeance belongeth unto me, I will recompense.[130] And again, The Lord shall judge his people.[131]

31 It is a fearful thing to fall into the hands of the living God.

26–29 This passage was destined to have repercussions in Christian history beyond what our author could have foreseen. By "sinning wilfully" he means something like that sinning "with a high hand"[132] for which no pardon was provided by the Old Testament law of atonement. He has already emphasized that the despising of the saving message spoken by the Son of God must carry with it penalties even more severe than the sanctions attached to the law of Moses, "the word spoken through angels" (Ch. 2:2); and he repeats the same argument here. The context suggests that something much more serious is in his mind than what Paul calls being "overtaken in any trespass"[133]—after all, he has pointed out more than once that in Jesus Christians have a high priest who can succor them when they are tempted, sympathize with them in their infirmities and bear gently with them when they stray from the path through ignorance.[134] What he has in mind is rather that "falling away from the living God" of which he spoke in Ch. 3:12, that renunciation of Christianity against which he warned his readers in Ch. 6:4–8. To have received the knowledge of the truth[135] and then reject it is to give up the only

---

[130] Cod. A and a few other authorities add from Rom. 12:19 "saith the Lord" (so also TR, AV). The quotation from Deut. 32:35 here and in Rom. 12:19 takes a form different from that of MT ("vengeance is mine, and recompense") and LXX ("in the day of vengeance I will repay"), but in agreement with that of the Targum of Onqelos (Aramaic: *qodāmay pŏr'ānūthā wa'anā 'ashallēm*), and of the Palestinian and Pseudo-Jonathan Targums. Evidently our author (and Paul) derived this quotation, either directly or (more probably) by way of a collection of *testimonia*, from a Greek text-form varying from the LXX A and B types, related perhaps to the Theodotionic text (*cf.* O. Michel *ad loc.*, MK, p. 237, n. 1).

[131] Deut. 32:36 (*cf.* also Ps. 135:14, where, however, LXX [134:14] shows οἰκτείρει, "pities", as a strong variant for κρίνει or κρινεῖ).

[132] Num. 15:30 (*cf.* p. 28, n. 2). For the *a fortiori* argument see p. 29, n. 4.

[133] Gal. 6:1.

[134] *Cf.* Chs. 2:17f.; 4:15f.; 5:2.

[135] "The knowledge of the truth" (ἐπίγνωσις (τῆς) ἀληθείας) is a recurring phrase in the Pastoral Epistles (I Tim. 2:4; II Tim. 2:25; 3:7; Tit. 1:1; *cf.* I Tim. 4:3); similar language occurs in the Johannine writings (*cf.* John 8:32;

way of salvation. "There remaineth no more a sacrifice for sins" which can avail for those who have deliberately abandoned reliance on the perfect sacrifice of Christ. That outright apostasy is intended here seems plain from the language of verse 29; the man who has committed this wilful sin is described as having "spurned the Son of God, and profaned the blood of the covenant by which he was sanctified, and outraged the Spirit of grace" (RSV).

Our author is not given to wild exaggeration, and when he uses language like this, he chooses his words with his customary care. To spurn the Son of God, to trample Him underfoot (as the word literally means), "denotes contempt of the most flagrant kind";[136] to treat the covenant-blood of Christ, by which alone His people are sanctified, cleansed and brought to God,[137] as no better than the most common[138] death, is to repudiate decisively both His sacrifice and all the blessings which flow from it; to outrage the Spirit of grace[139] is, in the words of Jesus, to be "guilty of an

---

I John 2:21; II John 1). A study of the expression in relation to the thought and vocabulary of Qumran is presented by H. Kosmala in *Hebräer-Essener-Christen* (Leiden, 1959), pp. 135ff.; he is, however, certainly at fault in his view that "the knowledge of the truth" in Hebrews "does not yet include faith in Jesus Christ" (p. 137).

[136] J. Moffatt (ICC, p. 151); he recalls the Homeric phrase for oath-breaking (καταπατεῖν ὅρκια, lit. "to trample oaths underfoot") and more particularly the LXX of Zech. 12:3, where Jerusalem is described as "a stone trampled on (καταπατούμενον) by all the nations; every one who tramples on her (καταπατῶν αὐτήν) will utterly scorn her". But there is no indication that Zech. 12:3 was in our author's mind here, although he uses the same verb καταπατέω.

[137] *Cf.* Chs. 9:14; 10:10, 14, 19ff. for all that, to our author's mind, is involved in being "sanctified" by the covenant blood of Christ. For His blood as "covenant blood" *cf.* p. 177 with n. 69; pp. 204ff. with nn. 91-144. The phrase αἷμα διαθήκης appears in a context of liberation in Zech. 9:11, which, however, is less likely to have influenced the wording of this and similar NT passages than Ex. 24:8 (quoted in Heb. 9:20).

[138] Gk. κοινός, "common" and therefore "unholy" (*cf.* the use of the adjective in Acts 10:13f., 28, and of the derivative verb κοινόω in the sense of "defile" in Ch. 9:13, as also in Mark 7:15, 18, 20, 23 and parallels; Acts 21:28).

[139] Gk. τὸ πνεῦμα τῆς χάριτος ἐνυβρίσας. *Cf.* "the spirit of grace and of supplication" (πνεῦμα χάριτος καὶ οἰκτιρμοῦ) in Zech. 12:10; here, however, the Spirit is personal as in Ch. 6:4 (one might treat τῆς χάριτος as a Semitic adjectival genitive and render "the gracious Spirit") and Eph. 4:30 suggests itself as a close parallel.

eternal sin" (Mark 3:29).[140] Anyone who was convicted, on adequate testimony, of a breach of Israel's covenant law was liable to the death penalty: "thine eye shall not pity him", so ran the inexorable sentence.[141] But that was the penalty of *physical* death; the spiritual death which lies in store for the apostate under the new order is a "much sorer punishment".

It was commonly inferred in the Early Church from this and other passages in the epistle that forgiveness for all kinds of post-baptismal sin, inadvertent as well as deliberate, was ruled out. The fact, however, that baptized Christians did sin was patent. Was there then no hope for them? If so, the disciples' question to their Master might well be echoed: "Then who can be saved?" (Luke 18:26). In the Roman church (where, thanks to our epistle, the issue may have been a specially live one) the question was taken up a generation or so later by Hermas in *The Shepherd*.[142]

We shall not properly understand the anxiety which this problem caused unless we realize that the kind of sin which in practice aroused greatest concern was sexual irregularity. It was precisely here that the ordinary canons of everyday behavior differed most as between Christians and pagans. We may think today that equal attention ought to be paid to the other six deadly sins; the fact remains that this was the one which involved the greatest heart-searching in the Christian community. The writer to the Hebrews, indeed, did not dwell particularly on offences of this character;[143] and perhaps it was not sufficiently considered that sexual irregularity commonly lacks that element of premeditated policy which he condemns most severely. But experience showed that it was in

---

[140] The sin which our Lord thus described was a deliberate closing of one's eyes to the light; in the immediate context that sin took the form of seeing the works of mercy and power which He wrought by the Holy Spirit and ascribing them to the activity of Beelzebul. Many have compared the "sin unto death" of I John 5:16 (which, however, may be a sin which has resulted in the sinner's bodily death, in which case his friends are not urged to pray for him). As appears from the quotation from the Qumran literature on p. 251 (n. 109), rebellious apostasy was regarded as an unforgivable sin in the Qumran community (*cf.* also 1QS ii. 13f.: "his spirit, parched [for lack of truth] and watered [with falsehood] shall be destroyed without pardon").

[141] *Cf.* Deut. 13:8; 19:13, etc.

[142] It is going too far, however, to say with E. J. Goodspeed that it was the Epistle to the Hebrews that "had most definitely stirred him [Hermas] to write" (*The Apostolic Fathers* [London, 1962], p. 97).

[143] He warns against them in Chs. 12:16; 13:4.

this realm that post-baptismal sin was most prone to occur. Hermas, knowing in his heart how liable human nature is to yield to this form of temptation, even if it be confined to the thought-life,[144] and having received the assurance of divine forgiveness himself, taught (on the basis of a revelation imparted to him) that a second repentance was possible, but no more. According to him, baptism in Christ's name wipes out all previous sins, and baptized persons who keep the law of Christ consistently need not fear the last judgment.[145] But anyone who sinned once after baptism could, after due repentance, receive forgiveness once more, and be assured of ultimate salvation if he did not fall again.[146] This curious concession shows that Hermas and those who thought like him had really failed to grasp the real principle at stake, although they must be given credit for treating sin in believers as a very serious matter. The logic of the argument, however, left something to be desired, for if forgiveness was available once for post-baptismal sin properly repented of, why might it not be available twice or more often still? A rigorist like Tertullian appreciated the logic of the situation, and condemned Hermas for a concession which, as he saw it, was the thin end of a very dangerous wedge.[147] Others, less rigorist than Tertullian, also appreciated the logic of the situation, and extended Hermas's concession indefinitely, making it an essential element of the institution of penance. According to this institution, every baptized person is required periodically to seek, by confession and penance, absolution for sins committed to date.[148] The writer to the Hebrews might well have considered that this institution differed but little

---

[144] It might indeed be supposed that Hermas's thought, that he would be happy if he had a wife comparable to Rhoda for beauty and character (Vision i. 1. 2), would not be regarded by any healthy mind as sinful at all, and Hermas himself did not think of it as sinful until it was revealed to him that it was so (Vision i. 1. 8; i. 2. 4).

[145] Hermas, *Shepherd*, Vision iii. 5. 1ff.; Mandate iv. 3. 1ff.; Similitude v. 5. 3; v. 6. 3.

[146] Hermas, *Shepherd*, Vision ii. 2. 1ff.

[147] See p. 123, with n. 55; the whole exposition there of Ch. 6:4ff. is relevant to the present discussion.

[148] According to L. Goppelt (*op. cit.*, p. 201), "the reformation of Luther began at this point; it was Luther who first cracked the basis of the penitential system started by Hermas, namely, the presupposition that baptism is merely a closed historical act and repentance a subsequent act (*WA*, VI, 529)".

in principle from the Old Testament institution of the day of atonement, in which "there is a remembrance made of sins year by year" (Ch. 10:3). What he urges his readers to do is to avail themselves continuously of the intercessory offices of their enthroned high priest, who appears in God's presence on their behalf by virtue of His perfect self-offering presented and accepted once for all. He would probably have thought it preposterous that his stern words of warning should in due course give rise to a penitential procedure so similar to that which he dismisses as for ever superseded.

30 He drives his warning home with two quotations from the Song of Moses in Deut. 32. The Song of Moses furnished the early Christians with a remarkable number of *testimonia*—largely, but not exclusively, on the subject of Jewish unbelief.[149] The later writers of anti-Judaic apologies regarded it as a strong point in support of their argument that in this Song Moses himself (or God through the mouth of Moses) testifies against Israel.[150] It is God through the mouth of Moses in this Song who says "Vengeance is mine, I will repay" (RSV)—so our author quotes Deut. 32:35 in a version, attested in the Targums, which is followed also by Paul in Rom. 12:19.[151] Our author's application of the words is not inconsistent with their original context: God's own people are not exempt from His law that men reap what they sow.[152] And this is confirmed in the next verse of the Song (Deut. 32:36): "Jehovah will judge his people." This certainly

---

[149] *Cf.* the use of the Song in Rom. 10:19 (quoting verse 21); I Cor. 10:20, 22 (echoing vv. 16f.). Other quotations or allusions may be traced in Rom. 15:10 (quoting v. 43); Phil. 2:15 (echoing v. 5); Heb. 1:6 (see pp. 15f., with nn. 74–76). The Song, with its denunciation of Israel's apostasy, also played an important part in the thinking of the Qumran community; *cf.* the quotation of v. 28 in CD v. 17.

[150] *Cf.* Justin, *Dialogue with Trypho*, 20, 119, 130. See J. R. Harris, "A Factor of Old Testament Influence in the New Testament", *ExT* xxxvii (1925–26), pp. 6ff.; B. Lindars, *New Testament Apologetic* (London, 1961), pp. 244f., 258, 274.

[151] Paul quotes the words to show that Christians should not avenge themselves, since that would be encroaching upon the province of God. Similarly in the Qumran literature (CD ix. 5) the members of the community are instructed to leave vengeance to God, since He "taketh vengeance on his adversaries, and he reserveth wrath for his enemies" (Nahum 1:2).

[152] In the immediate context of this part of the Song the vengeance is evidently directed against Israel's enemies:

means that He will execute judgment on their behalf, vindicating their cause against their enemies, but also that, on the same principles of impartial righteousness, He will execute judgment against them when they forsake His covenant. The privileges which Israel enjoyed as God's covenant-people meant that their responsibilities were the greater and that retribution would be the more severe in their case if they gave themselves up to unrighteousness: "You only have I known of all the families of the earth: therefore I will visit upon you all your iniquities" (Amos 3:2). What was true then remains true for God's dealings with His people now.

31 Our author has a deep conviction of the awesome holiness of the divine majesty. "It is a fearful thing," he says, "to fall into the hands of the living God." These words have no doubt been used frequently as a warning to the ungodly of what lies in store for them unless they amend their ways; but their primary application is to the people of God. "It is a splendid, but it is an awful thing to say, 'We know that we are of God'."[153] This is what Isaiah meant when he said, after God had acted so signally in His people's behalf by removing the Assyrian menace from Jerusalem: "Who among us can dwell with the devouring fire? who among us can dwell with everlasting burnings?"[154] (Isa. 33:14). The revelation of the consuming righteousness of God which they had

---

"For the LORD will vindicate his people
  and have compassion on his servants,
when he sees that their power is gone,
  and there is none remaining, bond or free" (Deut. 32:36, RSV).
But much of the Song is an indictment of Israel's unfaithfulness and a warning of God's ensuing judgment against her; if in the end He crushes her enemies, who were the instruments of His judgment on her, it is for His own name's sake:
"I would have said, 'I will scatter them [Israel] afar,
  I will make the remembrance of them cease from among men,'
had I not feared provocation by the enemy,
  lest their adversaries should judge amiss,
lest they should say, 'Our hand is triumphant,
  the LORD has not wrought all this'" (Deut. 32:26f., RSV).
[153] G. G. Findlay, *Exp.* V. ix (1899), p. 91, in reference to I John 5:19 (in article "St. John's Creed", pp. 81ff.).
[154] With language like this we may compare the "fierceness of fire" of v. 27 (*cf.* p. 257, n. 125). *Cf.* Deut. 5:26, where the title "the living God" occurs in a context of fiery symbolism: "who is there of all flesh, that hath heard the voice of the living God speaking out of the midst of the fire, as we have, and

just witnessed spoke more loudly to them than it did to Sennacherib's warriors who had fallen before it; in that hour of judgment
Israel learned something new about the character of the God who
dwelt constantly in her midst.[155] Yet, when the question must be
faced, into whose hands would any one of the people of God more
readily fall than into His? When King David was commanded to
choose between three forms of judgment after his numbering of
the people, his wise reply was the fruit of his previous experience
of God: "let us fall now into the hand of Jehovah; for his mercies
are great" (II Sam. 24:14). Perhaps this very passage was in our
author's mind and suggested the form of words he chose: "to fall
into the hands of the living God".[156] For "the living God" appears
repeatedly in the Bible as a synonym of Yahweh.[157] And if our
author were asked why it is so fearful to fall into *His* hands, he
might well reply: "Because He is the *living* God."

"It is a fearful thing," said the translators of the AV in the
peroration of their preface,[158] "to fall into the hands of the living
God; but a blessed thing it is, and will bring us to everlasting
blessedness in the end, when God speaketh unto us, to hearken;
when he setteth his word before us, to read it; when he stretcheth
out his hand and calleth, to answer, Here am I, here we are to do
thy will, O God. The Lord work a care and conscience in us to
know him and serve him that we may be acknowledged of him
at the appearing of our Lord Jesus Christ, to whom with the Holy
Ghost be all praise and thanksgiving. Amen."

---

lived?" The same title recurs in the situation which forms the background of
Isa. 33:14; Sennacherib's doom is sealed when he sends his minister "to defy
the living God" (Isa. 37:4, 17). See pp. 384f.

[155] *Cf.* Isa. 31:9.

[156] David's words are echoed in Sir. 2:18:
"Let us fall into the hands of the Lord,
    but not into the hands of men;
  for as his majesty is,
    so also is his mercy."

[157] In addition to the passages mentioned on p. 263, n. 154, *cf.* Josh. 3:10;
I Sam. 17:26; Pss. 42:2; 84:2.

[158] *The Translators to the Reader*, compiled by one of their number, Miles
Smith, Canon of Hereford (later to be Bishop of Gloucester).

3. CALL TO PERSEVERANCE

Ch. 10:32-39

32 But call to remembrance the former days,[159] in which, after ye were enlightened, ye endured a great conflict of sufferings;

33 partly, being made a gazingstock[160] both by reproaches and afflictions; and partly, becoming partakers with them that were so used.

34 For ye both had compassion on them that were in bonds,[161] and took joyfully the spoiling of your possessions, knowing that ye have for yourselves[162] a better possession[163] and an abiding one.

35 Cast not away therefore your boldness, which hath great recompense of reward.

36 For ye have need of patience, that, having done the will of God, ye may receive the promise.

---

[159] Gk. τὰς πρότερον ἡμέρας. A few good minuscules (including 33 69 1739) and the Bohairic Coptic add ὑμῶν ("your former days"); ℵ* not only adds ὑμῶν but in place of ἡμέρας exhibits the odd reading ἁμαρτίας ("your former sins", perhaps through a vague reminiscence of II Pet. 1:9).

[160] Gk. θεατριζόμενοι (cf. Paul's use of θέατρον, "spectacle", in I Cor. 4:9); D* and the Sahidic Coptic read ὀνειδιζόμενοι ("being reproached") under the influence of ὀνειδισμοῖς ("reproaches") in the same clause; cf. the collocation of the same substantive and verb in Rom. 15:3 (quoting Ps. 69:9). The verb θεατρίζω (here only in the Greek Bible) was not attested elsewhere earlier than Gregory of Nazianzus until it was discovered on a Gerasa inscription of Trajan's reign (A.D. 98–117); cf. A. H. M. Jones in *JRS* xviii (1928), pp. 144f.

[161] Gk. τοῖς δεσμίοις (so P¹³ apparently, with A D 33 and other minuscules, the Latin and Syriac versions), for which P⁴⁶ Ψ 81 and Origen read τοῖς δεσμοῖς ("on the bonds"); attempts to make this latter reading intelligible are found in the Old Latin texts *d* and *e*, which read "on their bonds", and in ℵ with the majority of manuscripts and Clement of Alexandria (followed by TR and AV), which read τοῖς δεσμοῖς μου ("on my bonds")—a reading which evidently originated in Alexandria under the influence of the belief that the writer was Paul (cf. Col. 4:18b).

[162] Gk. ἑαυτοῖς (D K L and many other manuscripts); but the better attested reading is ἑαυτούς (P¹³ P⁴⁶ ℵ A 1912 with the Latin version, Clement and Origen), whence ERV: "knowing that ye yourselves have a better possession and an abiding one".

[163] A few authorities (including P 1739 and the Peshitta and Harclean Syriac, followed by TR) add ἐν οὐρανοῖς (whence AV: "ye have in heaven a better and an enduring substance").

265

37   For yet a very little while,[164]
     He that cometh shall come, and shall not tarry.

38   But my righteous one shall live by faith:[165]
     And if he shrink back, my soul hath no pleasure in him.[166]

39   But we are not of them that shrink back unto perdition;
     but of them that have faith[167] unto the saving of the soul.

32–34 Like the warning of Ch. 6:4–8, so the warning of Ch. 10:26–31 is followed by words of reassurance and encouragement. Our author does not wish to discourage his readers, but to embolden them so that they will emerge victorious from the present growing test of their faith. This he does now in the first place by reminding them of how they stood a severe test in the earlier days of their life as Christians, not long after their "enlightenment"—an expression repeated from Ch. 6:4.[168]

The identification of this earlier test, even if any independent information survives about it, must be precarious so long as we are uncertain of the place where the addressees of this epistle lived. The identification, however, is made a little easier if we link with the present passage the words of Ch. 12:4: "In your struggle against sin you have not yet resisted to the point of shedding your blood" (RSV, NEB).[169] It is a reasonable inference from these words that, while the people addressed had undergone persecution, none of them had thus far suffered martyrdom. This appears to

---

164 This phrase, introducing the quotation that follows, echoes Isa. 26:20 (see p. 273, n. 197).

165 Gk. ὁ δὲ δίκαιός μου ἐκ πίστεως ζήσεται. "Here the writer transferred the pronoun μου from after πίστεως to after δίκαιος—a small alteration of great consequence" (G. Zuntz, *The Text of the Epistles*, p. 173). D* and a few other authorities with the Syriac versions and Eusebius restore the LXX B text by transposing μου to follow πίστεως, giving the sense "by my faith(fulness)"; P13 with the majority of later MSS and TR omit μου altogether (under the influence of Rom. 1:17; Gal. 3:11), whence AV: "Now the just shall live by faith" (see p. 273, n. 196).

166 Hab. 2:3f. (see pp. 272ff.).

167 Literally: "we are not of withdrawing (ὑποστολῆς) unto perdition, but of faith (πίστεως) unto the saving (περιποίησιν, 'gaining', 'acquiring') of the soul". The two genitives are descriptive in effect; a class of people is denoted in either case.

168 Gk. φωτισθέντες (*cf.* p. 120, n. 39).

169 See p. 357 with nn. 62–64.

rule out, for example, the Church of Jerusalem. Members of that church had suffered death in the persecution that broke out immediately after Stephen's execution about A.D. 33,[170] as also in A.D. 44, under Herod Agrippa I, when James the son of Zebedee was beheaded,[171] and in A.D.62, when James the Just was stoned at the instance of the high priest Annas II[172] (if indeed the last-named incident had taken place by the writing of this epistle). It might also be thought to rule out any of the communities established through the witness of Hellenistic refugees from Jerusalem in A.D. 33 and the following years, though this would be by no means a conclusive inference.

Again, others have compared the language of our author here with the descriptions by Tacitus and Clement of the indignities inflicted on the Christians of Rome under Nero in A.D. 64. "Their death," says Tacitus, "was made a matter of sport: they were covered in wild beasts' skins and torn to pieces by dogs; or were fastened to crosses and set on fire in order to serve as torches by night when daylight failed."[173] Clement tells how Christian women had to "enact the parts of Dirce and the daughters of Danaus".[174] But in spite of the correspondence between these descriptions and our author's reminder that some of his readers had been "abused and tormented to make a public show" (NEB), it could never have been said to Roman Christians after A.D. 64 that they had "not yet resisted unto blood, striving against sin"; that is precisely what they had done, and right nobly. While they had literally been made "a public show", our author may use the term somewhat more figuratively, rather as Paul does in I Cor. 4:9 when he compares himself and his fellow-apostles to "men condemned to death in the arena, a spectacle to the whole universe" (NEB).[175]

If, however, our author is adressing a group of Roman Christians *before* A.D. 64, we may recall another occasion which could satisfy his terms. Shortly after Claudius became emperor in A.D. 41,

---

[170] Acts 8:1ff. That believers suffered death, as well as imprisonment and exile, in this persecution is suggested by Paul's words in Acts 26:10 ("when they were put to death" is more than a generalizing plural, and implies that Stephen was not the only martyr at this time).

[171] Acts 12:2.

[172] Josephus, *Antiquities* xx. 200.

[173] Tacitus, *Annals* xv. 44.

[174] I Clement 6:2.

[175] See p. xliii, n. 92; p. 265, n. 160.

he imposed certain restrictions on the Jewish colony in Rome.[176] These restrictions evidently did not accomplish the purpose for which they were imposed, so some eight years later he took the more drastic step of expelling them from the capital. According to the well-known account of Suetonius, he expelled them because "they were constantly indulging in riots at the instigation of Chrestus".[177] The common inference from Suetonius's account— that these riots resulted from the recent introduction of Christianity into the Jewish colony in Rome—is supported by the fact that two of the expelled Jews, Priscilla and Aquila (who settled in Corinth where Paul made their acquaintance in A.D. 50), were Christians at the time.[178] A large-scale eviction of this nature would inevitably have been attended by widespread looting by the city proletariat, together with many other kinds of insults and indignities. We have a vivid account in Philo of what happened in Alexandria in A.D. 38 when the Jews of that city were forced to leave their homes in four of its five wards and be herded together in one ward. "Their enemies overran the houses now left empty and began to loot them, dividing up the contents like spoils of war."[179] The looting was accompanied by other acts of public outrage and violence. While there is no reason to suppose that the Roman Jews in A.D. 49 suffered anything like the extremes of brutality suffered by the Alexandrian Jews eleven years earlier, their experiences would very probably have been such as to merit our author's description here.

The fact that these words could reasonably be interpreted with reference to the circumstances attendant on Claudius's expulsion of the Jews of Rome does not, of course, exclude the possibility, and indeed the high probability, that from time to time Jewish communities in other cities (and especially, perhaps, those members of such communities who were disciples of Jesus) had to endure persecution of much the same kind. After the outbreak of the Jewish revolt against Rome in A.D. 66 the Jewish communi-

---

[176] Dio Cassius, *Hist.* lx. 6: "He did not directly banish them, but forbade them to gather in accordance with their ancestral way of life."

[177] Suetonius, *Claudius* 25. 4.

[178] *Cf.* F. F. Bruce, "Christianity under Claudius", *BJRL* xliv (1961–62), pp. 309ff. If this interpretation is right, the Christians of Rome, being in a minority, would inevitably come off worst in the riots of which Suetonius speaks.

[179] Philo, *Flaccus* 56.

ties fo many cities throughout Syria and Palestine were the victims of riot and massacre,[180] and Jewish Christians would be in no way exempt from such assaults. But since most of these involved wholesale slaughter, they are excluded from consideration here. Besides, the statement that the readers suffered these things in their early Christian days, after they were "enlightened", may suggest that they suffered them on account of their adherence to the gospel. This could be said, no doubt, of the Jewish believers of Rome in A.D. 49, who may even have had some persecution to endure at the hands of the synagogue authorities in addition to the hostile attentions of the pagan population; it would not be so applicable to those occasions on which Jewish communities were attacked simply because they were Jewish. This, for example, rules out the events in Alexandria in A.D. 38, because in them the Jews were attacked as Jews (it is nowhere implied that Christianity had anything to do with that trouble);[181] in addition, many of the Alexandrian Jews lost their lives in the pogroms of that year.[182]

In short, the events of A.D. 49 at Rome could be referred to here; it is perfectly conceivable that events at some other time or place could be referred to,[183] but on these we are even less well informed than we are about the events at Rome.

At any rate, the readers had at one time "endured a great conflict of sufferings", as our author puts it, using an athletic metaphor.[184] They had met the challenge of these sufferings as good athletes of Christ, and stood firm. Those of them who had not been personally exposed to suffering showed their solidarity with those who were directly attacked, and so shared the public scorn. When some of their number were imprisoned, the others did not shrink from visiting them, although in this way they ran

---

[180]   Cf. Josephus, War ii. 457ff.

[181]   Claudius's rescript to the Alexandrians of A.D. 41 (H. I. Bell, Jews and Christians in Egypt [London, 1924], pp. 1ff.), with its reference to illegal Jewish immigration into Alexandria from Syria or other parts of Egypt, has sometimes been thought to refer to the coming of Christianity to that city; but this is a very precarious interpretation (cf. article cited in n. 178).

[182]   Philo, Flaccus 65ff.

[183]   If the reference is indeed to events at Rome, this might suggest that the author knew of them at first hand (e.g. Priscilla or Aquila) or at second hand (e.g. Apollos). Cf. p. 274, n. 199.

[184]   Cf. Ch. 12:1f.; such metaphors are a commonplace of ancient literature (for their Pauline use cf. I Cor. 9:24ff.; II Tim. 4:7f.).

the risk of being imprisoned themselves. They thus secured a place for themselves among those to whom the Son of Man says: "I was in prison, and ye came unto me" (Matt. 25:36). Prisoners who had no means of their own were liable to starve unless their friends brought them food and whatever other form of help they required; throughout the whole age of imperial persecution of the Church the visiting of their friends who were in prison was a regular, though dangerous, duty of Christian charity.[185]

They had accepted this persecution, too, in a spirit of Christian cheerfulness. "Blessed are ye," their Master had said, "when men shall hate you, and when they shall separate you from their company, and reproach you, and cast out your name as evil, for the Son of man's sake. Rejoice in that day, and leap for joy: for behold, your reward is great in heaven" (Luke 6:22f.). It was exactly in the sense of this exhortation that these Hebrew Christians took the plundering of their property not merely in a spirit of equanimity but joyfully; it was for such as they, as well as for himself, that Paul spoke when he said "we also rejoice in our tribulations" (Rom. 5:3).[186] The eternal inheritance laid up for them was so real in their eyes that they could lightheartedly bid farewell to material possessions which were short–lived in any case. This attitude of mind is precisely that "faith" of which our author goes on to speak. They manifested it in those earlier days, and that is why he is so confident that they will continue to manifest it, although the trials that confront them now are different from those that they faced then, and more subtle in character.

35 You showed your courage in those days, he says; do not abandon it now.[187] The word he uses has appeared three times already in this letter; ARV translates it uniformly by "boldness". In Chs. 4:16; 10:19 it is used of the confidence with which Christians may approach the throne of God since Christ is there as their prevailing high priest; in Ch. 3:6 it is used more generally of the

---

[185] Cf. Lucian, Death of Peregrinus 12; Aristides, Apology 15; Tertullian, To the Martyrs 1f.; Apology 39; Eusebius, Hist. Eccl. iv. 23. 10, etc.; A. Harnack, Mission and Expansion of Christianity (Eng. tr., London, 1908), i, pp. 162ff., ii, p. 117. See p. 391.

[186] Cf. Acts 5:41; I Peter 4:13.

[187] With our author's μὴ ἀποβάλητε οὖν τὴν παρρησίαν ὑμῶν Moffatt (ICC, p. 155) compares Dio Chrysostom's very similar δέδοικα μὴ τελέως ἀποβάλητε τὴν παρρησίαν (Oration xxxiv. 39); but Dio uses παρρησία here of the Tarsian citizens' right of free speech.

courageous confession which Christians should maintain without fail. It is in this last sense that it is used here, with special reference to steadfastness in adverse and disheartening circumstances: "it is, so to say, the content of the Christian attitude in the world, the security of God's salvation and the open confession amidst of opposition".[188] We may think of the "boldness" of Peter and John which made such an impression on the Sanhedrin (Acts 4:13); the forthrightness of their language evinced an inner confidence of heart and life. So it had been with these "Hebrews"; preserve that former confidence of yours, says our author, for it carries a great reward with it (using a word which is peculiar to him among biblical writers, and which is not known before his time).[189] This is the "reward" of which Jesus spoke in the words quoted above from Luke 6:23; it is the realization of the promise in the good of which men of faith already live.[190]

36 What they need is patience.[191] God will certainly fulfil His promise; they will enter into the utmost enjoyment of it; but in the meantime they must remain loyal, and not give up doing God's will. Their Master came expressly to do the will of God, as they have been told already (Ch. 10:7, 9f.), although the doing of that will involved suffering and death for Him; His servants can expect no easier path as they in their turn do the will of God and await the promised bliss. Sometimes the promised bliss seemed close at hand, as they saw "the day drawing nigh";[192] but at other times it looked as though it would never come, and they had to be reassured, like people to whom another New Testament letter was sent, that "the Lord is not slack concerning his promise" (II Peter 3:9). Let their heart take courage, as they wait for their Lord.

37-38 The exhortation to patience is supported by a quotation

---

[188] W. C. van Unnik, "The Christian's Freedom of Speech in the NT", *BJRL* xliv (1961-62), p. 485. *Cf.* p. 244, n. 82.

[189] Gk. μισθαποδοσία (*cf.* Chs. 2:2; 11:26); *cf.* μισθαποδότης, Ch. 11:6.

[190] *Cf.* Rabbi Tarphon in *Pirqe Aboth* ii. 21: "It is not for thee to finish the work, neither art thou free to desist therefrom; if thou hast studied much Torah, much reward will be given thee, and faithful is thy Employer to pay thee the reward of thy labor; and know that the recompense of reward (Heb. *mattan sākhār*) for the righteous is for the time to come."

[191] Gk. ὑπομονή, cognate with the verb ὑπεμείνατε ("ye endured") in v. 32; but there is probably no deliberate harking back to ὑπεμείνατε.

[192] See pp. 255ff.

271

from Old Testament prophecy. The prophet Habakkuk, in the later part of the seventh century B.C., cried out to God because of the oppression that was rife on every hand, and wondered when divine righteousness would at last be vindicated on earth. God answered his complaint and bade him be patient: the oppressor would at last reap the judgment which his heaven-defying ways had incurred and God's purpose would be accomplished; meanwhile, the righteous man would preserve his life by his loyal trust in God.[193]

> "For the vision is yet for the appointed time,
> and it hasteth toward the end, and shall not lie:
> though it tarry, wait for it;
> because it will surely come, it will not delay.
>
> Behold, his soul is puffed up, it is not upright in him;
> but the righteous shall live by his faith" (Hab. 2:3f.).[194]

In the Septuagint version as quoted by our author some of these words are given a different emphasis:[195]

> "Because the vision is yet for an appointed time,
> and it will appear at length and not in vain:
> if he is late, wait for him;
> because he will surely come, he will not delay.

---

[193] *Cf.* J. H. Eaton, *Obadiah, Nahum, Habakkuk, Zephaniah* (London, 1962), pp. 82ff.

[194] The Targum of Jonathan renders the passage: "Behold, the prophecy will be for an appointed time, and its term is fixed; it will not be in vain. If there is a long period of waiting for the event, keep looking out for it; behold, it will come in its appointed time, and will not be late. Behold, the wicked say to themselves, 'None of these things are happening'; but the righteous will be established by their truth."

[195] Not only is there a different emphasis in LXX; there are some points of textual divergence from MT. Heb. *'uppelāh* ("is puffed up", with *napshō*, "his soul", as subject) is rendered ὑποστείληται ("draws back"), perhaps because the *Vorlage* had *'ullephāh* ("faints"), which is actually read in some MSS, perhaps because *'āphal* was confused with its homophone meaning "be neglectful" (*cf.* Num. 14:44). (The latter alternative probably accounts for Aquila's rendering of the verb by νωχελεύομαι, "be sluggish".) Heb. *naphshō* ("his soul") is read as *naphshī* ("my soul"), while the rendering εὐδοκεῖ ("takes pleasure in") presupposes some such word as *rāṣethāh* in place of *yāsherāh* ("is upright"; *cf.* Aquila's rendering εὐθεῖα). The B text of LXX presupposes *'emūnāthī* ("my faith [fulness]") for *'emūnāthō* ("his faith [fulness]"). See next note.

If he draws back, my soul has no pleasure in him,
but my righteous one[196] will live by faith (faithfulness)."

Here it is not simply for the fulfilment of the vision that the prophet is told to wait, but for a person, presumably an expected deliverer. When this deliverer appears, he will vindicate the righteousness of God and put down the oppressor; if, however, he draws back, that will indicate that he is not God's chosen agent. But if he does not draw back, but shows himself to be indeed God's chosen agent, His "righteous one", then by his faithfulness he will win his life. The deliverer in question is not called "the Lord's anointed" in so many words, but the Septuagint interpretation of this passage is essentially messianic.

Our author, then, is but dotting the i's and crossing the t's of the Septuagint interpretation when he applies the prophecy to the second coming of Christ. The clause with which he introduces the quotation ("for yet a very little while")[197] is not taken from any otherwise attested text of Hab. 2:3, but it may be a reminiscence of the Septuagint version of Isa. 26:20 ("a little moment"). Then the identity of the expected deliverer is made clearer. In the Septuagint "he will surely come" is literally

---

[196] The LXX witnesses differ in their placing of the possessive pronoun "my"; the B text reads ὁ δὲ δίκαιος ἐκ πίστεώς μου ζήσεται ("but the righteous one will live by my faithfulness"), while the A text and 'C' group of MSS attest the reading ὁ δὲ δίκαιός μου ἐκ πίστεως ζήσεται ("but my righteous one will live by faith [fulness]"). (Cod. A itself, indeed, has μου in both positions, but this is self-evidently a secondary reading.) Most editors prefer the B reading; it has even been suggested that the A reading has been influenced by the present text of Hebrews (cf. B. Lindars, New Testament Apologetic [London, 1961], p. 231; see also G. Zuntz, as quoted on p. 266, n. 165). But the A reading is strongly defended by T. W. Manson in his article "The Argument from Prophecy" (JThS xlvi [1945], pp. 129ff.)—an article to which the exposition above is considerably indebted. "In view of the general sense of the passage as presented in the LXX version," he says (p. 134), "it is not difficult to decide between these alternatives"—the B alternative, "the solid foundation for all the hopes of the righteous man is the faithfulness of God", and the A alternative, "God's righteous one will live by faithfulness". "The leader who plays the coward," he goes on, "eo ipso shows that he is not God's chosen. The genuine choice of God, God's righteous one, will be faithful to his God, his people, and his task, and so he will win life." "My righteous one," that is to say, is the one who "will surely come and not delay."

[197] Gk. ἔτι γὰρ μικρὸν ὅσον ὅσον. Isa. 26:20, LXX, has μικρὸν ὅσον ὅσον for Heb. ki-me'aṭ regaʿ. For another echo of Isa. 26 cf. v. 27 above (p. 257, n. 125).

"coming he will come" (an imitation in Greek of a common Hebrew idiom).[198] Our author places the definite article before the participle "coming" so as to yield the messianic title "The Coming One"—the title used, for example, by John the Baptist[199] when he sent his disciples to Jesus with the question: "Are you the Coming One, or are we to expect someone else?" (Matt. 11:3//Luke 7:19). "The Coming One will come; He will not delay."[200]

In his quotation of Hab. 2:4 our author inverts the two parts of the verse: "my righteous one shall live by faith" is applied to the Christian believer, tempted to wonder if Christ will ever return in accordance with His promise; and the warning about the divine displeasure which will rest upon anyone who draws back is applied to him who yields to the temptation to relapse from his Christian profession into his earlier way of life. The reason for the inversion is not hard to determine: by this means "my righteous one" becomes the subject of both parts of the verse.[201] If he perseveres in faith he will gain his life; if he shrinks back he will prove himself reprobate.

The clause "the righteous shall live by his faith" is twice quoted by Paul (Gal. 3:11; Rom. 1:17) in a context which suggests that he gave it the meaning: "it is he who is righteous by faith that will live". Indeed, this clause might well be regarded as the "text" of the Epistle to the Romans, and along with Gen. 15:6 it forms a principal *testimonium* for the doctrine of justification by faith. There is no fundamental difference in this respect between Paul and the author of Hebrews;[202] but our author, reproducing this

---

[198]   *Cf.* the same construction in Ch. 6:14 (p. 129, n. 75).

[199]   "A fact which becomes the more interesting if, as I think is probable, the author of Hebrews is Apollos, who was a Johannite before he became a Christian" (T. W. Manson, *loc. cit.*, p. 134). *Cf.* p. 269, n. 183.

[200]   *Cf.* Article 18 of the Creed of Maimonides: "I believe with perfect faith in the coming of Messiah, and though he tarry, I will wait daily for his coming."

[201]   *Cf.* Matt. 24:45ff., where the possibility is envisaged that the same servant may turn out to be either "the faithful and wise servant" who is found doing his duty when his master comes, or "that evil servant" who misconducts himself because his master seems to be so long in coming.

[202]   Paul omits the possessive pronoun from the clause altogether. It is plain that our author does not take the quotation from Paul. C. H. Dodd suggests that the quotation was current as a *testimonium* to the coming of Christ in primitive Christian times, and that its use in this way is reflected independently both in Paul's writings and in Hebrews. That it was current as a *testimonium*

clause together with part of its context, emphasizes the forward-looking character of saving faith, and in fact includes in "faith" not only what Paul means by the word but also what Paul more often expresses by the companion word "hope".[203] If Paul speaks about being "saved through faith" (*e.g.*, Eph. 2:8), he also says: "in hope were we saved" (Rom. 8:24).[204] And we remember our Lord's words to His disciples when He warned them of coming days which would test their faith severely: "In your patience ye shall win your souls" (Luke 21:19; *cf.* RSV: "By your endurance you will gain your lives").[205] It is patient endurance of this kind that our author desires his readers to show, and he is persuaded, for all his solemn warnings, that they will indeed show it, and gain true life thereby.

39 For, says he, in a further affirmation of his essential confidence in them, and including himself among them, "we are not among those who shrink back and are lost; we maintain our faith and win through to life".[206] They had begun their Christian

---

even before Paul wrote Galatians is the more likely, he thinks, because Paul's argument is very much *ad hominem*, and would be all the more effective if it was already common ground between him and his opponents that when the Coming One came, the righteous would live by faith (*According to the Scriptures* [London, 1952], pp. 50f.). We may compare the exegesis of the same passage in the Qumran commentary on Habakkuk, where the statement "the righteous shall live by his faith" is applied to "all the doers of the law in the house of Judah, whom God will save from the place of judgment because of their toil and their faith in the Teacher of Righteousness" (1Q p Hab. viii. 1–3). It is plain that the Teacher of Righteousness "was not only a spiritual leader but a figure of eschatological significance. Acceptance of his teaching, loyally keeping to the path which he marked out for his followers—this was the way to eternal life" (F. F. Bruce, "The Dead Sea Habakkuk Scroll", *Annual of Leeds University Oriental Society* i [1958–59], p. 16; *cf. Biblical Exegesis in the Qumran Texts* [London, 1960], pp. 77, 82f.).

[203] "Faith is indeed the primary Christian virtue; but it is so, to our writer, not merely because it enables the believer to make real in himself the righteousness freely offered to him in the grace of the Lord Jesus, a sense which the word has so conspicuously in the Pauline letters and with which there is no reason whatever for thinking that our writer would not be in entire agreement, but also because it sustains and gives substance to hope and demonstrates the reality of the invisible" (R. V. G. Tasker, *The Gospel in the Epistle to the Hebrews* [London, 1950], p. 60). *Cf.* Ch. 11:1, with the whole exposition of faith that follows.

[204] *Cf.* F. F. Bruce, *Epistle to the Romans*, TNTC (London, 1963), pp. 171ff.

[205] Gk. κτήσεσθε τὰς ψυχὰς ὑμῶν (*cf.* εἰς περιποίησιν ψυχῆς in Heb. 10:39).

[206] The phrase εἰς περιποίησιν ψυχῆς here is a variant expression for ζήσεται in the Habakkuk quotation in v. 38.

career in that carefree spirit which accepts without questioning the assurance of Christ that "whosoever would save his life shall lose it; and whosoever shall lose his life for my sake and the gospel's shall save it" (Mark 8:35). Let them maintain that spirit of faith to the end, and they would certainly gain their souls and "lay hold on the life that is life indeed".[207] That this will prove true with our author and his readers alike is his firm assurance.

---

[207] I Tim. 6:19.

CHAPTER XI

4. THE FAITH OF THE ELDERS

Ch. 11:1-40

(a) Prologue: The Nature of Faith

Ch. 11:1-3

1 Now faith is assurance[1] of *things* hoped for, a conviction of things not seen.

2 For therein the elders had witness borne to them.

3 By faith we understand that the worlds[2] have been framed by the word of God, so that what is seen hath not been made out of things which appear.

1 Our author might well have proceeded from Ch. 10:39 to the exhortation, "Therefore ... let us run with patience the race that is set before us" (Ch. 12:1); but first he encourages his readers further by reminding them of examples of faith in earlier days. In Old Testament times, he points out, there were many men and women who had nothing but the promises of God to rest upon, without any visible evidence that these promises would ever be fulfilled; yet so much did these promises mean to them that they regulated the whole course of their lives in their light. The promises related to a state of affairs belonging to the future; but these people acted as if that state of affairs were already present, so convinced were they that God could and would fulfil what He had promised. In other words, they were men and women of faith. Their faith consisted simply in taking God at His word and directing their lives accordingly; things yet future so far as their experience went were thus present to faith, and things outwardly unseen were visible to the inward eye. It is in these terms that our author now describes the faith of which he has been speaking. It is, he says, the *hypostasis* of things that are hoped for.[3]

---

[1] Gk. ὑπόστασις (ERV "the assurance").

[2] Gk. αἰῶνες (literally "ages"), as in Ch. 1:2.

[3] The form of the definition (ἔστιν δὲ πίστις ...) is paralleled in Philo; *cf.* his definition of prayer: "Now prayer is (ἔστιν δὲ εὐχή) a request of good things from God" (*On the unchangeableness of God*, 87).

This word *hypostasis* has appeared twice already in the epistle. In Ch. 1:3 the Son was stated to be the very image of God's *hypostasis*; in Ch. 3:14 believers are said to be Christ's associates if they hold fast the beginning of their *hypostasis* firm to the end. In the former place it has the objective sense of "substance" or "real essence" (as opposed to what merely seems to be so).[4] In the latter place it has the subjective sense of "confidence" or "assurance".[5] Here it is natural to take it in the same subjective sense as it bears in Ch. 3:14, and so ARV and RSV render it "assurance".[6] There is, however, something to be said for the objective meaning, represented by AV ("faith is the substance of things hoped for"), ARV margin ("the giving substance to things hoped for") and NEB ("Faith gives substance to our hopes").[7] That is to say, things which in themselves have no existence as yet become real and substantial by the exercise of faith. But on the whole the subjective meaning "assurance" is the more probable, especially as this meaning chimes in well with the companion word "conviction". From another use of the word attested in the Hellenistic papyri Moulton and Milligan "venture to suggest the translation 'Faith is the *title-deed* of things hoped for' ".[8] In the instances which they cite from the papyri this meaning is indicated by the context. It might no doubt be said that if we adopt this meaning here, we have something comparable to Paul's language about the Holy Spirit as the "firstfruits" or "earnest" of the coming inheritance of believers;[9] but one would require stronger evidence from the present context before adopting it here. Our author is making much the same point as Paul makes in Rom. 8:24f.: "hope that is seen is not hope: for who hopeth for that which he seeth? But if we hope for that which we see not, then do we with patience[10] wait for it."

The word rendered "conviction" (Gk. *elenchos*) has the same twofold sense as the English word. In II Tim. 3:16 it occurs as

---

[4] See p. 6 with nn. 26, 27.

[5] See p. 67 with n. 67 (and particularly the work by H. Dörrie cited there).

[6] Tyndale, Coverdale and the Great Bible render it "sure confidence".

[7] Following Vulg. *substantia*. *Cf.* the Geneva rendering: "Faith is that which causeth those things to appear in deed which are hoped for."

[8] MM, pp. 659f.

[9] *Cf.* Rom. 8:23; II Cor. 1:22; 5:5; Eph. 1:14.

[10] Gk. ὑπομονή (*cf.* Heb. 10:36).

a variant reading for the cognate *elegmos* to denote the "conviction" or "refutation" of error which Holy Scripture provides; here it means "conviction" in much the same sense as "assurance" in the preceding phrase. Physical eyesight produces conviction or evidence of visible things; faith is the organ which enables people (like Moses in verse 27) to see the invisible order.[11] Philo similarly links "faith towards God" with "apprehension of the unseen".[12]

2 It was for faith of this kind that men and women of old[13] received the divine commendation, and this has been placed on permanent record as an example to their descendants. The record is surveyed in verses 4–38. This catalogue of spiritual heroism belongs to the same literary category as "The Praise of the Elders" in Sir. 44:1–50:21, beginning: "Let us now praise famous men, and our fathers that begat us."[14] Ben Sira celebrates at length all the commendable qualities of the men of God whom he commemorates; our author, more concisely, confines himself to those features of his heroes' careers which illustrate their faith in God, for the encouragement of those who come after them. In some ways a better parallel is presented by the last words of Mattathias, father of Judas Maccabaeus and his brothers, in which he stimulates the zeal of his sons by reminding them of the faithfulness under testing of Abraham, Joseph, Phinehas, Joshua, Caleb, David, Elijah, the three Hebrews who were saved from Nebuchadnezzar's fiery furnace, and Daniel (I Macc. 2:51–60).[15] Indeed,

---

[11] This "conviction of things not seen" ($\pi\rho\alpha\gamma\mu\acute{\alpha}\tau\omega\nu\ \emph{ἔ}λεγχος\ o\mathring{v}\ \beta\lambda\varepsilon\pi o\mu\acute{\varepsilon}\nu\omega\nu$) embraces things which are invisible because they belong to the spiritual order and things which are invisible because they belong to the future, like the fulfilment of God's promises (*cf.* F. R. Tennant, "The Central Problems of Faith", *ExT* xxxii [1920–21], pp. 561ff.).

[12] *On Dreams* i. 68; *cf. Planting*, 20: man's body was made erect so that he could look up to heaven and "apprehend clearly by means of what was visible that which was not visible".

[13] Gk. οἱ πρεσβύτεροι (lit. "the elders"); *cf.* "the fathers" in Ch. 1:1.

[14] *Cf.* also the illustrations of wisdom from early OT narratives in Wisdom 10:1ff., the list in CD ii. 16ff. of those who went astray through "guilty inclination and lustful eyes", the lists in I Clem. of those who suffered through envy and jealousy (4:1ff.), of those who were found faithful, obedient and hospitable (9:1ff.), of those who sacrificed themselves for the good of others (55:1ff.).

[15] So in IV Macc. 16:20ff. the mother of the seven martyr-brothers encourages her sons to faithful endurance by reminding them of Abraham, Daniel and the three Hebrews; in IV Macc. 18:11ff. she adds Abel, Isaac, Joseph and Phinehas as examples for them to follow.

279

the literary genre is by no means confined to the Judaeo-Christian tradition; it shares many characteristics with the *diatribé* of Stoic-influenced rhetoric, which was given to the accumulation of historical or legendary examples of the particular quality under discussion.[16] Our author, however, does not only accumulate a series of examples; he sets them in historical sequence so as to provide an outline of the redemptive purpose of God, advancing through the age of promise until at last in Jesus, faith's "pioneer and perfecter",[17] the age of fulfilment is inaugurated.

3 Before he proceeds to celebrate the faith of the elders, however, he illustrates in another way his statement that faith is "a conviction of things not seen". The visible universe, he says, was not made out of equally visible raw material; it was called into being by divine power. "By faith[18] we understand[19] that the worlds have been framed by the word of God." Here, as in Ch. 1:2, the "worlds" are the *aiōnes* (literally "ages"); in both places the universe of space and time is meant.[20] There God is said to have made the universe by the agency of the Son; here He is said to have fashioned it by His word. It is unlikely that "the word of God" here is hypostatized as in John 1:1–3, so as to be practically synonymous with "the Son of God"; for one thing, the Greek substantive translated "word" here is not *logos* (as in John 1:1ff.) but *rhēma*, referring to the utterance by which God summoned into existence what had no existence before.[21] He is thinking of the creative command "Let there be light" (Gen. 1:3), interpreting it and the following commands after the fashion of the psalmist:

---

[16] *Cf.* O. Michel, *Der Brief an die Hebräer*, MK (Göttingen, 1949), pp. 244f.; H. Thyen, *Der Stil der jüdisch-hellenistischen Homilie* (Göttingen, 1955), pp. 40ff.

[17] Ch. 12:2 (p. 351).

[18] Here begins the succession of sentences commencing with πίστει which "provides the finest example of anaphora in the whole Bible and perhaps in all literature, secular as well" (C. Spicq, *L'Épître aux Hébreux* [Paris, 1952], i. p. 362).

[19] Gk. νοοῦμεν. So in Rom. 1:20 Paul speaks of "the invisible things" of God as "being perceived (νοούμενα) through the things that are made, even his everlasting power and divinity". Moffatt (ICC, p. 161) quotes A. T. Goodrick's note on Wisdom 13:4 (where this verb occurs) to the effect that "νοεῖν is in Hellenistic Greek the current word for the apprehension of the divine in nature".

[20] See p. 4 with nn. 17, 18.

[21] *Cf.* ῥῆμα in Ch. 1:3 (p. 6); note also the quotation from Philo, *On Flight and Finding* 137, on p. 121, n. 43.

"By the word of Jehovah were the heavens made,
And all the host of them by the breath of his mouth ...
For he spake, and it was done;
He commanded, and it stood fast."[22]

Thus "the visible came forth from the invisible" (NEB). But how do we know this? By faith, says our author. Greek speculation about the formation of the ordered world out of formless matter had influenced Jewish thinkers like Philo and the author of the Book of Wisdom;[23] the writer to the Hebrews is more biblical in his reasoning and affirms the doctrine of *creatio ex nihilo*, a doctrine uncongenial to Greek thought. The faith by which he accepts it is faith in the divine revelation; the first chapter of Genesis is probably uppermost in his mind,[24] since he is about to trace seven living examples of faith from the subsequent chapters of that book.

---

[22]   Ps. 33:6, 9 (LXX 32:6, 9).

[23]   "Just as nothing comes into being out of that which has no existence, so nothing is destroyed into that which has no existence" (Philo, *The Eternity of the World*, 5, where Empedocles and Euripides are quoted in this sense). Elsewhere Philo express himself more biblically, as when he says that "God, the begetter of all things, not only brought them into sight, but even made things which previously had no existence, being not merely an artificer but the Creator Himself" (*On Dreams* i. 76). *Cf.* Wisdom 11:17, where the "all-powerful hand" of God "created the world out of formless matter (ἐξ ἀμόρφου ὕλης)". The author of Wisdom might have appealed to *tōhū wā-bōhū* in Gen. 1:2 (see n. 24 for the LXX rendering); but the idea of imposing form on pre-existent matter is Greek rather than Hebrew in origin.

[24]   He may have thought of the LXX rendering of Gen. 1:2, "the earth was invisible (ἀόρατος) and unfurnished", although in the Greek this seems to refer to the condition of the earth after its creation. With his language we may further compare II Macc. 7:28, where the mother of the seven martyrs reminds her youngest son how God made the world "out of things that had no existence" (ἐξ οὐκ ὄντων); II Baruch 21:4, "O thou ... that hast fixed the firmament by the word, ... that hast called from the beginning of the world that which did not yet exist"; II Enoch 25:1ff., "I commanded ... that visible things should come down from invisible". *Creatio ex nihilo* is an inference from Gen. 1:1ff., and not an unambiguous statement of those verses; neither Heb. *bārā'* nor Gk. κτίζω in itself bears this meaning. Indeed, even in the passage now under consideration our author does not in so many words assert *creatio ex nihilo*, but that is practically what is implied in his denial that the universe was created out of things phenomenal. *Cf.* A. Ehrhardt, "Creatio ex Nihilo", in *The Framework of the NT Stories* (Manchester, 1964), pp. 200ff.

(b) The Faith of the Antediluvians

Ch. 11:4–7

4 By faith Abel offered unto God[25] a more excellent sacrifice[26] than Cain, through which he had witness borne to him that he was righteous, God bearing witness in respect of his gifts:[27] and through it he being dead yet speaketh.[28]

---

[25] P^{13} and apparently P^{46} omit "unto God" ($τῷ θεῷ$); the phrase is omitted also by Clement of Alexandria and the Armenian version of Ephrem's commentary (cf. G. Zuntz, The Text of the Epistles [London, 1953], p. 33, for an argument that the omission is original).

[26] Gk. $πλείονα θυσίαν$. C. G. Cobet's "brilliant conjecture"—as Professor Zuntz calls it (op. cit., p. 16)—of $ΗΔΕΙΟΝΑ$ for $ΠΛΕΙΟΝΑ$, i.e. $ἡδίονα$ ("more pleasant") for $πλείονα$ ("more abundant") was accepted by J. M. S. Baljon and F. Blass in their critical editions of the text. The point is, as Zuntz says, that Abel's offerings were "more agreeable" and not "more" in quantity. The corruption of $ἥδιον$ into $πλεῖον$ is established for Demosthenes, Prooemium 23 (as Moffatt points out ad loc.); as for the sense, Justin says that God accepts the sacrifices of believing Gentiles more gratefully ($ἥδιον$) than those of the Jews (Dialogue, 29), while Josephus uses the cognate verb $ἥδεται$ when he describes God as being "more pleased" with Abel's sacrifice than with Cain's (Ant. i. 54). The received reading has been supported by an appeal to Matt. 6:25 with its parallel Luke 12:23, where life is said to be "more" ($πλεῖον$) than food (cf. R. V. G. Tasker, NTS i [1954–55], p. 183, on the "qualitative rather than quantitative significance" of $πλεῖον$ here), and to Matt. 12:41f. with the parallel Luke 11:31f., where "something more" ($πλεῖον$) than Solomon or Jonah is said to be present—the "something more" being presumably the kingdom of God. See J. D. Maynard, "Justin Martyr and the Text of Hebrews xi, 4", Exp., VII. vii (1909), pp. 164ff.; G. Zuntz, op. cit., pp. 16, 285.

[27] Gk. $μαρτυροῦντος ἐπὶ τοῖς δώροις αὐτοῦ τοῦ θεοῦ$. This reading, which is that of our Byzantine witnesses, is confirmed by $P^{13*} P^{46}$ with the Latin, Syriac, Coptic and Armenian versions; it is so plainly the true reading that, if it had disappeared from the textual tradition completely, it would have been an obvious and certain conjectural emendation. The statement of ARV margin, "The Greek text in this clause is somewhat uncertain", is due to the fact that the Byzantine reading has opposed to it the authority of $ℵ^*$ A D and a few other witnesses, which exhibit $τῷ θεῷ$ for $τοῦ θεοῦ$ (either by "mechanical permutation", as Hort says, or under the influence of $τῷ θεῷ$ earlier in the verse [cf. n. 25], as Zuntz suggests). Another variant, attested by a corrector of P^{13} and Clement of Alexandria, is $αὐτῷ τοῦ θεοῦ$ for $αὐτοῦ τοῦ θεοῦ$—also due, in all probability, to "mechanical permutation", although Hort and Moffatt, rather oddly, give it their vote as the true reading. Cf. F. J. A. Hort in Westcott and Hort, The New Testament in the Original Greek, ii (Cambridge and London, 1882), Appendix, p. 131; G. Zuntz, The Text of the Epistles, pp. 33, 51.

[28] Gk. $λαλεῖ$, for which D with the majority of later manuscripts and TR reads $λαλεῖται$. If this is intended to be middle voice, it does not alter the sense

5 By faith Enoch was translated that he should not see death; and he was not found, because God had translated him: for he hath had witness borne to him that before his translation he had been well-pleasing unto God:[29]

6 and without faith it is impossible to be well-pleasing *unto him;* for he that cometh to God must believe that he is, and *that* he is a rewarder of them that seek after him.[30]

7 By faith Noah, being warned *of God* concerning things not seen as yet, moved with godly fear, prepared an ark to the saving of his house; through which he condemned the world, and became heir of the righteousness which is according to faith.

4 The first example of faith that our author finds in the biblical record is Abel. According to the narrative of Gen. 4:3ff., Abel and his elder brother Cain brought their offerings to God at the appropriate season; Abel brought "of the firstlings of his flock and of their fat portions", since he was a shepherd, while Cain, the agriculturalist, brought "an offering of the fruit of the ground". In either case the material of the offering was suitable to the offerer's vocation; yet "the LORD had regard for Abel and his offering, but for Cain and his offering he had no regard". Why was there this discrimination? Cain was dejected because his offering was disregarded, but God pointed out to him the way of acceptance: "If you do well, will you not be accepted? And if you do not do well, sin is couching at the door; its desire is for you, but you must master it" (Gen. 4:7, RSV). This rendering of the Massoretic text is quite in line with the later prophetic teaching about sacrifice; sacrifice is acceptable to God not for its material content, but in so far as it is the outward expression of a devoted and obedient heart.[31] Let Cain gain the mastery over the sin that threatens to be his un-

---

(*cf.* AV "speaketh") but would be a pointless change; probably it was intended to be taken as a passive ("is spoken of"), from an inability to understand how Abel could still be speaking.

29 Gen. 5:24, following LXX text (see p. 287).

30 Gk. τοῖς ἐκζητοῦσιν αὐτὸν μισθαποδότης γίνεται. The substantive μισθαποδότης is cognate with μισθαποδοσία of Chs. 2:2; 10:35; 11:26. For ἐκζητοῦσιν P¹³ and P have the simple verb ζητοῦσιν. (*Cf.* the similar variant in v. 14, p. 303, n. 111.)

31 See p. 233 with n. 36.

doing,[32] and his sacrifice will be accepted as readily as Abel's was.

The Septuagint version however, suggests that there was a ritual reason for the rejection of Cain's sacrifice; according to it, God says to Cain: "Have you not sinned if you offer it rightly without dividing it rightly?" (Gen. 4:7).[33] Other ancient interpretations explained its rejection, in contrast to the acceptance of Abel's sacrifice, in terms of the substance of the two offerings. So Philo: "Abel's offering was living, Cain's was lifeless. His was prior in age and quality, Cain's was inferior. His was superior in strength and fatness, Cain's was weaker."[34] Similarly Josephus: "The brothers having decided to sacrifice to God, Cain brought the fruits of the cultivated ground and of trees, while Abel brought milk and the firstlings of his flocks. This latter offering gave the greater pleasure to God, who is honored by those things which grow spontaneously and in accordance with nature, and not by those things which are forcibly produced by the ingenuity of covetous man"[35]—a far-fetched distinction indeed, although Josephus was not the last commentator on this passage to suggest that the shepherd's life involves less expenditure of energy than that of the agriculturalist! "Cain brought of the fruits of the earth, that is to say, less valuable things", says the Midrash *Genesis Rabba*,[36] while the Palestinian Targum makes Abel say to Cain: "The fruits of my works were better than yours and took precedence over yours; so it was my sacrifice that was accepted as

---

[32] In Gen. 4:7 the word which ARV translates "coucheth" is Heb. *rōbēṣ*, which is cognate with Akkadian *rabiṣu*, the name of a demon. Sin is depicted as a maleficent power lying in wait to pounce upon its prey, but it is powerless against a man of righteous life.

[33] Gk. οὐκ ἐὰν ὀρθῶς προσενέγκῃς, ὀρθῶς δὲ μὴ διέλῃς, ἥμαρτες; Theodotion's Greek version implies that the divine acceptance or non-acceptance of the offering was shown by the falling or withholding of fire (as in the sacrificial ordeal of I Kings 18:21ff.), since it translates Heb. *shā'āh* (ARV "had regard") in Gen. 4:4f. by ἐνεπύρισεν ("set on fire"). Another view of the way in which the acceptance or non-acceptance was shown is suggested by S. H. Hooke: "At the time when such rituals were practised only one criterion of success or failure was recognized, namely the pragmatic test of increased fertility or the opposite. The shepherd's flocks increased and multiplied while the unfortunate tiller of the soil saw his crops wither as the heat of the year increased in strength towards the summer" (*The Siege Perilous* [London, 1956], p. 68).

[34] *The Sacrifices of Abel and Cain*, 88.

[35] *Ant.* i. 54.

[36] *Gen. Rabba* 22 (on Gen. 4:3).

well-pleasing." A more recent variation on these accounts sees the
distinction in that Abel's offering involved the shedding of blood,
apart from which, as our author has said above, the law knows
no remission (Ch. 9:22);[37] but it is nowhere suggested in the
Genesis narrative that it was a sin-offering that the two brothers
brought; it was in either case the appropriate presentation of
the firstfruits of their increase. The unvarnished Massoretic text
makes the situation plain enough; since Cain was told that
he would be accepted if he did well, it follows that Abel was
accepted because he did well—because, in other words, he was
righteous. And in fact the righteousness of Abel is emphasized
elsewhere in the New Testament: our Lord refers to "the blood
of Abel the righteous" (Matt. 23:35)[38] and John tells us that
Cain killed his brother "because his works were evil, and his
brother's righteous" (I John 3:12).[39] To the same effect our author
says that Abel "had witness borne to him that he was righteous".
How? Because God bore this witness to him "by accepting his
gifts" (RSV). This echoes the Septuagint rendering of Gen. 4:4,
"God looked [*i.e.* with pleasure] upon Abel and upon his gifts".[40]
The abiding principle of Scripture in this regard is summed up

---

[37] So, for example, the seventeenth-century Puritan scholar John Owen
says that Abel's faith was "testified in the kind of his sacrifice, which was by
death and blood; in the one owning the death which himself by reason of sin
was liable unto; in the other the way of atonement, which was to be by blood,
the blood of the promised Seed" (*Hebrews: The Epistle of Warning* [abridged
edition, Grand Rapids, 1953], p. 218). Contrast Calvin's more disciplined
exegesis: "Abel's sacrifice was preferred to his brother's for no other reason
than that it was sanctified by faith; for surely the fat of brute animals did not
smell so sweetly, that it could, by its odour, pacify God. The Scripture indeed
shows plainly why God accepted his sacrifice, for Moses' words are these: 'God
had respect to Abel and to his gifts'. It is hence obviously to be concluded that
his sacrifice was accepted because he himself was graciously accepted. But how
did he obtain this acceptance, save that his heart was purified by faith?"
(*Commentary on Hebrews, ad loc.*).

[38] The adjective (δίκαιος) is absent from the parallel in Luke 11:51.

[39] So Josephus says that Abel "had a concern for righteousness" (δικαιοσύνης
ἐπεμελεῖτο) while Cain "was very wicked and has an eye for nothing but gain"
(*Ant.* i. 53). In Wisdom 10:3 Cain is "an unrighteous man" (ἄδικος) who "in
anger revolted against wisdom and perished in his fratricidal fury". Tanhuma
(*Balak*, 16) gives Abel second place in a list of "seven righteous men who built
seven altars, from Adam to Moses". See B. Lindars, *NT Apologetic* (London,
1961), pp. 20f.

[40] Gk. ἐπεῖδεν ὁ θεὸς ἐπὶ ᾿Αβὲλ καὶ ἐπὶ τοῖς δώροις αὐτοῦ.

in the words of Prov. 15:8, "The sacrifice of the wicked is an abomination to Jehovah; but the prayer of the upright is his delight."

But how could it be known that it was "by faith" that Abel brought God a more acceptable sacrifice than his brother? Probably the close association between righteousness and faith in Ch. 10:38, "my righteous one shall live by faith", was ground sufficient in our author's eyes for his statement about Abel's faith; moreover, his affirmation in verse 6 below, while primarily applicable to Enoch, is equally applicable to Abel: "without faith it is impossible to please" God—and since Abel manifestly pleased Him, it follows that Abel lived and acted by faith.

Through his faith, too, Abel continues to speak, even in death. When God accused Cain of Abel's murder, He said: "The voice of your brother's blood is crying to me from the ground" (Gen. 4:10, RSV).[41] Our author's point appears to be that Abel is still appealing to God for vindication, until he obtains it in full in the judgment to come. The idea in that case is paralleled in Rev. 6:9ff., where the souls of the martyrs cry aloud for vindication, and are told that they must wait until the full tale of martyrs is complete. It has been held, on the other hand,[42] that our author simply means that Abel, by his faith, bears abiding witness to succeeding ages; but that more than this was in his mind is suggested by Ch. 12:24, where he says that the purifying blood of Christ "speaks more graciously than the blood of Abel" (RSV)—a clear reference to Gen. 4:10.

5 The second example of faith is Enoch. All that the Hebrew Bible has to say of him[43] is that "Enoch lived sixty and five years, and begat Methuselah: and Enoch walked with God after he

---

41 Philo, continuing his allegorical interpretation of the story of Cain and Abel as a conflict between self-love and the love of God, paradoxically asserts that while, superficially speaking, Cain "slew him" (ἀπέκτεινεν αὐτόν), i.e. his brother, he really "slew himself" (ἀπέκτεινεν ἑαυτόν), and that Abel only seemed to die, since in fact "he is clearly found making use of his voice and crying out what things he has suffered at the hands of a wicked brother—for how could he speak if he no longer existed?" (*The Worse attacks the Better*, 47f.).

42 *Cf.* Moffatt (ICC, p. 164). See further on Ch. 12:24 (p. 379).

43 Apart from the statement that he was born to Jared when the latter was 162 years old (Gen. 5:18). *Cf.* I Chron. 1:3.

begat Methuselah three hundred years,[44] and begat sons and daughters: and all the days of Enoch were three hundred sixty and five years: and Enoch walked with God: and he was not; for God took him" (Gen. 5:21-24). In the Septuagint the repeated clause "Enoch walked with God" is rendered "Enoch was well-pleasing to God"[45]—from a desire, no doubt, to make the language less anthropomorphic—and the words "he was not; for God took him" are rendered "he was not found, because God translated him".[46] Our author follows the Septuagint here as elsewhere.

In one well-known strand of Jewish and Christian tradition Enoch appears as the recipient of special revelations about the spirit-world and the ages to come;[47] in this rôle he appears once in the New Testament, when Jude (verses 14f.) quotes the prophecy of "Enoch, the seventh from Adam", about the coming of the Lord with His holy myriads to execute judgment on the ungodly (I Enoch 1:9). More generally he is said to have been "the first among men that are born on earth who learned writing and knowledge and wisdom" (Jubilees 4:17). Of all this our author has nothing to say; he is more in line with the school of thought which regarded Enoch as the typically righteous man. Ben Sira, for example, says:

"Enoch was found perfect, and he walked with Yahweh, and was taken;
a sign of knowledge to every generation" (Sir. 44:16).

---

[44] In LXX Enoch is 165 years old at Methuselah's birth and the interval between that event and Enoch's "translation" is correspondingly reduced to 200 years.

[45] Gk. εὐηρέστησεν ... τῷ θεῷ, whence our author says μεμαρτύρηται εὐαρεστηκέναι τῷ θεῷ.

[46] Gk. οὐχ ηὑρίσκετο, ὅτι μετέθηκεν αὐτὸν ὁ θεός, words which our author quotes verbatim. Moffatt (ICC, p. 165) quotes from Epictetus iii. 5.5f. an instance of εὑρίσκεσθαι in the sense of "die" ("be found" by death), and suggests the rendering here: "did not die". Josephus (Ant. i. 85) paraphrases "God translated him" by saying that he "withdrew to the divine" (Gk. ἀνεχώρησε πρὸς τὸ θεῖον)—a phrase which he uses also to describe the mysterious passing of Moses (Ant. iv. 326; cf. iii. 96). Cf. I Clem. 9:3.

[47] Cf. in particular the compilation of Enoch-literature called the First Book of Enoch, extant in toto only in Ethiopic, for about one third of its compass in Greek, and fragmentarily in the original Aramaic. The Aramaic fragments form part of the manuscript discoveries at Qumran; among them all the sections of I Enoch are represented except Chs. 37–71, the "Similitudes of Enoch". This

His grandson, turning these words into Greek, conformed them to the sense of the Septuagint:

> "Enoch pleased[48] the Lord, and was translated;
> he was an example of repentance to all generations."

In this last clause the reference to Enoch's translation appears to be interpreted of a *moral* change in his life—an interpretation which we find also in Philo.[49]

More striking still is the account of Enoch in Wisdom 4:10ff.:

> "There was one who pleased God and was loved by him,
> and while living among sinners he was translated.
> He was caught up lest evil change his understanding
> or guile deceive his soul.
> For the fascination of wickedness obscures what is good,
> and roving desire perverts the innocent mind.
> Being perfected in a short time, he fulfilled long years;
> for his soul was pleasing to the Lord,
> therefore he took him quickly from the midst of wickedness.

> Yet the peoples saw and did not understand,
> nor take such a thing to heart,
> that God's grace and mercy are with his elect,
> and he watches over his holy ones."

Here Enoch is brought forward as the *beau idéal* of righteousness, type of the man who, according to his enemies, "professes to have knowledge of God, and calls himself a child of the Lord" (Wisdom

---

section, containing the "Son of Man" passages with New Testament affinities, may thus be later than the others (see p. 289, n. 50). The other sections narrate such things as Enoch's journey through other worlds and his dream-visions of world-history from the creation to the author's day. Similar, but later compilations are II Enoch ("The Book of the Secrets of Enoch"), composed in Greek but extant only in a Slavonic version, and III Enoch, a Hebrew work of the 3rd or 4th century A.D. edited by H. Odeberg (Cambridge, 1928).

[48] Gk. εὐηρέστησεν, as in Gen. 5:22, 24, LXX.

[49] "Concerning him it is said that 'Enoch was well-pleasing to God and was not found, for God translated (μετέθηκεν) him'; for 'translation' (μετάθεσις) denotes turning and changing, and that a changing for the better ..." (*On Abraham*, 17f.). On the same passage Philo elsewhere says: "By 'translation' is clearly signified the new home [granted to him 'who escaped the insurrections of the body and deserted to the side of the soul'], and by 'not found' the solitary life" (*On Rewards and Punishments*, 17). See p. 291, n. 57; p. 292, n. 67.

2:13). So, in Jubilees 10:17, Enoch is perfect in righteousness, excelling even Noah in this respect, "for Enoch's office was ordained for a testimony to the generations of the world, so that he should recount all the deeds of generation unto generation, till the day of judgment" (here Enoch's righteousness is linked with his prophetic ministry). And in I Enoch 71:14, in the conclusion of the section commonly called the *Similitudes of Enoch*, Enoch is acclaimed by the interpreting angel as the ideal just man:

> "Thou art the Son of Man born unto righteousness;
>   and righteousness abides upon thee;
>   yea, the righteousness of the Head of Days forsakes thee
>   not."[50]

It is, however, specifically as an example of *faith* that our author adduces Enoch here. Righteousness and faith, as we have seen already, are inseparably associated in his mind. If he is asked why Enoch should be regarded as a man of faith, his answer is that otherwise God would have had no pleasure in him.[51] But the record makes it plain that Enoch did please God;[52] the Septuagint paraphrase of the Hebrew idiom "walked with God"[53] is completely consistent with the teaching of the prophets, according to which walking humbly with God, together with the practice of justice and lovingkindness, is God's fundamental requirement of man.[54]

---

[50] M. Black, "The Son of Man Problem in Recent Research and Debate", *BJRL* xlv (1962-63), pp. 305ff., suggests that while I Enoch 71 belongs to the section called the "Similitudes", which is now commonly given a date in the Christian era (see p. 287, n. 47), this particular chapter may be earlier.

[51] *Cf.* Ch. 10:38b.

[52] A nice point of interpretation hangs on the question whether the adverbial phrase "before his translation" belongs with "he had been well-pleasing unto God" (so ARV, NEB) or with "he hath had witness borne to him" (so ARV margin, "before his translation he hath had witness borne to him that he had been well-pleasing unto God"; *cf.* AV, RSV). The former construction fits the facts better; Gen. 5:24 (LXX) bears witness that he had pleased God before he was translated, but the witness itself (*i.e.* the witness of the biblical record) was borne to him *after* his translation.

[53] Similarly of Noah (Gen. 6:9); so also the expression "walk before God" is rendered εὐαρεστεῖν ἐναντίον (ἐνώπιον) τοῦ θεοῦ (κυρίου, etc.), "to be well-pleasing before God", of Abraham (Gen. 17:1; 24:40), of Abraham and Isaac (Gen. 48:15); of the pious Israelite (Ps. 56:13 [LXX 55:13]; 116:9 [LXX 114:9]).

[54] Mic. 6:8.

6 Apart from faith neither Enoch nor anyone else could ever have been pleasing to God. The faith which our author has in mind embraces belief in the invisible spiritual order, and belief in the promises of God which have not yet been fulfilled. Belief in the invisible spiritual order involves, first and foremost, belief in Him who is "King of the ages, immortal, invisible, the only God" (I Tim. 1:17); and belief in God carries with it necessarily belief in His word. It is not belief in the existence of *a* God that is meant, but belief in the existence of *the* God who once declared His will to the fathers through the prophets and in these last days has spoken in His Son. Those who approach[55] Him can do so in full confidence that He exists, that His word is true, and that He will never put off or disappoint the soul that sincerely seeks Him. For all that He has revealed of Himself, whether through the prophets or in His Son, assures us that He is altogether worthy of His people's trust.

> "The God who created the skies,
>   The strength and support of His saints,
> Who gives them all needful supplies,
>   And hearkens to all their complaints:
>
> This, this is the God we adore,
>   Our faithful, unchangeable Friend,
> Whose love is as large as His power,
>   And neither knows measure nor end."[56]

The reward desired by those who seek Him is the joy of finding Him; He Himself proves to be their "exceeding joy" (Ps. 43:4).

No doubt our author states the basic principle, as revealed by the record of Enoch, for the benefit and encouragement of his readers. Of their desire to please God he has no doubt; he insists, however, that they cannot please Him apart from faith—the faith which not only believes that He exists but waits patiently and confidently for the reward promised to those who seek Him.

7 The next example of faith illustrates this willingness to believe that what God has promised He will certainly perform. Noah was a righteous man, like Abel; he walked with God, as did

---

[55] Gk. προσέρχεσθαι, as used already in Chs. 4:16; 7:25; 10:22.
[56] Joseph Hart (1712–1768).

Enoch;[57] but what is emphasized here is that when God announced that He would do something unprecedented in the experience of Noah and his contemporaries, Noah took Him at His word, and showed that he did so by making practical preparations against the day when that word would come true. Noah received a divine communication[58] that a deluge would sweep over the earth. Such a catastrophe had never been known before, but Noah's faith took the form of "a conviction of things not seen".[59] The building of an ark far inland must have seemed an absurd procedure to his neighbors; but in the event his faith was vindicated and their unbelief was condemned: "through his faith he put the whole world in the wrong" (NEB). He paid careful heed[60] to the divine admonition and got ready the means by which his household and himself would be kept safe when the deluge broke; thus he became a living witness to the truth of the scripture already cited: "my righteous one shall live by faith" (Ch. 10:38). Thus, says our author, he "became heir of the righteousness which is according to faith"; if the Genesis narrative represents God as saying to him, "thee have I seen righteous before me in this generation" (Gen. 7:1), it was because of his ready acceptance of what God had said. Of him as of Enoch the statement is true: "without faith it is impossible to be well-pleasing" to God.[61]

The Jewish wisdom writers not unnaturally found in Noah an outstanding example of true wisdom. "When the earth was flooded," says the author of the Book of Wisdom, "wisdom saved it again, steering the righteous man in a cheap structure of wood" (Wisdom 10:4). Ben Sira speaks at greater length:

---

[57] Gen. 6:9 (see p. 289, n. 53). Philo, having mentioned Enoch as the ideal example of repentance (see p. 288, n. 49), goes on to mention Noah as the ideal lover of God (or man loved by God) and lover of virtue (θεοφιλῆ καὶ φιλάρετον) (On Abraham, 27). In Jewish lore Noah, like Enoch, was the recipient of divine revelations apocalyptic in character (Jubilees 7:20ff.); these were embodied in a now lost "Book of Noah", fragments of which have been incorporated in I Enoch. Two accounts of his birth describe him as a wonder-child (1Q Genesis Apocryphon ii. 1ff.; I Enoch 106:2ff.). Cf. I Clem. 9:4.

[58] Gk. χρηματισθείς (cf. Chs. 8:5; 12:25), regularly of a divine oracle.

[59] With περὶ τῶν μηδέπω βλεπομένων here cf. πραγμάτων ... οὐ βλεπομένων in v. 1.

[60] Gk. εὐλαβηθείς, with which cf. the cognate substantive εὐλάβεια in Chs. 5:7; 12:28. See p. 101, n. 61.

[61] Cf. Gen. 6:9 (LXX), τῷ θεῷ εὐηρέστησεν Νῶε (cf. p. 289, n. 53).

"Noah was found perfect[62] and righteous;
  in the time of wrath he was taken in exchange;
therefore a remnant was left to the earth
  when the flood came.
Everlasting covenants were made with him
  that all flesh should not be blotted out by a flood."[63]

In other places in the New Testament the flood of Noah's day is an illustration of sudden judgment, a foreshadowing of the advent of the Son of Man;[64] his safe passage through the waters which overwhelmed others is a figure of Christian baptism;[65] he himself is described as a preacher of righteousness.[66] But here it is his faith that is set in relief, and it cannot be said that our author had to look far to discover faith in the Old Testament story of Noah. The great gospel terms righteousness and grace appear first in relation to him, so far as the canonical order of Scripture goes;[67] and the quality of his faith was proved by his prompt obedience: "Thus did Noah; according to all that God commanded him, so did he" (Gen. 6:22).

(c) The Faith of Abraham and Sarah

Ch. 11:8–12

8 By faith Abraham, when he was called,[68] obeyed to go out unto a place which he was to receive for an inheritance; and he went out, not knowing whither he went.

---

62 *Cf.* Gen. 6:9, "Noah was ... perfect in his generations".

63 Sir. 44:17f. *Cf.* Gen. 9:8–17 for the covenant with Noah.

64 *Cf.* Luke 17:26f.; Matt. 24:37–39.

65 *Cf.* I Peter 3:20f.

66 *Cf.* II Peter 2:5; Josephus, *Ant.* i. 74; Sibylline Oracles i. 125ff.

67 "Noah was a righteous (Heb. *ṣaddîq*, Gk. δίκαιος) man" (Gen. 6:9); "Noah found grace (Heb. *ḥēn*, Gk. χάρις) in the eyes of Jehovah" (Gen. 6:8). Philo points out that Noah is "the first man recorded as righteous in the sacred scriptures" (*Preliminary Studies* 90); indeed, he gives "righteous" alongside "rest" as the etymology of his name (*On Abraham*, 27). He explains the name Enoch as meaning "recipient of the grace of God" (κεχαρισμένος), linking this with his presentation of Enoch as the ideal repentant man (*On Abraham*, 17). (See p. 288, n. 49; p. 291, n. 57.)

68 Gk. καλούμενος, to which P⁴⁶ A D* 33 1739 and a few other authorities preface the definite article ὁ, yielding the sense "he who was called" (instead of "when he was called")—the reference would then be to the divine changing

9 By faith he became a sojourner in the land of promise, as in a *land* not his own, dwelling in tents, with Isaac and Jacob, the heirs with him of the same promise:

10 for he looked for the city which hath the foundations, whose builder and maker is God.

11 By faith even Sarah herself[69] received power to conceive seed[70] when she was past age,[71] since she counted him faithful who had promised:

12 wherefore also there sprang[72] of one, and him as good as dead, *so many* as the stars of heaven in multitude, and as the sand, which is by the sea-shore, innumerable.[73]

8 Of Abraham's title to be included in this catalogue there can be no question. The faith of Abel, Enoch and Noah might have to be inferred from what is recorded of them (although for all three of them it is a certain inference); but Abraham's faith is explicitly attested in the Genesis narrative: "he believed in Jehovah; and he reckoned it to him for righteousness" (Gen.

---

of his name from Abram to Abraham (Gen. 17:5). But the reference is certainly not to God's renaming him, but to His first calling him to leave his home and seek the promised land.

[69] The construction of αὐτὴ Σάρρα as nominative, as though Sarah were the subject of this sentence and not Abraham (see pp. 300ff., nn. 96–103), has given rise to a number of early glosses, *Schlimmbesserungen* ("false improvements"), as G. Zuntz calls them (*op. cit.*, p. 170). Thus P⁴⁶ D* Ψ with the Latin and Syriac versions add here στεῖρα ("barren"), 69 1739 and the Coptic versions add ἡ στεῖρα ("she who was barren"), P 1912 and some other authorities add στεῖρα οὖσα ("being barren").

[70] Gk. δύναμιν εἰς καταβολὴν σπέρματος ἔλαβεν (for its proper sense see p. 301 with n. 99). A further *Schlimmbesserung* is the insertion here of εἰς τὸ τεκνῶσαι ("so as to give birth") in D* P 69 and a number of other manuscripts with the Vulgate Cod. L and the Harclean Syriac.

[71] Gk. καὶ παρὰ καιρὸν ἡλικίας, "even beyond the season of life". K L P and the bulk of Byzantine manuscripts, followed by TR, construed καί as the conjunction "and" and after ἡλικίας added the verb ἔτεκεν (so AV, "and was delivered of a child when she was past age").

[72] Gk. ἐγενήθησαν, for which ℵ 1739, with the bulk of later manuscripts and TR, read ἐγεννήθησαν ("were begotten").

[73] Gen. 15:5; 22:17; 32:12. P⁴⁶ D* Ψ with the Ethiopic version omit ἡ παρὰ τὸ χεῖλος ("which is by the shore"), leaving the shorter phrase ὡς ἡ ἄμμος τῆς θαλάσσης ("as the sand of the sea").

15:6). Our author has already referred to Abraham's faith in the promise of God and his patient waiting for its fulfilment;[74] here he enlarges on the same theme. Repeatedly throughout his career Abraham acted as a man who walked by faith and not by sight, and made good his claim to be recognized by all subsequent ages as the father of the faithful. The Levites' prayer of confession in the days of Nehemiah and Ezra recalled God's dealings with him in these terms: "Thou ... didst choose Abram, and broughtest him forth out of Ur of the Chaldees, and gavest him the name of Abraham, and foundest his heart faithful before thee, and madest a covenant with him to give the land of the Canaanite, ... to give it unto his seed, and hast performed thy words; for thou art righteous" (Neh. 9:7f.). Ben Sira includes this panegyric on Abraham in his "Praise of the Elders":

> "Abraham was the great father of a multitude of nations,
>   and no one has been found like him in glory;
> he kept the law of the Most High,
>   and was taken into covenant with him;
> he established the covenant in his flesh,
>   and when he was tested he was found faithful.
> Therefore the Lord assured him by an oath
>   that the nations would be blessed through his posterity;
> that he would multiply him like the dust of the earth,
>   and exalt his posterity like the stars,
> and cause them to inherit from sea to sea
>   and from the River to the ends of the earth" (Sir. 44:19–21).

The author of the Book of Wisdom refers to Abraham when he says that "Wisdom ... recognized the righteous man and preserved him blameless before God" (Wisdom 10:5). Paul invokes the example of Abraham in support of his claim that the gospel way of righteousness by faith is "witnessed by the law and the prophets" (Rom. 3:21); if a man is justified by his works, then Abraham of all men has something of his own to glory in, but the testimony of Holy Scripture is clear that it was his faith in God that was reckoned to him for righteousness (Rom. 4:3ff.; Gal. 3:6ff.). Stephen begins his defence before the Sanhedrin by reminding them how "the God of glory appeared unto our father Abraham, when he was in Mesopotamia, before he dwelt in Haran, and said

---

[74] Ch. 6:13ff. See pp. 128ff.

unto him, 'Get thee out of thy land, and from thy kindred, and come into the land which I shall show thee'. Then came he out of the land of the Chaldaeans, and dwelt in Haran: and from thence, when his father was dead, God removed him into this land, wherein ye now dwell: and he gave him none inheritance in it, no, not so much as to set his foot on: and he promised that he would give it to him in possession, and to his seed after him, when as yet he had no child" (Acts 7:2–5).[75] Stephen's point is that, even in the promised land, Abraham lived a pilgrim life; and our author makes precisely this point in the exposition that follows.

Abraham's faith was manifested first of all by the readiness with which he left his home at the call of God, for the promise of a new home which he had never seen before and which, even after he entered it, he never possessed in person. "By faith Abraham ... obeyed"; faith and obedience are inseparable in man's relation to God. If the patriarchal narrative says in one place that Abraham was justified because he *believed* God, in another place God confirms to Isaac the promise made to Abraham "because that Abraham *obeyed* my voice, and kept my charge, my commandments, my statutes, and my laws" (Gen. 26:5). He would not have obeyed the divine call had he not taken God at His word; his obedience was the outward evidence of his inward faith. So Philo: "impelled by an oracle calling him to leave his native land and family and paternal home, and move to another country, he made eager haste to do so, considering that speed in giving effect to the command was as good as its full accomplishment; in fact, it looked as though he were returning to his homeland from foreign parts and not leaving his homeland for foreign parts".[76] Philo, after his fashion, interprets the story of Abraham's call and migration in a thoroughgoing allegorical manner, to denote the experiences "of a virtue-loving soul in its quest for the true God".[77] But he gives all due prominence to the part of faith in Abraham's response to God; pointing out that in Gen. 12:1 God speaks to Abraham in the future tense of "the land that I *will show* thee", he says: "This is a testimony to the faith which the soul placed in God, manifesting its gratitude not on the basis of accomplished

---

[75] *Cf. Acts,* NICNT (Grand Rapids, 1953), pp. 145ff.

[76] *On Abraham,* 62.

[77] *On Abraham,* 68.

facts but on the basis of expectation of things to come. For the soul, utterly dependent on good hope and considering those things which are not present to be indubitably present already because of the trustworthiness of Him who has promised, has won as its guerdon that perfect blessing, faith; as it is said farther on: 'Abraham believed God' [Gen. 15:6]."[78]

Our author points out that Abraham did not receive the promise of the inheritance at the time of his first call; the land to which he was directed to go was the "place which he was to receive for an inheritance"; the promise of the inheritance was not given until he had returned from Egypt and Lot had chosen the well-watered circuit of Jordan to settle in (Gen. 13:14ff.); it was reaffirmed to him along with the promise of an heir (Gen. 15:18ff.), and again after the bestowal of the covenant of circumcision (Gen. 17:8). The divine bidding was sufficient for him at his first call,[79] "and he went out, not knowing whither he went". The promise of the inheritance was not in the first instance an incentive to obedience; it was the reward of his obedience.

9 Even when he received the promise of the inheritance, it was the promise that he received, not the visible possession of the land; but to Abraham the promise of God was as substantial as its realization. He lived thereafter in the good of that promise. Year after year he pitched his moving tent amid the settled inhabitants of Palestine,[80] "in them but not of them", commanding their respect as "a prince of God",[81] but owning not a square foot of the country until he bought the field of Machpelah near Hebron from Ephron the Hittite as a family burial-ground. Yet, living like a resident alien[82] in the land which had been promised to him

---

[78] *Migration of Abraham*, 43f. He emphasizes that God said to Abraham δείξω, "I will show". and not δείκνυμι, "I am showing".

[79] So Philo: "he removed the moment he was bidden" (ἅμα τῷ κελευσθῆναι μετανίστατο)—although he immediately shows his allegorical understanding of the passage by saying that "his migration was one of soul rather than of body, for heavenly love (ἔρως οὐράνιος) tamed his desire for mortal things" (*On Abraham*, 66).

[80] "Abram the Hebrew" (Gen. 14:13) is rendered in LXX Ἀβρὰμ ὁ περάτης ("Abram the migrant"). *Cf.* H. Braun, "Der Fahrende", *ZThK* xlviii (1951), pp. 32ff. See also p. xxiv, n. 9.

[81] Gen. 23:6.

[82] Gk. παρῴκησεν, "he lived as a πάροικος (sojourner)", or, to give full force to the following preposition εἰς, "he migrated to" (not κατῴκησεν, "he settled down"). The verb occurs in one other place in NT, Luke 24:18, where the two

and his descendants, he did not grow impatient. Some visible tokens of the word of God he did indeed receive, in Isaac the promised child of his old age, and even in Isaac's son Jacob, through whom the line of promise was to run.[83] But Isaac and Jacob in their turn did not live to see the fulfilment of the promise that the land would be theirs;[84] they remained nomads like Abraham himself.

10 What was the secret of Abraham's patience? This, says our author: the commonwealth on which his hopes were fixed was no transient commonwealth of this temporal order. He was looking for a city of a different kind: the city with the eternal foundations,[85] planned and built by God.[86] Just as the true rest of God is not the earthly Canaan into which the first Joshua led the people of Israel (Ch. 4:8), so Abraham kept his eyes fixed on the well-established city of God which was to be revealed in the time of fulfilment.

---

disciples on the Emmaus road ask the unrecognized Jesus: "Are you the only visitor (παροικεῖς) to Jerusalem who does not know the things that have happened there in these days?" (*Cf.* p. 304, n. 114.) For πάροικος *cf.* Ex. 2:22, where Moses says πάροικός εἰμι ἐν γῇ ἀλλοτρίᾳ (compare ὡς ἀλλοτρίαν here); also Acts 7:6, 29; Eph. 2:19; I Pet. 2:11; for παροικία *cf.* Acts 13:17; I Pet. 1:17. So much did the early Christians pattern themselves on the patriarchs in this respect that the terminology of pilgrimage became part of their habitual language and survived long after its original force had disappeared; it is from Gk; παροικία, for example, that we get the word "parish". *Cf.* p. 306, n. 123.

[83] According to the chronology of the received text of Genesis, Abraham's grandsons Esau and Jacob were fifteen years old when he died (*cf.* Gen. 21:5; 25:7, 26), although Abraham's death is recorded before the birth of Esau and Jacob.

[84] *Cf.* v. 13, where Isaac and Jacob are included with Abraham.

[85] Gk. ἐξεδέχετο γὰρ τὴν τοὺς θεμελίους ἔχουσαν πόλιν (translated literally in ARV, "he looked for the city which hath the foundations", *i.e.* the only city with enduring foundations). C. F. D. Moule suggests that our author has in mind Ps. 87:1, "His foundation (LXX θεμέλιοι) is in the holy mountains"; he refers to C. Gore's point (in *The Reconstruction of Belief* [London, 1926], p. 770) that in Gal. 4:26 ("the Jerusalem that is above ..., which is our mother") Paul is echoing v. 5 of the same psalm (LXX Ps.86, μήτηρ Σιών), and compares also Phil. 3:20 (*The Birth of the New Testament* [London, 1962], p. 45).

[86] Gk. ἧς τεχνίτης καὶ δημιουργὸς ὁ θεός. Elsewhere in NT (Acts 19:24, 38; Rev. 18:22) τεχνίτης means "craftsman" or "artificer"; here it is used of God in much the same sense as the verb κατασκευάζω in Heb. 3:4, "he that built all things is God". In Wisdom 13:1 idolaters are condemned (much as in Rom. 1:19ff.) for failing to "recognize the Artificer (τεχνίτης) while paying heed to

Here certainly our author may be said to allegorize—to discern in the promise to Abraham that the earthly Canaan would be his and his descendants' an underlying promise of a richer and eternal inheritance. With his statement that Abraham looked for "the city with firm foundations" (NEB) we may compare Philo's description of the land which God promised to give Abraham as "a city good and wide and very prosperous, for the gifts of God are very great".[87] To Philo this city is the abode of the individual soul which spends its time in the contemplation of the universe and cultivation of the knowledge of God; it is the natural habitat of the true philosopher.[88] To our author it is the heavenly Jerusalem,[89] the commonwealth of God in the spiritual and eternal order, now effectively made accessible by the completion of Christ's high-priestly work, to which all the men and women of faith come to be enrolled as free citizens. In Philo's treatment not only the promised land but Abraham himself is allegorized; our author is content to treat Abraham and all the others listed in this catalogue as real

his works". As for the other word δημιουργός (literally "public workman", "constructor"), this is its only NT occurrence. It (or one of its derivatives) is used repeatedly in Philo along with τεχνίτης (or τεχνιτεύω) in reference to God as Creator. For example: "Through this power the Father who is Begetter and Artificer (τεχνιτεύσας) appointed the universe, so that 'I am thy God' is tanta-mount to 'I am Maker and Constructor' (δημιουργός)" (*On Change of Names*, 29); "It is said, 'Let us make man in our image', in order that, if the wax receives ... a noble impress, it should appear to be the construction (δημιούργημα) of Him who is the Artificer (τεχνίτης) of noble and good things alone" (*ib.*, 31); "The Artificer (τεχνίτης) ... constructed (ἐδημιούργει) the world" (*Who is the heir*, 133). Other Philonic references are given by C. Spicq, *L'Épître aux Hébreux* (Paris, 1952), i, p. 44. The *Epistle to Diognetus* (7:2), perhaps echoing the present passage in Hebrews, describes Jesus as "the very artificer and constructor (τεχνίτης καὶ δημιουργός) of the universe, by whom God created the heavens". In Gnostic thought δημιουργός was used of the divine power who created the material universe, envisaged as an inferior deity to the Supreme God. See G. W. H. Lampe (ed.), *A Patristic Greek Lexicon* (fasc. 2, Oxford, 1962), p. 342 (*s.v. δημιουργός*).

[87] *Leg. Alleg.* iii. 83.

[88] *Cf.* Philo on Jacob's dream at Bethel (Gen. 28:15); God's promise to bring Jacob back to the promised land may "hint at the doctrine of the im-mortality of the soul, which, leaving its heavenly abode ..., entered the body as if it were a foreign land; but the Father who gave it being says that He will not allow it to remain imprisoned for ever, but will take pity on it and loose its chains and conduct it in freedom and security to its mother-city (μητρόπολις)" (*On Dreams*, i. 181).

[89] *Cf.* Ch. 12:22 (pp. 373f. with nn. 146–151).

historical characters from whose experience later generations can learn. Nor was his insight at fault in discerning in the promise to Abraham something more abiding than the fairest earthly possession. To those who place their trust in Him God gives possessions of real and incorruptible value. Since, in our Lord's words, Abraham, Isaac and Jacob "live unto" God (Luke 20:38), their true heritage must be based in the being of God; if the New Testament writers are not misguided in portraying them as the ancestors of the family of faith, their essential blessings must be of the same order as the blessings enjoyed by their spiritual children under the new covenant.[90] "The Old Testament is not contrary to the New: for both in the Old and New Testament everlasting life is offered to Mankind by Christ, who is the only Mediator between God and Man, being both God and Man. Wherefore they are not to be heard, which feign that the old Fathers did look only for transitory promises."[91]

11 According to the transmitted text, as commonly translated, we now have a statement about the faith of Sarah. There are difficulties in the way of the traditional interpretation, some of them less weighty and some of them more so.

(i) Sarah, it is said, is not a good example of faith.[92] According to Gen. 18:12 she laughed when she overheard the divine promise that she would give birth to a son, and the comment of God on her laughter (Gen. 18:13f.) makes it plain that it was the laughter of incredulity. Chrysostom indeed, in dealing with this difficulty, suggests that her subsequent denial of her laughter was "by faith";[93] but of course it was nothing of the kind: "Sarah denied, saying, I laughed not; *for she was afraid*" (Gen. 18:15). Yet according to promise she gave birth to Isaac nevertheless.[94] No

---

[90]   "There is *an instinct of immortality* in saintship. He who lives to God *knows* that he must live for ever ... Canaan *could* not be the *goal* of one who walked with God" (C. J. Vaughan, *The Epistle to the Hebrews* [London, 1890], p. 221).

[91]   The Thirty-Nine Articles: Article VII.

[92]   "The mention of Sarah with Abraham is an astonishment to the expositor", says J. R. Harris, who finds her inclusion a possible token of feminine authorship of the epistle (*Side-lights on New Testament Research* [London, 1908], pp. 154f.). But see I Pet. 3:6.

[93]   *Homilies on Hebrews*, xxiii.

[94]   One might ask what the character of Abraham's laughter was when he received the promise of God that Sarah would bear a son (Gen. 17:17); even in the Genesis narrative, however, he is not blamed for laughing, and we may be

doubt when Isaac was born she laughed in a manner that betokened no incredulity but exulting wonder: "God hath made me to laugh; every one that heareth will laugh with me" (Gen. 21:6).[95] But our author speaks of an act of faith that preceded her conception of Isaac. Still, this is not an insuperable objection. Our author elsewhere in this chapter can see faith where most people would not, and there may be something in Professor Tasker's comment:[96] "It is surely just the paradoxical character of the illustration which is a sign of its genuineness; and *kai autē* ['even herself'] so far from making a poor connexion, as Zuntz asserts,[97] may well give us the insight we need into the author's thought about Gen. xviii. *Even* Sarah's acceptance of a promise which at first she seemed to hear with indifference is to the mind of the *auctor ad Hebraeos* a venture into the unseen world which faith makes real."[98]

(ii) In verse 12 it is still Abraham's faith that is the subject, so that verse 11, if it refers to Sarah, is a digression. Even so, it would not be an irrelevant digression; Sarah was very much involved in the fulfilment of the promise that Abraham would have a son.

(iii) The Genesis narrative lays stress on the quality of Abraham's faith in accepting God's promise that he would have descendants when he was still childless. It is in this particular context that Abraham "believed in Jehovah; and he reckoned it to him for righteousness" (Gen. 15:6). Paul, following the Genesis narrative here, emphasizes how Abraham, "looking unto the promise of God, ... wavered not through unbelief, but waxed strong through faith, giving glory to God, and being fully assured

---

intended to infer that this laughter was due to his appreciation of the divine absurdity of the situation.

[95] Philo, commenting on Sarah's laughter at Isaac's birth, allegorizes the incident in terms of Virtue's giving birth to Happiness (*Leg. Alleg.* ii. 82; *cf. Preliminary Studies*, 1ff.).

[96] *NTS* i (1954–55), pp. 182f. (in an article "The Text of the 'Corpus Paulinum'," pp. 180ff., a review of G. Zuntz's *The Text of the Epistles*).

[97] "καὶ αὐτή makes a poor connexion (it is typical of 'Scholiasten Griechisch'): 'likewise' is the only admissible translation. This makes nonsense of the context: who else had been said to have received, through faith, δύναμιν εἰς καταβολὴν σπέρματος?" (Zuntz, *op. cit.*, p. 16, n. 4).

[98] On this last point reference is made to A. Nairne, *The Epistle of Priesthood* (Edinburgh, 1913), p. 395.

that what he had promised, he was able also to perform" (Rom. 4:20f.). But on the usual reading of our present passage the author of Hebrews has nothing to say about this signal demonstration of Abraham's faith. If the language of verse 11 were unambiguous, we should simply have to accept this situation; but in fact the language of verse 11 points in another direction.

(iv) The one firm argument against taking verse 11 as a statement of Sarah's faith lies in the fact that the phrase translated "to conceive seed" just does not mean that; it refers to the father's part in the generative process, not the mother's. A literal translation would be "for the deposition of seed";[99] it does not denote the receiving or conception of seed. This is a straightforward matter of the natural sense of a Greek word, and had it not been for the apparent presence of "Sarah" as subject of the sentence no one would ever have thought of finding a reference to conception here.[100] Professor Tasker describes this objection to the traditional interpretation as a "notorious difficulty"; but adds: "do we know enough about Greek usage at the time to say definitely that an active noun of this kind could not also carry a passive sense?"[101] All that we know of the usage of *this* Greek noun at the time renders it in the highest degree improbable that it would be employed in the sense of "conception", especially by one so sensitive to Greek usage as our author is. But Professor Tasker is probably right in saying that the solution proposed by Professor Zuntz and others "seems a too drastic cutting of the knot". They suggest that the words "Sarah herself" should be rejected as a very early addition to the text; the verse would then be rendered: "By faith he [Abraham] also received power to beget a child when he was past age, since he counted him faithful who had promised".[102] But it is not necessary to cut out "Sarah herself" from the text;

---

[99] Gk. εἰς καταβολὴν σπέρματος. The expression "for the conception of seed" would be εἰς σύλληψιν σπέρματος.

[100] Of course the addition of ἔτεκεν in TR (see p. 293, n. 71) would compel us to take καταβολή in the sense of "conception"; but it is so clearly a later insertion that there is no question of such compulsion.

[101] He mentions Moulton and Milligan's reference to the first-century papyrus attestation of καταβολαῖος in the sense of "store-place"; but καταβολαῖος (sc. τόπος) used thus is "a place where one deposits (καταβάλλει) things".

[102] Zuntz, *op. cit.*, pp. 16, 170; F. Field, *Notes on Translation of NT* (Cambridge 1899), p. 232; H. Windisch, *Der Hebräerbrief*, HNT (Tübingen, 1931), p. 101.

all that is required is to construe the words in the dative case instead of the nominative,[103] and the verse then runs: "By faith he [Abraham] also, together with Sarah, received power to beget a child when he was past age, since he counted him faithful who had promised"—and verse 12 follows on very naturally.

12 Thus from this one man Abraham, when he was already "as good as dead" so far as the hope of founding a family was concerned,[104] there sprang a host of descendants, in fulfilment of the divine promises that his offspring would be as numerous as the stars in the sky (Gen. 15:5; 22:17) and "as the sand which is upon the seashore" (Gen. 22:17).[105] The word rendered "as good as dead" is the same perfect participle passive as Paul uses in reference to the same subject when he says that Abraham, on receiving the promise of God, weighed up all the adverse circumstances—"without being weakened in faith he considered his own body now *as good as dead*[106] (he being about a hundred years old), and the deadness of Sarah's womb" (Rom. 4:19)—and yet concluded that the certainty of God's word far outweighed them all.[107] "Wherefore also," adds Paul, "it was reckoned unto him for righteousness" (Rom. 4:22);[108] and our author is in full agreement. The point of verse 12, however, is all the more clearly made if Abraham is the subject of verse 11.

---

[103] Reading αὐτῇ Σάρρᾳ, not αὐτὴ Σάρρα, with E. Riggenbach, *Der Brief an die Hebraer*, ZK (Leipzig, 1913), pp. 356ff.; O. Michel, *Der Brief an die Hebräer*, MK (Göttingen, 1949), p. 262; A. Snell, *New and Living Way* (London, 1959), pp. 138f. The dative is "dative of accompaniment".

[104] What, it might be asked, of his sons by Keturah (Gen. 25:1ff.)? It is reading too much into the text to suppose that he married her after Sarah's death; in I Chron. 1:32 she is called "Abraham's concubine".

[105] This pair of similes appears in classical literature; cf. Plato, *Euthydemus* 294b; Catullus vii. 3ff., lxi. 206ff.

[106] Gk. νενεκρωμένος. The only other NT occurrence of νεκρόω is in Col. 3:5, in the sense "put to death" (ARV) or rather "reckon as dead".

[107] "In a hopeless situation Abraham hoped in God" (C. K. Barrett, *From First Adam to Last* [London, 1962], p. 37).

[108] Echoing Gen. 15:6, which comes immediately after God's promise that Abraham's offspring would be as numerous as the stars. (Abraham's obedience, faith and hospitality are celebrated also in I Clem. 10:1ff.; 31:2.)

(d) The City of God the Homeland of the Faithful

Ch. 11:13-16

13 These all died in faith, not having received[109] the promises, but having seen them[110] and greeted them from afar, and having confessed that they were strangers and pilgrims on the earth.

14 For they that say such things make it manifest that they are seeking[111] after a country of their own.

15 And if indeed they had been mindful[112] of that *country* from which they went out, they would have had opportunity to return.

16 But now they desire a better *country*, that is, a heavenly: wherefore God is not ashamed of them, to be called their God; for he hath prepared for them a city.

13 "These all"—more particularly, those mentioned in the five preceding verses, Abraham (with Sarah), Isaac and Jacob— "died in faith",[113] as they had lived in faith. Their lives were regulated by the firm conviction that God would fulfil the promises He had given them, and in death they continued to look forward to the fulfilment of these promises, as is evident from the words in which Isaac and Jacob bestowed their final blessings on their sons

---

[109] There is a curious variation in the Greek word rendered "having received"; P^{46} D 1739 with the majority of later MSS and TR read λαβόντες, ℵ I P 326 and others read κομισάμενοι, while A reads προσδεξάμενοι. The original reading is probably λαβόντες (*cf.* Ch. 9:15); the reading κομισάμενοι may have been influenced by Chs. 10:36; 11:39, and προσδεξάμενοι possibly by v. 35. *Cf.* G. Zuntz, *op. cit.*, pp. 52f.; F. W. Beare, *JBL* lxiii (1944), p. 394.

[110] 1518 with a few MSS and TR add καὶ πεισθέντες (whence AV "and were persuaded of them").

[111] P^{46} D* and a few other MSS. have the simple verb ζητοῦσιν, the majority reading is the compound ἐπιζητοῦσιν (for a similar variation in v. 6 see p. 283, n. 30).

[112] P^{46} ℵ* D* 1739 and a few other authorities read the present μνημονεύουσιν, 33 and a few others read the aorist ἐμνημόνευσαν, A and the remaining witnesses read the imperfect ἐμνημόνευον. The present tense, as the more difficult reading, is probably to be preferred (*cf.* Zuntz, *op. cit.*, p. 119; see also p. 305, n. 120).

[113] Here the author departs from his anaphoric use of πίστει and says κατὰ πίστιν, simply by way of literary variation. We have had κατὰ πίστιν already in v. 7, but in the attributive position (τῆς κατὰ πίστιν δικαιοσύνης).

or grandsons, as verses 20 and 21 indicate. But more generally it is true of all the men and women of God in Old Testament days that they "died in faith, not having received the promises, but having seen them and greeted them from afar", as indeed our author affirms in verse 39, at the end of his honors list. It was Abraham, Isaac and Jacob, however, who lived preeminently as "strangers and pilgrims[114] on the earth" in a sense which is inapplicable to those Israelites of later generations after the settlement in Canaan. To Abraham, Isaac and Jacob Canaan remained a "promised" land to the end of their days; their descendants saw the fulfilment of what was a promise to the patriarchs. But to the patriarchs that promise was sure, because it was God's promise; and they staked everything on its certainty. In one sense, as our author has said earlier, Abraham, "having patiently endured, ... obtained the promise" (Ch. 6:15)[115]—he obtained the promised son, not only by his birth but also by his restoration from death "in a figure", as verse 19 puts it—but the full realization of the promises had to await the day of Christ. "I am a stranger and a sojourner[116] with you", said Abraham to the sons of Heth (Gen. 23:4); he recognized and accepted his status as a pilgrim. So too Jacob, in old age, speaks of the long course of his life as "the days of the years of my pilgrimage"[117] (Gen. 47:9).

14 When the patriarchs used language like this, says our author, they made it plain[118] that the place of their sojourning was not their home.[119] Their "pilgrim's progress" through this world had as its goal a home elsewhere. Canaan was no more their home as they sought the country of their heart's desire than

---

[114] Gk. ξένοι καὶ παρεπίδημοι. Cf. Gen. 23:4, LXX, where Abraham describes himself as πάροικος καὶ παρεπίδημος (MT gēr we-tōshāb); Ps. 39:12 (LXX 38:13), where the psalmist says πάροικος (MT gēr) ἐγώ εἰμι ἐν τῇ γῇ καὶ παρεπίδημος (MT tōshāb); it is probably from this passage that our author derives his ἐπὶ τῆς γῆς, "on the earth" (cf. Ps. 119 [LXX 118]: 19). See p. 296, n. 82; p. 306, n. 123.

[115] See p. 129 with n. 76. Cf. the description of Abraham in v. 17 as "he that had gladly received (ἀναδεξάμενος) the promises" (where the promises themselves, not their fulfilment, should be understood).

[116] See n. 114 above.

[117] LXX ἃς παροικῶ (MT megūrai). Cf. p. 296, n. 82.

[118] Gk. ἐμφανίζουσιν, "they make it manifest" (cf. the passive of the same verb, rendered "to appear", in Ch. 9:24).

[119] What they seek is a πατρίς, their native land or home town (cf. Luke 4:23f.); the fact that they still seek it is proof that they have not found it here.

the wilderness was the home of their descendants in Moses' day who journeyed from Egypt to Canaan.

15 It is equally plain that, although they spoke of themselves as pilgrims in a foreign land, they did not think[120] of the land they had left as being their true home. In that case, they could easily have gone back there. But in fact they had no thought of doing so.[121] When Abraham's servant suggested to his master that Isaac might have to go to Mesopotamia in person to persuade his bride to come to Canaan, Abraham said: "Beware thou that thou bring not my son thither again" (Gen. 24:6). In the following generation Jacob had to flee to Mesopotamia from the anger of his brother Esau, but his vision at Bethel on the first night of his journey there made it impossible for him ever to think of Mesopotamia as his home; Canaan, to which his returning steps were directed twenty years later, was now the "land of his fathers" (Gen. 31:3), even if in it he had no settled abode.

16 The truth is,[122] their true homeland was not on earth at all. The better country on which they had set their hearts was the heavenly country. The earthly Canaan and the earthly Jerusalem were but temporary object-lessons pointing to the saints' ever-lasting rest, the well-founded city of God. Those who put their trust in God receive a full reward, and that reward must belong not to this transient world-order but to the enduring order which

---

[120] Gk. μνημονεύουσιν (see p. 303, n. 112). The verb is used in v. 22 below, where Joseph is said to have "made mention of" or "referred to" Israel's exodus from Egypt, and probably has much the same sense here. We might paraphrase: "In describing themselves as pilgrims and strangers in Canaan the patriarchs show that they are journeying to another country, their true home-land. It is equally clear that *they are not referring to* the former Mesopotamian home which they had left, for then they could have gone back there." See G. Zuntz, *op. cit.*, p. 119: "Discussing the quotation in ver. 13, the writer argues: 'the reference is not to the country they had left: this interpretation is excluded by the fact that they did not turn about. Their longing in fact is for a better country', &c."

[121] "Who else [other than the 'proper' (ἀστεῖος) man] would not have felt it burdensome both to leave his own country and to be driven from every civilized community (πόλις) into pathless places most difficult for the traveller to penetrate? Who would not have turned right about and retraced his homeward way, paying but little heed to future hopes but making haste to escape the present difficulty, thinking it folly to choose acknowledged ills in hope of good things which he could not see?" (Philo, *On Abraham*, 86).

[122] Gk. νῦν δέ at the beginning of v. 16 means "but as it is".

participates in the life of God. The example of the patriarchs is intended to guide the readers of the epistle to a true sense of values; like the elect sojourners of the Dispersion addressed in I Peter they are to live in this world as "aliens and exiles"[123] (I Pet. 2:11, RSV), and like the Philippians to whom Paul wrote, their "citizenship"[124] is in heaven" (Phil. 3:20). This ideal has proved too high for many Christians throughout the centuries of our era; yet there has never failed a distinguished succession of men and women possessed of this pilgrim attitude who have sung with Henry Francis Lyte:

> "It is not for me to be seeking my bliss
> And building my hopes in a region like this;
> I look for a city which hands have not piled,
> I pant for a country by sin undefiled."

Yet those who have shared most truly the otherworldliness of the patriarchs have not been unpractical people, too heavenly-minded to be of any earthly use. Abraham's neighbors were enriched by the presence of this wandering stranger in their midst; when the territory of some of them was devastated by an invading army on one occasion, it was "Abram the Hebrew"[125] who took immediate and effective action to deal with the situation.[126] There have indeed many occasions when practical men of the world have been thankful to saints and mystics for timely help in an emergency beyond their own power to cope with.

"Them that honor me I will honor", says God (I Sam. 2:30). The patriarchs honored God by putting their faith in Him; He honored them by calling Himself "the God of Abraham, the God of Isaac, and the God of Jacob" (Ex. 3:6).[127] What higher honor

---

[123] Gk. παροίκους καὶ παρεπιδήμους, as in Gen. 23:4, LXX (cf. p. 296, n. 82, p. 304, n. 114). In Eph. 2:19, "ye are no more strangers and sojourners" (Gk. ξένοι καὶ πάροικοι), the words are used in a different setting; there the point is that Gentile believers are no longer aliens but fellow-citizens with the people of God.

[124] Gk. πολίτευμα.

[125] See p. 296, n. 80.

[126] Gen. 14:8ff.; cf. pp. 134ff. above (on Ch. 7:1ff.).

[127] On the identification (and self-identification) of God as "God of the fathers" cf. A. Alt, Der Gott der Väter (Leipzig, 1929); B. Gemser, Vragen rondom de Patriarchenreligie (Groningen, 1958); F. M. Cross, Jr., "Yahweh and the God of the Patriarchs", HThR lv (1962), pp. 225ff.

than this could be paid to any mortal? These three patriarchs were not faultless, but God is not ashamed to be called their God, because they took Him at His word. It is noteworthy that, while Jacob is in many ways the least exemplary of the three, God is called the God of Jacob much more frequently in the Bible than He is called the God of Abraham or of Isaac. For all his shortcomings, Jacob had a true sense of spiritual values which sprang from his faith in God.[128] For these men, then, and for all who tread the same path of faith, God has prepared His city, His commonwealth.[129] There is, of course, no difference between the heavenly country[130] and the city of God. Words could hardly make it clearer that the patriarchs and the other men and women of God who lived before Christ have a share in the same inheritance of glory as is promised to believers in Christ of New Testament times.[131]

---

[128]   See note on Esau, described *per contra* as a "profane person" (Ch. 12:16f.), on p. 367.

[129]   It is probably on a passage like this or v. 10 or Ch. 13:14 (see p. 404) that Hermas depends when he tells how the angel said to him: "You know that you, the servants of God, live in a foreign land, for your city is far from this city. If then you know your city, in which you are going to dwell, why do you prepare here fields and costly establishments and buildings and dwellings which are to no purpose? He who prepares these things for this city cannot go back home to his own city" (*Shepherd*, Similitude i. 1).

[130]   With the "heavenly" (ἐπουράνιος) homeland prepared by God for the patriarchs Moffatt (ICC, p. 176) compares II Macc. 3:39, where God is described as the one whose dwelling is "heavenly" (ἐπουράνιος). It is to God's own dwelling, indeed, that men and women of faith are admitted as free burgesses, just as it has been emphasized earlier (Chs. 3:11; 4:3ff.) that it is God's own "rest" that may be attained by faith and forfeited by unbelief.

[131]   *Cf.* B. W. Newton's retort to those who pressed an unscriptural distinction between the people of God in Old Testament days and those of the present age: "Are we to say that Abraham hath 'THE promises', and yet that the chiefest results of those promises he hath *not*? Are we to say that Abraham belongs to that heavenly city whose maker and builder is God, ... and yet that he hath not the blessings which pertain to that city?" (*The Old Testament Saints not to be Excluded from the Church in Glory* [London, 1887], p. 14).

(e) More about the Faith of the Patriarchs

Ch. 11:17–22

17 By faith Abraham, being tried, offered up Isaac:[132] yea, he that had gladly received[133] the promises was offering up[134] his only begotten son;[135]

18 *even he* to whom it was said, In Isaac shall thy seed be called:[136]

19 accounting that God *is* able to raise up,[137] even from the dead; from whence he did also in a figure receive him back.

---

[132] Gk. πίστει προσενήνοχεν 'Αβραὰμ τὸν 'Ισαὰκ πειραζόμενος. P⁴⁶ with a few later authorities omits 'Αβραάμ. The perfect tense προσενήνοχεν may denote the completeness of the sacrifice so far as Abraham's resolution was concerned; cf. n. 134 below. The participle πειραζόμενος echoes ἐπείραζεν of Gen. 22:1 (LXX); cf. also Sir. 44:20, ἐν πειρασμῷ εὑρέθη πιστός (p. 294).

[133] Gk. ἀναδεξάμενος. The only other occurrence of ἀναδέχομαι in NT is Acts 28:7, where Publius, chief man of Malta, "received" Paul, Luke and their companions. The addition of "gladly" in the rendering of the verb is unnecessary.

[134] Here, by contrast with the preceding clause (cf. n. 132 above) the imperfect tense προσέφερεν is used, indicating that, so far as outward action was concerned, the sacrifice of Isaac was not completed by his death; we might render the verb here: "was on the point of offering up".

[135] Gk. τὸν μονογενῆ, corresponding to Heb. yāḥīd in Gen. 22:2 (so Aquila's version and Josephus, *Ant.* i. 222). LXX renders yāḥīd here by ἀγαπητός, "beloved", while Symmachus renders by μόνος, "only". The Hebrew adjective combines the two ideas (adding to its proper force "only" that of yādīd, "beloved"); hence Philo speaks of Isaac (in his allegorizing way) as "the beloved and only (ἀγαπητὸν καὶ μόνον) trueborn offspring of the soul" (*On the Unchangeableness of God*, 4). There are three instances of μονογενής in reference to an only child in Luke (7:12; 8:42; 9:38); its best-known NT usage, however, is its application to Christ, the Son of God, in the Johannine writings (John 1:14, 18; 3:16, 18; I John 4:9), where it is practically synonymous with ἀγαπητός in Mark 1:11; 9:7 (and parallels) and ἐκλελεγμένος in Luke 9:35. Cf. also the Parable of the Vineyard, where the proprietor "had yet one, a beloved son" (Mark 12:6), and Paul's echo of Gen. 22:2 in Rom. 8:32, "He that spared not his own Son" (where Gk. ἴδιος represents Heb. yāḥīd, as also, probably, in Acts 20:28, where God purchased the church "with the blood of His own", *i.e.* "of His only-begotten").

[136] Gen. 21:12.

[137] Gk. ἐγείρειν, for which a few authorities (A P etc.) have ἐγεῖραι, the aorist infinitive, as though the reference was to Abraham's faith that God could raise *Isaac*; the present infinitive implies Abraham's faith that God could raise *the dead*.

20 By faith Isaac blessed Jacob and Esau, even[138] concerning things to come.

21 By faith Jacob, when he was dying, blessed each of the sons of Joseph; and worshipped, *leaning* upon the top of his staff.[139]

22 By faith Joseph, when his end was nigh, made mention of the departure[140] of the children of Israel; and gave commandment concerning his bones.

17-18 The "Binding of Isaac",[141] as the story of Gen. 22 has traditionally been called among the Jews, is treated in Jewish interpretation as the classic example of the redemptive efficacy of martyrdom.[142] Its influence is probably to be traced in several New Testament passages,[143] but only in two places is the story expressly referred to—here and in Jas. 2:21ff.—and in both of these places it is set forth as an example of faith, faith manifested in action. "Was not Abraham our father justified by works," asks James, "in that he offered up Isaac his son upon the altar? Thou seest that faith wrought with his works, and by works was faith

---

[138] Gk. καί, omitted by א K L P etc., followed by TR (*cf.* AV); omitted also by the Syriac and Coptic versions.

[139] Gen. 47:31 (LXX); *cf.* pp. 313f.

[140] Gk. ἔξοδος.

[141] Heb. *ʿaqēdath yiṣḥāq*, from Gen. 22:9.

[142] In the Additional Service for the Jewish New Year these words occur: "Remember unto us, O Lord our God, the covenant and the loving-kindness and the oath which thou swarest unto Abraham our father on Mount Moriah; and may the binding with which Abraham our father bound his son Isaac on the altar appear before thee, how he overbore his compassion in order to perform thy will with a perfect heart." *Cf.* also the prayer in *Leviticus Rabba* xxix. 8: "If the sons of Isaac walk in rebellion and wicked works, remember the binding of their father Isaac, and leave the throne of judgment and sit on the throne of mercy" (this example is selected by C. K. Barrett, *From First Adam to Last* [London, 1962], pp. 27f., from the collection of relevant passages in N. Johansson, *Parakletoi* [Lund, 1940], pp. 168ff.); *cf.* also H. Riesenfeld, *Jésus transfiguré* (Uppsala, 1947), pp. 87ff.; H. J. Schoeps, *Aus frühchristlicher Zeit* (Tübingen, 1950), pp. 229ff.; I. Maybaum, *The Sacrifice of Isaac* (London, 1959).

[143] Rom. 8:32 (ὅς γε τοῦ ἰδίου υἱοῦ οὐκ ἐφείσατο) echoes Gen. 22:16 (LXX, οὐκ ἐφείσω τοῦ υἱοῦ σου τοῦ ἀγαπητοῦ). H. J. Schoeps, not too convincingly, finds other traces of the Binding of Isaac in Pauline soteriology (*Paul* [Eng. tr., London, 1961], pp. 141ff.). John 8:56 possibly alludes to a phase of the story (*cf.* p. 312 with n. 152).

made perfect; and the scripture was fulfilled which saith, And Abraham believed God, and it was reckoned unto him for righteousness;[144] and he was called the friend of God."[145] James's emphasis is in line with his general argument in that context; but he is in essential agreement with our author: Abraham's offering up of Isaac was a signal demonstration of his faith. Not only so, but this interpretation is consistent with the original narrative, in which God's command to Abraham to offer up Isaac was intended to "prove" him (Gen. 22:1),[146] and Abraham's ready obedience attested the unreserved quality of his allegiance to God. "When he was tested he was found faithful", says Ben Sira, plainly in reference to this incident (Sir. 44:20), while the author of Wisdom says that it was wisdom that "kept him strong in the face of his compassion for his child" (Wisdom 10:5).[147] In IV Maccabees the mother of the seven martyrs appeals to this example when pleading with her sons to preserve their faithfulness to God in face of deadly threats; it was for God's sake, she says, that "our father Abraham hastened to sacrifice his son Isaac, the ancestor of our nation, and was not overcome by fear at the sight of his own paternal hand descending on him with the knife" (16:20; cf. also 18:11).

What our author emphasizes, however, is Abraham's indomitable faith in the promises of God. God promised Abraham, long after the hope of progeny had receded for himself and Sarah, that

---

[144] Gen. 15:6 (quoted also by Paul in Gal. 3:6; Rom. 4:3). The counting of Abraham's faith to him for righteousness preceded the sacrifice of Isaac by many years, but his sacrifice of Isaac showed how implicit was his faith in God's promise (of Gen. 15:5) and in God's power to fulfil His promise, come what might.

[145] A reference to Isa. 41:8, "Abraham my friend"; cf. II Chron. 20:7, "Abraham thy friend".

[146] "With ten trials our father Abraham was tried, and he stood firm in them all, to make known how great was our father Abraham's love" (*Pirqē Aboth* 5:4). The ten are enumerated one by one in *Pirqē de-Rabbi Eliezer* 26–30 and in the Jewish morning service for the second day of the New Year; the Binding of Isaac is the tenth and greatest of them. In Jubilees 17:16ff. God's command to Abraham to sacrifice Isaac is the result of a challenge presented to Him by Mastema, the prince of evil, just as the trials of Job were the result of a challenge presented to Him by Satan.

[147] This point is made also by Philo in his account of the incident (*On Abraham*, 167ff.): "mastered by his love for God, he mightily overcame all the names and loving tokens of kinship" (170).

he would have a numerous posterity, and at last the long-awaited son was born—the son on whose survival the fulfilment of God's promises to Abraham depended. In this regard Ishmael and any other sons of Abraham did not count, for the word of God was quite specific: "Through the line of Isaac your posterity shall be traced" (NEB). Isaac was unique and irreplaceable—this is the point of the epithet rendered "only begotten"; he was, in God's own words to Abraham, "thine only son, whom thou lovest, even Isaac" (Gen. 22:2).[148] And it was *Isaac* who had to be sacrificed! The ethical problem which the story presents to twentieth-century readers[149] is not the problem on which our author concentrates. The problem to which he invites his readers' attention is this: The fulfilment of God's promises depended on Isaac's survival; if Isaac was to die, how could these promises be fulfilled? And yet Abraham had no doubt that the One who had given the promises required the sacrifice of Isaac. What was he to do? It was Abraham's problem; apart from the dictates of natural affection, how could the promise of God and the command of God be reconciled? Later writers, reflecting on the incident, make much of the turmoil in Abraham's heart, although the biblical narrative has little enough to say on this score. Indeed, the impression which we get from the biblical narrative is that Abraham treated it as God's problem; it was for God, and not for Abraham, to reconcile His promise and His command. So, when the command was given, Abraham promptly set about obeying it; his own duty was clear, and God could safely be trusted to discharge *His* responsibility in the matter.

19 Our author's statement that Abraham believed in God's ability to raise the dead[150] is not a gratuitous reading into the narrative of something that is not there. When Abraham left his servants behind while he and Isaac went to the place of sacrifice, he said to them: "The boy and I will go on there and worship, and we will come back to you" (Gen. 22:5). The plain meaning of the text is that Abraham expected to come back with Isaac. But how

---

[148] See p. 308, n. 135.

[149] *Cf.* S. Kierkegaard, *Fear and Trembling* (Eng. tr., Oxford, 1939); E. Wellisch, *Isaac and Oedipus* (London, 1954).

[150] *Cf.* Philo, *On Abraham*, 175, where Abraham's reply to Isaac in Gen. 22:8 is expanded by the words: "but know that to God all things are possible, including those that are impossible and impracticable for human beings".

could he come back with Isaac, if Isaac was to be offered up as a burnt-offering? Only if Isaac was to be raised from the dead after being sacrificed. Abraham reckoned, says our author, that since the fulfilment of the promises depended on Isaac's survival, then God was bound (as He certainly was able) to restore Isaac's life if his life had to be taken. And in fact, so far as Abraham's resolution was concerned, Isaac was as good as dead, and it was practically from the dead that he received him back when his hand was arrested in mid-air and the heavenly voice forbade him to proceed further. He received him back from the dead, says our author, "in a figure"[151]—meaning, probably, in a manner that prefigured the resurrection of Christ. Is it this incident that is referred to in the words of Christ in John 8:56: "Your father Abraham rejoiced to see my day; and he saw it, and was glad"?[152]

20 In some strands of Jewish interpretation the attitude of Isaac himself, in submitting to being bound by his father with a view to his sacrifice, is commended as an example of obedience, not only to his father but to God.[153] On this our author says

---

[151] Gk. ἐν παραβολῇ. The sacrifice of Isaac was early treated by Christians as a detailed parable of the sacrifice of Christ. "Our Lord ... was Himself going to offer the vessel of the spirit as a sacrifice for our sins, for the fulfilment of the type established in Isaac, who was offered upon the altar" (*Epistle of Barnabas* 7:3). According to Irenaeus (*Heresies* iv. 5. 4) and many later writers, Isaac carrying the wood is a type of Christ carrying the cross.

[152] Alternatively, these words may refer to Abraham's reply to Isaac: "God will provide himself the lamb for the burnt-offering" (Gen. 22:8). Since this is the only statement which Abraham is recorded in canonical scripture as having made to Isaac (apart from "Here am I, my son" in the preceding verse), this is presumably the statement referred to in the *Testament of Levi* (18:6), where it is said of the priest of the new age: "The heavens shall be opened, and from the temple of glory shall come upon him sanctification, with the Father's voice as from Abraham to Isaac." *Cf.* M. Black, "The Messiah in the Testament of Levi XVIII", *ExT* lx (1948–49), pp. 321f.

[153] *Cf.* IV Macc. 13:12 ("Isaac endured to be slain for the sake of piety"). Josephus, after the long and tasteless speech which he puts into Abraham's mouth at this moment, tells how Isaac made answer in terms of exemplary duty, and "rushed to the altar to be slain" (*Antiquities* i. 232). Similarly Clement of Rome: "Isaac, knowing with confidence what was about to be, was gladly brought as a sacrifice" (I Clem. 31:3). Several writers underline the reality of Isaac's cooperation by emphasizing that he was a grown man at the time—23 years old, according to Jubilees (*cf.* 16:12 with 17:15); 25, according to Josephus (*Antiquities* i. 227); 37, according to *Seder 'Olam*. His age is not recorded in Genesis, but the impression is given that he was but a boy.

nothing; the one incident from Isaac's career which he mentions as a token of his faith is his blessing of Jacob and Esau[154]—their names are given in this order and not in the order of seniority, perhaps because this was the order in which they received their father's blessing. Nothing is said about the deception practised on Isaac, in consequence of which the blessing which he had intended for Esau was bestowed on Jacob. The line of promise ran through Isaac, and as Isaac himself had received from God a reaffirmation of the promised blessings after Abraham's death,[155] so he determined to transmit these blessings to the following generation. When he learned that Jacob had received the blessing intended for Esau, he made no attempt to revoke it; rather he confirmed it: "yea, and he shall be blessed" (Gen. 27:33). Yet he did reserve a blessing for Esau, and although it was not the blessing bound up with the promise, yet it was a blessing "even concerning things to come", as truly as Jacob's blessing was. Isaac, like his father, believed God, and his faith too was an "assurance of things hoped for, a conviction of things not seen".

21 Jacob in his turn demonstrated similar faith. Isaac was misled by the plotting of his wife and younger son into giving the younger son the blessing which he had designed for the elder; but when Jacob on his deathbed blessed the two sons of Joseph he deliberately bestowed the greater blessing on Ephraim, the younger son.[156] But he blessed both of them "concerning things to come", as he himself had been blessed by Isaac; and thus, while his earlier career had been marked by anything but faith, as he endeavored repeatedly by his own scheming to gain advantages for himself, yet at the end of his days he recognized the futility of all his scheming, and relied on the faithfulness of the "Mighty One of Jacob".

The statement that he "worshipped, leaning upon the top of his staff", is based on the Septuagint version of Gen. 47:31.[157] The Massoretic text says that "Israel bowed himself upon the bed's head";[158] but the Septuagint translators read Hebrew *miṭṭāh*,

---

154 Cf. Gen. 27:27ff., 39f.; cf. p. 368 (on Ch. 12:17).
155 Gen. 26:2ff.
156 Gen. 48:14, 19.
157 Gk. καὶ προσεκύνησεν 'Ισραὴλ ἐπὶ τὸ ἄκρον τῆς ῥάβδου αὐτοῦ.
158 Cf. I Kings 1:47, where King David "bowed himself upon the bed (*mishkāb*)"; here LXX renders ἐπὶ τὴν κοίτην.

"bed", as though it were *maṭṭeh*, "staff". The picture of the patriarch sitting on his bed and leaning on his staff is convincing enough; the same cannot be said for the mistranslation in the Latin New Testament, which makes him worship the top of his staff[159]—a form of words from which some curious inferences have been drawn.[160]

22 Joseph also, at the end of his days, showed the same firm faith in the fulfilment of God's promises. Joseph's career certainly presents instances of faith in abundance, such as his steadfastness under temptation and his patience under unjust treatment:

> "Joseph was sold for a servant:
> His feet they hurt with fetters:
> His neck was put in a collar of iron,
> Until the time that his word came to pass,
> The word of Jehovah tried him."[161]

He endured his trials nobly and triumphed over them, for (as Stephen puts it) "God was with him, and delivered him out of all his afflictions, and gave him favor and wisdom before Pharaoh king of Egypt; and he made him governor over Egypt and all his house" (Acts 7:9f.). Other writers enlarge on his righteousness, his fortitude and his wisdom;[162] but the one incident singled out by our author to illustrate his faith belongs to the end of his life, because, above everything else recorded of him, it expresses his conviction regarding "things to come". "I die," he said to his kinsmen, "but God will surely visit you, and bring you up out of this land unto the land which he sware to Abraham, to Isaac, and to Jacob. ... God will surely visit you, and ye shall carry up my

---

[159] Vg. *adorauit fastigium uirgae eius*; whence Rheims-Challoner, "adored the top of his rod". In Gen. 47:31 Jerome translates from the Hebrew: *adorauit Israel Deum, conuersus ad lectuli caput*. He revised the Old Latin NT (outside the Gospels) with a light touch.

[160] *E.g.*, R. A. Knox gives the rendering "made reverence to the top of Joseph's staff", and explains in a footnote that the staff or sceptre was a symbol of the tribe (the Hebrew words *maṭṭeh* and *shēbeṭ* doing duty for both "staff" and "tribe").

[161] Ps. 105:17-19; *cf.* Wisdom 10:13f.; I Macc. 2:53; IV Macc. 18:11.

[162] *E.g.*, Philo, *On Joseph*; Josephus, *Antiquities* ii. 9ff.; and such pseudepigrapha as the *Testament of Joseph* and *Joseph and Asenath* (also *Qur'ān*, Sura 12). Indeed, we might carry the bibliography down to our own day to include Thomas Mann's cycle of *Joseph* books.

bones from hence" (Gen. 50:24f.). Joseph had spent the whole of his long life, apart from the first seventeen years, in Egypt; but Egypt was not his home. Even when the rest of his family came down to Egypt at his invitation, he knew that their residence there would be but temporary. Just as his father Jacob had insisted on being carried back to the promised land for burial, so Joseph made his relatives swear that they would perform the like service for him. He "made mention of the departure—literally, the exodus— of the children of Israel," says our author, "and gave commandment concerning his bones." And in due course the coffin which contained his embalmed body was carried from Egypt when the Israelites left that land under the guidance of Moses,[163] and was buried at Shechem after the settlement in Canaan.[164]

(f) The Faith of Moses

Ch. 11:23-28

23 By faith Moses, when he was born, was hid three months by his parents, because they saw he was a goodly child; and they were not afraid of the king's commandment.[165]

24 By faith Moses, when he was grown up, refused to be called the son of Pharaoh's daughter;

25 choosing rather to share ill treatment with the people of God, than to enjoy the pleasures of sin for a season:

26 accounting the reproach of Christ greater riches than the treasures of Egypt: for he looked unto the recompense of reward.

27 By faith he forsook Egypt, not fearing the wrath of the king: for he endured, as seeing him who is invisible.

---

[163] Ex. 13:19.

[164] Josh. 24:32.

[165] Gk. διάταγμα, for which A and a few other manuscripts have δόγμα ("decree"). This verse is followed in D* 1827 and many Latin MSS by the insertion: "By faith Moses, when he was grown up, slew (ἀνεῖλεν) the Egyptian when he saw the oppression (κατανοῶν τὴν ταπείνωσιν) of his brethren." This incident is recorded in Ex. 2:11f., and is referred to by Stephen in Acts 7:23ff. (cf. Acts, NICNT, p. 150). The insertion here is quite without authority.

28 By faith he kept[166] the passover, and the sprinkling of the blood, that the destroyer of the first-born should not touch them.[167]

23 The next example of faith is Moses, whose whole life is marked by awareness of the presence and power of the unseen God, and believing obedience to His word. In Jewish legend the achievements of Moses were magnified far beyond the biblical account.[168] A more sober summary of his career is given in Stephen's speech (Acts 7:20-44). Stephen mentions that "Moses was instructed in all the wisdom of the Egyptians; and he was mighty in his words and works" (Acts 7:22); but he lays chief emphasis on the fact that Moses was God's appointed messenger and redeemer to the people of Israel, the man who "led them forth, having wrought wonders and signs[169] in Egypt, and in the Red Sea, and in the wilderness forty years" (Acts 7:36). Our author's assessment of Moses is closely akin to Stephen's. He has already spoken of his faithfulness as a servant in God's house (Ch. 3:2, 5); here he singles out those features from the history

---

[166] Gk. πεποίηκεν, ARV mg. "he instituted"; NEB "he celebrated". A. Nairne explains the perfect tense as meaning: "he has left us the institution of the Passover" (*The Epistle of Priesthood* [Edinburgh, 1913], p. 400).

[167] A non-Vulgate Latin insertion at this point reads: "By faith they spoiled the Egyptians at their departure" (so the ninth-century *Codex Harleianus*) or "By faith they spoiled the Egyptians because they believed they would not return to Egypt" (so the eighth or ninth-century commentator Sedulius Scotus).

[168] Josephus (*Antiquities* ii. 230f.) enlarges on Moses' outstanding wisdom and exceptional beauty of stature, and (*ibid.* ii. 238ff.) describes a victorious expedition which he led against the Ethiopians as Egyptian commander-in-chief. Philo (*Life of Moses*, i. 20ff.) credits him with proficiency in arithmetic, geometry, poetry, music, philosophy, astrology, and all branches of education. Eupolemus, a Hellenistic Jewish writer, makes him the inventor of the alphabet, which the Phoenicians acquired from him, and the Greeks from them; Artabanus, another Hellenistic Jew, says that Egypt owed her civilization to him; others of the same school put Homer and Plato in his debt for whatever of truth and goodness their writings contain. See Justin, *First Apology* 59f.; Eusebius, *Preparation* vii. 14; ix. 26f.; xiii. 12. See also W. Nowack in *JE* ix (New York, 1905), *s.v.* "Moses", pp. 46ff.

[169] *Cf.* Wisdom 10:16, where Wisdom is said to have inspired him: "she entered the soul of a servant (θεράπων, as in Heb. 3:5) of the Lord, and withstood dread kings with wonders and signs". (For "wonders and signs" see p. 30 with n. 6.) See also the encomium of Moses in Ben Sira's "Praise of the Elders" (Sir. 45:1-5).

of Moses which best illustrate his present theme of faith in God.

The faith which was shown at Moses' birth was, of course, not his own but his parents'.[170] He was born in Egypt, soon after the reigning Pharaoh, to restrict the rapidly increasing numbers of the Israelites in his realm, had issued a decree ordering that all male children born to them should be put to death at birth. But, according to the Exodus narrative, when Moses' mother saw "that he was a goodly child, she hid him three months" (Ex. 2:2), and after that she placed him in a basket of bulrushes on the brink of the Nile, where he was found by Pharaoh's daughter. While the Hebrew text makes his mother the active party in thus circumventing the royal decree, the Septuagint says that both his parents hid him for three months,[171] and it is the Septuagint account that is followed by our author, as also by Philo[172] and Josephus.[173] Nature itself might suggest that his mother took the initiative, with the acquiescence of his father. Had their defiance of the law been discovered, the penalty would have been severe; but "they were not afraid of the king's commandment".

Wherein precisely did their "faith" lie? Probably the statement that Moses was a "goodly"[174] child means more than that he was a beautiful baby. We are perhaps intended to infer that there was something about the appearance of the child which indicated that he was no ordinary child,[175] but one destined under God to accomplish great things for his people. Our author does not repeat the story of the divine revelation to this effect which, according to

---

[170] Gk. πατέρες (literally "fathers").

[171] In Ex. 2:2b, LXX, the verbs are plural: ἰδόντες δὲ αὐτὸ ἀστεῖον, ἐσκέπασαν αὐτὸ μῆνας τρεῖς.

[172] Philo, *Life of Moses* i. 9. Philo says that their nerve failed after three months and they wished that they had exposed the child at birth.

[173] *Antiquities* ii. 218.

[174] Gk. ἀστεῖος, from Ex. 2:2, LXX (Heb. *ṭôb*, "good"). Stephen (Acts 7:20) says the child was ἀστεῖος τῷ θεῷ ("exceeding fair", literally "fair to God"); Philo, also using this adjective, describes him (*Life of Moses*, i. 9) as of a "more beautiful appearance than ordinary (ὄψιν ... ἀστειοτέραν ἢ κατ' ἰδιώτην)".

[175] Calvin (*ad loc.*) says that it was not the external beauty of the child that moved them, since faith, like God Himself, does not look on the outward appearance but on the heart (*cf.* I Sam. 16:7); rather "there was some mark, as it were, of future excellency imprinted on the child, which gave promise of something out of the ordinary". We may compare the descriptions of Noah's beauty at his birth (*cf.* p. 291, n. 57).

Josephus,[176] was given in a night vision to Moses' father Amram; but some appreciation of the divine purpose to be fulfilled through Moses is implied in his ascription of faith to Amram and Jochebed.

24 When Pharaoh's daughter found the infant Moses by the Nile, she adopted him and brought him up as her own son. But "when Moses was grown up,[177] ... he went out unto his brethren, and looked on their burdens" (Ex. 2:11). Stephen makes him "well-nigh forty years old" at the time, thus dividing his life of 120 years into three clearly demarcated periods of forty years each. According to Stephen, Moses presented himself to his fellow-Israelites as their champion, supposing "that his brethren understood that God by his hand was giving them deliverance; but they understood not" (Acts 7:25). Our author reads the Exodus narrative as Stephen did, and concludes that, by thus identifying himself with the downtrodden Israelites, Moses renounced the status which he enjoyed in Egypt as a member of the royal household. He could not identify himself both with the Israelites and with the Egyptians; he had to choose the one or the other. To choose the side of a slave-nation, with all the contempt and privation which that entailed, in preference to the very real advantages and prospects which were his as "the son of Pharaoh's daughter",[178] must have seemed an act of folly by all worldly standards. It is, however, an act which has been repeatedly re-

---

[176] *Antiquities* ii. 210ff.; *cf.* also *Mekhilta*, tractate *Shirata* 2, where the revelation is given to Amram not in a dream but by his daughter Miriam in her rôle as a prophetess (*cf.* Ex. 15:20).

[177] Gk. μέγας γενόμενος, LXX, as also here. An anticipation of Moses' adult renunciation of royal status in Egypt appears in Josephus's tale of the infant Moses throwing Pharaoh's crown to the ground and standing on it (*Antiquities* ii. 233f.; *cf. Mekhilta* and *Tanḥuma* for variants of the tale).

[178] We have no means of identifying this princess. One tradition, found in Jubilees 47:5 and Josephus (*Antiquities* ii. 224ff.), calls her Tharmuth or Thermuthis (a daughter of Rameses II, 1292–1225 B.C.); another, attested by Artabanus (Eusebius, *Preparation* ix. 27), calls her Merris (*cf.* Meri, a daughter of Ramses II by his Hittite wife, who was, however, in all probability younger than Moses himself). Some writers of more recent times have toyed with the improbable idea that she might have been Hatshepsut (*c.* 1500 B.C.), princess and queen-regnant of the Eighteenth Dynasty, daughter of Tuthmosis I (so J. Feather, "The Princess who rescued Moses: who was she?" *ExT* xliii [1931–32], pp. 423ff.; C. Marston, *The Bible is True* [London, 1934], pp. 179f.). That her father was an early king of the Nineteenth Dynasty (*c.* 1300 B.C.) is probable; more than that cannot be said.

produced in our day by outstanding members of subject nations
who have stood well with the imperial power, but have preferred
to cast in their lot with their own people even if this involved them
in loss, discomfort and imprisonment.

25 It was "by faith" that Moses made his great refusal, with
all that it cost him in material terms. His people were being ill-
treated, but he chose to share their ill-treatment[179] "rather than
enjoy the transient pleasures of sin"[180] (NEB). The privileges and
advantages which are attached to high rank and political power
are not sinful in themselves; they can indeed be used very effectively to promote the well-being of others and to help the under-
privileged. Moses might have argued to himself that he could do
much more for the Israelites by remaining in Pharaoh's court and
using his influence there on their behalf than by renouncing his
Egyptian citizenship and becoming a member of a depressed
group with no political rights. But for *Moses* to do this, when once
he had seen the path of duty clear before him, would have been
sin—the crowning sin of apostasy, against which the recipients of
this letter required so insistently to be warned. Even if (as some
have imagined) the crown of Egypt was within Moses' reach had
he remained where he was,[181] and his name had been perpetuated
in history as the greatest and wisest of the rulers of that land, he
would never have attained such a reputation as he did by making
the great refusal. But when Moses made that refusal he did not
foresee the reputation which he was going to establish for himself;
he had nothing to look forward to but privation, danger, scorn and
suffering—with Israel's liberation, please God. To have remained

---

[179] Gk. συνκακουχεῖσθαι, a hapax legomenon. For the simple verb see v. 37.
[180] Gk. πρόσκαιρον ἔχειν ἁμαρτίας ἀπόλαυσιν (literally, "have a temporary
enjoyment of sin"). For ἀπόλαυσις cf. I Tim. 6:17; for its use here cf. the verb
ἀπολαύειν in IV Macc. 5:8, where a pious Jew is upbraided for refusing "to
enjoy what is pleasant without being disgraceful" (by Gentile standards, that is).
The adjective πρόσκαιρος is used in Matt. 13:21 and Mark 4:17 of converts
who give up their confession as soon as persecution arises; in II Cor. 4:18 it is
used of the transience of the visible world by contrast with the eternity of the
invisible.
[181] This is naturally the opinion of those who make him the adopted son of
Hatshepsut (see n. 178 above). Philo says that Pharaoh's daughter was her
father's only child who, though now married for a long time, was childless
herself; Moses was thus heir to the throne (*Life of Moses*, i. 13). To this idea
neither the biblical narrative nor Egyptian history gives any color.

at Pharaoh's court would have been lasting dishonor, and that dishonor would be a price too high to pay for material advantages which at best would be but short-lived.

26 Moses weighed the issues in his mind, and decided that the temporal wealth of Egypt was far less valuable than "the stigma that rests on God's Anointed"[182] (NEB). What others would have considered as something to be shunned at all costs he esteemed as a prize to be eagerly sought. Like Paul after him, what things were gain to him, these he counted loss for Christ.[183] The identification of Christ with His people is noteworthy. The words which the God of Israel put in Moses' mouth when he went to Pharaoh to demand his people's release, "Israel is my son, my firstborn" (Ex. 4:22), are as applicable to Jesus personally as they are to Israel corporately. The Messiah is one with the messianic people, bone of their bone and flesh of their flesh.[184] "In all their affliction he was afflicted" (Isa. 63:9), and in the fulness of time He too, like His people before Him, was called out of Egypt[185] and had His Exodus to accomplish.[186] The "stigma" and disrepute which the people of God bore were borne in concentrated form by the Lord's Anointed; to Him the New Testament applies the psalmist's cry to God: "the reproaches of them that reproach thee are fallen upon me" (Ps. 69:9).[187] The national history of Israel, which began under Moses' leadership, led on to Christ; by his obedience to the heavenly vision Moses, like Abraham at an earlier date, looked forward to the day of Christ.

To readers whose perseverance was in danger of faltering because of the stigma attached to the name of Christ[188] the example of

---

[182] Gk. τὸν ὀνειδισμὸν τοῦ χριστοῦ. Cf. Ps. 89:51 (LXX 88:50f.): "Remember, O Lord, the reproach (ὀνειδισμός) of thy servants ... wherewith thy enemies have reproached (ὠνείδισαν), O Lord, wherewith they have reproached thy Anointed by way of recompense" (literally, "have reproached the recompense of thy Anointed, ὠνείδισαν τὸ ἀντάλλαγμα τοῦ χριστοῦ σου").

[183] Cf. Phil. 3:7.

[184] It is doubtful whether there is a veiled reference here to the belief that Jesus, so long before His incarnation, accompanied the Israelites through the wilderness (cf. p. 63 with n. 46).

[185] Cf. the quotation of Hos. 11:1 in Matt. 2:15, where the implication is that Messiah recapitulates in His own experience the experiences of His people.

[186] Cf. Luke 9:31, where Jesus' "decease which He was about to accomplish at Jerusalem" (ARV) is, in the Greek, His ἔξοδος.

[187] Quoted in Rom. 15:3 (οἱ ὀνειδισμοὶ τῶν ὀνειδιζόντων σε ἐπέπεσαν ἐπ' ἐμέ).

[188] Cf. Ch. 13:13, where they are urged to bear His "reproach" (ὀνειδισμός).

Moses was calculated to be a challenge and encouragement. It would help them to fix their eyes on the "recompense of reward"[189] held out to faith if they remembered how Moses weighed the issues of time in the balances of eternity: "his eyes were fixed[190] upon the coming day of recompense" (NEB). To have such a secure place in the history of redemption might have been reckoned reward enough; but to our author's mind Moses, as truly as the patriarchs, looked for his perfect recompense in the well-founded city of God.

27 With this forward-looking faith Moses abandoned[191] Egypt. His heart-renunciation of Egypt, with all that Egypt had to offer him, was the essential act of faith; but our author probably thinks of the occasion when he left Egypt to live in the wilderness of Midian,[192] a stranger in a strange land.[193] A difficulty may be felt here, since the Exodus narrative tells how Moses was afraid when he realized that his killing of the Egyptian whom he saw ill-treating a Hebrew was public knowledge. "Moses feared, and said, Surely the thing is known. Now when Pharaoh heard this thing, he sought to slay Moses. But Moses fled from the face of Pharaoh, and dwelt in the land of Midian" (Ex. 2:14f.).[194] Our author, who follows the biblical record so closely, certainly does not intend to contradict it, but rather to interpret it. "The fear of Moses is not immediately connected with his flight in the

---

[189] Gk. μισθαποδοσία, here as in Ch. 10:35 (see p. 271); it is the reward that comes from God, the great μισθαποδότης (cf. v. 6).

[190] Gk. ἀπέβλεπεν (ARV "he looked unto"), used of keeping one's attention fixed on something, as an artist keeps his fixed on the object or model that he is reproducing in painting or sculpture; cf. ἀφοράω, Ch. 12:2 (p. 351 with n. 33).

[191] Gk. κατέλιπεν, a verb which may denote physical departure (cf. n. 197 below), but also heart-renunciation, as when Levi (Matthew) the tax-collector "forsook all" (καταλιπὼν πάντα) to follow Jesus (Luke 5:28). So Philo (Life of Moses i. 149) says that Moses "abandoned the government of Egypt" (τὴν Αἰγύπτου κατέλιπεν ἡγεμονίαν).

[192] Ex. 2:15.

[193] Cf. Ex. 2:22, where he gives his firstborn son the name Gershom ("a stranger there") in acknowledgment of his impermanent status as a sojourner in a foreign land (cf. Acts 7:29; see also p. 296, n. 82; p. 304, n. 114).

[194] Philo emphasizes that Ex. 2:15 (LXX) says that Moses "withdrew" (ἀνεχώρησεν) from the face of Pharaoh (although the Hebrew text says quite plainly wayyibraḥ, "and he fled"). "Moses does not flee (φεύγει) from Pharaoh, for then he would have run away (ἀπεδίδρασκεν) without returning, but 'withdraws' (ἀναχωρεῖ), like an athlete taking an interval to regain his breath" (Leg.

321

Hebrew story, so that the author may have felt warranted by this in denying that the flight was due to fear."[195]   He was afraid, admittedly, but that was not why he left Egypt; his leaving Egypt was an act of faith. "By faith he left Egypt, and not because he feared the king's anger" (NEB). By his impulsive act of violence he had burned his boats so far as the court of Egypt was concerned; but he might have raised a slaves' revolt there and then.   By faith, however, he did nothing of the kind; "he had the insight to see that God's hour had not yet struck, and therefore he resolutely turned his back on the course he had begun to tread, and retraced his steps till he entered on the harder way.   For it was harder to live for his people than it was to die for them."[196]

Some commentators, however, have preferred to see here a reference to Moses' departure from Egypt at the time of the Exodus.[197]   One argument in favor of this view is the statement that "he endured, as seeing him who is invisible", which might be understood as an allusion to his experience at the burning bush.[198]   Against it, however, is the consideration that a reference to the Exodus here, before the institution of the Passover in verse 28, would be out of its natural order, as well as the consideration that fear of the king's wrath[199] would be irrelevant to this later departure from Egypt, since the king and his people alike then

---

Alleg. iii. 14).   He contrasts him with "any other who was running away (ἀποδιδράσκων) from a king's relentless wrath" (*Life of Moses* i. 49). Josephus (*Antiquities* ii. 254ff.) says nothing about Moses' killing of the Egyptian, but describes him as escaping from Egypt because of an envious plot against his life: "he left the land taking no supply of food, proudly confident of his power to endure (καρτερία)".

[195]   A. S. Peake, *The Heroes and Martyrs of Faith* (London, 1910), p. 118.

[196]   Peake, *op. cit.*, pp. 120f.

[197]   So Calvin (*ad loc.*), although he agrees that the reference could be to Moses' earlier departure, the mention of his fear in Ex. 2:14 notwithstanding; Weštcott also (*ad loc.*) concedes the possibility that his earlier departure is meant, but concludes that "it is however more likely that the words refer to the Exodus". He compares the use of καταλείπω in Josephus, *Antiquities* ii. 318, in reference to the Exodus: "they left (κατέλιπον) Egypt in the month Xanthicus ..." (but see n. 191 above).   He also suggests that the perfect πεποίηκεν in v. 28 (see p. 316, n. 166) "helps to explain the historical transposition".

[198]   Ex. 3:1ff.; *cf.* Acts 7:30ff.

[199]   The king at the time of the Exodus was not the Pharaoh from whom Moses fled earlier; that Pharaoh died while Moses was in Midian (Ex. 2:23).

urged Moses and the Israelites to get out as quickly as they could.[200]
As for Moses' endurance, "seeing him who is invisible",[201] this
need not be taken as a specific allusion to the burning bush, but
to the fact that Moses paid more attention to the Invisible King
of kings than to the king of Egypt. If faith is "a conviction of
things not seen", it is first and foremost a conviction regarding the
unseen God, as has been emphasized already in the affirmation
that he who comes to God must believe that He is (verse 6). Our
author probably means that Moses' lifelong vision of God was the
secret of his faith and perseverance.[202] Philo describes Moses as
the "beholder of that world of nature which cannot be seen",[203]
by contrast with Pharaoh, who "did not acknowledge any deity
that could be discerned by the mind alone, or any apart from those
that could be seen".[204] Here again there is a suggestion to the
readers of the epistle that the invisible order is the real and
permanent one, and not such a visible but transient establishment
as Judaism enjoyed up to A.D. 70.

28 It was by faith, too, that Moses instituted the Passover in
accordance with the divine command. The Passover became a

---

[200] Ex. 12:31ff. Several other attempts at reconciling our present passage
with Ex. 2:14f. have been made. A. B. Davidson (*ad loc.*) says: "So far as his life
was concerned he feared, but in a higher region he had no fear; he took steps
to save his life in faith of a time when God in accordance with His promises
would interpose to redeem His people, just as in this faith he had already acted
in opposition to the king." C. J. Vaughan (*ad loc.*) explains that "the two fears
are different: the one is the fear arising from the discovery of his slaying the
Egyptian, the other is the fear of Pharaoh's anger on discovering his flight".
C. Spicq (*ad loc.*) follows H. von Soden in seeing a reference to the whole series
of interviews and disputes with Pharaoh from Moses' return from Midian to
the Exodus (Ex. 5:1-15:21).

[201] Gk. τὸν γὰρ ἀόρατον ὡς ὁρῶν ἐκαρτέρησεν. G. H. Whitaker, in a note on
this passage (*ExT* xxvii [1915-16], p. 186), quotes examples from Plutarch
where καρτερέω, in association with a verb of seeing, means "to behold without
wavering".

[202] For Moses' perseverance *cf.* Josephus's use of καρτερία in *Antiquities* ii. 256,
quoted at the end of n. 194 (p. 322); although our author means something more
than the ability to go without food!

[203] *Change of Names*, 7: "Moses' entry into the darkness (Ex. 20:21) is
explained as denoting that essence which is invisible (ἀόρατος) and incorporeal."
Elsewhere Philo, in reference to Moses' prayer that he might see the divine
glory (Ex. 33:13), speaks of that purified and initiated mind which, "lifting its
eyes above and beyond creation, receives a clear vision of the Uncreated" (*Leg.
Alleg.* iii. 100f.; *cf. Life of Moses* i. 158).

[204] *Life of Moses* i. 88.

THE EPISTLE TO THE HEBREWS

perpetual memorial[205] for Israel of the last night that their fore-fathers spent in Egypt, when the angel of death[206] passed through the land destroying the firstborn in every home, apart from those whose doorways were marked by the blood of the paschal lamb, for at the threshold of those dwellings the God of Israel Himself stood guard and prevented the destroyer from entering.[207] Else-where in the New Testament Jesus is presented as the antitype of the paschal lamb;[208] if our author does not press this corre-spondence, it may be that he did not wish to detract from the correspondence between the death of Jesus and the annual sacrifice on the Day of Atonement.

(g) Faith at the Exodus and Settlement

Ch. 11:29-31

29 By faith they passed through the Red sea as by dry land: which the Egyptians assaying to do[209] were swallowed up.[210]

30 By faith the walls of Jericho fell down, after they had been compassed about for seven days.

---

[205] This is probably the force of the perfect tense πεποίηκεν (cf. p. 316, n. 166).

[206] Called here "the destroyer" (ὁ ὀλοθρεύων), after Ex. 12:23, LXX. In Wisdom 18:15 the agent of destruction is the "all-powerful word" (λόγος) of God, leaping down from His throne into the doomed land, "a stern warrior carrying the sharp sword of thy authentic command" (cf. p. 81). In the Exodus narrative the agent of the destruction is for the most part left out and the work is ascribed directly to Yahweh, as is also the protection of the Israelites.

[207] "When I see the blood, I will pass over you" (Ex. 12:13; cf. 12:23) means "I will cross over your threshold" (from the Hebrew verb pāsaḥ used in this clause is derived the name pesaḥ given to the feast, taken over into Greek as the loanword πάσχα, "passover", as here).

[208] I Cor. 5:7; the same thought underlies John's passion narrative (cf., e.g., John 19:36, quoting Ex. 12:46).

[209] Gk. ἧς πεῖραν λαβόντες οἱ Αἰγύπτιοι, literally: "of which [the sea] the Egyptians making trial". They ventured upon the sea without faith and were drowned. See p. 339, n. 278 (on v. 36).

[210] Gk. κατεπόθησαν (as in Ex. 15:4, LXX), "were swallowed up" (aorist passive of καταπίνω). A few minuscules, including 104 and 1912, have κατεποντίσθησαν, "were plunged or drowned in the sea".

31   By faith Rahab the harlot[211] perished not with them that
were disobedient,[212] having received the spies with
peace.[213]

29   The crossing of the Red Sea—the "Sea of Reeds",[214] as
the Hebrew has it—was the immediate sequel to the keeping of
the Passover. It might well have been cited as a further instance
of Moses' faith, but here "all they that came out of Egypt by
Moses" (Ch. 3:16) are associated with him in this act of faith.
Nevertheless it was Moses' faith that inspired them to move
forward into the sea; they were full of fear and complaint as they
saw the water before them and the pursuing Egyptian army
overtaking them from the rear, until at Moses' command they
advanced and saw "the salvation of Jehovah" (Ex. 14:13). For
the Sea of Reeds receded in front of them by reason of the strong
east wind which blew all that night,[215] and they were able to walk
across as on dry land.[216] But the pursuing Egyptians were but
half-way across when the sea returned to its usual place and
overwhelmed them. This great victory which Yahweh won for
His people was celebrated in the "Song of the Sea" preserved in
Ex. 15:1ff., and commemorated elsewhere in terms of the pri-
maeval cosmic triumph of the Creator over the forces of chaos.[217]
It supplied a pictorial form of language for describing later
deliverances, like the release from the Babylonian exile;[218] and is

---

211   Gk. ἡ πόρνη, for which ℵ* reads ἡ ἐπιλεγομένη πόρνη, "she who was
called the harlot" or "the so-called harlot", as though to tone down the un-
compromising wording of the text. Cf. I Clem. 12:1. See p. 328, n. 228.

212   Gk. τοῖς ἀπειθήσασιν, for which P46 reads τοῖς ἀπιστήσασιν (cf. Ch. 3:18
for the same variant).

213   That is, in a friendly manner. "Peace" may refer to the customary
greeting Shālōm ("Peace be upon you" or "Peace be upon this house"), which
was honored in action as well as in word (cf. Luke 10:5f.).

214   Heb. yam sūph (Ex. 13:18, etc.), used of the Gulfs of Suez and Aqaba, in
this instance of a northern extension of the Gulf of Suez. LXX renders it ἡ ἐρυθρὰ
θάλασσα ("the Red Sea").

215   Ex. 14:21.

216   Philo exaggerates the miracle by telling how the sea-bed between the
two walls of water "dried up and became a broad highway capable of carrying
a host of people" (Life of Moses i. 177).

217   Cf. Isa. 51:9–11.

218   Cf. Isa. 35:6ff.; 40:3ff.; 44:27; Jer. 23:7f.

used in the New Testament as a type of Christian baptism.[219] But our author is concerned with it for its bearing on the theme of faith. Why did the sea recede before the Israelites so that they passed over dry-shod? At one level it was an act of God;[220] at another level it could be ascribed to the east wind; but our author ascribes it to the Israelites' faith. It was none the less an act of God, who used the east wind to accomplish His saving purpose, but it was by faith that they appropriated the deliverance thus procured for them. And why were the Egyptians drowned when they tried in their turn to cross the sea? At one level this also was an act of God;[221] at another level it could be ascribed to the abating of the east wind, coupled with the sinking of their chariots in the mud;[222] but our author implies that they came to grief because they had no faith.

The Israelites' faith on this occasion consisted in their willingness to go forward at God's word,[223] although it seemed impossible to get across the sea. Moses assured them that their God would act on their behalf, and although they could not see how He would do so, they obeyed. But no further act of faith is recorded here throughout the wilderness wanderings. These forty years have already been described in the epistle as a period of unbelief, throughout which God was displeased with that generation.[224] Reference might have been made to Caleb and Joshua's encouraging minority report when they came back from surveying the promised land (Num. 13:30; 14:38); but our author is not attempting to exhaust the biblical examples of faith. Even of Moses' patience throughout those years nothing is said, although indeed the words "he endured, as seeing him who is invisible" (verse 27) belong to this final phase of his life at least as much as to the earlier phases.[225] But the closing obituary testimony of the

---

[219] I Cor. 10:1f.

[220] Cf. Ex. 14:14: "Jehovah will fight for you, and ye shall hold your peace."

[221] Cf. Ex. 15:1: "The horse and his rider hath he thrown into the sea."

[222] Cf. Ex. 14:25.

[223] Cf. Ex. 14:15: "Speak unto the children of Israel, that they go forward."

[224] Cf. Ch. 3:7ff. (pp. 60ff.).

[225] According to the original text of the now incompletely preserved *Assumption of Moses* (early first century A.D.), the final reward of Moses' fidelity was that his body was taken to heaven after his death (there is an allusion to this in Jude 9; cf. Clement of Alexandria, *Comments on Jude*; Origen, *First Principles* iii. 2. 1).

Pentateuch, "there hath not arisen a prophet since in Israel like unto Moses, whom Jehovah knew face to face" (Deut. 34:10), would have been regarded by our author as no longer valid, now that a greater than Moses had come and established a better covenant than that of Moses' day.

30   The record of faith, then, is suspended for forty years and resumed with the entry into Canaan. By whose faith did the walls of Jericho fall down? Primarily by Joshua's; he believed and obeyed the divine instructions given him when he saw the angel "prince of the host of Jehovah" (Josh. 5:14). But the people's faith was involved as well, for they carried out faithfully the instructions which Joshua communicated to them, until the city fell. But they could not see how it would fall; on the face of it, nothing could seem more foolish than for grown men to march round a strong fortress for seven days on end, led by seven priests blowing rams' horns. Who ever heard of a fortress being captured that way?[226] Nevertheless, when they marched round the city seven times on the seventh day and heard the last blast on the rams' horns, they "shouted with a great shout, and the wall fell down flat, so that the people went up into the city, every man straight before him, and they took the city" (Josh. 6:20).

Archaeology can throw much light on the collapse of ancient cities—although in the case of Late Bronze Age Jericho it has thrown much less light than might have been hoped, less indeed than was at one time believed.[227] But the forces that operate in the unseen realm, such as the power of faith, cannot be dug up by the excavator's spade. We may now never discover in material terms what made the walls of Jericho fall, whether earthquake or subsidence or something else, but our author ascribes their fall

---

[226] The Egyptian of Acts 21:38 promised his followers that the walls of Jerusalem would fall before them at his word (Josephus, *Antiquities* xx. 169ff.; cf. *War* ii. 261ff.).

[227] The discoveries on the site made under the direction of J. Garstang from 1929 onwards relate for the most part not, as was thought at the time (cf. J. Garstang, *The Story of Jericho* [London, 1940]), to Joshua's Jericho, but to earlier settlements on the site. The destruction of Late Bronze Age Jericho is very difficult to date archaeologically, owing to the considerable erosion of the site during the four centuries that elapsed before the foundation of Iron Age Jericho (I Kings 16:34), but it cannot be fixed before the second half of the fourteenth century B.C. Cf. K. M. Kenyon, *Digging up Jericho* (London, 1957); *Archaeology in the Holy Land* (London, 1960), pp. 209ff.

to the power of that faith which found expression in Joshua's submissive reply to the divine messenger: "What saith my lord unto his servant?" (Josh. 5:14). It is by this same faith that other Jerichoes, both large and small, can still be overthrown. "The weapons we wield," says Paul, "are not merely human, but divinely potent to demolish strongholds; we demolish sophistries and all that rears its proud head against the knowledge of God; we compel every human thought to surrender in obedience to Christ" (II Cor. 10:4f., NEB).

31 The next example of faith is the most surprising that we have met thus far—Rahab, the harlot[228] of Jericho. Yet this is not the only place in the New Testament where she receives honorable mention for her faith: in Jas. 2:25 her kindly treatment of Joshua's spies is one of two arguments for the thesis that faith without works is dead, the other argument being Abraham's offering up of Isaac. In fact Rahab, despite her antecedents, enjoys a place of esteem in Jewish and Christian records. The two scouts whom Joshua sent to spy out Jericho found a night's lodging in Rahab's house, and when the authorities discovered where they were, she concealed them and then helped them to escape, stipulating only that her life should be saved when Jericho fell into their hands. For, as she told them, the news of the Exodus and of Israel's victories in Transjordan had already reached Jericho and caused great alarm and despondency there; "for Jehovah your God, he is God in heaven above, and on earth beneath" (Josh. 2:11). Jericho's fall was therefore a foregone conclusion. They promised to protect her, and so, when Jericho was taken, she and the members of her household were saved from the massacre when the city was "devoted" to Israel's God, and incorporated in the commonwealth of Israel (Josh. 6:25). It was self-evidently her faith in the God of Israel that moved her to behave as she did, and led to her preservation. Indeed, she is probably mentioned in yet another place in the New Testament, for (in spite of a

---

[228] Heb. *zōnāh* (Josh. 2:1), *i.e.* a secular harlot, not a temple prostitute (*qedēshāh*). Attempts were made in antiquity to give her a more respectable calling (*cf.* p. 325, n. 211); thus Josephus (*Antiquities* v. 7ff.) makes her the keeper of an inn (καταγώγιον), as does also the Targum of Jonathan at Josh. 2:1 (Aram. *pundeqīthā*, a loanword from Gk. πανδοκεύτρια, "innkeeper"). Rashi in his commentary makes her a seller of food. *Cf.* D. J. Wiseman, "Rahab of Jericho", *Tyndale House Bulletin* (Cambridge, June 1964), pp. 8ff.

difference of spelling)[229] there can be little doubt that she is the Rahab who appears in Matt. 1:5 as the wife of Salmon, prince of Judah, the mother of Boaz, the ancestress of King David and therefore also of our Lord.[230] The earliest Christian writer outside the New Testament canon, Clement of Rome, recounts the story of Rahab to illustrate the virtues of faith and hospitality, and makes her a prophetess to boot, since the scarlet rope by which she let the spies down from her window on the city wall,[231] and by which her house was identified at the capture of the city, foreshowed "that through the blood of the Lord all who trust and hope in God shall have redemption" (I Clem. 12:7).[232]

(h) Further Examples of Faith

Ch. 11:32-38

32 And what shall I more say? for the time will fail me if I tell[233] of Gideon, Barak, Samson, Jephthah; of David and Samuel and the[234] prophets:

33 who through faith subdued kingdoms,[235] wrought righteousness, obtained promises, stopped the mouths of lions,

---

229 'Ραχάβ in Matt. 1:5 as against 'Ραάβ here and in Jas. 2:25, but the χ of 'Ραχάβ represents more accurately the ה of Heb. רָחָב.

230 According to TB *Megillah* 14b she married into another illustrious house, becoming the wife of Joshua and the ancestress of eight priests who were also prophets, including Jeremiah and Huldah. (How descendants of the Ephraimite Joshua and the Canaanite Rahab could be priests in Israel is quite a problem.)

231 Her house was on the city wall (Josh. 2:15), so their egress from Jericho was comparable to Paul's from Damascus (Acts 9:25; II Cor. 11:33). Sir Charles Marston mentions the fancy that a charred piece of cord found in the course of Garstang's excavations on the site might be a relic of this scarlet rope (*The Bible Comes Alive* [London, 1937], pp. 86f.).

232 So also Justin, *Dialogue with Trypho*, 111; Irenaeus, *Heresies* iv. 20. 12, and many another since their day.

233 Gk. ἐπιλείψει με γὰρ διηγούμενον ὁ χρόνος. For the bearing of the masculine participle διηγούμενον on the authorship of the epistle see p. xl, n. 78.

234 Before "prophets" (προφητῶν) a few minuscules (*e.g.* 69, 1288) with the Peshitta and Harclean Syriac and several other eastern versions add "other" (ἄλλων).

235 Gk. βασιλείας, for which P⁴⁶ reads βασιλεῖς ("kings").

34 quenched the power of fire, escaped the edge of the sword, from weakness were made strong,[236] waxed mighty in war, turned to flight armies of aliens.

35 Women[237] received their dead by a resurrection: and others were tortured,[238] not accepting their deliverance; that they might obtain a better resurrection:

36 and others had trial of mockings and scourgings, yea, moreover of bonds and imprisonment:

37 they were stoned, they were sawn asunder, they were tempted,[239] they were slain with the sword: they went about in sheepskins, in goatskins; being destitute, afflicted, ill-treated

38 (of whom the world was not worthy), wandering in[240] deserts and mountains and caves, and the holes of the earth.

32 The comparative detail in which examples of faith have been adduced from the earlier period of Old Testament history now gives place to a more summary account covering the later period. With a rhetorical transition[241] our author goes on, first

---

[236] Gk. ἐδυναμώθησαν, for which אᶜ with many later witnesses and TR have the compound ἐνεδυναμώθησαν (cf. Rom. 4:20). Cf. p. 336, n. 262.

[237] Gk. γυναῖκες (nom.), which is certainly the required form here (so the Byzantine text and TR against P¹³ א* A D* 33 1912, which exhibit the accusative γυναῖκας, impossible in this context).

[238] Gk. ἐτυμπανίσθησαν, for which D* has the classical compound ἀπετυμπανίσθησαν. The martyrs here referred to were stretched on a frame, as skin is stretched on a drum (τύμπανον), and beaten to death (see pp. 337f.).

[239] Gk. ἐπρίσθησαν ἐπειράσθησαν. So P¹³ A 1739 and many other Greek witnesses with the Latin and Armenian versions and TR. The order of the verbs is reversed in א L 326 and the Harclean Syriac. Probably ἐπειράσθησαν represents a false dittography and the true reading is ἐπρίσθησαν alone; so P⁴⁶ 2 327 (2423*?) with the Syriac Peshitta and Sahidic versions (cf. Calvin, ad loc.; G. Zuntz, The Text of the Epistles, pp. 47f.). A variant spelling of ἐπρίσθησαν, the itacistic ἐπρήσθησαν, appears in the minuscule 1923 and is implied in the Bohairic rendering ("they were burned"), as though it were aorist passive of πίμπρημι and not of πρίζω. See p. 341, n. 290.

[240] Gk. ἐν, for which several ancient witnesses have ἐπί (P¹³ א A P 33 etc.); the two prepositions were easily confused in uncial writing.

[241] Gk. καὶ τί ἔτι λέγω; (cf. τί δεῖ πλείω λέγειν; Josephus, Antiquities xx. 257). The following turn of phrase, "for the time will fail me if I tell ..." (ἐπιλείψει με γὰρ διηγούμενον ὁ χρόνος), has no lack of parallels in the classical orators and in Philo (cf. Spicq, ad loc.).

of all, to mention six men by name spanning the interval between the settlement in Canaan and the early monarchy. The six names are not given in strict chronological order (or the order in which they appear in the biblical narrative); in fact, if we arrange them in three pairs, the two men in each pair are named here in the reverse order to that of their Old Testament appearance, for in the Old Testament Barak appears before Gideon, Jephthah before Samson, and Samuel before David. The reversal of the order of Samuel and David may be intended to bring Samuel into closer contact with "the prophets" who are mentioned immediately after, Samuel being the first in the continuous "prophetic succession" of the age of the Hebrew monarchy.[242] The four figures from the book of Judges who here precede "David and Samuel" remind us of the four who are listed in I Sam. 12:11, where Samuel, in a speech to the people after they have chosen Saul to be their king, recalls how in their earlier times of distress "Jehovah sent Jerubbaal, and Bedan, and Jephthah, and Samuel, and delivered you out of the hand of your enemies on every side". Jerubbaal is another name for Gideon, and if Bedan is identical with Barak (as the Septuagint and Peshitta versions indicate), then Gideon and Barak appear in the same order as here. (The inclusion of Samuel in this way alongside the others may seem strange, since Samuel is the speaker; but it not unparalleled: in our own day General de Gaulle refers to himself in the third person when he is speaking historically. It is interesting, however, that for "Samuel" the Syriac Peshitta reads "Samson".)[243] On three out of these four—Gideon (Judg. 6:34), Jephthah (Judg. 11:29) and Samson (Judg. 13:25, etc.)—the Spirit of Yahweh is said to have come, and this could be taken as conclusive evidence of their faith.

Gideon was Israel's champion against the beduin Midianites; his small force of three hundred men, equipped with torches in earthenware jars, and trumpets, threw the host of Midian into

---

[242] David was a prophet (Acts 2:30; cf. II Sam. 23:2), but he was not reckoned in the prophetic "succession", still less was he a member of any prophetic guild.

[243] The Peshitta of I Sam. 12:11 replaces "Jerubbaal" by his more familiar name "Gideon"; hence it lists the four as Gideon, Barak, Jephthah and Samson. But its insertion of Deborah between Gideon and Barak shows that we are dealing with a targum of the original and not with the kind of translation that could be used for textual criticism.

panic and won a signal victory.[244] Barak was commander of the army of the tribes of Israel who united against Sisera, commander of the confederate Canaanite chariot-force, and defeated him and his followers "in Taanach by the waters of Megiddo" (Judg. 5:19). It is surprising to find Barak mentioned here as an example of faith rather than the prophetess Deborah, not to mention Jael, "the wife of Heber the Kenite, blessed ... above women in the tent" (Judg. 5:24). For Barak refused to take the field against Sisera when Deborah commanded him, in Yahweh's name, to do so, unless she went with him.[245] Yet his very refusal may have been, in its way, a token of faith; his insistence on having Deborah with him was perhaps an expression of his faith in the God whose servant and spokeswoman Deborah was. And when he was told by her that the expedition which he was undertaking would not be for his own honor, he led it none the less; it was not his own honor, but the triumph of Yahweh and His people, that he sought.

Samson, who championed Israel's cause against the Philistines in his own single-handed way, may strike one as an odd choice among illustrations of faith; yet the narrative of Judges portrays him as one who was deeply conscious of the invisible God, and of his own call to be an instrument in God's hand against the enemy.[246] And what of Jephthah, commander of the Transjordanian tribes against the Ammonites? Posterity remembers him chiefly for his rash vow; yet, rash as it was, it was a token of his sincere though uninstructed devotion to the God of Israel. The message which he sent to the king of Ammon (Judg. 11:14–27), with its historical retrospect reaching back to the Exodus and wilderness wanderings, expresses his appreciation of Yahweh's guidance of His people in those early days and his confidence that Yahweh will judge their cause today.

David is the only king to be mentioned by name; his record displays faults enough, but it also displays a humble readiness to repent and seek pardon from God, and a conviction of God's providence and faithfulness.[247] He made an earnest endeavor to put into practice the ideal of kingship portrayed in the poem

---

[244] Judg. 7:7ff.
[245] Judg. 4:8.
[246] *Cf.* especially Judg. 14:4.
[247] *Cf.* II Sam. 12:13; 24:10–14.

which has come down to us with the title "The last words of David":

"When one rules justly over men,
    ruling in the fear of God,
he dawns on them like the morning light,
    like the sun shining forth upon a cloudless morning,
    like rain that makes grass to sprout from the earth.
Yea, does not my house stand so with God?
    For he has made with me an everlasting covenant,
    ordered in all things and secure" (II Sam. 23:3ff., RSV).

Like Abraham and others before him, he too received promises from God, promises regarding his house "for a great while to come" (II Sam. 7:19), "the sure mercies of David" which found their fruition, as did the promises to Abraham, with the coming of Christ.[248]

None can question Samuel's fitness for inclusion here.

"Samuel, beloved by his Lord,
    a prophet of the Lord, established the kingdom
    and anointed rulers over his people.
By the law of the Lord he judged the congregation,
    and the Lord watched over Jacob.
By his faithfulness he was proved to be a prophet,
    and by his words he became known as a trustworthy seer"
                          (Sir. 46:13ff.).

Samuel's name is well worthy to stand alongside those of Moses, Joshua and David in the annals of Israel. He manifested the prophetic gift in his youth, and when the central sanctuary at Shiloh was destroyed by the Philistines, and the ark of the covenant, the palladium of Israel's nationhood, taken into captivity, it was he who proved equal to the task of rallying the shattered morale of his people. He showed them that God was still in their midst, even if the ark was in the hands of the Philistines; and indeed, when the ark was restored, he left it in an obscure place, lest the people's faith should once more be reposed in it instead of God. He went annually in circuit as judge in Israel,

---

248 In Isa. 55:3f. "the sure mercies of David" are bound up with the sending of "a witness to the peoples, a leader and commander to the peoples", who must be identified both with the Davidic king of Isa. 11:1ff. and with the Servant of Yahweh of Isa. 42:1ff. (*cf.* Acts 13:34).

and undertook priestly duties as the nation's representative with widespread acceptance. The central sanctuary was no more, but one man, under God, served as the focus of national life. He recalled Israel to its covenant-loyalty, and thanks to his inspiring leadership they defeated the Philistines on the very field of their earlier disaster.[249] Not without cause has Samuel been described as "God's emergency man".[250]

It is in the time of Samuel that we first meet prophetic guilds,[251] and from then on to post-exilic days the Old Testament narrative presents us with a sequence of prophets who not only spoke but acted for God—Elijah and Elisha, Amos and Hosea, Isaiah and Jeremiah, and others who, not expressly named by our author, were certainly in his mind as he penned these words.

33 The exploits of these warriors and messengers of God are listed in general terms. The subduing of kingdoms, beginning with the overthrow of Sihon and Og in the wilderness, goes on through the period of Joshua and the judges, and reaches its climax in the reign of David, whose empire stretched from the Egyptian frontier to the Euphrates.[252] Those rulers of Israel also established righteousness within the areas they controlled, in the spirit of that ancient "coronation oath" preserved to us as Psalm 101. This they did through faith[253] in God, whose own throne is founded on "righteousness and justice" (Ps. 97:2). They "obtained promises"[254] that God would be with them as they served His cause in faith, and obtained the fulfilment of His promises in the event; the promises made to David, as we have seen, had regard not only to his personal fortunes but to the destiny awaiting his house. It was of these latter promises that Paul spoke in the syna-

---

[249] I Sam. 7:3–16.

[250] In the title of a book by W. W. Fereday, *Samuel: God's Emergency Man* (Kilmarnock, 1945).

[251] *Cf.* I Sam. 10:5, 10f.; 19:20.

[252] The verb καταγωνίζομαι, "subdue", is used by Josephus of David's subduing the Philistines, καταγωνισαμένῳ Παλαιστίνους (*Antiquities* vii. 53).

[253] In vv. 33, 39 διὰ πίστεως is a variation on the recurrent πίστει of this chapter (*cf.* κατὰ πίστιν in vv. 7, 13).

[254] Gk. ἐπέτυχον ἐπαγγελιῶν, as in Ch. 6:15 (see p. 129 with n. 76). Whether the verb is ἐπιτυγχάνω, as here, or λαμβάνω, as in v. 13 (see p. 303, n. 109), or ἀναδέχομαι, as in v. 17, or κομίζομαι, as in v. 39, it is the context that must determine whether the receiving of the promise itself is meant, or the experiencing of its fulfilment, or both.

gogue at Pisidian Antioch when, after telling how God raised up
David to be Israel's king, he continued: "Of this man's seed hath
God according to promise brought unto Israel a Saviour, Jesus"
(Acts 13:23).

As for stopping the mouths of lions, we recognize immediately
the reference to Daniel, thrown into the lions' den for his fidelity
to God, but protected from their attacks "forasmuch" (in his own
words) "as before him innocency was found in me" (Dan. 6:22).[255]

34   Those who "quenched the power of fire" were Shadrach,
Meshach and Abednego, who refused to fall down and worship
Nebuchadnezzar's great golden image. They knew that their God
was able to deliver them from the furnace, but they had no means
of knowing whether He would in fact deliver them or not—"but
if not", said they, "be it known unto thee, O king, that we will not
serve thy gods, nor worship the golden image which thou hast set
up" (Dan. 3:18).[256] Had they received a special revelation that
their lives would be preserved, it would have called for considerable
faith to act upon it in face of the burning fiery furnace; but to
behave as they did without any revelation of the kind called for
much greater faith. The people to whom this epistle was sent
might well have a fiery ordeal[257] to face in the near future, but
whether life or death was their portion they could be sure of divine
companionship in the midst of it such as the three Hebrews
enjoyed.

We can think of several prophets and others who "escaped the
edge of the sword": Elijah was delivered from Jezebel,[258] Elisha
from her son Jehoram,[259] Jeremiah from Jehoiakim.[260] (But not
all were delivered, as verse 37 reminds us.)

It could be said of many of the judges and prophets that "from

---

255   *Cf.* the references to this incident in I Macc. 2:60 (where Mattathias on
his deathbed reminds his sons how "Daniel because of his innocence was
delivered from the mouth of the lions"); IV Macc. 16:3, 21; 18:13 (in the
martyrology of the seven brothers and their mother).

256   *Cf.* I Macc. 2:59; IV Macc. 13:9; 16:3; 18:12. In IV Macc. 16:21f.
the mother reminds her seven sons how Daniel and his three companions
"endured (ὑπέμειναν) for God's sake" and exhorts them: "You also, then, having
the same faith toward God, be not embittered."

257   *Cf.* the πύρωσις of I Pet. 4:12.

258   I Kings 19:2ff.

259   II Kings 6:31ff.

260   Jer. 36:19, 26.

weakness they were made strong". Gideon was least in his father's house, by his own account, and his family was the poorest in Manasseh;[261] yet Gideon and his three hundred were used by God to accomplish a great deliverance. The earliest comment on these words is provided by Clement of Rome. Clement was well acquainted with the Epistle to the Hebrews; in particular, he had studied this chapter and attempted to identify some of the heroes of faith who are here referred to anonymously. On the words "from weakness were made strong" he comments: "Many women have been made strong[262] through the grace of God and have accomplished many deed of valor"(I Clem. 55:3). He goes on to instance Judith and Esther.[263] What he says of Judith suggests that he thought of her as one in whom the remaining words of this verse came true: "waxed mighty in war, turned to flight armies of aliens".[264] "The blessed Judith," he says, "when her city was besieged, asked the elders to let her go out into the camp of the aliens.[265] So, exposing herself to danger, she went out for love of her country and people when they were being besieged, and the Lord delivered Holofernes into the hand of a woman" (I Clem. 55:4f.). But what was true of Judith in literature, was equally true of many Israelites in history, from the days of Joshua and the judges down to the war of independence led by Judas Maccabaeus and his brothers; they and their followers had their "weakness ... turned to strength, they grew powerful in war, they put foreign armies to rout" (NEB). They knew, in the words of Jonathan, that "there is no restraint to Jehovah, to save by many or by few" (I Sam. 14:6); they believed that the battle was not theirs but God's,[266] and therefore one of them chased a thousand, and two put ten thousand to flight.[267]

---

[261] Judg. 6:15.

[262] Gk. ἐνδυναμωθεῖσαι, the same verb as here (ἐδυναμώθησαν) with the prefix ἐν (both forms are found elsewhere in NT). See p. 330, n. 236.

[263] He describes Esther as exposing herself to danger on her people's behalf because she was "perfect in faith" (ἡ τελεία κατὰ πίστιν).

[264] Gk. ἐγενήθησαν ἰσχυροὶ ἐν πολέμῳ, παρεμβολὰς ἔκλιναν ἀλλοτρίων. (The Gentile foes are repeatedly called ἀλλότριοι in I Maccabees.)

[265] Gk. εἰς τὴν παρεμβολὴν τῶν ἀλλοφύλων, using παρεμβολή in the sense of "camp" (cf. Heb. 13:11, 13), whereas here our author uses it in the sense of "army", a sense which it bears very frequently in I Maccabees.

[266] Cf. II Chron. 20:15.

[267] Cf. Josh. 23:10; Deut. 32:30; also Lev. 26:8.

35 The women who "received their dead by a resurrection" were the poor widow of Zarephath and the wealthy woman of Shunem; the son of the former was restored to her by Elijah, the son of the latter by Elisha.[268] In the former instance the faith was Elijah's rather than the woman's; when her son died, she could only think that the prophet was a visitant of judgment to her house, bringing nemesis in this form for her sin. But Elijah's prayer of faith, "O Jehovah my God, I pray thee, let this child's soul come into him again" (I Kings 17:21), was heard and the boy was restored to his mother. The woman of Shunem was an Israelite (not a foreigner, like the widow of Zarephath), and when her little son died, she showed what spirit she was of by hasting to Mount Carmel to lay her plaint before the man of God. Elisha matched her faith with his own, and by prayer and appropriate action he brought the child back to life. Both these incidents are described as a resurrection;[269] nowadays we sometimes distinguish between the resuscitation of a body to mortal life and the resurrection of the dead to life immortal; but no such distinction is made in the biblical vocabulary. The distinction is nevertheless real, though not verbal; our author goes on to speak of some who sought a "better resurrection"[270] than that experienced by the two boys just mentioned, this "better resurrection" being a rising to the life of the age to come.

"Others were tortured," he says, "not accepting their deliverance,[271] that they might obtain a better resurrection." The particular form of torture indicated by the Greek verb is being stretched on the rack and beaten to death.[272] This was precisely the punishment meted out to Eleazar, one of the noble confessors

---

[268] I Kings 17:17ff.; II Kings 4:17ff.

[269] Gk. ἐξ ἀναστάσεως.

[270] Gk. ἵνα κρείττονος ἀναστάσεως τύχωσιν.

[271] Gk. ἀπολύτρωσις (which normally means "redemption", as in Ch. 9:15). For the more general sense of "deliverance" cf. Dan. 4:32 (LXX), where Nebuchadnezzar tells how, after his madness, "the time of my deliverance (ἀπολύτρωσις) came". "But even here the deliverance not accepted resolves itself into a ransom refused, the price of recantation, and in *Daniel*, as with Ahab [I Kings 21:27–29], reformation is viewed as the price of the prolongation of Nebuchadnezzar's tenure of power" (E. K. Simpson, *Words Worth Weighing in the Greek New Testament* [London, 1946], p. 8, n. 1). Cf. p. 201, n. 84 (on the uncompounded λύτρωσις in Ch. 9:12).

[272] Gk. τυμπανίζω (cf. p. 330, n. 238).

of Maccabaean days, who willingly accepted death rather than forswear his loyalty to God.[273] In II Maccabees the story of his martyrdom is followed by the record of the mother and her seven sons who endured this and other forms of torture sooner than transgress the law of God.[274] In this story one brother after another declares his readiness to accept torture and death because of the hope of resurrection. One says to the king: "You accursed wretch, you dismiss us from this present life, but the King of the universe will raise us up to an everlasting renewal of life, because we have died for his laws" (II Macc. 7:9). Another holds out his limbs to be mutilated, saying: "I got these from heaven, and because of his laws I disdain them, and from him I hope to get them back again" (II Macc. 7:11). And yet another at the point of death says: "One cannot but choose to die at the hands of men and to cherish the hope that God gives of being raised again by him. But for you there will be no resurrection to life!" (II Macc. 7:14). The resurrection to which they looked forward was "better" than that to which the boys of Zarephath and Shunem had been raised by Elijah and Elisha. Those boys were restored to mortal life, and in due course died; the resurrection for which the Maccabaean martyrs hoped was a resurrection to endless life. They could have avoided torture and death and accepted "deliverance" had they been prepared to compromise with the idolatrous requirements of Antiochus Epiphanes and his officers, but they knew that, if they did so, resurrection to life could never be theirs. They remained faithful unto death, and have been honored ever since by all who set loyalty to God above all else. In the Christian calendar the first day of August is marked as the festival of the "martyrdom of the holy Maccabees"; the Kontakion in the *Horologion* or office book of the Greek Church calls them the "greatest martyrs before the martyrs".[275]

---

[273] *Cf.* II Macc. 6:19, 28, where Eleazar goes willingly and unhesitatingly to the rack (τύμπανον) rather than taste unlawful food. In IV Maccabees it is on the wheel (τροχός) that Eleazar and the seven young men are tortured, in a manner reminiscent of the mediaeval penalty of breaking on the wheel (IV Macc. 5:32; 8:13; 9:12, 17, 19, 20; 10:7; 11:10, 17; 15:22).

[274] II Macc. 7:1ff.; IV Macc. 8:1ff.

[275] Gk. πρὸ μαρτύρων μέγιστοι μάρτυρες. Gregory of Nazianzus defended their enrolment among Christian martyrs on the ground that "if they suffered so courageously before the coming of Christ, their achievement would have been so much greater still, if they had lived after Him and had His death for

The Old Testament has but little to say about the future life. Long life in the land which the Lord their God had given them bulked more largely in the eyes of pious Israelites throughout most of the Old Testament period than the life of the world to come. Even at the beginning of the second century B.C. Ben Sira regards posterity's remembrance of a good man's virtues as the kind of immortality that ought chiefly to be desired.[276] But when the persecution broke out under Antiochus Epiphanes, the fear of the Lord was more likely to lead to an early and painful death than to length of days. The martyrs had the faith to perceive that death and the gloom of Sheol could not be the final issue of their loyalty to God. The hope of resurrection blazed up and burned brightly before their eyes, giving them added courage to endure their torments. While the doctrine of resurrection was implicit in the biblical revelation at a much earlier date—Jesus pointed out that it is involved in God's designation of Himself as the God of Abraham, Isaac and Jacob in Ex. 3:6[277]—it did not receive general acceptance among the Jews until the age of persecution, but from then on it became a cardinal doctrine in Judaism (except among the Sadducees, whose party, however, did not survive the catastrophe of A.D. 70).

36 When the recipients of the letter read of some who experienced[278] "mockings and scourgings, ... bonds and imprisonment", they might well think of members of their own community who had suffered some of these things in earlier days, as our author had already reminded them. And if similar experiences awaited them again, it might help them to realize that they were not the first to tread this path. The martyrs referred to in verse 35 experienced mockery and scourging before they died;[279] and so did

---

their example" (Oration 15: *Panegyric on the Maccabees*, 1). On the Christian commemoration and elaboration of their martyrdom see M. Simon, "Les saints d'Israël dans la dévotion de l'église ancienne", *RHPR* xxxiv (1954), pp. 98ff.; B. M. Metzger, *An Introduction to the Apocrypha* (New York, 1957), pp. 147ff.

[276] This is the main point of the passage entitled "The Praise of the Elders" (Sir. 44:1ff.). (*Cf.* p. 279.)

[277] Mark 12:26f. and parallels.

[278] Gk. πεῖραν ἔλαβον (*cf.* πεῖραν λαβόντες in v. 29, p. 324, n. 209).

[279] The same word as is used here for "mocking" (ἐμπαιγμός) appears in II Macc. 7:7 ("they brought forward the second [brother] for their *sport*"); the cognate verb ἐμπαίζω is similarly used in II Macc. 7:10. The word used here for "scourging" (μάστιξ), with its derivative verb μαστιγόω, appears

the pioneer and perfecter of faith Himself. Since, however, the subject of this verse is "others",[280] our author probably had in mind others than the martyrs alluded to in verse 35. And one Old Testament figure of whom he may very well have thought was Jeremiah, the prophet of the new covenant. On one occasion Jeremiah was beaten and put in the stocks,[281] and complained that he had been made a laughingstock and an object of mockery not only by the public at large but by members of his own family.[282] At a later date he was beaten again and put in prison,[283] from which he was taken out and thrown into the muddy cistern from which he was rescued by Ebed-melech the Ethiopian.[284]

37a Jeremiah may also have been in our author's mind when he speaks of those who were stoned; this was his fate, according to tradition, at the hands of the Jews in Egypt who could not abide his protest against their continuing idolatry.[285] Jerusalem itself had a reputation, our Lord Himself being witness, for killing the prophets and stoning those who were sent to her;[286] and our author may have in mind (among others) the example actually mentioned by Jesus: the priest-prophet Zechariah, who was stoned to death at the instance of King Joash "in the court of the house of Jehovah" (II Chron. 24:21).[287]

As for being "sawn asunder", this was the traditional fate of the prophet Isaiah during Manasseh's reign. The apocryphon called the *Ascension of Isaiah*, which records the prophet's death,[288] is a composite work, Christian in its completed form; but the record

---

repeatedly in the martyrologies of Eleazar and the seven brothers in both II and IV Maccabees.

[280] Gk. ἕτεροι.

[281] Jer. 20:2.

[282] Jer. 20:7ff.

[283] Jer. 37:15.

[284] Jer. 38:6ff.

[285] Tertullian, *Scorpion Antidote* 8; Jerome, *Against Jovinian* ii. 37; cf. C. C. Torrey (ed.), *Lives of the Prophets* (Philadelphia, 1946), pp. 21, 35; H. J. Schoeps, "Die jüdischen Prophetenmorde", *Aus frühchristlicher Zeit* (Tübingen, 1950), pp. 126ff.

[286] Matt. 23:37; Luke 11:49ff.; 13:33f.; cf. Acts 7:52.

[287] Luke 11:51 (called in Matt. 23:35 "Zechariah son of Barachiah"; cf. Zech. 1:1; Josephus, *War* iv. 335ff.). In the *Protevangel of James* 23:1–24:4 he is confused with Zechariah the father of John the Baptist. Cf. p. 379, n. 178.

[288] Cf. also TB *Yebamoth* 49b; *Sanhedrin* 103b; Justin, *Dialogue with Trypho* 120; Tertullian, *On Patience* 14; Torrey, *op. cit.*, pp. 20, 34.

of Isaiah's martyrdom which it incorporates (especially parts of Chs. 1:1–3:12; 5:1b–14) is of Jewish origin and exhibits affinities with the Qumran literature.[289] It tells how Isaiah, to avoid the wickedness rampant in Jerusalem under Manasseh, left the capital for Bethlehem and then withdrew to the hill country. There he was seized and sawn in two with a wooden saw; before his death he commanded his disciples to escape the persecution by going to Phoenicia, "because", he said, "for me only has God mingled the cup" (Ch. 5:13).[290]

Some through faith, we have been told, "escaped the edge of the sword", but some through faith "were slain with the sword". Elijah escaped Jezebel's vengeance, but other prophets of the Lord were "slain ... with the sword" at that time (I Kings 19:10). If Jeremiah was delivered from Jehoiakim when that king sought his life, his fellow-prophet Uriah was not so fortunate; he foretold the doom of Judah and Jerusalem in similar terms to Jeremiah, and when he fled to Egypt he was extradited from there and brought before Jehoiakim, "who slew him with the sword, and cast his dead body into the grave of the common people" (Jer. 26:23). By faith one lived, and by faith the other died. So too in the apostolic age Herod Agrippa I "killed James the brother of John with the sword" (Acts 12:2); but when he tried to do the same to Peter, Peter escaped his hands.

37b–38 The following words are echoed by Clement of Rome when he exhorts his readers to be "imitators of those who 'went about in sheepskins and goatskins', announcing the advent of Christ"; he refers, he says, to the prophets Elijah and Elisha, and also Ezekiel (I Clem. 17:1). Elijah, we know, wore "a garment of

---

[289] *Cf.* D. Flusser, "The Apocryphal Book of *Ascensio Isaiae* and the Dead Sea Sect", *IEJ* iii (1953), pp. 30ff.

[290] Our author's reference is scarcely to the solitary LXX instance of πρίζω in Amos 1:3. On the text here see p. 330, n. 239. If the itacistic spelling of ἐπρίσθησαν as ἐπρήσθησαν were taken as the aorist passive of πίμπρημι and rendered "they were burned", we might think of the incident in II Macc. 6:11, where some pious Jews who had gathered in caves to observe the sabbath day secretly were betrayed to the Seleucid authorities and "were all burned together (συνεφλογίσθησαν), because their piety kept them from defending themselves, in view of their regard for that most holy day" (conceivably a variant account of the incident of I Macc. 2:29–38, mentioned on p. 342). Even if this incident is not in our author's mind, it is nevertheless true that while some through faith "quenched the power of fire" (v. 34), others through faith endured death by fire.

haircloth" (II Kings 1:8, RSV);[291] and in the *Ascension of Isaiah* those who accompanied Isaiah to his wilderness retreat "were all clothed in garments of hair" (Ch. 2:10). But the whole description of those who, roughly clad like this, endured destitution, affliction and ill-treatment as they wandered in desolate places and sought the shelter of caves, reminds us especially of those godly Jews who fled from the persecution under Antiochus Epiphanes—the "wise among the people" who, in Daniel's vision, fell "by the sword and by flame, by captivity and by spoil, many days" (Dan. 11:33).[292] Such were the "many who were seeking righteousness and justice" who, in the narrative of I Macc. 2:29-38, "went down to the wilderness to dwell there" with their families, "because evils pressed heavily upon them". When they were besieged in their hiding-places they refused to break the law by offering resistance or leaving their caves on the sabbath day, but died "in their innocence" to the number of a thousand persons. "*C'était magnifique, mais ce n'était pas la guerre*"; these were indeed men and women "of whom the world was not worthy". They were outlawed as people who were unfit for civilized society; the truth was that civilized society was unfit for them.[293] They might well take on their lips the psalmist's cry to God:

"For thy sake are we killed all the day long;
We are accounted as sheep for the slaughter."[294]

Faith in God carries with it no guarantee of comfort in this world: this was no doubt one of the lessons which our author wished his readers to learn. But it does carry with it great "recompense of reward" in the only world that ultimately matters.

---

[291] This may have been the "mantle" which Elisha inherited (II Kings 2:13f.). Gregory of Nazianzus speaks of it as "Elisha's fair inheritance, the sheepskin mantle, accompanied by the spirit of Elijah" (*Panegyric on Basil*, 74). A "hairy mantle" appears to have been the recognized uniform of the prophets (Zech. 12:4); we may compare John the Baptist's garment of camel's hair (Mark 1:6). But such raiment was voluntarily worn by the prophets; our author here is describing instances of privation and harsh necessity.

[292] *Cf.* I Macc. 2:28; II Macc. 5:27; 6:11; 10:6 ("they had been wandering in the mountains and caves like wild animals").

[293] But, in the words of Wisdom 3:5, "God tested them and found them worthy of himself".

[294] Ps. 44:22 (LXX 43:23); *cf.* Rom. 8:36.

(i) Epilogue: Faith's vindication comes with Christ

Ch. 11:39-40

39 And these all,[295] having had witness borne to them through their faith, received not the promise,[296]

40 God having provided some better thing concerning us, that apart from us they should not be made perfect.

39 From "righteous Abel" to those whose faith was so nobly manifested on the very eve of the coming of Christ, they all "won their record for faith"[297] (Moffatt). Some of them, as we were told in verse 33, "obtained promises", but none of them received *the* promise in the sense of witnessing its fulfilment. They lived and died in prospect of a fulfilment which none of them experienced on earth; yet so real was that fulfilment to them that it gave them power to press upstream, against the current of their environment, and to live on earth as citizens of that commonwealth whose foundations are firmly laid in the unseen and eternal order. Their record is on high, and on earth as well, for the instruction and encouragement of men and women of later days.

40 But now the promise has been fulfilled; the age of the new covenant has dawned; the Christ to whose day they looked forward has come and by His self-offering and His high-priestly ministry in the presence of God He has procured perfection for them—and for us. "With us in mind, God had made a better plan,[298] that only in company with us should they reach their

---

[295] Gk. καὶ οὗτοι πάντες (*cf.* οὗτοι πάντες in v. 13). P⁴⁶ 1739 with the Sahidic Coptic omit οὗτοι (so Clement of Alexandria and Augustine). G. Zuntz expresses the view that while οὗτοι is necessary in v. 13 after ἀπέθανον, it is intolerable in v. 39 after καί. He adds that a full stop before the present clause "ruins the context"; the clause continues straight on from the preceding ones: "and although they all had won their record because of their faith ..." (*op. cit.*, p. 34).

[296] Gk. οὐκ ἐκομίσαντο τὴν ἐπαγγελίαν. A I with a few minuscules and the Sahidic Coptic read the plural τὰς ἐπαγγελίας (after v. 13).

[297] Gk. μαρτυρηθέντες, "having had their names entered on the record" (*cf.* NEB: "These also, one and all, are commemorated for their faith").

[298] Gk. τοῦ θεοῦ ... τι προβλεψαμένου. As used thus, προβλέπω is best translated "provide" ("God had made some better provision with us in view"). MM compare its use in the active voice in a sepulchral inscription where a man, knowing how prone one's heirs are to forgetfulness, provides (προβλέπων) a tomb

perfection" (NEB). They and we together now enjoy unrestricted access to God through Christ, as fellow-citizens of the heavenly Jerusalem. The "better plan" which God had made embraces the better hope, the better promises, the better covenant, the better sacrifices, the better and abiding possession, and the better re-surrection[299] which is their heritage, and ours.

> "E'en now by faith we join our hands
>   With those that went before,
> And greet the blood-besprinkled bands
>   On the eternal shore."[300]

---

for himself and his family (G. Kaibel, *Epigrammata Graeca ex lapidibus conlecta* [Berlin, 1878], 326). *Cf.* J. Moffatt (ICC, *ad loc.*): "God in his good providence reserved the messianic τελείωσις of Jesus Christ until we could share it."

[299] Chs. 7:19, 22; 8:6; 9:23; 10:34; 11:35. In all these (and other) passages the comparative adjective used is κρείττων, as here.

[300] C. Wesley.

CHAPTER XII

5. JESUS, THE PIONEER AND PERFECTER OF FAITH

Ch. 12:1-3

1 Therefore[1] let us also, seeing we are compassed about with so great a cloud of witnesses, lay aside every weight, and the sin which doth so easily beset[2] us, and let us run with patience the race that is set before us,

2 looking unto Jesus, the author and perfecter of *our* faith, who for the joy that was set before him endured the cross,[3] despising shame, and hath sat down at the right hand of the throne of God.

3 For consider him that hath endured[4] such gainsaying of sinners against himself,[5] that ye wax not weary, fainting[6] in your souls.

---

[1] Gk. τοιγαροῦν. Although none of the three component elements of this word can stand at the head of a Greek sentence, this compound itself does so stand in classical Greek, as also in both its NT occurrences (*cf.* I Thess. 4:8).

[2] Gk. εὐπερίστατος (see pp. 349f. with nn. 28, 29). Against this, the reading of all other authorities, P⁴⁶ has εὐπερίσπαστος, to be understood here in its transitive sense "easily distracting" (*cf.* AG, p. 324; F. W. Beare, *JBL* lxiii [1944], pp. 390f.), which, says G. Zuntz, "suits the context of Hebrews supremely, or even uniquely, well: as ὄγκος is liable to hamper the Christian athlete, thus sin is liable to divert him from his goal. The meanings which can be attached to the rival reading are so far inferior to this as to make it justifiable, nay necessary, to regard the reading of P⁴⁶ as original" (*The Text of the Epistles* [London, 1953], p. 28). *Cf.* NEB mg., "the sin which all too readily distracts us."

[3] Or "endured a cross"; the majority of witnesses have anarthrous σταυρόν here (τόν is prefixed, however, by P¹³ P⁴⁶ D* with the Sahidic Coptic and Armenian versions).

[4] Gk. τόν ... ὑπομεμενηκότα (P¹³ P⁴⁶ D* omit τόν, the sense then being "one who has endured").

[5] Gk. εἰς ἑαυτόν (αὐτόν, αὑτόν): so A P Dᶜ K L with the bulk of later MSS and TR. ARV margin renders "against themselves" [*cf.* ἑαυτοῖς in Ch. 6:6], which ERV places in the text; this reading, Gk. εἰς ἑαυτούς (αὐτούς, αὑτούς), has ancient and weighty attestation, being exhibited by P¹³ P⁴⁶ ℵ D* 256 1288 1319 1739 2127 and several early versions. (The aberrant *in uobis* found in d can be ignored.) "The singular is the only imaginable reading that fits the context, yet there is no ancient evidence for it. It looks like a correct conjecture. The plural is established as being the old recoverable reading by the consensus of all the ancient witnesses and of most versions. The attempts at making sense of it only prove its absurdity. It would, then, have to be put down as one more instance

1 In surveying the men and women whose faith was exhibited so signally in pre-Christian ages, our author has said repeatedly that they "had witness borne to them" by virtue of their faith; to them all, as to Abel, God Himself bore witness. But now they in turn are called witnesses. A "cloud" of witnesses is a good classical locution for a "host" of witnesses.[7] But in what sense are they "witnesses"? Not, probably, in the sense of spectators,[8] watching their successors as they in their turn run the race for which they have entered; but rather in the sense that by their loyalty and endurance they have borne witness to the possibilities of the life of faith. It is not so much they who look at us as we who look to them—for encouragement. They have borne witness to the faithfulness of God; they were, in a manner of speaking, witnesses to Christ before His incarnation, for they lived in the good of that promise which has been realized in Him. "The divinely inspired prophets", said Ignatius, "lived according to Jesus Christ. That is precisely why they were persecuted, being inspired by His grace, so as to convince the disobedient that there

---

of that 'primitive corruption' which Westcott and Hort recognized in this epistle" (G. Zuntz, *op. cit.*, p. 120). Westcott found in the phrase "sinners against themselves" an echo of Num. 16:38 (17:3 in MT and LXX); but the LXX rendering of the phrase, τῶν ἁμαρτωλῶν τούτων ἐν ταῖς ψυχαῖς αὐτῶν, would scarcely have suggested to our author the locution τῶν ἁμαρτωλῶν εἰς ἑαυτούς. Besides, the phrase εἰς ἑαυτούς or εἰς ἑαυτόν is placed here in the attributive position and therefore is to be taken closely with ἀντιλογίαν. That being so, εἰς ἑαυτόν yields the only tolerable sense in the context, as is recognized by RSV and (presumably, though not expressly) by NEB. Riggenbach does not exaggerate when he describes the plural reading as "very strongly attested, but absolutely meaningless" (*ad loc.*, ZK, p. 391).

[6] Gk. ἐκλυόμενοι (present participle middle or passive), for which P[13] P[46] D* 1739 read the perfect participle ἐκλελυμένοι, which F. W. Beare (*JBL* lxiii [1944], p. 395) and G. Zuntz (*op. cit.*, p. 118) incline to prefer.

[7] Gk. νέφος, as in Herodotus viii. 109, νέφος τοσοῦτο ἀνθρώπων ("so great a host of men").

[8] The word (Gk. μάρτυς) is capable of this sense, which it probably bears, *e.g.*, in I Tim. 6:12, "thou ... didst confess the good confession in the sight of many witnesses" (ἐνώπιον πολλῶν μαρτύρων). In Heb. 10:28 (*cf.* p. 257, n. 127) both senses of "witness" are implied: the "two or three witnesses" testify to what they have personally seen or heard. In IV Macc. 17:11ff., where the sufferings of the martyrs under Antiochus are described in agonistic terms, the verb used of the spectators is θεωρέω, not μαρτυρέω (in 16:16 the διαμαρτυρία is borne by the martyrs themselves).

is one God, who has manifested Himself through Jesus Christ His Son ..." (*Magnesians* 8:2).[9]

This is one of the early examples of the beginning of the semantic change by which the ordinary Greek word for "witness" acquired its distinctive Christian sense of "martyr"—a change which we find so thoroughly established by the time we come to Origen's *Exhortation to Martyrdom* (c. A.D. 235) that he uses the word, without feeling himself under any necessity to explain why he so uses it, of "one who of his own free choice chooses to die for the sake of religion" rather than save his life by renouncing it.[10] Other New Testament occurrences of the word which could have encouraged this semantic change are found in Acts 22:20, where Paul in prayer speaks of "the blood of Stephen thy witness", and in Rev. 2:13, where the glorified Christ, addressing the Pergamene church, mentions "Antipas my witness, my faithful one, who was killed among you". T. W. Manson, in an important article on this subject,[11] points out that the association between faithful witness and martyrdom goes back well before New Testament days; he illustrates his point with a reference to Neh. 9:26, where the Levites, in their prayer of confession to God, recall how the people of Israel "slew thy prophets that testified[12] against them to turn them again unto thee". And certainly the testimony and sufferings of the prophets play a prominent part in our author's survey of men and women of faith towards the end of Ch. 11.

There they are, then, and with their record to encourage us let us in our turn cultivate endurance like theirs as we run "the race

---

[9] *Cf.* Irenaeus, *Heresies* iv. 35:10: "For since they [the prophets] themselves were members of Christ, it was as such that each of them delivered his prophecy. Many as they were, they all prefigured One; their message referred to One."

[10] Origen, *Exhortation to Martyrdom* 5, 22. *Cf. Protevangel of James* 23:3 (see p. 340, n. 287), where Zechariah, father of John the Baptist, says "I am a martyr for God" (μάρτυς εἰμὶ τοῦ θεοῦ).

[11] "Martyrs and Martyrdom", *BJRL* xxxix (1956–57), pp. 463ff. He traces the introduction of the idea of suffering into the meaning of μάρτυς and its cognates back to the Jewish traditions about the persecution of the prophets, men who were "witnesses" in the twofold sense that they testified to what they saw and heard when they "stood in the council of Jehovah" (Jer. 23:18, 22). *Cf.* C. C. Torrey (ed.), *Lives of the Prophets* (Philadelphia, 1946); H. J. Schoeps, *Aus frühchristlicher Zeit* (Tübingen, 1950), pp. 126ff.

[12] Heb. *hēʿîdū*, LXX διεμαρτύραντο.

for which we are entered" (NEB).[13] Even those who have greeted
the promise to which Old Testament saints looked forward, who
live in the age of fulfilment and have experienced "the powers of
the age to come" (Ch. 6:5), continue to "have need of patience"
(Ch. 10:36).[14] Christ has appeared on earth, in fulfilment of the
promise of God, and has "put away sin by the sacrifice of himself"
(Ch. 9:26); but now He is no longer present on earth in visible
form, for He is exalted above the heavens. His people therefore,
while they wait for His second appearing "apart from sin, ... unto
salvation" (Ch. 9:28), must still endure, like Moses, "as seeing
him who is invisible" (Ch. 11:27). True, they have greater
incentive and fuller encouragement than any of their predecessors
who lived before Christ came, but they too have their contest to
engage in, their race to run. The description of the good life in
terms of an athletic engagement is readily paralleled both within
the New Testament[15] and outside it.[16] It may have suggested
itself the more readily to our author's mind at this point because
of the athletic or agonistic terminology in which the sufferings of the
martyrs under Antiochus Epiphanes are repeatedly portrayed in
IV Maccabees—an Alexandrine treatise of which there are several
echoes in the present context of our epistle. The martyrs contend[17]
in a contest[18] in which the pagan king is their antagonist,[19] and

---

[13]   Gk. τὸν προκείμενον ἡμῖν ἀγῶνα. Cf. Herodotus ix. 60 (ἀγῶνος μεγίστου
προκειμένου); Plato, Laches 182a (ὁ ἀγὼν πρόκειται); IV Macc. 15:2 (δυοῖν
προκειμένων); Philo, Agriculture 112 (προτεθέντα ἀγῶνα); Epictetus iii. 25 (ὁ ἀγὼν
πρόκειται), Testament of 40 Martyrs, 1, etc.

[14]   The word there and here is ὑπομονή. See n. 21 below.

[15]   Cf. Luke 13:24 (ἀγωνίζεσθε); but especially the Pauline instances of this
language (I Cor. 9:24–27; Gal. 2:2; Eph. 6:10ff.; Phil. 1:30; 2:16; Col. 1:29;
2:1; 4:12; I Thess. 2:2; I Tim. 6:12; II Tim. 2:3ff.; 4:7; cf. Acts 20:24). While
our author here uses ἀγών in the sense of "race" (as the context indicates), Paul
uses it in the more general sense of "contest"; when he means "race", he says
δρόμος (II Tim. 4:7; cf. Acts 13:25; 20:24) or στάδιον (I Cor. 9:24).

[16]   Cf. examples quoted in n. 13 above and others in Moffatt and Spicq,
ad loc. Such language is common in Christian martyrology; cf. I Clem. 5:2ff.
(of Peter and Paul and other victims of the Neronian persecution); Eusebius,
Hist. Eccl. v, praef. 4; 1. 19 (of Blandina and other victims of the persecution in
the Rhone valley in A.D. 177); see further G. W. H. Lampe (ed.), A Patristic
Greek Lexicon (Oxford, 1961), s. vv. ἀγών and derivatives, ἀθλέω and derivatives.

[17]   ἀγωνίζομαι (IV Macc. 17:13); Eleazar προηγωνίζετο.

[18]   ἀγών (11:20; 13:15; 15:29; 16:16; 17:11).

[19]   ἀντηγωνίζετο (17:14); cf. Heb. 12:4.

[20]   θεοσέβεια, which "crowned her own athletes" (17:15).

true religion[20] wins the victory by their endurance;[21] the universe
and the whole race of mankind are the spectators,[22] while Virtue
occupies the president's box. The prize with which the martyrs
are crowned is eternal life.[23]

So in the Christian contest the prize is assured to all who
compete lawfully[24] and run with patient endurance. "Even so
run," said Paul to the Corinthians, "that ye may attain" (I Cor.
9:24); and our author's advice to his readers is to the same effect.

The athlete must discipline himself;[25] he must divest himself of
all superfluous weight,[26] not only of heavy objects carried about
the body but of excess bodily weight. There are many things
which may be perfectly all right in their own way, but which
hinder a competitor in the race of faith; they are "weights" which
must be laid aside. It may well be that what is a hindrance to
one entrant in this spiritual contest is not a hindrance to another;
each must learn for himself what in his case is a weight or impediment. But there are other things which are not perfectly all right
in their own way but are essentially wrong; there is "sin which
doth so easily beset us". Our author is not referring so much to
some specific "besetting sin", in the common use of the phrase,
but to sin itself, as something which will inevitably encumber the
runner's feet and trip him up before he has taken more than a
step or two.[27] This appears to be the sense of the common reading
here, the adjective *euperistatos*. "Some have indeed fancifully
rendered it "the sin which men admire', inasmuch as *peristatos* may
convey the sense of being gaped at.[28] But that supposition is

---

[21]   ὑπομονή (17:12), a word which occurs 11 times in IV Maccabees, while
the verb ὑπομένω in a similar context occurs 15 times.

[22]   17:14.

[23]   ἠθέλετε γὰρ τότε ἡ ἀρετὴ ... δοκιμάζουσα τὸ νῖκος ἐν ἀφθαρσίᾳ, ἐν ζωῇ
πολυχρονίῳ (17:12).

[24]   II Tim. 2:5.

[25]   Cf. I Cor. 9:25ff.

[26]   The word here used is ὄγκος, which does not otherwise appear in the
Greek Bible. It was used in Greek metaphorically in the sense of "pride", in
addition to its literal sense; and in that sense the Sahidic Coptic version renders
it, but wrongly; the athletic terminology demands the sense "weight" or
"impediment".

[27]   RSV "sin which clings so closely"; NEB (less accurately) "every sin to
which we cling".

[28]   From the use of the verb περίσταμαι in the sense of standing around and
gaping at: "περίστατος is, from classical times onwards, a synonym for

utterly foreign to the context. The surest clue to the expression presents itself in the twofold meaning of *peristasis* and its cognate verb, which has been explicitly noticed both by Epictetus (ii.6) and Marcus Aurelius (ix.13). It can either indicate the *circumstantia* or surroundings of a person or event, or else be used in a pejorative acceptation of a state of beleaguerment, of exigencies and straits, in like fashion with *thlipsis*, 'a squeeze', or the Latin *angustiae*. This latter sense dominates our *euperistatos*." So writes E. K. Simpson,[29] adding that a constricting environment "may work for good or ill". "The difference in effect", he says, "is akin to that of a girdle or a shackle respectively. The girdle braces its wearer, the shackle impedes him. *Euperistatos* presents the latter spectacle by way of warning, the picture of *besetting* sin that has become a household word and a salutary admonition to the Christian athlete. The sin *so prone to hamper* or *trammel* would be our version," he concludes.

The alternative reading *euperispastos*, attested by our oldest extant witness for the text of the epistle, would bear the sense "easily distracting" in this context.[30] Anything that distracts an athlete from the contest in which he is competing will quickly put him out of the running.

2 Everything that would encumber him or divert his attention must therefore be put away, and the athlete must keep his eye fixed on the goal towards which he is pressing. In IV Macc. 17:9f. the unknown Alexandrine writer suggests as an epitaph for the Maccabaean martyrs the following words: "Here an aged priest and an aged woman and seven sons lie buried through the violence of a tyrant who wished to destroy the Hebrews' polity. They

---

περίβλεπτος ('noted', 'famous'). Consequently εὐπερίστατος (ον) is he, or that, which is 'surrounded by many', primarily in admiration. This in fact is the only notion of our adjective for which evidence independent of Hebrews can be adduced" (G. Zuntz, *op. cit.*, pp. 25f.).

[29] *Words Worth Weighing in the Greek New Testament* (London, 1946), pp. 26f. He further instances Polybius, θλιβόμενος ὑπὸ τῆς περιστάσεως (ii. 48), where "he appears to be envisaging this image of a clogging encumbrance", and ἀπερίστατοι ῥαστῶναι (vi. 44), for which the rendering "unshackled *laissez-faire*" is suggested; Epictetus (iv. 1. 159), who describes Diogenes as ἀπερίστατος ("unencumbered"); Diodorus Siculus, who "represents a throttling or stifling environment as συμπνιγὴς περίστασις" (iii. 51).

[30] See p. 345, n. 2. *Cf* ἀπερισπάστως in I Cor. 7:35 with the passive sense "undistractedly".

verily vindicated our nation, keeping their eyes fixed on God[31] and enduring torments even unto death."[32] In language reminiscent of this our author now exhorts his readers to keep their "eyes fixed on Jesus,[33] on whom faith depends from start to finish" (NEB). The earlier witnesses supply incentive in abundance; but in Jesus we have one who is *par excellence* "the faithful witness" (Rev. 1:5).[34] He is faith's "pioneer and perfecter" (RSV). In Greek the definite article stands before "faith"; in AV, ERV, ARV and RSV this is represented by the possessive pronoun "our". But more probably we should recognize here the regular Greek usage of the article before an abstract noun,[35] where English as regularly omits it. Jesus, that is to say, is presented as the one who has blazed the trail of faith and as the one who Himself ran the race of faith to its triumphant finish. But in what sense is He the trail-blazer or pathfinder of faith? We can understand how He is called the pioneer of salvation in Ch. 2:10;[36] apart from Him there is no Savior. We can understand, too, how for His people in the Christian age He provides a better example and incentive in running the race of faith than all who went before Him. But, when we consider that they did go before Him, how can He be called the *pioneer* of faith? Our author's answer might well be that they did not really go before Him; *He* went before *them* as truly as He has gone before us. "Jesus, who saved a people out of the land of Egypt" (as Jude most probably says),[37] who accompanied and nourished that same people in the wilderness (as Paul quite explicitly says),[38] is perhaps envisaged here as having led all the people of God, from earliest times, along the path of faith, although, since His incarnation and passion, His personal example makes His leadership available to His people in a way that was impossible

---

[31] Gk. εἰς θεὸν ἀφορῶντες.

[32] Gk. μέχρι θανάτου. *Cf.* μέχρις αἵματος in v. 4 below (p. 357 with nn. 62–64).

[33] Gk. ἀφορῶντες εἰς Ἰησοῦν. *Cf.* Ch. 11:26, ἀποβλέπω (p. 321, n. 190).

[34] *Cf.* Rev. 3:14, where Jesus speaks in the rôle of "the Amen, the faithful and true witness".

[35] Especially where, as here, the substantives which govern "faith" in the genitive case themselves have the article: τὸν τῆς πίστεως ἀρχηγὸν καὶ τελειωτήν.

[36] For ἀρχηγός see p. 40, n. 50; p. 43, n. 60. In *Acts of Thomas* 39 Jesus is the "true and undefeated athlete (ἀθλητής)".

[37] Jude 5 (see pp. 62f. with n. 46).

[38] I Cor. 10:3f. (see p. 62).

before. Moreover, since our author clearly regards Jesus as the one to whom all the prophets and martyrs bore witness, from Abel, who "being dead yet speaketh", right on to those who won their record through faith on the very eve of the Incarnation, Jesus could well be considered as having provided them in some degree with the incentive and encouragement that they needed in running their race with patience, as He has provided His people ever since with similar incentive and encouragement in the fullest degree.

Not only is Jesus the pioneer of faith; in Him faith has reached its perfection. "He trusts in God,"[39] they said as they stood by His cross; the implication was: "Much good His trust in God is doing Him now!" The words, though not their implication, were truer than they knew. The whole life of Jesus was characterized by unbroken and unquestioning faith in His heavenly Father, and never more so than when in Gethsemane He committed Himself to His Father's hands for the ordeal of the cross with the words: "not what I will, but what thou wilt" (Mark 14:36). It was sheer faith in God, unsupported by any visible or tangible evidence, that carried Him through the taunting, the scourging, the crucifying, and the more bitter agony of rejection, desertion and dereliction. "Come down from the cross, and we will believe," they said.[40] Had He come down, by some gesture of supernatural power, He would never have been hailed as the "perfecter of faith" nor would He have left any practical example for others to follow.

No; He "endured the cross, despising shame".[41] To die by crucifixion was to plumb the lowest depths of disgrace; it was a punishment reserved for those who were deemed of all men most unfit to live, a punishment for sub-men. From so degrading a death Roman citizens were exempt by ancient statute; the dignity of the Roman name would be besmirched by being brought into association with anything so vile as the cross.[42] For slaves, and

---

[39] Matt. 27:43 (RSV), echoing Ps. 22:8.
[40] Mark 15:30, 32.
[41] Gk. ὑπέμεινεν σταυρὸν αἰσχύνης καταφρονήσας. Christ is thus the supreme example of ὑπομονή as well as of πίστις. The martyrs under Antiochus are repeatedly said to have "despised" their sufferings for the sake of the law of God: thus "the seven brothers despised their pains even unto death" (τῶν μέχρι θανάτου πόνων ὑπερεφρόνησαν, IV Macc. 13:1; cf. 6:9; 8:28; 14:1, 11; 16:2). Cf. p. 351, n. 32; p. 357, n. 63.
[42] Cf. Cicero, Pro Rabirio 5: "Let the very mention of the cross be far

criminals of low degree, it was regarded as a suitable means of execution, and a grim deterrent to others. But this disgrace Jesus disregarded, as something not worthy to be taken into account when it was a question of His obedience to the will of God. So He brought faith to perfection by His endurance of the cross—and now the place of highest exaltation is His. The pioneer of salvation has been made perfect through sufferings,[43] and has therefore taken His seat "at the right hand of the throne of God".[44] His exaltation there, with all that it means for His people's wellbeing and for the triumph of God's purpose in the universe, is "the joy that was set before him", for the sake of which[45] He submitted to shame and death.

It is not difficult to trace an affinity between the joy of which our author speaks here and the joy to which Jesus Himself makes repeated reference in the upper room discourses of the Fourth Gospel. He tells His disciples there of His desire that His joy may be in them, so that their joy may be complete (John 15:11; cf. 16:20, 21, 22, 24); and in His high-priestly prayer He asks the Father "that they may have my joy made full in themselves" (John 17:13). So here, "the joy that was set before him" is not something for Himself alone, but something to be shared with those for whom He died as sacrifice and lives as high priest.[46] The throne of God, to which He has been exalted, is the place to which He has gone as His people's forerunner.[47] That is the goal of the

---

removed not only from a Roman citizen's body, but from his mind, his eyes, his ears".

[43] Cf. Chs. 2:10; 5:8f.

[44] Cf. Chs. 1:3; 8:1 (p. 161 with n. 2); 10:12. Here the tense is perfect (κεκάθικεν), indicating that He is still there; in the three other references it is aorist (ἐκάθισεν).

[45] The preposition ἀντί has here the same force as in v. 16 below, where Esau sold his birthright for (ἀντί) a single helping of food. The interpretation according to which Christ accepted suffering and death instead of the joy which might otherwise have been His, whether a continuation of His pre-incarnate joy or joy without suffering in His incarnate life, is much less suitable in the context. It was in order to secure the joy set before Him (τῆς προκειμένης αὐτῷ χαρᾶς) that He ran the race set before Him (τὸν προκείμενον ... ἀγῶνα). The "joy" here corresponds to the "glories" in I Pet. 1:11 ("the sufferings of Christ, and the glories that should follow them"; cf. Luke 24:26).

[46] Cf. John 17:24: "Father, I desire that they also whom thou hast given me be with me where I am, that they may behold my glory ...".

[47] Cf. Ch. 6:20 (pp. 131f.).

pathway of faith; the Pioneer has reached it first, but others who triumph in the same contest will share it with Him.[48] Our author would have found himself in perfect sympathy with the terms of the promise given to the Laodicean church in Rev. 3:21: "He that overcometh, I will give to him to sit down with me in my throne, as I also overcame, and sat down with my Father in his throne."[49]

> Captain of Israel's host, and guide
>   Of all who seek the land above,
> Beneath Thy shadow we abide,
>   The cloud of Thy protecting love;
> Our strength, Thy grace; our rule, Thy word;
> Our end, the glory of the Lord.
>
> By Thine unerring Spirit led,
>   We shall not in the desert stray;
> We shall not full direction need,
>   Nor miss our providential way;
> As far from danger as from fear,
> While love, almighty love, is near.
>
> We've no abiding city here,
>   But seek a city out of sight;
> Thither our steady course we steer,
>   Aspiring to the plains of light,
> Jerusalem, the saints' abode,
> Whose founder is the living God.
>
> Patient the appointed race to run,
>   This weary world we cast behind;
> From strength to strength we travel on
>   The new Jerusalem to find;
> Our labour this, our only aim,
> To find the new Jerusalem.
>
> Through Thee, who all our sins hast borne,
>   Freely and graciously forgiven,
> With songs to Zion we return,
>   Contending for our native heaven;
> That palace of our glorious King,
> We find it nearer while we sing.

---

[48] In IV Macc. 17:18 the martyrs under Antiochus "now stand beside the divine throne and lead a blessed life" (cf. Rev. 7:9, 15).

[49] Cf. Luke 22:29f.

Raised by the breath of love divine,
We urge our way with strength renewed;
The Church of the first-born to join
We travel to the mount of God,
With joy upon our heads to rise,
And meet our Captain in the skies.[50]

3 Christ has thus become His people's supreme inspirer of faith. When they become weary on the way, and grow faint at heart because there seems no end to the trials they have to endure, let them consider[51] Him. He suffered uncomplainingly the hostility and malevolence of sinful men; the recipients of this epistle had not been called upon to endure anything like their Master's sufferings.

The variant reading, which described our Lord's opponents as "sinners against themselves",[52] for all the strength of its attestation does not seem to have much point in this context. Attempts to give it point—such as the observation that "He, whom we so often 'contradict', is our true self"[53]—do not commend themselves as successful or convincing.

6. DISCIPLINE IS FOR SONS

Ch. 12:4-11

4 Ye have not yet[54] resisted unto blood, striving against[55] sin:

5 and ye have forgotten the exhortation which reasoneth with you as sons,[56]

---

[50] C. Wesley.

[51] Gk. ἀναλογίσασθε (the only NT instance of this verb); it conveys the idea of comparison as well as considering, and thus goes beyond κατανοήσατε of Ch. 3:1.

[52] See p. 345, n. 5.

[53] W. R. Inge, *Things New and Old* (London, 1933), p. 14.

[54] Gk. οὔπω. D L and a few minuscules, with the Armenian and Coptic versions, add γάρ ("for").

[55] Gk. ἀνταγωνιζόμενοι, for which P[13] P[46] with 69 and a few other authorities have the simple verb ἀγωνιζόμενοι. The agonistic language is continued, although it is warfare with sin rather than a race to be run that is now envisaged.

[56] The following words are quoted from Prov. 3:11f., LXX (A-text).

My son,[57] regard not lightly the chastening of the Lord,
Nor faint when thou art reproved of him;

6 For whom the Lord loveth he chasteneth,
And scourgeth every son whom he receiveth.

7 It is for chastening that ye endure;[58] God dealeth with
you as with sons; for what son is there whom *his* father
chasteneth not?

8 But if ye are without chastening, whereof all have been
made partakers, then are ye bastards, and not sons.

9 Furthermore, we had the fathers of our flesh to chasten
us, and we gave them reverence: shall we not much
rather[59] be in subjection to the Father of spirits,[60] and
live?

10 For they indeed for a few days chastened *us* as seemed
good to them; but he for *our* profit, that *we* may be
partakers of his holiness.

11 All chastening[61] seemeth for the present to be not joyous
but grievous; yet afterward it yieldeth peaceable fruit
unto them that have been exercised thereby, *even the fruit*
of righteousness.

57 Gk. υἱέ μου. D* 69 81 and some other minuscules with Clement, Augustine, and the Latin version of Origen omit μου, in harmony with LXX.

58 Gk. εἰς παιδείαν ὑπομένετε, where (so far as the form is concerned) the verb may be either present indicative or present imperative. D reads the aorist imperative ὑπομείνατε (which is unambiguous) and makes it the first word in the sentence, for it attaches the phrase εἰς παιδείαν to the preceding quotation (so as to yield the sense: "and scourgeth every son whom he receiveth for chastening"). For εἰς, 35 241 and the majority of later minuscules, with TR, read εἰ ("if"), whence AV: "If ye endure chastening, God dealeth with you as sons." (This reading is probably influenced by the following conditional sentence in v. 8.)

59 Gk. οὐ πολὺ μᾶλλον ... After πολύ P13 P46 D* 1739 add δέ, probably to balance the preceding μέν. "Proto-Alexandrian" reading though it is, this δέ is unacceptable (cf. G. Zuntz, op. cit., p. 189).

60 For πνευμάτων ("of spirits") the minuscule 440 reads πνευματικῶν ("of spiritual beings"), while 88 and a few others read πατέρων (as though the sense were "the Father of [our] fathers").

61 Gk. πᾶσα παιδεία (D* and a few other authorities). After πᾶσα ℵ* P 33 1739 and several other minuscules add μέν. P13 P46 A and the majority of MSS, with the Syriac versions and Latin Vulgate, most Coptic texts, and TR, add δέ, which is probably the true reading, μέν having arisen by anticipation of μέν in the phrase πρὸς μὲν τὸ παρόν ("for the present"). Cf. Zuntz, op. cit., p. 190.

4 In His endurance of the hostility of sinners Christ suffered death.[62] So too did many of the heroes of faith celebrated in Ch. 11. Some of them are described as having "resisted even to the torments of death for the sake of the law".[63] The recipients of this epistle had in earlier days endured severe persecution for their faith, but they had not yet been called upon to seal their testimony with their blood.[64] (This, as we have seen, may give us some limited help in deciding who they were and at what time they could be addressed in these terms.)[65] They might yet have to meet fiercer trials than had come their way thus far; but this was no time to be discouraged, when they thought of others who remained steadfast amid sufferings much worse than theirs. They ought rather to realize that their present hardships were a token of their heavenly Father's love for them, and the means by which He was training them to be more truly His sons.

5–8 Let them recall the words of wisdom in Prov. 3:11f., and they would be able to view their troubles in their proper perspective. These words remind the man who would be truly wise that when hardship is his lot he should accept it as God's method of training and disciplining him, and as a token that he is really a beloved son of God.[66] A father would spend much care and

---

[62] Cf. Phil. 2:8, where He is said to have maintained His obedience to God μέχρι θανάτου ("even unto death"); cf. other instances of this phrase listed in n. 63 below alongside μέχρις αἵματος here; also ἄχρι θανάτου, Rev. 2:10; 12:11.

[63] Spoken of Eleazar in IV Macc. 6:30, μέχρι τῶν τοῦ θανάτου βασάνων ἀντέστη ... διὰ τὸν νόμον (with which cf. ἀντικατέστητε, "ye have ... resisted", here; cf. also IV Macc. 17:14, p. 348 with n. 19, for ἀνταγωνιζόμενοι, "striving against", here). Cf. μέχρι θανάτου in IV Macc. 13:1 (quoted p. 352, n. 41); 17:10 (quoted p. 351 with n. 32); similarly IV Macc. 5:37; 6:21; 7:8, 16; 13:27; 15:10; 16:1; 17:7; also II Macc. 13:14, γενναίως ἀγωνίσασθαι μέχρι θανάτου περὶ νόμων ... ("to contend nobly unto death for the laws ...").

[64] The phrase μέχρις αἵματος is used of mortal combat in Heliodorus, Aeth. vii. 8. Some commentators take the phrase in Heb. 12:4 as referring not to the yielding up of life in martyrdom but to engaging in a conflict which involves the risk of wounds (cf. J. Behm in TWNT i [Stuttgart, 1933], s.v. αἷμα, p. 173). In the light of Ch. 11:35–38 actual martyrdom seems much more probable. See also Riggenbach ad loc. (ZK, p. 393).

[65] See pp. xliif, 266ff.

[66] In the second half of Prov. 3:12 LXX deviates from MT, which reads: "Even as a father the son in whom he delighteth." The deviation is very slight: it consists in reading ūke'āb ("even as a father") as weyak'īb ("and inflicts pain on") or the like. LXX may well represent the original sense (cf. Midrash Tehillim on Ps. 94, in a reference to Prov. 3:12).

357

patience on the upbringing of a true-born son whom he hoped to make a worthy heir; and at the time such a son might have to undergo much more irksome discipline than an illegitimate child for whom no future of honor and responsibility was envisaged, and who therefore might be left more or less to please himself.[67]

Philo quotes this passage from Proverbs to much the same effect as our author does. "So profitable a thing is some sort of hardship", he says, "that even its most humiliating form, servitude, is reckoned a great blessing."[68] Then he argues that Esau's servitude to his brother Jacob, foretold in their father Isaac's blessing, was intended for Esau's good, and continues: "For this reason, it seems to me, did one of Moses' disciples, a man whose name means 'peaceable',[69] who is called Solomon in our ancestral tongue, say:

'Son, regard not lightly the chastening of the Lord,
Nor faint when thou art reproved of him;
For whom the Lord loveth he chasteneth,
And scourgeth every son whom he receiveth.'

So, then, reproof and admonition are counted such a good thing, that by their means confession of God becomes kinship with him; for what relationship is closer than that of a father to his son, or a son's to his father?"[70]

All sons have to be disciplined,[71] our author says; he has already said that even Christ, Son though He was, "learned obedience by the things which he suffered" (Heb. 5:8).[72]

9-10 Our earthly fathers, he continues, disciplined us[73] for the limited period of years which preceded our coming of age, and received proper respect from us. We accepted the discipline

---

[67] A classical parallel to "then are ye bastards, and not sons" (ἄρα νόθοι καὶ οὐχ υἱοί ἐστε) is supplied by Aristophanes, *Birds* 1650-2, νόθος γὰρ εἶ κοὐ γνήσιος ... ὢν γε ξένης γυναικός ("for you are illegitimate and no trueborn son, since your mother is a foreign woman"), where, however, the νόθος is the child of a mixed marriage which was not recognized as legal in Athens of the fifth century B.C.

[68] Philo, *Preliminary Studies*, 175.

[69] Gk. εἰρηνικός (see p. 361 with n. 86, on v. 11).

[70] Philo, *ibid.*, 177.

[71] Gk. παιδείας, ἧς μέτοχοι γεγόνασιν πάντες (v. 8), echoing πάντα υἱόν in the quotation from Proverbs in v. 6.

[72] See pp. 102f. with nn. 65-69.

[73] Literally, "we had the fathers of our flesh as our discipliners *or* correctors (παιδευτάς)"; παιδευτής occurs in one other place in NT, in Rom. 2:20: "a corrector of the foolish".

because it was their province to impose it and our duty to submit to it; they knew, or thought they knew, what was best for us and subjected us to the discipline that commended itself to them.[74] If our heavenly Father also imposes discipline on us, shall we not accept it willingly from Him? Our earthly fathers may sometimes have been mistaken in their estimate of the discipline that we needed; our heavenly Father, in the perfection of His wisdom and love, can be relied upon never to impose any discipline on us that is not for our good.[75] The supreme good that He has in view for His children is this, that they should share His holiness.[76]

Here it is positive holiness of life that is meant; the emphasis is rather different from that found earlier in the epistle where the sanctification procured for believers by the sacrifice of Christ is that cleansing of conscience which fits them to approach God in worship.[77] That was the initial gift of holiness; the holiness mentioned here is rather the goal for which God is preparing His people[78]—that entire sanctification which is consummated in their manifestation with Christ in glory.[79] But this consummation is not attained "sudden, in a minute"; as Paul and Barnabas told the young churches of South Galatia, "through many tribulations we must enter into the kingdom of God" (Acts 14:22).

The designation of God as "the Father of spirits"[80] is unique. We may compare it with the phrase "the God of the spirits of all flesh" in Num. 16:22; 27:16, and with the frequent designation of God as "the Lord of spirits" in the *Similitudes of Enoch* (I Enoch 37:2, etc.).[81] But in the present context its force is plain: as "the

---

[74] Gk. κατὰ τὸ δοκοῦν αὐτοῖς (v. 10); NEB "according to their lights". The argument from earthly fathers to the heavenly Father appears repeatedly in the teaching of Jesus (*cf.* Matt. 7:9ff.; Luke 11:11ff.); in this connection G. K. Chesterton speaks of His "furious use of *a fortiori* argument" (quoted by H. J. Cadbury, *The Peril of Modernizing Jesus* [London, 1962], p. 58). *Cf.* p. 2, n. 6; p. 29, n. 4.

[75] *Cf.* I Cor. 10:13; with the testing is given the power to endure it.

[76] Gk. ἁγιότης (in NT also at II Cor. 1:12); commoner NT words for this concepts are ἁγιασμός (*cf.* v. 14) and ἁγιωσύνη.

[77] *Cf.* Chs. 9:13; 10:10, 14, 29.

[78] *Cf.* v. 14 (p. 364).

[79] *Cf.* I Thess. 5:23; Rom. 8:18, 21, 30; Col. 3:4.

[80] Gk. τῷ πατρὶ τῶν πνευμάτων. ARV margin rightly translates τῶν as "our".

[81] *Cf.* also II Macc. 3:24, "the Sovereign of spirits and of all authority" (ὁ τῶν πνευμάτων καὶ πάσης ἐξουσίας δυνάστης).

fathers of our flesh" are our physical (or earthly) fathers, so "the Father of (our) spirits" is our spiritual (or heavenly) Father. To try to trace metaphysical implications in the phrase is unwarranted.

11 "Discipline, no doubt, is never pleasant; at the time it seems painful, but in the end it yields for those who have been trained by it the peaceful harvest of an honest life" (NEB). The pedagogical value of suffering finds classical expression in Elihu's interposition in the debate between Job and his friends (Job 32:2–37:24). Elihu does not speak the last or greatest word on suffering in the Old Testament, but he represents a marked advance on the traditional position taken up by Job's three friends. If a man does not heed the admonition of God given in night-visions and the like, then:

> "Man is also chastened with pain upon his bed,
>   and with continual strife in his bones;
> so that his life loathes bread,
>   and his appetite dainty food.
> His flesh is so wasted away that it cannot be seen;
>   and his bones which were not seen stick out.
> His soul draws near the Pit,
>   and his life to those who bring death.
> If there be for him an angel,
>   a mediator, one of the thousand,
>   to declare to man what is right for him;
> and he is gracious to him, and says,
>   'Deliver him from going down into the Pit,
>   I have found a ransom;
> let his flesh become fresh with youth;
>   let him return to the days of his youthful vigor';
> then man prays to God, and he accepts him,
>   he comes into his presence with joy.
> He recounts to men his salvation,
>   and he sings before men, and says:
> 'I sinned, and perverted what was right,
>   and it was not requited to me.
> He has redeemed my soul from going down into the Pit,
>   and my life shall see the light' " (Job 33:19–28, RSV).

Similarly one of the psalmists could say:

> "Before I was afflicted I went astray;
>   But now I observe thy word ...

It is good for me that I have been afflicted;
That I may learn thy statutes" (Ps. 119:67, 71).[82]

Our Lord bade His disciples rejoice when they were persecuted for righteousness' sake, because the kingdom of heaven was theirs (Matt. 5:10-12; cf. Luke 6:22f.). Paul similarly tells the Christians of Thessalonica that the persecutions endured by them, while they are a token of God's righteous judgment on their persecutors, are the means by which they themselves are fitted for the kingdom of God (II Thess. 1:4ff.).[83] So too, when four rabbis visited Rabbi Eliezer as he lay sick in bed, three of them praised him for his piety, but Rabbi Aqiba comforted him with the assurance that "chastisements are precious"—and supported his statement by an argument which included a reference to the Proverbs of Solomon.[84] A modern restatement of much the same argument is made by Professor C. S. Lewis in *The Problem of Pain*.[85]

It may be that our author's description of the "fruit of righteousness" as "peaceable" represents nothing more than a coincidence with Philo's explanation of Solomon's name as meaning "peaceable", in the quotation given above.[86] Even so, it is an interesting coincidence in view of our author's quotation of Prov. 3:11f. The man who accepts discipline at the hand of God as something designed by his heavenly Father for his good will cease to feel resentful and rebellious; he has "stilled and quieted" his soul,[87] which thus provides fertile soil for the cultivation of a righteous life, responsive to the will of God.

---

[82] *Cf.* also Lam. 3:19-39. Several further parallels, biblical and extra-biblical, are mentioned by Moffatt, ICC, *ad loc.*

[83] *Cf.* II Pet. 2:9a.

[84] TB *Sanhedrin* 101a. Aqiba argued from Prov. 25:1 that Hezekiah must have taught his young son Manasseh the proverbs of Solomon, but added that it was not this instruction that brought him to repentance but his affliction recorded in II Chron. 33:11ff. A different emphasis from Aqiba's is found in the words of the righteous martyr in *Leviticus Rabba* 32 (on Lev. 24:10) and *Mekhilta* on Ex. 20:6, "These wounds have endeared me to my Father in heaven" (based on a misinterpretation of Zech. 13:6).

[85] "God whispers to us in our pleasures, speaks in our conscience, but shouts in our pains: it is His megaphone to rouse a deaf world" (C. S. Lewis, *The Problem of Pain* [London, 1940], p. 81).

[86] *Cf.* p. 358; εἰρηνικός is used in both places.

[87] *Cf.* Ps. 131:2.

7. LET US THEN BE UP AND DOING

Ch. 12:12-17

12 Wherefore lift up the hands that hang down, and the palsied knees;[88]

13 and make[89] straight paths for your feet,[90] that that which is lame be not turned out of the way, but rather be healed.

14 Follow after peace[91] with all men, and the sanctification without which no man shall see the Lord:

15 looking carefully lest *there be* any man that falleth short of the grace of God; lest any root of bitterness springing up trouble[92] *you*, and thereby the many[93] be defiled;

16 lest *there be* any fornicator, or profane person, as Esau, who for one mess of meat sold his own birthright.

17 For ye know[94] that even when he afterward desired to inherit the blessing, he was rejected; for he found no place for a change of mind *in his father*, though he sought it diligently with tears.

---

[88] *Cf.* Isa. 35:3.

[89] The weight of early Greek witnesses (P⁴⁶ ℵ* P 33 etc.) favors the present imperative ποιεῖτε, for which A D with the majority of later MSS and TR have the aorist ποιήσατε. Prov. 4:26 (LXX) has the present imperative, but in the singular (ποίει). The aorist ποιήσατε may be due to assimilation with the tense of ἀνορθώσατε ("lift up") in v. 12; on the other hand, it could be argued that the aorist is stylistically better (*cf.* G. Zuntz, *op. cit.*, p. 64).

[90] Prov. 4:26, LXX. With the inferior reading ποιήσατε the clause makes a perfect hexameter: καὶ τροχιὰς ὀρθὰς ποιήσατε τοῖς ποσὶν ὑμῶν (in such a careful stylist as our author this might be regarded as an argument *against* ποιήσατε).

[91] *Cf.* Ps. 34:14 (quoted in I Pet. 3:11).

[92] Gk. μή τις ῥίζα πικρίας ἄνω φύουσα ἐνοχλῇ, the last word of which seems to have risen by metathesis from ἐν χολῇ ("in gall") in Deut. 29:18 (LXX), μή τις ἐστὶν ἐν ὑμῖν ῥίζα (A F add πικρίας) ἄνω φύουσα ἐν χολῇ καὶ πικρίᾳ. See pp. 365f. with nn. 105-108.

[93] Gk. διὰ ταύτης μιανθῶσιν οἱ πολλοί. For διὰ ταύτης P⁴⁶ A H P 33 al. have δι᾽ αὐτῆς (as in Chs. 11:4; 12:11). The article is omitted by P⁴⁶ D P 1739 with the majority of later MSS and TR (whence AV "and thereby many be defiled"). See p. 365 with n. 104. G. Zuntz regards πολλοί as preferable here (*op. cit.*, pp. 53f.).

[94] Gk. ἴστε, a classical form (*cf.* Eph. 5:5; Jas. 1:19), for which NT usually has the Hellenistic οἴδατε (*cf.* the use of the classical ἴσασιν and not the Hellenistic οἴδασιν in Acts 26:4).

362

12-13 Reverting to his athletic figure of speech, our author bids his readers brace their flagging limbs and press on to the goal. Some of their number were feeling specially discouraged and disinclined to make the necessary effort; the others should do everything possible to help them. The exhortation is couched in Old Testament language—drawn partly from from words of encouragement addressed to exiled Jews who felt that the promised deliverance and restoration would never come and partly, like the exhortation of verses 5 and 6, from the book of Proverbs. The aptness of the Isaiah quotation needs no emphasizing:

"Strengthen the weak hands,
and make firm the feeble knees.[95]
Say to those who are of a fearful heart,
'Be strong, fear not!
Behold, your God will come ...
He will come and save you' " (Isa. 35:3f., RSV).

The context of the quotation, if not the words actually reproduced, repeats the assurance of Ch. 10:37 that in "a very little while, He that cometh shall come, and shall not tarry". The precise meaning of the Hebrew verb in Prov. 4:26a is uncertain,[96] but the Septuagint is here used (with the singular number replaced by the plural) to urge the smoothing of the way[97] for those who are weak and spiritually lame, and who might be prevented from continuing their course if they were tripped up and permanently disabled. The verb translated "be ... turned out of the way"[98] should rather be rendered "be put out of joint" (ARV margin, RSV, NEB); it is dislocation and not deviation that is suggested by the following words, "but rather be healed". Sprains and similar injuries must

---

[95] LXX reads ἰσχύσατε χεῖρες ἀνειμέναι καὶ γόνατα παραλελυμένα, "Be strong, ye relaxed hands and palsied knees"; the quotation here approximates more closely to the Hebrew construction. For the form παρειμένας used by our author in place of LXX ἀνειμέναι cf. Sir. 25:23, χεῖρες παρειμέναι καὶ γόνατα παραλελυμένα ... ("Drooping hands and weak knees are caused by the wife who does not make her husband happy").

[96] Heb. pallēs (AV "ponder"; ARV "make level"; RSV "take heed to").

[97] The Greek word here used for "path" (τροχιά) is found nowhere else in NT, and in LXX is confined to Proverbs (and Ezek. 27:19 in a different sense). Etymologically it means "wheel-track"; but that is not its meaning in Biblical Greek.

[98] Gk. ἐκτραπῇ, second aorist subjunctive passive of ἐκτρέπω, lit. "turn out" or "turn away". The sense of "dislocation" is attested in Hippocrates and other medical writers.

363

be bound up, so that the whole community may complete the
course without loss.

14 The athletic metaphor is now abandoned, and the same
teaching is expressed in straightforward ethical terms.[99] Peace
with all men must be sought. We recall our Lord's benediction on
the peacemakers, "for they shall be called sons of God" (Matt.
5:9), and Paul's injunction to the Roman Christians: "If it be
possible, as much as in you lieth, be at peace with all men" (Rom.
12:18).[100] It might not be possible, for their persecutors might
refuse to countenance "peaceful coexistence" with them; but they
themselves must remain peaceable in attitude and conduct and
never take the initiative in stirring up strife. If this was their duty
with regard to mankind in general, how much more was it their
duty to "be at peace one with another" (Mark 9:50).

"The sanctification[101] without which no man shall see the Lord"
is, as the words themselves make plain, no optional extra in the
Christian life but something which belongs to its essence. It is the
pure in heart, and none but they, who shall see God (Matt. 5:8).
Here, as in verse 10, it is practical holiness of life that is meant,
the converse of those things against which a warning is uttered in
the verses which follow. We are reminded of Paul's words to the
Thessalonians: "This is the will of God, even your sanctification,
that ye abstain from fornication ..." (I Thess. 4:3)—for the things
that are *unholy* effectively debar those who practise them from
inheriting the kingdom of God (I Cor. 6:9f.). Our author is as
far as Paul was from encouraging antinomianism in his readers.
Those who are called to be partakers of God's holiness must be
holy themselves; this is the recurring theme of the Pentateuchal
law of holiness, echoed again in the New Testament: "Ye shall
therefore be holy, for I am holy" (Lev. 11:45, etc.; *cf.* I Pet. 1:15f.).
To see the Lord is the highest and most glorious blessing that

---

[99] Moffatt (ICC, *ad loc.*) points out a similar train of thought in the *Testament of Simeon* 5:2f.: "Make your hearts good before the Lord, and your ways straight before men, and ye shall find grace before the Lord and men. Beware, therefore, of fornication, for fornication is mother of all evils, separating from God, and bringing near to Beliar."

[100] See also p. 362, n. 91.

[101] Gk. ἁγιασμός, here only in this epistle (other NT occurrences are Rom. 6:19, 22; I Cor. 1:30; I Thess. 4:3, 4, 7; II Thess. 2:13; I Tim. 2:15; I Pet. 1:2). See p. 359, n. 76.

mortals can enjoy, but the beatific vision is reserved for those who are holy in heart and life.[102]

15 If such sanctification is to be pursued, then care must be taken to detect and nip in the bud any tendency that would be inimical to it. Let them see to it that none of them fails to attain[103] the grace of God. If it is the grace of God that sets a man's feet at the entrance of the pathway of faith, it is equally the grace of God that enables him to continue and complete that pathway. Paul too found it necessary to beg some of his converts not to "receive ... the grace of God in vain" (II Cor. 6:1) and to warn others who had begun to run well but had come up against an obstacle at an early stage that they had "fallen away from grace" (Gal. 5:4, 7). "Grace to help in time of need" (Ch. 4:16) is constantly available to the people of Christ, and Peter urges his readers to have their hope securely fixed "on the grace that is to be brought to you at the revelation of Jesus Christ" (I Pet. 1:13). If nevertheless some of them fall short of the grace of God, it is not because His grace was inaccessible, but because they would not avail themselves of it, and have therefore failed to reach the goal which is attainable only by His grace—the vision of God of which our author has just spoken.

If some incipient sin manifests itself in their midst, it must be eradicated at once; if it is tolerated, this is a sure way of falling short of God's grace, for the whole community[104] will then be contaminated. Such a sin is called a "root of bitterness",[105] in language borrowed from Deut. 29:18, where Moses warns the

---

102 *Cf.* Rev. 22:4. Philo regards the vision of God as the goal of the contemplative life; thus, commenting on the change of Jacob's name to Israel (which he interprets as "he who sees God", as though its etymology were Heb. 'īsh rō'eh 'Ēl), he says: "The task of him who sees God is not to leave the holy contest uncrowned, but to carry off the prizes of victory. And what garland composed of fairer flowers or more suited to its purpose could be woven for the victorious soul than that which will enable him to behold the Existent One with clear vision? Glorious indeed is the prize held out to the athlete-soul, that it should be blessed with eyes to apprehend clearly the One who alone is worthy to behold" (*On Change of Names*, 81f.).

103 Gk. ὑστερῶν ("falling short of").

104 Gk. οἱ πολλοί (on the text see p. 362, n. 93). We may compare Heb. hā-rabbîm, "the many", used in the Qumran literature to denote the general membership of the community; but no closer contact can be inferred from such a comparison. *Cf.* also τὸ πλῆθος in Acts 4:32, etc., and οἱ πλείονες in II Cor. 2:6.

105 NEB "no bitter, noxious weed".

Israelites against any inclination to fall into the idolatrous practices of Canaan, "lest there should be among you a root that beareth gall and wormwood" (or, with RSV, "a root bearing poisonous and bitter fruit").[106] Deut. 29:18 with its context plays a similar admonitory part in the literature of the Qumran community; for example, in one of the *Hymns of Thanksgiving* it is said of the opponents of the community: "A root breeding gall and wormwood is in their thoughts; and in the stubbornness of their hearts they go astray, and inquire of thee amid their idols."[107] But perhaps the best commentary on our author's words here is his earlier warning in Ch. 3:12: "Take heed, brethren, lest haply there shall be in any one of you an evil heart of unbelief, in falling away from the living God."[108]

16 In telling them to make sure that they have no fornicator among them, he may conceivably be following Old Testament usage in employing this terminology to denote idolatry or apostasy;[109] but most probably he has in mind the literal sense of the word. It may be that Esau is mentioned only as an example of a "profane person",[110] since in the Old Testament record Esau is not charged with fornication—unless the meaning of the term be stretched to cover his marriage with two daughters of Heth, who made life bitter for his parents (Gen. 26:34f.).[111] Post-biblical tradition, however, makes Esau a vicious character. Philo interprets the statement that "Esau was a skilful hunter, a man of the field" (Gen. 25:27) to mean that "vice, which hunts after the passions, is unfit by nature to dwell in the city of virtue, but

---

[106] *Cf.* Lam. 3:19 LXX, πικρία καὶ χολή μου μνησθήσεται ("my wormwood and gall will be remembered"); Acts 8:23, εἰς χολὴν πικρίας ("in the gall of bitterness").

[107] 1QH iv. 14. The words of Deut. 29:19, "Peace be mine, though I walk in the stubbornness of my heart", are quoted in 1QS ii. 13f. with reference to the violator of the Qumran covenant; *cf.* p. 170 with n. 48.

[108] *Cf.* p. 66, with n. 60 (the "evil root" of IV Ezra mentioned there is relevant to the present context too).

[109] Judg. 2:17, etc.

[110] Gk. βέβηλος, applied in LXX to Zedekiah because of his breach of oath to the king of Babylon (Ezek. 21:25).

[111] In Jub. 25:1 Rebekah complains that all the deeds of Esau's two Canaanite wives "are fornication and lust"; in v. 8 Jacob tells her that Esau has often urged him to marry a sister of his Canaanite wives, but that he has always refused, "for with regard to lust and fornication Abraham my father gave me many commandments" (v. 7).

pursues a boorish and undisciplined life in complete senseless-ness".[112] Elsewhere he says, with reference to the description of Esau in Gen. 27:11, that "the 'hairy man' is the unrestrained, lecherous, impure and unholy man".[113] The Palestinian Targum on Gen. 25:29 enlarges on Esau's coming home exhausted on the day that he sold Jacob his birthright by saying that "in that day he had committed five transgressions", one of which consisted in adultery with a betrothed maiden. Similar accusations against him are recorded in other places in rabbinical literature.[114] Whether our author had Esau in mind as a fornicator is not at all certain;[115] it is certain, however, that he judged it necessary to warn his readers against harboring any such person, for he reverts to the subject again in Ch. 13:4: "Fornicators and adulterers God will judge."

The incident which he does recall from Esau's career illustrates not fornication but "profaneness", that is to say, the lack of any sense of spiritual values. Nothing is related of him in Genesis which is positively to his discredit; he is the "hunting, shooting, fishing" type of man whose chief concerns are the material interests of the moment. When Jacob by deceit received the blessing intended for Esau, Esau fell into a towering rage, and threatened his brother's life; but he soon forgot his resentment, together (possibly) with the cause of it. Compared with such a sportsman, Jacob in some respects cuts a poor figure. Yet, even in his most disreputable moments, Jacob showed an appreciation of the heritage promised by God to his family and a determination not to miss that heritage; and at the end, as we have seen, he won his record for faith.[116] On the other hand, so little did Esau value the birthright with which that heritage was bound up that in a moment of hunger he sold it "for a mess of pottage".[117] "So Esau

---

[112] Leg. Alleg. iii. 2.
[113] Questions and Answers on Genesis, iv. 201.
[114] Cf. Genesis Rabba 70 d, 72 a; Exodus Rabba 116 a.
[115] Delitzsch (ad loc.) says that if our author had meant to designate Esau as βέβηλος only, and not πόρνος, he would have written μή τις πόρνος ἢ ἢ βέβηλος. But since he leaves the subjunctive of the verb "to be" to be understood, we cannot be sure where he would have placed it if he had expressed it. Westcott (ad loc.) is more probably right in referring βέβηλος only of the two words to Esau; cf. E. Elliot, "Esau", ExT xxix (1917–18), pp. 44f.
[116] Ch. 11:20f. (pp. 313f.).
[117] This proverbial phrase occurs in the Pilgrimage of Perfection (1526), in

despised his birthright" is the summing up of that incident in the Old Testament record (Gen. 25:34).

17 He did, indeed, regret his hasty action later. Our author sees a close link between his despising of his birthright in Gen. 25:29–34 and his losing the blessing due to the firstborn in Gen. 27:1–40. It may be implied in the Genesis narrative itself that if Esau had not sold his birthright Jacob would not have found it so easy to steal the blessing from him. But, when he came in from the field to receive the blessing, he found himself "disqualified",[118] and though he wept loudly and bitterly[119] there was no way of retrieving the situation. His father could not and would not call back the blessing pronounced on Jacob: "yea, and he shall be blessed" (Gen. 27:33). ARV interprets the "repentance" for which Esau found no opportunity as a change of mind on Isaac's part, but this is not the natural construction of the words. "He found no way open for second thoughts" (NEB). The pronoun "it"[120] in the clause "though he sought it diligently with tears" most probably refers to the blessing.

The application is plain; it is a reinforcement of the warning given at an earlier stage in the argument, that after apostasy no second repentance is possible. "Let us fear therefore, lest haply, a promise being left of entering into his rest, any one of you should seem to have come short of it" (Ch. 4:1).[121]

---

the headings to Gen. 25 in the Bibles of 1537, 1539 and 1560, and in the last paragraph of the AV translators' address to the reader. The termination -ετο in the aorist ἀπέδετο, "sold" (classical ἀπέδοτο), illustrates the Hellenistic tendency for the ω-conjugation to encroach on the μι-conjugation.

[118] Gk. ἀπεδοκιμάσθη.

[119] Although Esau's weeping (Gen. 27:38b, MT) is omitted from the best authenticated LXX text, his "exceeding great and bitter cry" (v. 34) would give adequate ground for our author's statement about his tears.

[120] Gk. αὐτήν, which might refer to μετανοίας ("repentance"), as NEB takes it ("he found no way open for second thoughts, although he strove, to the point of tears, to find one"), but more probably to εὐλογίαν ("blessing"), in the light of Gen. 27:34, 38. Cf. R. T. Watkins, "The New English Bible and the Translation of Hebrews xii. 17", ExT lxxiii (1961–62), pp. 29f.; he suggests a slight modification of the NEB wording: "you know that although he wanted afterwards to claim the blessing, he was rejected; though he begged for it to the point of tears, he found no way open for second thoughts." ARV margin and ERV indicate that what Esau sought was the blessing by printing the clause "for he found no place of repentance" as a parenthesis.

[121] One commentator on Hebrews, G. H. Lang, was led by this mention of the Esau incident to his distinctive interpretation that the "rest" which may be

8. THE EARTHLY SINAI AND THE HEAVENLY ZION

Ch. 12:18-24

18 For ye are not come unto *a mount*[122] that might be touched,[123] and that burned with fire, and unto blackness, and darkness, and tempest,[124]

19 and the sound[125] of a trumpet, and the voice of words;

forfeited in Chs. 3:11–4:11, like the "blessing" or "grace of God" of which some may fall short here, is the millennial reign of the resurrected saints with Christ (*cf.* his *Firstborn Sons: their Rights and Risks* [London, 1936], p. 217 *et passim*). See p. 75 with n. 21.

[122] Gk. ὄρει ("a mount") appears only in inferior manuscripts (D K L P 69 and the bulk of later codices) with the Sixto-Clementine Vulgate, Harclean Syriac and TR; but it is to be understood here from v. 22 (Σιων ὄρει). So far as the construction goes, the absence of ὄρει makes possible the rendering of ARV margin, "a palpable and kindled fire" (ψηλαφωμένῳ καὶ κεκαυμένῳ πυρί), which is preferred by Westcott; but the idea of a fire that could be "handled" is strange; the contrast is between the material mountain of Sinai which could indeed be touched (since the people were forbidden to do so) and the spiritual and heavenly hill of Zion.

[123] Gk. ψηλαφωμένῳ. The verb ψηλαφάω is not used in LXX to render Heb. *nāga'* ("touch") in Ex. 19:12 (where the LXX uses ἅπτομαι and θιγγάνω); its verbal adjective ψηλαφητός is used, however, in Ex. 10:21, of the "darkness which may be felt". In our author's mind the darkness of the ninth plague of Egypt may have been associated with the "thick darkness" of Sinai. E. C. Selwyn ("On ψηλαφωμένῳ in Heb. 12:18", *JThS* xii [1911], pp. 133f.) offers the conjectural emendation πεφεψαλωμένῳ, "calcined" (*cf.* Aeschylus, *Prometheus Vinctus* 363); he refers to A. P. Stanley's description of "the vast heaps, as of calcined mountains", of "what seemed to be the ruins, the cinders, of mountains calcined to ashes" (*Sinai and Palestine* [London, 1887], pp. 21, 71), and suggests that the author of Hebrews may have visited the site of Sinai. This emendation is quite unnecessary (and indeed improbable), as is also that offered by G. N. Bennett (*Classical Review* vi [1892], p. 263) of ὕψει νενεφωμένῳ ("a beclouded height") in place of ψηλαφωμένῳ—an emendation which, he says, "would fit in exactly with the Old Testament accounts, which represent the summit as burnt with fire, while lower down it was enveloped in a dense cloud". On ψηλαφάω here see E. Norden, *Agnostos Theos* (Leipzig, 1912), p. 15.

[124] Gk. γνόφῳ καὶ ζόφῳ καὶ θυέλλῃ. In Deut. 4:11 LXX uses the three words σκότος γνόφος θύελλα for the dark storm-cloud in which God was enshrouded on Sinai (*cf.* Ex. 10:22; 20:21). It may be under the influence of this passage that several authorities here read σκότει (P⁴⁶ Ψ) or σκότῳ (‮אc‬ 4 1739 with the majority of later MSS and TR) for ζόφῳ.

[125] Gk. ἤχῳ. LXX (Ex. 19:16, 19; 20:18) has φωνή (or φωναί) τῆς σάλπιγγος, but the verb ἠχέω appears in Ex. 19:16, "the voice of the trumpet sounded (ἤχει) loud". The substantive ἦχος is probably used here by our author rather than φωνή since φωνή is used in the following phrase for the voice of God on Sinai. (as in LXX of Ex. 19:5, 13, 16, etc.).

THE EPISTLE TO THE HEBREWS

which *voice* they that heard entreated that no word more should be spoken unto them;[126]

20 for they could not endure that which was enjoined, If even a beast touch the mountain, it shall be stoned;[127]

21 and so fearful was the appearance, *that* Moses said, I exceedingly fear[128] and quake:[129]

22 but ye are come unto mount Zion, and unto the city of the living God, the heavenly Jerusalem, and to innumerable hosts of angels,[130]

23 to the general assembly[131] and church of the firstborn who are enrolled in heaven,[132] and to God the Judge of all, and to the spirits[133] of just men made perfect,[134]

24 and to Jesus the mediator of a new covenant, and to the blood of sprinkling that speaketh better[135] than *that of* Abel.[136]

---

126 Gk. παρῃτήσαντο μὴ προστεθῆναι αὐτοῖς λόγον. The negative particle μή is idiomatic, but not essential to the sense; it is lacking in ℵ* P and a few other MSS.

127 Ex. 19:13. A few MSS, followed by TR, complete the quotation by adding ἢ βολίδι κατατοξευθήσεται ("or thrust through with a dart", AV).

128 Deut. 9:19. See p. 372, n. 140.

129 Gk. ἔντρομος (ℵ D* ἔκτρομος).

130 Gk. μυριάσιν ἀγγέλων ("myriads of angels"), for which D* reads μυρίων ἁγίων ἀγγέλων ("ten thousand holy angels"); cf. Deut. 33:2; Jude 14.

131 Gk. πανηγύρει, which should probably be taken closely with the preceding phrase as a circumstantial dative ("myriads of angels in festal array"). This construction is favored by those MSS which indicate punctuation, and by the Latin and Syriac versions. Moffatt deduces from citations in Ambrose, Augustine, Rufinus's Latin translation of Origen, and from the Bohairic Coptic version, that there was a variant reading πανηγυριζόντων (so F. Blass).

132 Gk. ἀπογεγραμμένων ἐν οὐρανοῖς. The Byzantine text has the order ἐν οὐρανοῖς ἀπογεγραμμένων, which is shown by 0228 to go back to the end of the 4th century (G. Zuntz, op. cit., p. 160).

133 Gk. πνεύμασι, for which D* and the Sixtine Vulgate read the singular πνεύματι.

134 Gk. τετελειωμένων, for which D* and Hilary read the curious variant τεθεμελιωμένων ("founded").

135 Gk. κρεῖττον, for which P46 33 and a few other MSS, followed by TR, read κρείττονα ("better things", AV).

136 Gk. παρὰ τὸν Ἀβελ, "in comparison with Abel", a compendious construction for "in comparison with Abel's". But P46 L and some other MSS read παρὰ τὸ Ἀβελ, "in comparison with that of Abel".

370

18-19 Our author reverts to the contrast already pointed in Ch. 2:2-4 between the giving of the law and the reception of the gospel. Awesome as were the circumstances of the giving of the law in Moses' day, more awesome by far are the privileges associated with the gospel, if they are despised or refused. Those who wholeheartedly believe the gospel and gladly embrace its privileges need have no fear; they are urged to enter the heavenly sanctuary with "boldness" through the blood of Jesus.[137] The stern note of warning is for those who, having begun to make an approach, fall back. They are reminded that the consequences of despising the gospel are even more dreadful than were the consequences of despising the law.

The description of the terrors of Sinai is based on the account in Ex. 19:16-19; 20:18-21, with Moses' recollection of the scene forty years later in Deut. 4:11f. The mountain was so charged with the holiness of the God who manifested Himself there that for man or beast to touch it meant certain death. "Mount Sinai was wrapped in smoke, because the LORD descended upon it in fire; and the smoke of it went up like the smoke of a kiln, and the whole mountain quaked greatly. And as the sound of the trumpet grew louder and louder, Moses spoke, and God answered him in thunder" (Ex. 19:18f., RSV).[138] Then, "when all the people perceived the thunderings and the lightnings and the sound of the trumpet and the mountain smoking, the people were afraid and trembled; and they stood afar off, and said to Moses, 'You speak to us, and we will hear; but let not God speak to us, lest we die' " (Ex. 20:18f., RSV).

20 If even a beast accidentally touched or trespassed on the hill of God, it contracted so much holiness from it that it became highly dangerous to touch itself; it must be killed from a safe distance—stoned, or (as AV adds, reproducing a later text amplified on the basis of the Exodus narrative) "thrust through with a dart".[139]

21 And not only were the people terrified; even Moses,

---

[137] Ch. 10:19ff.

[138] On the nature of these phenomena *cf.* W. J. Phythian-Adams, *The Call of Israel* (Oxford, 1934), pp. 145ff.

[139] A. H. McNeile explains the injunction to kill the trespassing beast from a distance in that to touch it would involve transgressing the barrier (*The Book of Exodus*, WC [London, 1931], p. 112).

THE EPISTLE TO THE HEBREWS

privileged as he was to press up into the thick darkness where God
was, was filled with numinous awe at the *mysterium tremendum et
fascinans*. His words, "I exceedingly fear and quake",[140] are not
recorded in the Pentateuchal descriptions of the Sinai theophany;
the closest Old Testament parallel is in Deut. 9:19, where he
reminds the people of his supplication for them after the incident
of the golden calf: "For I was afraid of the anger and hot displeasure, wherewith Jehovah was wroth against you to destroy
you." Another parallel appears in Stephen's speech, where in
face of the theophany at the burning bush "Moses trembled, and
durst not behold" (Acts 7:32). Our author may have been acquainted with a haggadic account of the Sinai theophany which
made explicit mention of Moses' fear and trembling on this
occasion too.

22 The events of the Exodus and the wilderness wanderings,
as we have seen before, are treated in the apostolic age as parables
of Christian experience.[141] But Christians have come to no sacred
mountain which can be touched physically but to the heavenly
dwelling-place of God, the true and eternal Mount Zion. "Ye are
come" may denote their conversion to Christianity; the Greek
verb is that from which "proselyte" is derived,[142] and while it is
such a common verb that normally no such implication could be
read into it, the particular form used in this particular context
carries with it overtones of conversion. Philo uses this same perfect
tense of the verb in question when, in a meditation on Moses'
vision of God in Ex. 33:13ff., he says that all kindred souls to
Moses who refuse fables and embrace truth obtain the approval
of God, whether this has been their attitude from the beginning
or they have been converted to it subsequently.[143] These last, he
goes on, Moses "calls 'proselytes' because they 'have come to' a
new and God-loving commonwealth".[144] So, by virtue of their
accepting the gospel, the readers of this epistle had come to that
spiritual realm some of whose realities are detailed in the following
clauses.

---

[140] Gk. ἔκφοβός εἰμι καὶ ἔντρομος. *Cf.* I Macc. 13:2, "the people were
trembling and fearful" (ἔντρομος καὶ ἔμφοβος).
[141] See pp. 62ff.
[142] Gk. προσεληλύθατε, προσήλυτος.
[143] *Special Laws* i. 51.
[144] Gk. τούτους δὲ καλεῖ προσηλύτους ἀπὸ τοῦ προσεληλυθέναι κτλ. The per-

372

Mount Zion was the site of the Jebusite stronghold which David captured and made his royal residence in the seventh year of his reign.[145] He made it the religious centre of his kingdom by installing there "the ark of God, which is called by the Name, even the name of Jehovah of hosts that sitteth above the cherubim" (II Sam. 6:2). Thus Zion became the earthly dwelling-place of God, "the city which Jehovah had chosen out of all the tribes of Israel, to put his name there" (I Kings 14:21). For (in the words of an Asaphite psalm):

"He chose the tribe of Judah,
Mount Zion, which he loves.
He built his sanctuary like the high heavens,
like the earth, which he has founded for ever"
(Ps. 78:68f., RSV).

When later Solomon built his temple on the hill to the north of Zion, and installed the sacred ark there, the name Zion was extended to include this further area, and became in practice synonymous with Jerusalem—

"Jerusalem, built as a city
which is bound firmly together,
to which the tribes go up,
the tribes of the LORD,
as was decreed for Israel,
to give thanks to the name of the LORD" (Ps. 122:3f., RSV).

As the earthly Zion was the meeting point for the tribes of the old Israel, so the heavenly Zion is the meeting point for the new Israel.[146] Their heritage, the place of their solemnities, is "the city of the living God, the heavenly Jerusalem". If the movable tabernacle in the wilderness was constructed according to the pattern of the sanctuary on high, so the temple and city of Jerusalem were material copies of eternal archetypes.[147] Both in Jewish

---

fect tense here as in our Hebrews passage is significant, denoting a permanent status resulting from the conversion event.

[145] II Sam. 5:6-9.

[146] *Cf.* Rev. 14:1, where "Mount Zion" on which the Lamb stands with the hundred and forty-four thousand is the heavenly Zion, since they sing their new song "before the throne, and before the four living creatures and the elders" (v. 3).

[147] *Cf.* I Chron. 28:11-19, where the plan of the temple given by David to Solomon is made clear "by the writing from the hand of the LORD concerning it" (RSV).

and in Christian thought the heavenly counterpart of the earthly Jerusalem is familiar—the rabbis inferred the existence of the heavenly archetype from the words of Ps. 122:3 (quoted above), which they rendered: "Jerusalem which is built like the city that is its fellow"[148]—the oldest approximately datable reference to it being Paul's words in Gal. 4:26, "the Jerusalem that is above is free, which is our mother".[149] In the Syriac *Apocalypse of Baruch*, which is to be dated soon after A.D. 70, Baruch is told on the eve of the destruction of the First Temple that this is not the true city of God; the true city was revealed by God to Adam before his fall, to Abraham when God made a covenant with him, and to Moses at the same time as he was shown the pattern in the mount.[150] In Rev. 21:2 "the holy city, new Jerusalem", which has existed eternally in heaven, is seen coming down to earth, so that henceforth "the tabernacle of God is with men, and he shall dwell with them" as their covenant-God.[151] This is not our author's perspective: the new Jerusalem has not yet come down to men, but

---

148 Heb. *ke 'ir she-ḥubberāh lāh*, vocalized as *ke 'ir she-ḥabērāh lāh*. *Cf.* Targum and *Midrash Tehillim* on Ps. 122:3.

149 The manner in which Paul introduces the figure suggests that it was no novelty to him, nor yet, perhaps, to his readers. *Cf.* p. 297, n. 85.

150 II Baruch 4:2ff. (*cf.* 32:2ff.). According to TB Ḥagigah 12b, Rabbi Meir (*c.* A.D. 150) said that of the seven heavens, the fourth is called *zebūl*, "in which are Jerusalem and the temple, and an altar is built, at which Michael the great prince stands and offers sacrifice, as it is said: 'I have surely built thee a house of habitation, a place for thee to dwell in for ever' [I Kings 8:13]. And how do we know that it [*zebūl*] is called heaven? Because it is written: 'Look down from heaven, and behold from the habitation of thy holiness and of thy glory' [Isa. 63:15]."

151 *Cf.* Rev. 3:12; IV Ezra 7:26; 8:52 (quoted above, p. 79); 13:36; I Enoch 90:29; *Test. Dan* 5:12, for the New Jerusalem of the future. The Qumran texts include several fragments of a New Jerusalem apocalypse—an Aramaic work based mainly on Ezek. 40-48. The fragments from Caves 1, 2 and 5 have been published (1Q 32, 2Q 24, 5Q 15); see *Discoveries in the Judaean Desert* i [Oxford, 1955], pp. 134f.; iii, Texte [Oxford, 1962], pp. 84ff., 184ff.). Just how the Qumran community envisaged the new Jerusalem cannot be satisfactorily determined until the fragments from Caves 4 and 11 are published. The Cave 2 fragments at least seem to describe a literal city with material temple and animal sacrifices (like the purified city and temple of 1QM ii); but all this may have been given a spiritual meaning. *Cf.* M. Baillet, *Discoveries in the Judaean Desert*, iii, Texte, p. 85: "It must moreover be remembered that for the sect the temple is susceptible of identification with the community (*cf.* 1QS viii. 5-9; ix. 5-6) and that it is a replica of heaven: see *Revue Biblique* lxiii, 1956, p. 394." *Cf.* J. Strugnell, *VT Supplement* vii (Leiden, 1960), p. 320.

in the spiritual realm they already have access to it. They have
become fellow-citizens with Abraham of that well-founded city for
which he looked; it is the city or commonwealth which comprises
the whole family of faith, God's true dwelling-place. Even now
this city has not been manifested in its fulness; it is still in one sense
"the city which is to come" (Ch. 13:14), but the privileges of its
citizenship are already enjoyed by faith. The people of God are
still a pilgrim people, treading the "highways to Zion", but by
virtue of His sure promise they have already arrived there in spirit.
Our author may retain the symbolism of "up there"[152] when he
speaks of God, but he makes it clear that His people need not
climb the heavenly steeps to seek Him, for He is immediately
accessible to each believing heart, making His dwelling in the
fellowship of the faithful.[153]

You have come, he continues, "to myriads of angels in festal
gathering".[154] The myriads of angels remind us of the "ten
thousands of holy ones" who attended God at the giving of the
law on Sinai (Deut. 33:2), or of the "thousand thousands" whom
Daniel saw serving God, and "ten thousand times ten thousand"
who stood before Him (Dan. 7:10).[155] In the Qumran *Hymn of
the Initiants* a man who knows himself justified by God proclaims
that God has caused him and his fellow-believers "to inherit the
portion of the Holy Ones; He has joined their assembly to the sons
of heaven, to be a council of the community, a foundation of the
holy building, an eternal planting in all time to come".[156] Our
author goes farther than this. He knows that the attendant angels

[152] J. A. T. Robinson, *Honest to God* (London, 1963), pp. 11ff.
[153] *Cf.* Ch. 3:6 (pp. 58f.). Since in OT God dwells in Zion (Ps. 87:1; Isa.
18:7; 31:9; Amos 1:2; Mic. 4:7f.) and "with him also that is of a contrite and
humble spirit" (Isa. 57:15; *cf.* 66:1f.), the identification of the spiritual abode
of God with the community of His people is not far-fetched. See further E.
Lohse, *TWNT* vii (Stuttgart, 1961), pp. 281ff. (*s.v. Σινα*); G. Fohrer and E.
Lohse, *ib.*, pp. 291ff. (*s.v. Σιων*); Pseudo-Cyprian, *De montibus Sina et Sion*;
Strack-Billerbeck, *Komm. zum NT* iii (Munich, 1926), p. 796; K. L. Schmidt,
"Jerusalem als Urbild und Abbild", *Eranos Jahrbuch*, 1950; J. Schreiner, *Sion-
Jerusalem Jahwes Königssitz* (Munich, 1963); T. C. Vriezen, *Jahwe en zijn Stad*
(Amsterdam, 1962).
[154] For the construction and punctuation see p. 370, n. 131.
[155] *Cf.* I Enoch 40:1; Rev. 5:11 (see also Ch. 2:2, p. 28 with n. 3).
[156] 1QS xi. 8f. *Cf.* 1QSa ii. 8f.; 1QM vii. 6.; also J. Strugnell, "The an-
gelic liturgy at Qumran", *VT Supplement* vii (Leiden, 1960), pp. 318ff. Important
NT parallels are I Cor. 11:10; Eph. 3:10.

are sent to minister to the heirs of salvation;[157] how exalted the status of the heirs of salvation is may be gauged from the fact that the Son of God passed by angels in order to partake of flesh and blood with mankind.[158] When, therefore, believers come to the myriads of angels it is not to worship *them*, but to worship the God whose servants they are.[159]

23 How then are we to understand the "church of the firstborn who are enrolled in heaven"? One interpretation is that this is another way of designating the elect angels, called "firstborn" because they were created before men.[160] So, when Hermas asked about the six young men whom he saw building the tower, the ancient lady told him that they were "the holy angels of God who were first created"—the myriads of other men whom he saw bringing up stones for the building being also "holy angels of God", but inferior in rank to the six.[161] But against this interpretation is the description of these "firstborn" ones as "enrolled in heaven". The idea of enrolment in the heavenly book is regularly associated with men.[162] "Rejoice that your names are written in heaven", said Jesus to His disciples (Luke 10:20); and in the Apocalypse repeated reference is made to those whose names are inscribed in "the Lamb's book of life" (Rev. 21:27, etc.).[163] If, then, believers in Christ are said to have come to "the church of the firstborn" in this sense, the reference may be to those men and women who lived and "died in faith" before Christ came, but who "apart from us" could not attain perfection.[164] If so, the phrase is synonymous with "the spirits of just men made perfect" at the end of this verse. But more probably the reference is to the

---

157 Ch. 1:14 (pp. 24f.).

158 Ch. 2:16 (p. 51).

159 *Cf.* Rev. 19:10; 22:9, where the interpreting angel refuses homage from John because he is his fellow-servant.

160 So Spicq, *ad loc.*; he compares Ps. 89:7 (LXX 88:6), where the angels are the βουλὴ ἁγίων (Heb. *sōd qedōšīm*), and the *Extracts of Theodotus* 37:3f., where the highest angels are called πρωτόκτιστοι, "first-created" (quoted by E. Käsemann, *Das wandernde Gottesvolk* [Göttingen, 1938], p. 28).

161 Hermas, *Shepherd*, Vision iii. 4. 1.

162 *Cf.* Westcott and Windisch, *ad loc.*

163 *Cf.* Acts 13:48 (*Acts*, NICNT, p. 283, n. 72); Phil. 4:3.

164 *Cf.* Calvin, *ad loc.*: "The description *firstborn* is not given here to the children of God indiscriminately, as Scripture sometimes does, but he gives this distinction to honour particularly the patriarchs and the other prominent men of the old Church" (W. B. Johnston's translation).

whole communion of saints, including those who, while "militant
here in earth", are enrolled as citizens of heaven.[165] To this
community believers have come—not merely into its presence (as
they have come into the presence of angels innumerable), but into
its membership. All the people of Christ are the "firstborn"
children of God, through their union with Him who is The Firstborn *par excellence*;[166] their birthright is not to be bartered away,
as was Esau's.[167]

Further, the readers have come to "God the Judge of all"—or,
as the phrase is more precisely rendered in RSV, to "a judge
who is God of all".[168] The designation of God as "the Judge of all
the earth" goes back to early biblical times (Gen. 18:25). The
mention of God as judge in this context is calculated to emphasize
the solemnity of the Christian's responsibility; it echoes an earlier
reference to the one "with whom we have to do", before whom
our inmost being lies open to view (Ch. 4:13), and the warning of
Ch. 10:30f. that, since the judgment of His people is God's
prerogative, it is "a fearful thing" to fall into His hands.[169] If we
recognize a continuance of proselyte terminology here, we may
recall Boaz's words of blessing on Ruth: "a full reward be given
thee of Jehovah, the God of Israel, under whose wings thou art
come to take refuge" (Ruth 2:12).[170] The living God to whom

---

165 *Cf.* Westcott, *ad loc.*: "Christian believers in Christ, alike living and dead,
are united in the Body of Christ." So in the eschatological conflict envisaged by
the Qumran community "not only will the angels fight side by side with the
earthly 'holy people' ([1QM] xii, 7–8), but also the 'elect of the holy people', i.e.
former earth-dwellers now in heaven, will fight side by side with the angels"
(Y. Yadin, *The Scroll of the War of the Sons of Light against the Sons of Darkness*
[Oxford, 1962], pp. 241f.).

166 *Cf.* Chs. 1:6, where Jesus is the πρωτότοκος (as against the plural
πρωτότοκοι here); 2:13ff.; Rom. 8:29; Col. 1:15, 18; Rev. 1:5.

167 The birthright in v. 16 is πρωτοτόκια, literally "right of the firstborn".

168 Gk. κριτῇ θεῷ πάντων, but the word order may have only stylistic
significance.

169 The suggestion that God is here designated as the "vindicator" or
"avenger" of His people against their enemies (so Delitzsch, Riggenbach, *ad loc.*)
may be admitted, if we also bear in mind the recurrent emphasis throughout this
epistle that even His people (or indeed, *especially* His people) will incur His
judgment if they rebel against Him or despise His saving message. See also
Moffatt, Spicq, *ad loc.*, and *cf.* Chs. 9:27; 13:4.

170 Ruth did not merely live in Israel as a resident alien but as a religious
proselyte, as witness her words to Naomi: "thy God [shall be] my God" (Ruth

believers come is indeed the refuge and strength of His people, but the intimacy of their covenant-union with Him is not unmixed with awe before His pure holiness. As for "the spirits of just men made perfect",[171] they are surely believers of pre-Christian days, like those mentioned in Ch. 11:40, who could not be "made perfect" until Christ came in the fulness of time and "by one offering ... perfected for ever them that are sanctified" (Chs. 10:14; 11:40). If it was the divine plan that "apart from us they should not be made perfect", it is equally true that apart from them we could not be made perfect; by coming to God we have also come to those who in earlier times came to Him believing "that he is, and that he is a rewarder[172] of them that seek after him" (Ch. 11:6). They fulfilled the promise of Ch. 10:38, "my righteous one shall live by faith"; and the words of Wisdom 3:1 have come true for them: "the souls of the righteous are in the hand of God".[173] No distinction in meaning can be pressed between "spirits" here and "souls" there. Our author's lack of reference to the coming resurrection does not mean that it found no place in his creed (we recall his words in Ch. 11:35 about a "better resurrection"); but it is plain that, for him, the souls of believers do not need to wait until the resurrection to be perfected. They are perfected already in the sense that they are with God in the heavenly Jerusalem.[174]

24 They have come to God; they have come to "the spirits of just men"; and they have come to Him who is the mediator between God and men, "Jesus the mediator of a new covenant". Their ancestors in Moses' day had been borne on eagles' wings and brought to God Himself[175] in terms of the old covenant; that old

---

1:16; the Targum makes Naomi tell her in detail all that becoming a proselyte involves).

[171] In I Enoch 22:9 (cf. 41:8) a place of refreshment in the realm of the dead is reserved for "the spirits of the righteous" (τὰ πνεύματα τῶν δικαίων). Cf. also Hermas, *Shepherd*, Mandate xi. 1. 15, for the phrase πνεύματα δικαίων, where, however, living men of God in a Christian congregation are meant.

[172] Gk. μισθαποδότης, with which Spicq correlates κριτής in this verse.

[173] Gk. δικαίων δὲ ψυχαὶ ἐν χειρὶ θεοῦ.

[174] Cf. the *Westminster Shorter Catechism*, Answer to Question 37: "The souls of believers are at their death made perfect in holiness, and do immediately pass into glory; and their bodies, being still united to Christ, do rest in their graves, till the resurrection."

[175] Cf. Ex. 19:4.

covenant, as we have already learned, has now been antiquated by the new one, of which Jesus is mediator. A different word for "new" is used here from that employed in the similar phrase in Ch. 9:15, but the different word is to be accounted for in terms of rhythm and not because of any distinction in meaning.[176] Since Jesus' sacrifice of Himself, those who come to God must "draw near unto God through him" (Ch. 7:25).

To "draw near unto God through him" means "to enter into the holy place by the blood of Jesus" (Ch. 10:19); accordingly, believers are further said to have come to "the blood of sprinkling". This may remind us of "the sprinkling of the blood" at the time of the first passover (Ch. 11:28);[177] but more probably our author is thinking of the covenant-blood of Christ as the antitype of the blood sprinkled at the inauguration of the old covenant. By the blood of the new covenant, symbolically applied, believers' hearts are "sprinkled from an evil conscience" (Ch. 10:22). The removal of an evil conscience does away with the barrier between them and God; the sacrifice of Christ thus "has better things to tell than the blood of Abel" (NEB). Abel's blood cried out to God from the ground, protesting against his murder and appealing for vindication;[178] but the blood of Christ brings a message of cleansing, forgiveness and peace with God to all who place their faith in Him.

---

[176] Here $\delta\iota\alpha\theta\dot{\eta}\varkappa\eta\varsigma$ $\nu\dot{\epsilon}\alpha\varsigma$ as against $\delta\iota\alpha\theta\dot{\eta}\varkappa\eta\varsigma$ $\varkappa\alpha\iota\nu\tilde{\eta}\varsigma$ in Ch. 9:15. The conventional distinction between $\varkappa\alpha\iota\nu\acute{o}\varsigma$ ("new in character") and $\nu\dot{\epsilon}o\varsigma$ ("new in respect of time") cannot be universally pressed; cf. the $\varkappa\alpha\iota\nu\grave{o}\varsigma$ $\ddot{\alpha}\nu\theta\varrho\omega\pi o\varsigma$ of Eph. 4:24 as against the $\nu\dot{\epsilon}o\varsigma$ $\ddot{\alpha}\nu\theta\varrho\omega\pi o\varsigma$ of Col. 3:10 (Moffatt points out that the new Jerusalem of Test. Dan 5:12 is $\nu\dot{\epsilon}\alpha$, whereas elsewhere it is $\varkappa\alpha\iota\nu\dot{\eta}$).

[177] "Was the author of Hebrews, when writing these words, aware of the Jewish tradition that the offering of Cain and Abel took place on the 14th of Nisan, i.e. on the same day on which the blood of Jesus was shed (Targum Jonathan on Gen. 4:3)?" (E. Nestle, ExT xvii [1905–6], p. 566).

[178] Cf. Ch. 11:4 (p. 286). In I Enoch 22:6f. Enoch asks Raphael whose spirit it is "whose voice goes forth and makes suit to heaven"; Raphael answers: "This is the spirit which went forth from Abel, whom his brother Cain slew; he makes his suit against him till his seed is destroyed from the face of the earth, and annihilated from among the seed of men." So, in TB Sanhedrin 96b, the blood of Zechariah the son of Jehoiada (II Chron. 24:24; cf. p. 340) cried from the ground for vengeance and would not be appeased until the blood of many Jews was shed by Nebuzaradan, thus atoning for his murder.

9. PAY HEED TO THE VOICE OF GOD!

Ch. 12:25-29

25 See[179] that ye refuse not him that speaketh. For if they escaped not[180] when they refused him that warned *them* on earth,[181] much more *shall not* we *escape* who turn away from him that *warneth* from heaven:

26 whose voice then shook the earth: but now he hath promised, saying, Yet once more will I make to tremble[182] not the earth only, but also the heaven.[183]

27 And this *word*,[184] Yet once more, signifieth the removing of those things that are shaken,[185] as of things that have been made, that those things which are not shaken may remain.

28 Wherefore, receiving a kingdom that cannot be shaken, let us have[186] grace,[187] whereby we may offer service[188] well-pleasing[189] to God with reverence and awe:[190]

29 for our God is a consuming fire.[191]

---

[179] Gk. βλέπετε, as in Ch. 3:12.

[180] Gk. εἰ γὰρ ἐκεῖνοι οὐκ ἐξέφυγον, with οὐκ instead of μή since emphasis is laid on the fact that they did not escape. For ἐξέφυγον (cf. Ch. 2:3, ἐκφευξόμεθα) a few authorities (Ν^c D K L M Ψ etc.) have the uncompounded ἔφυγον.

[181] Gk. ἐπὶ γῆς παραιτησάμενοι τὸν χρηματίζοντα, where ἐπὶ γῆς, while it modifies χρηματίζοντα, is thrown back to the beginning of the phrase for emphasis in contrast with the following ἀπ᾽ οὐρανῶν. The manuscript tradition shows variations in the word order.

[182] Gk. σείσω (LXX συσσείσω, "I will shake together"), for which a few authorities (D K L P etc.) read the present σείω (probably under the influence of the similar oracle in Hag. 2:21).

[183] Hag. 2:6, LXX.

[184] Gk. τὸ δέ, introducing a quoted phrase, as in Eph. 4:9.

[185] Gk. τὴν τῶν σαλευομένων μετάθεσιν (Ν* A C 33 and a few authorities); τήν is omitted by P⁴⁶ D* 1739, whose reading is preferred by G. Zuntz (*op. cit.*, pp. 117f.). L P and the bulk of later manuscripts read τῶν σαλευομένων τὴν μετάθεσιν.

[186] Gk. ἔχωμεν (P^{46c} A D etc., with the Syriac Peshitta and Coptic versions, 3 Vulgate MSS, and TR), for which P^{46*} Ν P 33 69 and the bulk of later MSS, with the Latin and Harclean Syriac versions, read ἔχομεν, "we have". This variation between the indicative and subjunctive is a common textual phenomenon, the pronunciation of the two forms being practically identical, and a decision must be reached mainly on the ground of context, which here unquestionably demands ἔχωμεν.

[187] Better, "let us be grateful" (RSV), "let us therefore give thanks to God" (NEB). This is the regular force of Gk. χάριν ἔχω (like Lat. *gratiam habeo*).

25 It is not suggested in the Exodus narrative that there was anything culpable in the people's request to Moses that God should not speak to them directly, but through an intermediary. That request sprang from their terror at the awe-inspiring circumstances of the theophany. When our author warns his readers not to "refuse ... him that speaketh", he uses the same verb for refusing as he did in verse 19,[192] where the people "entreated that no word more should be spoken unto them"—or, as it might be rendered, "refused to have any further word spoken to them". But, whatever was the people's attitude when God spoke at Sinai, the Pentateuchal record makes it plain that time and again throughout their wilderness wanderings they failed to pay heed to the commandments of God, and suffered for their disobedience. This has formed the basis of a solemn warning in the earlier part of the epistle (Ch. 3:7ff.), and the warning is repeated here. The Israelites in the wilderness did not escape judgment when they disregarded the voice—the voice of God, surely[193]—that thundered from Sinai. But if it was from an earthly hill that God proclaimed

---

[188] Either aorist subjunctive λατρεύσωμεν with P⁴⁶ or, more probably, present subjunctive λατρεύωμεν with A D L 33, the Latin versions and TR (the present indicative λατρεύομεν, in ℵ P and the bulk of later MSS, is a further example of the common phenomenon mentioned in n. 186 above).

[189] Gk. εὐαρέστως, "acceptably", here only in NT.

[190] Gk. μετὰ εὐλαβείας καὶ δέους, with P⁴⁶ ℵ A D* and a few other MSS, the Syriac Peshitta and Armenian versions. Variant readings are μετὰ εὐλαβείας καὶ αἰδοῦς (M P 1739 etc., with the Latin and, apparently, Harclean Syriac versions) and μετὰ αἰδοῦς καὶ εὐλαβείας (K L with the majority of later MSS and TR, whence AV, "with reverence and godly fear"). For εὐλάβεια cf. Ch. 5:7 (p. 101 with n. 61). This is the only NT instance of δέος, "fear".

[191] Gk. καὶ γὰρ ὁ θεὸς ἡμῶν πῦρ καταναλίσκον, from Deut. 4:24, LXX: ὅτι κύριος ὁ θεός σου πῦρ καταναλίσκον ἐστίν ("for the Lord thy God is a consuming fire").

[192] Gk. παραιτέομαι, not used in the Greek version of the Exodus narrative here referred to. Windisch (HNT, p. 113) thinks our author does represent the Israelites' παραίτησις as wicked.

[193] Gk. τὸν χρηματίζοντα (cf. the passive uses of the same verb in Chs. 8:5; 11:7, where God is the speaker). Moffatt (ICC, ad loc.) argues that the one "that warned them on earth" is Moses, since in the Pentateuchal narrative God is repeatedly said to have spoken to Israel from heaven (Ex. 20:22; Deut. 4:36); he translates τὸν χρηματίζοντα as "their instructor" (comparing Acts 7:38, where Moses "received living oracles to give unto us"). But while the Sinaitic revelation was given from heaven, it was an earthly revelation in comparison with the revelation given in the gospel.

the statutes which formed the basis of the old covenant, it is
from the heavenly Zion, from His unseen throne, that He speaks
in the gospel. The "how much more" argument of Chs. 2:2f. and
10:29 is pressed home again: to disobey the gospel incurs judgment more certain and terrible even than that incurred by disobedience to the law.

26 When God spoke from Sinai, "the whole mount quaked"
(Ex. 19:18). This earthquake remained deeply rooted in the
national memory, and is celebrated in the Psalter and other Old
Testament poems.

"O God, when thou wentest forth before thy people,
When thou didst march through the wilderness,
The earth trembled, the heavens also dropped rain
At the presence of God:
Yon Sinai[194] trembled at the presence of God,
The God of Israel" (Ps. 68:7f.).[195]

In the Old Testament earthquake is also expected to mark the
coming day of the Lord, "when he ariseth to shake mightily the
earth" (Isa. 2:19, 21); and not only earthquake, but the shaking
of heaven too: "I will make the heavens to tremble, and the earth
shall be shaken out of its place, in the wrath of Jehovah of hosts,
and in the day of his fierce anger" (Isa. 13:13). In similar language
the prophet Haggai conveys an oracle of assurance to Zerubbabel
the governor and Joshua the high priest[196] at the dedication of the
Second Temple (516 B.C.): "Yet once, it is a little while, and I will
shake the heavens, and the earth, and the dry land; and I will
shake all nations; and the precious things of all nations shall come;
and I will fill this house with glory, saith Jehovah of hosts" (Hag.
2:6f.). In their context these words declare God's purpose, in the
day when He rises in vindication of His cause, to put down Gentile
dominion, to exalt the throne of David, and to make Jerusalem

[194] Heb. *zeh sīnai* (*cf.* Judg. 5:5), perhaps a divine title: "He of Sinai". The
translation will then be: "at the presence of God, the God of Sinai; at the
presence of God, the God of Israel". *Cf.* A. Weiser, *Die Psalmen* (Göttingen,
1955), p. 326.
[195] *Cf.* also Judg. 5:4f.; Pss. 77:18; 114:4, 7. It may have been on one of
these poetical passages that our author depended here, since the LXX of Ex.
19:18 speaks not of the quaking of the earth but of the terror of the people.
[196] *Cf.* p. 77, n. 28.

and its temple the centre of worship and allegiance for all nations.[197] Our author interprets them of the end of the present world-order; the picture is similar to that in the Apocalypse, where earth and heaven flee away from the face of the Judge on the great throne, to be replaced by a new heaven and a new earth (Rev. 20:11; 21:1).[198]

27–29 When, in accordance with the divine promise, this cosmic convulsion takes place—when (in Dryden's words)

"the last and dreadful hour
This crumbling pageant shall devour"—

the whole material universe will be shaken to pieces, and the only things to survive will be those that are unshakable. To this unshakable order, however, belongs the kingdom which believers in Christ share with Him—a kingdom, because their great high priest is a *royal* priest.[199]

In the current debate whether the created world[200] was eternal or not our author stands right within the Hebrew tradition. He

---

[197] *Cf.* the similar oracle in Hag. 2:21f.

[198] *Cf.* Rev. 6:12ff.; 16:18f.; II Pet. 3:10; I Enoch 60:1; II Baruch 32:1; 59:3. There is no need to suppose that this language was suggested to our author by some recent earthquake, like that at Antioch in A.D. 115 (so W. L. Dulière, "Les chérubins du troisième Temple à Antioche", *Zeitschrift für Religions- und Geistesgeschichte* xiii [1961], pp. 201ff.).

[199] The term "kingdom" may have been suggested to our author because in the oracle of Hag. 2:21f., a companion to that quoted in v. 26, God promises to "overthrow the throne of kingdoms" and "destroy the strength of the kingdoms of the nations"—although in both clauses LXX says "kings" (βασιλέων) and not "kingdoms" (βασιλειῶν). The phrase βασιλείαν παραλαμβάνω is a common one for receiving (or succeeding to) a kingdom (*cf.* Dan. 5:31, LXX and Theod.); in Dan. 7:18 (LXX and Theod.) it is used of the receiving of the kingdom by the saints of the Most High (and for the sense we may compare Luke 12:32; 22:29, although different verbs are used with βασιλεία there). As in Dan. 7:27 the kingdom which the saints receive is "an everlasting kingdom", so here it is unshakable, ἀσάλευτος, an adjective used by Philo to describe the laws of Moses (*Life of Moses*, ii. 14). Our author thus shows himself conversant with the primitive gospel vocabulary, although for the most part he communicates the saving truth in a new idiom. The present participle παραλαμβάνοντες suggests that the people of Christ have not finally entered into their royal heritage with Him, although it is already theirs by promise.

[200] "The shaking of these created things (ὡς πεποιημένων) means their removal" (NEB).

has already[201] quoted with approval the passage in Ps. 102:25ff. which emphasizes the transitoriness of all created things:

"They shall pass away, but thou endurest;
Like clothes they shall all grow old;
Thou shalt fold them up like a cloak;
Yes, they shall be changed like any garment" (NEB).

Philo tries, rather awkwardly, to mediate between the biblical doctrine and the Platonic doctrine of the eternity of the world;[202] but our author is quite forthright. Earlier he has emphasized the transitoriness of the world in order to set in contrast the eternity of the Son of God; now he emphasizes it again in order to set in contrast the eternity of that new order into which the Son of God has brought His people.

"Let us be thankful," he says, "that the kingdom which we receive is unshakable; and in that spirit of thankfulness let us offer acceptable worship to God." To the grace of God the proper response is a grateful heart, and the words and actions that flow from a grateful heart are the sacrifices in which God takes delight.[203]

At the same time, such sacrificial worship must be offered with a due sense of the majesty and holiness of the God with whom we have to do: not only thankfulness, but reverence and awe must mark His people's approach to Him; "for our God is a consuming fire".[204] He who descended on Mount Sinai in fire and spoke to His people from the midst of that fire still consumes in the white heat of His purity everything that is unworthy of Himself.[205] On Isa. 33:14 George Adam Smith wrote:

"To Isaiah life was so penetrated by the active justice of God, that he described it as bathed in fire, as blown through with fire. Righteousness was no mere doctrine to this prophet:

---

[201] Ch. 1:10–12 (pp. 21ff.).

[202] The world, according to Philo, is indestructible, not *per se*, but by the will of its Creator. "The world has come to be, and its coming to be is the beginning of its dissolution, even if by the providence of its Maker it is rendered immortal; and there was once a time when it was not" (*Decalogue*, 58). The authenticity of the treatise *On the Eternity of the World*, a treatise ascribed to Philo in which the world appears to be treated as uncreated and inherently indestructible, is suspect.

[203] *Cf.* Ch. 13:15f. (pp. 405ff.).

[204] See p. 381, n. 191. *Cf.* Ch. 10:27, 31 (p. 257, n. 125; p. 263, n. 154).

[205] *Cf.* I Cor. 3:13–15.

it was the most real thing in history; it was the presence which pervaded and explained all phenomena. We shall understand the difference between Isaiah and his people if we have ever for our eyes' sake looked at a great conflagration through a coloured glass which allowed us to see the solid materials— stone, wood, and iron—but prevented us from seeing the flames and shimmering heat. To look thus is to see pillars, lintels, and cross-beams, twist and fall, crumble and fade; but how inexplicable the process seems! Take away the glass, and everything is clear. The fiery element is filling all the interstices that were blank to us before, and beating upon the solid material. The heat becomes visible, shimmering even where there is no flame. Just so had it been with the sinners in Judah these forty years .... Isaiah alone faced life with open vision, which filled up for him the interstices of experience and gave terrible explanation to fate. It was a vision that nearly scorched the eyes out of him. Life as he saw it was steeped in flame—the glowing righteousness of God. Jerusalem was full *of the spirit of justice, the spirit of burning. The light of Israel is for a fire, and his Holy One for a flame.*[206] ... So Isaiah saw life, and flashed it on his countrymen. At last the glass fell from their eyes also, and they cried aloud, *Who among us shall dwell with the devouring fire? Who among us shall dwell with everlasting burnings?*"[207]

It is an aspect of the character of God as revealed in the Bible that plays little part in much present-day thinking about Him; but if we are to be completely "honest to God", we dare not ignore it. Reverence and awe before His holiness are not incompatible with grateful trust and love in response to His mercy.

Who can behold the blazing light?
Who can approach consuming flame?
None but Thy wisdom knows Thy might;
None but Thy word can speak Thy name.[208]

---

[206] Isa. 4:4; 10:17; *cf.* also Isa. 30:33.
[207] G. A. Smith, *The Book of Isaiah* ii (London, 1927), pp. 350f.
[208] I. Watts.

CHAPTER XIII

VII. CONCLUDING EXHORTATION AND PRAYER
Ch. 13:1–21

Our author's argument has now been rounded off, and if his work had been a written homily and nothing more, there would have been no need for anything further. What follows in Ch. 13 resembles the usual assortment of ethical and practical admonition and personal information with which New Testament epistles tend to close. Why this document should end like an epistle although it does not begin like one is a general problem of introduction.[1] One thing is certain: Ch. 13 is an integral part of the text of the document, and there is no reason in either internal or external evidence why it should be regarded as in some way a separate composition. Odd theories have been advanced from time to time, suggesting, for example, that Ch. 13 or part of it was written in deliberate imitation of Paul's epistolary style in order to secure acceptance for the whole work as a Pauline epistle,[2] or that it was written by Paul himself as a "letter of commendation" to validate the author's thesis,[3] or that it was a fragment of a Pauline letter accidentally and mistakenly tacked on to a work with which it really had nothing to do.[4] These theories can be given no higher

---

[1] See pp. xxiii, xlviif.

[2] *Cf.* W. Wrede, *Das literarische Rätsel des Hebräerbriefs* (Göttingen, 1906). Such arguments have been based, *inter alia*, on the presence of several Pauline words in Heb. 13 which do not appear in Heb. 1–12. C. R. Williams ("A Word-Study of Hebrews XIII", *JBL* xxx [1911], pp. 129ff.) counts 25 such words, but points out that the chapter also contains several words which are not Pauline, or are used in a different sense from that which Paul gives them. *Cf.* also C. Spicq, "L'authenticité du chapitre xiii de l'Épître aux Hébreux", *Coniectanea Neotestamentica* xi (1948), pp. 226ff.

[3] *Cf.* G. A. Simcox, "Heb. xiii; 2 Tim. iv", *ExT* x (1898–99), pp. 430ff. F. J. Badcock suggested that vv. 23–25 were Paul's postscript to a latter which was substantially the work of Barnabas (*The Pauline Epistles and the Epistle to the Hebrews in their Historical Setting* [London, 1939], pp. 199f.); *cf.* p. xxxvii, n. 62.

[4] E. D. Jones ("The Authorship of Hebrews xiii", *ExT* xlvi [1934–35], pp. 562ff.) argues that this chapter was the end of Paul's "severe letter" to Corinth. He points out that a Corinthian destination and Pauline authorship for Heb. 13:23–25 were defended by T. W. Ll. Davies (*Pauline Readjustments* [London, 1927]), who, however, went on to argue that, since this section is integral to the whole epistle, the whole epistle was written by Paul to the Corinthians, and

status than that of curiosities of literary criticism. The reversion
in verses 10–16 to the main theme of the epistle is sufficient
evidence, if evidence were required, of the integrity of Ch.
13 with the foregoing chapters.

1. ETHICAL INJUNCTIONS

Ch. 13:1-6

1 Let love of the brethren continue.

2 Forget not to show love unto strangers: for thereby some
have entertained angels unawares.[5]

3 Remember them that are in bonds, as bound with them;
them that are ill-treated, as being yourselves also in the
body.

4 *Let* marriage *be* had in honor among all, and *let* the bed
be undefiled:[6] for fornicators and adulterers God will judge.

5 Be ye free from the love of money; content[7] with such

---

is, in fact, the "previous letter" referred to in I Cor. 5:9! A reply to E. D.
Jones's argument by R. V. G. Tasker ("The Integrity of the Epistle to the
Hebrews", *ExT* xlvii [1935–36], pp. 136ff.) is a good defence of the integrity
of Ch. 13 with the rest of the epistle.

5 Gk. ἔλαθόν τινες ξενίσαντες ἀγγέλους, an excellent classical idiom.

6 Since the verb is left to be understood (*cf.* the literal Rheims rendering,
"Marriage honourable in all, and the bed undefiled"), it may be understood
as indicative (so AV, "Marriage is honourable in all, and the bed undefiled"),
in which case we should have a defence of holy matrimony as against an insistence on the superiority of celibacy; or as imperative (as in ARV, etc.), in which
case we have an admonition to safeguard the sanctity of marriage against
adulterous encroachments and the like. The latter is the more probable construction, both because of the following clause ("for fornicators and adulterers
God will judge") and also because the parallel construction at the beginning of
v. 5 (ἀφιλάργυρος ὁ τρόπος) implies the imperative mood, "Let your way of life
be free from love of money" (the indicative, "Your way of life is free from love
of money", would be inappropriate).

7 Gk. ἀρκούμενοι τοῖς παροῦσιν, probably an imperatival use of the participle,
common in such lists of ethical admonitions (*cf. Ephesians-Colossians*, NICNT
[Grand Rapids, 1957], p. 280, n. 99, on Col. 3:13; and see D. Daube, "Appended Note: Participle and Imperative in I Peter", in E. G. Selwyn, *The First
Epistle of St. Peter* [London, 1946], pp. 467ff.; N. Turner, *A Grammar of NT
Greek* [ed. J. H. Moulton], iii [Edinburgh, 1963], p. 343, with bibliography in
n. 1). For the plural ἀρκούμενοι P⁴⁶ and 1739 (with M = 0121) read the
singular ἀρκούμενος (a reading present also in manuscripts used by Augustine)—

387

things as ye have: for himself hath said, I will in no wise fail thee, neither will I in any wise forsake thee.[8]

6 So that with good courage we say,[9]
The Lord is my helper; I will not fear:
What shall man do unto me?[10]

Like Paul and the other writers of New Testament epistles, our author is alive to the ethical implications of Christian doctrine. He does not systematize his ethical injunctions as some of them do[11] (his readers had probably been well grounded already in the early catechesis of Christian *didachē*), but he urges upon them certain Christian virtues which he presumably knew it was desirable to emphasize in their present situation—brotherly love, hospitality, help to those in need, chastity and contentment.

---

probably by mechanical conformity to τρόπος (the plural is an elegant "sense construction"). See G. Zuntz, *The Text of the Epistles* (London, 1953), p. 42. E. K. Simpson ("Vettius Valens and the NT," *EQ* ii [1930], pp. 389ff.) points out (p. 392) an example of the phrase in Vettius Valens, *Anthologiarum Libri* (ed. W. Kroll), 220. 25: ἀρκοῦνται τοῖς παροῦσιν, and suggests that the construction in our present passage, which he regards as anacoluthic, is due to the fact that the expression was proverbial (which is confirmed by its occurrences elsewhere).

[8] Josh. 1:5, where there is an echo of Deut. 31:6, 8. The Greek (οὐ μή σε ἀνῶ οὐδ᾽ οὐ μή σε ἐγκαταλίπω) does not correspond exactly to any surviving LXX text, but precisely the same form of the quotation appears in Philo (*Confusion of Tongues*, 166). P. Katz, referring also to Philo, *On Dreams*, i. 3, 179–181, concludes that Philo and our author quote a variant LXX reading of Gen. 28:15, expanded from Deut. 31:6, 8 (*Biblica* xxxiii [1952], pp. 523ff.).

[9] Gk. ὥστε θαρροῦντας ἡμᾶς λέγειν. P[46] Ψ 1739 omit ἡμᾶς ("this is hardly more than a scribal slip", says Zuntz, *op. cit.*, p. 42).

[10] Ps. 118:6. Before "I will not fear" (οὐ φοβηθήσομαι) P[46] A D with the majority of later MSS and TR insert "and" (καί); so AV, which also subordinates the following clause to "I will not fear". The ARV construction is much preferable.

[11] Cf. *Ephesians-Colossians*, NICNT, pp. 264ff. O. Michel, however, sees evidence of topical arrangement in the injunctions of vv. 1–6; he discerns four pairs: (i) brotherly love and hospitality (vv. 1, 2); (ii) care for prisoners and others in trouble (v. 3); (iii) honor of wedlock and avoidance of unchastity (v. 4); (iv) avoidance of covetousness and cultivation of contentment (vv. 5, 6), and concludes that this chapter is no mere postscript but a section which has its distinctive contribution to make to the structure of the complete epistle. Future commentators on Hebrews, he suggests, should pay more attention to the artistic form of the epistle than has generally been paid in the past (*Der Brief an die Hebräer*, MK [Göttingen, 1949], pp. 328f.).

1 "Love of the brethren" was a virtue highly esteemed in antiquity. The Byzantine anthologist Stobaeus gathers together a number of quotations from ancient authors under the caption: "That brotherly love and a proper disposition towards one's kinsfolk is an excellent thing, and that it is necessary." In the biblical area the classic passage is Ps. 133:1, "Behold, how good and how pleasant it is for brethren to dwell together in unity!" The word used here *(philadelphia)* appears in the Pauline writings and in both the Petrine epistles; and the grace of brotherly love itself, whatever terms be used, is inculcated throughout the New Testament. "Concerning love of the brethren,"[12] writes Paul to the Thessalonians, "ye have no need that one write unto you: for ye yourselves are taught of God to love one another; for indeed ye do it ..." (I Thess. 4:9f.). Such brotherly love is no mere sentiment; it can be a very costly thing, as John emphasizes: "Hereby know we love, because he laid down his life for us: and we ought to lay down our lives for the brethren. But whoso hath the world's goods, and beholdeth his brother in need, and shutteth up his compassion from him, how doth the love of God abide in him?" (I John 3:16f.). If a weakening of faith and resolution among the recipients of this epistle led to a weakening of the bonds that united them to their fellow-Christians, this would add urgency to the plea that brotherly love should *continue* among them. Some specific forms of brotherly love are enjoined in the following verses.

2 Strangers, and especially strangers belonging to the Christian brotherhood, must be shown hospitality. Among Jews and Gentiles alike hospitality to strangers ranked high as a virtue; it was, indeed, a religious obligation. Among the Greeks, strangers were under the special protection of Zeus, in his rôle as Zeus Xenios, "Zeus the patron of strangers". On occasion, indeed, Zeus or one of the other gods was believed to have assumed the disguise of a wayfarer and brought great blessing to those who treated him hospitably, not realizing whom they were entertaining.[13] Among the Jews Abraham was regarded as outstanding for his hospitality as for his other virtues;[14] a true son of Abraham

---

[12] Gk. φιλαδελφία, as here.

[13] As in the story of Philemon and Baucis (*cf. Acts*, NICNT [Grand Rapids, 1954], pp. 291f.).

[14] According to Resh Laqish (TB *Soṭa* 10a) it was to refresh weary travellers that Abraham planted a tamarisk tree at Beersheba (Gen. 21:33). Some rabbis

must be hospitable too. In the New Testament hospitality is incumbent on all Christians,[15] and Christian leaders in particular must be "given to hospitality" (I Tim. 3:2; Tit. 1:8). Christians travelling from one place to another on business would be specially glad of hospitality from fellow-Christians. Inns throughout the Roman Empire were places of doubtful repute, as the reader of Petronius and Apuleius is well aware, and would provide very uncongenial company for Christians.

The opportunity of free board and lodging might tempt some unscrupulous characters to masquerade as Christians. Proteus Peregrinus in Lucian's satire comes to mind;[16] and the necessity of some rough-and-ready rule of thumb for detecting impostors is implied in the *Didache*: "Let every apostle who comes to you be received as the Lord, but he must not stay more than one day, or two if it is absolutely necessary; if he stays three days, he is a false prophet. And when an apostle leaves you, let him take nothing but a loaf, until he reaches further lodging for the night; if he asks for money, he is a false prophet."[17] Some Christians who had been deceived by such impostors might be chary of offering hospitality too readily next time they were asked for it, but here they are encouraged with the remark that some who have given hospitality to passing strangers found that they were entertaining "angels unawares". Those who are given to hospitality find that such happy experiences far outweigh the unhappy ones.

The reference is no doubt primarily to Abraham's experience when he entertained "three men" so hospitably by the terebinth of Mamre,[18] and found that one of them was no other than

---

elaborated the story by saying that he planted a whole orchard, others that he erected an inn. He called there on the name of "Jehovah, the Everlasting God" (*'Ēl 'Ôlām*), it was added, in order that all who passed that way might name His name.

15   *Cf.* Matt. 25:35f.; Rom. 12:13; I Pet. 4:9, etc.

16   Lucian, *The Death of Peregrinus*, 11ff.

17   *Didache* 11:4–6.

18   Gen. 18:1ff. At the wedding of the son of Rabban Gamaliel II, the bridegroom's father poured wine for the guests, some of whom thought it unfitting that they should be waited upon thus by so distinguished a scholar. They remembered, however, that Abraham, a greater man than Gamaliel, had waited upon others. "Ah!" said someone, "but these were ministering angels." "Yes", was the reply, "but Abraham did not know that; to him they looked like

Yahweh,[19] who promised Abraham and Sarah that they would have a son the following year. When Yahweh stayed to speak with Abraham, His two angelic companions went on to Sodom and were entertained there in the house of Lot, to whom they brought deliverance from the catastrophe that overwhelmed the city next day.[20] The incidents of Gideon[21] and Manoah,[22] and Tobit[23] at a later date, may also have been in our author's mind. He is not necessarily encouraging his readers to expect that those whom they entertain will turn out to be supernatural beings travelling incognito; he is assuring them that some of their visitors will prove to be true messengers of God to them, bringing a greater blessing than they receive.

3 The community addressed in this epistle had already, in earlier days, shown practical sympathy with their imprisoned friends.[24] Here they are urged to go on remembering this Christian duty. Lucian no doubt gives a fairly accurate account of Christian practice in this regard when he describes how Proteus Peregrinus, during his period of association with the Christians, was imprisoned: the Christians "left no stone unturned in their endeavor to procure his release. When this proved impossible, they looked after his wants in all other matters with untiring solicitude and devotion. From earliest dawn old women ('widows,' they are called[25]) and orphan children might be seen waiting about the prison-doors; while the officers of the church, by bribing the jailors, were able to spend the night inside with him. Meals were brought in, and they went through their sacred formulas."[26] This picture, satirical as it is in intention, can be duplicated many times over from other records of the concern which Christians showed

---

Arabs" (TB *Qiddushin* 32*b*). *Cf.* Josephus, *Ant.* i. 196 ("he thought they were strangers"); Philo, *Abraham*, 107ff.

19 To be understood, no doubt, as the "angel of the LORD" (*mal'akh Yahweh*), the executive agent or personification of God's relation of grace to His people.

20 Gen. 19:1ff.

21 Judg. 6:11ff.

22 Judg. 13:3ff.

23 Tobit 3:17; 5:4ff.

24 *Cf*. Ch. 10:32ff. (pp. 269f.).

25 *Cf*. I Tim. 5:3ff.

26 *The Death of Peregrinus*, 12. Lucian probably models his account on the behavior of Christians at various places where Ignatius broke his journey (*c*. A.D. 115) on the way from Syrian Antioch to the amphitheatre in Rome.

for those who were in prison or otherwise suffering for their faith, ignoring the personal risks involved.[27]

In saying, "Remember them that are in bonds, as bound with them", our author need not imply that his readers have themselves suffered imprisonment (this might be true of some, but not of all); we need see no more in his words than a specific application of the Pauline principle that if "one member suffereth, all the members suffer with it" (I Cor. 12:26).[28] A capacity for putting oneself in another's place and exercising imaginative sympathy is part of true charity. This same imaginative sympathy should be extended to all who were ill-treated;[29] those who are themselves "in the body" are in a position to imagine how they would feel if the same ill-treatment were meted out to them. The phrase "in the body" should not be interpreted to mean "in the body of Christ (as fellow-members)".[30]

4 The injunction to honor the marriage union and abstain from sexual sin may also be brought under the general heading of brotherly love; chastity is not opposed to charity,[31] but is part of it. Here is no exaltation of celibacy as something inherently superior to marriage; the marriage union is divinely ordained, and its sacred precincts must not be polluted by the intrusion of a third party, of either sex. Fornication and adultery are not synonymous in the New Testament: adultery[32] implies unfaithfulness by either party to the marriage vow, while the word translated "fornication"[33] covers a wide range of sexual irregularities, including unions within bounds prohibited by law.[34] Our author agrees with other New Testament writers that those who are guilty of such practices incur the judgment of God. "Let no

---

[27] See p. 270 with n. 185.

[28] The *Epistle to Diognetus* (6:7) speaks of Christians as "confined in the world as in a prison" as the soul is imprisoned in the body, but that is hardly the thought here; the prefix συν- in συνδεδεμένοι implies some form of sharing in the lot of those who were actually in prison.

[29] Gk. κακουχούμενοι, as in Ch. 11:37. *Cf.* also p. 319, n. 179.

[30] This "interpretation ...—beautiful as the thought is—is inadmissible" (B. F. Westcott, *ad loc.*).

[31] As against G. M. Carstairs, *This Island Now* (London, 1963), p. 50.

[32] Gk. μοιχεία.

[33] Gk. πορνεία (*cf.* Ch. 12:16, pp. 366f.). On the whole question see O. A. Piper, *The Biblical View of Sex and Marriage* (New York, 1960).

[34] *Cf. Acts*, NICNT, p. 315 with n. 51.

man deceive you with empty words," says Paul; "for because of these things cometh the wrath of God upon the sons of disobedience"[35] (Eph. 5:6).

5–6 When Paul speaks like this, he includes among "these things" unchastity and covetousness. Covetousness, indeed, in its New Testament connotation can refer to illicit sexual desire as well as to love of money.[36] It was therefore a natural transition of thought for our author to pass from his injunction about chastity to his plea to his readers not to live for money. Here too he is in line with the pervasive teaching of the New Testament. Our Lord warned His hearers that they could not serve God and Mammon,[37] and that "a man's life consisteth not in the abundance of the things which he possesseth" (Luke 12:15). We forget this warning every time we ask how much a man is worth, when we really mean how much he owns. The adjective which our author uses here, meaning "free from love of money",[38] occurs in one other place in the New Testament, where it is laid down that a "bishop" or leader in a Christian church must be "no lover of money" (I Tim. 3:3); "for the love of money[39] is the root of all evils; it is through this craving that some have wandered away from the faith and pierced their hearts with many pangs" (I Tim. 6:10, RSV).

The chief pang which pierces the heart of the lover of money

---

35   *Cf.* Col. 3:5f.; I Cor. 6:9f.; I Thess. 4:3-6.

36   *Cf.* I Thess. 4:6, "that no man ... wrong (πλεονεκτεῖν) his brother in the matter"—*sc.* of conceiving a sinful desire and committing a trespass against another man's family circle, by illicit relations with one of his womenfolk.

37   Matt. 6:24; Luke 16:13. *Cf.* Dante, *Purgatorio* xix. 70ff., where the avaricious (including Pope Adrian V) cry out, "My soul cleaveth unto the dust" (Ps. 119:25), like Bunyan's man with the muck-rake. *Cf.* also Milton (*Paradise Lost* i. 679ff.):

"Mammon, the least erected spirit that fell
From heaven; for e'en in heaven his looks and thoughts
Were always downward bent, admiring more
The riches of heaven's pavement, trodden gold,
Than aught divine or holy else enjoyed
In vision beatific."

(Milton's reference to heaven's "pavement" may have been suggested by the Vulgate of Ps. 119:25, quoted in Latin by Dante, *loc. cit.*, line 73: *adhaesit pauimento anima mea.*)

38   Gk. ἀφιλάργυρος.

39   Gk. φιλαργυρία.

is gnawing anxiety. The greedy man can never be a happy man, but the opposite of covetousness is contentment. Here too there is a close affinity between this passage and I Timothy: "There is great gain in godliness with contentment;[40] for we brought nothing into the world, and we cannot take anything out of the world; but if we have food and clothing, with these we shall be content" (I Tim. 6:6-8, RSV). Behind both documents lies our Lord's teaching: "Do not be anxious, saying, 'What shall we eat?' or 'What shall we drink?' or 'What shall we wear?' For the Gentiles seek all these things; and your heavenly Father knows that you need them all. But seek first his kingdom and his righteousness, and all these things shall be yours as well" (Matt. 6:31-33). "Be content with what you have," says our author. But the carefree contentment of which he speaks is not an irresponsible improvidence; it springs from an intelligent trust in God and acceptance of His promises. If to each one of His people God gives the assurance, "I will never leave you or desert you" (NEB), their reasonable response may well be made in the words of the psalmist: "Jehovah is on my side; I will not fear: what can man do unto me?" (Ps. 118:6).

2. EXAMPLES TO FOLLOW

Ch. 13:7-8

7 Remember them that had the rule over you, men that spake unto you the word of God; and considering the issue of their life, imitate their faith.

8 Jesus Christ *is* the same yesterday and to-day, *yea* and for ever.

7 Three times in this chapter mention is made of their guides or leaders.[41] In verse 17 they are told to obey them; in verse 24 they are asked to convey the writer's greetings to them; here they are exhorted to remember them. In verses 17 and 24 the reference plainly is to leaders who are still alive and active;

---

[40] Gk. αὐτάρκεια. *Cf.* Phil. 4:11, "I have learned, in whatsoever state I am, therein to be content (αὐταρκής)."

[41] Gk. οἱ ἡγούμενοι. Here the present participle may have imperfect force.

here the reference seems rather to be to those who led them in earlier days but have now completed their service; the whole course of their lives, from start to finish, now lies before their disciples and followers for review and imitation. By precept and example they showed the right path to tread; being dead they yet speak, and the record of their faith is still alive in the memory of those who knew them. In Chapter 11 the faith of men and women of earlier generations is presented for emulation, but there is something in the vivid recollection of a life that we have seen which cannot be conveyed by a record that has come to us only by reading or hearing. Those who planted this community of Christians and fostered it by the ministry of the word of God[42] and the example of a life of faith had run the race unwavering to the end; what they had done their followers could also do. It is not necessary to suppose that they had suffered martyrdom;[43] but like the heroes of Chapter 11 they "died in faith".

8 Yet they died; they lived on in the memory of those who had known them, but they were no longer available for consultation and wise guidance as they had once been. Jesus Christ, by contrast, was always available, unchanging from year to year, "the same yesterday and today and for ever". In Ch. 1:12 the words of Ps. 102:27 were applied to Him: "thou art the same, and thy years shall not fail". These words, we saw, in their original context were addressed to the God of Israel; but this is not the only instance in which we find such a spontaneous transition of reference from the Father to the Son. "I am he," says God to His people in Isa. 48:12; "I am the first, I also am the last"[44]— language which in the New Testament is taken over and applied to Jesus without any sense of incongruity.[45] *Yesterday* Jesus "offered

---

42 The same persons are probably referred to in Ch. 2:3, where the gospel "was confirmed unto us by them that heard". "Does not ... the aorist ἐλάλησαν ["spake"] in v. 7 refer to the *original* proclamation of the word of God to the hearers?" (R. V. G. Tasker, *ExT* xlvii [1935-36], p. 138).

43 So Tasker, *loc. cit.* ("whose leaders have already suffered martyrdom"); Moffatt, *ad loc.* ("They had laid down their lives as martyrs"). Moffatt compares "the issue (ἔκβασις) of their life" with Wisdom 2:17, where the wicked say of the righteous man, whom they propose to persecute and kill, "let us test what will happen at the end of his life (τὰ ἐν ἐκβάσει αὐτοῦ)".

44 *Cf.* Isa. 41:4; 44:6.

45 *Cf.* Rev. 1:17 (also 2:8; 22:13), where the glorified Christ says "I am the first and the last". A purely verbal near-coincidence appears in the Egyptian

up prayers and supplications with strong crying and tears unto him that was able to save him from death" (Ch. 5:7); *today* He represents His people in the presence of God, a high priest who is able to sympathize with them in their weakness, because He was "in all points tempted like as we are, yet without sin" (Ch. 4:15); *for ever* He lives, this same Jesus, "to make intercession for them" (Ch. 7:25). His help, His grace, His power, His guidance are permanently at His people's disposal; why then should they lose heart? Others serve their generation by the will of God and pass on; "but he, because he abideth for ever, hath his priesthood unchangeable" (Ch. 7:24). He never needs to be replaced, and nothing can be added to His perfect work.

3. THE TRUE CHRISTIAN SACRIFICES

Ch. 13:9-16

9 Be not carried away[46] by divers and strange teachings: for it is good that the heart be established by grace; not by meats, wherein they that occupied themselves[47] were not profited.

10 We have an altar, whereof they have no right to eat[48] that serve the tabernacle.

11 For the bodies of those beasts whose blood is brought into the holy place by the high priest *as an offering* for sin,[49] are burned without the camp.

Book of the Dead, ed. E. A. W. Budge (London, 1913), i, p. 177, where the deceased who has been assimilated to Osiris says, "I am yesterday, today and tomorrow" ('nk sf dw' bk').

[46] Gk. μὴ παραφέρεσθε. For παραφέρεσθε ("be carried along") K L etc. with the Coptic versions and TR read περιφέρεσθε ("be carried about", AV), perhaps under the influence of Eph. 4:14 ("carried about with every wind of doctrine").

[47] Literally "they that walked".—Gk. οἱ περιπατοῦντες (P46 ℵ* A D*), for which ℵc K L with the majority of MSS and TR read οἱ περιπατήσαντες.

[48] Gk. ἐξ οὗ φαγεῖν οὐκ ἔχουσιν ἐξουσίαν. D* M (and John of Damascus) omit ἐξουσίαν. The omission is a scribal slip, but as it happens the remaining words give reasonably good sense: "whereof they cannot eat" (for ἔχω with infinitive *cf.* Ch. 6:13). See G. Zuntz, *op. cit.*, p. 140, n. 3.

[49] Gk. περὶ ἁμαρτίας (*cf.* p. 234, n. 42, on Ch. 10:6).

12 Wherefore Jesus also, that he might sanctify the people through his own blood, suffered without the gate.[50]

13 Let us therefore go forth unto him without the camp,[51] bearing his reproach.

14 For we have not here an abiding city, but we seek after *the city* which is to come.

15 Through him then[52] let us offer up a sacrifice of praise to God continually, that is, the fruit of lips[53] which make confession to his name.

16 But to do good and to communicate forget not: for with such sacrifices God is well pleased.

9 The reminder that "Jesus Christ is the same" links what precedes it with what follows it. Because "Jesus Christ is the same," says our author, "do not be swept off your course by all sorts of outlandish teachings;[54] it is good that our souls should gain their strength from the grace of God, and not from scruples about what we eat, which have never done any good to those who were governed by them" (NEB). The language here suggests something more than a relapsing into orthodox Judaism; it reminds us of Paul's appeal to the Colossian Christians not to let any one sit in judgment on them in respect of food or drink, because things like these disappeared in the very act of being used; regulations and prohibitions regarding such evanescent things provided no spiritual support or defence.[55] "Food will not commend us to God," says Paul elsewhere: "neither, if we eat not, are we the worse; nor, if we eat, are we the better" (I Cor. 8:8). Our author makes the same point. It is by divine grace[56], and not by rules about food, that the

---

50 Gk. ἔξω τῆς πύλης. For πύλης P⁴⁶ P read παρεμβολῆς ("camp"), under the influence of v. 13; 436 and the Syriac Peshitta read πόλεως, "city" (a reading possibly implied by Tertullian, *Reply to the Jews*, 14: "One of the goats, begirt with scarlet, amid cursing and universal spitting, and tearing and piercing, was ejected by the people into perdition outside the city [*extra ciuitatem*]").

51 Gk. ἔξω τῆς παρεμβολῆς, from Lev. 16:27, LXX.

52 Gk. οὖν, omitted (by haplography, according to Zuntz, *op. cit.*, p. 192) by P⁴⁶ ℵ* D* P Ψ and the Peshitta.

53 From Hos. 14:2, LXX; *cf.* p. 405, n. 90.

54 Gk. διδαχαῖς ποικίλαις καὶ ξέναις.

55 Col. 2:16, 21ff.; *cf. Ephesians-Colossians*, NICNT, pp. 243ff.

56 Gk. χάρις. In view of the force of this word in Ch. 12:28, it may be permissible to include here the idea of gratitude—gratitude in response to the grace of God.

heart—that is to say, the spiritual life—is nourished; rules about food, imposed by external authority, have never helped people to maintain a closer walk with God. (Voluntary fasting, in the spirit of our Lord's instruction in Matt. 6:16ff., is quite a different matter; but that is not the subject here.) The strange teaching which laid such insistence on food was probably some form of syncretistic gnosis, perhaps with Essene or quasi-Essene affinities.[57] This kind of thing was so widespread at the time that the vague allusion to it here (vague to modern readers, not to the original readers, who probably understood the allusion perfectly) provides no clue to the destination of the epistle. It was current in Asia Minor, we know; but even to the Roman Christians[58] Paul judged it necessary to point out that "the kingdom of God is not eating and drinking, but righteousness and peace and joy in the Holy Spirit"[59] (Rom. 14:17). To put such indifferent matters in a place of central religious importance would diminish the sovereignty of Jesus Christ, the same yesterday and today and for ever.

Since the word translated "meats" is the same as that used in Ch. 9:10,[60] where "meats and drinks and divers washings" are listed among the "regulations for the body imposed until the time of reformation", it is possible that a reference to sacrificial meals of some kind is included here. In any case, food regulations of all kinds, whether positive or negative, are catalogued by our author among those external ordinances which Christianity has rendered null and void.

10-11 In fact, the whole principle of attaching religious value to material food was inconsonant with the essence of Christianity.

---

[57] Cf. the outline of the Colossian heresy in *Ephesians-Colossians*, NICNT, pp. 165ff. T. W. Manson, because of the similarity between that heresy and the "strange teachings" implied here, suggested tentatively that this epistle might have been addressed to Christians in the Lycus valley when the heresy was in a less developed state than it had attained by the time Paul wrote Colossians (*Studies in the Gospels and Epistles* [Manchester, 1962], pp. 242ff.).

[58] Cf. the evidence that Roman Judaism (the matrix of Roman Christianity) had nonconformist affinities (pp. xxix, 115f.).

[59] Cf. I Tim. 4:3ff.

[60] Gk. $\beta\rho\dot{\omega}\mu\alpha\tau\alpha$. Although these are the only two places where the word occurs in this epistle, it is used in the singular ($\beta\rho\ddot{\omega}\mu\alpha$) or plural repeatedly in NT in the most general sense of food(s); cf. Matt. 14:15; Mark 7:19; Luke 3:11; 9:13; John 4:34; Rom. 14:15, 20; I Cor. 3:2; 6:13; 8:8, 13; 10:3; I Tim. 4:3.

The sacrifice of Christ was the antitype of the sacrifice offered on the great day of atonement, and the flesh of the animals slaughtered in the course of that ritual was not eaten; their bodies were "carried forth without the camp" and there completely burned[61] (Lev. 16:27). There were other sin-offerings in which this was not done; when the blood was not presented to God in the holy of holies, the flesh was eaten by the priests in the sanctuary.[62] But since the blood of the bullock which made atonement for Aaron and his family, and of the goat which made atonement for the people, was carried into the holy of holies on the day of atonement, their bodies were incinerated. In other words, "they ... that serve the tabernacle"[63] have no permission to eat from the altar which typically foreshadows the sacrifice of Christ. But the sacrifice of Christ is a better sacrifice, not only because the spiritual antitype is superior to the material type, but also because those who enter the heavenly sanctuary "by the blood of Jesus" (Ch. 10:19) know that the One who became their perfect sin-offering is permanently available as the source of their spiritual nourishment and refreshment, as they feed on Him in their hearts by faith.[64]

The word "altar" is used by metonymy for "sacrifice"—"as

---

[61]   So also with the sin-offerings of Ex. 29:14; Lev. 4:12; 8:17;9:11
[62]   *Cf.* Lev. 10:16ff.
[63]   Not only the priests, but all who participate in the "tabernacle" worship. The σκηνή here is surely the tabernacle in the wilderness, or, by extension, every phase of the earthly sanctuary which that tabernacle constituted in wilderness days. Windisch and Moffatt (*ad loc.*) take οἱ τῇ σκηνῇ λατρεύοντες to mean the worshippers under the new order, in which case the σκηνή must be the heavenly tabernacle: "we *have* an altar", our author would then say, "but it is not one from which we can derive material food; it is a figurative altar in the heavenly sanctuary which is the locus of our worship". But the reference to the Levitical sin-offering which follows immediately makes it almost certain that the σκηνή is the material tabernacle. J. M. Creed was disposed to follow Windisch and Moffatt here ("Hebrews xiii. 10", *ExT* 1 [1938–39], pp. 13ff.); but see J. P. Wilson ("The Interpretation of Hebrews xiii. 10", *ibid.*, pp. 380f.).
[64]   "Our great sin-offering, consumed in one sense outside the gate, is given to us as our food. The Christian, therefore, who can partake of Christ, offered for his sins, is admitted to a privilege unknown under the old Covenant" (B. F. Westcott, *ad loc.*). "In reality the only food that matters is the spiritual food of the sacrifice offered upon that altar to which, while they remain in the Mosaic stage, they have no access" (C. F. D. Moule, *JThS* NS i [1950], p. 38, in the course of an article "Sanctuary and Sacrifice in the Church of the New Testament", pp. 29ff.).

when, *e.g.*, we say that a man keeps a good *table*, meaning thereby good *food*".[65] Our author, who insists throughout that Christians have something better than an earthly sanctuary and animal sacrifices, certainly does not suggest that they have a material altar. It has, indeed, been thought by some commentators that by "we" in "we have an altar" he means "we Hebrews" and not "we Christians".[66] In that case the reference would be simply to the Levitical sacrifice prescribed for the day of atonement, as though he wished to say: "There is a sacrifice prescribed in the Levitical ritual which those who minister in the tabernacle have no right to eat." But "we have" here must surely have the same force as "we have" in Ch. 8:1, "we have such a high priest".[67]

Christians had none of the visible apparatus which in those days was habitually associated with religion and worship—no sacred buildings, no altars, no sacrificing priest. Their pagan neighbors thought they had no God, and called them atheists; their Jewish neighbors too might criticize them for having no visible means of spiritual support. So Archbishop Laud, when he came to Scotland in attendance on King Charles I in 1633, found that its benighted inhabitants had "no religion at all that I could see—which grieved me much".[68] The way in which Irenaeus expounds the nature of true Christian sacrifices suggests that he knew of people who said: "You Christians have no real religion, for you have no sacrifices".[69] If there were people in the first century who said, "You Christians have no altar", our author replies: "We *have* an altar—and a better one than the Jews had

---

[65] R. Anderson, *The Buddha of Christendom* (London, 1899), p. 302. It is unlikely that our author refers to the heavenly mercy-seat—a view proposed by A. S. Peake (Cent. B., *ad loc.*) and approved by J. P. Wilson (*loc. cit.*)—for the mercy-seat is never called a θυσιαστήριον. In the spiritual antitype certainly both altar and mercy-seat can be used by metonymy for the sacrifice of Christ, but this is not the same as saying that the mercy-seat is specifically intended here.

[66] R. Anderson, *op. cit.*, pp. 301ff.; *The Hebrews Epistle* (London, 1911), pp. 119ff.; W. H. Spencer, "Hebrews xiii. 10", *ExT* 1 (1938–39), p. 284. The latter appeals to A. C. Downer, *The Principle of Interpretation of the Epistle to the Hebrews* (London, 1928).

[67] *Cf.* C. F. D. Moule, *loc. cit.*, p. 37. In this article Heb. 13:10 is interpreted as part of a Christian apologetic answering the charge that Christians had neither priesthood nor altar, neither sacrifice nor sanctuary.

[68] Quoted by T. Carlyle, *Cromwell's Letters and Speeches*, introduction.

[69] Irenaeus, *Heresies* iv. 17f.

400

under the Levitical order." The Christian altar was the sacrifice of Christ, the benefits of which were eternally accessible to them. Material food, even if it was called sacred, perished with the using;[70] in this new and spiritual order into which they had been introduced by faith, Christ was perpetually available, "the same yesterday and today and for ever".

What connection is there between this passage and the Eucharist? No direct connection at all. It is remarkable how our author avoids mentioning the Eucharist when he has every opportunity to do so; for example, it would have been easy for him to derive some eucharistic significance from the bread and wine which Melchizedek brought to Abraham when he met him "returning from the slaughter of the kings" (Ch. 7:1); but he does not even mention the bread and wine (cf. p. 135 with n. 10). His failure to mention them, let alone discern some Christian meaning in them, can scarcely be accidental. If we had any independent knowledge of the community addressed, it might give us some clue to the omission of eucharistic references from his argument. It has, indeed, been suspected that they treated the Eucharist as a sacred meal[71] rather after the Essene or Qumranic fashion,[72] and did not appreciate that "the Body of Christ is given, taken, and eaten, in the Supper, only after an heavenly and spiritual manner", and that "the means whereby the Body of Christ is received and eaten in the Supper is Faith".[73] But this suspicion can be nothing

---

[70] Cf. Col. 2:20ff., with Ephesians-Colossians, NICNT, pp. 252ff.

[71] Cf. O. Holtzmann, "Der Hebräerbrief und das Abendmahl", ZNW x (1909), pp. 251ff.; J. Moffatt, ICC, ad loc., for the view that our author is engaging in a polemic against a rising "sacramentarianism" which interpreted the Eucharist as an "eating" of the body of Christ. "When θυσιαστήριον is identified with the Lord's table, it becomes possible to hear ... an early protest against the realistic sacramental view of the Lord's supper which sought to base its efficacy on conceptions of communion popular among the pagan mysteries" (J. Moffatt, Introduction to the Literature of the NT [Edinburgh, 1918], pp. 454f.). But it is not until a much later date that we find the Lord's Table spoken of as an altar—once doubtfully in Irenaeus (Heresies iv. 18. 6), once or twice in Tertullian (On Prayer, 19; Exhortation to Chastity, 10), and then regularly from Cyprian onwards. Cf. Westcott's "Additional Note ... on the History of the Word θυσιαστήριον" in his Hebrews, pp. 455ff.; J. B. Lightfoot, Philippians (London, 1913), p. 265, n. 2.

[72] Cf. K. G. Kuhn, "The Lord's Supper and the Communal Meal at Qumran", The Scrolls and the NT, ed. K. Stendahl (London, 1958), pp. 65ff.; M. Black, The Scrolls and Christian Origins (London, 1961), pp. 102ff.

[73] The Thirty-Nine Articles, Article XXVIII.

more than a tentative inference from the general tenor of the epistle.

The most that can be said is that our author may be pointing to the truth of Christian experience which is independently attested in the Eucharist—that Christ is both the sacrifice and the sustenance of His people, and that as sacrifice and as sustenance alike He is to be appropriated by faith.[74]

12 The fact that the bodies of the animals sacrificed on the day of atonement were burned outside the camp suggests a parallel to the fact that Jesus was crucified outside one of the city gates of Jerusalem.[75] The parallel may seem inexact, since the animals of the sin-offering were actually slaughtered within the camp; our author may, however, have also in mind the fact that the red heifer, which was a kind of sin-offering, was slaughtered outside the camp.[76] Jesus died[77] in order to "sanctify the people"—bring them to God as worshippers purified in conscience—by means of His blood, the willing sacrifice of His life.[78] And the practical implication of His dying "without the gate" is made plain in the exhortation that follows.

13 "Let us then go to him outside the camp, bearing the stigma that he bore" (NEB). Jesus was led outside Jerusalem to be crucified, and this is regarded as a token of His rejection by all that Jerusalem represented. To have His messianic claims rejected by the leaders of the people was in itself a stigma; to be cast out and crucified added to that stigma. But, as Moses in his day "considered the stigma that rests on God's Anointed greater wealth than the treasures of Egypt" (Ch. 11:26, NEB), so the call came now to the people of Christ to consider that same stigma greater wealth than anything they could hope to gain by declining to burn their boats and commit themselves unreservedly to Him. Our author may have recalled an Old Testament

---

[74] *Cf.* John 6:48ff., with the interpretative principle in vv. 63f. Apart from the records of the institution, it is noteworthy how infrequently the Eucharist is mentioned in NT—much less frequently than baptism.

[75] *Cf.* John 19:20, "the place where Jesus was crucified was nigh to the city" —but therefore outside it.

[76] Num. 19:3 (*cf.* pp. 202f. with n. 88).

[77] Gk. ἔπαθεν, "suffered". *Cf.* for the absolute use of this verb in reference to the death of Christ Luke 22:15; 24:46; Acts 1:3; 17:3; I Pet. 2:21; and also Ch. 9:26 above.

[78] *Cf.* Ch. 10:10, 14, and (especially) 29.

occasion when, according to the Septuagint version which he knew, God was rejected in the camp of Israel and manifested His presence outside. For, after the incident of the golden calf, "Moses took his tent and pitched it outside the camp, far off from the camp, and it was called 'The Tent of Testimony'; and so it was, that everyone who sought the Lord would go out to the tent which was outside the camp".[79] Now, in the person of Jesus, God had again been rejected in the camp; His presence was therefore to be enjoyed outside the camp, where Jesus was, and everyone who sought Him must go out and approach Him through Jesus. In this context the "camp" stands for the established fellowship and ordinances of Judaism. To abandon them, with all their sacred associations inherited from remote antiquity, was a hard thing, but it was a necessary thing. They had been accustomed to think of the "camp" and all that was inside it as sacred, while everything outside it was profane and unclean.[80] Were they to leave its sacred precincts and venture on to unhallowed ground?[81] Yes, because in Jesus the old values had been reversed. What was formerly sacred was now unhallowed, because Jesus had been expelled from it; what was formerly unhallowed was now sacred, because Jesus was there. "Let us then go outside the camp" might be a hard exhortation; "Let us then go to him" should not be hard for any Christian; to whom else should they go? True, to be associated with Him meant bearing the stigma that He bore; it

---

[79] Ex. 33:7, LXX. Philo (*Giants*, 53f.) characteristically interprets this to mean the abandonment "of all created things and of the inmost veil and wrapping of mere opinion" so as to come to God with the mind unimpeded; Moses, in other words, "set up his judgment where it could not be deflected", outside the whole array of physical things, and then only began to worship God aright.

[80] The bodies of Nadab and Abihu were carried outside the camp after they were burned as a result of offering "strange fire" (Lev. 10:4f.); the blasphemer was stoned to death outside the camp (Lev. 24:14, 23); Miriam had to spend the seven days of her leprosy "shut up without the camp" (Num. 12:14f.). The scapegoat (although the precise phrase is not used in connection with it) was taken as far outside the camp as possible, laden with the sins of the people (Lev. 16:20–22; see p. 193).

[81] This aspect of the exhortation is well brought out by H. Koester, "Outside the Camp: Hebrews 13:9–14", *HThR* lv (1962), pp. 299ff. He points out, *inter alia*, that, whereas the man who burned the carcases of the animals sacrificed on the day of atonement was permitted to come back into the camp after the due washing of his body and clothes (Lev. 16:28), the recipients of the epistle are commanded to stay outside the camp.

THE EPISTLE TO THE HEBREWS

meant taking up the cross and following Him; it meant leaving
the shelter of a *religio licita*[82] for a fellowship which invited the
hostile attention of imperial law; but if, like Moses, they "looked
unto the recompense of reward", they would see that the stigma
carried eternal glory with it.[83] There, "without the camp", stood
Jesus, calling them to follow Him. Inside they felt secure; they
knew where they were amid its familiar installations; they were
psychologically insulated from the world outside. But Jesus claimed
the world outside for Himself. Other Jewish Christians, Hellenists
like themselves, had taken the initiative in evangelizing the Gentile
world. The future lay not with the "camp" but with the Gentile
mission;[84] let them exchange the imagined security of their old
associations for the new venture to which Jesus was leading His
followers out. Time and again in the history of the people of God
a similar call has come when a new advance must be made into
the unknown and unfamiliar, to occupy fresh territory under the
leadership of Jesus. There is nothing static about Him or His
cause; to stand still is to fall behind Him.

"New occasions teach new duties;
   Time makes ancient good uncouth:
They must upward still and onward
   Who would keep abreast of truth."[85]

14 Moreover, the old securities to which their hearts clung
were themselves insecure; the old order was about to crash. By
responding to the call to go out, they would be the gainers; they
would be leaving a "city" which was doomed to pass away for
"the city which hath the foundations, whose builder and maker is
God"[86] (Ch. 11:10). At present, the heavenly city was yet to
come; but by faith those who went forth to Christ were already
enrolled in its register of burgesses. Every earthly institution
belongs to "those things that are shaken" (Ch. 12:27); in none
of them can the spirit of man find permanent rest. "The city of
God remaineth."

---

[82] *Cf.* S. L. Guterman, *Religious Toleration and Persecution in Ancient Rome*
(London, 1951), pp. 103ff.
[83] *Cf.* Ch. 11:26 (pp. 320f. with n. 188).
[84] *Cf.* W. Manson, *The Epistle to the Hebrews* (London, 1951), p. 151.
[85] J. R. Lowell.
[86] *Cf.* p. 297, n. 85; p. 374, nn. 148–151.

15 Were they told that they had no sacrifices and no altar? But of course they still had sacrifices to offer, even if there remained no more sacrifice for sin. The sacrifice of thanksgiving had once been accompanied by an animal sacrifice in the temple—it was a form of peace-offering, according to Lev. 7:12.[87] Animal sacrifices had been rendered forever obsolete by the sacrifice of Christ, but the sacrifice of thanksgiving might still be offered to God, and indeed should be offered to Him by all who appreciated the perfect sacrifice of Christ.[88] No longer in association with animal sacrifices, but through Jesus, the sacrifice of praise was acceptable to God. The dissociation of this sacrifice from animal sacrifices had already been adumbrated in an Asaphite psalm:

"If I were hungry, I would not tell thee;
For the world is mine, and the fulness thereof.
Will I eat the flesh of bulls,
Or drink the blood of goats?
Offer unto God the sacrifice of thanksgiving;
And pay thy vows unto the Most High;
And call upon me in the day of trouble;
I will deliver thee, and thou shalt glorify me."[89]

The sacrifice of praise is further described as "the fruit of lips which make confession to his name", in language borrowed from the Septuagint version of Hos. 14:2. In the Massoretic text of that passage the sacrifice of praise is a substitute for animal sacrifices; so ARV translates it: "so will we render as bullocks the offering of our lips".[90] In this spirit the Qumran *Rule of the*

---

[87] With ἀναφέρωμεν θυσίαν αἰνέσεως here, *cf.* Lev. 7:2, LXX: ἐὰν μὲν περὶ αἰνέσεως προσφέρῃ αὐτήν, καὶ προσοίσει ἐπὶ τῆς θυσίας τῆς αἰνέσεως ἄρτους ἐκ σεμιδάλεως ... ("If he offers it [the peace-offering] for praise, then he shall bring for the sacrifice of praise loaves of fine flour ..."). (Lev. 7:2, LXX, corresponds to Lev. 7:12, MT, ARV, etc.) Our author's argument practically amounts to saying that, for Christians, their sin-offering is also their peace-offering—something that was impossible under the old order.

[88] *Cf.* I Pet. 2:9, where Christians, as "a royal priesthood" (*cf.* Ex. 19:6), "show forth the excellencies" of their Savior God (*cf.* Isa. 43:21).

[89] Ps. 50:12–15 (LXX 49:12–15). *Cf.* Ps. 141:2 (LXX 140:2), for the sacrificial value of prayer and heart-worship.

[90] MT *pārīm sephāthēnū*; LXX καρπὸν χειλέων ἡμῶν (whence our author derived καρπὸν χειλέων here) implies a different division of the Hebrew words, *viz. perī missephāthēnū*, "fruit from our lips". (In MT and LXX this verse appears as Hos. 14:3.) It is a disputed point which interpretation should be regarded

405

Community declares that when the prescriptions of the community are carried out in Israel, "to obtain favor for the land apart from the flesh of burnt-offerings and the fat of sacrifice, then the oblation of the lips according to right judgment shall be as a sweet savor of righteousness, and the perfection of one's ways as an acceptable free will offering".[91] At Qumran, however, this did not involve a total repudiation of animal sacrifices on principle. Similarly, while Philo provides parallels to this insistence on the sacrificial value of thanksgiving and deeds of piety, and holds that sacrifice is acceptable only if it is the expression of true heart-devotion, he does not suggest that the sacrificial ritual itself can be dispensed with.[92] Our author's treatment of the sacrificial ritual as antiquated is due to his understanding of the finality and perpetual efficacy of the sacrifice of Christ.[93]

16 To the sacrifice of praise is added the sacrifice of kind and loving action.[94] "Never forget to show kindness and to share what you have with others; for such are the sacrifices which God approves" (NEB). Here we have the proper ritual of Christianity. James expresses the same thing when he says: "The kind of religion which is without stain or fault in the sight of God our Father is this: to go to the help of orphans and widows in their distress and

---

as representing the prophet's meaning; RSV ("the fruit of our lips") follows LXX, but MT "bullocks" is appropriate to the sacrificial context.

[91] 1QS ix. 4f.; see also p. 177 and the reference to 4Q *Florilegium* 12 (p. 219, n. 153). *Cf.* 1QH i. 28: "Thou hast determined the fruit of the lips before ever they were." *Cf.* M. Mansoor, "Thanksgiving Hymns and Massoretic Text", *Revue de Qumran* iii (1961–62), No. 11, pp. 391f.

[92] *Cf.* Philo, *Noah's Planting* 126ff. (on the primacy of praise); *Special Laws* i. 267ff. (where he expounds the spiritual significance of the red heifer ceremony); *Migration of Abraham* 89ff. (where he criticizes the view that the literal observance of ceremonial laws may be abandoned if their spiritual lessons are learned and practised). *Cf.* p. 196, n. 63.

[93] On "the sacrifice of praise" A. Snell says: "If any one wants to find here a reference to our Eucharist, he may be right in doing so" (*New and Living Way* [London, 1959], p. 161). Contrariwise J. A. Bengel says here in his succinct way: "*Nil de missa*" (*Gnomon, ad loc.*). The sacrifice of praise always accompanies the Eucharist, but is not restricted to it.

[94] *Cf.* Philo, *On Flight and Finding*, 18f., for the sacrificial quality of "the virtues and the modes of action that are in accordance with them" (by way of a remarkable exegesis of Ex. 8:26, "we will sacrifice the abominations of Egypt to the Lord our God").

keep oneself untarnished by the world"[95] (Jas. 1:27, NEB). To the same effect, too, is Peter's statement that those who come to Christ, the chief corner-stone, themselves "as living stones, are built up a spiritual house,[96] to be a holy priesthood, to offer up spiritual sacrifices, acceptable to God through Jesus Christ" (I Pet. 2:5), as is also Paul's plea to the Roman Christians to present their bodies "a living sacrifice, holy, acceptable to God, which is your spiritual service" (Rom. 12:1). Christianity is sacrificial through and through; it is founded on the one self-offering of Christ, and the offering of His people's praise and property, of their service and their lives, is caught up into the perfection of His acceptable sacrifice, and is accepted in Him.

4. SUBMISSION TO LEADERS

Ch. 13:17

17   Obey them that have the rule over you,[97] and submit[98] *to them*: for they watch in behalf of your souls, as they that shall give account;[99] that they may do this with joy, and not with grief: for this *were* unprofitable[100] for you.

17 The leaders referred to here are probably the successors of those whose memory they are exhorted to cherish in verse 7. Our author evidently has as much confidence in the present leaders as in their predecessors. Perhaps they were leaders in the wider city church from whose fellowship and jurisdiction the group addressed in the epistle was tempted to withdraw. At any rate, the leaders carried a weighty responsibility; they were accountable for the spiritual well–being of those placed in their care. No wonder that they lost sleep[101] over this responsibility—for

---

95   *Cf.* Hermas, *Shepherd*, Similitude i. 8ff., where the true wealth which believers are urged to acquire consists of "afflicted souls"—*i.e.*, they should "go to the help of widows and orphans".

96   For this conception of a living house or household *cf.* Heb. 3:6 (pp. 57ff).

97   Your ἡγούμενοι, as in vv. 7, 24.

98   Gk. ὑπείκω, here only in NT; in LXX only in IV Macc. 6:35.

99   Gk. ὡς λόγον ἀποδώσοντες. D* reads ὡς λόγον ἀποδώσονται περὶ ὑμῶν ("because they will render an account concerning you"). *Cf.* p. 83, n. 58.

100   Gk. ἀλυσιτελής, a classical word, not elsewhere in the Greek Bible.

101   Gk. ἀγρυπνέω.

the "watching" could well involve this as well as general vigilance —if some of their flock were in danger of straying beyond their control. The readers are invited to cooperate with their leaders, to make their responsible task easier for them, so that they could discharge it joyfully and not with sorrow.[102] The idea is on the same lines as Paul's exhortation to the Philippian Christians to lead such lives in this world "that I may have whereof to glory in the day of Christ, that I did not run in vain neither labor in vain"[103] (Phil. 2:16).

There would always be a tendency throughout the churches for visitors who came purveying new and esoteric doctrines to be regarded as much more attractive and interesting personalities than the rather humdrum local leaders, who never taught anything new, but were content with the conservative line of apostolic tradition. Nevertheless it was those local leaders, and not the purveyors of strange teaching, who had a real concern for the welfare of the church and a sense of their accountability to God in this respect. If the discharge of their responsibility and the ultimate rendering of their account were made a burden to them, the resultant disadvantage would fall on those who were led as well as on the leaders.

5. REQUEST FOR PRAYER

Ch. 13:18-19

18 Pray[104] for us: for we are persuaded[105] that we have a good conscience, desiring to live honorably in all things.
19 And I exhort *you* the more exceedingly[106] to do this, that I may be restored to you the sooner.

---

[102] Gk. στενάζοντες, "groaning". Moffatt (*ad loc.*) quotes Sir Edward Denny's lines:
"O give us hearts to love like Thee,
Like Thee, O Lord, to grieve
Far more for others' sins than all
The wrongs that we receive."
[103] *Cf.* I Thess. 2:19f.
[104] D and Chrysostom read an intrusive καί ("also"), as though to say, "Pray for them, and pray for us (me) too".
[105] Gk. πειθόμεθα, changed to the singular πείθομαι ("I am persuaded") in a few minuscules (256, etc.) and to the perfect πεποίθαμεν in ℵ^c C^c D Ψ *et al.*
[106] Gk. περισσοτέρως, as in Ch. 2:1.

18 The terms of our author's request for prayer for himself[107] may suggest that he himself occupied, or had occupied, some position of responsibility in regard to his readers. But what this position might be we can only surmise. The good conscience[108] of which he speaks is probably the fruit of a sense of duty done, a responsibility well discharged. Like Paul he could say: "our conscience assures us that in our dealings with our fellow-men, and above all in our dealings with you, our conduct has been governed by a devout and godly sincerity, by the grace of God and not by worldly wisdom.... In order that our service may not be brought into discredit, we avoid giving offence in anything" (II Cor. 2:12; 6:3, NEB).

19 He had hoped to renew his former personal association with them, but had not been able to do so thus far; however, he hopes that the way for a reunion would soon be opened up, and he invites them to redouble their prayers for him to this end. It is difficult to be sure how much should be read between the lines of this petition. Does he suspect a certain spirit of resentment against him for some reason or other—perhaps because he has been so long away? Is there an element of personal apologia in his request for prayer and his protestation of conscientious and honorable behavior? And what was the nature of the restraint which prevented him from coming to see them sooner? Some have thought of imprisonment; but in that case he might have said so explicitly, and the reference to Timothy's release in verse 23 suggests that he himself is not in custody.

6. PRAYER AND DOXOLOGY

Ch. 13:20–21

20 Now the God of peace, who brought again from the dead the great shepherd of the sheep with the blood of an eternal covenant, *even* our Lord Jesus,[109]

---

[107] That the plural is purely literary (*cf.* Chs. 5:11; 6:9, 11) is suggested by the immediate transition to the singular in v. 19. But see p. xl with n. 82.

[108] *Cf.* p. 196, n. 62 (on Ch. 9:9).

[109] D* Ψ 33 etc., with some Latin authorities and the Syriac Peshitta, add "Christ" (a characteristic Western expansion).

21 make you perfect in every good thing[110] to do his will,
working[111] in us[112] that which is well-pleasing in his sight,
through Jesus Christ; to whom *be* the glory for ever and
ever.[113] Amen.

20, 21 This prayer has the general structure of a collect[114]
in the third person, consisting of *(a)* the invocation ("Now the
God of peace"), *(b)* an adjective clause setting forth the ground
on which the following petition is based ("who brought again
from the dead the great shepherd of the sheep with the blood of
an eternal covenant, even our Lord Jesus"), *(c)* the main petition
("make you perfect in every good thing to do his will"), *(d)* a
subsidiary petition ("working in us that which is well-pleasing in
his sight"), *(e)* a pleading of the mediatorial merit of Christ
("through Jesus Christ"), *(f)* a doxology ("to whom be the glory
for ever and ever"), and *(g)* the "Amen".

The fact that God is invoked as "the God of peace"[115] may
suggest that the community was troubled by disunity, which
required to be healed if the pleasure of God was to be wrought
out in their midst. It is true that in the Old Testament "peace"
has the fuller sense of well-being and salvation, but the Greek
sense of the word would come more readily to our author's mind
than the Hebrew sense.

This is the only place in the epistle where the title "shepherd"
is given to Jesus; but it is a title which comprehends the other

---

[110] Gk. ἐν παντὶ ἀγαθῷ, to which C with the majority of later MSS, the
Syriac Peshitta and TR, add ἔργῳ (*cf.* AV, "in every good work"), while A adds
ἔργῳ καὶ λόγῳ (probably under the influence of II Thess. 2:17, "in every good
work and word").

[111] Gk. ποιῶν, to which the unintelligible αὐτῷ is prefixed by ℵ* A C 33
etc., αὐτό by P⁴⁶ and αὐτός by 1912 (*cf.* d, *ipso faciente*). Hort argued that αὐτός
was the original reading, αὐτῷ being a corruption of it; it is much more probable
that we have to do with a dittography of the preceding αὐτοῦ (in τὸ θέλημα
αὐτοῦ, "his will"). *Cf.* G. Zuntz, *op. cit.*, p. 62.

[112] Gk. ἐν ἡμῖν, attested by P⁴⁶ ℵ D K M and the majority of MSS, with
the Peshitta; A and some other MSS with the Latin versions and TR, read
ἐν ὑμῖν ("in you").

[113] Gk. εἰς τοὺς αἰῶνας τῶν αἰώνων. P⁴⁶ D H and some other authorities
omit τῶν αἰώνων, and this shorter reading may be original, since the tendency
was always to expand such doxologies (*cf.* Zuntz, *op. cit.*, pp. 120ff.).

[114] A prayer-form characteristic of the Western Church, from Latin *collecta
oratio* ("a gathered-together prayer").

[115] *Cf.* Rom. 15:33; 16:20; I Thess. 5:23.

rôles which are here assigned to Him. Indeed, Markus Barth goes so far as to say, in a study of our author's use of the Old Testament, that for him "exegesis is the endeavor to help people in need by telling them what the Bible says of their shepherd Jesus Christ".[116] The form of the title is derived from the Septuagint version of Isa. 63:11: "Where is he that brought up from the sea the shepherd of the sheep?" The words in their original context refer to Moses—or, if the plural "shepherds" be read, to Moses and Aaron, in the sense of Ps. 77:20, "Thou leddest thy people like a flock by the hand of Moses and Aaron". Here they are applied to Jesus as the second Moses, who was brought up not from the sea but from the realm of the dead.[117] (In the Exodus typology of the New Testament the "sea of reeds" which Israel crossed on the way out of Egypt is a token of the death and resurrection of Christ into which His people are baptized.)

This is the only reference to our Lord's resurrection in the epistle; elsewhere the emphasis is on His exaltation to the right hand of God, in keeping with the exegesis of Ps. 110:1, 4, and the exposition of Jesus' high priesthood.[118]

Jesus was brought up from death "by the blood of the eternal covenant" (AV, RSV, NEB); that is to say, His resurrection is the demonstration that His sacrifice of Himself has been accepted by God and the new covenant established on the basis of that sacrifice. The phrase "the blood of the eternal covenant" echoes Ch. 9:20, where Moses speaks of "the blood of the covenant" confirmed by God with Israel on the basis of the law.[119] But now a better sacrifice has been offered, and the new covenant ratified thereby is superior to the older one in this respect among others,

---

[116] *Current Issues in NT Interpretation*, ed. W. Klassen and G. F. Snyder (New York, 1962), p. 58.

[117] For other NT applications of ποιμήν to Jesus *cf.* Mark 14:27 (quotation of Zech. 13:7); John 10:11, 14, 16 (echoing Ezek. 34, where Yahweh speaks of "my servant David", *i.e.* the coming Messiah, as the true shepherd of His own people Israel); I Pet. 2:25; 5:4 (ἀρχιποιμήν). The ideal of the shepherd-king goes back to the beginnings of Greek literature, and appears earlier still in the literature of other Near Eastern peoples. Philo depicts God as the supreme Shepherd (*cf.* Ps. 23:1), who entrusts His flock, the universe, to the shepherd care of the Logos, His firstborn Son (*Agriculture*, 51; *Change of Names*, 115f.).

[118] See pp. lvi, 50f.

[119] *Cf.* p. 208, n. 109. The preposition ἐν here is instrumental, used in much the same sense as διά in Ch. 9:12 (see pp. 200f.).

that it endures for ever. (There may also be an echo here of Zech. 9:11, where God promises Zion that He will release her captives from the waterless pit "because of the blood of thy covenant"; if so, it is but a verbal echo, but one may think of the rôle of the shepherd in the following chapters, Zech. 11:4ff.; 13:7.)

The prayer, then, is that the people addressed may be spiritually equipped[120] for every form of good work, and thus fulfil God's will as He operates in them "both to will and to work, for his good pleasure", as Paul would put it (Phil. 2:13).

The adjective clause which concludes this prayer ("to whom be the glory for ever and ever") is probably to be taken as an ascription of glory to God, the subject of the sentence (as is suggested by the punctuation of ARV), rather than as referring to "Jesus Christ" as its immediate antecedent. Our author has already made it plain in verse 15 that it is through Christ that glory is to be given to God.

---

[120] Gk. καταρτίζω, "put into a proper condition" or "make complete".

VIII. POSTSCRIPT

Ch. 13:22-25

1. PERSONAL NOTES

Ch. 13:22-23

22 But I exhort you, brethren, bear with[121] the word of exhortation: for I have written unto you in few words.

23 Know ye[122] that our[123] brother Timothy hath been set at liberty; with whom, if he come shortly, I will see you.

22 The "word of exhortation"[124] refers to the whole of the preceding epistle. In Acts 13:15, where the rulers of the synagogue at Pisidian Antioch send a message to Paul and Barnabas inviting them to pass on any "word of exhortation" that they may have for the assembled company, the phrase clearly denotes a homily; it is thus a very suitable description for this epistle, which is a homily in written form, with some personal remarks added at the end. But could a document of this length be appropriately spoken of as written "in few words"?[125] It might be a long letter, but not a long homily; it can be read aloud within one hour. At one point the writer has said "we have many things to say" (Ch. 5:11); but at another point he indicates that he could have said much more (Ch. 9:5b). Even if we regard it as a letter, it is not so long as Romans and I Corinthians. There is no need to suppose that the "word of exhortation" might be confined to the concluding admonitions of Ch. 13:1-19; they are so brief that no writer would think it necessary to ask his readers to bear with them[126] (the added

---

[121] Gk. ἀνέχεσθε (imperative), for which D* Ψ 33 and a few other authorities read ἀνέχεσθαι (infinitive, dependent on παρακαλῶ, "I exhort").

[122] Gk. γινώσκετε, in form indicative or imperative; the imperative is required by the sense here.

[123] Gk. ἡμῶν ("our") is omitted by K P with the majority of later MSS and TR, but even so it is understood (cf. the italicized "our" in AV).

[124] Gk. λόγος παρακλήσεως. See p. xlviii.

[125] Gk. διὰ βραχέων ἐπέστειλα ὑμῖν, "I have sent you a letter [ἐπιστέλλω being the verb corresponding to the substantive ἐπιστολή, 'epistle', 'letter'] by means of a few (words)".

[126] G. A. Simcox, however, distinguishes the "word of exhortation" (Chs. 1-12) from the "few words" (Ch. 13:1-19); see p. 386, n. 3. R. Anderson similarly takes the "few words" to refer to Ch. 13, written as a covering letter

413

remark about "few words" makes it clear that it is the length of the exhortation, not its content, that our author thinks the readers might begin to find wearisome).

23 Timothy is almost certainly Paul's friend of that name. We have no other account of his imprisonment. (It is just possible to argue that "set at liberty" means not "released from prison" but "sent away on some commission";[127] but it is very unlikely that the verb, used absolutely as it is here, has this latter meaning.) The place of his imprisonment was at some distance from the author's residence at the time, yet nearer to the author than to his readers, since he has news of Timothy's release before his readers are likely to know of it, and if Timothy joins him where he is they can travel together to visit them. Timothy was with Paul when Philippians, Colossians and Philemon were written; that is to say (so far as the last two epistles are concerned, at least), he was with him in Rome. I Tim. 1:3 may indicate a later residence of Timothy at Ephesus, from which Paul summons him (to Rome, presumably) in II Tim. 4:9ff. Rome or Ephesus would satisfy the present conditions, but they do not exhaust the possibilities.[128]

---

to accompany the treatise (*The Hebrews Epistle* [London, 1911], p. 12). But the identity of the "word of exhortation" with the few "words" is implied by the structure of this sentence. "The writer surely means ... that he has refrained from developing his great theme at undue length, as he was writing a 'word of exhortation' and not a merely academic treatise" (R. V. G. Tasker, *ExT* xlvii [1935–36], p. 138).

[127] The verb is ἀπολελυμένον (perfect participle passive of ἀπολύω). It is used, *e.g.*, in Acts 13:3 of the action of the Antiochene church in "releasing" Paul and Barnabas for a more extended apostolic ministry. E. D. Jones (*ExT* xlvi [1934–35], p. 566) argues that the meaning here is that Timothy has already set out from the place where the writer is to go to Corinth *via* Macedonia (in the light of his theory mentioned on p. 386, n. 4); but "it must be confessed that the more obvious meaning of the word is 'released', and that the sentence refers to some otherwise unknown imprisonment of Timothy" (R. V. G. Tasker, *loc. cit.*).

[128] Various suggestions have been made by commentators in harmony with their general views on the provenience and destination of the epistle. Thus A. Nairne hazards "the guess that both the author and Timothy may have been brought to Italy by the peril of their master S. Paul—that S. Paul has perished in Nero's persecution, that Timothy has been imprisoned, and that the freedom of both Timothy and the author is now assured" (*The Epistle of Priesthood* [Edinburgh, 1913], p. 432). W. F. Howard similarly suggests that Timothy, having been summoned to Rome by Paul (II Tim. 4:9ff.), was compromised by

them nothing in this situation; only attachment to the unchanging and onward-moving Christ could carry them forward and enable them to face a new order with confidence and power. So, in a day when everything that can be shaken is being shaken before our eyes and even beneath our feet, let us in our turn give thanks for the unshakable kingdom which we have inherited, which endures forever when everything else to which men may pin their hopes disappears and leaves not a wrack behind.

INDEX OF PERSONS AND PLACES

419

INDEX OF CHIEF SUBJECTS

424

INDEX OF AUTHORS

427

xlii, xlvi, 2, 254, 267, 312, 329, 336, 341, 356
Clements, R. E., 166
Cobet, C. G., 282
Cole, A., 199
Connolly, R. H., xxxviii
Coppens, J., xxix
Creed, J. M., 35, 399
Cross, F. L., 62
Cross, F. M., 16, 165, 306
Cullmann, O., lii f., 58, 101
Curtis, A. H., 86
Cyprian, 135
Cyril, 128

Dalman, G., 246
Daniélou, J., xxviii, 24, 62, 116
Dante, 127, 392
Darby, J. N., xlii, 237
Davidson, A. B., xii, 82, 131, 158, 241, 248, 323
Davidson, S., xxxiii
Davies, T. W. L., 386
Davies, W. D., 16, 35
Daube, D., 116, 387
Debrunner, A., 103
Deissmann, A., 42, 211, 415
de Jonge, M., 144
Delitzsch, F., xli, 188 f., 204, 232 f., 367, 377
Delling, G., 109
Demosthenes 282
Denny, Edward, 408
Denney, J., lv, 206, 234, 236
Didymus, 128
Dillmann, A., 91
Dio Cassius, 268
Diodorus Siculus, 350
Diogenes Laertius, 102
Dionysius of Alexandria, xlv
Dionysius of Corinth, 126
Dix, G., 116
Dodd, C. H., lvii, 11, 16; 35, 42, 45 f., 80, 119, 133, 246, 274
Dörrie, H., 67, 103
Downer, A. C., 400
Driver, G. R., 19
Driver, S. R., 42
Dryden, J., 383
Duhm, B., 96, 172
Dulière, W. L., 191, 383
du Plessis, P. J., 44

Eaton, J. H., 272
Ehrhardt, A., lviii, 122, 147, 155, 281

Eliezer, Rabbi, 361
Elliot, E., 367
Ellison, H. L., 34 f., 96, 171, 179, 205, 230
Empedocles, 281
Ephrem, xlv
Epictetus, 109, 287, 348, 350
Eupolemus, 316
Euripides, 81, 132, 281
Eusebius, xxiii, xxxiv, xxxvi, xxxviii, xlv, 105, 126, 128, 266, 270, 316, 348

Feather, J., 318
Fereday, W. W., 334
Festugière, A. J., 82
Field, F., 301
Findlay, G. G., 263
Fitzmyer, J., 107
Flusser, D., xxviii, 341
Focke, F., 2
Fohrer, G., 375
Fridrichsen, A., 62
Friedlaender, M., 107

Gaius of Rome, xxxviii, xlvi
Gandy, S. W., 50
Garstang, J., 327, 329
Garvie, A. E., 6, 37 f., 43, 98, 100, 226
Gaster, M., 203
Gelb, I. J., 134
Gemser, B., 306
Goguel, M., liii
Goldberg, P. S., 204
Goodenough, E. R., 183
Gooding, D. W., 187
Goodrick, A. T., 280
Goodspeed, E. J., 260
Goppelt, L., 255 f., 261
Gore, C., 297
Gosse, Sir Edmund, xi
Grant, R. M., 1
Gregory, C. R., xxxvii
Gregory of Elvira, xxxvii
Gregory of Nazianzus, 265, 338, 342
Grobel, K., 52
Guilding, A. E., xlviii, 188
Gunkel, H., 97
Guterman, S. L., 404

Harnack, Adolf, xxxv, xl, 32, 100 f., 103, 241, 254, 270
Harris, J. R., xl, 5, 46, 62, 77, 82, 86, 262, 299
Hart, Joseph, 290
Hatch, E., 211

INDEX OF SCRIPTURE REFERENCES

OLD TESTAMENT

433

435

436

444

NON-BIBLICAL BOOKS